OSBORN'S
CONCISE LAW DICTIONARY

OSBORN'S

CONCISE

LAW DICTIONARY

ELEVENTH EDITION

Edited by

MICK WOODLEY

Associate Dean, School of Law, Northumbria University

with contributions from:

Jenny Adams   Russell Hewitson
Liane Atkin   Adam Jackson
Jonathan Bainbridge   Philip Judd
Joanne Clough   Sue Wolf
Judith Gowland

(all at Northumbria University)

SWEET & MAXWELL   THOMSON REUTERS

First Edition	1927
Second Edition	1937
Third Edition	1947
Fourth Edition	1954
Second Impression	1958
Third Impression	1960
Fourth Impression	1962
Fifth Impression	1963
Sixth Impression	1963
Fifth Edition	1964
Second Impression	1970
Third Impression	1974
Sixth Edition	1976
Seventh Edition	1983
Second Impression	1986
Third Impression	1987
Fourth Impression	1990
Fifth Impression	1990
Eighth Edition	1993
Second Impression	1994
Third Impression	1996
Fourth Impression	1998
Ninth Edition	2001
Second Impression	2004
Tenth Edition	2005
Eleventh Edition	2009

Published in 2009 by Thomson Reuters (Legal) Limited
(Registered in England & Wales, Company No 1679046.
Registered Office and address for service:
100 Avenue Road, London NW3 3PF)
trading as Sweet & Maxwell

For further information on our products and services, visit
www.sweetandmaxwell.co.uk

Typeset by YHT Ltd, London
Printed in the UK by CPI William Clowes Beccles NR34 7TL

A CIP catalogue record for this book is available from The British Library
ISBN 9781847033086

No natural forests were destroyed to make this product;
only farmed timber was used and re-planted.

PREFACE

In compiling the entries for this, the eleventh edition of Osborn's Law Dictionary, my colleagues and I have once again been struck by the extent and the occasional impenetrability of the legislation that Parliament has passed since our publishers last called upon our services. As to the former we have no control but in the case of the latter we hope to have provided at least some enlightenment. Amongst the many statutes that have reached the statute book in recent years is the Companies Act 2006, a veritable magnum opus (great work), which, with its 1300 sections and 16 Schedules, is the largest single piece of legislation to be enacted by the UK Parliament. Inevitably with such bulk only selected definitions can be provided, but this Act is also illustrative of a further difficulty that the hard-pressed compiler faces, namely commencement dates. By the time that this edition reaches the shelves most, but not all, of those 1300 sections and 16 Schedules will be in force. For the purposes of clarity we have done as most student texts on Company Law have done and assumed that the 2006 Act is fully in force as it is planned to be by October 1, 2009. In making this decision (the responsibility for which I, as editor, accept the blame) we are conscious that there always remains a risk, and a look back at the tenth edition provides a salutary reminder of that fact. The Constitutional Reform Act 2005 established a Supreme Court in place of the judicial functions of the House of Lords and the existing Supreme Court Act 1981 was renamed the Senior Courts Act 1981, or at least this was anticipated to be the case. However, we await the new court and the renaming of the former statute. Although this is expected to occur towards the end of 2009, the references in this edition remain that of the Supreme Court Act 1981.

Elsewhere we have once again endeavoured to reflect the variety of new terms that are to be found across the full range of the judicial and parliamentary landscape, whilst amending those that have changed and removing those that have passed their sell-by-date. The legislature cannot be accused of being idle and this edition has sought (inter alia) to provide entries that capture the fundamental reforms that are taking place in the provision of legal services and in the structure of the tribunal system in addition to the developments in both the criminal and civil law.

My thanks go to my fellow contributors and the nameless colleagues who have assisted us in our task and also to our publishing editor, Constance Sutherland, without whose patient forbearance our task would have been so much harder.

Subject to the caveat provided above, the law is as stated on October 1, 2008.

Mick Woodley

CONTENTS

vii

A

CONCISE

LAW DICTIONARY

A

A1 at Lloyd's A ship entered in Lloyd's Register of Shipping as of the highest class.

A and B Lists See CONTRIBUTORY.

ACAS See ADVISORY, CONCILIATION and ARBITRATION SERVICE.

ADR See ALTERNATIVE DISPUTE RESOLUTION.

AIM See ALTERNATIVE INVESTMENT MARKET.

ASBO See ANTISOCIAL BEHAVIOUR ORDER.

a coelo usque ad centrum [From heaven to the centre of the earth] In principle, the extent of the right of the owner of property. See CUJUS EST SOLUM, ETC.

a fortiori [Much more; with stronger reason]

a mensa et thoro [From board and bed]

a posteriori [From the effect to the cause] Inductive reasoning.

a priori [From the cause to the effect] Deductive reasoning.

a verbis legis non est recedendum [You must not vary the words of a statute]

a vinculo matrimonii [From the bond of matrimony] See DIVORCE.

Ab.:Abr. Abridgment (*q.v.*).

ab initio [From the beginning] A phrase added to the term, void, to indicate the time from which a purported contractual transaction is of no effect. See NULLITY; TRESPASS AB INITIO; VOID.

abandonment The relinquishment of an interest, claim or thing. In marine insurance when there is a constructive total loss (*q.v.*) the insured may abandon the subject matter insured to the insurer or underwriter by giving notice of abandonment to him within a reasonable time. Thereupon the insured is entitled to the insurance moneys and the insurer or underwriter to the subject matter insured.

An easement (*q.v.*) may be lost by abandonment, of which non-user for 20 years may be sufficient evidence.

There is abandonment of an action when it is no longer proceeded with, or of an appeal when it is withdrawn. See DISCONTINUANCE.

Abandonment of a child means leaving it to its fate. This is an offence (Children and Young Persons Act 1933 s.1).

1

abatement A reduction, allowance, or rebate. An abatement pro rata is a proportionate reduction of the amount of each of a number of debts or claims, as where a fund or estate is insufficient for payment of all in full.

abatement notice Where a local authority is satisfied that a statutory nuisance (*q.v.*) exists or is likely to exist in its area the authority shall serve an abatement notice on the person responsible for the nuisance or the owner or occupier of the premises from which the nuisance has occurred. An abatement notice may require the abatement (bringing to an end) of the said nuisance or the execution of works and taking of specified steps. It is a criminal offence not to comply with an abatement notice without reasonable excuse. Appeals against abatement notices may be made to the magistrates' court. (See Pt III of the Environmental Protection Act 1990.) See ABATEMENT OF NUISANCE; NUISANCE.

abatement of claim (formerly abatement of action) Formerly a suspension or termination of proceedings in an action for want of proper parties or owing to a defect in the writ or service. Almost every change of interest after the commencement and before the termination of proceedings caused an abatement. Now, where a party to a claim dies or becomes bankrupt but the cause of action survives, the claim shall not abate by reason of the death or bankruptcy. Criminal proceedings are not terminated by the death either of the prosecutor or of the Sovereign, but on the death of the accused the proceedings drop. See PLEAS IN ABATEMENT.

abatement of legacies The receipt by legatees of none or part only of their legacies owing to insufficiency of assets. General legacies not given in payment of a debt due to the legatee or in consideration of the legatee abandoning any right or interest, abate proportionately between themselves, unless the intention is clear that any particular legacy shall be paid in full. Specific legacies take priority over general legacies, and are liable to abatement only if the assets are insufficient for the payment of debts.

Demonstrative legacies are not subject to abatement unless the assets are insufficient for payment of debts, or until the fund out of which payment is directed becomes exhausted. See LEGACY.

abatement of nuisance To remove or put an end to it, as an alternative to bringing an action. An occupier of land may terminate by his own act any nuisance by which that land is injuriously affected, e.g. by cutting off overhanging branches of trees. Notice may be necessary to the other party if it is necessary to enter on his land to abate the nuisance (*q.v.*), except in case of emergency.

A public nuisance may be abated by anyone to whom it does a special injury, but only to the extent necessary to prevent such injury, e.g. to remove a fence unlawfully erected across a highway.

Local authorities have statutory powers to secure abatement notices in respect of statutory nuisances (*q.v.*). See, e.g. the Environmental Protection Act 1990 ss.79–82.

abatement of purchase-money The reduction of the agreed purchase price by way of compensation, when a vendor has misdescribed property and is unable to convey it as described.

abator One who abates, or terminates, a nuisance by his own act.

abbreviatio placitorum A collection of cases decided in the superior courts from the reign of Richard I down to the commencement of the Year Books.

abdication Renunciation, particularly of an office or responsibility. Royal Abdication, i.e. abdication of the throne, can only be effected by Act of Parliament. See, e.g. His Majesty's Declaration of Abdication Act 1936.

abduction The wrongful taking away of a person. The Sexual Offences Act 1956 contained various sexual offences connected with abduction. See Sexual

Offences Act 1956 ss.17, 19, 20 and 21. These sections have been repealed by the Sexual Offences Act 2003 and replaced in that Act with a new criminal code of sexual offences.
   Under the Child Abduction Act 1984 as amended, it is an offence for a person connected with a child under the age of 16 (e.g. the child's parent), to take or send a child out of the United Kingdom without the appropriate consent. It is also an offence for a person who is not connected to a child to take or detain a child so as to remove or keep that child from the lawful control of someone entitled to such control.

abet See AID AND ABET; ACCESSORY.

abeyance The condition of an inheritance which has no present owner, e.g. a peerage.

abeyance of seisin An interruption in the tenancy of a freehold. It was a rule of the common law that the seisin must always be "full", e.g. the tenancy of the freehold be uninterrupted, and any attempted disposition of land which would produce an abeyance of the seisin was void. This rule ceased to operate when the Law of Property Act 1925 came into effect.

abjuration Forswearing or renouncing by oath: an oath to leave the realm for ever, taken by a person who had claimed sanctuary (*q.v.*).

abode Habitation or place of residence; the place where a person ordinarily lives and sleeps at night. For purposes of immigration law a person has "the right of abode" in the United Kingdom in the circumstances set out in the Immigration Act 1971 s.2 (as amended by British Nationality Act 1981 s.39), i.e. either that he is a British citizen (*q.v.*) or that he was a Commonwealth citizen (*q.v.*) having the right of abode under s.2(1)(d) or s.2(2) of the Act of 1971 immediately before the commencement of the 1981 Act and has not ceased to be a Commonwealth citizen in the meantime.

abominable crime The term that was used in the Offences against the Person Act 1861 s.61, to describe the felonies of sodomy and bestiality. See BUGGERY; SEXUAL OFFENCES.

abortion A miscarriage or expulsion of a human foetus before gestation is completed. Until 1967 procuring or causing an abortion was an offence. Under the Abortion Act 1967 procuring an abortion is not an offence where the pregnancy is terminated by a registered medical practitioner and two registered medical practitioners are of the bona fide opinion that one of the grounds set out in s.1(1)(a), (b), (c), or (d) of the Abortion Act 1967 (as reformulated by the Human Fertilisation and Embryology Act 1990) exists.

abrogate To repeal, cancel, or annul.

abscond To go away secretly, to evade the jurisdiction of the court. Under the Bail Act 1976 as amended, absconding by a person released on bail is an offence. See BAIL.

absence If a person has not been heard of for seven years, and the circumstances are such that, if alive, he would have been heard of, the presumption of death arises, but not as to the date of death (*Re Phene's Trusts* (1869) L.R. 5 Ch.App. 139). The court may, however, order that death be presumed at any time if sufficient evidence is shown. See the Matrimonial Causes Act 1973 s.19. See also BIGAMY.

absence beyond the seas Absence from the United Kingdom (*q.v.*).

absente reo [The defendant being absent]

absolute Complete and unconditional. (1) A rule or order which is complete and becomes of full effect at once, e.g. decree absolute, charging order (*q.v.*) absolute, garnishee order (*q.v.*) absolute. Contrast and see NISI.
   (2) An estate which is not defeasible before its natural expiration.

3

absolute assignment An assignment of a whole debt (and not merely a portion of it), free from conditions but including an assignment by way of mortgage, or by way of trust. See ASSIGNMENT OF CHOSES IN ACTION.

absolute discharge (1) Imposed when the court has convicted an offender but is of the opinion that it would be inexpedient to inflict punishment on them, the court having had regard to the circumstances of the case, including the nature of the offence and the character of the offender (Powers of Criminal Courts (Sentencing) Act 2000 s.12(1)).

(2) Both the Secretary of State and the Mental Health Review Tribunal can direct absolute discharge from hospital of a restricted patient (*q.v.*) within the meaning of the Mental Health Act 1983 ss.42, 73.

(3) A disposal option available to the Crown Court where: (a) a special verdict is returned that the accused is not guilty by reason of insanity; or (b) findings have been made that the accused is under a disability and that he did the act or made the omission charged against him (Criminal Procedure (Insanity) Act 1964 s.5, as substituted by the Domestic Violence, Crime and Victims Act 2004 s.24(1).

absolute interest Full and complete ownership; a vested right of property which is liable to be determined only by the failure of appropriate successors in title.

absolute title (1) In relation to freehold estates, a person may be registered with absolute title if the Registrar is of the opinion that the person's title to the estate is such as a willing buyer could properly be advised by a competent professional adviser to accept (Land Registration Act 2002 s.9(2)).

(2) In relation to leasehold estates, a person may be registered with absolute title if (a) the Registrar is of the opinion that the person's title to the estate is such as a willing buyer could properly be advised by a competent professional adviser to accept, and (b) the Registrar approves the lessor's title to grant the lease (Land Registration Act 2002, s.10(2)). See LAND REGISTRATION; CHIEF LAND REGISTRAR.

absolve To free from liability or guilt.

absque hoc [Without this, that] The commencing words of a traverse, or denial, in the old pleadings.

absque impetitione vasti [Without impeachment of waste (*q.v.*)]

absque tali causa [Without the alleged cause] See DE INJURIA.

abstract of title A chronological statement of the instruments and events under which a person is entitled to property, showing all incumbrances to which the property is subject. It is only relevant where the land is unregistered. Overreached interests are not to be included in an abstract (Law of Property Act 1925 s.10). See also EPITOME OF TITLE.

abstraction The removal or abstraction of water from a water supply such as a river, stream or underwater source. Generally the abstraction of water is prohibited save in pursuance of an abstraction licence granted by the Environment Agency (*q.v.*) under the provisions of Pt II of the Water Resources Act 1991.

abundante cautela [Out of great caution] A reference to a statement included to make sure that a matter is plain or understood.

abuse Vulgar abuse, insult, or vituperation afford in general no ground for an action for defamation.

abuse of distress Where animals or chattels lawfully distrained are worked or used. It is a ground for an action of conversion.

abuse of position of trust Offences involving the abuse of a position of trust are created by the Sexual Offences Act 2003. These are: sexual activity with a child; causing or inciting a child to engage in sexual activity; sexual activity in the presence of a child; causing a child to watch a sexual act (Sexual Offences Act 2003 ss.16–19).

The following are exceptions to what would otherwise be an abuse of a position of trust: the marriage exception; sexual relations which pre-date the position of trust (Sexual Offences Act 2003 ss.23–24). See also POSITIONS OF TRUST; SEXUAL OFFENCES.

abuse of process The court may strike out a statement of case if it appears to the court that the statement of case is an abuse of the court's process, e.g. where the claim is the same as a claim which has already between adjudicated upon between the parties. It is a power "which any court of justice must possess to prevent misuse of its procedure in a way which, although not inconsistent with the literal application of its procedural rules, would nevertheless be manifestly unfair to a party to litigation before it, or would otherwise bring the administration of justice into disrepute among right-thinking people": per Lord Diplock in *Hunter v Chief Constable of the West Midlands Police* [1982] A.C. 529. See VEXATIOUS ACTIONS; STRIKING OUT.

abuttals The bounds of land; the parts at which it abuts on other lands.

ac etiam [And also]

acceleration Where an estate or interest in any property in remainder or expectancy falls into possession sooner than it otherwise would, by reason of the preceding interest being or becoming void or determined by surrender, merger, lapse, or extinguishment. The disclaimer of a peerage shall not accelerate the succession to that peerage (Peerage Act 1963 s.3(1)).

acceptance (1) Tacit acquiescence or agreement imported by failure to reject a thing offered; thus acceptance of rent may create a tenancy or waive a notice to quit.

(2) The act of assenting to an offer. Acceptance of an offer to create a contract must be made while the offer still subsists by the offeree who must know of the offer; it must conform with the offer and must either be communicated to the offerer or the requisite act must be done.

(3) Acceptance of goods within the Sale of Goods Act 1979 s.35 is: (a) where the buyer intimates to the seller that he has accepted them; or (b) where the goods have been delivered to him and he does any act in relation to them which is inconsistent with the ownership of the seller; or (c) when, after the lapse of a reasonable time, he retains the goods without intimating to the seller that he has rejected them. Note however that a buyer who has not previously examined goods is not deemed to have accepted them until he has had a reasonable opportunity of examining them for the purpose of ascertaining whether they are in conformity with the contract.

acceptance of a bill of exchange When the person on whom the bill is drawn writes his signature across the bill, with or without the word "accepted", he thereby engages to pay the bill when due (Bills of Exchange Act 1882 ss.17–19). Acceptance supra protest is where a bill of exchange has been protested for non-acceptance by the drawee; anyone may thereupon accept it for honour of the drawer or indorsers (ibid. ss.65–68).

acceptance of service Where a solicitor: (a) is authorised to accept service on behalf of a party; and (b) has notified the party serving the document in writing that he is so authorised, a document must be served on the solicitor unless personal service is required by an enactment, rule, practice direction or court order (CPR 6.4(2)).

acceptance of service

Formerly, when a solicitor wrote on a writ of summons that he accepted service of the writ on behalf of the defendant, personal service was not required and the writ was deemed to have been served on the day the indorsement was made (Ord. 10, r.1(2)).

access (1) The opportunity of sexual intercourse between husband and wife. It is a presumption of law that a child born during lawful wedlock or within the period of gestation after its termination is legitimate, but evidence that access by a husband to his wife at the necessary time was impossible or highly improbable will rebut the presumption. The evidence of a husband or wife is admissible in any proceedings to prove that marital intercourse did or did not take place between them during any period (Matrimonial Causes Act 1973 s.48).

(2) Access to children, i.e. the right of a non-custodial parent, grandparent or other person to see and share the company of children of the family, usually after divorce or separation proceedings. Access to children is a basic right of a parent and is only refused in the most unusual circumstances (*S v S* [1962] 1 W.L.R. 445). Access orders ceased to be available under the Children Act 1989. See now CONTACT ORDER.

Access by the child to the parent is considered to be a right of the child, to be refused only in unusual circumstances.

(3) Approach or the means of approach, e.g. there is a right of access to a highway by the owner of adjoining land.

access order Where a person wishes to carry out works to land and, for the purposes of carrying out those works, needs to enter onto adjoining or adjacent land but does not have consent to enter that land, then an application may be made to the County Court for an access order under the Access to Neighbouring Land Act 1992 s.1.

accessible record The definition of data (*q.v.*) under the Data Protection Act 1998 includes data which, whilst not falling within other parts of the definition, forms part of an accessible record as defined in s.68 of that Act. The latter defines accessible records as health records, educational records or accessible public records.

accessio The doctrine of Roman law, founded on the right of occupancy, that the additions to property by growth or increase belonged to the owner of that property. In English law possession of a thing may give good title to other things which are the natural product and expected increase of the thing possessed, e.g. lambs born to ewes possessed under a hire-purchase contract (*Tucker v Farm and General Investment Trust Ltd* [1966] 2 Q.B. 421). See ACCESSIO CEDIT PRINCIPALI.

accessio cedit principali [An accessory thing when annexed to a principal thing becomes part of the principal thing] The accessory thing becomes the property of the owner of the principal thing; as, e.g. in alluvion, dereliction, and the addition of buildings and plants to the soil, the birth of offspring of animals, etc. There is also *accessio* in the combination of things belonging to different persons in a single article; e.g. the shoeing of A's horse with B's horseshoes. In principle, the ownership of chattels is not divested, but possession may be awarded at the discretion of the court to the person whose interest in the combined or new chattel is the more substantial, on the terms that he pays the value of the other's interest.

accession (1) Succeeding to the Throne. "The King never dies", and the heir to the throne accedes immediately on the death of the reigning Sovereign. The new Sovereign makes a declaration as prescribed by the Accession Declaration Act 1910. See ACT OF SETTLEMENT.

(2) A mode by which original acquisition of territory may take place, without any formal act of taking possession (see *The Anna* (1807) 5 C.Rob. 373).

6

accessory A person, other than the actual perpetrator, who is a party to the commission of a criminal offence. Prior to the Criminal Law Act 1967 s.1, which abolished the distinction between felony and misdemeanour and assimilated the law to that applicable to misdemeanour, a person who procured the commission of a felony but was not present at its commission was known as an accessory before the fact (if present, such a person was a principal in the second degree). A person who, knowing a felony had been committed, afterwards gave assistance to the perpetrator, was an accessory after the fact.

Since the Criminal Law Act 1967, the classification of parties as accessories before the fact and principals in the second degree has ceased and they are known generally as secondary parties (although sometimes referred to as accessories), with their liability being governed by the Accessories and Abettors Act 1861 s.8 (as amended by the Criminal Law Act 1977):

"whosoever shall aid, abet, counsel or procure the commission of any indictable offence ... shall be liable to be tried, indicted and punished as a principal offender".

The Magistrates' Courts Act 1980 s.44 makes similar provision in relation to summary offences. See SECONDARY LIABILITY.

Liability as an accessory after the fact has lapsed, with the creation of a new offence under the Criminal Law Act 1967 s.4 of assisting a person who has committed an arrestable offence.

accessory liability Knowing assistance in breach of trust. Unlike recipient liability (*q.v.*) it is not restitution based but requires a person who dishonestly procures or assists in a breach of trust or fiduciary obligation to make good any resulting loss. Dishonesty involves proof not on a criminal standard but even so a high level of probability beyond that which the reasonable man ought to have appreciated (See *Royal Brunei Airlines Sdn Bhd v Tan* [1995] 2 A.C. 378).

accident In the popular and ordinary sense, accident denotes an unlooked-for mishap or an untoward event which is not expected or designed (*Fenton v Thorley* [1903] A.C. 443 at 448, 451). Inevitable accident means an accident the consequences of which were not intended and could not have been foreseen by the exercise of reasonable care and skill. It is, in general, a ground of exemption from liability in tort. See ACT OF GOD.

In equity, accident means such an unforeseen event, misfortune, loss, act, or omission as is not the result of any negligence or misconduct by the party applying for relief. If a deed or negotiable security were lost, equity would enforce the claimant's rights under the document on his giving, if necessary, a proper bond of indemnity to the defendant.

In criminal law, on a charge of murder, the defence of accident may be a complete defence, or may justify a conviction for manslaughter only. Note the distinction drawn between accidental killing and killing by recklessness or gross negligence.

accident cases The fact that serious injuries have been incurred in accidents is not a "special circumstance" so as to lead to a trial by jury. The judges have evolved scales of damages with which juries would be unfamiliar (*Sims v William Howard & Son Ltd* [1964] 2 Q.B. 409, CA).

accommodation agencies These are regulated by the Accommodation Agencies Act 1953. See *Saunders v Soper* [1975] A.C. 239.

accommodation bill A bill of exchange which a person has signed as drawer, acceptor, or indorser, without receiving value therefor and for the purpose of lending his name to some other person (Bills of Exchange Act 1882 s.28(1)).

accommodation land Land occupied or used in conjunction with other land or premises, as a matter of convenience.

accommodation works Gates, bridges, fences, etc. constructed and maintainable by a railway or canal concern, for the accommodation of the owners or occupiers of adjoining lands.

accomplice Any person who, either as a principal or as an accessory, has been associated with another person in the commission of any offence. The evidence of an accomplice is admissible, but the judge must warn the jury of the danger of convicting on such evidence unless corroborated, and if this warning is omitted a conviction may be quashed. See ACCESSORY; CORROBORATION.

accord and satisfaction The purchase of a release from an obligation, whether arising under contract or tort, by means of any valuable consideration, not being the actual performance of the obligation itself. The accord is the agreement by which the obligation is discharged. The satisfaction is the consideration which makes the agreement operative (*British Russian Gazette Ltd v Associated Newspapers Ltd* [1933] 2 K.B. 616 at 643–644). Thus there is accord and satisfaction where the parties to a contract agree that one of them shall give, and the other shall accept, something different in kind from what he was bound to give or accept under the contract. The general rule is that accord without satisfaction does not discharge a contract after breach, but the promise of something different will discharge the original cause of action, provided the intention was that the new promise itself should be taken in satisfaction and not the actual performance of it (*Morris v Baron* [1918] A.C. 1 at 35).

account, claim for (formerly an action for an account) Proceedings for an account may arise in administrative claims, claims for specific performance and partnership claims. They are assigned to the Chancery Division by the Supreme Court Act 1981 s.61 and Sch.1. The procedure for a claim is governed by CPR Pts 24 and 25.

account, current A running account kept between parties with items on both sides; e.g. a banking account. See APPROPRIATION.

account on the footing of wilful default An account taken on the footing that the accountable party is liable not only for sums actually got in, but for all moneys which, without his wilful neglect or default, might have been possessed or received. Thus, where it is proved that a debt was due to a trust estate, the burden is thrown on the trustee or executor to show why he did not get it in. Similarly, a mortgagee in possession is liable to account not only for the rents and profits he actually receives, but for those he would have received if he had used the greatest possible care.

account payee (or a/c payee) A direction, written or printed on a cheque, to a collecting banker to apply the proceeds to the account of the payee designated on the face of the cheque. Originally the words did not affect the transferability of the cheque. However, the Cheques Act 1992 inserts a new s.81A into the Bills of Exchange Act 1882 by which such cheques cease to be transferable and are valid only between the original parties. The same section preserves the statutory protection of both paying and collecting bankers who have acted honestly and without negligence.

account, settled Settled accounts are accounts that are agreed between the parties. A settled account will be a defence to a claim for an account. There are various grounds upon which a settled account may be reopened including common mistake and fraud.

account stated (1) An admission of a sum of money being due from one person to another, who are under no duty to account to each other, from which a promise to pay is implied by law; e.g. an IOU. It is not necessarily binding: it may be shown to have been given in mistake, or for a debt for which the consideration has failed or was illegal.

8

(2) An account which contains entries on both sides of it, and in which the parties have agreed that the items on one side should be set against the items on the other side, and the balance should be paid. The items on the smaller side are set off and deemed to be paid by the items on the larger side, from which arises a promise for good consideration to pay the balance.

accountable receipt An acknowledgment of the receipt of money, or of any chattel, to be accounted for by the person receiving it.

accountant-general The officer of the Supreme Court in whom funds paid into court are vested: the Clerk of the Crown (*q.v.*) (Supreme Court Act 1981 s.97).

accountant to the Crown Any person who has received money belonging to or for and on behalf of the Crown, and is accountable therefor. See CROWN DEBTS.

accounting, false It is an offence for a person dishonestly or with a view to gain or with intent to cause loss to another (1) to destroy, deface, conceal or falsify any account or any record or document made or required for any accounting purpose; or (2) in furnishing information for any purpose to produce or make use of any account, or any such record or document which to his knowledge is or may be misleading, false or deceptive in a material particular (Theft Act 1968 s.17).

accounts and inquiries Where a claimant, in his claim form, seeks a remedy which includes taking an account or making an inquiry, an application can be made under CPR Pt 24 (claim for summary judgment) by any party to the proceedings for an order directing any necessary accounts or inquiries to be taken or made.

The court may also, by powers given to it under CPR Pt 25 to grant orders for interim remedies, direct that accounts be taken and inquiries made.

Further provisions as to orders for accounts and inquiries are contained in CPR Pt 40.

accounts, falsification of Falsification of accounts is an indictable offence under the Theft Act 1968 ss.17–20.

accredit To furnish a diplomatic agent with papers, called credentials or letters of credit, which certify his public character.

accretion The act of growing on to a thing; usually applied to the gradual accumulation of land from out of the sea or a river. If the accretion to land is imperceptible, it belongs to the owner of the land, but if sudden and considerable it belongs to the Crown. Accretions from the sea are annexed to the relevant parish or community (Local Government Act 1972 s.72). See ACCESSIO; ALLUVION; DERELICTION.

accrual A right is said to accrue when it vests in a person, especially when it does so gradually or without his active intervention, e.g. by lapse of time, or by the determination of a preceding right. When a fund or other property is increased by additions which take place in the ordinary course of nature or by operation of law, the additions are said to accrue either to the original fund or property, or to the person entitled to it. Limitation periods begin to run from the date on which a cause of action accrues. See CAUSE OF ACTION; LIMITATION, STATUTES OF.

accumulation The continual increase of principal by the reinvestment of interest. By the Law of Property Act 1925, replacing the Accumulations Act 1800, accumulation of income is restricted to: (a) the life of the settlor; (b) 21 years thereafter; (c) the duration of the minority of any person or persons living or *en ventre sa mere* at the death of the settlor; (d) the duration of the minority of any person or persons who would have been entitled to the income if of full age (s.164); and (in respect of instruments taking effect on or after July 16, 1964) (e) a term of 21 years from the date of the making of the disposition; and (f) the duration of the minority or respective minorities of any person or persons in

9

being at the date of the disposition (Perpetuities and Accumulations Act 1964 ss.13, 15(5)). If the purpose is the purchase of land, then (d) is the only period admissible (Act of 1925 s.166). The restrictions do not apply to the accumulations for the payment of debts of the settlor, for raising portions for children, and in respect of the produce of timber or wood (ibid. s.164). So far as the direction to accumulate is void for excess, the income belongs to those who would have been entitled thereto if such accumulation had not been directed.

A beneficiary may put an end to a trust for accumulation which is exclusively for his benefit and demand the property when he comes sui juris. The exercise of his right is facilitated by s.14 of the Act of 1964. See PERPETUITY.

accumulative sentence A sentence of imprisonment, which is to commence at the end of another sentence already imposed.

accusare nemo se debet; accusare nemo se debet nisi coram Deo [No one is bound to accuse himself except to God] A witness is not bound to answer any question which in the opinion of the court would incriminate him.

accusatorial procedure Sometimes known as the adversary procedure. The common law principle which places the responsibility for collecting and presenting evidence on the party who seeks to introduce that evidence. Furthermore by the common law system of pleading (*q.v.*) the defendant is bound only to refute the allegations made by the claimant in the pleadings in order to succeed. Contrast and see INQUISITORIAL PROCEDURE See also STATEMENT OF CASE.

accused One charged with an offence.

acknowledgement of debt An admission in writing signed by the debtor or his agent, that a debt is due, which revives a debt which is statute barred. By the Limitation Act 1980 s.29, where a right of action has accrued in respect of a debt and there is such an admission made, the right of action is deemed to have accrued on the date of the acknowledgement. See LIMITATION, STATUTES OF.

acknowledgement of right to production of documents A writing given by a person who retains possession of title deeds which cannot be delivered over to a purchaser. The possessor is obliged to produce them for proving or supporting the title of any person entitled to the benefit of the acknowledgement, and to deliver to him true copies of or extracts from them (Law of Property Act 1925 s.64).

acknowledgement of service Where particulars of claim have been served upon a defendant he will receive a response pack which includes a form for acknowledging service of the claim. The defendant may by CPR 10.1(3) file an acknowledgement of service where he is unable to file a defence within 14 days after service of the particulars of claim, or where he wishes to dispute the court's jurisdiction. By CPR 10.3(1) the acknowledgement of service must be filed within 14 days of service of the claim form, where the particulars of claim are served on or with the claim form, or within 14 days of service of the particulars of claim where they are served after the claim form.

For many years an Acknowledgement of Service has been the document by which service of a Petition for divorce in the county court (*q.v.*) was acknowledged, see Family Proceedings Rules 1991 as amended, r.2.9.

acknowledgement of wills If a will is not signed in the presence of witnesses, the testator must acknowledge his signature in their presence (Wills Act 1837 s.9).

acquiescence Assent to an infringement of rights, either expressed, or implied from conduct, by which the right to equitable relief is normally lost. See LACHES.

acquis communautaire The body of European Community (*q.v.*) law and practice which applies to all Member States (*q.v.*).

acquittal Discharge from prosecution upon a verdict of not guilty, or on a successful plea of pardon or of autrefois acquit or autrefois convict (*q.v.*). Acquittal is a bar to any such subsequent prosecution.

acquittance A written acknowledgment of the payment of a sum of money or debt due.

act in law An act of a party or person having legal effect; e.g. the making of a contract or conveyance. See also ACT OF LAW.

act in pais [Act in the country] An act or transaction done or made otherwise than in the course of a record or deed.

act of attainder See ATTAINDER.

act of God An accident or event which happens independently of human intervention and due to natural causes, such as storm, earthquake, etc. which no human foresight can provide against, and of which human prudence is not bound to recognise the possibility. It will relieve from absolute liability in tort.

act of grace An Act of Parliament giving a general and free pardon.

act of indemnity An Act passed to legalise transactions which, when they took place, were illegal, or to exempt particular persons from pecuniary penalties or punishments for acts done in the public service, as in time of war, which were breaches of the law. The Indemnity Act 1920 restricted the taking of legal proceedings in respect of such acts.

act of law The effect of the operation of law, e.g. succession of property or intestacy. See also ACT IN LAW.

Act of Parliament The legislative decree of the Queen in Parliament; a statute. There are the following kinds of Acts: Public, General, Local, Personal and Private. Acts are now given chapter numbers by reference to the calender year in which they are passed (Acts of Parliament Numbering and Citation Act 1962).
  An Act comes into force on the day on which it receives the Royal Assent (*q.v.*) unless otherwise provided, with effect from the last moment of the previous day (Acts of Parliament (Commencement) Act 1793). See APPOINTED DAY; ROYAL ASSENT; STATUTE.
  Legislation coming before Parliament must now be accompanied by a statement from the relevant Minister indicating whether or not it is compatible with Convention rights (*q.v.*) under the European Convention on Human Rights. See HUMAN RIGHTS; STATEMENT OF COMPATIBILITY.

Act of Settlement 1700 The statute (12 & 13 Wm. 3 c.2), which enacted:
  (a) That after the death of William III and of Princess Anne (afterwards Queen Anne) and in default of issue of either of them, the Crown should descend to Sophia, Electress of Hanover and the heirs of her body, being Protestants.
  (b) That the Sovereign shall be a member of the Church of England as by law established and shall vacate the throne on becoming or marrying a Roman Catholic.
  (c) That judges should hold office during good behaviour and be paid fixed salaries, but might be removed from office on the address of both Houses of Parliament. See now, Supreme Court Act 1981 s.11.
  (d) That no pardon under the Great Seal of England should be pleadable to an impeachment (*q.v.*).

act of state An act of the Executive as a matter of policy performed in the course of its relations with another state, including its relations with the subjects of that state, unless they are temporarily within the allegiance of the Crown. It is an exercise of sovereign power which cannot be challenged, controlled or interfered with by municipal courts. Its sanction is not that of law but that of sovereign power and whatever it be, municipal courts must accept it, as it is, without question (*Salaman v Secretary of State for India* [1906] 1 K.B. 613 at 639; *Sobhuza II v Miller* [1926] A.C. 518). It includes an act done by an agent of the Crown whether previously authorised, or subsequently ratified (*Buron v Denman* [1848] 2 Exch. Rep. 167).

Act of Supremacy The statute (1 Eliz. 1 c.1), passed in 1558 to establish the supremacy of the Crown in ecclesiastical matters.

Act of Uniformity An Act of Parliament regulating Public Worship. See particularly the statute (14 Car. 2 c.4) passed in 1662, which legalised the Book of Common Prayer and which was repealed (except for ss.10 and 15) by the Church of England (Worship and Doctrine) Measure 1974 which permits the General Synod (*q.v.*) to sanction alternative forms of service.

acte clair A term used to refer to a matter which is claimed to be "so clear" as not to require argument.

actio [Roman law] An action; the right of suing before a judge for what is due. Also proceedings or form of procedure for the enforcement of such right. The main forms of actio were as follows:

arbitraria: the formula directed the judge, if he found the plaintiff's claim valid, to make an order that the defendant should make amends to the plaintiff; e.g. to give up the thing claimed, and at the same time fixing the sum that the defendant ought to pay the plaintiff in case he should fail to make amends as ordered.

bonae fidei: an equitable action. The formula required the judge to take into account considerations of what was fair and right as between the parties.

directa: an action based immediately on the very text of the law, or arising from an essential part of the execution of a contract.

hypothecaria or *quasi-Serviana*: allowed in all cases where an owner retained possession, but agreed that his property should be a security for a debt.

in personam: a personal action, in which the plaintiff claimed that the defendant ought to give, do or make good, something to or for him.

in rem: a real action, in which the plaintiff claimed that, as against all the world, the thing in dispute was his.

(in rem) confessoria: an action to try a right to a servitude, brought by the owner of the dominant land against the owner of the servient land.

(in rem) negativa: an action brought by the owner of the servient land, who alleged that his adversary was not entitled to a servitude which he claimed; or that he himself was entitled to his land free from the servitude claimed.

mixta: a mixed action; an action with a view both to the recovery of a thing and to the enforcement of a penalty that was both real and personal, or rather that was entirely personal but in one respect more or less similar to a real action; e.g. *familiae excisundae*, which involved the adjudication of particular things to the parties. "Actions are mixed in which either party is plaintiff."

noxalis: an action brought against a master for delicts committed by his slave, or for damage done from wantonness, heat or savage nature, by his tame animals. The master could free himself from liability by delivering up the offending slave or animal to the person aggrieved.

praejudicialius: an action preliminary to proceedings with a view to ascertaining a fact which it was necessary to establish before going on with the case; as whether a man was free or a freedman, or was the son of his reputed father.

quod metus causa: open to a person who had alienated property or undertaken an obligation under the constraint of intimidation (*metus*) or violence (*vis*).

serviana: an action which gave the landlord of a farm a right to take possession of the stock of his tenant for rent due, when the tenant had agreed that the stock should be a security for the rent.

stricti juris: strict law; the formula limited the attention of the judge to the purely legal considerations involved.

utilis: an action granted by the Praetor, in the exercise of his judicial authority, by means of an extension of an existing action to persons or cases that did not come within its original scope.

actio personalis moritur cum persona [A personal action dies with the person] No executor or administrator could sue or be sued for any tort committed against, or by, the deceased in his lifetime (except injuries to property); the right of action in tort was destroyed by the death of the injured or injuring party, because an act of tort was regarded originally as purely punitive and only later as compensatory. The rule is now confined to causes of action for defamation (Law Reform (Miscellaneous Provisions) Act 1934 s.1(1), as amended). Exemplary damages are not recoverable (s.1(2), as amended).

action Replaced in the Civil Procedure Rules (CPR) (*q.v.*) by the claim (*q.v.*). Prior to the CPR it was a civil proceeding commenced by writ or in such other manner as was prescribed by rules of court.

In early times actions were divided into criminal and civil, the former being proceedings in the name of the Crown, and the latter those in the name of a subject.

"Action" generally meant a proceeding in one of the common law courts, as opposed to suit in equity. Actions were divided into real, personal, and mixed: real (or feudal) actions being those for the specific recovery of lands or other realty; personal actions, those for the recovery of a debt, personal chattel, or damages; and mixed actions, those for the recovery of real property, together with damages for a wrong connected with it.

A plaintiff at common law had to sue by one or other of certain forms of actions or writs. They were: (1) on contract: (a) covenant, being on a deed alone; (b) assumpsit, being on simple contract only; (c) debt, being either on a deed or a simple contract; (d) *scire facias*, being on a judgment; (e) account; and (f) annuity; (2) in tort: (g) trespass *quare clausum fregit*, to real property, and trespass *de bonis asportatis*, to goods, and trespass *vi et armis*, to the person; (h) case; (i) trover; (j) detinue; and (k) replevin; (3) the mixed action of ejectment.

The Common Law Procedure Act 1852 provided that it should not be necessary to mention any form or cause of action in any writ of summons, and all forms of action are now abolished. See also ACTIONS, REAL; ACTIONS, SUCCESSIVE; EJECTMENT; PENAL ACTION.

action area An area designated by a local authority as an area selected for the commencement, during a prescribed period, of comprehensive treatment by development, redevelopment or improvement. See also SIMPLIFIED PLANNING ZONE; ENTERPRISE ZONE.

action in rem An action in the Admiralty Court commenced by the arrest of the res, the ship.

action on the case The writ of trespass was issuable for wrongs done to person, land, or chattels, and also in a number of unclassified cases, when the writ was said to be issued *super casum* [on the case], because the particular circumstances of the case were set out in the writ. Later, the writs of trespass and trespass on the case separated out, and the action of trespass on the case was called "action on the case". From this action, "the fertile mother of actions" a number of actions were evolved not coming under specific heads. See IN CONSIMILI CASU.

actiones nominatae The approved forms of writs. See ACTION ON THE CASE.

actions, real Proceedings at common law by means of which a freeholder could recover his land: (1) actions commenced by the Writ of Right to decide the question of title to land. Actions were delayed by dilatory pleas (essoins), and trial by battle was possible; (2) Possessory Assizes, to decide questions of disseisin, or recent dispossession; (3) Writs of Entry. The real actions were displaced by the action of ejectment (*q.v.*) and were largely abolished by the Real Property Limitation Act 1833. See ACTION.

actions, successive All damages from the same cause of action must be recovered in one action, except: (1) where there is unaccrued or unknown damage at the time the first action is brought; (2) where there is the violation by the same act of more than one distinct right; (3) where there are distinct wrongful acts; (4) where there are continuing injuries; in which cases further, or successive, actions may be brought. It is possible for there to be an award of provisional damages in personal injuries actions, where it is probable that the condition of the claimant will change significantly at some time after judgment is given, Supreme Court Act 1981 s.32A.

active trust A trust calling for actual duties by the trustee. See BARE TRUSTEE.

Acts of Union With (1) Wales: the statute 1536 (27 Hen. 8 c.26); (2) Scotland: 1706, 1707; (3) Ireland: 1800. See DEVOLUTION; WELSH ASSEMBLY.

actus non facit reum, nisi mens sit rea See ACTUS REUS; MENS REA.

actus reus The elements of an offence excluding those which concern the mind of the accused. The phrase:
"derives, I believe, from a mistranslation of the Latin aphorism *Actus non facit reum nisi mens sit rea* Properly translated this means 'an act does not make a man guilty of a crime unless his mind be also guilty.' It is thus not the *actus* which is *reus* but the man and his mind respectively."
(*Haughton v Smith* [1973] 3 All E.R. 1109, per Lord Hailsham, L.C.)

ad avizandum [To be deliberated upon]

ad colligenda bona [To collect the goods] A form of grant of administration where the estate is of a perishable or precarious nature, and where regular administration cannot be granted at once.

ad diem [To the day appointed]

ad eundum [To the same class]

ad hoc [For this purpose]

ad idem [Of the same mind; agreed] See CONSENSUS AD IDEM.

ad interim [In the meanwhile]

ad litem [For the suit] See GUARDIAN AD LITEM; LITIGATION FRIEND.

ad medium filum viae (or aquae) [To the middle line of the road (or stream)] The normal boundary of lands separated by a road or river.

ad quod damnum [To what damage] A writ formerly issued to a sheriff: (a) before the Crown granted a right to hold a fair, market, etc. within the bailiwick or area, for which the sheriff acted: it directed the sheriff to inquire what damage might be done by such grant; (b) before a licence was given by the Crown to alienate lands in mortmain; the licence did not issue unless a return *ad damnum nullis* was made so as to show that no man would be injured; (c) before a licence to make or divert a road was given.

ad referendum [For further consideration]

ad rem [To the point]

ad sectam [At the suit of]

ad summam [In conclusion]

ad terminum qui preterit Writ of entry which lay for a lessor and his heirs when a lease had been made for a term of years or for a life or lives, and after the expiration of the lease, the lands were withheld from the lessor or his heirs by the tenant or by some other person. Abolished by the Real Property Limitation Act 1833 s.36.

ad valorem [According to the value] Duties which are graduated according to the value of the subject-matter taxed.

adaptation It is an infringement of copyright to adapt a literary, dramatic or musical work, a computer program or a database, without the permission of the copyright owner. Adaptation in relation to a literary or dramatic work means: (i) a translation of the work; (ii) a version of a dramatic work in which it is converted into a non-dramatic work, or of a non-dramatic work which is converted into a dramatic work; (iii) a version of the work in which the story or action is conveyed wholly or mainly by means of pictures in a form suitable for reproduction in a book, or in a newspaper, magazine or similar periodical.

Adaptation in relation to a computer program means an arrangement or altered version of the program or a translation of it.

Adaptation in relation to a database means an arrangement or altered version of the database or a translation of it.

Adaptation in relation to a musical work means an arrangement or transcription of the work (Copyright, Designs and Patents Act 1988 s.21).

additionality The principle in Community law whereby the governments of Member States receiving moneys from Community funds, earmarked for specific purposes, must treat those moneys as funds additional to any moneys or grants the government of a Member State may disburse for the same purposes. The UK Government now recognises this principle, albeit reluctantly.

address for service This is the address for service within the jurisdiction where all documents, other than those to be personally served, must be served.

A party must give an address for service within the jurisdiction (CPR 6.5(2)).Where a party (a) does not give the business address of his solicitor as his address for service; and (b) resides or carries on business within the jurisdiction, he must give his residence or place of business as his address for service (CPR 6.5(3)).

Where (a) a solicitor is acting for the party to be served; and (b) the document to be served is not the claim form, the party's address for service is the business address of his solicitor (CPR 6.5(5)).

Where (a) no solicitor is acting for the party to be served and (b) the party has not given an address for service, the document must be sent or transmitted to, or left at, the place shown in the Table contained in CPR 6.5(6), (CPR 6.5(6)).

The defendant's address for service of the claim form may be the business address of the defendant's solicitor if he is authorised to accept service on behalf of the defendant but not otherwise (CPR 6.13(2)).

Prior to the CPR the address for service was the address, within the jurisdiction, where writs, notices, summonses, orders, etc. could be served. An address for service as regards the plaintiff had to be stated in the endorsement upon the writ (Ord. 6, r.5); and as regards the defendant, in the acknowledgment of service (Ord. 12, r.3).

ademption The complete or partial extinction or withholding of a legacy (but not of a devise of real estate) by some act of the testator during his life other than revocation by a testamentary instrument; e.g. the state of an object specifically bequeathed. Where a father or person in loco parentis provides a portion by his will by a legacy, and subsequently in his life makes or covenants to make another gift also amounting to a portion, the legacy is adeemed, either wholly or in part.

adherent Being adherent to the Queen's enemies in the realm, giving them aid or comfort in the realm, or elsewhere, is treason (Treason Act 1351). See *R. v Casement* [1917] 1 K.B. 98 at 137.

adjectival or adjective law So much of the law as relates to practice and procedure. (Bentham.)

adjourned summons A summons which stands adjourned for further hearing.

adjournment The suspension or putting off of the hearing of a case to a future time or day. See SINE DIE.

adjudication (1) A judgment or decision of the court.

(2) The decision of the Commissioners of Inland Revenue as to the liability of a document to stamp duty.

(3) A form of Alternative Dispute Resolution (*q.v.*). It is used widely in the construction industry and allows disputes to be determined by an adjudicator comparatively swiftly while work progresses. The adjudicator's decision is binding, unless and until the dispute is finally determined by legal proceedings, arbitration (*q.v.*) or the agreement of the parties. The parties may, however, accept the adjudicator's decision as finally determining the dispute. By virtue of the Housing Grants, Construction and Regeneration Act 1996 there must be an adjudication provision in every "construction contract" (as defined by the Act). In default of such a contractual provision the legislation supplies an adjudication scheme (see Scheme for Construction Contracts (England and Wales) Regulations 1998).

Adjudicator to HM Land Registry The Lord Chancellor must appoint an Adjudicator to HM Land Registry. Disputed applications to the Land Registry are to be referred to the Adjudicator. The Adjudicator has power to determine the matter in dispute, or to direct the commencement of court proceedings for the purpose of obtaining the court's decision on the matter (Land Registration Act 2002 Pt 11). The process for referrals to the Adjudicator is set out in the Land Registration (Referral to the Adjudicator to HM Land Registry) Rules 2003.

adjunctio [Roman law] A form of *accessio*; the joining of materials belonging to one person with something belonging to another; e.g. when one wove another's purple into his own vestment.

adjusters Average adjusters are employed by marine insurers to compute the general average and particular average losses arising out of an insured marine loss. There is a small profession of people engaged in the assessment of fire damage claims known as loss adjusters.

adjustment The operation of settling and ascertaining the amount which the assured, after allowances and deductions are made, is entitled to receive under a policy of marine insurance, and some fire insurance policies, and of fixing the proportion which each underwriter is liable to pay. See AVERAGE.

admeasurement of dower The writ in an action formerly brought by an heir against the widow of an ancestor who was alleged to withhold more land for her dower than she was entitled to.

admeasurement of pasture The writ in an action formerly brought by one commoner against another commoner alleged to have put more beasts on the common than was lawful.

administration action Prior to the CPR, an action assigned to the Chancery Division to secure the due administration of the estate of a deceased person by the court. Proceedings could be begun by a writ or an originating summons taken out by a creditor or any person interested in the estate as legatee, devisee, next-of-kin, etc. or by the personal representative (*q.v.*) himself (Ord. 85).

The effect of an order of the court for the general administration of the estate was that the personal representatives could not exercise their powers without the sanction of the court and the creditor could not sue the personal representatives for a debt. The court could require the administrator to produce sureties: See Supreme Court Act 1981 s.120; no such guarantee was required from an executor. See ADMINISTRATION CLAIM.

administration claim A claim for the administration under the direction of the court of the estate of a deceased person or for the execution under the direction of the court of a trust (CPR Pt 64).

Prior to the CPR, it was the practice to commence proceedings by writ or originating summons. Proceedings may now be commenced by claim form (*q.v.*) under CPR Pts 7 and 8. See ADMINISTRATION ACTION.

administration of estates The collection of the assets of a deceased person, payment of the debts, and distribution of the surplus to the persons beneficially entitled by the deceased's personal representatives (*q.v.*).

Small estates may be administered by the Public Trustee (*q.v.*) if he sees no reason to the contrary. If the estate is insolvent it may be administered in bankruptcy, in accordance with the rules made under s.421 of the Insolvency Act 1986. See ADMINISTRATION ACTION.

The order in which the assets of the deceased are applied in payment of debts, where the estate is solvent, is (subject to directions in the will):

(1) Property undisposed of by will.

(2) Property not specifically devised or bequeathed, but included in a residuary gift.

(3) Property specifically appropriated or devised or bequeathed for the payment of debts.

(4) Property charged with the payment of debts.

(5) The fund retained to meet pecuniary legacies.

(6) Property specifically devised.

(7) Property appointed by will under a general power.

Where the assets are insufficient for the payment of debts, i.e. where the estate is insolvent, the debts are payable in the following order:

(1) Funeral, testamentary and administration expenses.

(2) As in bankruptcy, see Insolvency Act 1986 s.421 and the orders made thereunder.

administration order (1) An order providing for the administration by the county court (*q.v.*) of a debtor's estate. The total debts must not exceed the limit of the current county court limit. See County Courts Act 1984 s.112.

(2) An order of the court appointing a person as administrator of a company. The court may make an administration order only if satisfied that: (a) the company is or is likely to become unable to pay its debts and (b) that the administration order is reasonably likely to achieve the purpose of the administration. Insolvency Act 1986 Sch.B1, paras 10 & 11 (as substituted by the Enterprise Act 2002 s.248 and Sch.16). See ADMINISTRATOR.

Administrative Court The Administrative Court is that part of the High Court which deals with applications for judicial review. If the claim is proceeding in London then the documents must be filed at the Administrative Court of the Queens Bench Division. See CPR Pt 54.

Administrative Justice & Tribunals Council Set up under the Tribunals, Courts and Enforcement Act 2007 to replace the Council on Tribunals (*q.v.*) the AJTC's principal functions are to keep under review the administrative justice system and to consider ways to make the system accessible, fair and efficient. It will also review and report on the constitution and working of listed tribunals and of statutory inquiries.

administrative law The law relating to the organisation, powers and duties of administrative authorities (Dicey). The subordinate branch of constitutional law consisting of the body of rules which govern the detailed exercise of executive functions by the officers or public authorities to whom they are entrusted by the Constitution; for example, the law relating to town and country planning.

administrative receiver A receiver or manager of the whole, or substantially the whole of a company's property appointed by the holder of any debenture of the company secured by a floating charge (*q.v.*) or by such a charge and other securities, Insolvency Act 1986 s.29. Administrative receivership is an insolvency procedure, see ibid. Pt III.

administrative tribunals Tribunals (*q.v.*) concerned with administrative law (*q.v.*). They form part of the machinery of state but function as adjudicative bodies, e.g. Rent Tribunal, Employment Tribunal. See the Tribunals and Inquiries Act 1992, as amended by the Tribunals, Courts and Enforcement Act 2007.

administrator (1) A person appointed to manage the property of another, e.g. the person to whom a grant of administration is made. See LETTERS OF ADMINISTRATION.
(2) A person appointed to manage the affairs, business and property of a company: Insolvency Act 1986 s.8 and Sch.B1 para.1(1) (as substituted by the Enterprise Act 2002 s.248 and Sch.16). See ADMINISTRATION ORDER.

administratrix A female person to whom letters of administration are granted.

Admiral or Lord High Admiral An officer entrusted by the Crown with the charge of the seas, with jurisdiction over naval and maritime matters and over wrongful acts committed on the high seas or in navigable rivers, exercised by means of the Court of the Admiral. The criminal jurisdiction of this court was ultimately transferred to the Central Criminal Court and the Judges of Assize. The civil jurisdiction of the court, which became the High Court of Admiralty, is vested in the Admiralty Court (*q.v.*). The naval functions of the Lord High Admiral have, since 1827, been exercised by the commissioners for executing the office, i.e. the Admiralty (*q.v.*).

Admiralty The Lords Commissioners of the Admiralty who have succeeded to the administrative or naval functions, but not the judicial, of the Lord High Admiral. The Board of Admiralty consisted of the First Lord of the Admiralty, who was a member of the Government, the First, Second, Third and Fourth Sea Lords, who were naval officers, and a civilian, the Civil Lord of the Admiralty. They are now merged in the Ministry of Defence.

Admiralty Court A court, within the Queen's Bench Division of the High Court, created by the Administration of Justice Act 1970 and now governed by ss.20–24 of the Supreme Court Act 1981. Its jurisdiction comprises the Admiralty and prize business formerly the function of the Probate, Divorce and Admiralty Division of the High Court. Certain county courts, designated by the Lord Chancellor, have a limited Admiralty jurisdiction under ss.26 and 27 of the County Courts Act 1984.

Admiralty, droits of When a state of war exists, enemy goods seized in English ports go to the Crown as *droits* of Admiralty. Formerly, derelict ships and wreckage on the high seas were condemned as *droits* of Admiralty; they are now dealt with under the Merchant Shipping Acts.

admission order A disposal option available to the Crown Court following findings that (a) the accused is unfit to plead; and (b) did the act or made the omission charged (Criminal Procedure (Insanity) Act 1964 s.5, as amended by Criminal Procedure (Insanity and Unfitness to Plead) Act 1991 s.3, and Domestic Violence, Crime and Victims Act 2004 s.24(1)). The effect of an admission order is comparable to that of a hospital order made under Mental Health Act 1983 s.37. The option is also available to both the Crown Court and the Magistrates

Court following the special verdict of not guilty by reason of insanity. See supervision and treatment order.

admissions A party to proceedings may admit the truth of the whole or any part of another party's case at any stage of the proceedings (CPR 14.1(1)). He may do this by giving evidence in writing, such as in a statement of case or by letter (CPR 14.1(2)). Where a party makes an admission the other party is entitled to apply for judgment on the admission (CPR 14.3(1)). Judgment shall be such judgment as it appears to the court that the applicant is entitled to on the admission (CPR 14.3(2)).

Where the admission is in relation to a money claim and is made within 14 days of service of the claim form, or, where the particulars of claim are served after the claim form, within 14 days of service of the particulars of claim, there are additional rules providing a mechanism for agreeing the rate and time by which the admitted claim is to be paid (CPR 14.2, 14.4, 14.5, 14.6, 14.7).

Prior to the CPR, admissions could be made by or on behalf of a party to suit orally, in writing, or could be inferred from conduct. They were admissible in evidence, if relevant, as against his interest. They could be either formal or informal. (1) Formal admissions for the purpose of the trial could be made on pleadings, as, e.g. where a contract and the breach were admitted (Ord. 27). (2) Informal admissions could be made before or during the proceedings.

In criminal proceedings admissions may be by plea of guilty, by a statement of facts by the accused, or in the form of a confession (*q.v.*).

admittance The lord of a manor was said to admit a person as a tenant of copyhold lands forming part of the manor when he accepted him as tenant of those lands in place of the former tenant; e.g. on the surrender, devise, or death intestate of the former tenant. Copyholds were abolished by the Law of Property Act 1922 on January 1, 1926.

admittendo clerico A writ directed to the bishop requiring him to admit a clerk.

adopted child A child in respect of which an adoption order has been made. See ADOPTION OF CHILDREN.

adoptio [Roman law.] The transfer of a person from the *potestas* of one man to that of another: (1) by imperial rescript, under which a man may adopt men or women sui juris (*adrogatio* (*q.v.*)); (2) by the authority of a magistrate, under which a man may adopt men or women *alieni juris*.

adoption of children Adoption is the legal process by which a child becomes a permanent and full member of a new family. Adoption in England and Wales is governed by the Adoption and Children Act 2002 and related secondary legislation. Adoption is effected by a court order which vests parental responsibility (*q.v.*) for a child in the adopter or adopter(s) and extinguishes the parental responsibility of the birth parents (Adoption and Children Act 2002 s.46). An adopted child is treated in law (save for limited purposes such as affinity under the Marriage Act 1949, under the Sexual Offences Act 2003 and under the provisions of the British Nationality Act 1981) as if he had been born as a child of the adopters (s.67, 2002 Act).

adoption of contract The acceptance of it is binding, notwithstanding some defect which entitles the party to repudiate it.

adoptive act An Act of Parliament which does not become operative until adopted by a public body or a particular number of voters in an area.

adrogatio [Roman law] The oldest form of adoption, applicable only in adoption of persons sui juris. Originally it took place under the sanction of the Pontifex, and in the *comitia curiata*, as an act of legislation; superseded under the Empire by the imperial rescript.

adult See FULL AGE.

adulteration The mixing with any substance intended to be sold, of any ingredient which is dangerous to health, or which makes the substance something other than that as which it is sold or intended to be sold. It is an offence under the Food and Drugs Acts and other Acts.

adultery Voluntary sexual intercourse between persons of the opposite sex, one of whom is married to a third party.

That the respondent has committed adultery and the petitioner finds it intolerable to live with the respondent may constitute proof that a marriage has broken down (Matrimonial Causes Act 1973 s.1). See DIVORCE.

In any civil proceedings the fact that a person has been found guilty of adultery in any matrimonial proceedings is admissible in evidence (Civil Evidence Act 1968 s.12).

Adultery was formerly a tort actionable by writ of trespass in an action of criminal conversation (*q.v.*). The action was abolished by the Law Reform (Miscellaneous Provisions) Act 1970 s.4.

advancement, equitable doctrine of If a purchase or investment is made by a father, or person in loco parentis, in the name of a child or by any person under an equitable obligation to support or make provision for another, a rebuttable presumption arises that it was intended as an advancement (that is, for the benefit of the child), so as to rebut what would otherwise be the ordinary presumption in such cases of a resulting trust in favour of the person who paid the money. The doctrine also applies to a purchase made in the name of a wife (*Tinker v Tinker* [1970] 1 All E.R. 540).

advancement, power of Trustees of trusts constituted after 1925 may apply capital moneys for the advancement or benefit, as they think fit, of any person entitled to the capital of the trust property; provided that the advancement does not exceed one-half of the presumptive or vested share or interest of the beneficiary in the trust property, and is brought into account as part of such share, if and when, the beneficiary becomes entitled to a share of capital (Trustee Act 1925 s.32). Land may be advanced (*Re Collard's Will Trusts* [1961] Ch. 293).

adventure Formerly, the sending of goods abroad at owner's risk in a ship in the charge of a supercargo or agent who was to dispose of them to the best advantage. An adventure in the nature of trade is treated as a trade under Sch.D to the Income and Corporation Taxes Act 1988 s.832(1).

adverse possession An occupation of land inconsistent with the right of the true owner: the possession of those against whom a right of action has accrued to the true owner. It is actual possession in the absence of possession by the rightful owner, and without lawful title. Time does not begin to run under the Statutes of Limitation unless there is some person in adverse possession of the land (Limitation Act 1980 s.15, Sch.1, para.8).

If the adverse possession continues, the effect at the expiration of the prescribed period is that not only the remedy but the title of the former owner is extinguished (ibid. s.17). The person in adverse possession gains a new possessory title which cannot normally exceed in extent or duration the interest of the former owner. See LIMITATION, STATUTES OF.

adverse witness A witness adverse to the party examining him: he may with leave of the court be cross-examined by the party calling him. See HOSTILE WITNESS.

advertisements Offering a reward for the return of stolen property and promising that no questions will be asked, constitutes an offence. The printer and publisher are also liable. (Theft Act 1968 s.23). An advertisement of goods for sale is an invitation to make offers, and is not itself an offer. The display of advertisements is subject to control under the Town and Country Planning legislation. See PLANNING.

Many forms of advertisement are subject to control or prohibition, in the public interest. These include: regulation of advertisements relating to consumer credit and consumer hire, Consumer Credit Act 1974 ss.43–47, and Consumer Credit (Advertisement) Regulations 2004; regulation of advertising of insurance, deposit taking and investment falls within the financial promotion regime under the Financial Services and Markets Act 2000.

Discriminatory advertisements are unlawful under the Race Relations Act 1976, the Sex Discrimination Act 1975, the Disability Discrimination Act 1995 and the Employment Equality (Age) Regulations 2006.

advice See BARRISTER'S OPINION.

advice, letter of A letter from one merchant or banker to another concerning a business transaction in which both are engaged.

advice note The document sent by a railway undertaking to the consignee intimating that his goods have arrived and informing him that if the goods are not fetched away the railway undertaking will only keep them as warehousemen and not as carriers, thereby reducing their liability to liability only for negligence.

Advisory, Conciliation and Arbitration Service (ACAS) A body originally set up under the Employment Protection Act 1975 whose function is to improve industrial relations, Trade Union and Labour Relations (Consolidation) Act 1992 ss.209–214. It conciliates, arbitrates and advises in industrial disputes and may issue codes of practice (ibid., ss.199–202).

advocate One who pleads the cause of another in a judicial tribunal; barristers or solicitors. Formerly, a member of the College of Advocates, with the exclusive right of practising in the Ecclesiastical and Admiralty Courts. The College of Advocates was abolished by the Court of Probate Act 1857.

advocate, Crown Formerly the second law officer of the Crown in the Court of Admiralty.

Advocate General An officer of the Court of Justice of the European Communities (*q.v.*). The position has no exact parallel in common law jurisdictions save possibly amicus curiae (*q.v.*), since the Advocate General is neither a judge nor an advocate for one of the parties. He ranks as a member of the court, and makes reasoned submissions to the judges on matters before the court for decision.

Advocate, Lord See LORD ADVOCATE.

Advocates, Faculty of The body which has the exclusive right of appointing advocates or members of the Scottish Bar.

advow, avow, or avouch To vouch; to call on the feudal lord to defend his tenant's right.

advowson The perpetual right of presentation to a church or benefice being a rectory or vicarage. It is the right of patronage. An advowson is an incorporeal hereditament which will pass on a conveyance and previously could be registered at HM Land Registry. A right of patronage of a benefice is not capable of sale and any transfer for valuable consideration is void (see Patronage (Benefices) Measure 1986 s.3(1)). A right of patronage vested in an ecclesiastical corporation shall not be transferred to any body or person unless (a) the consent of the bishop or, if the bishop is the proposed transferor, the consent of the archbishop has been obtained; or (b) the transfer is made by a pastoral scheme or order (Patronage (Benefices) Measure 1986 s.3(2)). See also ADVOWSON APPENDANT; ADVOWSON IN GROSS.

advowson appendant An advowson annexed to a manor or some corporeal hereditament. Every advowson which immediately before January 1, 1989 (the date the Patronage (Benefices) Measure 1986 s.32(1) came into force) is appendant to any land or manor is severed from that land or manor and becomes an advowson in gross which (a) in the case of land belonging at that date to a charity belongs to that charity; (b) in any other case belongs in his personal capacity to the person who at that date is the owner in fee simple of that land or the land of that manor (Patronage (Benefices) Measure 1986 s.32(1)). Every advowson which immediately before January 1, 1989 was appendant to any rectory, not being a rectory with cure of souls, is severed from that rectory and becomes an advowson in gross belonging in his personal capacity to the person who at that date is the rector of that rectory (Patronage (Benefices) Measure 1986 s.32(2)). See also ADVOWSON; ADVOWSON IN GROSS.

advowson in gross An advowson belonging to an individual, and not annexed to a corporeal hereditament. See also ADVOWSON; ADVOWSON APPENDANT.

aequitas Equity (*q.v.*).

aequitas sequitur legem [Equity follows the law]

affidavit Defined in the Glossary to the CPR as "a written sworn statement of evidence". The person making the statement is called the deponent. The affidavit must indicate which of the statements made in it are made from the deponent's own knowledge, which are matters of information or belief, and the source for any matters of information or belief. See CPR Pt 32 PD.

Evidence must be given by affidavit instead of or in addition to a witness statement if this is required by the court, by a provision contained in any other rule, by a practice direction or by any other enactment. A witness may give evidence by affidavit at a hearing other than the trial if he chooses to do so but may not be able to recover the additional costs of using an affidavit without a court order. See CPR 32.15.

affidavit of documents See DISCOVERY.

affiliation order This was an order that a man adjudged to be the father of the illegitimate child of a single woman, a widow or married woman living apart from her husband, should pay a weekly sum for the maintenance and education of the child (Affiliation Proceedings Act 1957). Such affiliation proceedings were abolished by the Family Law Reform Act 1987, except that orders made before April 1, 1989 remain in force. These affiliation proceedings and orders are replaced by maintenance proceedings and orders under the Children Act 1989 Sch.1 and the Child Support Acts 1991 and 1995.

affinity Relationship by marriage; the relationship between a husband and his wife's kindred, and between the wife and her husband's kindred; but there is no affinity between a person and the relations by marriage of his or her spouse. The degrees of affinity within which a marriage is void are set out in the Marriage Act 1949 s.1, Sch.1, as amended most recently by the Marriage (Prohibited Degrees of Relationship) Act 1986, and the Civil Partnership Act 2004.

affirm (1) To elect to abide by a voidable contract; (2) to uphold a judgment; (3) to be allowed to give evidence without taking the oath, either on the ground that taking an oath is contrary to the person's religious belief, or that the person has no religious belief (Oaths Act 1978 s.5(l)). An affirmation may be made where it is not practicable to administer an oath as required by a person's religious belief.

affray A person is guilty of affray if he uses or threatens unlawful violence towards another and his conduct is such as would cause a person of reasonable firmness present at the scene to fear for his personal safety. Affray may be committed in private as well as public places (Public Order Act 1986 s.3).

affreightment A contract made either by charterparty or by bill of lading, by which a shipowner agrees to carry goods in his ship for reward. See also FREIGHT.

after-care under supervision Also known as Supervised Discharge. Where a patient (who has attained 16 years) is liable to be detained in hospital for treatment for his or her mental disorder, he or she may be made liable to be supervised on leaving hospital with a view to him or her securing those after-care services which must be provided for him or her by reason of s.117 of the Mental Health Act 1983, provided the criteria set out in s.25A of the Mental Health Act 1983 are satisfied. The Mental Health Act 1983 does not define "after-care services".

age discrimination Discrimination in employment and vocational training on the basis of age is unlawful under the Employment Equality (Age) Regulations 2006. See also RETIREMENT AGE.

age, full See FULL AGE.

agent A person employed to act on behalf of another. An act of an agent, done within the scope of his authority, binds his principal. If a person professes to contract as agent on behalf of another as principal, although without the latter's authority, the latter may subsequently ratify the contract. Otherwise if a person represents himself to have authority to act as agent when he has none, he is liable for breach of an implied warranty of authority (*Collen v Wright* (1857) 7 E. & B. 301).

Once an agent has brought his principal into contractual relations with another, he drops out, and his principal sues or is sued on the contract. Agents are:

(1) Universal, appointed to act for the principal in all matters, e.g. where a party gives another a universal power of attorney.

(2) General, appointed to act in transactions of a class, e.g. a banker, solicitor. The scope of authority of such agent is the authority usually possessed by such agents, unless notice is given to third parties of some limitation.

(3) Special, appointed for one particular purpose. The agent's scope of authority is the actual authority given him.

See also DEL CREDERE AGENT; FACTOR; POWER OF ATTORNEY; COMMERCIAL AGENT.

agent of necessity A person who in urgent circumstances acts for the benefit of another, there being no opportunity of communicating with that other. Thus a person may be bound by a contract made by another on his behalf, but without his authority; e.g. the master of a ship, in an emergency, may contract and bind the owner. The implied authority of a deserted wife to pledge her husband's credit as agent of necessity was abrogated by the Matrimonial Proceedings and Property Act 1970 s.41.

agent provocateur The admissible limits in the involvement of the police with informers for the purpose of obtaining evidence were considered in *R. v Birtles* [1969] 1 W.L.R. 1047 at 1049; *R. v McCann* (1972) 56 Cr.App.R. 359; *R. v McEvilly* (1974) 60 Cr.App.R. 150; and *R. v Sang* [1979] 3 W.L.R. 263.

aggravated burglary See BURGLARY.

aggravated damages Damages (*q.v.*) awarded where the injury to the claimant (e.g. mental distress or injury to feelings) results from, or has been increased by, the conduct of the defendant, whether before or after the original wrong. Such damages will not be awarded for breach of contract (*q.v.*) or the tort of negligence (*q.v.*) but have been awarded for various other torts (*q.v.*) such as defamation (*q.v.*), discrimination (*q.v.*), malicious prosecution (*q.v.*) and nuisance (*q.v.*). See EXEMPLARY DAMAGES.

aggravated vehicle taking An offence under the Theft Act 1968 s.12A (as inserted by the Aggravated Vehicle Taking Act 1992), involving the basic offence under s.12 of taking a mechanically propelled vehicle but where, between the taking and recovery of the vehicle: it was driven dangerously on a road or other public place; owing to the driving, an accident occurred causing injury to any person or to any property other than the vehicle; damage was caused to the vehicle.

aggressive commercial practice An aggressive commercial practice is an unfair commercial practice under the Consumer Protection from Unfair Trading Regulations 2008 reg.3(5)(c). A commercial practice may be aggressive if it significantly impairs or is likely significantly to impair the typical consumer's freedom of choice or conduct in relation to the product concerned through the use of harassment, coercion or undue influence; and it thereby causes or is likely to cause the typical consumer to take a transactional decision he would not have taken otherwise (see Consumer Protection from Unfair Regulations 2008 reg.7).

agistment Where a person takes in and feeds or pastures horses, cattle or similar animals upon his land for reward. An agister is, therefore, a bailee for reward, and is liable for damage to the cattle if he uses less than ordinary diligence.

agnates Kinsmen related through males. In Roman law, *agnati* were persons so related to a common ancestor that, if they had been alive together with him, they would have been under his *potestas*. See COGNATI.

agreement The concurrence of two or more persons in affecting or altering their rights and duties. An agreement is an act in the law whereby two or more persons declare their consent as to any act or thing to be done or forborne by some or one of those persons for the benefit of the others or other of them. Such declaration may take place by (a) the concurrence of the parties in a spoken or written form of words as expressing their common intention; (b) an offer made by some one of them and accepted by the others or other of them (Pollock). The requisites of an agreement are: two or more persons, a distinct intention common to both, known to both, referring to legal relations and affecting the parties (Anson). See CONTRACT.

agricultural holding The aggregate of the agricultural land comprised in a contract of tenancy, not being a contract under which the said land is let to the tenant during his continuance in any office, appointment or employment held under the landlord (Agricultural Holdings Act 1986 s.1). An agricultural tenant must have 12 months' notice to quit at the end of a year of the tenancy.

agriculture Includes horticulture, fruit growing, seed growing, dairy farming and livestock breeding and keeping (Agricultural Holdings Act 1986 s.96). See also COMMON AGRICULTURAL POLICY.

aid and abet Denotes secondary participation in the commission of a criminal offence. The words tend to be used together. To aid is to assist, help or give support in the commission of a crime. To abet is to aid, instigate or encourage. (See *Att Gen's Reference (No. 1 of 1975)* [1975] 2 All E.R. 684.) See ACCESSORY SECONDARY LIABILITY.

aid by verdict Defects in the old common law pleadings, if not demurred, could not be objected to after verdict, unless of a very serious kind. They were said to be aided or cured by the verdict.

aids Payments from feudal tenants by military or socage tenures to their lords for: (1) ransoming the lord's body; (2) knighting the lord's eldest son; (3) marrying the lord's eldest daughter. Abolished by 12 Car. 2 c.24.

aiel A grandfather.

air The enjoyment of air is a natural right. There is no absolute right in the owner of land to the enjoyment of an uninterrupted passage of air over the land of another, but the right to a defined current of air can be acquired as an easement (*q.v.*). The owner of land is entitled to the ownership and possession of the column of space above the surface ad infinitum. See AIR NAVIGATION.

An action in respect of air pollution may be brought under the rule in *Rylands v Fletcher* (*q.v.*) (see *Halsey v Esso Petroleum Co Ltd* [1961] 1 W.L.R. 683). Certain emissions into the air may also constitute a statutory nuisance (*q.v.*) under Pt III of the Environmental Protection Act 1990. Air pollution is tackled by means of various legislative provisions. In order to release emissions into the air certain industrial installations require an authorisation under Pt 1 of the Environmental Protection Act 1990. (The system of authorisations is gradually being replaced by a system of permits under the Pollution Prevention Control Act 1999.) Various other air pollution offences are created by the Clean Air Act 1993 which provides a separate air pollution regime from that contained in Pt 1 of the Environmental Protection Act 1990. The Secretary of State is required to publish a national air quality strategy which will enable the United Kingdom to meet international and European Community obligations in respect of atmospheric pollution. See ENVIRONMENT; AIR QUALITY; STATUTORY NUISANCE.

Air Force The Air Force was constituted by the Air Force (Constitution) Act 1917. The enlistment discipline of the RAF was provided for in the Air Force Act 1955. This was continued in force by Order in Council under the Armed Forces Act 2001 s.1(2) until December 31, 2006. The Armed Forces Act 2006 provides for the Act to continue in force for one more year and for Orders in Council to continue it in force until, but not beyond, the end of 2011.

The Air Council which controlled the Air Force is merged in the Ministry of Defence.

air navigation This is controlled under the Civil Aviation Acts 1980, 1982 and 2006. No action lies in respect of trespass or nuisance by reason only of the flight of aircraft over any property at a reasonable height, but the owner of aircraft is liable for all actual damage done while in flight, whether to person or property, without proof of negligence. Such liability, however, is subject to certain limitations of amount, and third party risks must be insured against (Civil Aviation Act 1982 s.76).

The Civil Aviation (Eurocontrol) Act 1962 gave effect to the Eurocontrol Convention of 1960 relating to European co-operation for safety of air navigation. This is now governed by the Civil Aviation Act 1982 and the Civil Aviation (Eurocontrol) Act 1983. As to aviation security see the Aviation Security Act 1982, as amended by the Civil Aviation Act 2006, and the Aviation and Maritime Security Act 1990.

air quality The Secretary of State has a duty under s.80 of the Environment Act 1995 to draw up a national air quality strategy containing policies with respect to the assessment or management of the quality of air. Such strategy may also contain policies for implementing obligations under European Community and International law. The strategy must include statements with respect to standards relating to air quality (air quality standards) and air quality objectives. Local authorities are required to review compliance with any air quality standards and objectives (*q.v.*) and designate air quality management areas (*q.v.*) where such standards and objectives are not being achieved (Pt IV, Environment Act 1995).

air quality management areas Where, as a result of an air quality review, it appears to a local authority that any air quality standards or air quality objectives (*q.v.*) are not being achieved or are not likely to be achieved within the relevant time, the local authority is under a duty to designate the relevant area as an air quality management area (see Environment Act 1995 ss.82–84).

air quality standards and air quality objectives Air quality standards are the standards for air quality prescribed by the Secretary of State under the Environment Act 1995 s.87(2)(a). Air quality objectives, also to be prescribed in regulations by the Secretary of State, impose targets for the restriction of the levels at which particular substances are present in air. Local authorities are under a duty to conduct air quality reviews (Environment Act 1995, s.82) to assess whether air quality standards and objectives are being achieved or are likely to be achieved within the relevant time period. See AIR QUALITY MANAGEMENT AREAS.

air space State sovereignty in air space extends to the air space above its land territory and its territorial sea. See Civil Aviation Act 1982.

There is a possible trespass (*q.v.*) created by intrusion into another's airspace. An easement (*q.v.*) in respect of a right to a free flow of air through a defined channel, e.g. a ventilator, may be acquired.

alba firma White rents: quit-rents payable in silver or white money, in contra-distinction to "black rents", i.e. reserved in work, grain, etc.

alcohol Means spirits, wine, beer, cider or any other fermented, distilled or spirituous liquor, but does not include: (a) alcohol which is of a strength not exceeding 0.5 per cent at the time of the sale or supply in question; (b) perfume; (c) flavouring essences recognised by the Commissioners of Customs and Excise as not being intended for consumption as or with dutiable alcoholic liquor; (d) the aromatic flavouring essence commonly known as Angostura bitters; (e) alcohol which is, or is included in, a medicinal product; (f) methylated spirits; (g) methyl alcohol; (h) naphtha; or (i) alcohol contained in liqueur confectionery (Licensing Act 2003 s.191(1)).

The sale by retail of alcohol, the supply of alcohol by or on behalf of a club or to the order of a member of a club, are licensable activities under the Licensing Act 2003.

Alderman (originally Ealdorman (*q.v.*)). An alderman is now either an alderman of the City of London or an honorary alderman of a county.

aleatory contract A wagering contract.

alia enormia [Other wrongs] The concluding allegation in declarations in the action of trespass, consisting of the general words "and other wrongs to the plaintiff then did".

alias (alias dictus) [Otherwise called] A false name.

alias writ A second writ, issued after a former one had proved ineffectual.

alibi [Elsewhere] A defence where an accused alleges that at the time when the offence with which he is charged was committed, he was elsewhere. Notice of intention to raise an alibi must be given (Criminal Justice Act 1967 s.11). See *R. v Lewis* [1969] 2 Q.B. 1.

alien At common law an alien is a subject of a foreign state who was not born within the allegiance of the Crown. "Alien" now means a person who is neither a Commonwealth citizen (*q.v.*) nor a British Protected Person nor a citizen of the Republic of Ireland (British Nationality Act 1981, s.50(1)). An alien has full proprietary capacity, except he may not own a British ship nor may he exercise the franchise. See DEPORTATION; IMMIGRATION; NATURALISATION.

alien ami or friend The subject of a foreign state with which this country is at peace.

alien enemy The subject of a foreign state with which this country is at war, or one who is voluntarily resident or carries on business in enemy territory including enemy-occupied territory (*Sovfracht's Case* [1943] A.C. 203). A company is an alien enemy if it is controlled by persons who are alien enemies (*Daimler Co Ltd v Continental Tyre and Rubber Co Ltd* [1916] 2 A.C. 307).

Enemy aliens resident in the enemy country cannot sue in the English Courts (*Porter v Freudenberg* [1915] 1 K.B. 857), but enemy alien civilians resident in this country with licence of the Queen may sue (*Schaffenius v Goldberg* [1916] 1 K.B. 184). An alien enemy has no right to a writ of habeas corpus.

Trading with the enemy was a common law misdemeanour, but the provisions of the Trading with the Enemy Act 1939 now apply. See also the Distribution of German Enemy Property Act 1949.

alienation The power of the owner or tenant to dispose of his interest in real or personal property. Alienation may be voluntary, e.g. by conveyance or will; or involuntary, e.g. seizure under a judgment order for debt.

alieni juris [Roman law] A person under *potestas*, *mantis* or *mancipium* as opposed to sui juris (*q.v.*).

alimentary trust A protective trust (*q.v.*).

alimony Alimony was the term used to describe the allowance to a married woman when she was under the necessity of living apart from her husband. The term is no longer used in matrimonial causes and is replaced by maintenance pending suit and permanent financial provision thereafter. See MAINTENANCE.

alio intuitu With a motive other than the ostensible and proper one.

aliquis non debet esse judex in propria causa quia non potest esse judex et pars [No man ought to be a judge in his own cause, because he cannot act as a judge and at the same time be a party]

aliter [Otherwise]

aliud est celare, aliud tacere [Silence is not the same thing as concealment] But active concealment is equivalent to a positive statement that the fact does not exist, and is a deceit.

aliunde [From elsewhere] From another place or person.

all fours, on Strictly analagous.

allegans suam turpitudinem non est audiendus [A person alleging his own infamy is not to be heard]

allegation A statement or assertion of fact made in any proceeding; particularly a statement or charge which is, as yet, unproved.

allegiance The tie which binds the subject to the Queen in return for that protection which the Queen affords the subject; the natural and legal obedience which every subject owes to his Sovereign. Breach of allegiance is the basis of the crime of treason (*q.v.*). Local allegiance is the allegiance owed by every alien while he continues within the dominions and the protection of the British Crown, and even after that protection is temporarily withdrawn, owing to the occupation of the British territory by the enemy in time of war (*De Jager v Att Gen of Natal* [1907] A.C. 326). Allegiance is also owed by an alien who receives and retains a passport from the Crown; and this is so even after the alien has left the realm (*Joyce v DPP* [1946] A.C. 347).

The oath of allegiance has to be taken on appointment by judges and justices of the peace, and by Members of Parliament on taking their seats, and clergymen before ordination.

allocation Appropriation of a fund to particular persons or purposes. See APPROPRIATION. See ALSO TRACK ALLOCATION.

allocation questionnaire The form which the court sends to both parties when a case is defended. The questionnaire requires each party to provide information which will assist in the allocation of the case to the appropriate track. The court may dispense with the need for a questionnaire if it considers it already has enough information (CPR 26.3). See TRACK ALLOCATION.

allocatur [It is allowed] The certificate of the taxing master as to the amount of costs allowed.

allocutus The demand of the court to a prisoner convicted of treason on indictment as to what he has to say as to why the court should not proceed to pass judgment upon him. It is an essential step in a trial.

allodium Lands not held of any lord or superior, in which, therefore, the owner had an absolute property and not a mere estate.

allonge A slip of paper annexed to a bill of exchange for endorsements when there is no room for them on the bill (Bills of Exchange Act 1882 s.32(1)).

allotment (1) The allocation or appropriation of property to a specific person (or persons), called the "allottee", e.g. the partition of land held jointly among the several owners.

(2) The appropriation to an applicant by a resolution of the directors of a company of a certain number of shares in the company, in response to an application. This is generally done by sending to the applicant a letter of allotment, informing him of the number of shares allotted to him. A return of allotments, including a statement of the company's capital (*q.v.*), has to be made to the Registrar of Companies (Companies Act 2006 s.555). Shares are allotted once a person acquires the unconditional right to be entered in the company's register of members in respect of those shares.

(3) Lands held by a local authority under the Allotments Acts 1922–1950 for the purpose of providing residents in their area with small plots of land for cultivation.

Alluvio [Roman law] Alluvion: an imperceptibly gradual deposition of soil from a river or the sea.

alteration A material alteration of an instrument, e.g. an alteration of the date of a bill of exchange whereby payment would be accelerated, invalidates the instrument. Alterations in deeds are presumed to have been made before execution; in wills, after, and are ignored unless duly executed or proved to have been made in fact before execution of the will.

alternative averments The statement in the same count of an indictment of an offence in an alternative form in conformity with the enactment constituting the offence (Indictment Rules 1971 r.7).

alternative business structure Under the terms of the Legal Services Act 2007, once fully implemented, lawyers and non-lawyers will be able to provide services to consumers as a single business entity and solicitors and barristers will also be allowed to operate in the same firm. Those wishing to form such a business must be licensed to do so by the approved regulators.

alternative dispute resolution (ADR) A "catch-all" phrase to describe various schemes which complement the current court system, e.g. conciliation, mediation, negotiation, arbitration. By using an alternative method to resolve the dispute, the parties may avoid the need to go to court.

Defined in the Glossary to the Civil Procedure Rules 1998 as "A collective description of methods of resolving disputes otherwise than through the normal trial process". The court may, in furtherance of the overriding objective of actively managing cases, encourage the parties to proceedings to use an alternative means of dispute resolution (CPR 1.4(2)(e)).

Alternative Investment Market (AIM) An alternative market of the London Stock Exchange. It has less onerous requirements than for those companies on the Official List (*q.v.*) and was launched in 1995 to provide a market for young and growing companies. See STOCK EXCHANGE.

alternative, pleading in the Either party may include in his pleading (now referred to as a statement of case (*q.v.*), see CPR) two or more inconsistent sets of material facts and claim relief thereunder in the alternative.

amalgamation The merger of two or more companies or their undertakings. See the Companies Act 2006 ss.899-901. See also RECONSTRUCTION.

ambassadors Diplomatic agents residing in a foreign country as representatives of the states by whom they are dispatched. See DIPLOMATIC PRIVILEGE; EXTRA TERRITORIALITY.

ambiguity (1) A double meaning; (2) Ambiguities in the meaning of a statute or other legislation are resolved by recourse to rules of construction and interpretation. The current preferred approach of statutory interpretation is the unified contextual approach (Cross, *Statutory Interpretation*, (2nd ed.); and *Maunsell v Olins* [1975] A.C. 373, at 391). See STATUTORY INTERPRETATION.

ambulatory Revocable for the time being; a provision whose operation is suspended until the happening of some event upon which the provision becomes operative and binding. A will is ambulatory until the death of the testator.

amendment The correction of some error or omission, or the curing of some defect, in judicial proceedings.

A party may amend his statement of case at any time before it is served on any other party. Once served, it can only be amended with the consent of all the other parties or with the permission of the court (CPR 17.1).

Even where a party has amended his statement of case with the permission of all the other parties and where the permission of the court was therefore not required, the court may disallow the amendment (CPR 17.2). It is a matter for the discretion of the court, exercising the overriding objective and its case management powers, as to whether or not to allow the amendment.

Prior to the CPR, in civil proceedings in the High Court, the court could, at any stage of the proceedings, and on any terms as to costs or otherwise amend any defect or error in any proceedings, and all necessary amendments could be made. A writ or statement of claim could be amended once without leave (Ord. 20).

In criminal proceedings, the amendment of indictments is governed by the Indictments Act 1915, s.5 as amended by Prosecution of Offences Act 1985 s.31(b) Sch.2.

The Crown Court may, in the course of hearing an appeal, correct any error or mistake in the order or judgment under appeal (Supreme Court Act 1981 s.48(1)).

amends, tender of An offer to pay a sum of money by way of satisfaction for a wrong alleged to have been committed.

amenity That which is conducive to comfort or convenience. See, e.g. "loss of amenity" in connection with personal injury claims.

amicus curiae [A friend of the court] One who calls the attention of the court to some point of law or fact which would appear to have been overlooked; usually a member of the Bar. On occasion the law officers are requested or permitted to argue a case in which they are not instructed to appear.

amnesty A pardon for offences granted by an Act of Parliament which is originated by the Crown.

amortisation Provision for the paying off of a debt, or for the wasting of an asset (e.g. a lease), by means of a sinking fund.

amotion Removal from office.

Amsterdam, Treaty of See TREATY OF AMSTERDAM.

an, jour et waste See YEAR, DAY, AND WASTE.

ancestor Any of those relatives from whom descent by blood may be traced, whether through the father or mother; the person prior to 1926, to whose property an heir succeeded on intestacy. By the fifth rule of intestate succession to realty (based on the Inheritance Act 1833), on failure of lineal descendants or issue of a purchaser, the land "descended" to his nearest lineal ancestor.

ancient demesne The manors which were in actual possession of the Crown during the reigns of Edward the Confessor and William the Conqueror, and which in Domesday (*q.v.*) are styled *terrae regis* or *terrae regis Eduardi* The tenants in ancient demesne originally could sue or be sued on questions affecting their lands only in the Court of Common Pleas or the Court of Ancient Demesne of the manor. Abolished by the Law of Property Act 1925 s.128.

ancient documents Documents which are at least 20 years old and which, when produced from proper custody, and are otherwise free from suspicion, prove themselves, no evidence of their execution needing to be given. Prior to the Evidence Act 1938 the period was 30 years.

ancient lights The right to access of light to any building, actually enjoyed for the full period of 20 years without interruption, when the right becomes absolute and indefeasible, unless enjoyed under some express grant (Prescription Act 1832 s.3). The acquisition of a prescriptive right to light may be prevented by the registration of a local land charge (Rights of Light Act 1959 and Local Land Charges Act 1975).

ancient monuments Protection is afforded by the Ancient Monuments and Archaeological Areas Act 1979 and they come under the control of the Historic Buildings and Monuments Commission for England, established by the National Heritage Act 1983. The 1979 Act defines a monument as: (1) any building, structure or work, whether above or below the surface of the land and any cave of excavation; (2) any site comprising the remains of any such building, etc.; and (3) any site comprising or comprising the remains of, any vehicle, vessel or aircraft or part of it which neither constitutes nor forms any part of any work which is a monument within head (1). The Secretary of State must compile and maintain a schedule of monuments.

ancients The former name of the older barristers of an Inn of Court. Certain of the senior barristers of the Middle Temple are still called ancients, but only for dining purposes.

ancillary Auxiliary or subordinate, e.g.:
(1) Ancillary relief, i.e. subservient or incidental relief. Where a claimant seeks to recover damages and an injunction, the injunction is by way of ancillary relief.
(2) Ancillary relief in matrimonial causes (*q.v.*), i.e. where a party to proceedings for divorce, nullity or judicial separation seeks an order for financial provision (*q.v.*) (see Matrimonial Causes Act 1973 ss.23, 24, 24B, 25B and 25C). See FINANCIAL PROVISION ORDERS.
(3) Ancillary credit business, i.e. business relating to credit brokerage, debt adjusting, debt counselling, debt collecting or the operation of a credit reference agency. See Consumer Credit Act 1974 s.145(1).

angary, right of The right of the belligerent state in time of war, and in case of necessity, of seizing the property of neutrals, subject to payment of compensation. See *The Zamora* [1916] 2 A.C. 77.

animals In law, an animal is any creature of the animal world, not belonging to the human race. Animals are divided into two classes, domestic and wild. It is a question of law to which class a particular animal belongs (*McQuaker v Goddard* [1940] 1 K.B. 687).
There may be absolute property in domestic animals and a qualified property in wild animals. Domestic animals are capable of being stolen and, in some circumstances, wild animals also may be the subject of theft (Theft Act 1968 ss.1, 4).

30

The common law rules relating to liabilities for damage done by animals *ferae naturae* (*q.v.*) were abolished by the Animals Act 1971. The keeper of an animal of a dangerous species is generally liable. In the case of the animal not of a dangerous species, the keeper is liable for damage which that particular animal is likely to cause (s.2).

Straying animals may be detained and the damage caused by them is recoverable with the expense of keeping them. The common law remedy of distress damage-feasant has been abolished (Animals Act 1971 ss.4–7).

Certain species of animals are protected by law in the interests of conservation (see Wildlife and Countryside Act 1981, as amended.)

animus cancellandi [The intention of cancelling]

animus dedicandi [The intention of dedicating] At common law the ownership of the soil of a highway is in the adjacent owners, they having dedicated it to the public.

animus deserendi [The intention of deserting (a spouse)] See DESERTION.

animus furandi [The intention of stealing] See THEFT.

animus manendi [The intention of remaining] One of the necessary elements of domicile (*q.v.*).

animus revertendi [The intention of returning] Animals accustomed to go and return, e.g. pigeons in a dovecote, continue to be the property of their owner until they lose the *animus revertendi*.

animus revocandi [The intention of revoking] e.g. a will.

animus testandi [The intention of making a will]

annates Synonymous with first fruits or *primitae*, the first year's whole profits of every spiritual preferment; originally payable to the Pope, then by the statute 26 Hen. 8 c.3, to the Crown, and from 1703 to the Commissioners of Queen Anne's Bounty (*q.v.*). By the First Fruits and Tenths Measure 1926, as from July 16, 1926, first fruits and tenths were either extinguished or provision was made for their redemption.

anni nubiles The marriageable age of women. At common law 12 years of age. Now it is 16 years of age (Marriage Act 1949). Parental consent is now required to the marriage of persons under 18 years old, but a magistrates' court, county court or the High Court may give such consent where parents refuse. Application may also be made to a court in accordance with the Family Proceedings Rules 1991 r.3.20.

annual return A document which a limited company (*q.v.*) must file annually with the Registrar of Companies (*q.v.*). It must be filed within 28 days after the end of the period to which it refers (Companies Act 2006 ss.854–859). It must be in the prescribed form and signed by a director or the secretary of the company. Filing may be carried out electronically (ibid. s.1068 and Sch.5).

annual value The value placed on land or hereditaments for rating purposes. The gross value is the rack-rent, i.e. the rent for which the property is worth to be let by the year, the landlord paying for repairs, insurance and expenses, the tenant paying the rates. The net annual value, or rateable value, is the gross value less the statutory deductions. General domestic rating was abolished by the Local Government Finance Act 1988 which introduced the community charge. The community charge (*q.v.*) is replaced by the council tax (*q.v.*), which is based for domestic premises on the capital value of the premises.

annuity A yearly payment of a certain sum of money. If charged on real estate it is commonly called a rentcharge.

31

Annuities given by will are pecuniary legacies payable by instalments, and where the will directs the purchase of an annuity for A for life, A is entitled to take the purchase-money instead.

Only the interest portion of a purchased annuity is liable to income tax.

annul To deprive a judicial proceeding of its operation, either retrospectively or only as to future transactions.

annulment See NULLITY OF MARRIAGE.

anonymous work A literary, dramatic, musical or artistic work in which copyright is not infringed by an act done or arrangements made at a time when (a) it is not possible by reasonable inquiry to ascertain the identity of the author; and (b) it is reasonable to assume either: (i) that copyright has expired; or (ii) that the author died 70 years or more before the beginning of the calendar year in which the act is done or the arrangements are made (Copyright, Designs and Patents Act 1988 s.57(1)).

Where the work is (a) a work in which Crown copyright subsists; or (b) a work in which copyright vested in an international organisation by virtue of s.168 of the Act and in respect of which an Order has been made specifying a copyright period longer than 70 years, then s.57(1)(b)(ii) will not apply (Copyright, Designs and Patents Act 1988 s.57(2)).

Where the work is a work of joint authorship (a) the reference in s.57(1) to being able to ascertain the identity of the author is to be construed as a reference to it being possible to ascertain the identity of any of the authors; and (b) the reference in s.57(1)(b)(ii) to the author having died is to be construed as a reference to all the authors having died (Copyright, Designs and Patents Act 1988 s.57(3).

answer (1) Prior to the CPR, an answer to interrogatories (*q.v.*) (Ord. 26, r.1).

(2) The defence of a party to a petition of divorce (Family Proceedings Rules 1991 r.2.12).

ante-date To date back. See Bills of Exchange Act 1882 s.13.

ante litem motam Before litigation was in contemplation. Declarations by deceased relatives made *ante litem motam* are admissible to prove matters of family pedigree or legitimacy.

antenatus A child born before the marriage of its parents.

ante-nuptial Before marriage.

anticipation The act of assigning, charging or otherwise dealing with income before it becomes due. See RESTRAINT ON ANTICIPATION.

anti-competitive practices (1) Were defined as a course of conduct likely to restrict, distort or prevent competition under the Competition Act 1980 (now replaced by the Competition Act 1998 and the Enterprise Act 2002).

(2) Generally they are practices that harm the competitive structure of a market and are forbidden under articles 81 and 82 of the Treaty of Rome or ss.2 and 18 of the Competition Act 1998. See COMPETITION COMMISSION; COMPETITION POLICY.

antiqua statuta or vetera statuta Old statutes passed before the reign of Edward III.

antisocial behaviour order (ASBO) An antisocial behaviour order may be made prohibiting acts by persons over the age of 10 which cause or are likely to cause harassment, alarm or distress to one or more persons not of the same household as the perpetrator of the behaviour. Application for an order is made by the local authority by complaint to a magistrates' court (*q.v.*). On a breach of the order the perpetrator may be convicted of a summary offence punishable with imprisonment for up to six months, or a fine, or both, or of an indictable offence punishable with imprisonment for up to five years, or a fine, or both (Crime and Disorder Act 1998 s.1).

antitrust law The term used in the USA for competition law (*q.v.*).

Anton Piller See PILLER, ANTON.

apology In actions for libel contained in newspapers, etc. it is a defence to publish an apology accompanied by payment of money into court by way of amends. An apology may be pleaded in mitigation of damages in any action for defamation (Libel Acts 1843, 1845).

In cases of unintentional defamation, an offer of amends may be made, consisting of the publication of a suitable correction of the words complained of and a sufficient apology to the party aggrieved by them (Defamation Act 1996 s.2).

apostasy The total renunciation of Christianity by one who has been educated in or professed that faith within this realm.

appeal Any proceeding taken to rectify an erroneous decision of a court or tribunal by bringing it before a higher court. The only rights of appeal are those expressly provided for by statute. An appellate court may substitute its own decision against which the appeal is brought. Compare and contrast the procedure for judicial review (*q.v.*). In many instances, leave is required to bring an appeal, granted by either the court of trial or the appellate court itself. Appeals may lie to the High Court on a point of law only, against the decisions of tribunals and decisions taken following public inquiries. In these cases it is necessary to refer to the machinery provided by the statute creating the tribunal or providing for the holding of a public inquiry, in order to determine the extent of the right to an appeal.

Appeal, Court of See COURT OF APPEAL.

appeal of felony An accusation of having committed a felony made by one person against another. The person charged had the right to trial by battle, which took place between him and the accuser, the combatants being each armed with a leather shield and a cudgel, and having to fight for a day, or until one of them gave in. Abolished by the statute 59 Geo. 3 c.46. See BATTLE, TRIAL BY.

appearance The formal step formerly taken by a defendant to a High Court action after he had been served with the writ. See now ACKNOWLEDGEMENT OF SERVICE.

appellant One who appeals. See APPEAL.

appendant Incorporeal hereditaments are appendant if they arose originally because the land over which they are enjoyed, and the land to which they are annexed, formed part of the same manor, e.g. a right of common, of pasture. See APPURTENANT.

appendix The matter bound up with the parties' cases, in appeals to the House of Lords, or Privy Council, and consisting of the evidence, judgments, etc. given in the courts below. See *Practice Direction (HL) (House of Lords Documents)* [1964] 1 W.L.R. 424.

applicable law See PRIVATE INTERNATIONAL LAW.

applicant The person who makes an application. See APPLICATION.

application The process by which a person in civil proceedings applies for a court order. An application may be made where court proceedings have already been commenced, or the proceedings may be commenced by means of an application. CPR r.23 sets out the general provisions for making applications. An application must usually be made by application notice (CPR r.23.3). The circumstances where an application may be made without an application notice are described in CPR PD 23 para.3.

application notice The document in which the applicant states his intention to seek a court order (CPR r.23.1).

apply, liberty to A direction by a judge or master enabling parties to come to the court again without issuing new proceedings.

appointed day The day fixed for an Act of Parliament to come into operation.

appointee One in whose favour a power of appointment is exercised.

appointment, power of A power, given by deed or will, to appoint a person or persons to take an estate or interest in property, whether real or personal.

The person to whom the power is given is called a donee of the power, and when he exercises it he is called the appointor. The person in whose favour it can be exercised is the object of the power. A true power is discretionary, not imperative, as is a trust. A general power of appointment is one where the donee may appoint to anyone including himself; a special power is one where the donee can only appoint in favour of specified objects. There is also a third class of power which is not special in the sense that there is a distinct class of objects specified among which a power to appoint is given, and yet is not general because some persons are excluded; e.g. a power to appoint to any person other than the donee of the power. Uncertainty as to the distinction between general and specified powers for the purpose of the rule against perpetuities (see PERPETUITY) is removed by the Perpetuities and Accumulations Act 1964 s.7.

Powers must be exercised in the way indicated (if any); e.g. by a deed, but equity may assist the defective execution of a power, i.e. where prescribed formalities for executing the power are not complied with. An excessive execution of a power is where the interests attempted to be created are either illegal or outside the scope of the power. A fraud on a power is where the power is exercised by the donee, not in accordance with the true purpose of the power, but to benefit himself, and may be set aside. An exclusive power is one enabling the appointor to select from amongst the specified objects of the power; a non-exclusive power is one which does not permit the entire exclusion of any one member; in the latter case a merely nominal or negligible appointment to one or more of the objects of the power was called an illusory appointment, and was invalid. Now, however, an appointment is not invalidated by the exclusion of any object, unless the power declares the amount of the share from which any object is not to be excluded (Law of Property Act 1925 s.158). See POWER.

apportionment Division in proportion; the assignment of a share. At common law, where the owner of land died between two dates of payment of rent, the rent was not divisible and the executors of the deceased owner were not entitled to any rent for the broken period. The rent was either not payable, or went to the reversioner.

This rule was altered by the Apportionment Act 1870, which enacted that all rents, annuities, dividends, and other periodical payments in nature of income should, like interest on money lent, be considered as accruing from day to day, and should be apportionable accordingly. The Act may, however, be excluded by the will.

apportionment of contract The division of contract into several distinct acts, or parts, the performance of one or more of which may give the right to enforce the contract to that extent against the other party. If some parts are lawful and some unlawful, the lawful parts can be enforced, while the unlawful are void, unless the consideration is illegal, when the whole contract is void. See also SEVERANCE.

appraisement The valuation of goods or property, in particular of goods seized in execution, or by distraint, or under order of the court. Real property is usually valued by surveyors.

appraiser A valuer; one who makes an appraisement.

apprentice One who binds himself to serve and learn for a definite time from an employer, who on his part covenants to teach his trade or calling. A minor's contract of apprenticeship, if substantially for his advantage, is binding on him.

approbate and reprobate To blow hot and cold; a person is not allowed to take a benefit under an instrument and disclaim the liabilities imposed by the same instrument.

appropriate person Under Pt IIA of the Environmental Protection Act 1990 in relation to contaminated land (*q.v.*), the local authority (or Environment Agency (*q.v.*) in respect of a special site (*q.v.*)) is required to determine who is the appropriate person or persons to bear responsibility for anything which is to be done by way of remediation (*q.v.*) to the land in question (Environmental Protection Act 1990 s.78A(9)). The question of who is an appropriate person is determined in accordance with s.78F which places initial responsibility on the person who causes or knowingly permits the relevant contaminating substances to be in on or under the land. Where after reasonable enquiry no such persons can be found then liability for remediation falls to the current owners or occupiers who become the appropriate persons for remediation. See CONTAMINATED LAND; SPECIAL SITES; REMEDIATION.

appropriation Making a thing the property of a person.

(1) The setting apart of goods or moneys out of a larger quantity as the property of a particular person; e.g. appropriating goods to a contract.

(2) Appropriation by a personal representative is the application of the property of the deceased in its actual condition in satisfaction of a legacy (Administration of Estates Act 1925 s.41).

(3) Appropriation of payments to debts. Where a debtor owes more than one debt to a creditor, any payment made can be applied in extinction of any of the debts at the option of the debtor, exercised at the time of payment; otherwise the creditor may appropriate up to the last moment. Where there is an account current between the parties the law presumes that they intended to apply the first item on the credit side to the first item on the debit side and so on. For example, in a banking account it is assumed that the sums first paid in are exhausted by the sums first paid out (*Clayton's Case* (1816) 1 Mer. 572). As to appropriation of payments under a hire-purchase, conditional sale or consumer hire agreement, see the Consumer Credit Act 1974 s.81(2).

(4) Appropriation of supplies is the legalisation of the expenditure of public money by means of the annual Appropriation Act.

(5) The attachment of an ecclesiastical benefice to the perpetual use of some religious house, or dean and chapter, or other spiritual person.

(6) The Theft Act 1968 s.3 defines appropriation as any assumption by a person of the rights of an owner. By s.1 of the Act any such dishonest appropriation of property belonging to another with the intention of permanently depriving the other of it is theft (*q.v.*).

approval, on When goods are delivered to a buyer on approval, the property in the goods passes to the buyer:

(a) when he signifies his approval or acceptance to the seller or does any other act adopting the transaction;

(b) if he does not signify his approval or acceptance to the seller but returns the goods without giving notice of rejection then, if a time has been fixed for the return of the goods, on the expiration of that time and, if no time has been fixed, on the expiration of a reasonable time (Sale of Goods Act 1979 s.18, r.4).

approved clinician A person approved by the Secretary of State to act as an approved clinician for the purposes of the Mental Health Act 1983 (see Mental Health Act 1983 s.145, as amended by the Mental Health Act 2007). Drawn from a range of professionals in nursing, occupational health, psychology, social as well as from medical practitioners, they will have primary responsibility for the care of those with mental disorders (*q.v.*). See also RESPONSIBLE CLINICIAN.

approved schools See COMMUNITY HOMES.

approved social worker An officer of a local social services authority appointed to act as an approved social worker for the purposes of the Mental Health Act 1983. ASWs have certain powers and duties under the Act. The post of approved social worker is to be abolished and replaced by the approved mental health practitioner (see Mental Health Act 1983 s.114, as amended by the Mental Health Act 2007). See APPROVED MENTAL HEALTH PROFESSIONAL.

approved mental health professional A person approved by a local social services authority to act as an approved mental health professional for the purposes of the Mental Health Act 1983 (see Mental Health Act 1983 s.114, as amended by the Mental Health Act 2007).

approvement The inclosure of part of a common by the lord of the manor, sufficient being left for the commoners.

approver An accomplice who turns Queen's evidence (*q.v.*).

appurtenant Such incorporeal interests as are not naturally and originally appendant to corporeal hereditaments, but have been annexed to them either by some express deed of grant, or by prescription; e.g. rights of common or of way. See APPENDANT.

aqua cedit solo [Water passes with the soil] As water is land covered with water, ownership of the water goes with ownership of the land covered by it.

aqua et ignis interdictio [Roman law] Forbidding the use of fire and water; an indirect mode of depriving of citizenship.

arbitration The determination of disputes by the decision of one or more persons called arbitrators. Many commercial contracts contain an arbitration agreement by which the parties agree, in the event of a dispute between them, that the dispute will be referred to arbitration. An arbitration is a legally effective adjudication of a dispute otherwise than by the ordinary procedure of the courts. The parties choose the arbitrator, and he is usually a specialist in the relevant field. The arbitrator is required to act in a judicial manner. The decision of the arbitrator is called an award, and is usually binding on the parties. If legal proceedings are instituted in contravention of submission to arbitration the defendant may apply to the court to stay the proceedings. See the Arbitration Act 1996.

Certain organisations offer arbitration services, e.g. the Chartered Institute of Arbitrators, and various trade associations, e.g. ABTA, offer arbitration schemes for claims by consumers against members of the association.

Archbishop The chief of the clergy within his province. The Archbishop of Canterbury is styled Primate of all England, and the Archbishop of York Primate of England. They are spiritual lords of Parliament.

Archdeacon An ecclesiastical superior who is a visitor of the clergy in his district.

Arches, Court of Canterbury The ecclesiastical court of appeal of the Archbishop of Canterbury. Within the province of York the appellate court is the Chancery Court of York. See the Ecclesiastical Jurisdiction Measure 1963. See ECCLESIASTICAL COURTS.

Areas of Outstanding Natural Beauty Under the National Parks and Access to the Countryside Act 1949 the former Countryside Commission (now Agency) had the power to designate land, outside National Parks, as areas of outstanding natural beauty. Now regulated by the Countryside and Rights of Way Act 2000 which enables the designation of land outside the National parks where this is desirable in order to conserve and enhance the natural beauty of the area. Once designated any decisions taken by public bodies, including planning authorities, in relation to the land must have regard to the prime aim of conserving and enhancing the natural beauty of the area.

arguendo [In the course of his argument]

argumentum ab inconvenienti plurimum valet in lege [An argument based on inconvenience is of great weight in the law]

armed forces The Army Act 1881, which was required to be reviewed annually, recited that a standing army in time of peace was illegal without the consent of Parliament. It was replaced by the Army Act 1955 which, together with the Air Force Act 1955 and the Naval Discipline Act 1957, was amended and continued in force by the Armed Forces Acts 1986, 1991, 1996 and 2001 until December 31, 2006. The Armed Forces Act 2006 provides for the Acts to continue in force for one more year, and for Orders in Council to continue them in force until, but not beyond, the end of 2011.

armistice A temporary but total suspension of hostilities by agreement between the governments of the belligerents. A truce is a suspension of hostilities arranged by military commanders in the field.

arm's length, at The relationship which exists between parties who are strangers to each other and who bear no special duty, obligation, or relation to each other; e.g. vendor and purchaser. See UNDUE INFLUENCE.

Army Council The body, created by letters patent in 1904, which administered the Army. It is merged in the Ministry of Defence.

arraign To call a prisoner to the bar of the court by name, to read to him the substance of the indictment, and to ask him whether he pleads guilty or not guilty. See the Criminal Law Act 1967 s.6(1).

arrangement, scheme of See SCHEME OF ARRANGEMENT.

array, challenge to See CHALLENGE OF JURORS.

array, commission of Writs issued under the Assize of Arms 1181 to impress men for military service for defence of the realm.

arrears Debts not paid at the due date.

arrest To arrest a person is to deprive him of his liberty by some lawful authority, for the purpose of compelling his appearance to answer a criminal charge, or as a method of execution. An arrest may be lawfully made by a person authorised to make it by a warrant (*q.v.*) which is lawfully issued and signed by a justice of the peace (*q.v.*) or other judicial authority. Part III of the Police and Criminal Evidence Act 1984 divides powers of arrest without warrant into four categories: arrest without warrant by constables, arrest without warrant by other persons, other statutory powers of arrest and arrest for fingerprinting.

Section 24 of the Police and Criminal Evidence Act 1984 (as amended by s.110 of the Serious Organised Crime and Police Act 2005) confers upon a constable the power to arrest without warrant anyone who is about to commit an offence, anyone who is in the act of committing an offence, anyone whom he has reasonable grounds for suspecting to be about to commit an offence, anyone whom he has reasonable grounds for suspecting to be committing an offence. The power of summary arrest conferred upon a constable by s.24 is only exercisable if the constable believes that any of the "general arrest conditions" specified in s.24 are satisfied. The general arrest conditions are complex but include the fact that where the name of the person concerned is unknown to the constable, the constable has reason for doubting whether a name provided by that person is his real name. A person other than a constable may arrest without

37

warrant anyone who is in the act of committing an indictable offence or anyone whom he has reasonable grounds for suspecting to be committing an indictable offence.

There are also other statutory powers of arrest set out in Sch.2 to the Police and Criminal Evidence Act 1984 and within other statutes, e.g. a power of arrest may be attached to an occupation order (*q.v.*) made under the Family Law Act 1996.

There remain certain powers of arrest under the common law, e.g. any person may arrest anyone whom he sees committing or about to commit a breach of peace (*q.v.*) for sufficient time to prevent the commission of the offence.

arrest of judgment In criminal cases the accused may at any time between conviction and sentence move that judgment be not pronounced because of some technical defect in the indictment.

arrestable offence The classification of offences as "non arrestable", "arrestable" and "serious arrestable" was removed by the Serious Organised Crime and Police Act 2005 which amended previous provisions in the Police and Criminal Evidence Act (PACE) 1984. As a result of the amendments all offences are now arrestable subject to the conditions set out in the amended provisions of PACE (see Code of Practice G).

arretted Accused.

arson Without lawful excuse, the intentional or reckless destruction or damage by fire of any property belonging to another (Criminal Damage Act 1971 s.1).

Article Each section of the EC Treaty is referred to as an article. For example, the aims of the European Community (*q.v.*) are stated in art.3 EC Treaty. The Amsterdam Treaty 1997 reorganised the numbering of the Treaty articles, and since that time it is common practice to cite both the post-Amsterdam and pre-Amsterdam notation (For example, art.81 EC (ex art.85)).

articled clerk A clerk under written articles of agreement to serve a practising solicitor in consideration of being initiated into the profession. Now known as a trainee solicitor who enters a training contract with a firm of solicitors. See SOLICITOR.

articles Clauses of a document; in addition the word "articles" sometimes means the document itself, e.g. articles of agreement, articles of partnership, etc.

articles of association See ASSOCIATION, ARTICLES OF.

articles of the peace The complaint on oath of a person that he feared with reasonable cause that another person would do or cause to be done bodily harm to him or to his wife or child or burn his house; and the court, if satisfied that there were reasonable grounds of fear, was bound to require sureties for the peace. See now the Magistrates' Courts Act 1980 s.115 which provides for binding over (*q.v.*) to keep the peace or to be of good behaviour.

articles of war The rules for the government of troops on active service issued under the prerogative of the Crown, prior to the Mutiny Act 1803. See MILITARY LAW.

articuli super chartas The statute 1300, (28 Edw. 1), confirming Magna Carta and Charta de Foresta.

artificial insemination The placing of sperm inside a woman's vagina or uterus by means other than by sexual intercourse. The sperm may be that of the woman's husband (AIH—artificial insemination by husband), partner (AIP) or some third party donor (AID). Human artificial insemination by donor and other forms of assisted conception are regulated by the Human Fertilisation and Embryology Act 1990, as amended. See IN VITRO FERTILISATION.

artificial person An association which is recognised by law as having legal personality, e.g. a corporation (*q.v.*) or company (*q.v.*).

artistic craftsmanship, a work of One of the categories of artistic work capable of copyright protection under the Copyright, Designs and Patents Act 1988. Generally covering limited edition hand-crafted items rather than mass produced products. See ARTISTIC WORK.

artistic work (a) a graphic work, photograph, sculpture or collage, irrespective of artistic quality; (b) a work of architecture being a building or a model for a building; or (c) a work of artistic craftsmanship (Copyright, Designs and Patents Act 1988 s.4). See ARTISTIC CRAFTSMANSHIP; COPYRIGHT.

ascertained goods Goods identified and agreed on after the contract of sale of goods is made. Compare with unascertained goods (*q.v.*) and specific goods (*q.v.*). See Sale of Goods Act 1979.

asportation The "carrying away" which was an essential ingredient of the common law offence of larceny. It included any removal of anything from the place which it occupied. The requirement of taking and carrying away does not form part of the definition of theft in the Theft Act 1968 s.1.

asportavit [Did carry away]

assault An assault is any act committed intentionally or recklessly, which leads another person to fear immediate personal violence. An assault becomes a battery (*q.v.*) if force is applied without consent. Common assault is a summary offence (Criminal Justice Act 1988 s.39). The more serious forms of assault are indictable offences (*q.v.*).

Assault is also a tort consisting of an act of the defendant which causes the claimant reasonable fear of the infliction of battery on him by the defendant.

assault by penetration A person (A) commits an offence if: (a) he intentionally penetrates the vagina or anus of another person (B) with a part of his body or anything else; (b) the penetration is sexual; (c) B does not consent to the penetration; and (d) A does not reasonably believe that B consents (Sexual Offences Act 2003 s.2).

assay The testing of the quality of an article, e.g. bread or silver, or the accuracy of weights and measures.

Assembly, European Now known as the European Parliament (*q.v.*).

assembly, unlawful See UNLAWFUL ASSEMBLY.

assent, of executor A document which acknowledges the right of a legatee or a devisee to property under a will. An assent to the vesting of a legal estate must be in writing, signed by the personal representative (*q.v.*), and must name the person in whose favour it is given, and it operates to vest in that person the legal estate to which it relates (s.36(4) of the Administration of Estates Act 1925). It relates back to the date of the testator's death (unless a contrary intention appears) as, e.g. in the case of a specific legacy, but not in the case of residue, which does not come into existence until ascertained.

assent, royal See ROYAL ASSENT.

assessment (1) To quantify or fix the amount of damages, or the value of property.

(2) The ascertainment of a person's liability to taxation; the formal evidence of such ascertainment.

assessor (1) One who assists a court or tribunal in trying or hearing a scientific or technical question (other than criminal proceedings by the Crown) but who has no voice in the decision.

(2) A person employed by an insurer to investigate and assess the amount of loss.

assets Property, notably available for the payment of debts and inheritance. Real assets are real property, and personal assets are personal property. Legal assets comprise everything which an executor takes by virtue of his office, and with which he would have been charged in an action at law. Equitable assets are such as could only be reached in a court of equity.

Since January 1, 1926, the rule has been that real and personal estate, whether legal or equitable, of a deceased person, together with property over which a general power of appointment is exercised by will, are assets for payment of debts whether by specialty or simple contract (s.32 of the Administration of Estates Act 1925). See ADMINISTRATION OF ESTATES.

assets by descent Land which descended to an heir charged with the debts of his ancestor. The heir was liable for specialty debts in which he was bound, to the extent of the assets descending to him.

assets, marshalling of See MARSHALLING.

assign (1) To assign (transfer) property.
(2) An assignee (*q.v.*).

assignatus utitur jure auctoris [An assignee is clothed with the right of his principal]

assignee A person to whom an assignment is made. A creditor's assignee was the equivalent of the modern trustee in bankruptcy (*q.v.*).

assignment A transfer of property, most commonly of a lease or a chose in action (*q.v.*) but also of a contractual liability or benefit.

assignment of choses in action Choses in action (*q.v.*) were not assignable at common law, but choses in action, both legal and equitable, were assignable in equity. If the chose in action were legal, the assignee could only sue in the name of the assignor, but if equitable he could sue in his own name.

Negotiable instruments (*q.v.*) became assignable by the law merchant (*q.v.*), and policies of insurance by statute. By the Judicature Act 1873 s.25, all legal choses in action were made assignable by law. Now by the Law of Property Act 1925 s.136(1) any absolute assignment by writing under the hand of the assignor (not purporting to be by way of charge only) of any debt or other legal thing in action, of which express notice in writing has been given to the debtor or trustee, is effectual in law (subject to equities having priority over the right of the assignee) to pass and transfer from the date of such notice: (a) the legal right to such debt or thing in action; (b) all legal and other remedies for the same; and (c) the power to give a good discharge for the same without the concurrence of the assignor. Assignments of equitable choses in action are untouched by that Act, and the assignee can still bring an action in his own name. See ABSOLUTE ASSIGNMENT; CHOSES IN ACTION; EQUITABLE ASSIGNMENT; NOTICE.

assignment of contract The general rule is that liabilities under a contract cannot be assigned. But they may be assigned with the consent of the other party to the contract to whom the liability is owed and the parties may make them assignable, either expressly or impliedly. The original contracting party normally can procure (hence discharge) the performance of the contract by someone else, but if his personal performance is essential under the contract, e.g. as in a contract to sing in an opera, the liability to perform the contract cannot be assigned.

Rights or benefits under a contract may be assigned by legal assignment, equitable assignment, statute, or by operation of law. See ASSIGNMENT OF CHOSES IN ACTION; NOVATION; PRIVITY OF CONTRACT.

assignment of dower Before a widow could take possession of any of her husband's land as tenant in dower, her part had to be assigned to her, either by agreement between her and the heir, or by the sheriff in execution of a judgment obtained by her.

assignor One who assigns, or transfers.

assisa cadera [A non-suit]

assisa vertitur in juratam [The assize turned into the *jurata*] Anciently, the original writ commencing an action summoned an assize, but after the introduction of pleadings the jury was summoned after joinder of issue by writ of *venire facias*, and was known as the *jurata*.

assistance, writ of A High Court writ in aid of execution. Ord. 46, r.1. See also POSSESSION, WRIT OF.

assize [A sitting or session] (1) A legislative enactment, e.g. the Assize of Clarendon.
An assize passed in the reign of Henry II provided for the trial of questions of seisin and title to land by a recognition or inquiry of 16 men sworn to speak the truth, called the Grand Assize. Hence the proceedings, and the recognitors themselves, became known as the assizes.
(2) Assize Courts.
Magna Carta provided that assizes of *novel disseisin (q.v.)* and *mort d'ancestor (q.v.)* should be taken only in the shire where the land lay, and for this purpose justices were sent into the country once a year; hence they were called justices of assize. Afterwards, the Statute of Nisi Prius (13 Edw. 1 c.30) enacted that the justices of assize should try issues in ordinary actions in the counties in which they arose and return the verdict to the court at Westminster.
Courts of assize were abolished as part of the court reforms following a Royal Commission Report on Assizes and Quarter Sessions. The civil business of assizes was allocated to the High Court and their criminal jurisdiction is now exercised by the Crown Court (*q.v.*).

Assize of Clarendon (1166) Provided that 12 legal men from each hundred district must present to the judges the crimes of which they knew. If the accused failed to clear themselves by ordeal (*q.v.*), they were punished. This was effectively the origin of the grand jury (*q.v.*).

assize of mort d'ancestor A real action which lay to recover land of which a person had been deprived on the death of his ancestor by the abatement or intrusion of a stranger. It extended the remedy introduced by *novel disseisin* to the case of persons claiming through the disseisee.

Assize of Northampton (1176) A re-enactment and enlargement of the Assize of Clarendon (*q.v.*).

assize of novel disseisin A real action which lay to recover land which a person had recently disseised, i.e. lost possession of.

assize, petty The assizes of *darrein presentment, mort d'ancestor (q.v.), novel disseisin (q.v.)*, and *utrum (q.v.)*. Abolished by the Real Property Limitation Act 1833.

assize rents Fixed and certain rents.

assize utrum A real action for trying the question whether land was a lay-fee (*q.v.*) or held in frankalmoign (*q.v.*).

associates Officers of the common law courts, who were appointed by and held office at the pleasure of the Chief Justice or Chief Baron of each court, and whose duties were to keep the records of the court, to attend nisi prius (*q.v.*)

sittings, make out the list of cases, conduct the jury ballot, note the judgment, make up the *postea* (or certificate of the result of trial) and deliver the record to the proper party. Now, associates are officers of the Queen's Bench Division of the High Court.

association, articles of A document which, together with certain other resolutions, comprises the constitution of a company (*q.v.*). It provides regulations concerning the management and internal affairs of a company (see the Companies Act 2006 ss.18-20). Model sets of articles are provided by regulations made by the Secretary of State. Thus Table A provides a model set of articles for a company limited by shares and to the extent that such a company does not exclude or restrict Table A when it is registered, then Table A will apply (ibid. s.20). The current model Table A (as amended) is that passed under the Companies Act 1985 pending full implementation of the 2006 Act. The Companies Act 1985 (Electronic Communications) Order 2000 made significant changes to Table A to facilitate the use of electronic communication, e.g. to allow electronic sending of notices and appointment of proxies. See LIMITED COMPANY; PRIVATE COMPANY; PUBLIC COMPANY; VOTING.

association, memorandum of Formerly the principal document of a company which set out a company's constitution and objects but under the Companies Act 2006 this document has reduced significance. Those wishing to form a company under the 2006 Act must still subscribe to a memorandum of association (s.8) and comply with the requirements for registration (ss.9-13). The details to be registered are the company's proposed name, the situation of its registered office, whether the liability of its members is to be limited and, if so, whether limitation is by shares or guarantee and whether the company is to be a private (*q.v.*) or public company (*q.v.*). Where a company is to have share capital, certain information about the amount and distribution of that capital must also be registered (s.10). It is no longer necessary for the memorandum to record the objects for which a company has been formed. Indeed s.31 provides that unless a company's articles specifically restrict the objects of the company, its objects are unrestricted. See COMPANY; LIMITED COMPANY; PRIVATE COMPANY; PUBLIC COMPANY; ULTRA VIRES

assumpsit [He promised or undertook] The common law action which grew out of the action of trespass on the case. It was brought for the breach of an undertaking, a cause of action analogous to deceit (*q.v.*) It gradually supplanted the action of debt and came into general use for the enforcement of an agreement not under seal (a simple contract), and for which an action of covenant would not therefore lie. Actions assumpsit were divided into *indebitatus* (common or money counts) and special counts. The former were brought to recover debts arising from contract, the latter for damages for breach of contract. They were abolished by the Judicature Acts 1873–1875.

assurance (1) A surrender, conveyance, assignment or appointment of property. (2) Insurance (*q.v.*).

assured shorthold tenancy An assured tenancy (*q.v.*) under which the landlord has an extra mandatory ground for obtaining possession against the tenant, i.e. on expiry of the fixed term with notice. See the Housing Act 1988, as amended.

assured tenancy A tenancy defined in s.1 of the Housing Act 1988 under which the tenant has security of tenure (*q.v.*).

asylum Originally a place in which there was safety from pursuit, then a place for the reception and treatment of the insane. The Mental Treatment Act 1930 provided that asylums were to be called "mental hospitals".

asylum, right of (1) The right of vessels of a belligerent power to insist on admission to neutral ports when their vessels are in distress.

(2) The refusal of extradition, or to deliver up to the territorial sovereign, a person who has taken refuge in an embassy or place enjoying diplomatic immunity.

(3) A claim for asylum in the United Kingdom, particularly by political refugees, is to be considered under domestic legislation as well as the United Kingdom's obligations under the Convention relating to the Status of Refugees and the European Convention on Human Rights (*q.v.*) and their respective Protocols. See ASYLUM-SEEKER; POLITICAL ASYLUM.

asylum-seeker The Immigration and Asylum Act 1999 defines an asylum-seeker as: "a person who is not under 18 and has made a claim for asylum which has been recorded by the Secretary of State but which has not been determined."

This, together with the Immigration Act 1971, provides generally for asylum-seekers and their dependants to obtain leave to enter and/or remain in the United Kingdom, rules as to adjudication on these and other issues, as well as regulating support to asylum-seekers and their dependants whilst in the United Kingdom. See also SI 2000/704 and SI 2000/541. See POLITICAL ASYLUM; ASYLUM, RIGHT OF.

attachiamenta bonorum Distress of a man's goods and chattels for debt.

attachment (1) To attach a person is to arrest him under an order of committal (*q.v.*). It is employed in ordinary cases of disobedience to an order, judgment, etc. or other contempt of court committed in the course of a suit or otherwise.

(2) Attachment of debts. See GARNISHEE PROCEEDINGS.

(3) Attachment of earnings. An attachment of earnings order may be obtained from a court which directs an employer to deduct specified sums from the earnings of one against whom judgment or certain orders have been made. The order requires that such deductions be paid to the court. See Attachment of Earnings Act 1971, as amended.

(4) See also FREEZING INJUNCTIONS.

attainder That extinction of civil rights and capacities which formerly took place when judgment of death or outlawry was recorded against a person who had committed treason or felony. It involved the forfeiture and escheat of the land and goods belonging to the criminal, and the corruption of his blood, i.e. he became incapable of holding or inheriting land, or of transmitting a title by descent. It also resulted from Acts of Parliament known as Bills of Attainder. Abolished by the Forfeiture Act 1870. See BILL OF ATTAINDER; ATTAINT.

attempt At common law, attempt was an act done with intent to commit a crime and forming part of a series of acts which would constitute its actual commission if it were not interrupted. The common law of attempt has been abolished and attempt is now a statutory offence under the Criminal Attempts Act 1981, as amended. Attempt occurs if:
"with intent to commit an offence ... a person commits an act which is more than merely preparatory to the commission of the offence".

A person may be guilty of an attempt even though the facts are such that the commission of the offence is impossible or even though the true facts are such that no offence would have been committed (ibid. s.1 and s.1A).

attendance allowance Non-contributory national insurance benefit originally paid to those so disabled that they required constant attendance. The benefit was largely replaced by the care component of the disability living allowance (*q.v.*). Attendance allowance is still payable in respect of those who were aged 65 or more when they first qualified for the benefit. See Social Security Contributions and Benefits Act 1992 ss.63–65 and SI 1991/2740 (as amended).

attendance centres Offenders under 21 years of age can be required by a court to attend a centre and be given occupation or instruction, under supervision, for a specified number of hours up to a maximum of 36, depending on the age of the offender and the gravity of the offence (Powers of Criminal Courts (Sentencing) Act 2000 s.60, as amended by the Criminal Justice Act 2003).

attendant term Where a long term of years created a freehold for the purpose which later had become satisfied was vested in trustees for the protection of the owner of the freehold, it was said to be kept on foot "in trust to attend the inheritance". See SATISFIED TERM.

attest To witness any act or event, e.g. the signature or execution of a document, such as a will (*q.v.*).

attestation clause The statement in a deed (*q.v.*) or will (*q.v.*), etc. that it has been duly executed in the presence of witnesses.

attested copy A copy of a document which is certified correct by a person who has examined it.

attorney (1) A person appointed by another to act in his place or represent him (See POWER OF ATTORNEY).

(2) Formerly persons admitted to practise in the superior courts of common law representing suitors who did not appear in person.

Attorney-General The principal law officer of the Crown, and the head of the Bar. He is appointed by letters patent and holds at the pleasure of the Crown. He is usually a member of the House of Commons, but not normally of the Cabinet, and changes with the government. In his absence the Solicitor General (*q.v.*) will act for him.

Civil proceedings by or against the Crown may be instituted by or against the Attorney-General in lieu of the appropriate Government Department. After proceedings have been instituted he may be substituted for the authorised Government Department, or vice versa (Crown Proceedings Act 1947 s.17). See NOLLE PROSEQUI; RELATOR.

attornment (1) The agreement by the tenant of land to hold his land from the transferee of the owner of the fee, or reversion, which was formerly necessary to the validity of the grant of the reversion. He was said to attorn tenant to the new reversioner. By s.151 of the Law of Property Act 1925, the conveyance of a reversion is valid without attornment, and attornment without the lessor's consent is void.

(2) Attornment may also arise in relation to goods. At common law, where a bailee (*q.v.*) attorns to a person who is not the original bailor (*q.v.*), he becomes the bailee of that other person, holding the goods on the same terms as they were held originally.

auction A process whereby a person, the auctioneer, sells or offers for sale goods or land where a person bids against competition to purchase. Unless there is a reserved price which is not met, the purchaser will generally be the highest bidder. A bid is generally accepted when the auctioneer's hammer falls and thus a contract is created, *Payne v Cave* (1789) 3 T.R. 148. See MOCK AUCTION.

auctioneer One who conducts an auction (*q.v.*).

auctoritas [Roman law] The authorisation of a tutor, the legal capacity in virtue of which the tutor completed the legal capacity of his pupil.

audi alteram partem [Hear the other side] That no one shall be condemned unheard nor without prior notice of allegations against him is one of the principles of natural justice (*q.v.*).

audience, right of The right to appear as advocate in court proceedings.

Audit Commission A Commission for Local Authorities and the National Health Service in England whose members are appointed by the Secretary of State. The

Commission's main purpose is to undertake or promote comparative or other studies designed to enable it to make recommendations for improving economy, efficiency and effectiveness in the exercise of the functions of best value authorities and the provision of services provided by other bodies subject to audit. See the Audit Commission Act 1998 (as amended). In Wales these powers have been devolved to the Welsh Assembly (*q.v.*) under the Local Government and Public Involvement in Health Act 2007.

auditors Originally officers of the Exchequer; examiners of accounts.

With certain exceptions, every company must ensure that its accounts are audited (s.475, Companies Act 2006) and to this end the shareholders in general meeting will appoint an auditor by ordinary resolution. In order to be eligible for appointment as an auditor a person must be a member of a recognised supervisory body and be eligible for appointment under the rules of that body (s.1212 Companies Act 2006).

The auditor's principal duty is to prepare and submit a signed report on the company's accounts for a financial year (*q.v.*). Auditors must report to the company's members on the annual accounts of a company and state whether, in the auditor's opinion, the annual accounts give a true and fair view and have been properly prepared (s.495). The report may be qualified or unqualified. In addition the auditor must consider whether the information given in the directors' report for the financial year is consistent with the accounts; if not, the auditor must state that in the report (s.496). The auditors will also have certain statutory rights, notably to have access to the company's books, accounts and vouchers (s.499).

aula regis [The Hall of the King or King's Court] After the Conquest this was the King's Court or *Curia Regis* From it all the courts of justice emanated, as did the High Court of Parliament and the Privy Council.

author For copyright (*q.v.*) purposes, the author is the person who creates the work. This is taken to be the producer of a sound recording, the producer and principal director of a film, the person making a broadcast, the publisher in the case of a typographical arrangement of a published edition. For computer-generated literary, dramatic, musical or artistic work, the author is taken to be the person making the arrangements necessary for creation of the work. With the notable exception of where the author is an employee acting in the course of his employment, the author is the first owner of any copyright in a work (Copyright, Designs and Patents Act 1988).

authorised guarantee agreement (AGA) An agreement by which a tenant guarantees the performance of the covenants in the lease by the assignee (s.16 Landlord and Tenant (Covenants) Act 1995). Such an agreement lasts only until the assignee assigns the lease.

authority (1) Delegated power; a right or rights invested in a person or body. An authority is a body charged with the power and duty of exercising prescribed functions, e.g. a local planning authority. A person vested with authority is usually termed an agent (*q.v.*), and the person for whom he acts, the principal (*q.v.*). A bare authority is an authority which exists only for the benefit of the principal, which the agent must execute in accordance with his directions. An authority coupled with an interest is where the person vested with the authority has a right to exercise it, partly or wholly, for his own benefit. A mere authority is revocable by the grantor at any time; one coupled with an interest is not.

(2) A decided case, judgment, textbook of repute or statutory enactment cited as an exposition or statement of the law. See PRECEDENT.

authorship See AUTHOR.

automatism A state of mind which renders a person incapable of voluntary action.

Automatism is a defence to criminal offences, but if it is self-induced (e.g. by alcohol consumption) the defence may not succeed, depending on whether the crime requires basic intent or specific intent. A diabetes sufferer wishing to run a defence of automatism due to a hypoglycaemic attack would have to establish that he could not reasonably have avoided the attack by advance testing and advance warning (see *R v C* [2007] All E.R. (D) 91). If automatism is caused by disease of the mind, e.g. epilepsy, the defence is one of insanity (*q.v.*). See INTENTION.

autre droit, in [In right of another] For example, an executor holds the deceased's property in right of the persons entitled to his estate.

autre vie [The life of another] See TENANT PUR AUTRE VIE.

autrefois acquit [Previously acquitted] A special plea in bar to a criminal prosecution that the accused has already been tried for the same offence before a court of competent jurisdiction and has been acquitted. The plea can only succeed where the accused was in jeopardy on the first proceedings (the "double jeopardy" principle (*q.v.*)), i.e. that the merits of the prosecution's case were gone into, so that the decision of the court was that there was insufficient evidence to support the prosecution. See also the Criminal Law Act 1967 s.6(5). See Case C–187/01 *Criminal proceedings against Gözütok*; Case C–385/01 *Criminal proceedings against Brügge* [2003] 2 C.M.L.R. 59, ECJ on the prohibition on convicting a defendant twice on the same facts in two different Member State jurisdictions which are parties to the Convention implementing the Schengen Agreement (*q.v.*). See AUTREFOIS CONVICT.

autrefois convict [Previously convicted] A special plea in bar to a criminal prosecution by which the accused alleges that he has already been tried and convicted for the same offence before a court of competent jurisdiction. For a full examination of the doctrine see *Connelly v DPP* [1964] A.C. 1254; *R. v Beedie* [1998] Q.B. 356. See also AUTREFOIS ACQUIT

auxiliary jurisdiction of equity Before the Judicature Act 1873, the jurisdiction of equity by which aid was lent to the plaintiff in a common law action, as by compelling discovery of documents.

auxilium An aid. See AIDS.

aver To affirm, allege or assert in pleading to state facts positively.

average (1) The apportionment of loss incurred in mercantile transactions, such as contracts of affreightment (*q.v.*) or insurance, between the person suffering the loss and other persons concerned or interested; the contribution payable by such others to the person so suffering the loss (sometimes the term is applied to the loss or damage itself).

General average is any loss or damage voluntarily incurred for the general safety of the ship and cargo; e.g. where goods are thrown overboard in a storm for the purpose of saving the ship and the rest of the cargo. The several persons interested in the ship, freight and cargo must contribute rateably to indemnify the person whose goods have been sacrificed against all but his proportion of the general loss.

Particular average is loss or damage to the ship or cargo caused by a peril insured against (e.g. damage to goods due to sea-water), which loss falls on the persons incurring the loss. For statutory definitions and the insurance position relating to such loss see the Marine Insurance Act 1906 s.66.

(2) Some petty charges, such as towage (*q.v.*), beaconage, etc. for which the owner or consignee of goods shipped on board a vessel is bound to reimburse the master or shipowner.

(3) A service of working with his beasts, which a tenant owed to his lord.

avoid To make void. A person is said to avoid a contract when he repudiates it and sets up, as a defence in any legal proceeding taken to enforce it, some defect which prevents it from being enforceable, such as a misrepresentation or lack of capacity. Alternatively, the contract may be rescinded by the innocent party. Reasonable steps must be taken to give notice of avoidance of the contract within a reasonable time: *Car and Universal Finance Co Ltd v Caldwell* [1961] 1 Q.B. 525. See REPUDIATION; RESCISSION.

avoidance Setting aside or vacating. A bond is said to be conditioned for avoidance when it contains a condition providing that it shall be void on a certain event. See AVOID.

avow To admit or confess.

avowtry Adultery *(q.v.)*.

avulsion The cutting off of land from the property to which it belongs, as may happen if a river changes its course. The ownership of the land remains unchanged. Compare ALLUVIO *(q.v.)*.

award The finding or decision of an arbitrator or compensation awarded in respect of legal liability. See ARBITRATION; BASIC AWARD.

away-going crop See WAY-GOING CROP.

B

BATNEEC Best available technique not entailing excessive cost *(q.v.)*.

BPEO Best Practicable Enviromental Option *(q.v.)*.

BPM Best Practicable Means *(q.v.)*.

Babanaft proviso A term incorporated into a freezing injunction *(q.v.)* for the protection of third parties abroad. The proviso means that such parties will not be affected until the injunction is validated by the appropriate foreign court (*Babanaft International Co SA v Bassatne* [1990] Ch. 13).

back bond A bond of indemnity given to a surety *(q.v.)*.

back freight Expenses claimable from the owner in respect of the carriage of goods returned by a master to the port of loading because the master is unable to deliver the goods to the consignee.

backing a warrant Formerly the indorsement by a magistrate of a warrant *(q.v.)* issued by a magistrate of another district or jurisdiction to enable execution within the jurisdiction of the indorser. Now the Criminal Law Act 1977 ss.38A and 38B provide for the execution of unindorsed warrants throughout the United Kingdom. Similar provisions under the Insolvency Act 1986 s.426, allow for unindorsed warrants to be issued pursuant to insolvency.

backwardation A sum paid by a seller of stock to the purchaser for the privilege of delaying delivery. Compare CONTANGO.

bad Wrong in law, ineffectual, inoperative, or void.

bad character evidence In relation to the rules of admissibility of evidence, evidence of, or a disposition towards, misconduct on the part of a person in criminal proceedings (whether defendant or non-defendant), other than evidence which relates to the alleged facts of the offence which the defendant is charged or which is evidence of misconduct in connection with the investigation or prosecution of that offence (Criminal Justice Act 2003 s.98).

Misconduct means the commission of an offence or other reprehensible behaviour (ibid. s.112). See PREVIOUS CONVICTIONS.

bail The release from the custody of officers of the law or the court of an accused or convicted person, or one whose extradition is sought in respect of an offence, who undertakes to subsequently surrender to custody. Bail may be unconditional or granted upon some security or other condition, such as to reside in a bail hostel or, for a child or young person, to submit to electronic tagging. The grant of bail in criminal proceedings by a custody officer, constable, justice of the peace or Crown Court judge is primarily governed by the Bail Act 1976. The Supreme Court Act 1981 s.81 also regulates the Crown Court's powers to grant bail. The Police and Criminal Evidence Act 1984 Pt IV regulates the granting of bail by a custody officer, who may also impose conditions. The conditions for electronic tagging have been amended by the Criminal Justice and Immigration Act 2008.

The Bail Act 1976 established a general presumption in favour of bail (s.4), it may only be withheld in general prescribed circumstances, e.g. that there are substantial grounds for believing that the defendant, if released on bail, would fail to surrender to custody or would commit an offence or interfere with witnesses (Sch.1). However, amendments made by the Criminal Justice Act 2003 stipulate certain circumstances where bail may not normally be granted, particularly in relation to those who have tested positive for Class A drugs.

The person granted bail cannot be required to give any recognizance (*q.v.*) (Bail Act 1976 s.3(2)), but failure to surrender to custody is a separate offence (s.6). A person who absconds or fails to comply with any condition whilst on bail is liable to arrest (s.7). To agree to indemnify sureties is an offence (s.9).

bail bond A bond with sureties entered into by a defendant to a sheriff, on arrest upon a writ of *capias ad respondendum* (*q.v.*), conditioned for the defendant's appearance within the required period upon which he was entitled to discharge. See ARREST.

A bail bond is also a sworn undertaking by sureties in respect of a defendant's adjudged liability in proceedings in the Admiralty Court (*q.v.*).

bail court An auxiliary court of King's Bench at Westminster, wherein points connected more particularly with pleading and practice were argued and determined. Also called the Practice Court (*q.v.*).

bailee A person taking possession of goods with the consent of the owner, or the owner's agent, where there is no intention to transfer ownership.

Any person is a bailee who, otherwise than as an employee, either receives or holds possession of a thing for another, upon an undertaking with that other to keep and return or deliver it to him or to a third party according to his directions.

A bailee has a special property or qualified ownership in the goods bailed and may recover damages from a person who wrongly injures the goods.

The bailment is determined and the right to possess the goods reverts to the bailor if the bailee does an act entirely inconsistent with the terms of the bailment. Loss caused by an act not authorised by the terms of the bailment, though not otherwise negligent, will fall on the bailee, unless inevitable in any case. A bailee is bound to take care of the goods bailed and is liable for negligence. The standard of duty of care varies according to the type of bailment.

A bailee whose original possession was innocent could not be convicted of larceny (*q.v.*) at common law unless and until he committed a trespass by breaking bulk, but a bailee may now be guilty of theft (*q.v.*) under the Theft Act 1968 s.1. See BAILMENT; BULK GOODS.

bailiff Formerly an officer entrusted with the local administration of justice. Now a sheriff's officer appointed by a high sheriff to execute writs and processes.

Because the sheriff is legally responsible for their acts, his bailiffs are annually bound to him in a bond with sureties for the due execution of their office and known as bound bailiffs or "bum bailiffs".

County Court bailiffs are employed by the county courts to enforce court orders by recovering money owed under a county court judgment.

bailiwick The area within which an under-sheriff exercises jurisdiction (Under-Sheriffs' Bailiwicks Order SI 1974/222, art.2(1), made under Local Government Act 1972 s.219). These areas do not necessarily correspond with the boundaries of the county areas covered by high sheriffs. This results in some counties having more than one bailiwick and some bailiwicks spanning more than one county.

bailment The transfer of possession of goods, but not ownership, by the bailor on a condition, expressed or implied, that the goods shall be returned by the bailee to the bailor, or according to his directions, as soon as the purpose for which they are bailed has been fulfilled. Examples of bailment include: hire or lease of goods; delivery of goods for repair or under a pledge.

Bailments were divided into six classes by Holt C.J. in *Coggs v Bernard* (1703) 2 Ld. Raym 909, but essentially they are either gratuitous or contractual, i.e. for good consideration. See BAILEE; BAILOR.

bailor One who entrusts goods to a bailee (*q.v.*). The bailor has the general property in, or general ownership of, the goods bailed.

balance order An order obtained by a liquidator making a call on contributories in the course of the winding up (*q.v.*) of a company. See the Insolvency Act 1986.

ballot System of secret voting. Secret ballot was introduced for the purpose of parliamentary elections by the Ballot Act 1872. The Representation of the People Act 1983, a consolidating statute, regulates ballots for both parliamentary and local government elections and preserves the right to secrecy (s.66). This right is extended to European Parliamentary elections by virtue of European Parliamentary Elections Regulations, SI 1999/1214 reg.3(1) and Sch.1.

The Government of Wales Act 1999 and SI 1999/450 regulate ballots in respect of the Welsh Assembly and ballots to the Scottish Parliament are regulated by the Scotland Act 1998 and SI 1999/787.

In the field of industrial relations, secret ballots must be held to validate the election of members to a trade union executive committee and trade union strike or other industrial action (see Trade Union and Labour Relations (Consolidation) Act 1992).

banc, or banco, sitting in Prior to the Judicature Acts (*q.v.*) coming into force, sittings held at Westminster by judges of the King's or Queen's Bench, Common Pleas and the Exchequer exclusively to determine questions of law. These were held both during term and on other appointed days. When judges of these courts sat at nisi prius (*q.v.*) or on circuit they dealt only with questions of fact. Four judges normally sat together *in banc*, while at nisi prius or on circuit, judges sat singly.

banishment The compulsory quitting and forsaking of the realm. This may arise by abjuration (*q.v.*) or by authority of Parliament.

bank holidays Traditionally the days (other than Saturdays and Sundays) on which the banks and other commercial institutions were closed. Under the Banking and Financial Dealings Act 1971 s.1 and Sch.1, the bank holidays in England and Wales are Easter Monday, the last Mondays in May and August, December 26th (if not a Sunday), December 27th in a year in which December 25th or 26th is a Sunday and any other day appointed by proclamation. Since 1974, January 1st (or 2nd if appropriate) has been so proclaimed, as has the first Monday in May since 1978. Good Friday and Christmas Day, whilst generally considered to be bank holidays, are common law holidays in England and Wales.

bank notes Defined in the Currency and Bank Notes Act 1954 s.3 as "notes of the Bank of England payable to bearer on demand". This Act authorises the Bank of England to issue bank notes of such denominations as the Treasury (*q.v.*) might approve (s.1(1)). Similarly, the Treasury is empowered to call in bank notes which it declares to cease being legal tender (s.1(5)).

banker Defined in the Bills of Exchange Act 1882 as including "a body of persons whether incorporated or not who carry on the business of banking" (s.2). In practice a banker receives the money of its customers on deposit and pays it out again in accordance with the customers' instructions. The relation between banker and customer is that of debtor (banker) and creditor, not of trustee and cestui que trust (*q.v.*). There is an additional obligation arising out of the custom of bankers to honour the written instructions of customers and in following these instructions the banker acts as agent for the customer. The banker owes a duty of secrecy to its customers.

Under the amended Companies Act 1985 ss.255–255B, s.255D and Sch.9, special provisions apply to the disclosure of information and accounting standards required of banking companies and groups. The Financial Services and Markets Act 2000 removed the distinction between banking and other forms of financial services and regulates all financial services.

bankers' books Under the Bankers' Books Evidence Act 1879, as amended, these include ledgers, day books, cash books, account books and other records used in the ordinary business of a bank (including that undertaken now by a building society, National Savings Bank and the Post Office). These may be written records or on microfilm, magnetic tape or other forms of data retrieval mechanism (s.9(2)). Case law has excluded from this definition paid cheques and paying-in slips retained by a bank after the transaction to which they relate has been concluded (*Williams v Williams; Tucker v Williams* [1987] 3 All E.R. 257; [1987] 3 W.L.R. 790, CA).

A copy of any entry in a banker's book is, in legal proceedings, prima facie evidence of the contents of the entry and of the matters, transactions and accounts recorded therein (ibid. s.3). Upon application by a party to legal proceedings a court or judge may order bankers' books to be made available to that party for the purpose of such proceedings (ibid. s.7 and see Financial Services and Marketing Act 2000).

banker's draft A draft (*q.v.*) drawn by a banker on himself, payable on demand at the head office or other office of his bank. Such drafts are not bills of exchange (*q.v.*) nor cheques, but, nevertheless, may be effectively crossed and the banker handling them protected under the Bills of Exchange Act 1882 and the Cheques Act 1957.

bankrupt An individual who has been adjudged bankrupt and whose estate is administered by a trustee in bankruptcy for the benefit of the bankrupt's creditors. A bankrupt must co-operate in the administration of his estate with the trustee in bankruptcy. An undischarged bankrupt is subject to a number of disqualifications which include holding a solicitor's practising certificate and being a Member of Parliament. There are several bankruptcy offences, e.g. obtaining credit above the prescribed amount without disclosing status as a bankrupt. General provisions governing bankrupts are contained in the Insolvency Acts 1986 and 2000 and the Enterprise Act 2002.

bankruptcy The process by which an insolvent individual is made bankrupt and his estate administered for the benefit of his creditors (Insolvency Act 1986 Pt IX). Bankruptcy proceedings are initiated by a petition upon which the court may make a bankruptcy order (*q.v.*). A petition may be presented by: a creditor or creditors; the debtor; the supervisor of a voluntary arrangement or a party to that arrangement; the official petitioner or any person specified in the order where a criminal bankruptcy order has been made; a temporary administrator; a liquidator. After a bankruptcy order is made, the official receiver becomes the receiver and manager of the bankrupt's estate. The estate is administered by a trustee in bankruptcy (*q.v.*), who may be either a qualified insolvency practitioner or the official receiver. On his appointment the debtor's estate vests automatically in the trustee, who is then responsible for the administration of the estate. Most bankruptcies are automatically discharged one year after the date of the bankruptcy order.

Bankruptcy is generally regulated by the Insolvency Act 1986, the Insolvency Act 2000 and the Enterprise Act 2002.

bankruptcy order An order issued by the High Court or county courts under which an individual is made bankrupt. See BANKRUPTCY.

bankruptcy restriction order (BRO) The court can make a bankruptcy restriction order for between 2 to 15 years if it thinks it appropriate having regard to the conduct of the bankrupt before or after the making of the bankruptcy order. The order will usually take effect on discharge of the bankrupt and restrictions include prohibitions on the individual acting as an insolvency practitioner, or as a company director without leave of the court, or from obtaining credit over £500 without disclosing that a BRO is in force; or from trading other than in the name under which that person was adjudged bankrupt (Insolvency Act 1986 as amended by the Enterprise Act 2002).

banning order An order made under the Football Spectators Act 1989 ss.14–14J. Significant amendments were made to this Act by the Football (Disorder) Act 2000, including the imposition of banning orders, and banning orders are regulated by the Anti-social Behaviour Act 2003 and the Violent Crime Reduction Act 2006. The order may be made on conviction or complaint of a relevant offence where the magistrates believe that the order would "help to prevent violence or disorder at or in connection with certain association football matches" (s.1 of the 2000 Act). The Football Spectators Act 1989 allows the order to be made to prevent attendance by an individual at a regulated football match in England and Wales by prohibiting their attendance and outside England and Wales by requiring an individual to report to a police station prior to a match. In the latter case the individual subject to the order may be required to surrender his passport. A person who fails to comply with the terms of a banning order will be guilty of a criminal offence. See also ANTISOCIAL BEHAVIOUR ORDER; DRINKING BANNING ORDER.

banns of marriage The publication in church of an intended marriage between the persons named. This is one of four different methods of procedure which must precede the solemnisation of a valid marriage according to the rites of the Church of England under s.5 of the Marriage Act 1949. The banns must be published in accordance with the Act's provisions (ss.6–14).

bar (1) A partition across a court of justice.

(2) In the Houses of Lords and Commons the bar forms the boundary of the House and, therefore, all persons who have to address the House appear at the bar for that purpose.

(3) To bar a legal right is to destroy or end it, e.g. bar an entail or cause of action under the Limitation Act 1980.

Bar The professional body of barristers, so called because they are "called to the bar" when admitted into practice.

Bar Council See general council of the bar of England and Wales.

Bar Standards Board Established in 2006 as the independent regulatory board of the Bar Council (*q.v.*), its responsibilities include setting the education and training requirements for becoming a barrister, setting standards of conduct for barristers and handling complaints against barristers. Where necessary it will take disciplinary action.

Bar Vocational Course The vocational stage of qualification prior to a person being called to the Bar. This provides instruction in skills, knowledge and attitudes required to practise as a barrister and is recognised by the Bar Council.

bare licensee A person who, for his own purposes, is permitted by the occupier of property to go or be upon that property, so as not to be a trespasser (*q.v.*). The bare licensee has no contractual right to use the land and the occupier may revoke the licence at any time.

bare trustee A simple or naked trustee (*q.v.*). One who merely holds property on trust with no present interest in or duty as to the trust property, except to convey it when required according to the directions of the beneficial owner.

Barmote courts Ancient courts comprising the Great Barmote Courts and the Small Barmote Courts of High Peak. Still in existence, their jurisdiction relates to mining rights in parts of the High Peak in Derbyshire. These courts of record are regulated by statute, their judge is called a steward (or deputy steward) and the officers are barmasters (or their deputies). The Barmote Courts of Wirksworth and adjacent liberties are similar to those of the High Peaks.

baron [Man] "Baron and feme" meant husband and wife.

Before the Judicature Acts (*q.v.*), judges of the Court of Exchequer were called barons and the chief judge of that court was called the Lord Chief Baron of the Exchequer.

One of the five degrees of peerage. See BARONY.

baronetcy An hereditary dignity founded in 1611 by James I. Baronets take precedence of knighthoods other than those of the Order of the Garter. Baronets are entitled to the title "Sir".

barony The rank of a baron, the lowest rank in the peerage. A writ of summons to Parliament, followed by an actual sitting therein, formerly created a barony.

They are now created by letters patent (*q.v.*) Baronies created by writ descend to the heirs of the original baron, and are consequently held by a number of females. Baronies by letters patent descend according to the provisions of the patent.

barratry (1) The former common law offence of habitually moving, exciting or maintaining suits, abolished by the Criminal Law Act 1967 s.13.

(2) Any wrongful act wilfully committed by the master or crew of a ship to the prejudice of the owner or charterer without the latter's knowledge or connivance, e.g. sinking the ship or stealing the cargo. Barratry is one of the perils of the sea generally insured against in policies of marine insurance, Marine Insurance Act 1906 Sch.1.

barrister A member of one of the four Inns of Court (*q.v.*) who has been called to the Bar by his Inn. The ordinary work of a barrister is to supply legal services, including legal advice, representation (advocacy), drafting or settling statements of case, witness statements and affidavits (*q.v.*). A barrister intending to practise must spend 12 months as a pupil. The professional conduct of barristers is regulated by the General Council of the Bar of England and Wales (*q.v.*).

Barristers' fees at common law are *honoraria* and no action lies to recover such fees.

Barristers were formerly immune against actions for negligence arising out of their presentation of cases in court (see *Rondel v Worsley* [1969] 1 A.C. 191; *Saif Ali v Sydney Mitchell & Co* [1980] A.C. 198, HL; and s.62 of the Courts and Legal Services Act 1990). However, in *Arthur J.S. Hall & Co (a firm) v Simons* [2000] 3 All E.R. 673 the House of Lords held that advocates no longer enjoyed immunity from suit in respect of their conduct of civil and criminal proceedings (see *Awoyami v Radford* [2007] All ER (D) 183).

barrister's opinion The term used to describe a document written by a barrister commenting upon various issues within a legal matter, e.g. on evidential or procedural issues.

base courts Inferior courts (*q.v.*), or those not of record (*q.v.*).

base fee (1) An estate which has some qualifications attached and which determines whenever such qualification occurs.
(2) Specifically, the estate created by a tenant in tail barring the entail (*q.v.*) by executing a disentailing assurance (*q.v.*).

base rate The interest rate set by the Bank of England and which is used as the basis for the rates of interest charged by other banks. It is important in considering interest to be paid on, e.g. damages.

base tenure A tenure under which land was held by base services, e.g. villein tenure, the former equivalent of copyhold tenure. See SERVICE.

basic award A sum payable by an ex-employer to the successful claimant in an unfair dismissal (*q.v.*) claim. The amount is calculated on the basis of the claimant's age, gross weekly pay and length of service at the effective date of termination. Pay and years of service are subject to statutory maximum figures set out in the Employment Rights Act 1996 ss.119–122 and s.227.

bastard Commonly, a child born out of wedlock: an illegitimate child. See LEGITIMACY.

bastardise Formerly if the court made a decree of nullity of marriage, the effect was to make illegitimate any children of the marriage, or to bastardise them. Since 1959 the child of a void marriage is treated as the legitimate child of his parents if at all material times both or either of them reasonably believed that the marriage was valid (now Legitimacy Act 1976 s.1 as amended by the Family Law Reform Act 1987 s.28.) The relevant time under s.1 is "the insemination resulting in the birth, or where there was no such insemination, the child's conception". See LEGITIMACY

bastardy order Formerly an affiliation order governing the obligations of the adjudged father of an illegitimate child. Abolished by the Family Law Reform Act 1987. See LEGITIMACY.

battery The direct or indirect application of unlawful force by one person upon another. This may be intentional or reckless, but must amount to a positive act (*Fagan v Metropolitan Police Commissioner* [1969] 1 Q.B. 439). Battery may occur through the medium of a third party: *Haystead v Chief Constable of Derbyshire* [2000] 3 All E.R. 890, DC.

battle, trial by Method of trying accused persons, determining appeals or settling certain civil disputes. The two opposing parties engaged in physical combat, each armed with a leather shield and a cudgel and continued fighting until the stars came out or one of them submitted. The defeated party was thus found guilty or failed in his claim or appeal. The parties originally fought in person (with some exceptions, e.g. children) but eventually all civil litigants were permitted to be represented by champions. This form of trial was introduced by the Normans, becoming virtually obsolete during the fourteenth century. It was abolished in 1819 by statute (59 Geo. 3 c.46), after its attempted invocation in the murder case of *Ashford v Thornton* (1818) 1 B. & Ald. 405, where the challenge was declined.

In 1985 an unsuccessful attempt was made to challenge the Lord Advocate in battle by a defendant claiming that the 1819 Act did not change the law in Scotland.

beadle A common law parish officer chosen by the vestry *(q.v.)* to hold office as its messenger and servant. Now largely obsolete and replaced by the sexton or verger.

bear One who sells stocks or shares "short" on the Stock Exchange, i.e. without possessing what he sells, but intending to buy in later when the price has fallen and make a profit of the difference. Contrast bull.

bearer The person in possession of a bill of exchange *(q.v.)* or promissory note *(q.v.)* which is payable to the bearer (Bills of Exchange Act 1882 s.2). Payment of a bearer security may be claimed by anyone who presents it.

bees Bees are *ferae naturae (q.v.)* so there is no property in them until they are hived. After hiving the hiver retains property in them even if the swarm leaves the hive as long as the swarm can be seen and followed.

The Bees Act 1980 gave wide powers to the Minister of Agriculture Fisheries and Food (now Department for Environment, Food and Rural Affairs) to make provision to control pests and diseases affecting bees. These powers can be invoked to, inter alia prohibit or regulate the importation of bees, bee combs, or hives into Great Britain, authorise examination of bees, etc. and order the destruction of infected bees, etc. The Bee Diseases and Pests Control Orders 2006 were passed in pursuance of these powers to restrict the spread of named diseases of bees.

begin, right to The right of the party to a suit on whom the main burden of proof rests to open his case first.

behaviour See UNREASONABLE BEHAVIOUR.

belief See RELIGION.

bench The judges of a court of law, including magistrates.

Benchers, or Masters of the Bench The governing body of each of the four Inns of Court *(q.v.)*, having control over the property of their respective Inn. They have power to determine the admission of students, calls to the Bar, disbarring members and disbenching their colleagues. Disciplinary authority with respect to external matters rest with the Council of the Inns of Court. See GENERAL COUNCIL OF THE BAR OF ENGLAND AND WALES

benefice An ecclesiastical living of the Church of England, e.g. rectory, vicarage, perpetual curacy, whereby the incumbent has a freehold interest in the emoluments of that benefice until his death or vacation of the office. The freehold of the benefice is held by a patron, e.g. bishop. As to the creation, alteration and dissolution of benefices, see the Pastoral Measure 1983 and the amended Incumbents (Vacation of Benefice) Measure 1977.

beneficial interest The interest of a beneficial owner *(q.v.)* or beneficiary under a trust.

beneficial owner The person who enjoys or who is entitled to the benefit of property being entitled both at law and in equity. In a conveyance of land for valuable consideration (other than a mortgage) by a person who conveys and is expressed to convey as beneficial owner it is implied that it is conveyed with full title guarantee or with limited title guarantee (or their Welsh equivalent), s.9 of the Law of Property (Miscellaneous Amendments) Act 1994 (as amended).

beneficiary [Cestui que trust *(q.v.)*] Person entitled in equity to property held on trust.

beneficium [Roman law] A privilege or benefit: (1) *competentiae*: the privilege of having the *condemnatio* limited to the extent of a person's means so that he should not be reduced to want; (2) *inventarii*: the full inventory made by the heir which, under Justinian, released him from all personal liability beyond the value of the estate; (3) *separationis*: the advantage of having a clear separation made between the property of testator and of heir.

benefit of clergy Exemption of members of the clergy from criminal process. An accused cleric was handed over by the secular court to the bishop to be tried under canon law (*q.v.*) in the ecclesiastical courts. The privilege was extended during the 14th and 15th centuries to all able to read, literacy being demonstrated by the accused or convicted person's recital of the neck verse (*q.v.*). Laymen could claim the benefit only once, after which they were branded on the thumb to prevent them claiming it again.

Many statutes were passed making felonies punishable without benefit of clergy. Originally women could not claim the benefit, but it was later extended to them. Benefit of clergy could be claimed neither in treason nor in other cases provided for by particular statutes. It was abolished in 1827 by statute 7 & 8 Geo. 4 c.28.

benevolences An early mode of raising money for the Crown. They purported to be voluntary loans, but were in reality forced contributions not intended to be repaid. They were afterwards levied as an anticipation of the lawful revenue. Prohibited by the Petition of Right 1627.

benevolent society A society formed for benevolent or charitable purposes and one of six types of society subject to the provisions of the Friendly Societies Acts, notably of 1974 and 1992. Subject to regulation by the Financial Services Authority (*q.v.*).

benignae faciendae sunt interpretationes et verba intentioni debent inservire [Liberal interpretation should be the rule, and the words should be made to carry out the intention]

bequeath Give personal property by will (*q.v.*).

bequest A gift of personal property by will (*q.v.*). A residuary bequest is a gift of the residue of the testator's personal estate. A specific bequest is a bequest of property of a certain kind, e.g. a watch.

Berne Convention 1886 The international convention for the protection of literary and artistic copyright, subsequently amended. The Copyright Act was passed in 1911 to give effect to the Convention in English law. Now, the Copyright, Designs and Patents Act 1988 (as amended) restates the law on inter alia copyright (*q.v.*). The Act concerns the protection of intellectual property rights generally and has been amended to cover such forms of property as computer programs, databases and satellite broadcasts.

best available technique not entailing excessive cost (BATNEEC) It is a requirement of s.7 of the Environmental Protection Act 1990, that certain prescribed processes which require authorisation under Pt I of the 1990 Act use the best available techniques not entailing excessive cost in order to prevent the release of prescribed substances into any environmental medium (air, water and land) or, where that is not practicable, to reduce the release of such substances and to render them harmless to the environment. The Environment Agency (*q.v.*) may impose whatever conditions are necessary to achieve the standard of BATNEEC. The concept of BATNEEC involves a balance between the costs of using the best available pollution abatement techniques and the benefits that accrue to the environment from using them. BATNEEC is usually expressed as emission limits for the prescribed substances released by the process. See INTEGRATED POLLUTION CONTROL; BEST PRACTICABLE ENVIRONMENTAL OPTION; BEST AVAILABLE TECHNIQUES.

best available techniques In setting the conditions of an Integrated Pollution Prevention Control (IPPC) permit the regulator should seek to ensure that all appropriate preventative measures are taken against pollution, in particular through the application of the best available techniques (s.11(2) of the Pollution Prevention and Control Regulations 2000). Section 3 of the regulations provides that the best available techniques means the most effective and advanced stage in the development of activities and their methods of operation which indicates the practical suitability of particular techniques for providing in principle the basis for emission limit values (*q.v.*) designed to prevent and, where that is not practicable, generally to reduce emissions and the impact on the environment as a whole. See INTEGRATED POLLUTION PREVENTION CONTROL.

best practicable environmental option (BPEO) In framing the conditions of an IPC (*q.v.*) authorisation, the Environment Agency (*q.v.*) must impose the necessary conditions in order to achieve the minimisation of pollution (*q.v.*) to the environment (*q.v.*) as a whole having regard to the best practicable environmental option available. This is the option that provides the most benefit or least damage to the environment as a whole, at acceptable cost, in the long as well as the short term (Royal Commission on Environmental Pollution). See BATNEEC; BPM; INTEGRATED POLLUTION CONTROL.

best practicable means (BPM) A standard frequently used in environmental law, for example, in relation to certain statutory nuisances (*q.v.*) arising on trade and industrial premises. It is a ground for defence in respect of non-compliance with an abatement notice (*q.v.*) to prove that the best practicable means were used to prevent or counteract the effects of the nuisance (Environmental Protection Act 1990 s.80(7)). Best practicable means is not a fixed standard but means reasonably practicable having regard to among other things local conditions and circumstances, the current state of technical knowledge and the financial implications (EPA 1990 s.79(9)).

bestiality Formerly the crime of buggery (*q.v.*) committed with an animal. See now Sexual Offences Act 2003 s.69. See SEXUAL OFFENCES.

betterment Increasing the value of property by public improvements effected in its vicinity, and for which the owners may be required to contribute towards the cost.

betting Risking one's money or other value against another's on the result of a sporting or other event, the outcome of which is uncertain. Betting agreements, including wager (*q.v.*) agreements, are void at common law.

The Gambling Act 2005 has repealed the existing legislation on gaming, betting and participating in lotteries and replaced it with a new unified framework. Under the 2005 Act, s.9 betting means making or accepting a bet on: (a) the outcome of a race, competition or other event or process; (b) the likelihood of anything occurring or not occurring; (c) whether anything is or is not true. See GAMBLING; GAMING; LOTTERY; WAGER.

betting house This was a "house, office room or other place" used for betting (Betting Act 1853, repealed). Under the Act it was unlawful to keep a betting house. In *Powell v Kempton Park Racecourse Co Ltd* [1899] A.C. 143 a betting house was held to be confined to indoor places. See BETTING OFFICE.

betting levy A levy introduced in 1961 payable by bookmakers (*q.v.*) and now the Horserace Totalisator Board (due to be dissolved by the Horse Race Betting and Olympic Lottery Act 2004) on their turnover derived from betting on horse races. The levy is assessed and collected by the Horserace Betting Levy Board (originally due to be dissolved by the Horse Race Betting and Olympic Lottery Act 2004 but now expected to survive until 2009), which is empowered to use the funds so raised for the improvement of breeds of horses and horse racing and the advancement or encouragement of veterinary science or veterinary education.

betting office Licensed premises to which persons may resort for the purpose of betting with the holder of a betting premises licence. Formerly regulated by the Betting, Gaming and Lotteries Act 1963, this Act has been repealed by the Gambling Act 2005. The Act introduces a single regulator for gambling in Great Britain, the Gambling Commission, and a new licensing regime for commercial gambling. It also establishes a Gambling Appeals Tribunal to hear appeals from decisions made by the Commission.

bias See NATURAL JUSTICE.

bid A contractual offer (a) to buy at a bidden price a lot which is displayed at auction (*Payne v Cave* (1789) 3 Term Rep. 148); or (b) made in response to an invitation to tender (*Harvela Investments v Royal Trust Co of Canada* [1986] A.C. 207).

bigamy The offence committed by any person who, being validly married and while the marriage subsists, marries any other person during the life of the existing spouse, whether the second marriage takes place in England or elsewhere (Offences Against the Person Act 1861 s.57 as amended). It is a defence that the existing wife or husband has been absent for seven years at the date of subsequent marriage and has not been known by the spouse to be living during that time. Even if seven years have not elapsed, bona fide belief, on reasonable grounds, of death is a good defence (*R. v Tolson* (1889) 23 Q.B.D. 168). An honest belief on reasonable grounds of the invalidity of the previous marriage or of the death of the spouse (*R. v King* [1964] 1 Q.B. 285) or that a decree absolute has dissolved the previous marriage (*R. v Gould* [1968] 2 Q.B. 65) is also a defence.

bill (1) A letter or written document.

(2) A parliamentary measure which, having been passed by both Houses and receiving the Royal Assent (*q.v.*), becomes an Act of Parliament (*q.v.*).

(3) A document by which legal proceedings were formerly commenced, e.g. a Bill in Chancery.

bill of attainder Formerly a bill formulating an accusation against a peer, or other high personage, in a matter of public importance, declaring him to be attainted and his property forfeited. See ATTAINDER.

bill of costs A statement or account delivered to his client by a solicitor setting out in detail the work done on behalf of the client and showing the amount charged for each item, including disbursements. The bill of costs to be enforceable must be signed by the solicitor or a duly authorised employee of the solicitor or in a duly signed letter referring to the bill. The bill may be delivered to the party to be charged personally, or by post to, or left for him at, his place of business, dwelling house or last known place of abode, or by electronic means where the party to be charged has so agreed. (Solicitors Act 1974 s.69, as amended by the Legal Services Act 2007). For bills of costs in contentious work, see ibid. s.64. No action to recover the costs can be brought until one month after delivery, except in cases of imminent insolvency, etc. of the client. See COSTS.

bill of entry The account deposited with Customs giving particulars of goods imported or exported, Customs and Excise Management Act 1979 ss.35, 53 (as amended).

bill of exceptions A statement of the objections of a party to a suit to the decisions of the judge on matters of law, which was then argued before a court of error. Abolished by the Common Law Procedure Act 1852.

bill of exchange A form of negotiable instrument:

"an unconditional order in writing, addressed by one person to another, signed by the person giving it, requiring the person to whom it is addressed to pay on demand or at a fixed or determinable future time a sum certain in money to or to the order of a specified person, or to bearer" (Bills of Exchange Act 1882 s.3).

A bill is given by the drawer, and addressed to the drawee, who becomes the acceptor by signing the bill. The bill is payable to the payee, who must be named or indicated with reasonable certainty (ibid. s.7(1)). If the payee is a fictitious or non-existing person the bill may be treated as payable to bearer (ibid. s.7(3)).

bill of health A document given to the master of a ship by the consul of the port from which he comes, describing the sanitary state of the place. It may be a clean, suspected, or foul bill. The vessel may be considered unseaworthy without a bill of health.

bill of indictment A written or printed accusation of crime made at the suit of the Crown against one or more persons. Formerly it was a draft written accusation presented to a grand jury (*q.v.*), which, if of the opinion that there was sufficient ground to put the accused on trial before the petty jury, endorsed "true bill" on the back of it. On presentment by the grand jury it became an indictment. Otherwise the words "we do not know" were endorsed and the bill was thrown out. If a bill is not duly signed, there can be no valid trial on indictment (see *R. v Clarke* [2008] 2 All E.R. 665 (HL)). See INDICTMENT.

bill of lading A document signed and delivered by the master of a ship or other authorised person to the shippers on goods being shipped to acknowledge their receipt. The bill is conclusive evidence against the carrier of the shipment of the goods or their receipt for shipment (s.1 and s.4 of the Carriage of Goods by Sea Act 1992). Copies are kept by the master, the shipper and the consignee. It is a document of title transferable by indorsement and delivery, giving the holder the right to sue thereon, but it is not a negotiable instrument (*q.v.*) so that a transferee obtains no better title than the transferor has.

Bill of Middlesex The procedure contrived in the 15th century to avoid using the writ system and the unpopular Court of Common Pleas, whereby the Court of King's Bench acquired jurisdiction in civil disputes. The bill was issued to the sheriff of Middlesex commanding him to arrest the defendant for an imaginary trespass (in which the court had jurisdiction) and bring him before the court. Then he was proceeded against for any cause of action. If the defendant was not found in Middlesex the sheriff made a return of *non est inventus* (*q.v.*), whereupon the court issued the process of *latitat* to the sheriff of the county in which he *latitat et discurrit* ("lurks and runs about"). The latitat commanded the sheriff to arrest the defendant. *Latitat* was abolished by the Uniformity of Process Act 1832.

bill of pains and penalties A bill, usually introduced in the House of Lords, for the punishment of a named person without trial in the ordinary way. Such person could defend himself by counsel and witness. The last such bill was against Queen Caroline in 1820.

bill of particulars A written statement of what a claimant sought to recover in an action, being an amplification of the claim as set out in the declaration of summons. Now particulars of claim (*q.v.*).

bill of peace A bill which could be filed in Chancery for the grant of a perpetual injunction to restrain all further proceedings at law by the litigants, or those claiming under them upon the same title. The object was to prevent multiplicity of suits.

Bill of Rights The declaration delivered by the Lords and Commons to the Prince and Princess of Orange and afterwards enacted as the statute (1 Will. & Mary sess. 2 c.2), which inter alia abolished the dispensing and suspending of power and provided for freedom of speech in Parliament. The political campaign to enact a new Bill of Rights in the United Kingdom to enshrine the fundamental rights of the individual led eventually to the formal adoption of the European Convention on Human Rights through the passing of the Human Rights Act 1998. See HUMAN RIGHTS.

bill of sale A written document to transfer property in chattels (*q.v.*) where possession is not intended to be transferred (but excluding inter alia bills of lading) (definition contained in the Bills of Sale Act 1878 s.4). Regulated by the Bills of Sale Act 1878 and the Bills of Sale (1878) Amendment Act 1882.

billeting Formerly the quartering of soldiers and their horses in the house or premises of a subject. The Petition of Right 1628 contained protests against the billeting of soldiers upon the property of private persons, and it was declared illegal. Billeting of soldiers was subsequently legalised by the Mutiny Acts. Now, the Army Act 1955 and the Air Force Act 1955 empower the proper authorities of the armed forces to issue billeting requisitions. These can require occupiers of prescribed premises to provide accommodation for members of Her Majesty's forces or their vehicles.

binding over (1) Requiring a person to enter into a recognisance *(q.v.)* to perform some act, e.g. to prosecute or to give evidence.

(2) Magistrates have power on complaint to bind a person over to keep the peace or to be of good behaviour (Magistrates' Courts Act 1980 s.115). Binding over to be of good behaviour, without any finding that the defendant has breached the peace, has been held to be a violation of the European Convention on Human Rights, see *Hashman and Harrup v UK* (2000) 30 E.H.R.R. 241.

Proceedings under s.115 have been held by the European Court of Human Rights to amount to criminal proceedings giving rise to the due process rights in Art.6 of the Convention, see *Steel and Others v UK* (1998) 28 E.H.R.R 603. The power under the Criminal Justice Act 1991 s.58 for the binding over of a parent or guardian of a juvenile offender has been abolished by the Powers of Criminal Courts (Sentencing) Act 2000 Sch.12.

(3) The Crown Court has a common law power where, instead of imposing a punishment on a convicted person (other than one convicted for murder), it may require him to enter into recognisances with or without sureties to come up for judgment when called upon. He is usually also bound over to keep the peace and be of good behaviour.

(4) Any court of record *(q.v.)* having criminal jurisdiction has an auxiliary power to bind over to be of good behaviour a person (including a witness) whose case is before the court by requiring him to enter into his own recognisances or to find sureties or both and committing him to prison if he does not comply (Justices of the Peace Act 1968 s.1(7)).

biometric immigration document In the case of a person subject to immigration control a document which records information about that person's external physical characteristics (UK Borders Act 2007).

biometric information In the case of a person subject to immigration control information about that person's external characteristics including his fingerprints and features of his iris or any other part of his eyes (UK Borders Act 2007 s.15).

Birmingham Six The six men sentenced to life imprisonment after conviction in 1975 of murder arising out of a Birmingham pub bombing the previous year in which 21 people were killed. After an unsuccessful appeal, commenced in 1987, their case was again referred to the Court of Appeal by the Home Secretary in 1990. Their convictions were quashed as "unsafe and unsatisfactory" in 1991 and they were released after spending 16 years in prison. Their release coincided with the setting up of the Royal Commission on Criminal Justice which reported in 1993. The Report led to significant legislative change, including the establishment of the Criminal Cases Review Commission *(q.v.)*, which investigates suspected cases of miscarriages of justice and has the power to refer cases back to the Court of Appeal. The Commission's powers, etc. are regulated by Pt II of the Criminal Appeal Act 1995. See MISCARRIAGE OF JUSTICE.

birretum The black cap or coif (*q.v.*) formerly worn by judges and Serjeants-at-Law (*q.v.*).

birth Legal duties are imposed concerning the notification and registration of the birth of babies, including still-births. Notification by the father or other attendant at the birth is regulated under s.269 of the National Health Service Act 2006. This provision also lays down the duties of the registrar of births and deaths to notify the appropriate Primary Care Trust of a birth. Registration and particulars of the birth must also be lodged with the registrar of births and deaths under the Births and Deaths Registration Act 1953. See CONCEALMENT OF BIRTH.

bishop A legally ordained minister of the Church of England appointed by the Crown as chief ecclesiastical officer in a diocese or archdiocese in the case of archbishop. The legal process of appointing a bishop upon a vacancy occurring is prescribed in the Appointment of Bishops Act 1533 (as amended, notably by the Statute Law Revision Act 1888 and the Cathedrals Measure 1999). After confirmation of the appointment, the bishop is consecrated and installed under the 1533 Act. Senior bishops are summoned to the House of Lords and known as the lords spiritual.

bishop, suffragan A bishop who assists a diocesan bishop. Appointed by the Crown from two nominees forwarded by the diocesan bishop in conformity with the Suffragan Bishops Acts 1534 and 1898 and the Suffragans Nomination Act 1888.

black cap A square black cap worn over the wig by a judge of the High Court on solemn or state occasions. Historically judges donned the black cap when passing the death sentence.

black list A list of persons or corporations with whom no dealings are to be had by those circulated with the list. Of particular importance in the context of traders and unpaid debts (*Thorne v Motor Trade Association* [1937] A.C. 797).

Black Rod The Gentleman Usher of the Black Rod is the chief officer of the Order of the Garter. He attends the House of Lords during its sittings and his other duties include the execution of the orders of the House in taking offenders into custody and assisting in ceremonies. In his capacity of Serjeant-at-Arms of the House of Lords he attends the Lord Chancellor (*q.v.*) or the lord acting as Speaker. His deputy is the Yeoman Usher.

blackleg (1) One who wins money at cards or betting by dishonest practices.
(2) One who continues to work during an industrial strike (also known as a "scab").

blackmail Originally rent payable in cattle, labour or produce (*niger redditus*), as distinguished from rent payable in silver or white money. Subsequently it meant the toll levied by freebooters along the Scottish border.
A person commits blackmail:
"if, with a view to gain for himself or another or with intent to cause loss to another, he makes any unwarranted demand with menaces" (Theft Act 1968 s.21).
See MENACES.

blank, acceptance in An acceptance written before the bill is filled up. It is an authority to fill up the paper as a complete bill for any amount (Bills of Exchange Act 1882 s.20.) See INDORSEMENT.

blank transfer A transfer of shares which is executed without the name of the transferee. Such a transfer, with the certificates of the shares, is frequently lodged as security for money, the intention being that the purchaser or mortgagee may later on fill in the blank and perfect his security by getting himself registered.

blasphemy The publication of contemptuous, reviling, scurrilous or ludicrous matter relating to (Christian) God, Jesus Christ, the Bible or Book of Common Prayer. It is a common law indictable offence. If written, the words constitute blasphemous libel, where the defendant's intention is irrelevant to conviction (*R. v Lemon* [1979] A.C. 617, HL). An attack on Islamic religion has been held not to be blasphemy (*R. v Chief Metropolitan Stipendiary Magistrate Ex p. Choudhury* [1990] 3 W.L.R. 986).

blended fund A fund derived from a variety of sources, e.g. where a testator directs his real and personal estate to be sold and disposes of the proceeds as one aggregate.

block exemption An exemption granted to certain categories of agreement which would otherwise be prohibited by art.81 EC Treaty and the Competition Act 1998 (as amended). See COMPETITION; COMPETITION POLICY.

blockade In international law, an act of war carried out by a belligerent to prevent access to or departure from the whole or part of an enemy's coast or ports by any vessel of any nation. Under the Declaration of Paris 1856 a blockade is binding if effective and a neutral ship is affected by having actual or constructive notice of the blockade. The penalty for breach of blockade by a neutral ship is confiscation of the vessel, whose cargo may be condemned by a prize court (*q.v.*).

blockade, pacific The temporary suspension, during peace, of the commerce of an offending or recalcitrant state by the closing of access to its coasts or of some particular part of its coasts, but without recourse to other hostile measures, save in so far as may be necessary to enforce this restriction. A pacific blockade is of dubious legality in light of the United Nations Convention on the Law of the Sea, which provides that ships of all states are entitled to innocent passage through the territorial sea.

blodwyte or bloodwit A fine or composition for the shedding of blood and payable to the lord. Contrast with *wergild* (*q.v.*), which was payable to the injured party or, if deceased, his relatives.

blood (1) Persons connected by blood relationship, i.e. by descending from one or more common ancestors. This is important in the context of inheritance, permitted marriage and incest (*q.v.*).

(2) The relationship enabling a person to take property by descent. One person is said to be of the whole blood to another when they are both descended from the same pair of ancestors, e.g. two brothers who have the same parents. Persons are said to be of the half blood to one another when they are descended from one common ancestor only, e.g. two brothers who have the same father but different mothers. Formerly, relations by the half blood were incapable of inheriting from one another, but this disability was removed by the Inheritance Act 1833. Since 1925 the half blood take on intestacy immediately after the whole blood of the same degree, Administration of Estates Act 1925, as amended. See CONSANGUINITY.

blood test Sample of blood to eliminate or otherwise a person from legal charges. Where the paternity of a child is in question in any civil proceedings a blood test or scientific test may be ordered by the court, Family Law Reform Act 1969 ss.20–25.

A blood sample may be ordered to be taken for comparison from a person held on suspicion of rape (*HM Advocate v Milford* [1975] Crim. L.R. 110).

A person arrested for driving under the influence of drink or drugs may be required to supply for laboratory test a specimen of his blood or urine, see Road Traffic Act 1988. See BREATH TEST.

blot on title A defect in title.

blowing the whistle See WHISTLEBLOWER.

Board of Green Cloth The Counting House of the Queen's Household. It consists of the Lord Steward, the Treasurer, the Comptroller and the Master of the Household, with their respective clerical assistants.

Board of Trade See TRADE, BOARD OF.

bodily harm (1) Actual bodily harm: it is an offence under s.47 of the Offences Against the Person Act 1861 to assault someone causing them actual bodily harm.

(2) Grievous bodily harm means serious injury short of death. Inflicting grievous bodily harm either maliciously or with intent is an indictable offence (Offences Against the Person Act 1861 s.20 and s.18 respectively).

body of deed The operative part of a deed as distinguished from the recitals (*q.v.*).

boilerplate clauses Clauses which are common to commercial contracts of a particular type and which usually deal with the operation of the contract.

bomb hoax The criminal offence of dispatching or placing any article (including any substance) with the intention of inducing in any other person a belief that it is likely to explode or ignite and cause personal injury or damage to property, Criminal Law Act 1977 s.51(1). It is also an offence to communicate information which is known to be false where the communicator intends to induce a similar belief (ibid. s.51(2)).

bona fide In good faith, honestly, without fraud, collusion or participation in wrongdoing.

bona gestura Good behaviour.

bona notabilia Goods situated in another diocese to that in which a deceased had died.

bona vacantia Goods without an apparent owner in which property vests in the Crown, e.g. fish royal (*q.v.*), shipwrecks, treasure trove. In default of any person taking an absolute interest in the property of an intestate it belongs to the Crown, Duchy of Lancaster, or Duke of Cornwall, as the case may be, as bona vacantia and in lieu of any right to escheat (*q.v.*) Administration of Estates Act 1925 s.46(1)(vi). In practice, the Treasury may grant such property to the person who appears to have the most meritorious claim. In Roman Law it was property left by a deceased person who had no successor.

bona waviata See WAIFS.

bond An instrument of indebtedness issued by companies and governments to secure the repayment of money borrowed by them. See also BAIL BOND; BOTTOMRY BOND.

bond washing A type of transaction which seeks to avoid tax by the sale and repurchase of securities.

bonded goods Dutiable goods in respect of which a bond for the payment of the duty has been given to the Commissioners of Customs and Excise.

bonded warehouse See EXCISE WAREHOUSE.

bondsman A surety (*q.v.*), or other person bound by a bond (*q.v.*).

boni judicis est ampliare jurisdictionem [It is the duty of a good judge to extend his jurisdiction]

bonorum emptio or venditio In Roman law the purchase or sale of an insolvent estate by or to one that offers to satisfy the largest proportion of the claims of the creditors. A praetorian mode of execution.

bonorum possessio [Possession of the property] In Roman law this was the praetorian situation corresponding to civil law *hereditas* (*q.v.*), whereby a universal successor succeeded by virtue of the intervention of the praetor.

bonorum possessor The praetorian heir. See BONORUM POSSESSIO.

bonus shares Shares (*q.v.*) allotted to the existing shareholders of a company and paid for out of profits which could otherwise be distributed as a dividend. Such an issue is often referred to as a capitalisation of profits (or of reserves). Bonus shares are capital and not income in the shareholders' hands. Similarly, unissued debentures may be issued as bonus debentures. Bonus shares or debentures can be issued if the articles of association (*q.v.*) so provide.

bookmaker A person who carries on the business of receiving or negotiating bets or conducting pool betting operations (whether as principal or agent) or holds himself out or permits himself to be held out, in the course of a business, as such a person (see Betting and Gaming Duties Act 1981 (as amended)).

booty of war Enemy property captured by a land force, including military arms, equipment and stores. This property belongs to the Crown and is subject to the High Court's prize jurisdiction.

borough Originally an area established as a royal stronghold against invasion. More recently a borough council is a district incorporated by Royal Charter with a common seal, chaired by a mayor. For the purpose of the administration of local government, boroughs outside Greater London were replaced by counties and districts by virtue of the Local Government Act 1972 ss.1, 20. London boroughs are listed in the London Government Act 1963 Sch.1. In Wales these were renamed principal areas and communities from April 1, 1996 (ibid. s.20 as amended by the Local Government (Wales) Act 1994). See GREATER LONDON AUTHORITY

borough court An inferior court of record for trying civil actions in a particular borough. These included local courts such as the Mayor's and City of London Court and the Liverpool Court of Passage. These courts, together with many other ancient courts, were abolished by a series of statutes, including the Courts Act 1971, the Local Government Act 1972 and the Administration of Justice Act 1977.

borough, English A customary mode of descent, under which the youngest son inherited land to the exclusion of his elder brothers ("*ultimogeniture*"). It was abolished by the Administration of Estates Act 1925 s.45.

borstal institutions Replaced by youth custody centres then young offender institutions (*q.v.*). See YOUTH JUSTICE BOARD.

botes Estovers (*q.v.*) or necessaries for husbandry (*q.v.*) which may be claimed as rights of common (*q.v.*), e.g. house-bote (wood to fuel or repair a house).

bottomry bond An agreement entered into by the owner of a ship or his agent, usually the ship's master, whereby, in consideration of money advanced for the purposes of the ship, the borrower undertakes to repay the same with interest if the ship terminates her voyage successfully. The debt is lost in the event of non-arrival of the ship. It binds or hypothecates the master, ship and freight, or the cargo. Under s.10 of the Marine Insurance Act 1906 the lender of money on bottomry has an insurable interest in respect of the loan. Although still within the jurisdiction of the Admiralty Court, bottomry bonds are effectively obsolete.

bought and sold notes Documents containing particulars of a transaction of sale or purchase delivered by an agent (*q.v.*) or broker (*q.v.*) to the principal (*q.v.*).

boundary An imaginary line, natural or artificial, marking the division of contiguous parcels of land. Boundaries are determined by acts of the owners, by statutes or orders or by legal presumption. It is important to determine boundaries in many types of legal actions including the recovery of land, trespass and nuisance.

Boundary Commissions One each for England, Wales, Scotland and Northern Ireland reviewing and reporting on the parliamentary constituencies within their respective areas as required by the Parliamentary Constituencies Act 1986 (as amended).

Boundary committees One each for England, Wales, Scotland and Northern Ireland and reporting to the Electoral Commission (*q.v.*) with the task of conducting electoral, structural or administrative boundary reviews in relation to local authorities within their respective spheres under the Political Parties, Elections and Referendums Act 2000.

bounty Money payable by the Crown as reward, inducement or by way of charity.

boycotting A deliberate refusal to have any dealings with another person (or state), named after Captain Boycott in Ireland.

Bracton The author of *De Legibus et Consuetudinibus Angliae* ["On the Laws and Customs of England"]. Died 1268.

branch Under the Companies Act 2006 s.1046, regulations may require an overseas company (*q.v.*) to provide specified documents if that company opens a branch in the UK. Branch means a branch within the meaning of the Eleventh Company Law Directive (89/666/EC) but the latter measure provides no definition. Section 1056 requires overseas companies that are credit or financial institutions with a branch in the UK to prepare, and have audited, accounts and directors' reports. For these purposes a "branch" is defined as "a place of business that forms a legally dependent part of the institution and conducts directly all or some of the operations inherent in its business".

brawling The former common law misdemeanour of creating a disturbance in a consecrated building, churchyard or burial ground. Now brawling and nuisance in churchyards is an offence punishable by virtue of s.2 of the Ecclesiastical Jurisdiction Act 1860, as amended.

breach The invasion of a right, or the violation of or omission to perform a legal duty. More specifically, for the purpose of the tort of negligence, the term breach of duty signifies:
"... the omission to do something which a reasonable man, guided upon those considerations which ordinarily regulate the conduct of human affairs, would do, or doing something which a prudent and reasonable man would not do" (*Blyth v Birmingham Waterworks Co* (1856) 11 Exch. 781, per Alderson B.).
See NEGLIGENCE; BREACH OF CONTRACT.

breach of close Trespass on land.

breach of condition notice A notice served by a local planning authority requiring compliance with conditions imposed on a grant of planning permission for the development of land subject to conditions, Town and Country Planning Act 1990 s.187A. Failure to comply with the notice is a summary offence. See DEVELOPMENT; PLANNING PERMISSION.

breach of confidence See CONFIDENTIALITY.

breach of contract Failure to fulfil a contractual obligation which entitles the innocent party to a remedy. The obligation, or term, may be agreed in writing, orally or by conduct and may be expressly agreed by the parties or implied at common law, by statute or statutory instrument (e.g. the Sale of Goods Act 1979 ss.12–15, as amended). See CONDITION; WARRANTY; INNOMINATE TERM; TERM.

breach of privilege Contempt of the High Court of Parliament, whether relating to the House of Lords or to the House of Commons, e.g. resistance to the officers of the House. Each House has power to imprison, suspend, reprimand or admonish a member who is in contempt.

breach of promise Refusal to fulfil a promise to marry. From the 16th century this gave the female a right of action for damages to compensate for her disappointment. This right was abolished by the Law Reform (Miscellaneous Provisions) Act 1970 s.1. The law relating to matrimonial property is applied to property disputes between parties who have broken off an engagement to be married. Legal presumptions apply to determine the ownership of wedding gifts and engagement rings.

breach of the peace Behaviour harming, likely to harm or putting a person in fear of harm to himself or, in his presence, to his property (see Watkins L.J. in *R. v Howell (Erroll)* [1981] 3 All E.R. 383). The common law power of arrest for breach of the peace is exercisable by all citizens and has not been removed by the Police and Criminal Evidence Act 1984. This was considered in *Williamson v Chief Constable of West Midlands Police* [2003] EWCA Civ. 337.

breach of trust An improper act on the part of a trustee in respect of the trust property which is in contravention or excess of his trust duties or is neglect or omission of those duties. A concurrence or acquiescence by a trustee of any of the preceding acts of another trustee is also a breach of trust. The trustee will be legally liable for any loss caused as a result of the breach. Any profit accruing from a breach of trust, e.g. improper speculation or trading with the trust assets, belongs to the trust estate. See TRUST; TRUSTEE.

breath test A preliminary test for the purpose of obtaining, by means of a device of a type approved by the Secretary of State, an indication whether the proportion of alcohol in a person's breath or blood is likely to exceed the prescribed limit, Road Traffic Act 1988 (as amended). Sections 6 and 6A set out the circumstances in which a breath specimen may be required.

breve [A short thing] A writ.

brevia testata Early forms of deeds of conveyance.

breviate A memorandum of the contents of a Bill.

brewster sessions Licensing sessions. The general annual meeting in each licensing district of the licensing justices. The Licensing Act 1964 s.2, required one general meeting and at least four transfer sessions to be held each year. The Act consolidated the law relating to licensing for retail sale and consumption of intoxicating liquor. The Act was repealed and replaced by the Licensing Act 2003 and power to grant licences was transferred to relevant licensing authorities (*q.v.*).

bribery Giving or offering any gift or reward to any person to influence his conduct. It is an offence at common law to bribe, inter alia, a judge, magistrate or other judicial officer. There are also statutory offences relating to bribery, e.g. bribery at elections, which also amounts to corruption, is an offence under the Representation of the People Act 1983 s.113.

bridleway or bridle-path Highway over which the public has a right of way on foot, on horseback or leading a horse, with or without a right to also drive animals along it (Highways Act 1980 s.329). Under the Countryside Act 1968 s.30 bicyclists (but not motorcyclists) are permitted to use bridleways, but should give way to pedestrians and horse-riders.

Bridlington Principles The principles of an agreement reached at the 1939 annual Trades Union Congress. Whilst declared not to be legally binding they are enforced by the TUC Disputes Committee. The main principle concerning inter-union transfer operated to permit exclusion or expulsion of individual members. It was effectively prohibited under s.174 of the Trade Union and Labour Relations (Consolidation) Act 1992 and the Bridlington Principles amended accordingly.

brief A concise statement. The instructions furnished by a solicitor or other authorised person to a barrister to enable him to represent the client in legal proceedings. A brief consists normally of a narrative of the facts of the case and a reference to the relevant law.

British citizen A person classified as such for political and other purposes under the British Nationality Act 1981 and, as such, has the right of abode in the United Kingdom. British national overseas citizens, formerly having different legal status, are included in this definition by virtue of the British Overseas Territories Act 2002. A person may acquire British citizenship by: (a) birth; (b) adoption; (c) descent; (d) registration; (e) naturalisation.

British Commonwealth See COMMONWEALTH.

British Council A body incorporated by Royal Charter in 1940 to promote knowledge of the United Kingdom and English language abroad and to develop cultural relations between the United Kingdom and other countries.

British dependent territories citizens Renamed British overseas territories citizens under the British Overseas Territories Act 2002 s.2. See BRITISH OVERSEAS TERRITORIES.

British Empire The territories over which the Crown exercised sovereignty and the inhabitants of which owed allegiance to the British Crown. These comprised the British Colonies and the British Dominions of Canada, Australia, New Zealand and the Indian Empire. The term was replaced by the "Commonwealth" (*q.v.*).

British Library Head of the national library system established by the British Library Act 1972 and managed by the British Library Board. There is a duty on publishers to submit to the British Library Board, within one month of publication, a copy of every book published in the United Kingdom, Legal Deposit Libraries Act 2003.

British Museum For constitution see the British Museum Act 1963, which separated the Natural History Museum from the British Museum. A copy of the script of any performance in Great Britain of a new play must be delivered to the Trustees of the British Museum (s.11 of the Theatres Act 1968).

British national (overseas) status A form of status created by the Hong Kong Act 1985 with the purpose of endowing limited British nationality on Hong Kong citizens prior to sovereignty passing from the United Kingdom to China in 1997. The status could only be acquired during a limited period and does not give the right of abode in the United Kingdom.

British overseas territories For the purposes of the British Nationality Act 1981 (see s.50 and Sch.6) include Bermuda, Cayman Islands, Falkland Islands, Gibraltar and Virgin Islands.

British overseas territories citizens Formerly British dependent territories citizens (*q.v.*).

broadcasting Publication for general reception by means of "wireless telegraphy", Broadcasting Act 1990 s.202. It is treated as publication in permanent form for the purposes of the law of libel (*q.v.*) and slander (*q.v.*) (ibid. s.166). Licensing of all forms of radio, television and cable networks is regulated by the Broadcasting Act 1990 with amendments and supplementary regulation by the Broadcasting Act 1996, which specifically applies to "digital form" of television and sound programme services, and the Communications Act 2003.

brocards Repertories of antithetical maxims of the civil law.

brokage A marriage brokage contract is one to procure a marriage for reward and is void at common law (*Hermann v Charlesworth* [1905] 2 K.B. 123). However it seems unlikely that a dating agency charging a fee to arrange introductions between its clients would fall foul of such unlawfulness.

broker A mercantile agent (*q.v.*) engaged to make contracts for the purchase or sale of goods or property, including stocks and shares. A broker does not have possession of the goods or property nor of their documents of title and is not normally personally liable on a resulting contract.

brokerage The commission payable to a broker for his services.

brothel At common law a place resorted to by persons of opposite sexes where women offer themselves to participate in physical acts of indecency, but not one where only one woman so offers herself. Under the Sexual Offences Act 1956 it is an offence to keep a brothel, or to manage a brothel, or to let premises for use as a brothel, or to permit them to be used as such (ss.33–35). The Sexual Offences Act 2003 makes the same acts unlawful in relation to a brothel used for prostitution (*q.v.*). The definition of brothel was extended under the Sexual Offences Act 1967 s.6 to include premises resorted to for homosexual practices. See DISORDERLY HOUSE; SEXUAL OFFENCES.

Brussels Common reference to the European Commission (*q.v.*) Parliament (*q.v.*), or their administration. The Commission is based in Brussels but, while the Parliamentary committee meetings are held there, the plenary sessions are held in Strasbourg and the secretariat and most of the Parliamentary staff are based in Luxembourg.

brutum fulmen An empty threat.

budget The annual financial statement made by the Chancellor of the Exchequer to the House of Commons reviewing the country's economy, estimating its income and expenditure for the next year, setting taxes, etc. In the budget speech the Chancellor also announces the government's long term expenditure plans. The speech is followed by the budget debate, then the resolutions, proposing the new taxation for the year, which are later embodied in the annual Finance Act.

buggery Sexual intercourse *per anum* between (1) a man and a woman or another man; or (2) *per anum* or *per vaginam* between a man or a woman and an animal. The act of buggery was punishable under the Sexual Offences Act 1956. Buggery no longer exists as a separate offence but, if not consensual, may amount to rape under s.1 of the Sexual Offences Act 2003 or, whether or not consensual, rape in the case of a child under 13 (ibid. s.5) or a child under 16 (ibid. s.9). See SEXUAL OFFENCES; RAPE; BESTIALITY.

building lease A lease "for any building purposes or purposes connected with building purposes", s.117(1) of the Settled Land Act 1925. Under such lease the lessee covenants to erect certain specified buildings on the land, and to insure and keep in repair such buildings during the term of the lease. At the end of the lease the buildings become the property of the lessor subject to the right of a lessee to acquire the freehold, Leasehold Reform Act 1967, as amended.

building society A body incorporated for the principal purpose of making loans which are secured on residential property and are funded substantially by its members and whose principal office is in the United Kingdom, see Building Societies Act 1986 s.5 as amended. Building societies' powers and limitations, including those relating to banking, are generally regulated by the 1986 Act and the Building Societies Act 1997. The Building Societies' (Distributions) Act 1997 amends the law in respect of distribution of assets on the take-over or conversion of a building society. Under the Building Societies (Funding) and Mutual Societies (Transfers) Act 2007 the Treasury (*q.v.*) may amend the 1986 Act to allow the funds of a society to be drawn more from the wholesale finance market and less from its own members, to place members on the same footing as creditors in the event of a society's insolvency and to ease the transfer of business between mutual societies.

bulk goods Under s.61 of the Sale of Goods Act 1979, "bulk" means a mass or collection of goods of the same kind which is contained in a defined space or area and is such that any goods in the bulk are interchangeable with any other goods therein of the same number or quantity.

In a contract for the sale of goods the pre-paying buyer of a specified quantity of unascertained goods (*q.v.*) in an identified bulk acquires ownership in an undivided share in the bulk and becomes an owner in common of the bulk, Sale of Goods Act 1979 s.20A.

bull One who buys stocks and shares intending not to take delivery but to resell at a higher price. See BEAR.

Bullock order In an action claiming relief against two or more defendants either severally or in the alternative, if the judge is satisfied that it was reasonable for both defendants to be joined, the claimant will be ordered to pay the costs of the successful defendant, and then add these costs to those which the unsuccessful defendant has to pay to the claimant (*Bullock v London General Omnibus Co* [1907] 1 K.B. 264). The power to join parties is contained in the Civil Procedure Rules, 19.

bundles Trial bundles are the documents which are likely to be referred to in trials and tribunal hearings. A bundle must be paginated and indexed. Several identical bundles must be prepared for use by the parties, the judge, etc.

burden of a contract The liability to perform a contract or discharge the obligations of a contract for the benefit of the other party to the contract or a third party. See PRIVITY.

burden of proof See PROOF.

burgage tenure A form of free land-holding, generally at a money rent, peculiar to boroughs, similar to the modern tenure in fee simple (*q.v.*), but subject to local custom. It was abolished by the Law of Property Act 1922. See BOROUGH, ENGLISH.

burgess The inhabitant of a borough or town who carried on a trade in that place.

burglary A person is guilty of burglary if (a) he enters any building or part of a building as a trespasser with intent to commit any such offence as is mentioned below; or (b) having entered any building or part of a building as a trespasser he steals or attempts to steal anything therein or inflicts or attempts to inflict on any person therein any grievous bodily harm, Theft Act 1968 s.9(1). The offences referred to above are offences of stealing, inflicting grievous bodily harm or doing unlawful damage (s.9(2)). Building includes an inhabited vehicle or vessel (s.9(3)). Burglary with firearms (including air guns) or imitation firearms or any offensive weapon or explosive is aggravated burglary (s.10).

burial The traditional method of disposing of a human body after death. Burial or interment need not be in any particular place and burial at sea is legally permissible. There is no legal requirement as to the type of ceremony, but Church of England burials are regulated by canon law and statutory provisions. See CREMATION.

business names A business name is a name which does not consist of the surname of a sole trader, the surnames or corporate names of all members of a partnership, or in the case of a corporate business, the name of the company concerned. The Business Names Act 1985 regulates the names under which persons may carry on business in Great Britain to ensure the true identity of persons running businesses is disclosed. It is due to be replaced by regulations passed under the Companies Act 2006 in October 2009.

business tenancy A tenancy where the property comprised in the tenancy is or includes premises which are occupied by the tenant for the purposes of a business carried on by him or for those and other purposes (s.23 of the Landlord and Tenant Act 1954). Section 23(1A) extends the meaning to include occupation or the carrying on of a business (a) by a company in which the tenant has a controlling interest; or (b) where the tenant is a company, by a person with a controlling interest in the company. Business tenancies, with certain exceptions, are protected under Pt II of the 1954 Act, although this has been significantly amended by the Regulatory Reform (Business Tenancies) (England and Wales) Order 2003.

BVC See BAR VOCATIONAL COURSE.

byelaws Rules made by some authority (subordinate to the legislature) for the regulation, administration or management of a certain district, property, undertaking, etc. and binding on all persons who come within their scope.

Byelaws are the means by which local authorities exercise their regulative functions under a wide variety of statutes. Such byelaws usually require confirmation by the appropriate Secretary of State. To be valid a byelaw must be within the powers of the local authority which makes it, must not be repugnant to the law of England, must be certain and positive in its terms and must be reasonable.

C

CAFCASS See CHILDREN AND FAMILY COURT ADVISORY AND SUPPORT SERVICE.

CIF Cost, insurance, freight. A contract for the sale of goods where the seller's duties are (1) to ship at the port of shipment within the time stated in the contract goods of the contract description; (2) to procure on shipment a contract of carriage under which the goods will be delivered at the destination contemplated by the contract; (3) to insure the goods for the benefit of the buyer; (4) to make out an invoice of the goods; (5) to tender to the buyer the bill of lading, the invoice, and the policy of insurance. It is the duty of the buyer to take up these documents and pay for them. The risk in the goods is prima facie the responsibility of the buyer from the time of shipment.

CPE See COMMON PROFESSIONAL EXAMINATION.

CPR Civil Procedure Rules 1998 (*q.v.*).

CrPR See CRIMINAL PROCEDURE RULES 2005.

ca. sa. See capias ad satisfaciendum.

cab-rank rule A rule or principle under which barristers (*q.v.*) theoretically should accept any cases within their specialised field, subject to their availability during the appropriate time, which are offered to them at a fair and proper fee. Its importance was emphasised by Lord Hobhouse of Woodborough in *Arthur J S Hall & Co v Simons* [2000] 3 All E.R. 673 at p.738.

Cabinet The committee of senior government ministers, all members of the Privy Council, presided over by the Prime Minister, whose functions are advisory and consultative. It determines government policy including the content and priorities of legislative proposals. The Cabinet first emerged in the reign of Charles II as a "meeting of His Majesty's Servants". Its existence depends on convention (*q.v.*). There are no rules prescribing its size or composition although all the main departments of state are normally represented.

By convention, all members of the Cabinet are collectively responsible for decisions taken. Any member unable to support Cabinet decisions should resign. The force with which this convention is observed has varied with the political climate.

cadit quaestio [The matter admits of no further argument]

caeteris paribus [Other things being equal]

Calderbank letter A letter containing an offer to settle litigation. Otherwise "without prejudice" (*q.v.*), the letter may be brought to the attention of the court on an issue as to costs (*Calderbank v Calderbank* [1975] 3 All E.R. 333, CA).

call A demand upon the holder of partly paid-up shares in a company for payment of the balance, or an instalment of it, by the company itself; or, if the company is in liquidation, by the liquidator.

call to the Bar The ceremony whereby a member of an Inn of Court (*q.v.*) is admitted as barrister (*q.v.*).

camera [Chamber] See IN CAMERA.

Campbell's Act, Lord Act (9 & 10 Vict. c.93), known as the Fatal Accidents Act 1846. This provided for damages to be paid to relatives of a deceased person provided that the deceased would have had a cause of action in respect of the wrongful act.

Campbell's Libel Acts, Lord The Libel Acts 1843 and 1845. See APOLOGY.

Cancellaria Curia The Court of Chancery.

cancellation (1) The drawing of lines across an instrument (*q.v.*) with the purpose of depriving it of effect.

(2) Certain classes of contract may be cancellable by virtue of statute, e.g. certain classes of agreement regulated by the Consumer Credit Act 1974 may be cancelled during a "cooling-off" period. The effect of cancellation through the statutory procedure is basically to treat a relevant contract as never having been made. Similar provisions apply to contracts for life insurance and timeshares and those involving investment agreements and doorstep selling.

canon (1) A rule of the canon law, or ecclesiastical law. Occasionally also a rule of the ordinary law, e.g. the canons of descent.

(2) A minor ecclesiastical dignitary, member of the bishop's advisory council, who assists the dean.

canon law (1) A body of ecclesiastical law, compiled from the opinions of the ancient Latin fathers, the decrees of general councils and the decretal epistles and bulls of the Holy See. It was codified in the 12th century by Gratianus, and added to by subsequent collections, and known as the *Corpus Juris Canonica*.

(2) The law of the Church of England. Unless subsequently receiving the authorisation of Parliament or merely declaratory of ancient customs, such

canons bind only the clergy and laymen holding ecclesiastical office, e.g. churchwardens *(q.v.)*.

capacity (1) In order to form a wholly valid contract *(q.v.)*, the parties must have legal capacity. Agreements made with certain groups of individuals may not be fully enforceable against them, for example those entered into with a minor (Minors' Contracts Act 1987) or with a person suffering from a mental disorder.
(2) In order to have the legal capacity to make a valid will *(q.v.)*, a person must generally be over 18 years of age, and be of sound mind, memory and understanding.
(3) An individual is presumed to have capacity to make a treatment decision unless that person: (a) is unable to take in and retain the information material to the decision especially as to the likely consequences of having or not having treatment; or (b) is unable to believe the information; or (c) is unable to weigh the information in the balance as part of a process of arriving at the decision (see para.15.10, Code of Practice to the Mental Health Act 1983 (1999), based on the judgments in *Re C (Refusal of Treatment)* [1994] 1 F.L.R. 3; and *Re MB* [1997] 2 F.L.R. 426). The Mental Capacity Act 2005 s.2 says that a person lacks capacity in relation to a matter if at the material time he is unable to make a decision for himself in relation to the matter because of an impairment of, or a disturbance in the functioning of, the mind or brain. The impairment or disturbance may be permanent or temporary. The Lord Chancellor *(q.v.)* has issued a Code of Practice under the 2005 Act providing guidance and information about how the Act works in practice.

capax doli Having capacity of committing crime.

cape A writ used in the "real" actions. See ACTION.

capias [That you take] A writ for the arrest of the person named therein.

capias ad audiendum judicium A writ to summon a defendant in a criminal prosecution to court to hear judgment pronounced against him.

capias ad respondendum A writ issued for the arrest of a person against whom an indictment for a misdemeanour had been found, in order that he might be arraigned. Abolished by the Crown Proceedings Act 1947 (Sch.1).

capias ad satisfaciendum, or ca. sa. A writ for the arrest of the defendant in a civil action when judgment had been recovered against such person for a sum of money and had not been satisfied. Abolished by the Supreme Court Act 1981 s.141.

capias extendi facias A writ of execution issuable against a debtor to the Crown, which commanded the sheriff to "take" or arrest the body, and "cause to be extended" the lands and goods of the debtor. Abolished by the Crown Proceedings Act 1947 s.13 (Sch.1). See EXTENT (WRIT OF).

capias in withernam A writ formerly used in cases where the defendant in an action of replevin *(q.v.)* had obtained judgment for the redelivery of the goods, and the sheriff had returned elongata, i.e. that the goods had been removed to unknown places. The writ commanded the sheriff to take other goods of the plaintiff to the value of the goods replevied, and deliver them to the defendant to be kept by him until the latter goods were returned.

capias pro fine A writ issued for the arrest of one who had been fined for an offence against a statute. The writ authorised his imprisonment until the fine was paid.

capita [Heads] See PER CAPITA.

capital The fund, or *corpus*, the yield of which is profits or income. A tenant for life is entitled to income and the remainderman to capital.

The capital of a company is the amount of principal with which a company is formed to carry on business. Under the Companies Act 2006 those forming a company with a share capital must deliver to the Registrar of Companies (*q.v.*) a statement of capital and initial shareholdings (ibid. s.10).

capital crimen [Roman law] An accusation affecting the caput (*q.v.*) of the accused.

capital gains tax Tax charged on capital or chargeable gains under the Taxation of Chargeable Gains Act 1992.

capital money Sums paid to trustees under the Settled Land Acts as a result of certain transactions relating to settled land or land held on trust for sale.

Capital moneys may be applied principally in investments in trustee securities, loans on mortgage, purchase of land, and expenditure on improvements as authorised by s.73 of the Settled Land Act 1925 as amended.

capital offences Offences punishable by sentence of death. Capital murder as defined by the Homicide Act 1957 s.5, was a capital offence. It was repealed by the Murder (Abolition of Death Penalty) Act 1965 which substitutes for the death penalty a sentence of life imprisonment or, in the case of a person under 18, a sentence of detention during Her Majesty's pleasure.

Piracy (*q.v.*) with violence or high treason (*q.v.*) remained capital offences until the Crime and Disorder Act 1998. The former statutory provisions allowing sentence of death to be passed by courts martial on offenders serving in the Navy, Army and Air Force were repealed by the Human Rights Act 1998.

capital punishment See CAPITAL OFFENCES.

capital transfer tax Now known as inheritance tax (*q.v.*).

capitalisation The conversion of profits or income into capital, as, e.g. by a resolution of a company. See *Blott's Case* [1921] 2 A.C. 171.

capite, tenure in Tenure "in chief". The holding of land direct from the Crown.

capitis diminutio [Roman law] A lessening of the legal status of the person by various legal acts, e.g. by enslavement or deportation.

capitula [Articles] See CAPITULATIONS.

capitulations Agreements, concluded between Christian states on the one hand and non-Christian countries on the other, under which certain immunities and privileges were secured to subjects of the former while in the territories of the latter. These subjects formed an extra-territorial community subject to the laws of their own country and outside the jurisdiction of the local law.

captator A person who obtains a gift or legacy through artifice.

caption The formal heading of a legal document, e.g. affidavit (*q.v.*), stating before whom it was taken or made. In the case of a coroner's inquest (*q.v.*) the caption is one of the three parts of the formal inquisition. It must set out various details including the place where the inquest is held, thereby establishing that the coroner (*q.v.*) has jurisdiction.

capture (1) A mode of acquiring property, e.g. a *res nullius*, by seizure.

(2) In international law, the seizure of enemy property in war.

caput [Roman law] The standing of a person in the view of the law in respect of his freedom, citizenship and family rights.

car tax A tax charged on vehicles made or registered in the United Kingdom. Abolished by the Car Tax (Abolition) Act 1992.

carat The measure indicating the proportion of fine gold in a manufactured article. The marking of gold and other precious metals is regulated by the Hallmarking Act 1973.

caravan sites The use of land as a site for caravans requires both planning permission under the Town and Country Planning Act 1990 and a licence under the Caravan Sites and Control of Development Act 1960 Pt I. The latter Act defines a caravan site as:
"land on which a caravan is stationed for the purpose of human habitation and land which is used in conjunction with land on which a caravan is so stationed".

The Caravan Sites Act 1968 was enacted primarily to afford some protection from eviction from caravan sites and to require local authorities to establish such sites for the "use of gipsies and other persons of nomadic habit". See also the Mobile Homes Act 1983, which provides protection for mobile home owners by prescribing the content of site agreements, as amended extensively by the Housing Act 2004.

care, duty of See DUTY OF CARE.

care and control Term formerly used in matrimonial proceedings to describe the powers and responsibility of the person with whom the child lived to control the child's day to day activities. See now CONTACT ORDER; RESIDENCE ORDER.

care home A care home provides accommodation, together with nursing or personal care for persons: who are or have been ill; who have or have had a mental disorder; who are disabled or infirm; who are or have been dependent on alcohol or drugs. Care homes are regulated by the Care Standards Act 2000.

care order A court order which places a child in the care of a local authority (see the Children Act 1989 s.31). Such order made prior to a final hearing is an interim care order, which may initially last for eight weeks and subsequently for a maximum of four weeks (ibid. s.38). A series of care orders may be made, renewable by the court.

careless or inconsiderate driving It is an offence under the Road Traffic Act 1988 s.2B (as amended by the Road Safety Act 2006), to cause a death by driving a mechanically propelled vehicle on a public road without due care and attention or without reasonable consideration for other persons using that road. See DANGEROUS DRIVING.

careless driving The Road Traffic Act 1988 s.3 provided that a person driving a motor vehicle (intended or adapted for use on roads) on a road without due care and attention, or without reasonable consideration for other persons using the road, was guilty of an offence. This was substituted by the Road Traffic Act 1991 by an offence of careless and inconsiderate driving which now extends to any mechanically propelled motor vehicle and to public places other than roads. It is also an offence under s.3A 1988 Act, to cause death by careless driving when under the influence of drink or drugs.

carer's allowance A non means tested benefit paid to claimants over 16 who spend more than 35 hours a week caring for a severely disabled person (formerly invalid care allowance).

cargo Anything carried in a ship or other vessel.

carriage by air International carriage of goods and persons by air is regulated by various international conventions, e.g. Warsaw (1929), Hague (1955) and Montreal (1975 and 1999). The conventions, inter alia, limit the liability of carriers and are implemented by domestic legislation, e.g. the Carriage by Air and Road Act 1979 and the Aviation Security Act 1982.

carrier A person who carries passengers or goods otherwise than for their own purposes or for purposes connected with their own trade or business. Carriers, who may act either gratuitously or for reward, can be common carriers, private carriers (who are bailees) or other special carriers, including carriers by air and sea. Carriers' rights and duties are determined according to their classification.

carry over The postponement of the completion of a contract to purchase or sell securities, by arranging to resell or repurchase for the current account and to sell or purchase for the new account in a later settlement period.

cartel (1) An agreement between states as to the exchange of prisoners during war.

(2) A manufacturers' agreement to maintain matters such as fixed prices or market shares. Section 188 of the Enterprise Act 2002 introduced cartel offences in the shape of price-fixing, limitation of production or supply, the sharing of markets, and bid-rigging. See RESTRICTIVE TRADE PRACTICES.

cartel ship A ship sailing during a state of war under safe conduct, protected from molestation or capture when voyaging for the purpose of the exchange of prisoners under a cartel (*q.v.*).

case See ACTION ON THE CASE.

case management Under the Civil Procedure Rules 1998 (*q.v.*) the courts must further the overriding objective (*q.v.*) of the Rules by active case management. The Employment Tribunals (Constitution and Rules of Procedure) Regulations 2004 provide for proactive case management in employment tribunal disputes (Sch.1, r.10).

case stated The statement of the relevant facts in a case for the opinion or judgment of another court. Such statements may arise, inter alia, in the following instances:

(1) After the hearing and decision of a case by magistrates a party may require a case to be stated for the opinion of the High Court, Magistrates' Courts Act 1980 s.111(1), on the ground that it is wrong in law or in excess of jurisdiction. The Crown Court in its appellate jurisdiction may be requested to state a case on similar grounds (Supreme Court Act 1981 s.28).

(2) Appeal to the Court of Appeal from a decision of the Lands Tribunal on a point of law.

(3) Appeal from other tribunals by way of case stated.

casino Under the Gaming Act 2005 an arrangement whereby people are given an opportunity to participate in a game of chance which is not equal chance gaming (s.7). See GAMING.

cassetur billa [Let the bill be quashed] An entry in the court records where an action commenced by a bill was discontinued.

cassetur breve [Let the writ be quashed] A method of discontinuing an action in the old common law practice.

casting vote The deciding vote which a returning officer or chair may have power to give when there is otherwise an equality of votes.

casual delegation A term adopted to describe the factual circumstances underlying a line of cases in which one who retained control of his chattel, e.g. a motor car, has been held liable for the negligence of another permitted to use it on his behalf (see *Wheatley v Patrick* (1837) 2 M. & W. 650).

casus belli An act justifying war.

casus omissus [An omitted case] A matter which should have been, but has not been, provided for in a statute or in statutory rules.

catching bargain Originally a contract for a loan, made on oppressive terms, with an expectant heir (*q.v.*). Equity granted relief on the ground of constructive fraud, i.e. that the parties were not on equal terms, of which unfair advantage had been taken, and a hard bargain made. See UNDUE INFLUENCE; EXTORTIONATE.

cathedrals See The Cathedrals Measure 1999.

cattle trespass See ANIMALS.

causa causans The immediate cause: the last link in the chain of causation. It is to be distinguished from *causa sine qua non*, which means some preceding link but for which the *causa causans* could not have become operative.

causa falsa [Roman law] An untrue ground or motive; a cause or title wrongly thought to be just or legal.

causa justa [Roman law] A true or just cause, means, motive, or ground; a legal title; a fact in conclusive proof.

causa liberalis [Roman law] An *actio praejudicialis* brought to try whether a man was or was not free. Prior to Justinian an *assertor libertatis* [claimant for freedom] acted for the person whose freedom was in question, but Justinian gave the action to the person directly claiming his freedom.

causa lucrativa [Roman law] A ground that is purely gainful. A mode of acquisition without valuable consideration.

causa mortis [Because of death] See DONATIO MORTIS CAUSA.

causa petendi Cause of action: the grounds on which an application originating proceedings before the European Court of Justice is based.

causa proxima non remota spectatur [The immediate, not the remote, cause is to be considered] Formerly used in the context of marine insurance policies. See Marine Insurance Act 1906 s.55.

causa sine qua non See CAUSA CAUSANS.

causation The relation of cause and effect which is important in establishing both criminal and civil liability and compensation.

cause An ordinary civil proceeding, an action.

Cause Lists The actions or other proceedings for trial or hearing before a specified judge or court are contained in the Daily Cause List of that judge or court.

cause of action The fact or combination of facts which gives rise to a right of action.

cautio juratoria [Roman law] A guarantee by oath (under Justinian); a promise on oath made by a defendant sued in his own name that he will remain in the power of the court up to the end of the suit.

caution (1) Under the Land Registration Act 2002 s.19 the registrar must keep a register of cautions against first registration. Where an application for registration under the Act relates to a legal estate which is the subject of a caution against first registration (*q.v.*), the registrar must give the cautioner notice of the application and of his right to object to it (ibid. s.16).
(2) A warning to a person concerning inter alia his response to questions put regarding his suspected involvement in a criminal offence (Police and Criminal Evidence Act 1984, Code of Practice for the Detention, Treatment and Questioning of Persons by Police Officers).

caution against first registration Under s.15 of the Land Registration Act 2002 a person is entitled to lodge a caution against the registration of title to an

75

unregistered legal estate if he claims to be the owner of a qualifying estate or entitled to an interest affecting a qualifying estate. See LAND REGISTRATION.

cautions register The Chief Land Registrar (*q.v.*) must keep a register of cautions against first registration (*q.v.*) under s.19 of the Land Registration Act 2002. See LAND REGISTRATION.

caveat A warning. An entry made in the books of the offices of a registry or court to prevent a certain step being taken without previous notice to the person entering the caveat (who is called the caveator).

caveat actor [Let the doer beware] He who does any act does it at his peril. Not a general rule. However, a man is usually presumed to intend the probable consequences of his acts.

caveat emptor [Let the buyer beware] At common law, when a buyer of goods had required no warranty he took the risk of quality upon himself, and had no remedy if he had chosen to rely on the bare representations of the vendor, unless he could show that representation to have been fraudulent. By statute, however, various terms are implied as to quality, e.g. by s.14(2) of the Sale of Goods Act 1979, where goods are sold in the course of a business, that they are of satisfactory quality (*q.v.*).

caveat venditor [Let the seller beware]

census The official collection of personal information about the inhabitants of dwellings in Great Britain or any part of Great Britain, principally for statistical purposes. The Census Act 1920 provides that a census may be directed by Order in Council, provided five years have elapsed since the last one. The Act also provides that a local authority may seek permission to hold a local census. The carrying out of a national census in England and Wales is now the duty of the Statistics Board (see Statistics and Registration Service Act 2007).

Central Criminal Court ["The Old Bailey"] The Crown Court (*q.v.*) when sitting in the City of London, which retains its former title of the "Old Bailey" and the privileges of the Lord Mayor and aldermen of the City of London as judges of the court (Courts Act 1971 s.29 Sch.2 and Supreme Court Act 1981 s.8).

Central Office The Central Office of the Supreme Court was established by the Judicature (Officers) Act 1879 to consolidate the offices of the masters and associates of the various divisions of the Supreme Court. This work is now performed by various departments within the Supreme Court Group, inter alia the Action Department and the Masters' Secretary's Department.

cepi corpus [I have taken the body] When a writ of *capias* (*q.v.*) or attachment is directed to the sheriff for execution, when he has the defendant in custody, he returns the writ with an indorsement stating that he has taken him. This is called a return of *cepi corpus.*

certificate A statement in writing by a person having a public or official status concerning some matter within his knowledge or authority.

certificate, land A certificate under the seal of the Land Registry containing a copy of the registered particulars of a certain piece of land. Abolished by s.24 of the Land Registration Act 2002.

certificate of lawful use or development A certificate issued by a local planning authority on application, where: (a) the authority is satisfied that the existing use of buildings or other land or operations which have been carried out on land would not be liable to the taking of enforcement proceedings; or (b) the authority is similarly satisfied as to the lawfulness of proposed development of land (Town and Country Planning Act 1990 ss.191–194, as amended). These certificates replaced established use certificates. See DEVELOPMENT; ENFORCEMENT NOTICE.

certificate of shares See SHARE CERTIFICATE.

certificate, trial by A mode of trial where the fact in issue was a matter of special knowledge, e.g. a custom of the City of London. Replaced by reference to arbitration.

Certification Officer An officer appointed under Trade Union and Labour Relations (Consolidation) Act 1992 s.254 to deal with the listing and certification of independent trade unions and functions relating to their funds. He also has judicial functions in respect of various matters concerning trade unions and their members. The Certification Officer took over the duties of the Commissioner for the Rights of Trade Union Members when this post was abolished by the Employment Relations Act 1999.

certified copy A copy of a public document, signed and certified as a true copy by the officer to whose custody the original is entrusted and admissible as evidence when the original would be admissible. Also, it is provided by various statutes that certified copies of certain documents and entries shall be receivable in evidence if properly authenticated.

certiorari Formerly a prerogative writ directed to an inferior court of record, commanding it to "certify". Now called a quashing order (*q.v.*). See JUDICIAL REVIEW.

certum est quod certum reddi potest [That which is capable of being made certain is to be treated as certain]

cessante causa, cessat effectus [When the cause ceases, the effect ceases]

cessante ratione legis, cessat ipsa lex [The reason of the law ceasing, the law itself ceases]

cessante statu primitivo cessat derivativus [The original estate ceasing, that which is derived from it ceases]

cessat executio [Suspending execution]

cesser The cesser of a term is when it comes to an end. It was formerly used for a provision in a settlement creating a long term of years to secure a sum of money, providing for when that term should cease, the trusts thereof being satisfied. This now occurs automatically (see Law of Property Act 1925 s.116).

cessio bonorum [Roman law] The surrender by a debtor of his property to his creditors.

cessio in jure [Roman law] A fictitious surrender in court by which a new title was conferred.

cession A mode of acquisition of territory. The transfer of territory by one state to another, under pressure of war or by arrangement.

cestui que trust A person for whom another is trustee: a beneficiary under a trust.

cestui que use A person to whose use or benefit lands or other hereditaments were held by another person; (*q.v.*) *cestui que trust.*

cestui que vie Where a person is entitled to an estate or interest in property during the life of another, the latter is called the *cestui que vie.*

chain of representation A rule whereby the executor of a sole or last surviving executor of a testator is himself the executor of that testator, and so long as the chain of such representation is unbroken, the last executor in the chain is the executor of every preceding testator.

challenge of jurors An objection to persons summoned to be jurors.

(1) A challenge to the array is an exception to the whole jury on the ground that the person responsible for summoning the jurors in question is biased or has acted improperly (Juries Act 1974 s.12(6)).

(2) Challenges for cause. These are challenges brought by either side on grounds of ineligibility or disqualification or alleged bias. The right of the defence to challenge jurors without giving any reason was known as peremptory challenge. This was abolished by the Criminal Justice Act 1988 s.118(1). On right to peremptory challenge under the Human Rights Act 2000 see *R. v Cruz* [1994] 2 L.R.C. 390.

challenge to fight To challenge a person to fight, either orally or by letter, or to bear or provoke such a challenge, was a common law misdemeanour. The offence was abolished by the Criminal Law Act 1967 s.13.

Chamberlain, Lord An officer of the Queen's Household, who changes with the Ministry of the day. He was formerly the censor of plays under the Theatres Act 1843. That function was removed by the Theatres Act 1968.

Chamberlain, Lord Great The officer in charge of the Houses of Parliament responsible for performing ceremonial duties.

chambers (1) Rooms attached to the courts in which sit the judges, the masters and district judges for the transaction of legal business which does not require to be done in court. A judge sitting in chambers can exercise the full jurisdiction vested in the High Court (Supreme Court Act 1981 s.67). Masters (*q.v.*) sit in chambers.

(2) Counsel's private offices, e.g. in the Temple or Lincoln's Inn.

(3) Barristers' chambers: the place from where self-employed barristers carry on their practices.

champerty or champarty A bargain between a party to legal proceedings and another who finances or assists these proceedings, that the latter will take as his reward for the assistance a portion of anything which may be gained as a result of the proceedings. The common law misdemeanour of champerty was abolished by the Criminal Law Act 1967 s.13. No person is liable in tort for champerty but it is contrary to public policy (s.14). Contrast conditional fee agreement.

chancellor The judicial officer of a King, Queen, Bishop, or University, etc.

Chancellor, Lord (High) Traditionally a cleric, he became "keeper of the King's conscience" and by 1474 began making decisions in response to pleas to intervene in equity. In modern times he has performed significant legislative, executive and judicial functions. He has acted as Speaker of the House of Lords and participates actively in the business of that House. He heads a major government department (formerly known as the Lord Chancellor's Department, now the Department of Constitutional Affairs) and is normally a member of the Cabinet. Until recently he was an active judge and the effective decision-maker in the most senior judicial appointments (technically made by the monarch) and actual appointee of many other judges.

The role of Lord Chancellor has become extremely controversial. Recent Lord Chancellors have adopted a higher political profile. The effect of the Human Rights Act 1998 has focused attention on the need for an independent judiciary and it was felt that his multi-functional role, which clearly breached the doctrine of separation of powers, left his decisions vulnerable to challenge.

The Government has attempted to address this by replacing the Lord Chancellor's Department with a Department of Constitutional Affairs (*q.v.*) and the passage of the Constitutional Reform Act 2005. This retains the post of Lord Chancellor, but will redistribute a number of his judicial functions: his role as head of the judiciary, representing the views of the judges, will be transferred to the Lord Chief Justice as President of the Courts of England and Wales (*q.v.*);

the powers in relation to the appointment of judges to the Judicial Appointments Commission; it is anticipated that new arrangements will be made in relation to the Speakership of the House of Lords. Whilst a number of his functions will be reallocated, he continues to exercise wide-ranging functions in relation to the administration of justice and regulation of the provision of legal services. There is no requirement that the Lord Chancellor is legally qualified.

Chancellor of the Duchy of Lancaster A member of the Cabinet with no departmental responsibilities.

Chancellor of the Exchequer An officer originally appointed to act as a check on the Lord Treasurer, and a judge of the Court of Exchequer sitting as a court of equity. Now he is nominally one of the Commissioners of the Treasury, but in practice is the Cabinet Minister at the head of the Treasury.

chance-medley Casual affray. Where a person is assaulted in the course of a sudden brawl or quarrel, and kills his adversary in self-defence. It was formerly regarded as excusable. It is now dealt with under the heads of justifiable homicide, self-defence, or provocation.

Chancery Court of York See ARCHES, COURT OF CANTERBURY; ECCLESIASTICAL COURTS.

Chancery Division See COURT OF CHANCERY.

change of parties The court may, in certain circumstances, add or substitute a party to proceedings or order that a person cease to be a party to proceedings (see CPR 19.2 and also CPR PD 19A—Addition and Substitution of Parties).

chapter The canons of a cathedral or the collegiate churches of Westminster Abbey and St George's Chapel, Windsor, including a deacon who is head of the chapter, who form the bishop's advisory council. The chapter and dean together form a corporation aggregate. The chapter cannot act without the dean.

Chapter Number The number assigned to a bill. Chapter numbers are issued in the numerical order in which the bills are signed.

character, evidence of Evidence relating to the good or bad character of a witness, where such evidence is admitted, is primarily relevant to the credibility of that witness. Formerly evidence of the bad character of an accused was generally not admissible, either for the purpose of tending to show guilt of the crime charged or, where he testifies, to undermine his credibility as a witness. Sections 98–110 and 112 of the Criminal Justice Act 2003 abolish the common law rules governing the admissibility of evidence of bad character in criminal proceedings save to the extent that in criminal proceedings a person's reputation is admissible for the purposes of proving his bad character. The Criminal Justice Act 2003 s.101 permits evidence of the defendant's bad character to be admitted in criminal proceedings if: all parties agree; the evidence is adduced by the defendant himself; it is important explanatory evidence; it is relevant to or has substantial probative value in respect of an important matter in issue between the defence and prosecution; it is evidence to correct a false impression by the defendant; the defendant has made an attack on another person's character. Evidence of the bad character of any other witness to criminal proceedings may only be admitted if it is important explanatory evidence, it has substantial probative value in relation to a matter which is in issue in the proceedings and is of substantial importance to the case, or all parties to the case agree to its admission (s.100).

charge (1) In property law a charge is a form of security for the payment of a debt or performance of an obligation, consisting of the right of a creditor to receive payment out of some specific fund or out of the proceeds of the realisation of specific property. The fund or property is said to be charged with the debt thus payable out of it. The only property charges capable of subsisting at law are: (i) a rentcharge (*q.v.*) in possession charged on land, being either perpetual or for a term of years absolute (*q.v.*); (ii) a charge by way of legal mortgage (*q.v.*); (iii) tithe (*q.v.*) rentcharge annuities or similar charge on land not created by an instrument (Law of Property Act 1925 s.1(2)). See FIXED CHARGE; FLOATING CHARGE

(2) In criminal law a charge is an accusation; a charge to the jury is the address of the presiding judge with regard to the duties of the jury.

charge by way of legal mortgage A legal charge (*q.v.*). A form of mortgage introduced by the Law of Property Act 1925 s.85(1) now governed by the Land Registration Act 2002 ss.48–57 and Sch.2.

chargé d'affaires A subordinate diplomatic agent, accredited to the Foreign Minister of the State where he resides.

charge sheet A document completed by a police officer listing the particular charges brought against the accused.

charge, statutory Where services have been provided by the Legal Services Commission (*q.v.*) for a client and money or property is recovered as a result, that money, etc. must be used to pay the client's legal costs if no order for payment of the assisted parties costs has been made, or the bill is more than the client's contribution, (if any). This is to prevent an assisted person making a profit. Accordingly, s.10(7) of the Access to Justice Act 1999 creates a statutory charge on any such funds recovered. See Community Legal Service (Costs) Regulations 2000 and the Community Legal Service (Financial) Regulations 2000, both as subsequently amended.

charges having equivalent effect Member States (*q.v.*) of the European Union (*q.v.*) are prohibited from introducing customs duties (*q.v.*) and charges having equivalent effect to customs duties (art.25 EC Treaty). The extension of the prohibition of customs duties to charges having equivalent effect is intended to supplement the prohibition against obstacles to trade and facilitate the free movement of goods. The European Court of Justice has held that a charge having equivalent effect to a customs duty includes any pecuniary charge, however small and whatever its designation and mode of application, which is imposed unilaterally on domestic or foreign goods by reason of the fact that they cross a frontier, and which is not a customs duty in the strict sense.

charging order A court order imposing a charge on a debtor's property to secure payment of any money due or to become due by virtue of a court order (Charging Orders Act 1979, s.1). See STOP ORDER.

charitable incorporated organisation (CIO) A body corporate formed under the Charities Act 1993 (as amended) with a constitution that states (inter alia) its name, its purposes, whether its principal office is in England or Wales and whether or not its members are liable to contribute to its assets if it is wound up and, if they are, up to what amount. Introduced by the Charities Act 2006, a CIO is designed to enable charities to gain incorporation without the need to register under the Companies legislation. A CIO must, however, register with the Charities Commission (*q.v.*) as must a charitable company, registered industrial and provident society (*q.v.*) or community interest company (*q.v.*) which wishes to convert to become a CIO.

charitable purpose A purpose that is for the public benefit (*q.v.*) and is included in either one of the twelve specific heads set out in the Charities Act 2006 s.2(2), or the general head in s.2(4). Among other purposes, the Act identifies the prevention or relief of poverty, the advancement of education, the advancement of amateur sport and the relief of those in need by reason of particular cause (e.g. youth or disability) as charitable purposes.

charitable trust There are four main heads of charity: trusts for the relief of poverty; trusts for the advancement of religion; trusts for the advancement of education; trusts for other purposes beneficial to the community. (This fourth head includes those purposes deemed to be charitable by virtue of the Recreational Charities Act 1958. See *Commissioner for Special Purposes of Income Tax v Pemsel* [1891] A.C. 531.)

To be a charity in law, a trust must be established for purposes which are exclusively charitable. That purpose must be directed to the public benefit. If a trust is established partly for non-charitable purposes it may in some circumstances be validated by the Charitable Trusts (Validation) Act 1954.

The charitable trust is not subject to the requirement of certainty or the perpetuity rule which applies to other trusts. Charities may claim a number of tax exemptions.

The administration and supervision of charities is governed by the Charities Act 1993. See also CHARITABLE PURPOSE; CY-PRÈS.

charities, register of The Charity Commission (*q.v.*) must maintain a register containing the name of every registered charity (subject to certain exceptions) and remove any institution which it no longer considers to be a charity and any charity which has ceased to exist or does not operate (Charities Act 1993 s.3 (as amended)).

charity Any institution, whether incorporated or not, that is established for charitable purposes (*q.v.*) only and is subject to the control of the High Court in the Court's exercise of its jurisdiction with respect to charities (Charities Act 2006 s.1).

Charity Commission A body corporate established under the Charities Act 1993 s.1A, to replace the Charity Commissioners. It is a non-Ministerial government department which has five objectives (s.1B), six general functions (s.1C) and six general duties (s.1D). For example, one of the five objectives is to increase public trust and confidence in charities and among its six general functions is the task of determining whether institutions are or are not charities. The Commission's duties include a requirement that in performing its functions it "must have regard to the need to use its resources in the most efficient, effective and economic way".

Charity Tribunal A tribunal established by the Charities Act 2006 to replace the jurisdiction previously exercised by the High Court to hear certain appeals and applications from decisions of the Charity Commission (see Charities Act 1993 s.2A) and references from the Attorney General (*q.v.*).

charter (1) Formerly any deed relating to hereditaments, especially deeds of feoffment (*q.v.*); now a royal charter, which is a grant by the Crown, in the form of letters patent under the Great Seal, to persons therein designated, of specified rights and privileges.

(2) A charter differs from a constitution in that the former is granted by the sovereign, while the latter is established by the people themselves: both are the fundamental law of the land.

(3) The act of the legislature creating a corporation is called its charter.

(4) In marine contract law, an agreement by which a vessel is hired by the owner to another is a charter.

charterparty [*Carta partita*, a deed cut in two] A written agreement by which a shipowner lets an entire ship, or a part of it, to the charterer for the conveyance of goods, binding himself to transport them to a particular place for a sum of money which the charterer undertakes to pay as freight for their carriage. The principal stipulations refer to the places of loading and delivery, the mode and time of paying the freight, the number of lay days (*q.v.*) and the rate of demurrage (*q.v.*). The charterparty may operate as a demise or lease (*q.v.*) of the ship itself with or without the services of the master and crew. The charterer then becomes for the time the owner of the vessel, and the master and crew become his agents or employees. The test is: has the owner parted for the time with the whole possession and control of the ship?

More commonly the charterparty is a simple charter under which the shipowner retains possession and control but the charterer has rights such as such as loading goods on board and deciding the ports of call. See TIME CHARTER; VOYAGE CHARTER.

chase A district of land privileged for wild beasts of chase, with the exclusive right of hunting therein. Franchises of free chase were abolished by the Wild Creatures and Forest Laws Act 1971. It differs from a park (*q.v.*) because it may be on another's ground and because it is not enclosed.

chattels [*catalla*, cattle] Any property other than freehold land. Leasehold and other interests in land less than freehold are termed chattels real, as they issue out of the realty. Chattels personal are movable, tangible articles of property and are objects, whether movable or immovable which belong immediately to the person. See also TRESPASS.

cheat The common law misdemeanour of fraudulently obtaining the property of another by any deceitful practice not amounting to felony, but of such a nature that it may directly affect the public at large. The common law offence of cheating was abolished by the Theft Act 1968 s.32(1), except as regards offences relating to the public revenue. It was an offence under s.25 of the Theft Act 1968 to go equipped for burglary, theft or cheat. For the purposes of s.25, cheat meant an offence under s.15 of the Theft Act 1968 (obtaining property by deception). The term "cheat" was removed from the 1968 Act by the Fraud Act 2006 s.6 of which makes it an offence for a person to have in his possession or under his control any article for use in the course of, or in connection with, any fraud.

cheque A cheque is a bill of exchange (*q.v.*) drawn on a banker, payable on demand (Bills of Exchange Act 1882 s.73). The person making the cheque is called the drawer (*q.v.*), and the person to whom it is payable is called the payee (*q.v.*).

Chief Baron of the Exchequer The judge who presided in the Court of Exchequer (*q.v.*). His powers are now exercised by the Lord Chief Justice (Constitutional Reform Act 2005 s.7).

chief clerks The old Masters in Chancery (*q.v.*). The Judicature Act 1873 transferred them to the Supreme Court and in 1897 they were entitled Masters of the Supreme Court.

Chief Constable The Chief Officer of any police force (apart from the Metropolitan Police Force) responsible for its direction and control (Police Act 1996 s.10). He is appointed by the police authority for the force, subject to the approval of the Secretary of State. See POLICE AUTHORITY.

Chief Land Registrar Her Majesty's Land Registry consists of the Chief Land Registrar, appointed by the Lord Chancellor, and the staff appointed by him (Land Registration Act 2002 s.99 and Sch.7).

Chief Justice of the Common Pleas The judge who presided, before the Judicature Act 1873, in the Court of Common Pleas, and subsequently in the Common Pleas Division. His powers are now exercised by the Lord Chief Justice (Constitutional Reform Act 2005 s.7).

chief-rent An annual or periodic sum issuing out of land. It now constitutes a Rentcharge (Rentcharges Act 1977 s.1). See RENTCHARGE.

child For the purpose of the Children Act 1989 and the United Nations Convention on the Rights of the Child this means a person under the age of

18. In criminal matters a child relates to an offender under the age of 14 (see Children and Young Persons Acts 1933 and 1969). See MINOR.

child assessment order An order made under the Children Act 1989 s.43, to enable the assessment of the state of a child's health or development, or of the way in which the child has been treated, to determine whether the child is suffering or is likely to suffer significant harm. See EMERGENCY PROTECTION ORDER.

child benefit A non-income or savings related benefit paid to those responsible for a dependent child or young person (see Social Security Contributions and Benefits Act 1992 s.14). The Child Benefit Act 2005 introduced wider definitions of the terms dependent child and young person.

child destruction The offence committed by any person who, with intent to destroy the life of a child capable of being born alive, by any wilful act causes a child to die before it has an existence independent of its mother (Infant Life (Preservation) Act 1929 s.1). Note, however, no person shall be found guilty if the act that caused the death was done in good faith to preserve the life of the mother. See also ABORTION.

Child Maintenance and Enforcement Commission A statutory body established under the Child Maintenance and Other Payments Act 2008, its main objective is to maximise the number of those children who live apart from one or both of their parents for whom effective maintenance arrangements are in place (s.2). The Commission has the following core functions: to encourage and support the making and keeping by parents of appropriate voluntary maintenance arrangements for their children; to support the making of applications for child support maintenance under the Child Support Act 1991; to secure compliance when appropriate with parental obligations under the 1991 Act. Under the new scheme, which is not expected to be fully in force until 2011, benefit claimants will be able to choose between private or statutory maintenance arrangements (presently operated by the Child Support Agency).

child minder A person acts as a child minder if they look after one or more children under the age of eight for reward, for total periods exceeding two hours in any one day: Children Act 1989 s.79A and B, as inserted by the Care Standards Act 2000. However, a person will not be a child minder if they are a parent (*q.v.*) or relative of the child, have parental responsibility (*q.v.*) for the child, are a local authority foster parent, are fostering (*q.v.*) a child who has been placed by a voluntary organisation or are fostering a child privately.

child of the family In relation to the parties to a marriage, it means: (a) a child of both parties; (b) any other child, not being a child who is placed with those parties by a local authority or voluntary organisation, who has been treated by both of those parties as a child of their family: Children Act 1989 s.105. See also Matrimonial Causes Act 1973. The Civil Partnership Act 2004 s.75 amended this definition and reference to a marriage should be read to also include reference to a civil partnership (*q.v.*).

child support A scheme introduced by the Child Support Act 1991 makes an absent parent responsible for paying the parent or person with care maintenance for his/her child. The amount of child support maintenance is fixed by a maintenance assessment and the scheme is administered and enforced by the Child Support Agency and Child Support Officers.

child tax credit A means-tested or income-related payment, administered by the HM Revenue and Customs, for families with dependent children or young persons (see Tax Credits Act 2002).

Child Trust Fund The Child Trust Funds Act 2004 makes provision for bank accounts to be opened with certain account providers approved by HM Revenue and Customs. Accounts must be held by children who were born after August 31, 2002 and who are otherwise eligible under the Act in their own names. An initial sum will be paid into this account by the HM Revenue and Customs. Further contributions may be made to the account by the child's parents.

Children and Family Court Advisory and Support Service (CAFCASS) Introduced by the Criminal Justice and Court Services Act 2000, this body came into operation on April 1, 2001. It is a non-departmental service and provides a single service to look after the welfare of children and their families in family court proceedings. It combines and replaces services formerly provided by various other bodies such as the Family Court welfare service, the local authority guardian ad litem and reporting officer service and the children's branch of the Official Solicitor's Office (*q.v.*). It is responsible for advising the court on child welfare matters, e.g. taking children into local authority care, adoption matters, applications for residence and contact. See CHILDREN AND FAMILY REPORTER; CHILDREN'S GUARDIAN.

Children and Family Reporter These individuals, employed by CAFCASS (*q.v*), report to the court under the Children Act 1989 s.7 on matters relating to the welfare of children involved in private law Children Act 1989 proceedings, e.g. residence and contact. See CONTACT ORDER; RESIDENCE ORDER.

Children's Commissioner Children's Commissioners have been appointed for England (Children Act 2004), Wales (Care Standards Act 2000), Scotland (Commissioner for Children and Young People (Scotland) Act 2003) and Northern Ireland (Commissioner for Children and Young People (Northern Ireland) Order 2003). All have duties to promote the views and interests of children, and investigative powers, but the specific powers and duties afforded to each Commissioner vary.

children's guardian The court may appoint a guardian for a child if the child has no one with parental responsibility for him/her (Children Act 1989 s.5(1)). Formally known as guardian ad litem (*q.v.*).

children's home A home which provides care and accommodation wholly or mainly for children: Care Standards Act 2000 s.1. There are three categories of children's home: community homes (*q.v.*), voluntary homes and registered children's homes. Health service hospitals, independent hospitals and clinics, residential family centres and schools which are intended to provide accommodation for no more than 295 days each year are excluded from this definition.

Chiltern Hundreds The Hundreds of Stoke, Desborough and Burnham in Bucks. An office of profit under the Crown. An M.P. cannot "retire" during the life of Parliament. If he wishes to vacate his seat he must disqualify himself. This is done by accepting an "office of profit under the Crown". The office of Bailiff of the Chiltern Hundreds is one such office and is granted to any member who wishes to retire. See HUNDRED.

chirograph In ancient times, a deed of two parts which were written on the same paper or parchment, with the word *chirographum* in capital letters between the two parts; the paper or parchment was then cut through the middle of the letters, and a part given to each party. If the cutting was indented, the deed was an indenture (*q.v.*).

chirographum apud debitorum repertum praesumitur solutum [A deed or bond found with the debtor is presumed to be paid]

chose A French word signifying thing; a chattel personal. A chose in possession is a movable chattel in the custody or under the control of the owner.

chose in action A right of proceeding in a court of law to procure the payment of a sum of money (e.g. on a bill of exchange (*q.v.*), policy of insurance), or to recover pecuniary damages for the infliction of a wrong or the non-performance of a contract. A legal chose in action is a right of action which could be enforced in a court of law; an equitable chose in action is a right which could only be enforced in the Court of Chancery, e.g. an interest in a trust fund or legacy. See ASSIGNMENT OF CHOSES IN ACTION.

Church Commissioners for England The body formed by the merger of the Ecclesiastical Commissioners (*q.v.*) and Queen Anne's Bounty (*q.v.*) (Church Commissioners Measure 1947; Church Commissioners Measure 1964). The Church Estates Commissioners are members of the Church Commissioners.

Church of England Since the Reformation it has been a separate national church independent of the Pope. As an established church, its law is part of the law of England, i.e. ecclesiastical law. See CANON LAW; MEASURES.

churchwardens Parochial officers of the Church. See the Churchwardens' Measure 2001; Synodical Government Measure 1969 Sch.3 para.11. The former duties of the churchwardens relating to church property are now a function of the parochial church council, Parochial Church Council (Powers) Measure 1956 s.4.

circuit judges See CROWN COURT.

circuits Divisions of the country for judicial business. Under the Courts and Legal Services Act 1990, s.72, the country is divided into six circuits: Midland and Oxford, North-Eastern, Northern, South Eastern (including London), Wales and Chester and Western.

circuity of action Where two or more proceedings were taken to effect the same result as might be effected by one: abolished in practice by the right to raise a counterclaim at the trial of an action.

circumstantial evidence A series of circumstances leading to the inference or conclusion of guilt when direct evidence is not available. Evidence, which although not directly establishing the existence of the facts required to be proved, is admissible as making the facts in issue probable by reason of its connection with or relation to them. It is sometimes regarded as of higher probative value than direct evidence, which may be perjured or mistaken.

citation (1) The calling upon a person who is not a party to an action or proceeding to appear before the court.
(2) The quotation of decided cases in legal arguments as authorities. In accordance with Practice Direction (Form of Judgments, Paragraph Marking and Neutral Citation) [2001] 1 W.L.R. 194 and Practice Direction (Neutral Citation) [2002] 1 W.L.R. 346 a system of neutral citation has been introduced whereby all judgments in every division of the High Court and the Court of Appeal are prepared for delivery, or issued as approved judgments, with single spacing, paragraph numbering (in the margins) but no page numbers to ensure uniformity of citation by advocates. See LAW REPORT.

citizenship Under the British Nationality Act 1981 there are three classes of citizenship: British Citizenship (*q.v.*); British Dependent Territories Citizenship (*q.v.*); and British Overseas Citizenship (*q.v.*). There are, in addition, the further categories of British National (Overseas) Citizens (*q.v.*); Commonwealth Citizens; and Citizens of the European Union. Only British citizens and citizens of the European Union are exempt from immigration controls.

Citizenship, European The Treaty on European Union established citizenship of the European Union. The provisions relating to citizenship are now found in arts 17–22 of the EC Treaty. Citizenship of the Union is conferred on every person holding the nationality of a Member State. Union citizenship complements, but does not replace, national citizenship. Citizens of the Union enjoy the rights conferred by the Treaty including a qualified right of movement and residency within the territory of the Member States. See, e.g. Case C–184/99 *Grzelczyk v Centre public d'aide sociale d'Ottignies-Louvain-la-Neuve* [2001] E.C.R. I-6193.

city A town corporate which has or has had a bishop, or which by letters patent has been created a city by prerogative of the Crown.

City of London Court A court having a local jurisdiction within the City of London; practically a county court. See MAYOR'S AND CITY OF LONDON COURT.

Civil as opposed to (i) ecclesiastical; (ii) criminal; (iii) military.

civil action Proceedings by way of action (*q.v.*) as contrasted with criminal proceedings.

civil death Loss of legal personality, as on banishment or profession of religion, when the possessions of the person concerned devolved as on actual death, or were forfeited.

civil debt Any sum of money recoverable on complaint to a magistrates' court, or declared by statute to be a civil debt recoverable summarily. See Magistrates' Courts Act 1980 ss.58 and s.96.

civil law [Roman law] The *Corpus Juris Civilis.*

Civil List A sum of money paid annually to the Queen and certain members of the Royal Family as a contribution to the salaries and expenses of the Royal Household. The amount, fixed in the Civil List Acts 1972–1975, is varied by regulation from time to time. In 1992 the Queen took over financial responsibility for most members of the Royal Family apart from the then Queen Mother, the Duke of Edinburgh and the Prince of Wales. See Civil List Act 1972 s.1(3).

civil partners Parties to a civil partnership (*q.v.*).

civil partnership As defined by the Civil Partnership Act 2004 (Interpretation Act 1978 s.5 Sch.1). A civil partnership is formed when two people of the same sex aged 16 or over register as civil partners of each other in England and Wales, Scotland, Northern Ireland or, in certain circumstances, when registered overseas. The Civil Partnership Act 2004 enables civil partners to refer property disputes to the court, and to apply for financial relief corresponding to the financial relief available to married couples under Pt 2 of the Matrimonial Causes Act 1973. The Civil Partnership Act 2004 also entitles the civil partners to apply to court for a s.8 order (*q.v.*) or for financial provision for children of the family (*q.v*). For the purposes of certain other Acts civil partners are to be treated as if they are married to one another. See CHILD OF THE FAMILY; FATAL ACCIDENT

Civil Procedure Rules (CPR) The Civil Procedure Rules 1998. The rules and procedures for the civil courts in England and Wales which came into effect on April 26, 1999 following the Woolf Report (*q.v.*). The overriding objective (*q.v.*) of the CPR is to enable the courts to deal with cases justly. This procedural code must be interpreted and applied so as to give effect to the overriding objective. A key feature of the CPR is active case management by the courts. Every defended claim will be allocated to a track by the courts. See TRACK ALLOCATION; SMALL CLAIMS; FAST TRACK; MULTITRACK.

civil restraint order An order restraining a party from: (a) making any further applications in current proceedings (a limited civil restraint order); (b) issuing certain claims or making certain applications in specified courts (an extended civil restraint order); or (c) issuing any claim or making any application in specified courts (a general civil restraint order) See CPR r.2.3.1.

civil servant A servant of the Crown, other than the holder of political or judicial office, who is employed in a civil capacity, and whose remuneration is paid wholly and directly out of moneys voted by Parliament. He is an officer employed in a department of the state or a state agency with the approval of the Treasury. A civil servant is a person holding his appointment directly from the Crown, or one who has been admitted into the Civil Service with a certificate from the Civil Service Commissioners. He holds his office during the royal pleasure.

civiliter mortuus [Civilly dead] See CIVIL DEATH.

claim The assertion of a right. An action in the civil courts is referred to as a claim. A policy of assurance becomes a claim when the event insured against happens. See also PARTICULARS OF CLAIM; STATEMENTS OF CASE.

claim form Civil court proceedings are initiated by issuing a claim form. This will have a concise statement of the nature of the claim and specify the remedy sought. See PARTICULARS OF CLAIM; STATEMENTS OF CASE.

claimant The person bringing an action at law or claim, formerly known as the plaintiff. See CLAIM; CLAIM FORM.

clam, vi, aut precario [By stealth, violence or entreaty] In order that the title of the owner of land may be barred under the Statute of Limitation in favour of a person in possession of the land, the occupier must hold neither secretly, forcibly nor by leave of the owner. See LIMITATION, STATUTE OF.

Clarendon, Assize of See ASSIZE OF CLARENDON.

Clarendon, Constitutions of (1164) Enactments passed to secure the jurisdiction of the King's Courts in certain matters of dispute between laymen and the Church, permitting punishment of the clergy by royal courts and otherwise lessening the autonomy of the Church.

Class A and Class B Persons Under the contaminated land (*q.v.*) regime in Pt IIA of the Environmental Protection Act 1990 the enforcement authority is responsible for determining who will be liable for the remediation (*q.v.*) of contaminated land. Principally liability falls upon the person or persons who caused or knowingly permitted the contaminating substances to be in, on or under land (ibid. s.78F(2)). The Statutory Guidance issued by the Secretary of State under the provisions of this Act refers to such persons as Class A persons. A group of Class A persons is referred to as a Class A Liability Group. If no such Class A person can be found for a particular pollutant linkage then liability is transferred to the owner or occupier of the land who in turn is referred to as a Class B person (ibid. s.78F(4)).

class action suit A lawsuit in which one or more parties file a complaint on behalf of themselves and all other people who are "similarly situated" (suffering from the same problem). Often used when a large number of people have comparable claims.

class closing rules Rules of construction, known as the rules in *Andrews v Partington* (1791) 3 Bro. C.C. 401, which artificially limit the members of a class who can take a class gift. Once the class closes, no one born after that date can enter the class. In the case of an absolute gift, the class closes when the document containing the gift takes effect or, if relevant, when all prior interests have ended. In the case of a contingent gift where no beneficiary has satisfied the contingency at the time when the class would normally close, the class closes when the first beneficiary satisfies the contingency.

clause A particular division which makes part of a treaty; of a legislative Bill; of a deed, written agreement, or other written contract or will. When a clause is obscurely written, it ought to be construed in such a way as to agree with what precedes and what follows, if possible.

clausulae inconsuetae semper inducunt suspicionem [Unusual clauses always excite suspicion]

clausum fregit [He broke the close] See CLOSE.

clean hands A suitor or plaintiff who is free from any taint of fraud, sharp practice, etc. One who sues in good faith. A man must come to equity with clean hands. If he has acted wrongly, morally or legally, he will not be helped by a court when complaining about the actions of the other party. See EQUITY, MAXIMS OF.

clear days Complete days; exclusive of named first or last days.

clearance A certificate by HM Revenue and Customs to the effect that a ship has complied with the customs and excise requirements and is at liberty to put to sea.

clergy Persons in Holy Orders or ordained for religious service. The parish clergy are rectors, vicars, perpetual curates and curates.

clerk Anciently, a priest or deacon, in Holy Orders or not, or a scholar, man who could read, a learned person or a man of letters. More recently denotes someone employed to keep records or accounts, as the clerk of the court or town clerk.

clerk of arraigns An assistant of the clerk of assize (*q.v.*). The office was abolished by the Judicature (Circuit Officers) Act 1946.

clerk of assize The principal officer attached to the assizes. Courts of assize and, with them, clerks of assize have been abolished. See ASSIZE.

Clerk of the Crown, or Clerk of the Crown in Chancery This officer performs the duties of the Clerk of the Hanaper (*q.v.*) and the Clerk of the Petty Bag (*q.v.*). He is Clerk of the court of the Lord High Steward, and Accountant-General (*q.v.*) of the Supreme Court (Supreme Court Act 1981 s.97). Duties include issuing writs of election or official notices of elections to be held in a constituency, and to read out the title of each Act when Royal Assent is given.

Clerk of the Hanaper [*Hanaperis*, a hamper] Formerly an officer on the common law side of the Court of Chancery who registered the fines that were paid on every writ, and saw that the writs were sealed up in bags (or hampers), in order to be opened afterwards and issued. He also took account of all patents, commissions and grants that passed the Great Seal. See now CLERK OF THE CROWN

Clerk of the House of Commons The Senior Official of the House of Commons, appointed by the Crown for life. The appointment, by letters patent (*q.v.*), styles him as "Under Clerk of the Parliaments, to attend upon the Commons". He reads whatever is required to be read in the House and signs the orders of the House, endorsing bills sent or returned to the House of Lords. He has custody of all records and other documents of the House. His duties include Chief Executive of the House of Commons Service and its 1,400 staff, and Corporate Officer (see Parliamentary Corporate Bodies Act 1992).

Clerk of the Parliaments One of the chief officers of the House of Lords. He is appointed by the Crown, by letters patent (*q.v.*). On entering office he makes a declaration to make true entries and records of the things done and passed in the Parliaments, and to keep secret all such matters, as shall be treated therein. He indorses on every Act the date on which it receives the Royal Assent.

clerk of the peace Formerly, an officer appointed by the Custos Rotulorum (*q.v.*) to keep the county records and to assist the justices of the peace in quarter sessions not only in drawing indictments, entering judgments, issuing process, etc. but also in administrative business. With the abolition of quarter sessions

(Courts Act 1971 s.3) the offices of clerk of the peace and deputy clerk of the peace were abolished on January 1, 1972 (ibid. s.44).

Clerk of the Petty Bag An officer of the Court of Chancery whose duty it was to record the return of all inquisitions out of every shire; to make out patents, summonses to Parliament, etc. See now CLERK OF THE CROWN.

Clerks of Records and Writs Officers formerly attached to the Court of Chancery, whose duties consisted principally in sealing bills of complaint and writs of execution, filing affidavits, keeping a record of suits, and certifying office copies of pleadings and affidavits. By the Judicature (Officers) Act 1879 they were transferred to the Central Office of the Supreme Court, under the title of Masters of the Supreme Court.

clerk to the justices or justice's clerk The clerk acts as legal adviser to the lay magistrates of the magistrates' court. The appointment and function of Justice's Clerks are governed by the Courts Act 2003.

clog on equity of redemption The doctrine of equity that no mortgage deed may contain any stipulation or provision fettering or impeding the mortgagor's right to redeem, e.g. which unduly delays the time for redemption, or which is unfair or unconscionable or which is inconsistent with or repugnant to the right to redeem. Collateral stipulations or advantages were formerly void as an evasion of the usury laws, but they are now valid provided they do not clog the equity.

close [Enclosed land] A trespass (*q.v.*) on a man's land was formerly described as a breach of his close, or trespass *quare clausum fregit.*

close company One which is under the control of five or fewer participators or of participators who are directors or of certain participators who together possess or are entitled to acquire the greater part of the assets available for distribution among the participators on winding up (Income and Corporation Taxes Act 1988 s.414). A company is not a close company if it is not resident in the United Kingdom, if it is controlled by the Crown or by a non-close company/companies, or if it is a registered industrial and provident society or building society. Special rules as to corporation tax apply to close companies.

close rolls and close writs Certain Royal letters sealed with the Great Seal and directed to particular persons, and not being proper for public inspection, were closed up and sealed on the outside. They were thence called writs close, and recorded in the close rolls.

close seasons The varying periods of the year during which it is forbidden to kill or take game or fish.

closed shop A term applied to a situation in which an employee may only obtain a particular job if, in relation to a specified trade union, he is an existing member (pre-entry closed shop) or he becomes and remains a member (post-entry closed shop) of that union. As a result of legislative changes during the 1980s and early 1990s, the negative protection afforded to closed shop agreements was removed. Whilst the closed shop as an institution is not unlawful, any attempt to enforce it is likely to be unlawful. (Trade Union and Labour Relations (Consolidation) Act 1992 Pt III.)

closed shop agreement An agreement whereby employers agree to employ only members of one or more specified trade unions. In legislation it was referred to as a union membership agreement.

closing order An order made by a local authority for closing a house which is unfit for habitation (e.g. under the Local Government and Housing Act 1989 s.165(1)(b) Sch.9 Pt II para.14).

closure A procedure whereby a debate or speech may be brought to an end. In Parliamentary debates, if the motion "that the question be now put" is carried (provided that not fewer than 100 members vote in favour), the debate must cease.

closure order An order requiring premises which are being used for the unlicensed sale of intoxicating liquor to be closed immediately: see Criminal Justice and Police Act 2001 ss.20–21.

club A voluntary association of persons for social or other purposes. It is not a partnership (*q.v.*), and must sue or be sued in the names of the members of the committee, or the officers, on behalf of themselves and all other members of the club. Members are liable only to the extent of their subscriptions. In a proprietary club the expenses are borne by a contractor, who receives the subscriptions of the members and makes his profit out of the difference.

A club is regulated by the rules agreed to by the members and for the time being in force. If a member is expelled from a club by a decision which has been arrived at without giving him an opportunity of being heard in his own defence, the court may grant an injunction, or give damages.

The sale or supply of intoxicating liquor in a club is regulated by the Licensing Act 2003 ss.60–90. As to racial discrimination against non-members: see Race Relations Act 1976 s.25.

club premises certificate A certificate granted under the Licensing Act 2003 Pt 4 by the relevant licensing authority in respect of premises occupied by, and habitually used for the purposes of, a club, certifying that the premises may be used by the club for one or more qualifying club activities specified in the certificate, and certifying that the club is a qualifying club in relation to each of those activities.

code The whole body of law; whether of a complete system of law, e.g. the Roman Law Code of Justinian or the Code Napoleon of France, or relating to a particular subject or branch of law, such as the Sale of Goods Act 1979, or Bills of Exchange Act 1882, which were statutes collecting and stating the whole of the law, as it stood at the time they were passed.

code of practice for victims See VICTIMS, CODE OF PRACTICE.

co-decision One of the available procedures in the European Union (*q.v.*) for the passage of legislation, and the one which allows for the greatest involvement of the European Parliament. The procedure is defined in art.251 of the EC Treaty and may involve the use of a conciliation committee (*q.v.*) which has the task of reaching agreement on a joint text. Following the Treaty of Amsterdam 1997 the co-decision procedure applies to the majority of policy areas in which Community legislation (*q.v.*) is adopted. Where the co-decision procedure is used the resulting act is adopted as a regulation, directive or decision of both the European Parliament (*q.v.*) and the Council (*q.v.*), signed by both Presidents.

codicil A codicil is an instrument executed by a testator for adding to, altering, explaining or confirming a will previously made by him. It becomes part of the will, and must be executed with the same formalities as a will (Wills Act 1837 ss.1 and 9). The effect of a codicil is to bring the will down to the date of the codicil, and thereby to make the same disposition of the testator's estate as if the testator had, at that date, made a new will, with the original dispositions as altered by the codicil.

coercion An act that is committed under physical coercion may not be a criminal offence as the defence of duress (*q.v.*) is available to all persons. Moral or spiritual coercion (as opposed to threat of death or injury required to prove duress) may provide a defence for a wife who commits an offence in the presence of, and under the coercion of, her husband.

It was a common law presumption that a married woman who committed a felony other than homicide in the presence of her husband acted under his coercion and was not guilty of an offence, but this presumption was rebuttable.

This doctrine was abolished by the Criminal Justice Act 1925 s.47, but it also provided that on a charge against a wife for any offence other than treason or murder, it is a good defence to prove that the offence was committed in the presence of, and under the coercion of, the husband.

cogitationis poenam nemo meritur [The thoughts and intents of men are not punishable] For the Devil himself knoweth not the mind of man (per Brian, C.J.).

cognati [Roman Law] Cognates. Persons related to each other by blood.

cognisance Judicial notice or knowledge; jurisdiction.

cognitor [Roman law] An agent appointed to act for another in an action. He was appointed by a set form of words in the presence of the opposite party. He need not be present at the ceremony, but he did not become cognitor unless and until he consented to take up office. See PROCURATOR.

cognovit actionem A written confession by a defendant in an action that he had no defence, on condition that he should be allowed a certain time for the payment of the debt or agreed damages. Now superseded by orders of the court made by consent for the entry of judgment or for the issue of execution at a future date.

cohabitants A couple who live together as husband and wife, but who are not married. See also COHABITATION; COMMON LAW SPOUSE.

cohabitation Living together as husband and wife, even if not married. Traditionally interpreted to mean two persons of opposite sex who although not married to each other live together as husband and wife. *Ghaidan v Mendoza* [2004] 3 W.L.R. 113, HL and the Domestic Violence Crime and Victims Act 2004, amending the Family Law Act 1996 s.62(1), extend this definition to mean either two persons of the opposite sex living as husband and wife or, if of the same sex, who live in an equivalent relationship. See COHABITANTS; COHABITATION AGREEMENT; COMMON LAW SPOUSE; CIVIL PARTNERSHIP.

cohabitation agreement Also called a living-together contract. A document that spells out the terms of a relationship and often addresses financial issues and how property will be divided if the relationship ends. No case decided in England and Wales has yet found a cohabitation agreement to be enforceable, although it is suggested (*Sutton v (1) Mishcon de Reya and (2) Gawor & Co* [2003] EWHC 3166) that provided usual contractual requirements are met there are no longer public policy reasons against enforceability.

cohaeredes sunt quasi unum corpus, propter unitatem juris quod habent [Co-heirs are regarded as one person on account of the unity of title which they possess] See, e.g. COPARCENER.

coif A white silk cap which serjeants-at-law (*q.v.*) wore in court.

collaborative law Increasingly used by family lawyers, it allows both parties to seek legal advice throughout the negotiation process with a solicitor who will be present with them during all meetings. In collaborative law the parties and their solicitors agree not to threaten or issue court proceedings, but if the latter are instructed to do so the process ends and they cannot continue to act. An agreement is signed reflecting this and everyone agrees to disclose all relevant documents and information on a voluntary basis. See also MEDIATION.

collateral [By the side of] A collateral assurance, agreement, etc. which is independent of, but subordinate to, an assurance or agreement affecting the same subject-matter. A collateral security is one which is given in addition to the principal security. Thus a person who borrows money on the security of a mortgage may deposit shares with the lender as collateral security.

collatio bonorum [Roman law] Bringing into hotchpot (*q.v.*).

collation To compare a copy with the original document in order to certify its correctness.

collective agreement Agreement or arrangement made by or on behalf of one or more trade unions and one or more employers or employers' associations and relating to specified employment issues. See Trade Union and Labour Relations (Consolidation) Act 1992 s.178(1); see also COLLECTIVE BARGAINING.

collective bargaining Negotiations relating to or connected with one or more employment related issues including terms and conditions of employment, allocation of work duties, discipline, membership of and facilities for officials of trade unions, procedures for negotiation and consultation about the above issues (Trade Union and Labour Relations (Consolidation) Act 1992 s.178(1)). See COLLECTIVE AGREEMENT.

collective enfranchisement Rights conveyed upon the qualifying tenants of certain premises to extend the term of their lease or to have the freehold acquired upon their behalf. Governed by the Commonhold and Leasehold Reform Act 2002.

college A corporation created for the promotion of learning and the support of members who devote themselves to learning.

College of Arms See HERALD'S COLLEGE.

colligenda bona See AD COLLIGENDA BONA.

collision statement of case See PRELIMINARY ACT.

collusion The arrangement of two persons, apparently in a hostile position or having conflicting interests, to do some act in order to injure a third person, defraud them of their rights, to obtain an objective forbidden by law, or deceive a court. In divorce, collusion was a bar to a decree but all the old bars to divorce, including collusion, were repealed by the Divorce Reform Act 1969. Collusion as a bar to a decree of nullity was abolished by the Nullity of Marriage Act 1971 s.6(1).

colony A British colony is any part of Her Majesty's Dominions outside the British Islands except: (a) countries having fully responsible status within the Commonwealth; (b) territories for whose external relations a country other than the United Kingdom is responsible; or (c) associated states (Interpretation Act 1978 s.5 Sch.1).

colour Any appearance, pretext or pretence, or fictitious allegation of a right; thus a person is said to have no colour of title when he has not even a prima facie title.

colourable That which is in appearance only, and not in substance, what it purports to be.

combination order Renamed the community punishment and rehabilitation order, an order made under the Powers of the Criminal Court (Sentencing) Act 2000 s.51, now replaced by a community order (*q.v.*) under Criminal Justice Act 2003.

comfort letter A commercial communication which is intended to assure another of bona fide (*q.v.*) intentions in relation to a prospective contract.
    In EC competition law formerly a letter from the Commission giving the view that a notified agreement did not contravene the competition provisions. It was an administrative letter and did not bind national courts or the Commission.

comitatus [A county]

comitia calata [Roman law] Special meetings of the *Comitia Curiata* or Curiate assembly, summoned twice a year, and presided over by the Pontiff.

comity of nations That body of rules which the states observe towards one another from courtesy or convenience, but which are not binding as rules of international law.

command papers Papers published by the authority of Parliament. They include green papers, which are discussion documents, and white papers, in which the government outlines policy and proposals for legislative change. Unlike green papers, white papers will indicate the government's proposed changes. See also LAW COMMISSION.

commencement In relation to an Act or enactment the time when the Act or enactment comes into force: Interpretation Act 1978 s.5 Sch.1.

commendation The act of an owner of land in placing himself and his land under the protection of a lord, so as to constitute himself a vassal or feudal tenant.

commercial agent Defined as a self-employed intermediary who has continuing authority to negotiate the sale or purchase of goods on behalf of another person (the principal), or to negotiate and conclude the sale or purchase of goods on behalf of and in the name of that principal, Commercial Agents (Council Directive) Regulations 1993. The Regulations provide rules governing the relations between commercial agents and their principals.

commercial cause Causes arising out of the ordinary transactions of merchants and traders. See COMMERCIAL LAW.

Commercial Court The Commercial Court was formally constituted by the Administration of Justice Act 1970 s.3 as part of the Queen's Bench Division of the High Court, thus giving statutory effect to the practice whereby, since 1895, commercial actions have been dealt with on a simplified procedure and expeditiously by a specialist judge. See now Supreme Court Act 1981 s.6. The judges of the Commercial Court are such of the puisne judges of the High Court as the Lord Chancellor *(q.v.)* may from time to time nominate to be Commercial Judges. Detailed procedure rules are contained in the CPR Pt 49, Practice Direction—Commercial Court PD (1999) 49D and the Commercial Court Guide which also contains other relevant Practice Directions and Statements. The judge of the Commercial Court may act as arbitrator in disputes of a commercial character entered in the commercial list, Supreme Court Act 1981 s.62(3). See PUISNE

commercial law The law of business contracts, bankruptcy, patents, trade marks, designs, companies, partnership, export and import of merchandise, affreightment, insurance, banking, mercantile agency and usages.

commercial practice Any act, omission, course of conduct, representation or commercial communication (including advertising and marketing) by a trader, which is directly connected with the promotion, sale or supply of a product to or from consumers, whether occurring before, during or after a commercial transaction (if any) in relation to a product: see the Consumer Protection from Unfair Trading Regulations 2008 reg.2.

commission (1) An order or authority to do an act or exercise powers, e.g. an authority to an agent to enter into a contract.

(2) The body charged with a commission, e.g. the Charity Commission.

(3) An agent's remuneration.

(4) One of the institutions of the European Community, its chief decision-making and executive body whose main responsibility is to ensure that the objectives set out in the treaties are attained.

commission, examination of witnesses on Used to obtain evidence from a witness outside the jurisdiction. The procedure in criminal cases is governed by the Crime (International Cooperation) Act 2003 and in civil proceedings by CPR Pt 34 r.8 and r.23.

Commission for Equality and Human Rights The Commission brings together the functions of the three previous equality commissions (the Equal Opportunities Commission, the Commission for Racial Equality and the Disability Rights Commission) and also takes on responsibility for the other aspects of equality: age, sexual orientation and religion or belief, as well as human rights.

Commission for Racial Equality (CRE) See COMMISSION FOR EQUALITY AND HUMAN RIGHTS; RACE RELATIONS.

commission of assize Formerly commissions issued to judges or Queen's Counsel, authorising them to sit at assizes for trial of civil actions. See ASSIZE.

commission of the peace This is the authority under which justices of the peace exercise their jurisdiction to preserve the peace and carry out their statutory duties (see Courts Act 2003 s.7). see LOCAL JUSTICE AREA.

Commissioner for victims and witnesses Appointed under the Domestic Violence Crime and Victims Act 2004 s.48, to promote the interests of victims and witnesses, encourage good practice in the treatment of victims and witnesses and keep under review the code of practice of victims (*q.v.*).

commissioners for oaths Persons entitled to administer oaths (*q.v.*) and take affidavits (*q.v.*). Originally appointed under the Commissioners for Oaths Act 1889. Every solicitor (*q.v.*) holding a practising certificate, every authorised person and every general notary (*q.v.*) or member of the Incorporated Company of Scriveners may use the title Commissioner for Oaths, see Courts and Legal Services Act 1990 s.113.

Commissioner for the Rights of Trade Union Members An officer appointed under the Trade Union and Labour Relations (Consolidation) Act 1992 s.266 who provided assistance to union members taking or contemplating legal proceedings against their union to enforce rights or duties owed to them (e.g. the right to be balloted on strike action under ibid. s.62). The office was repealed by the Employment Relations Act 1999.

Commissioners of Crown Lands Officers superseded by the Crown Estate Commissioners (Crown Estate Act 1961).

Commissioners for Her Majesty's Revenue and Customs Appointed by letters patent under the Commissioners for Revenue and Customs Act 2005, they replace the former Commissioners for Inland Revenue and for Customs and Excise. Under the Act a new integrated department has been formed. There is also a new statutory prosecutions office, the Revenue and Customs Prosecutions Office.

Commissions for Local Administration Bodies appointed under the Local Government Act 1974 s.23, charged with investigating complaints of maladministration (*q.v.*) by local authorities and those other bodies listed in s.25 of the Local Government Act 1974. See also OMBUDSMAN.

committal (1) The sending of a person to prison, generally for a short period, or temporary purpose, e.g. for contempt of court.

(2) Committal for trial to the Crown Court is the order made by the examining justices upon charges of indictable crime where they decide there is a strong enough case or sufficient evidence against the accused to warrant his being tried by jury. See Magistrates' Courts Act 1980 s.6(1) and Interpretation Act 1978 s.5 Sch.1.

committee (1) A person to whom the custody of the person or the estate of a mental patient was formerly committed or granted by the Lord Chancellor. See COURT OF PROTECTION.

(2) Persons to whom any matter or business is committed or referred.

committee of inspection A committee of creditors supervising the administration of a bankrupt's estate, now replaced by the creditors' committee (*q.v.*), Insolvency Act 1986 as amended by Insolvency Act 2000.

Committee of the Regions An advisory committee of the European Union established by the Treaty on European Union 1992 and now governed by arts 263–265 of the EC Treaty. The Committee is made up of representatives of regional and local bodies who either hold a regional or local authority electoral mandate or are politically accountable to an elected assembly. The EC Treaty specifies the instances in which the Council and Commission must consult with the Committee on legislative proposals. At present the Committee has 317 members and it may have no more than 350 members.

Committee of the Whole House This consists of all the members of the House of Commons sitting in committee without the Speaker in the chair. The effect is to allow the committee to follow a more informal procedure. Such a committee is used for the committee stage of public bills in exceptional circumstances, e.g. where the bill is of major constitutional importance. Until 1967 a large part of the financial business of the House of Commons was dealt with in a committee of the whole House. When performing this function the committee was known as the Committee of Ways and Means.

commixtio [Roman law] The mixing together of materials belonging to different owners, the product being held in common or divided in proportion to the shares contributed.

commodatum A kind of bailment (*q.v.*).

common A right of common is the right of taking some part of any natural product of the land or water belonging to another. It may be created by grant or claimed by prescription or arise from the custom of the manor. It is an incorporeal hereditament and a species of profit à prendre. The four principal rights of common are: (1) pasture, the right of feeding beasts upon the land of another; (2) piscary, the right of fishing in the waters of another; (3) estovers, the right of cutting wood, gorse or furze, etc. on the land of another; and (4) turbary, the right of digging turves on the soil of another.

The Commons Registration Act 1965 provides for the maintenance of registers by local authorities containing particulars: (a) of common land; (b) town and village greens; (c) rights of common and rights of ownership of common land. A register is conclusive evidence of those matters (ss.1 and 10). The 1965 Act is due to be replaced by the Commons Act 2006 (in force for pilot areas from October 2008). See COMMONS COUNCIL.

Any right of common originating in the forest law is freed from restrictions on its exercise (Wild Creatures and Forest Laws Act 1971).

A common is a piece of land subject to rights of common. The Secretary of State for the Environment has power to make rules to prevent further enclosures of commons or waste in urban areas, and to enable the public to have access for air and exercise (Law of Property Act 1925 ss.193, 194).

Common Agricultural Policy (CAP) Title II of the EC Treaty (arts 32–38) lays down the rules for the establishment of a common market in agricultural products. In particular art.32(4) requires that the operation and development of the common market for agricultural products must be accompanied by the establishment of a common agricultural policy. The objectives of the CAP are listed in art.33(1) and include increased agricultural productivity; a fair standard of living for the agricultural community; stable markets; secured supplies; and reasonable prices. On November 20, 2007, the Commission published, for consultation, proposals for change to the operation of the CAP, referred to as the 2008 CAP health check.

common assault An assault not amounting to an aggravated assault. See ASSAULT; battery.

common assurances The legal evidence of the transfer of property by which a person's estate is assured to him: (1) under the old common law on the actual land to be conveyed by handing over a symbol of it; (2) by matter of court record; (3) by special local custom; (4) by a deed; and (5) by will.

common bench The Court of Common Pleas (*q.v.*).

common carrier See CARRIER, COMMON

commons council A body corporate set up under the Commons Act 2006 to manage the agricultural activities, the vegetation and rights of common on an area of land. It may make rules relating to the leasing or licensing of rights of common, maintain a register of grazing and establish and maintain boundaries. See COMMON.

common counts Counts (*q.v.*) for money lent, for work done, etc.

Common Customs Tariff (CCT) Article 23(2) of the EC Treaty provides that products originating from countries outside the European Union (*q.v.*) shall benefit from the rules on the free movement of goods (*q.v.*) if the import formalities have been complied with and any customs duties which are levied have been paid. The CCT involves applying uniform customs duties to goods and products originating outside the European Union irrespective of where the goods enter the Union. See CUSTOMS UNION.

common employment The common law rule that a master was not liable to his servant for injuries resulting from the negligence of a fellow servant in the course of their common employment, unless there was on the part of the master want of care in selecting his servants, or personal negligence or omission to take reasonable precautions to ensure his servant's safety. Common employment meant work which necessarily and naturally in the normal course of events exposed servants engaged in that work to the risk of the negligence of the one affecting the other. The rule was modified by the Employers' Liability Act 1880, which placed a workman in certain cases in the same position as that of a stranger. It was abolished, and the Employers' Liability Act 1880, repealed, by the Law Reform (Personal Injuries) Act 1948.

Common Foreign and Security Policy (CFSP) One of the three pillars of the European Union (*q.v.*), established by the Treaty on European Union 1992. Under Title V of the Treaty on European Union, the European Union shall define and implement a common foreign and security policy covering all areas of foreign and security policy.

common informer A person who sued for a penalty under a statute which entitled any person to sue for it. Common informer procedure was abolished by the Common Informers Act 1951.

common injunction The injunction formerly granted in Chancery to prevent the institution or continuance of proceedings at common law which were inequitable, e.g. where an instrument sued on had been obtained by fraud. The injunction was addressed to the parties so proceeding, not to the common law court. It became obsolete after the Judicature Act 1873, when equitable defences could be pleaded in any court.

common jury A jury consisting of ordinary jurymen, as opposed (formerly) to a special jury. See SPECIAL JURY.

common law That part of the law of England formulated, developed and administered by the old common law courts, based originally on the common customs of the country, and unwritten. It is opposed to: equity (the body of rules administered by the Court of Chancery); statute law (the law laid down in Acts of Parliament); special law (the law administered in special courts such as ecclesiastical law, and the law merchant); and to the civil law (the law of Rome).

It is "the common sense of the community, crystallised and formulated by our forefathers". It is not local law, nor the result of legislation.

common law marriage and common law wife or husband (1) Colloquial terms sometimes used to denote the relationship of a man and woman who live together as if man and wife without having gone through a legal ceremony of marriage. The term has no legal significance in its everyday sense as above, but see (2) below.

(2) A marriage which does not comply with the normal requirements (for which see MARRIAGE) can be validly contracted in any place abroad where the English common law prevails, and where either the local law is inapplicable, or cannot be complied with, or the local law does not invalidate such a marriage. See COHABITATION.

Common Market The creation of the common market is one of the central tasks of the European Community, as prescribed by art.2 of the EC Treaty. The activities to fulfil this task are set down in art.3 EC and include the prohibition on customs duties, the prohibition on quantitative restrictions on exports and imports and the creation of a common commercial policy. In 1986 the Single European Act introduced the concept of the internal market, which is largely synonymous with the common market. See INTERNAL MARKETS; FUNDAMENTAL FREEDOMS.

common pleas Common law actions between subject and subject. See COURT OF COMMON PLEAS.

Common Professional Examination The educational stage preceding the vocational stage of training for a solicitor or barrister. It is a conversion course for graduates in disciplines other than law. The course is offered at various locations throughout England and Wales and is centrally regulated by the CPE Board. See BAR VOCATIONAL COURSE; LEGAL PRACTICE COURSE.

common recovery See RECOVERY.

Common Serjeant A judicial officer of the City of London, next below the Recorder, and a judge of the Central Criminal Court. The Common Serjeant is now a circuit judge (Courts Act 1971 Sch.2 para 2(2)).

common vouchee The crier of the court vouched to warranty in the common recovery. See RECOVERY.

commonable A thing over, by, or in respect of which a right of common (*q.v.*) may be exercised.

commonhold The Commonhold and Leasehold Reform Act 2002 Pt 1 introduces a scheme for the ownership of freehold land called commonhold. "Commonhold" was adopted as a term in order to convey both the notion of land ownership and the element of community of interests and co-operation in management which is intrinsic in the scheme: See *Commonhold: Freehold Flats and Freehold Ownership of other Interdependent Buildings: Report of a Working Group*, Cm. 179 (1987). Land which is held as commonhold is divided into units whose freehold is owned by unit-holders. Those parts of the land which are not held as units are held as common parts owned by the commonhold association. See COMMONHOLD ASSOCIATION; COMMONHOLD LAND.

commonhold association A commonhold association is a private company limited by guarantee, the memorandum of which states that an object of the company is to exercise the functions of a commonhold association in relation to specified commonhold land, and states £1 as the amount required to be specified as a member's guarantee (s.34 of the Commonhold and Leasehold Reform Act 2002). This association is charged with responsibility both for managing common parts and for enforcing rights and responsibilities between commonhold unit-holders.

commonhold community statement The relations between unit-holders and the commonhold association are defined by the commonhold community statement. It must comply with the requirements of the Commonhold and Leasehold Reform Act 2002 s.31, specifying rights and duties of the commonhold association and commonhold unit-holders.

commonhold land Land is commonhold land if: (a) the freehold estate in the land is registered as a freehold (*q.v.*) estate in commonhold land; (b) the land is specified in the memorandum of association of a commonhold association (*q.v.*) as the land in relation to which the association is to exercise functions; and (c) a commonhold community statement (*q.v.*) makes provision for rights and duties of the commonhold association and unit-holders (whether or not the statement has come into force) (see Commonhold and Leasehold Reform Act 2002 s.1). Flying freeholds, agricultural land and land subject to a contingent title cannot be commonhold land (Sch.2 to the Act).

commonhold unit A commonhold unit specified in a commonhold community statement (*q.v.*), and defined in that statement (Commonhold and Leasehold Reform Act 2002 s.11).

Commonwealth, The (1) The English state during the period 1649–1660 when there was no actual King, although Charles II was deemed to have reigned from 1649 when Charles I died.

(2) The association of the United Kingdom and the self-governing nations whose territories originally formed part of the British Empire (*q.v.*). The Commonwealth has not been recognised as an entity in international law. Each of the Member States has separate membership of the United Nations. Those states are equal in status and not subordinate one to another. The Queen is head of the Commonwealth. States became members of the Commonwealth from time to time by statutes granting them representative self-government. Some are republics within the Commonwealth. There are currently 53 members and 20 dependencies. South Africa, which withdrew in 1961, rejoined in 1994. In March 2002 Zimbabwe was suspended, after elections which observers said were marred by violence and intimidation. The suspension was extended indefinitely in December 2003. The Zimbabwean government responded by announcing the country was leaving the Commonwealth in the same month. In 2006 Fiji was suspended over a military coup and in 2007 Pakistan was suspended but readmitted in 2008.

commorientes Persons dying together on the same occasion where it cannot be ascertained by clear evidence which died first. By s.184 of the Law of Property Act 1925, death is presumed to have taken place in order of seniority. Section 184 does not apply between spouses when the elder dies intestate, Intestates Estates Act 1952 s.1(4). The statutory presumption is excluded by an express contrary provision in the will. For inheritance tax purposes, however, they are treated as having died at the same instant, Inheritance Tax Act 1984 s.4(2).

communis error facit jus [Common mistake sometimes makes law]

communities Districts in Wales are divided into communities (Local Government Act 1972 ss.20, 27–35). These continued to be part of the administration of local government in Wales after the Local Government (Wales) Act 1994.

community charge Local tax, colloquially known as the poll tax, now replaced by council tax (*q.v.*).

community homes Residential accommodation provided, managed, equipped and maintained by a local authority and accommodation provided by a voluntary agency under s.53(3) of the Children Act 1989. If provided by voluntary organisations but managed, equipped and maintained by a local authority they are designated "controlled community homes" (ibid. s.53(4)). If they are both provided and managed by a voluntary organisation they are designated "assisted community homes" (ibid. s.53(5)).

community interest company (CIC) A new type of limited liability company (*q.v.*) available to those who want to establish social enterprises to benefit the community. Such a company will have to comply with a community interest test and register as a community interest company with relevant memorandum and articles of association (*q.v.*). There is a cap on the payment of dividends and a restriction on distribution of assets to members. CICs will report to the Regulator of Community Interest Companies. See the Companies (Audit, Investigations and Community Enterprise) Act 2004.

Community Legal Advice. A free legal advice service funded by the Legal Services Commission (*q.v.*) and delivered in partnership with independent advice agencies (e.g. the Citizens Advice Service) and lawyers.

Community Legal Service (CLS) The Legal Services Commission (*q.v.*) has responsibility for developing and administering the Community Legal Service. Part of that service includes the Community Legal Service Fund which replaced the former scheme for civil legal aid. The Community Legal Service provides a framework which covers networks of funders including local authorities and charities as well as legal aid (*q.v.*) in order to provide a co-ordinated service.

In addition it aims to disseminate information and advice about legal rights and responsibilities and legal service provision. It has developed a range of initiatives, e.g. the Community Legal Service Partnerships which allow local funders and providers of services to plan for local community needs.

Community legislation Within the European Community legislation may be issued by the Council of the European Communities or by the Commission of the European Communities, art.240 (ex art.189) of the EC Treaty. It is of two principal types: Regulations and Directives. Regulations are directly applicable within Member States without further legislation by the Member State. The jurisprudence of the European Court of Justice (ECJ) (*q.v.*) makes it clear that Regulations can impose obligations and confer rights on individuals which must be applied by the courts of the Member States in preference to the state's municipal law. Directives impose an obligation on Member States to enact legislation to give effect to the terms of the Directive. In conditions laid down in the jurisprudence of the ECJ, a Directive may be of direct effect in Member States and confer rights on individuals against the state concerned and quasi-governmental entities in the state. See DECISION.

community of property Common ownership of the property existing between spouses. Community of property may be formed by express agreement in the marriage contract, or may take place when the parties make no agreement in the marriage contract but the law of the domicile at the time of the marriage imposes a regime of community of property. Property owned by spouses subject to a community of property regime is known as community property. To be compared with the English system of separation of assets where each spouse owns their own assets.

community order Where a person aged 16 or over is convicted of an offence, the court by or before which he is convicted may make an order known as a community order imposing on him any one or more of the following requirements: an unpaid work requirement, an activity requirement, a programme requirement, a prohibited activity requirement, a curfew requirement, an exclusion requirement, a residence requirement, a mental health treatment requirement, a drug rehabilitation requirement, an alcohol treatment requirement, a supervision requirement, or an attendance centre requirement (Criminal Justice Act 2003 s.177). Replaces the provisions of the Powers of Criminal Courts (Sentencing) Act 2000 Ch.3 of Pt 4, notably the provisions relating to community and rehabilitation orders, community punishment orders and community rehabilitation orders, which are repealed.

community sentence Under the Powers of Criminal Courts (Sentencing) Act 2000 s.33(2) and Criminal Justice Act 2003 s.147(1), defined as a sentence which consists of or includes a community order (*q.v.*) under Criminal Justice Act 2003 s.177 or one or more youth community orders as defined by the Criminal Justice Act 2003 s.147(2).

commutation (1) The conversion of the right to receive a variable or periodical payment into the right to receive a fixed or gross payment.
(2) The change of a punishment to which a person has been condemned into a less severe one. This can be granted only by the executive authority in which the pardoning power resides.

company An incorporated body with separate legal personality. Generally, an association of persons formed for the purpose of some business or undertaking carried on in the company's name. A private company limited by shares or guarantee can be formed by one person, Companies Act 2006. Most companies are formed by registration under the Companies Acts and are regulated by those Acts.
The Companies Act 2006 provides three basic types of company: companies limited by shares, companies limited by guarantee and unlimited companies (*q.v.*). Under the Companies Act 2006 s.3 these are in turn: (1) where the liability of the members is limited by its constitution to the amount, if any, unpaid on their shares; (2) where the liability of the members is limited by its constitution to such amount as the members undertake to contribute to the assets of the company in the event of its being wound up; and (3) where there is no limit to their liability. Under the Companies Act 2006 the principal constitutional document for a company will be its articles of association.
Every registered company is also classified as a private company (*q.v.*) or a public company (*q.v.*). A public company (Plc) must have a share capital satisfying the minimum amount and a statement in its certificate of incorporation that it is a public company and have complied with the requirements for a public company. Any company that does not meet the requirements for a public company is a private company. See now also community interest company. See ASSOCIATION, ARTICLES OF; ASSOCIATION, MEMORANDUM OF.

Company Names Adjudicators Company Names Adjudicators make decisions in disputes about opportunistic company name registrations under s.69(12) Companies Act 2006. The disputes are heard in the Company Names Tribunal (*q.v.*) which is part of the UK Intellectual Property Office.

Company Names Tribunal A new statutory body established under the Companies Act 2006 that allows complaints to be made where a company has been registered with the intention of extracting money from the complainant or to prevent him from registering a name in which he has goodwill ("opportunistic registration"). Complaints are made to what are known as Company Names Adjudicators (*q.v.*) through the newly established Company Name Tribunal.

company secretary A public company must have a secretary. If it appears to the Secretary of State that a public company is in breach of this requirement, he may give the company a direction. It is the duty of the directors of a public company to take all reasonable steps to secure that the secretary of the company is a person who appears to them to have the requisite knowledge and experience to discharge the functions of secretary of the company.

100

A private company is no longer required to have a company secretary, see Companies Act 2006 s.270(1). In the case of a private company without a secretary, anything authorised or required to be given or sent to, or served on, the company by being sent to its secretary may be given or sent to, or served on, the company itself, and if addressed to the secretary is to be treated as addressed to the company; and anything else required or authorised to be done by or to the secretary of the company may be done by or to a director, or a person authorised generally or specifically in that behalf by the directors.

company voluntary arrangement See VOLUNTARY ARRANGEMENT.

compass Contriving or imagining, e.g. the death of the reigning monarch; a mental intention or design, which must be manifested by some overt (open) act.

compensatio [Roman law] Set-off; when the defendant brings up his claims against the plaintiff in order to have them reckoned in reduction of the plaintiff's demand.

compensation A payment to make amends for loss or injury to person or property, or as recompense for some deprivation, e.g. compensation to the owner for the compulsory acquisition of his property. See, e.g. Land Compensation Acts 1961 and 1973.

compensation order A court by or before whom a person is convicted of an offence may make an order requiring him to pay compensation for the injuries, loss or damage he has caused (Powers of Criminal Courts (Sentencing) Act 2000 s.130 as amended by the Criminal Justice Act 2003 s.304 and the Violent Crime Reduction Act 2006 s.29).

competency (1) The mental ability to understand the general effect of a transaction or document. See also CAPACITY.

(2) The legal fitness or ability of a witness to be heard on the trial of a cause or to act as a competent witness in civil proceedings. All persons are competent to give evidence for prosecution or defence or to act as witness in civil proceedings, save children who have insufficient intelligence to testify or a proper appreciation of the importance of speaking the truth, mentally retarded or mentally ill persons who are incapable of testifying, those unable to communicate with others, and those who are temporarily incapable of understanding and giving rational answers. See GILLICK COMPETENCE.

Competition Commission Replaced the Monopolies and Mergers Commission. It investigates and reports on references made to it by the Secretary of State, the Office of Fair Trading (*q.v.*) and utility regulators and will also hear appeals under the Competition Act 1998 from decisions of the Office of Fair Trading or a regulator via its Appeals Tribunal.

competition policy The regime of Rules, Regulations and Directives adopted by the European Community in order to fulfil the objectives set out in art.3 of the EC Treaty, of instituting a system to ensure that competition in the common market is not distorted. The two principal articles in the Treaty dealing with competition policy are arts 81 and 82 (ex arts 85 and 86) EC. They are concerned with restrictive trade practices (*q.v.*) and abuses of dominant positions in the market respectively. The Community has also developed a policy on merger control. See ANTI-COMPETITIVE PRACTICES; COMPETITION COMMISSION; DGIV.

complainant One who makes a complaint to the justices.

complaint A complaint is a statement of the facts of a case before the magistrates' court, e.g. alleging non-payment of money due to the complainant under a periodic payment order. Part II of the Magistrates' Courts Act 1980, as amended by the Courts Act 2003, deals with the civil jurisdiction and procedure of the magistrates' courts and provides for the issue of a summons requiring a person to appear before the court to answer a complaint.

completion Completion of a contract for the sale of property consists on the part of the vendor in conveying with a good title the estate contracted for in the land sold and delivering up the actual possession or enjoyment thereof to the purchaser. On the purchaser's part, it lies in accepting such title, preparing and tendering a conveyance for the vendor's execution, and paying the purchase price.

compos mentis [Of sound mind]

composition An agreement between a debtor and his creditors for the satisfaction of his debts by the payment of a sum of money differing in amount or in mode of payment from what is owed. A debtor may, for example, propose a composition in satisfaction of his debts or a scheme of arrangement (*q.v.*) of his affairs as an individual voluntary arrangement (*q.v.*) to his creditors in satisfaction of his debts as an alternative to bankruptcy (*q.v.*). (See Insolvency Act 1986 Pt VIII, as amended by Insolvency Act 2000.)

A voluntary arrangement (*q.v.*) in the form of a composition or scheme of arrangement may also be agreed between a company and its members and creditor. (See Insolvency Act 1986 Pt I, as amended by the Insolvency Act 2000 and the Enterprise Act 2002.)

compound To agree to accept a composition.

compound settlement A settlement constituted by a number of documents, deeds or wills, extending over a period of time.

compounding a felony This offence has lapsed on the abolition of the distinction between felony (*q.v.*) and misdemeanour (*q.v.*). But concealing an offence may be an offence under the Criminal Law Act 1967 s.5.

compromise An agreement between parties to a dispute to settle it out of court.

comptroller One who controls or checks the accounts of others; originally by keeping a counter-roll or register.

Comptroller and Auditor General The public officer who controls the issue of money from the Consolidated Fund and the National Loans Fund and who, as head of the National Audit Office, examines the accounts of government departments and other public bodies to see that money is properly expended according to law, for the purposes for which it was voted, and that value for money has been obtained through resources being used economically, efficiently and effectively.

Appointment is by the Crown, the salary is charged on the Consolidated Fund, and the office is held during good behaviour. This is designed to show the independence of the office holder from the Executive and Parliament.

compulsory purchase order An order authorising the acquisition of land by compulsion. Such orders must be authorised by an enabling statute and are normally made under the procedure of the Acquisition of Land Act 1981. The order does not, of itself, acquire the land but makes it lawful for an acquiring authority to take further steps to achieve this end, i.e. the authority may serve a notice to treat (*q.v.*) or make a vesting declaration (*q.v.*).

compurgation Wager of law: a method by which the oaths of a number of persons as to the character of an accused person in a criminal case, or of a defendant in a civil case, were accepted as proof of his innocence in the one case or as proof in the other case that the claim made against him was not well founded. The persons who made such oaths were known as compurgators. It began to decline in the reign of Henry II, but continued available in the old actions of debt, detinue (*q.v.*) and account, until it was abolished by the Civil Procedure Act 1833.

computer misuse See HACKING; CRIMINAL DAMAGE; INTERCEPTION OF COMMUNICATIONS.

computer program [Software] A series of instructions, written in code, to a computer enabling it to perform a specific task. A computer program may be produced for sale as a standard package or designed for a specific application. Copyright (*q.v.*) exists in software as a literary work. It is unclear whether a computer program is goods or goods and services. For implied terms as to quality, performance, etc. See Supply of Goods and Services Act 1982 or Sale of Goods Act 1979. See COMPUTER MISUSE.

concealment Non-disclosure of a fact by a party to a contract. If active, and therefore fraudulent, it is a ground for rescission, but not otherwise, except in contracts uberrimae fidei, e.g. a policy of insurance.

concealment of birth A person who by any secret disposition of the dead body of a child, whether it died before, at, or after its birth, endeavours to conceal the birth is guilty of a misdemeanour (*q.v.*) (Offences Against the Person Act 1861 s.60).

concentration The EC Merger Regulation 139/2004 requires compulsory and exclusive (one-stop shop) prior notification to the European Commission of mergers, acquisitions and certain transaction that involve a change of control and meet certain turnover thresholds. If a concentration has a community dimension it is subject to scrutiny by the European Commission.

concerted practice Under art.81 EC or Pt I of the Competition Act 1998 concerted practices are forbidden. A concerted practice has been defined as the knowing substitution of practical co-operation for the risks of competition.

conciliation The bringing together of employers and employees in an endeavour to settle disputes. See ADVISORY, CONCILIATION AND ARBITRATION SERVICE.

conciliation committee In relation to the enactment of Community legislation some legislative procedures (co-decision (*q.v.*) and conciliation) require that a proposal is submitted to a conciliation committee. By art.251(4) of the EC Treaty the committee is made up of Members of the Council or their representatives and an equal number of representatives of the European Parliament. The committee is charged with reaching agreement on a joint text. See also CONSULTATION PROCEDURE.

concilium magnum regni The Great Council (*q.v.*).

concluded Estopped. See ESTOPPEL.

concubinatus [Roman law] Concubinage; the permanent cohabitation of one man and one woman which did not give the father *potestas* over the children born to him by the concubine.

concurrent jurisdiction of the Court of Chancery That part of equity which dealt with cases in which the common law courts recognised the right but granted no complete and adequate remedy, and where equity gave a better remedy, e.g. specific performance (*q.v.*) and injunction (*q.v.*).

concurrent sentences Where the defendant is convicted of several offences at the same trial, the court has, in general, power to direct that the sentences shall be served concurrently (i.e. together or at the same time). Sentences run consecutively if they follow one upon the other.

condemnation The adjudication of a Prize Court on a captured vessel that it has been lawfully captured, which divests the owner of the vessel of his property and vests it in the captor.

condictio [Roman law] The general term for a personal action; an action where the plaintiff alleges against another that something ought to be given to or done for him. Originally a formal notice to be present on the 30th day to choose a *judex*.

condition A provision which makes the existence of a right dependent on the happening of an event; the right is then conditional, as opposed to an absolute right.
A true condition is where the event on which the existence of the right depends is future and uncertain. An express condition is one set out as a term in a contract or deed. An implied condition is one founded by the law on the presumed intention of the parties, with the object of giving such efficacy to the transaction as the parties must have intended it should have.
A condition precedent is one which delays the vesting of a right until the happening of an event; a condition subsequent is one which destroys or divests the right upon the happening of an event.
A condition in a contract is a stipulation going to the root of the contract, the breach of which gives rise to a right to treat the contract as repudiated. See (and contrast) WARRANTY. See also CONDITIONS OF SALE.

conditional appearance Before 1981 a defendant could enter an appearance in qualified terms reserving the right to apply to the court to set aside the writ or service thereof for an alleged informality or irregularity. This has now been abolished.

conditional discharge Where a person has been found guilty of an offence, a court may make an order of conditional discharge if the court does not think it expedient to impose a punishment. The discharge is conditional on the person not committing any offence during the period specified by the court, Powers of Criminal Courts (Sentencing) Act 2000 s.12, as amended by Criminal Justice Act 2003 s.304 and s.332, and Criminal Justice and Immigration Act 2008 Sch.26(2) para.41. See also ABSOLUTE DISCHARGE.

conditional fee agreement An agreement with a person for advocacy or litigation services which provides that the fees for the service are paid only in certain circumstances, usually if the client wins. Such agreements are enforceable only in so far as they comply with s.58 of the Courts and Legal Services Act 1990 as amended by the Access to Justice Act 1999. Family proceedings cannot be the subject of such an agreement.

conditional fee simple A fee simple (*q.v.*) granted to a person with a condition that on the happening or non-happening of a specified event the grantor shall be entitled to re-enter the land; as, e.g. where the grantee is to take the name and arms of the grant or within a certain time. It is not a legal estate, not being a fee simple absolute. See ESTATE.

conditional sale agreement A contract for the sale of goods (*q.v.*) may be absolute or conditional, Sale of Goods Act 1979 s.2(3). A conditional sale agreement may also be a regulated consumer credit agreement within the Consumer Credit Act 1974 and that Act defines such an agreement as an agreement for the sale of goods or land under which the purchase price is payable by instalments and the property (*q.v.*) in the goods or land is to remain in the seller until the instalments are paid, ibid. s.189(1).

conditions of sale The terms on which the purchaser is to take property to be sold by auction. Conditions of sale implied by law in the absence of any stipulation or intention to the contrary in the contract of sale are contained in Law of Property Act 1925, s.45. Under ibid. s.46, the Lord Chancellor issued the Statutory Form of Conditions of Sale, which apply also to contracts by correspondence.

condonation Condonation of a matrimonial offence was formerly a bar to divorce but this is no longer the law (repealed by Divorce Reform Act 1969). Condonation remained a factor for consideration by magistrates exercising their matrimonial jurisdiction but this too has now been repealed (by the Domestic Proceedings and Magistrates' Court Act 1978).

conduct money Money given to a witness to defray his expenses of coming to, staying at, and returning from the place of trial.

conductio [Roman law] A hiring.

conference In its legal usage, a meeting between a barrister and a client to discuss issues relating to a case. The client can be a lay client, e.g. a defendant and/or a professional client, the person instructing the barrister, e.g. a solicitor. See also CONSULTATION.

confession An admission of guilt made to another by a person charged with a crime. The Police and Criminal Evidence Act 1984 s.76 makes any such confession inadmissible in evidence if obtained by oppression or if likely to be unreliable as a result of anything said or done. The Criminal Justice Act 2003 s.76A will permit a confession made by an accused to be used as evidence against their co-accused to the extent that it is relevant to a matter in issue in the proceedings.

confession and avoidance A pleading which confesses (i.e. admits) the truth of an allegation of fact contained in the preceding pleading, but avoids it (i.e. deprives it of effect) by alleging some new matter by way of justification.

confidential communications Legal privilege protects oral and written communications between a professional legal adviser and a client from being disclosed, even in court. The police cannot seize records of such communications as evidence, Police and Criminal Evidence Act 1984 s.9. By s.63 of the Courts and Legal Services Act 1990, the privilege extends to authorised conveyancers and certain persons providing advocacy and litigation services.
In healthcare a healthcarer is required to maintain the security of information obtained from a patient in the course of the healthcare relationship.

confidentiality The common law action of breach of confidence regulates the use of confidential information. There are three elements to the action:
(1) the information in question must have the necessary quality of confidence;
(2) the information must have been imparted in circumstances importing an obligation of confidence; and
(3) there must have been an unauthorised use of the information.
Particular rules govern the use of confidential information by employees. During the course of employment employees must not disclose information expressly or impliedly confidential to their employer; however, after employment is terminated, subject to the terms of the employment contract, employees may disclose any confidential information that does not amount to a trade secret (See *Faccenda Chicken v Fowler* [1987] Ch. 117). Various statutes impinge to some extent on the common law position. See for example the Data Protection Act 1998 and the Freedom of Information Act 2000.

confirmation A conveyance of an estate or right, whereby a voidable estate is made sure and unavoidable, or whereby a particular estate is increased. See FINES AND RECOVERIES ACT 1833.

confiscation The seizure and appropriation of property as a punishment for breach of the law, whether municipal or international.

confiscation order An order made under Pt 2 of the Proceeds of Crime Act 2002 requiring a defendant to pay a sum of money equivalent to the benefit derived from his crime.

conflict of interest Refers to a situation when someone, such as a lawyer or public official, has competing professional or personal obligations or personal or financial interests that would make it difficult to fulfil his duties fairly.

conflict of laws An alternative name for private international law (*q.v.*).

confusio [Roman law] The mixing of liquids belonging to different owners. The product was held in common or divided in proportion to the shares contributed.

confusion of goods The mixture of things of the same nature but belonging to different owners so that the identification of the things is no longer possible. The right to the ownership of the constituent parts is not, in general, lost by mixing, but possession of the mixture may be awarded to the party with the best right to it, subject, in a proper case, to compensating the owner of the other constituents.

congé d'elire [Permission to elect] A licence from the Crown to the dean and chapter of a bishopric to elect a bishop, accompanied by letters missive containing the name of the person to be elected.

congenital disability A child may have a cause of action if born with some disability as a result of a tortious act done to one of its parents before birth or conception (Congenital Disabilities (Civil Liability) Act 1976). Liability may extend to the child's mother if she was driving a motor vehicle at the time of the occurrence and the child was *in utero* (s.2).

conjugal rights A married person is entitled to the society and the cohabitation of his or her spouse, unless they are judicially separated, or have agreed to live apart. But the husband is not entitled to exercise force to claim his rights. The suit for restitution of conjugal rights was abolished by the Matrimonial Proceedings and Property Act 1970 s.20 (now repealed).

conjuration Conferring with evil spirits. It was an offence under s.4 of the Witchcraft Act 1735 for any person to pretend to exercise any form of witchcraft, conjuration, etc. but in this section conjuration was not limited to evil spirits only (*R. v Duncan* [1944] K.B. 713): the gist of the offence was in the pretence. The Witchcraft Act 1735 was repealed by the Fraudulent Mediums Act 1951 which in turn has been repealed by the Consumer Protection from Unfair Trading Regulations 2008. See MEDIUMS.

connivance An agreement or consent, indirectly given, that something unlawful shall be done by another, i.e. the intentional active or passive acquiescence by the petitioner in the adultery of the respondent. Connivance is no longer a bar to the grant of a decree of divorce.

connubium [Roman law] The legal power of contracting marriage. The parties were required to have citizenship; not be within the prohibited degrees of relationship; and have the consent of their *paterfamilias* (*q.v.*).

consanguinity [Of the same blood] Relationship by descent, either lineally, as in the case of father and son, or collaterally, by descent from a common ancestor; thus, cousins are related by collateral consanguinity, being descended from a common grandparent.

consecutive sentences Criminal sentences that must be served one after the other rather than at the same time.

consensus ad idem [Agreement as to the same thing] The common consent necessary for a binding contract.

consensus facit legem [Consent makes law] Parties to a contract are legally bound to do what they have agreed to do.

consensus non concubitus facit matrimonium [Consent and not cohabitation constitutes a valid marriage]

consensus tollit errorem [Consent takes away error] See ACQUIESCENCE.

consent Acquiescence, agreement. It is inoperative if obtained by fraud. Consent is a defence to a charge of rape, assault by penetration, sexual assault and causing a person to engage in sexual activity without consent. The Sexual Offences Act 2003 s.74 provides that a person consents if he agrees by choice, and has the freedom and capacity to make that choice. However, note also that for the purposes of this Act, in the circumstances described by s.75 including where the complainant was subject to violence, was asleep or was under a physical disability, it may be presumed that the complainant did not give consent. Under s.76, if the defendant intentionally deceived the complainant as to the nature of the act, or induced consent by impersonating another, it is also to be conclusively presumed that the complainant did not consent.

In medical law consent is required for medical, surgical or dental treatment, otherwise there is a prima facie case of trespass (*q.v.*) to the person.

Informed consent is a doctrine which requires that the amount of information given to a patient before that person consents to treatment, particularly invasive treatment, is to be determined not by the health carer but by what the patient would want to know.

conservation area An area designated as being of special architectural or historic interest. Since 1967 local planning authorities have had a statutory duty to determine which parts of their areas ought to be so designated and to take steps to safeguard the character of such areas. See Planning (Listed Buildings and Conservation Areas) Act 1990 Pt II.

conservation (of plants and animals) The Wildlife and Countryside Act 1981 repeals and re-enacts with amendments previous legislation relating to the protection of some wild animals, nature conservation, National Parks, public rights of way and related topics.

conservators of peace Officers appointed to maintain the public peace, e.g. the judges and sheriffs; justices of the peace (*q.v.*).

consideration To constitute a simple contract (*q.v.*) an agreement must amount to a bargain, each of the parties paying a price for that which he receives from the other. This price is referred to as consideration. In *Currie v Misa* (1875) L.R. 10 Ex. 162, consideration was defined as:

"some right, interest, profit or benefit accruing to one party, or some forbearance, detriment, loss or responsibility given, suffered or undertaken by the other".

If, therefore, one party, e.g. gives a right or benefit, he gives consideration. Equally, if a party incurs or undertakes responsibility, he gives consideration.

consignment Goods delivered by a carrier (*q.v.*) to a consignee at the instance of a consignor.

consilium [Roman law] A public body that, inter alia, considered proposals for manumission under the *Lex Aelia Sentia* It met on certain days at Rome and it held regular sessions in the provinces, on the last day of which manumission proposals were examined. See MANUMISSION.

consistory court The court of a diocese in the Anglican Church. Its jurisdiction is laid out in the Ecclesiastical Jurisdiction Measure 1963 (as amended) s.6.

Consolato del Mare A code of the maritime law of the Mediterranean, *temp* 14th century.

Consolidated Fund The fund formed by the public revenue and income of the United Kingdom. The National Loans Fund set up by the National Loans Act 1968 operates in conjunction with the Consolidated Fund.

Consolidation Acts Acts which sweep up and collect and re-enact in one statute the existing enactments on a certain subject. To be compared with codifying Acts which also incorporate common law rules not previously codified. The Consolidation of Enactments (Procedure) Act 1949 laid down a procedure for consolidation where at the same time incidental corrections and minor improvements ought to be made; they must be approved by the appropriate parliamentary committee and the Lord Chancellor (*q.v.*) and the Speaker. In interpreting a consolidation Act it is proper to look at the earlier provisions which it consolidated (*IRC v Hinchy* [1960] A.C. 748, per Lord Reid). See also Interpretation Act 1978 s.17(2)(a),(b).

consolidation of actions If several actions are pending in the same Division with reference to the same subject-matter, the court may order them to be tried together (see CPR r.3.1).

consolidation of mortgages The equitable doctrine that a mortgagee (*q.v.*) who holds several mortgages (*q.v.*) by the same mortgagor (*q.v.*) on several properties can insist on the redemption of all, if the mortgagor seeks to redeem any of them. The doctrine is now excluded by s.93 of the Law of Property Act 1925, unless a contrary intention is expressed in any of the deeds.

consortium The all-embracing term used to denote the association between a husband and wife whereby each is entitled to companionship, love, affection, comfort and support of the other. Enticement (*q.v.*) of a spouse formerly entitled the other to an action for damages for loss of consortium, but this general entitlement was abolished by the Law Reform (Miscellaneous Provisions) Act 1970. There remained the possibility of an action in tort in respect of the loss of consortium where a tortious act, for example, injured a wife and deprived the husband of her society and services. However, by s.2 of the Administration of Justice Act 1982, no person shall be liable in tort to a husband on the ground only of his having deprived him of the services or society of his wife.

conspiracy (1) With some exceptions the common law offence of conspiracy has been abolished by the Criminal Law Act 1977 s.5(1). The new statutory offence, created by the 1977 Act s.1(1) (as amended by the Criminal Attempts Act 1981 s.5) exists when any person agrees with any other person or persons that a course of conduct carried out in accordance with their intentions, either: (a) will necessarily amount to or involve the commission of any offence of offences by one or more of the parties to the agreement; or (b) would do so but for the existence of facts which render the commission of the offence or any of the offences impossible. The common law remains in respect of conspiracy to defraud and also conspiracy to engage in conduct which tends to corrupt public morals or outrage public decency.

(2) The tort of conspiracy consists of either: (a) conspiracy by lawful means, where two or more persons combine together to injure the claimant by use of means lawful in themselves but with the predominant purpose to harm the claimant rather than to advance the legitimate interests of those combining together; or (b) conspiracy to use unlawful means, where those combining together do so with intent to injure the claimant by use of means which are unlawful in themselves. (See *Allen v Flood* [1898] A.C. 1, HL; *Crofter Hand Woven Harris Tweed Co Ltd v Veitch* [1942] A.C. 435, HL; *Lonhro Plc v Fayed* [1992] A.C. 448, HL, *OBG v Allan* [2008] 1 A.C. 1.)

Section 219(2) of the Trade Union and Labour Relations (Consolidation) Act 1992 provides that an agreement or combination to do any act in contemplation or furtherance of a trade dispute (*q.v.*) is not actionable in tort if the act is one which, if done without such agreement or combination, would not be actionable.

constables Traditionally inferior officers of the peace. High constables were appointed at the court leet (*q.v.*) of the franchise or hundred over which they

constructive malice

presided. Their duty seems to have been to keep the peace within the hundred. Petty or parish constables were appointed by the justices in petty sessions for the preservation of the peace within their parish or township, and the service of the summonses and the execution of warrants of the peace. They have been superseded by the establishment of the modern police force, wherein police officers of the lowest rank are now named constables. See ARREST.

constat [It appears] A copy or exemplification.

constituency A geographical area for parliamentary and local government elections.

constituent A person who appoints another by power to do some act for him. Also a voter in a constituency (*q.v.*).

constitution (1) Those laws, institutions and customs which combine to create a system of government to which the community regulated by those laws accedes. (2) The written document embodying these laws.
Typically constitutional laws are to some degree entrenched, i.e. a special procedure must be used to change them. The United Kingdom does not have a written constitution, but has a body of rules that regulate the exercise of state power and the rights of the individual. These rules are to be found in statute law, case law, the law and custom of Parliament and constitutional conventions (*q.v.*) and have, in general, no higher status than any other laws. As a result the constitution of the United Kingdom is said to be flexible. As a result of membership of the European Union, Community law is to some degree entrenched in that it cannot be repealed by implication.

constitutional law All rules which directly or indirectly affect the distribution or exercise of sovereign power (Dicey). So much of the law as relates to the designation and form of the legislature, the rights and functions of the several parts of the legislative body, the construction, office and jurisdiction of the courts of justice (Paley). The rules which regulate the structure of the principal organs of government and their relationship to each other, and determine their principal functions. The rules governing the relationship between the individual and the state.

construction The process of ascertaining the meaning of a written document. "Construction of law" is a fixed or arbitrary rule by which a result follows from certain acts or words without reference to the intention of the parties.

constructive Adjective to be used where the law infers or implies (construes) a right, liability or status without reference to the intention of the parties. See some of the titles following this entry.

constructive desertion See DESERTION.

constructive dismissal A dismissal to be inferred from the fact that the employer's conduct is such that the employee has no choice but to resign. For the purposes of unfair dismissal (*q.v.*) and redundancy (*q.v.*), an employee may claim to be dismissed where the employee terminates the contract under which he is employed by the employer, with or without notice, in circumstances such that he is entitled to terminate it without notice by reason of the employer's conduct (Employment Rights Act 1996 ss.95(1)(c), 130(1)(c)). See EMPLOYER AND EMPLOYEE.

constructive fraud Conduct falling short of common law fraud (*q.v.*), but against which equity gives relief on the ground of general public policy or on some fixed policy of the law under four main heads: (1) undue influence (*q.v.*); (2) abuse of confidence; (3) unconscionable bargain (*q.v.*); (4) fraud on a power (*q.v.*).

constructive malice Where death resulted from an act of violence done in the course of, or in the furtherance of, a felony (*q.v.*) involving violence, e.g. rape

109

(*DPP v Beard* [1920] A.C. 479), although without actual malice aforethought (*q.v.*), it was held that there was constructive malice and the crime was murder (*q.v.*). Constructive malice, however, was abolished by the Homicide Act 1957 s.1, which provides that where a person kills another in the course of or in the furtherance of some other offence, the killing does not amount to murder unless done with malice aforethought.

constructive notice See NOTICE.

constructive total loss See TOTAL LOSS.

constructive treason The doctrine that a conspiracy to do some act in regard to the King which might endanger his life was an overt act of compassing the King's death, and treason. It led to the passing of the Treason Act 1795 (now repealed by Crime and Disorder Act 1998). See TREASON.

constructive trust A trust (*q.v.*) raised by equity to satisfy the demands of justice and good conscience without reference to any presumed intention of the parties. The concept is flexible but is applied in the following cases: (1) vendor's lien for unpaid purchase-money; (2) purchaser's lien for purchase-money paid; (3) where a person makes a profit in a fiduciary position or out of trust property; (4) where a stranger intermeddles in a trust; (5) where a mortgagee sells under his power of sale, he is a trustee of any surplus realised.

constructive trustee The person deemed to be a trustee in the case of a constructive trust (*q.v.*).

consuance Acknowledgment; jurisdiction.

consuetudo est altera lex [A custom has the force of law]

consuetudo est optimus interpres legum [Custom is the best interpreter of the laws]

consuetudo et communis assuetudo vincit legem non scriptam, si sit specialis; et interpretatur legem scriptam, si lex generalis [Custom and common usage overcome the unwritten law, if it be special; and interpret the written law, if it be general] See CUSTOM.

consul Agent appointed to watch over the interests of a State or its nationals in foreign parts. The duties and privileges of consular officers are set out in the Consular Relations Act 1968 (as amended by the International Organisations Act 1968; Post Office Act 1969; Diplomatic and Other Privileges Act 1971; British Nationality Act 1981; and Merchant Shipping Act 1995).

consultation A conference with two or more counsel (*q.v.*).

consultation procedure One of the available procedures used for the passage of legislation by the European Union. Originally the sole procedure by which the European Parliament was involved in the legislative process, it is now used as required by specific articles of the Treaty. The majority of decisions are taken by means of co-decision (*q.v.*) but the consultation procedure is reserved for certain legislative areas of a more politically sensitive nature including the competition rules under arts 81 and 82 of the EC Treaty.

consumer A term used to identify a class afforded special treatment in various statutes. There is no consistent definition. See, for example, the Unfair Terms in Consumer Contracts Regulations 1999, and the Consumer Protection (Distance Selling) Regulations 2000, and the Sale and Supply of Goods to Consumers Regulations 2002, which define a consumer as:
  "any natural person who, in contracts covered by these Regulations, is acting for purposes which are outside his trade, business or profession".

Under the Consumer Protection from Unfair Trading Regulations 2008 a consumer is: "any individual who in relation to a commercial practice is acting for purposes which are outside his business".

In the Unfair Contract Terms Act 1977 s.12 a person "deals as consumer" in relation to another party if: (a) he neither makes a relevant contract in the course of a business nor holds himself out as doing so; (b) the other party does so make the contract in the course of a business; and (c) in the case of a contract governed by the law of sale of goods (*q.v.*) or hire-purchase (*q.v.*) (or other analogous type contracts) the goods passing under or in pursuance of the contract are of a type ordinarily supplied for private use or consumption. If the party mentioned in (a) is an individual, paragraph (c) must be ignored. A buyer is not in any circumstances to be regarded as dealing as a consumer: (a) if he is an individual and the goods are second hand goods sold at public auction at which individuals have the opportunity of attending the sale in person; (b) if he is not an individual and the goods are sold by auction or by competitive tender.

consumer credit The Consumer Credit Act 1974 regulates agreements identified as consumer credit agreements (it also treats consumer hire agreements (*q.v.*) in a similar way). There is no definition of the word "consumer" in the Act but the Act distinguishes between "individuals" and others. For the purposes of the Act an individual includes a sole trader or a partnership. Thus, business or professional people are protected by the Act provided they are not incorporated bodies (See COMPANY). "Credit", for the purposes of the Act, includes a cash loan or any other form of financial accommodation, e.g. a hire purchase agreement (*q.v.*). To be regulated, a consumer credit agreement must not provide credit exceeding £25,000.

Consumer Guarantees Directive Directive 1999/44 dealing with aspects of the sale of consumer goods and associated guarantees. The Directive requires that in sales of consumer goods, the goods must be in conformity with the contract and if not that the remedies available to the consumer are; repair of the goods, replacement of the goods, rescission of the contract, price reduction depending upon the circumstances. The Directive was implemented into UK law by the Sale and Supply of Goods to Consumers Regulations 2002.

consumer hire agreement An agreement regulated by the Consumer Credit Act 1974 under which a person (a term which includes a company (*q.v.*)) enters an agreement with an individual (the hirer) for the bailment (*q.v.*) of goods, not being a hire purchase agreement (*q.v.*). To be regulated, the agreement must be capable of lasting more than three months and must not require the hirer to make payments exceeding £25,000.

Consumer Panel The Legal Services Board (*q.v.*) must establish a panel of persons to represent the interests of consumers (Legal Services Act 2007 s.8). The Panel may, inter alia, carry out research for and provide advice to the Board.

consummated Completed, e.g. a marriage is consummated when completed by ordinary and complete sexual intercourse (and not necessarily intercourse which may result in conception: ejaculation is irrelevant). If either party is impotent or wilfully refuses to consummate the marriage, such marriage is voidable by decree of nullity. See Matrimonial Causes Act 1973 s.12; see NULLITY OF MARRIAGE.

contact order An order requiring the person with whom a child lives, or is to live, to allow the child to visit or stay with the person named in the order or for that person and the child otherwise to have contact with each other, Children Act 1989 s.8.

contaminated land Part IIA of the Environmental Protection Act 1990 (inserted by s.57 of the Environment Act 1995) provides a statutory regime for the identification and remediation (*q.v.*) of contaminated land. Contaminated land is any land to be in such a condition, by reason of substances in, on or under the land, that significant harm is being caused or there is a significant possibility of such harm being caused; or pollution of controlled water (*q.v.*) is being or is likely to be caused. Local authorities must make a determination as to whether land is contaminated in accordance with the statutory guidance issued by the Secretary of State. Contaminated land may be classified as a special site (*q.v.*). See REMEDIATION; CLASS A AND CLASS B PERSONS.

contango A percentage paid by a buyer of stock, of which delivery is to be taken on a certain date, for being allowed to delay taking delivery until some other date. See BACKWARDATION.

contemporanea exposito est optima et fortissima in lege [The best way to construe a document is to read it as it would have read when made]

contempt of court The offence of contempt of court consists of conduct which interferes with the administration of justice or impedes or perverts the course of justice. Contempt may be civil or criminal. Civil contempt consists of a failure to comply with a judgment or order of a court or the breach of an undertaking to the court. Whilst being termed civil contempt, the offence is criminal in nature. Criminal contempt is a wider concept and encompasses activities both inside and outside the court. Such contempt may take the form of interrupting court proceedings, refusing to answer questions before a court without lawful excuse or scandalising the court. An important form of criminal contempt is unintentional conduct likely to prejudice a fair trial in particular proceedings. This is called the "strict liability rule" and is governed by the Contempt of Court Act 1981 ss.1, 2. The strict liability rule only applies to publications, which term includes speeches, writing or communications addressed to the public or a section of the public. It is still a contempt at common law to intend to impede or prejudice the administration of justice. The 1981 Act also makes it a contempt to tape record proceedings (s.9). Section 5 of the 1981 Act provides that a publication of discussion in good faith of public affairs or other matters of general public interest is not to be treated as contempt if the risk of impediment or prejudice to particular legal proceedings is merely incidental to the discussion.

contempt of Parliament An offence against the authority or dignity of a House of Parliament or of its members. A breach of parliamentary privilege is a contempt. Parliament has the power to punish for contempt.

contentious business Court proceedings in which there are opposed parties, particularly in probate (*q.v.*) actions where the validity of a will or the eligibility for a grant is contested (cf. common form proceedings or non-contentious business where there is no dispute). Contentious probate business is dealt with by the Chancery Division (Supreme Court Act 1981 Sch.1).

continental shelf The seabed, and subsoil, outside territorial waters. See the Continental Shelf Act 1964, as amended.

contingent That which awaits or depends on the happening of an event.

contingent interest See CONTINGENT REMAINDER.

contingent remainder A remainder limited so as to depend on an event or condition which may never happen or be performed, or which may not happen or be performed until some time after the determination of the preceding estate: e.g. to A for life, and then to B if he has attained 21. Every contingent remainder of an estate of freeholds had to vest either during the continuance of the prior particular estate, or at the very moment when that estate determined; or else fail. Thus, unless B was 21 when A dies, B could never take the property. The Contingent Remainders Act 1877, however, saved from the operation of this rule every contingent remainder which would have been valid if originally created as a shifting use, or executory devise. By the Law of Property Act 1925 Sch.1. Pt I all existing contingent remainders and all to be created subsequently are converted into equitable interests. See REMAINDER.

continuando [By way of continuing] Before the Judicature Acts 1872–75 an allegation in the old action of trespass, of an injury, continuing from day to day.

continuation If a buyer or seller of stock on the Stock Exchange is unable to complete the bargain on the next following Settlement Day, they may by agreement carry over or continue the bargain until the next account day.

continuity of employment A concept used in employment legislation for the purpose of determining when certain employment rights accrue. An employee must have a certain period of "continuous employment", e.g. for protection from unfair dismissal, the period is one year's continuous employment, in order to be entitled to certain statutorily created rights. To compute continuous employment, see Employment Rights Act 1996 Pt XIV.

continuous voyage The doctrine that goods which would be contraband if carried to an enemy port can be dealt with as contraband even though they are being carried to a neutral port, because they are intended to be forwarded either by land or sea from the neutral port to an enemy country. See CONTRABAND OF WAR.

contra bonos mores [Against good morals]

contra formam collationis (or feoffamenti) [Against the form of the gift (or feoffment)]

contra formam statuti [Against the form of the statute] Formerly a necessary ending to an indictment charging a statutory offence.

contra proferentem The doctrine that the construction least favourable to the person putting forwards a document should be adopted against him.

contraband of war Such articles as may not be carried by a neutral to a belligerent, because they are calculated to be of direct service in carrying on war.

contract An agreement enforceable at law. An essential feature of contract is a promise by one party to another to do, or forbear from doing, certain specified acts. The offer of a promise becomes a promise by acceptance. Contract is that species of agreement whereby a legal obligation is constituted and defined between the parties to it.
　For a contract to be valid and legally enforceable there must be: (1) capacity to contract; (2) intention to contract; (3) *consensus ad idem*; (4) valuable consideration; (5) legality of purpose; (6) sufficient certainty of terms. In some cases the contract or evidence of it must be in a prescribed form, i.e. in writing or by deed, and the rule that a contract must be supported by valuable consideration does not apply in the case of contracts of record or by deed.
　There are the following kinds of contract: (1) of record, entered into through the machinery of a court of justice, e.g. a recognisance; (2) specialty, by deed; (3) simple or parole, i.e. in writing or oral; (4) implied, founded by law on the assumed intention of the parties; (5) quasi (*q.v.*), founded by law on the circumstances, irrespective of the wishes of the parties.

contract for sale of land Such a contract can only be made in a written document signed by both parties which incorporates all the terms which the parties have expressly agreed. Where contracts are exchanged one part must be signed by each party (Law of Property (Miscellaneous Provisions) Act 1989 s.2).

contract for services See independent contractor; employer and employee; worker.

contract of employment See EMPLOYER AND EMPLOYEE.

contract of service See EMPLOYER AND EMPLOYEE.

contracting out Giving up the benefit of a statute in consideration of some alternative scheme or advantage. Statutes frequently restrict contracting out.

contracts re Contracts made *re* were one of the four types of basic contracts recognised by Gaius in classical Roman law. Contracts *re* were real contracts arising from the delivery by one party to another of a *res corporalis* Real contracts included *mutuum, commodatum, depositum* and *pignus.*

contribution The payment of a proportionate share of a liability which has been borne by one or some only of a number equally liable. See JOINT TORTFEASORS.

contributory Every person liable to contribute to the assets of a company in the event of the company being wound up, Insolvency Act 1986 s.79. The present and past members are liable in an amount sufficient for the payment of the company's debts and liabilities and the costs of the winding-up (*q.v.*), and for the adjustment of the rights of the contributories amongst themselves. The list of contributories is made out in two parts, A and B. The A contributories are the existing members of the company and are primarily liable; the B contributories are the past members who have ceased to be members within the year proceeding the winding-up, and are only liable to contribute after the A contributories are exhausted. But a B contributory is not liable in respect of any debt of the company contracted after he ceased to be a member.

Note, however, in the case of a company limited by shares, no contribution may exceed the amount of the unpaid liability on the shares. "Contributory" is nevertheless sometimes used to refer to persons holding fully paid shares, and in the wider sense means a member of the company.

contributory mortgage A mortgage where the mortgage money is advanced by two or more persons separately. A trustee must not join in a contributory mortgage since by doing so he parts with his exclusive control of the trust property.

contributory negligence The defence in an action at common law for damages for injuries arising from negligence, that the claimant's own negligence directly caused or contributed to his own injuries.

The original common law rule was if there was blame causing the accident on both sides, however small, the loss lay where it fell. This rule was mitigated by the doctrine of "last opportunity", i.e. that when both parties were negligent, the party which had the last opportunity of avoiding the result of the other's carelessness was alone liable.

The rule that contributory negligence operated as a complete bar to the claimant's claim did not apply to collisions at sea, whereby the fault of two or more vessels damage is caused to one or more of those vessels. The general rule of maritime law is that each vessel is liable for so much of the damage suffered by the other vessel as is proportional to its degree of fault, the remainder of the damage lying where it falls.

The law was altered by the Law Reform (Contributory Negligence) Act 1945, which provided that, where any person suffers damage as a result partly of his own fault and partly of the fault of others, a claim in respect of that damage is not to be defeated by reason of the fault of the person suffering the damage. The damages recoverable, however, are to be reduced to such extent as the court thinks just and equitable having regard to the claimant's share in the responsibility for the damage. But the court must first find and record the total damages that would have been recoverable if the claimant had not been at fault and the damages are apportioned according to the respective degrees of fault. See DANGER, ALTERNATIVE.

control order An order against an individual that imposes obligations on him for purposes connected with protecting members of the public from a risk of conversion

terrorism, Prevention of Terrorism Act 2005 s.1. The section was repealed on March 11, 2005 but has continued to be in-force by statutory instrument, see 2008/559 art.2. See DEROGATING CONTROL ORDER; NON-DEROGATING CONTROL ORDER .

controlled tenancy A protected or statutory tenancy of a dwelling house. Controlled tenancies were converted into regulated tenancies by s.18 of the Rent Act 1977 as amended. See REGULATED TENANCY.

controlled waste Household, industrial or commercial waste. Such waste is described as controlled for the purpose of Pt II Environmental Protection Act 1990.

controlled waters These include relevant territorial waters (three miles off shore), coastal waters (*q.v.*), inland freshwaters (*q.v.*) and ground waters (*q.v.*). See Water Resources Act 1991 s.104.

controlled work Legal help and representation provided under the contract system of legal aid established by the Access to Justice Act 1999.

contumacy Refusal to obey the order of an ecclesiastical court. Such a refusal is now a matter of censure (see the Jurisdiction Measure 1963, and the Clergy Discipline Measure 2003). A person convicted of contumacy under foreign law may be a fugitive criminal under the Extradition Act 1989.

convention award Under the Arbitration Acts 1950 and 1996 a foreign arbitration award. See the Convention on the Recognition and Enforcement of Foreign Judgments 1958 (New York Convention).

Convention compliant Legislation which is compatible with the European Convention on Human Rights. Section 19 of the Human Rights Act 1998 requires Ministers to certify whether the provisions of a Bill are compatible with the European Convention on Human Rights or not. Also used to describe an act of a public authority (*q.v.*) that is in accordance with the European Court of Human Rights (ECHR) (*q.v.*). See DECLARATION OF INCOMPATIBILITY; STATEMENT OF COMPATIBILITY.

convention, constitutional A non-legal rule of constitutional behaviour, considered binding upon those who operate the constitution but which is not enforced by the courts or by the presiding officers of Parliament. Examples of conventions are: the doctrine of cabinet collective responsibility; and that the Monarch is bound to exercise her legal powers according to the advice given by the Cabinet through the Prime Minister (*q.v.*).

Convention on the Future of Europe Established in 2002 to consider a European Constitution. Referenda on its acceptance are being held in the Member States of the European Union but with several States rejecting the Constitution its future is uncertain.

Convention rights The rights contained in arts 1–12 and 14 of the First Protocol and arts 1 and 2 of the Sixth Protocol of the European Convention on Human Rights and Fundamental Freedoms (*q.v.*) as read with arts 16–18 of the Convention. These rights are the basic human rights created by the European Convention and given domestic effect by virtue of the Human Rights Act 1998 which came into effect on October 2, 2000. The rights are set out in Sch.1 to the 1998 Act. They include: a right to life; a right to respect for private and family life; freedom of thought, conscience and religion; freedom of expression; no punishment without lawful authority. See also HUMAN RIGHTS.

conversion (1) The maxim that equity regards as done that which ought to be done means that money directed to be employed in the purchase of land, and land directed to be sold and turned into money, are to be considered as that

115

species of property into which they are directed to be converted. The effect of conversion is to turn realty (*q.v.*) into personalty (*q.v.*), and personalty into realty, for all purposes. It used to be an important point as the rules about the inheritance of realty and personalty differed. It occurs in three cases: (1) partnership land is treated as personalty; (2) under order of the court; (3) under a contract for sale or purchase of land was abolished in relation to trusts for sale of realty and personalty by s.3 of the Trusts of Land and Appointment of Trustees Act 1996.

(2) In tort, committed by a person who deals with chattels not belonging to him in a manner inconsistent with the rights of the owner. By s.1 of the Torts (Interference with Goods) Act 1977, conversion of goods, together with trespass to goods, negligence resulting in damage to goods and any other tort resulting in damage is classed as "wrongful interference with goods". Defences include the exercise of a right of distress, (*q.v.*) *ius tertii* (*q.v.*) or consent but contributory negligence is not a defence except in the case of actions against banks. See CONTRIBUTORY NEGLIGENCE; TROVER.

conveyance (1) An instrument (other than a will) that transfers land. See Law of Property Act 1925 s.205(1)(ii).
(2) The transfer of land.

conveyancer A barrister or solicitor who specialises in drawing conveyances.

conveyancer, licensed A person licensed by the Council of Licensed Conveyancers to provide conveyancing services.

convict Formerly, one sentenced to death or imprisonment for treason or felony. Now one found guilty of an offence and imprisoned.

conviction The finding of a person guilty of an offence after trial. Summary conviction is conviction by a magistrates' court. Evidence of conviction is admissible in civil proceedings (Civil Evidence Act 1968 s.11). The evidence is conclusive for the purposes of defamation actions (ibid. s.13).

cooling-off period See CANCELLATION.

co-operation procedure One of the available procedures used for the passage of legislation by the European Union. A number of provisions of the Treaty relating to Economic and Monetary Union (EMU) require that the Council acts in accordance with this procedure, which is defined in art.252 of the EC Treaty. In most policy areas where the co-operation procedure was in force the Amsterdam treaty has replaced it with the co-decision procedure. See CO-DECISION.

co-ownership Forms of ownership in which two people are entitled to possession at the same time. They include joint tenancy (*q.v.*); and tenancy in common (*q.v.*).

copyhold A form of tenure (*q.v.*) in land forming part of a manor, originally granted by the lord in return for agricultural services. Copyhold was so called because the evidence of the title to such land consisted of a copy of the court roll of the manor, in which all dealings with the land were entered. Copyhold tenure was abolished by the Law of Property Act 1922, and existing copyholds enfranchised and converted into freeholds.

copyright Copyright is an intangible property right. It consists of the exclusive right to reproduce in any form those works defined in s.1(1) of the Copyright Designs and Patents Act 1988. These are original literary, dramatic, musical or artistic works, sound recordings, films, broadcasts or cable programmes and the typographical arrangement of published editions. Under the Duration of Copyright and Rights in Performances Regulations 1995, copyright, in relation to literary, dramatic, musical or artistic works and films in general, lasts during the lifetime of the author and for 70 years after his death. Copyright is transmissible by assignment, testamentary disposition or by operation of law, as personal or moveable property. No assignment of copyright is valid unless in writing signed by or on behalf of the assignor. Licences may be granted in respect of copyright by the owner or under a licensing scheme. In addition to the remedies available to the copyright owner upon infringement of copyright, it is also a criminal offence to make or deal with an article which is, and which a person knows or has reason to believe is, an infringing copy of a copyright work (Copyright, Designs and Patents Act 1988).

Copyright Tribunal This tribunal replaced the Performing Right Tribunal (*q.v.*) as a result of the Copyright, Designs and Patents Act 1988. It has jurisdiction to hear and determine proceedings relating to licensing of copyright works and performances and rights in databases (*q.v.*).

cor: coram [In the presence of]

coram judice [In the presence of the judge] Before a properly constituted or appropriate court.

coram non judice [Before one who is not a judge] The proceedings are a nullity.

COREPER The Committee of Permanent Representatives prepares the work of the Council of the European Union. It carries out the tasks assigned to it by art.209(1) of the EC Treaty. It is made up of delegates from the Member States who are known as Permanent Representatives and are based in Brussels.

co-respondent A person called upon to answer a petition or proceeding jointly with another, e.g. in divorce.

corn rents Additional sums payable in relation to land wholly or partly in lieu of tithes. The Corn Rents Act 1963 provides for the making of a scheme by the Commissioners of Inland Revenue (now the Special Commissioners for HM Revenue and Customs) for the apportionment, redemption and, in certain cases, the extinguishment of corn rent.

coroner An officer of the Crown appointed from barristers, solicitors or qualified medical practitioners of at least five years standing. His function is to inquire into deaths suspected of being unnatural or violent. Most inquests are held without a jury. The coroner's procedure is inquisitorial, see Coroner's Act 1988.

corporate governance The system by which companies are directed and controlled. The subject of a wide-ranging debate from the 1990s aiming to improve the functioning of boards of companies. The work of three committees (Cadbury, Greenbury and Hampel) formed the basis of a set of principles subsequently consolidated into the Combined Code on Corporate Governance. Listed companies (*q.v.*) are required to comply with the Code.

corporate manslaughter Under the common law a company may be guilty of manslaughter by an unlawful act or gross negligence, but only if the company is identified with an individual guilty of the offence. See *AG's Reference No.2 of 1999* However the common law offence of manslaughter by gross negligence is abolished in its application to corporations by the Corporate Manslaughter and Corporate Homicide Act 2007 s.20. Under s.1 of the Act an organisation to which the section applies is guilty of an offence if the way in which its activities are managed or organised causes a person's death, and amounts to a gross breach of a relevant duty of care owed by the organisation to the deceased. A breach of a duty of care by an organisation is a "gross" breach if the conduct alleged to amount to a breach of that duty falls far below what can reasonably be expected of the organisation in the circumstances. The organisations to which the section applies include corporations, police forces and partnerships, trade unions and employers' associations, that are employers. An organisation is guilty of an offence under s.1 only if the way in which its activities are managed or organised by its senior management is a substantial element in the breach of duty. An organisation that is guilty of corporate manslaughter is liable on conviction on indictment to a fine. The offence of corporate homicide is indictable only in the High Court of Justiciary.

corporation A legal person created by Royal Charter, Act of Parliament, international treaty, or registration under a statutory procedure, e.g. under the Companies Acts (the commonest type). A corporation is a distinct legal entity, separate from such persons as may be members of it, and having legal rights and duties and perpetual succession. It may enter into contracts, own property, employ people and be liable for torts and crimes. See *Salomon v Salomon & Co Ltd* [1897] A.C. 22.

corporation sole A corporation (*q.v.*) consisting of a certain office (e.g. a bishop) which continues as a legal entity regardless of the human holder of that office.

corporation tax A tax payable by resident bodies corporate on their profits, both income and capital.

corporeal property Property which has a physical existence such as land or goods. See HEREDITAMENTS; INCORPOREAL PROPERTY.

corpus [Body] The capital of a fund, as contrasted with the income.

corpus delicti The facts which constitute an offence.

corpus juris canonici See CANON LAW.

corpus juris civilis The body of Roman law contained in the Institutes, Digest, and Code compiled by order of Justinian, together with the *Novellae*, or constitutions promulgated after the compilation of the Code.

corroboration Independent evidence which implicates a person accused of a crime by connecting him with it. Corroboration is not required by statute save in relation to treason, perjury, speeding and attempts to commit those offences. In relation to the evidence of certain types of witness, e.g. accomplices or children, a jury may need to be warned of the dangers of convicting on uncorroborated evidence.

corruption The bribing of an office holder is an offence at common law and there are various statutory provisions relating to corruption in local government and other public bodies.

corrupt practices Offences under the Representation of the People Act 1983 in connection with a parliamentary or other election, e.g. treating, undue influence, personation or the procuring thereof, bribery, or making a false declaration as to election expenses.

corruption of blood See ATTAINDER.

corsned [The accursed morsel] A piece of barley bread, weighing about one ounce, which an accused person, after certain quasi-religious invocations, was set to swallow. If he succeeded, he was held innocent: failure was proof of guilt.

cost book mining company A partnership formed for working a mine under local customs, e.g. in Derbyshire, Devon and Cornwall.

costs in civil proceedings The general rule is that a successful litigant in civil proceedings is entitled to his costs; costs follow the event. But costs are always at the discretion of the court and there may be statutory or other restrictions on the award of costs.

In awarding costs the court will take into account such factors as the outcome of the case, payments into court and the conduct of the parties.

Judges will usually assess costs summarily at the end of the trial or there will be a detailed assessment conducted at a later date, CPR Pts 44–48.

costs in criminal proceedings The court may order the costs of the prosecution or of the defence to be paid out of central funds or by the other side (see Prosecution of Offences Act 1985 as amended).

costs officer Means a costs judge, district judge or an authorised court officer from the Supreme Court Costs Office (*q.v.*). (Formerly a taxation officer.)

couchant See LEVANT AND COUCHANT.

Council of Europe An intergovernmental body established in 1949 and the body which developed the European Convention on Human Rights (*q.v.*).

Council of Law Reporting Set up in 1865 to produce the Law Reports, effectively replacing the earlier nominate reports.

Council of Legal Education The body once charged with regulating the examination of students of the Inns of Court for qualification for call to the Bar. This function ended in 1997 and was passed to the General Council of the Bar (*q.v.*). In 2006 the regulatory role was taken over by the Bar Standards Board (*q.v.*). See BARRISTER.

Council of the European Union The major decision making body of the European Union with a wide range of functions such as policy co-ordination. It consists of a representative from each of the Member States. That representative will be a government minister but the precise representative will vary from meeting to meeting depending on the nature of the business to be discussed (art.203 (ex art.146)). The presidency of the Council is held by each of the Member States in turn for a six-month period.

Council of the Inns of Court A body comprising representatives of the four Inns of Court (*q.v.*) and the General Council of the Bar (*q.v.*).

Council on Tribunals Established under Tribunals and Inquiries Act 1958 and governed by the Tribunals and Inquiries Acts 1971 and 1992, it was composed of between 10 and 15 members appointed by the Lord Chancellor (*q.v.*) and the Secretary of State. The Council had an advisory role. It was under a duty to keep under review the constitution and working of the tribunals specified in the 1992 Act. On November 1, 2007 the Council on Tribunals was replaced by the Administrative Justice & Tribunals Council (*q.v.*). See TRIBUNALS; TRIBUNALS SERVICE.

council tax Term used to refer to the system of local property taxation provided to replace the local tax known as the community charge, or colloquially as the poll tax (*q.v.*) (see the Local Government and Valuation Act 1991 and the Local Government Finance Act 1992).

counsel A barrister (*q.v.*) (generally, practising barristers).

count Paragraphs in an indictment (*q.v.*), each containing and charging an offence.

counterclaim A response by the defendant to a claim who alleges in his defence a claim, relief or remedy against the claimant, instead of bringing a separate action. A counterclaim may also be made against any other person who is liable to him together with the claimant in respect of the counterclaim or the original subject matter of the action, see Pt 20 CPR 1998. Accordingly a counterclaim is often referred to as a Pt 20 claim (*q.v.*).

counterfeit Made in imitation. To make a false instrument or to counterfeit currency notes or coins is an indictable offence under the Forgery and Counterfeiting Act 1981.

counter-marque Letters issued by one state as a reprisal for the issue of letters of marque (*q.v.*) by another state.

counterpart A lease is generally prepared in two identical forms, called the lease and the counterpart respectively. The lease is executed by the lessor alone, and the counterpart is executed by the lessee alone, and then the lease and counterpart are exchanged.

country, trial by Trial by jury. See IN PAIS; JURY.

county Originally a shire, or portion of the country comprising a number of hundreds, under the sheriff. There were, before local government reorganisation in 1974, 39 counties. After that England was divided into Greater London, six metropolitan counties and 39 non-metropolitan counties. The Greater London Council and the metropolitan councils were abolished and, generally, their functions transferred to the London Borough Councils and the metropolitan district councils, respectively in 1985. Wales is divided into eight counties.

county borough Boroughs of not less than 50,000 inhabitants were created county boroughs and administrative counties under the Local Government Act 1888, and the Local Government Act 1933. They have now ceased to exist (Local Government Act 1972).

county corporate A city or town which had by virtue of royal charters the privilege of being a county of itself, and not within any other county. This status has disappeared with the change in local government structure. See COUNTY.

county council The elective bodies for the administration of the local government of the counties, established in 1882 and replacing administration by the Justices of the Peace. Now governed by the Local Government Act 1972. See COUNTY.

county courts The modern County Courts, established by the County Courts Act 1846 are the busiest civil courts in the country. There are 220 County Courts, served by circuit judges (*q.v.*), and District Judges (*q.v.*). Both the High Court and the County Court operate the same process under the Civil Procedure Rules 1998 as amended. County Courts have unlimited jurisdiction for contract and tort claims but a claimant cannot bring a personal injury action in the High Court if its value is under £50,000 nor any other claim worth less than £15,000. In addition where statute requires a case to be brought there and specialist cases may only be started in the High Court. Cases are allocated to one of three tracks for hearing: small claims (generally under £5,000), fast track (generally between £5,000 and £15,000) and multi track (generally over £15,000 but, unlike the other two, without a standardised procedure).

county palatine A county, the owner of which had (in the Middle Ages) *jura regalia* (*q.v.*) or royal franchises and rights of jurisdiction similar to those possessed by the Crown in the rest of the kingdom, including the power of pardoning crimes and appointing judges and officers within his county. The three counties palatine were Chester (whose courts were abolished in 1830), Durham and Lancaster, which continued until 1971. See PALATINE COURT.

coupons Detachable slips of paper annexed to a bond or debenture payable to bearer for the purpose of providing for the periodical payment of interest on the principal, usually half-yearly. The interest is payable only on presentation and delivery to the paying agent of the coupon referring thereto.

court (1) A place where justice is administered; (2) the judge or judges who sit in a court; (3) an aggregate of separate courts or judges, as the Supreme Court of Judicature.

court baron A feudal manorial court, in which the free tenants or freeholders of the manor were the judges. It entertained suits concerning land held of the

120

manor, including copyholds (*q.v.*). The manorial courts were finally put down in 1977. See COURT LEET.

court expert An independent expert witness (*q.v.*) appointed by the court on an application by a party, in a non-jury case, to inquire into and report on any question of fact or opinion.

Court for Crown Cases Reserved Created by the Crown Cases Act 1848 for the decision of questions of law arising on the trial of a person convicted of crime, and reserved by the judge or justices at the trial at their discretion for the consideration of the court. It was abolished when a proper criminal appellate system was created in 1907.

court leet Developing from the pre-Conquest sherriff's tourn and coming into private hands, it maintained the "view of frankpledge" (tithing system) as a means of raising revenue for its owner and, before the development of the police force, elected constables. Abolished by the Law of Property Act 1922.

court-martial A court convened by or under the authority of the Crown to try an offence against military or naval discipline, or against the ordinary law, committed by a soldier or sailor in Her Majesty's service. There is an appeal to a Court-Martial Appeal Court under the Courts-Martial (Appeals) Act 1968 (as amended). Procedural changes to ensure compliance with the European Convention on Human Rights (*q.v.*) were introduced by the Armed Forces Discipline Act 2000.

Court of Appeal The Court of Appeal was created by the Judicature Act 1873. Its constitution, practice and procedure are now governed by the Supreme Court Act 1981. It consists of two divisions: the Criminal Division and the Civil Division. The Lord Chief Justice (*q.v.*) is the President of the Criminal Division and the Master of the Rolls (*q.v.*) is the President of the Civil Division. The Civil Division has vested in it the former jurisdiction of the Lord Chancellor (*q.v.*) and the Court of Appeal in Chancery and the Court of Exchequer Chamber (*q.v.*). The Court of Appeal consists of senior judges known as "Lord/Lady Justices of Appeal." Under the Administration of Justice Act 1999 a right to appeal is exercisable only with leave of the court.

For the Criminal Division see CRIMINAL APPEAL. See also SUPREME COURT.

The Court of Appeal is bound to follow decisions of the House of Lords, and the Civil Division is bound to follow its own previous decisions and those of the courts that it superseded. Where the previous decisions conflict, the Court of Appeal must decide which to follow. See PRECEDENT PER INCURIAM; APPEAL.

Court of Arches The ecclesiastical court of appeal for the archdiocese of Canterbury (cf. the Chancery Court of York). The five judges of the Court of Arches include the Dean of the Arches (Ecclesiastical Jurisdiction Measure 1963, as amended).

Court of Auditors An institution of the EC charged with overseeing the expenditure of the Community, art.247 EC Treaty.

Court of Chancery Developed in the Middle Ages as the court of the Lord Chancellor, dealing with questions relating to royal grants (on the Latin side) and complaints about interference with common law rights (on the English side). It was said to be a court of conscience and was less constrained by legal forms than the common law courts. From this developed the distinction between equity (*q.v.*) and common law (*q.v.*). By the 19th century its delays were legendary and reform led to the fusion of the common law and equity courts and remedies. It was merged in the High Court of Justice by the Judicature Act 1873 and is now known as the Chancery Division.

Court of Chivalry The court of the Lord High Constable and Earl Marshall in matters of honour and heraldry. The court has sat once only since 1737 to deal with a complaint by Manchester Corporation that their arms were being usurped ([1955] 1 All E.R. 387). It uses the procedure of the Civil Law.

Court of Common Pleas One of the courts into which the *Curia Regis* was divided. It was originally the only superior court of record having jurisdiction in ordinary civil actions between subject and subject. It consisted of the Lord Chief Justice and five puisne judges. It was transferred to the High Court of Justice by the Judicature Act 1873, and is now represented by the Queen's Bench Division (see the Judicature Act 1925 ss.18(1), 56(2); Supreme Court Act 1981 s.5(1)(b)).

Court of Criminal Appeal Created by the Criminal Appeal Act 1907, to replace the Court of Crown Cases Reserved. The court was abolished by the Criminal Appeal Act 1966, and its jurisdiction transferred to the Criminal Division of the Court of Appeal. See CRIMINAL APPEAL.

Court of Directors Directors of the Bank of England consisting of the Governor, two deputy governors and 16 directors, all of whom are appointed by the Queen and who manage the Bank's affairs.

Court of Ecclesiastical Cases Reserved A court of original jurisdiction in ecclesiastical matters (see Ecclesiastical Jurisdiction Measure 1963).

Court of Exchequer One of the courts into which the *Curia Regis* was divided. By the year 1200 it had a separate existence, but it continued to collect revenue in addition to trying cases, until the first Chief Baron was appointed in 1312. It was originally a court having jurisdiction only in matters concerning the public revenue, e.g. in suits by the Crown against its debtors; but it afterwards acquired, by the use of fictitious pleadings, jurisdiction in actions between subject and subject. It was formerly subdivided into a court of common law and a court of equity; but its equitable jurisdiction (except in revenue matters) was transferred to the Court of Chancery. Under the Judicature Act 1873, the jurisdiction of the Court of Exchequer was transferred to the High Court of Justice, Exchequer Division, until, in 1881, the three "common law" divisions of the High Court were merged into one. It is now represented by the Queen's Bench Division (Judicature Act 1925 ss.18(2), 56(2); Supreme Court Act 1981 s.5(1)(b)). See QUO MINUS.

Court of Exchequer Chamber See EXCHEQUER CHAMBER, COURT OF.

Court of First Instance (1) Where a case commences.
(2) A court of trial as opposed to an appellate court.

Court of First Instance of the European Communities (CFI) Established in 1988 and came into operation in September 1989. It consists of 25 members. The CFI is attached to the European Court of Justice and has jurisdiction to hear and determine at first instance certain classes of action, including proceedings brought by employees of the Community and judicial review actions brought by "natural and legal persons". The Court also deals with cases concerning EC competition law, merger control and state aid. The CFI has no jurisdiction to give preliminary rulings on the interpretation of Community law.
There is a right of appeal on a point of law to the European Court of Justice (see art.225 of the EC Treaty (ex art.168a)).

Court of Hustings The oldest of the ancient City of London Courts.

court of inquiry A court appointed by naval, military, air force authorities, etc. to ascertain the facts in some matter so that the propriety of instituting legal proceedings or taking disciplinary action may be considered. In relation to a trade dispute the Secretary of State may appoint such a court to inquire into the causes and circumstances of the dispute, s.215 of the Trade Union and Labour Relations (Consolidation) Act 1992. See also TRIBUNALS.

Court of Justice of the European Communities (ECJ) Established under the Treaty of Rome (*q.v.*) to ensure that in the interpretation and application of the EC Treaty the law is observed. The Court is based in Luxembourg and consists of 27 judges and is supported by eight Advocates General. The ECJ has jurisdiction, inter alia, to give preliminary rulings on the interpretation of the Treaty and the validity and interpretation of the acts of the institutions (primarily Regulations, Directives and Decisions) (art.234 EC (ex art.177)). For guidance on when a national court should consider it necessary or not to refer a matter to the ECJ, see the ECJ judgment in Case 283/81 *CILFIT v Ministry of Health* [1982] E.C.R. 3415. The Court can also declare that a Member State has failed to comply with Community law in an action brought by the European Commission (*q.v.*) or another Member State (*q.v.*), although the latter is very rare (see arts 226–228 EC (ex arts 169–171)).

See COURT OF FIRST INSTANCE OF THE EUROPEAN COMMUNITIES; COMMUNITY LEGISLATION.

Court of King's [Queen's] Bench The court originally held in the presence of the Sovereign. It was one of the superior courts of common law, having, ultimately, in ordinary civil actions concurrent jurisdiction with the Courts of Common Pleas and Exchequer. Its principal judge was styled the Lord Chief Justice of England. It also had special jurisdiction over inferior courts, magistrates and civil corporations by the prerogative writs (*q.v.*) of mandamus, prohibition and certiorari, and in proceedings by quo warrants and habeas corpus. It was also the principal court of criminal jurisdiction in England: informations might be filed and indictments preferred in it in the first instance. The King's [Queen's] Bench accordingly had two "sides" namely, the "plea side", for civil business, and the "Crown side", or "Crown Office", for the criminal and extraordinary jurisdiction. The court was merged in the Supreme Court by the Judicature Act 1873, of which it is now the Queen's Bench Division (see the Judicature Act 1925 ss.18(2), 56(2); Supreme Court Act 1981 s.5(1)(b)).

Today, the Queen's Bench Division has jurisdiction over actions in contract and tort. Within the Division there are specialist Commercial and Admiralty Courts. The Queen's Bench Division may be constituted as a Divisional Court (*q.v.*) to exercise supervisory jurisdiction or to hear criminal appeals by way of case stated, either directly from the magistrates' courts or via the Crown Court.

court of last resort A court from which there is no appeal.

Court of Probate Formed by the Court of Probate Act 1857 to take over the jurisdiction of church and other courts in the matter of wills. Transferred by the Judicature Act 1873 to the Supreme Court of Judicature, where it is represented by the Family Division of the High Court in relation to non-contentious business and by the Chancery Division of the High Court in relation to other probate business (mainly contentious business).

Court of Protection Formerly an office of the Supreme Court for the protection and management of property and affairs of persons under a mental disability (Mental Health Act 1983 s.93). It had a Master appointed by the Lord Chancellor (Supreme Court Act 1981 and Courts and Legal Services Act 1990). Under the Mental Capacity Act 2005 s.45 it has become a superior court (*q.v.*) with a jurisdiction which can be exercised by amongst others the President of the Family Division (*q.v.*), a puisne judge (*q.v.*) or a district judge (*q.v.*). It has the same powers, rights, privileges and authority as the High Court (*q.v.*). See PUBLIC GUARDIAN.

Court of Protection Visitor A person appointed by the Lord Chancellor (*q.v.*) either to a panel of Special Visitors (registered medical practitioners or those having suitable qualifications or training, or special knowledge of and experience in cases of impairment of or disturbance in the functioning of the mind or brain) or to a panel of General Visitors who need no medical qualification. The role of a Court of Protection Visitor is to provide independent advice to the court and the Public Guardian (*q.v*). A Visitor may be directed by the Public Guardian to visit a donee of a lasting power of attorney (*q.v.*).

court of record A court whereof the acts and judicial proceedings are enrolled for a perpetual memory and testimony, and which has authority to fine and imprison for contempt of its authority. The House of Lords, Court of Appeal, High Court and Crown Court are examples of superior courts of record. The County Court is an inferior court of record. Other inferior courts of record were abolished by the Courts Act 1971 s.43. Under the provisions of the Tribunals, Courts and Enforcement Act 2007 the Upper Tribunal (*q.v.*) is to be a superior court of record. See FIRST-TIER TRIBUNAL; SUPREME COURT.

court roll (1) A book in which all the proceedings of the customary court of a manor were entered.

(2) A record of any court.

Court service An executive agency created in 1995 to run all courts other than magistrates courts and coroners courts. Under the Courts Act 2003 it has been replaced by Her Majesty's Courts Service, an executive agency of the Ministry of Justice and by locally accountable courts boards (*q.v.*).

Courts Boards Established by the Courts Act 2003 on a geographical basis to scrutinise the Lord Chancellor's role in providing an efficient and effective court system.

courts, inferior See INFERIOR COURT.

covenant A promise made by deed. It may be positive, stipulating the performance of some act or the payment of money, or negative or restrictive, forbidding the commission of some act. Covenants may be used to serve the purpose of a bond (*q.v.*).

covenantee The person who benefits from the covenant and can enforce it.

covenantor The person who has to perform the promise.

covenant, action of The action which until the Judicature Acts 1873 and 1875 lay where a party claimed damages for breach of covenant (obsolete).

covenant to stand seised A covenant by a person seised of land in possession, reversion, or vested remainder in consideration of his natural love and affection, to stand seised of the land to the use of his wife, child or kinsman. By the Statute of Uses the use was converted into a legal estate, and the covenant operated as a conveyance (obsolete).

covenant, writ of A writ which lay for claiming damages for breach of covenant. Abolished by Real Property Limitation Act 1833.

covenants for title The covenants entered into by a seller in a conveyance of land on sale as to his title, giving the purchaser the right to an action for damages if the title subsequently proves to be bad. See FULL TITLE GUARANTEE; LIMITED TITLE GUARANTEE.

cracked trial One where the defendant does not plead guilty until the last moment, thus wasting time of the CPS, witnesses, court, etc.

credit (1) The right given by a creditor to a debtor to defer payment of his debt.

(2) Cross-examination as to credit means asking questions of a witness designed to test his credibility.

credit agreement There is no statutory definition but it is an agreement between a creditor and a debtor in which the creditor provides the debtor with a cash loan or other financial accommodation. See CONSUMER CREDIT.

credit broker The person who facilitates the granting of credit to individuals. Credit brokers must be licensed and are subject to regulation under the Consumer Credit Act 1974.

credit card A type of credit token (*q.v.*) issued by a bank or other financial institution, it can be used to buy goods or services from dealers who have entered into a merchant agreement with the network, compare charge cards (*q.v.*), debit cards (*q.v.*).

credit institution An undertaking whose business is to receive deposits from the public and to grant credits, e.g. a bank. See the Banking Consolidation Directive 2000/12 EC.

credit reference agency An organisation that collects and provides information on the financial status of individuals. A person has the right to find out whether a credit reference agency has been consulted about him in any credit transaction in which he is involved, and also to discover the information any credit reference agency has compiled about him and require it to be amended if necessary.

credit token A document or thing given to an individual by a person carrying on a consumer credit business regulated by the Consumer Credit Act 1974. The token is intended for production in transactions whereby cash, goods or services are obtained on credit. See CONSUMER CREDIT.

credit-sale agreement An agreement for the sale of goods under which title passes immediately to the buyer but the purchase price or part of it is payable by instalments, compare a conditional sale agreement (*q.v.*) (Consumer Credit Act 1974 s.189). Transactions under £25,000 come within s.8 of the Act unless exempt under s.16.

credit union An organisation made up of a group of people with a common interest who agree to become members and to save regularly in a common fund. The Credit Union can then make loans to members at a low rate of interest. They are governed by the Industrial and Provident Societies Acts 1965–1978 unless the Credit Unions Act 1979 provides otherwise.

creditor A person to whom a debt is owing.

creditors' committee A committee consisting of at least three and not more than five persons representing the creditors of a bankrupt (*q.v.*). The function of the committee is to supervise the administration of the bankrupt's property by the trustee (Insolvency Act 1986 s.301 and see Insolvency Rules 1986).

Where a company is in administrative receivership or subject to an administration order (*q.v.*), creditors of the company can appoint a committee of creditors to represent them (Insolvency Act 1986 ss.26, 49). Compare LIQUIDATION COMMITTEE (*q.v.*).

cremation The disposal of a dead body by burning in a crematorium (Cremation Act 1902; Cremation Act 1952).

CREST Introduced in 1996, CREST is an electronic system to record the ownership of shares and enable them to be traded on the Stock exchange. The title is recorded and is said to be uncertificated or dematerialised. Only listed companies need to have uncertificated shares. Transfers are made through a central securities depositary which is regulated by the Uncertificated Securities Regulations 2001. By 2005 there will be a single cross EU border settlement system.

crime A crime may be described as an act, default or conduct prejudicial to the community, the commission of which by law renders the person responsible liable to punishment by fine or imprisonment in special proceedings, normally instituted by officers in the service of the Crown, (cf. Aristotle's definition "an injury voluntarily inflicted in defiance of the law"). Indictable offences (other than treason) were formerly divided into felonies (*q.v.*) and misdemeanours (*q.v.*), but the distinction between the two was abolished by the Criminal Law Act 1967 s.1. Crimes are now classified as indictable, summary or either way offences (*q.v.*), definitions of which are to be found in the Interpretation Act 1978 s.5 Sch.1. Offences which may only be tried on indictment are tried by the Crown Court (*q.v.*) before a judge and jury; offences which are triable summarily will be tried before justices in a magistrates' court (*q.v.*); either way offences may be tried in the Crown Court or in the magistrates' court.

crimen falsi The common law offence of forgery (*q.v.*) and falsification.

crimen laesae majestatis [The crime of injured majesty] Treason and lesser offences against the Sovereign, e.g. insult.

criminal appeal Rights to appeal depend on whether the case was tried summarily or on indictment. A defendant convicted in a magistrates' court (*q.v.*) may appeal against conviction and/or sentence to the Crown Court (*q.v.*), which will rehear the case, or may appeal by way of case stated to the High Court (*q.v.*).

A defendant convicted at the Crown Court may, with leave of the Court of Appeal (*q.v.*) or a certificate of fitness from the trial judge, appeal to the Court of Appeal against conviction and/or sentence. Under the Criminal Appeal Act 1968, as amended by the Criminal Appeal Act 1995, the Court of Appeal must allow an appeal against conviction if it thinks the finding was unsafe and against sentence on the grounds that its either: (a) wrong in law, or (b) is manifestly excessive. A defendant may also appeal by way of case stated to the High Court. Under the Criminal Justice Act 2003 the prosecution may also appeal with leave of the court and may apply for an order quashing an acquittal and seeking a retrial for a qualifying offence (*q.v.*) under new provisions providing for an exception to the rule against double jeopardy (*q.v.*).

After determination by the High Court or the Court of Appeal either prosecution or defence may, with leave from the court below or the House of Lords (*q.v.*), appeal to the House of Lords, provided that the court below certifies that a point of law of general public importance is involved and that it is one which ought to be considered by the House of Lords.

An appeal from a Divisional Court of the Queen's Bench Division (*q.v.*) in a criminal cause or matter lies to the House of Lords (Administration of Justice Act 1960 ss.1–4). See SUPREME COURT.

criminal bankruptcy Where a person was convicted of an offence before the Crown Court (*q.v.*) and the loss or damage attributable to that offence exceeded £15,000, the court could make a criminal bankruptcy order against him (Powers of Criminal Courts Act 1973). The Act was repealed by the Powers of Criminal Courts (Sentencing) Act 2000.

Criminal Cases Review Commission Set up by the Criminal Appeal Act 1995, to investigate and process allegations of miscarriages of justice. The act abolished the Home Secretary's power to refer cases to the Court of Appeal (*q.v.*). The Commission may refer cases in respect of sentence and conviction on indictment to the Court of Appeal and may refer convictions and sentences imposed in the magistrates courts to the Crown Court.

criminal compensation See COMPENSATION ORDER; CRIMINAL INJURIES COMPENSATION.

criminal damage There are four main criminal damage offences: simple criminal damage, aggravated criminal damage (*q.v.*), arson (*q.v.*) and aggravated arson. Simple criminal damage occurs when a person who without lawful excuse destroys or damages any property belonging to another, intending to destroy or damage any such property or being reckless as to whether any such property would be destroyed or damaged (Criminal Damage Act 1971 s.1(1)). If committed by fire it may be charged as arson (*q.v.*). Criminal damage is generally triable either way but where the damage is less than £5,000 (unless caused by fire or aggravated) it is treated as triable only summarily. The maximum penalty for aggravated criminal damage is life imprisonment

Criminal Defence Service (CDS) Replaced the criminal legal aid scheme from 2001. It relies on contracting selected private solicitors to carry out the work. The firms are subject to periodic audits.

criminal injuries compensation A person who sustains a criminal injury may receive compensation for it under a tariff system established by the Criminal Injuries Compensation Act 1995. Under the Domestic Violence Crime and Victims Act 2004 there is provision for a scheme to be adopted that would allow the compensation paid to the victim to be recovered from the appropriate person. This latter scheme is not yet in force.

criminal libel At common law it is an offence to publish a defamatory libel, that is one which tends to vilify a person or bring him into hatred, contempt and ridicule, whether false or not. Where the prosecution is of a newspaper proprietor, etc. the leave of a judge in chambers is required. Law of Libel Amendment Act 1888.

criminal lunatic An inmate of a criminal lunatic asylum: a "Broadmoor patient" (Criminal Justice Act 1948 s.62 repealed). See BROADMOOR.

Criminal Procedure Rules 2005 Made under the Courts Act 2003 s.69, they are the first step in the creation of a consolidated criminal code. The rules apply in all criminal cases in magistrates' courts, crown courts and the criminal division of the Court of Appeal. They create an overriding objective that all criminal cases should be dealt with justly (CrPR r.1).

Criminal Procedure Rules Committee Set up under the Courts Act 2003 to develop rules and determine practices and procedures to be used in all criminal courts.

cross-appeals Where both parties to a case appeal.

crossbows The Crossbows Act 1987 establishes various summary offences relating to the sale, purchase, hiring and possession of a crossbow to or by a person under the age of 18.

cross-examination The questioning of a witness by the opponent of the party calling him or by any other party to the proceedings. Under the Youth Justice and Criminal Evidence Act 1999 certain witnesses may not be cross-examined by the accused in person.

cross-remainder Where land is given in undivided shares to A and B for limited estates so that, upon the determination of the particular estate in A's share, the whole of the land goes to B, and vice versa.

crossed cheque When a cheque bears across its face the words "and Company", or any abbreviation thereof, between two parallel transverse lines, it is said to be crossed generally, and when it bears across its face the name of a banker, it is said to be crossed specially (Bills of Exchange Act 1882 s.76). A generally crossed cheque can be paid only through a bank, and a specially crossed cheque only through the bank specified. A holder of a cheque crossed "not negotiable" cannot give a transferee a better title than he has (ibid. s.81). See CHEQUE; ACCOUNT PAYEE.

Crown The Monarch in his public capacity as a body politic. "The King never dies": there is no interregnum. The coronation is but an ornament or solemnity of power (*Calvin's Case* (1608) 7 Co. Rep. 1a). See ROYAL TITLE.

Crown

The Crown is the highest branch of the legislature, the head of Executive power, and the fountain of justice and honour. As "the King can do no wrong", the Crown was not liable in tort, nor was it liable for the torts of the Crown servants; they, however, are liable personally for their own torts. But a petition of Right (*q.v.*) lay against the Crown. By the Crown Proceedings Act 1947, the Crown was put as near as possible in the same position as the subject in litigation. See CROWN PROCEEDINGS.

Crown Court The Courts Act 1971 abolished the courts of Assize and Quarter Sessions and replaced them with a single Crown Court divided into six circuits. It is a part of the Supreme Court (*q.v.*), staffed by High Court judges for the most serious offences and by circuit judges (*q.v.*) and recorders (*q.v.*) for less serious ones. It hears all cases involving trial on indictment as well as appeals from those convicted by the magistrates. When the Crown Court sits in London it is known as the Central Criminal Court (*q.v.*) (ibid. s.8(3)).

Crown debts Debts due to the Crown in respect of, e.g. VAT, which took precedence over ordinary creditors in insolvency proceedings until the Enterprise Act 2002 removed this precedence.

Crown lands Land of the Crown surrendered at the beginning of the Monarch's reign in return for payments under the Civil List (*q.v.*). The Crown Estate Act 1961 provides for the management of such land now known as the Crown Estate by the Crown Estate Commissioners.

Crown Office The office in which all the ministerial business of the Court of the King's [Queen's] Bench in respect of its prerogative and criminal jurisdiction was transacted. Now part of the Central Office of the Supreme Court. See CLERK OF THE CROWN.

Crown privilege See PUBLIC INTEREST IMMUNITY.

Crown proceedings Legal proceedings instituted on behalf of the Crown to enforce the payment of sums or debts due to the Crown were formerly brought by way of Information on the Revenue side of the King's [Queen's] Bench Division, or by writ of summons in the High Court.

By the Crown Proceedings Act 1947, the Crown was, in general, made liable to be sued in contract or in tort, etc. as if it were a private person of full age and capacity, subject to the Crown's prerogative and statutory rights. Proceedings by or against the Crown are now brought by or against the appropriate government department, or the Attorney-General (*q.v.*). Judgment, however, cannot be enforced against the Crown; nor are injunctions or decrees or specific performance normally available against the Crown. In lieu, declaratory orders or judgments may be made against the Crown, and a certificate thereof given to the person in whose favour they are made.

Crown Prosecution Service (CPS) Formerly the instigation of prosecution was a matter for the police, but the Prosecution of Offences Act 1985 set up a national prosecution service under the Director of Public Prosecutions (*q.v.*) to undertake the task. In 1999 it was reorganised into 42 areas to match the boundaries of police forces, each headed by a Chief Crown Prosecutor. It is staffed and its workload conducted by barristers, solicitors and, under the Crime and Disorder Act 1998, designated caseworkers.

Crown Side The prerogative and criminal jurisdiction of the Queen's Bench Division. It had an ancient jurisdiction of supervising inferior courts.

Crown Solicitor The Director of Public Prosecutions (*q.v.*).

cruel, inhuman or degrading treatment A state which, as a matter of policy, practices or condones such treatment violates international law. See GENEVA CONVENTION.

cruelty Before the Divorce Reform Act 1969 cruelty was a matrimonial offence and a ground for divorce. Since the 1969 Act behaviour which would previously have been classed as cruelty would be described as unreasonable behaviour which is one of the current grounds for divorce. See DIVORCE; UNREASONABLE BEHAVIOUR.

cui in vita An action by which a widow could recover her lands if they had been aliened during the coverture of her husband.

cujus est dare ejus est disponere [He who gives anything can also direct how the gift is to be used]

cujus est instituere ejus est abrogare [He that institutes may also abrogate]

cujus est solum ejus est usque ad coelum [Whose is the soil, his is also the heavens]

culpa [Roman law] Wrongful default.

culpa lata [Roman law] Incurred by extreme negligence; negligence so gross that it cannot but seem intentional. It amounts to *dolus* (fraud (*q.v.*)).

culpa levis [Roman law] Incurred when a person falls short either of the care of a *bonus paterfamilias* (*in abstracto*) or the care that he ordinarily gives to his own affairs (*in concreto*).

cum liber erit [Roman law] The appointment of another man's slave as tutor is void, unless made with the condition "when he becomes free". Ulpian says that it is to be implied, if not inserted.

cum testamento annexo [With the will annexed] See LETTERS OF ADMINISTRATION.

cur. adv. vult. *Curia advisari vult* (*q.v.*).

cura; curatio [Roman law] The office or function of the curator.

curator [Roman law] A guardian appointed to a person past the age of puberty to manage his affairs, when from any cause he is unfit to manage them himself.

curator bonorum distrahendorum [Roman law] A curator appointed for the purpose of selling a debtor's property and distributing among the creditors the amount realised.

curfew order Where a person aged under 16 is convicted of an offence, a court may make an order requiring him to remain, for periods specified in the order, at a place so specified. The curfew order may be monitored by electronic tags so as to identify breaches of the order, see Powers of Criminal Courts (Sentencing) Act 2000 s.37, as amended by the Criminal Justice Act 2003.

curia advisari vult [The court wishes to be advised] In law reports contracted to c.a.v. It means that judgment was not delivered immediately, time being taken for consideration.

curia regis The King's Court. See AULA REGIS.

cursitors (clerici de cursu) The lowest grade of clerks in the Chancery who wrote out the standard form writs "of course".

curtain principle Under the Settled Land Act 1925, subject to certain exceptions, the purchaser of land is not entitled nor bound to see the details of the trust which are concealed behind the curtain of the vesting deed.

curtesy of England, tenure by See TENURE BY CURTESY OF ENGLAND.

curtilage A courtyard, garden, yard, field, backside or piece of ground lying near and belonging to a dwelling house (*Pilbrow v St Leonard, Shoreditch Vestry* [1885] 1 Q.B. 433).

custode admittendo; custode removendo Writs which anciently lay for the appointing or removing of a guardian.

custodes pacis [Conservators or keepers of the peace] Since 1368 called justices of the peace (*q.v.*) (42 Edw. 3 c.6).

custodial sentence In relation to an offender aged 21 years or over, a sentence of imprisonment and, under that age, detention in a young offender institution (*q.v.*) etc., Powers of Criminal Courts (Sentencing) Act 2000 s.76, as amended by the Criminal Justice Act 2003.

custodiam lease Anciently, a grant by the King, under the Exchequer Seal, by which Crown lands were demised or granted to some person as custodian or lessees thereof.

custodian trustee A trustee who has the custody and care of trust property, but not its management. See the Public Trustee Act 1906. He is not a "bare trustee" (*q.v.*).

custodianship order Order made under Children Act 1975 s.33 vesting legal custody of child in the applicant. Abolished by the Children Act 1989.

custody (1) Confinement or imprisonment, e.g. remand (of accused person) in custody.
(2) Control and possession of some thing or person, e.g. to surrender oneself into the custody of the court (Bail Act 1976 s.2(2)).

custody of children In its widest sense, custody was defined as "so much of the parental rights and duties as relate to the person of the child (including the place and manner in which his time is spent)" (Children Act 1975 s.86). Custody orders ceased to be available by virtue of the Children Act 1989 and were replaced by the concept of parental responsibility (*q.v.*) and residence orders (*q.v.*), contact orders (*q.v.*), prohibited steps orders (*q.v.*) and specific issues orders (*q.v.*) under s.8 of that Act.

custody officer A police officer appointed under the Police and Criminal Evidence Act 1984 (as amended by the Serious Organised Crime and Police Act 2005 ss.120–121) to have responsibility for safeguarding the rights of suspects detained at the police station following arrest. The main responsibilities of the officer are to determine whether the suspect's detention is valid; to determine whether there is sufficient evidence to charge the suspect; to keep a custody record (*q.v.*); to ensure the suspect is treated in accordance with the Codes of Practice made under the Act; and to inform the suspect of his rights, such as the right of access to a solicitor.

custody record A document which records the history of a suspect's detention in police custody, Police and Criminal Evidence Act 1984 s.39(1)(b) and PACE Code C which sets out the requirements for the detention, treatment and questioning of suspects not related to terrorism in police custody.

custom (1) A rule of conduct, obligatory on those within its scope, established by long usage. A valid custom must be of immemorial antiquity, certain and reasonable, obligatory, not repugnant to statute law, though it may derogate from the common law.
General customs are those of the whole country, as, e.g. the general custom of merchants. Particular customs are the usage of particular trades. Local customs are customs of certain parts of the country.
(2) A source of implication of terms in contracts.

customs The duties or tolls payable upon merchandise imported into the country. See Customs and Excise Management Act 1979.

Customs duties Member States of the European Union (*q.v.*) are prohibited from introducing between Member States any new customs duties on imports or exports or any charges having equivalent effect (*q.v.*). A customs duty is any charge of a fiscal nature that is imposed directly or indirectly on goods which cross a border.

Customs Union Article 23 of the EC Treaty provides that the [European] Community shall be based upon a customs union which shall cover all trade in goods. The customs union is made up of an internal and external element. Internally, within the European Union (*q.v.*), Member States (*q.v.*) are prohibited from introducing customs duties (and all charges having equivalent effect) on imports and exports (art.25 EC Treaty). Externally, goods originating outside the European Union are able to move freely within the Union once they have paid a common customs tariff (*q.v.*) on entry into one of the Member States. See COMMON CUSTOMS TARIFF.

custos brevium et recordorum The keeper of the writs and records. Abolished by Superior Courts Officers Act 1837.

custos rotulorum Keeper of the rolls or records. The first justice of the peace and first civil officer of the county for which he was appointed.

cy-près The doctrine that where a settlor or testator has expressed a general intention, and also a particular way in which he wishes it carried out, but the intention cannot be carried out in that particular way, the court will direct the intention to be carried out as nearly as possible in the way desired. The doctrine is more particularly applied to charities. Thus, whereas when a beneficiary predeceases a testator the gift will lapse, in the case of a charitable gift the cy-près doctrine will enable the property to be used for similar purposes. The Charities Act 1960, as replaced by the Charities Act 1993, extended to some extent the scope of the doctrine.

cybersquatters A term for those who deliberately and in bad faith register a domain name (*q.v.*) which infringes the trade mark of another business. See also WORLD INTELLECTUAL PROPERTY ORGANISATION.

D

DGIV Directorate General IV. The department is responsible for applying the European Community (*q.v.*) rules in support of free competition within the market and works closely with national governments. It has powers to deal with anti-competitive practices and restrictive agreements which affect trade between Member States (*q.v.*) of the European Community (*q.v.*) or in some instances the European Economic Area (*q.v.*). The directorates general have now been named after their functions so that DGIV is now known as DG Competition. It has exclusive powers to deal with certain large-scale mergers with a European dimension.

DNA Database DNA (or Deoxyribonucleic Acid) samples obtained for analysis from the collection of DNA at crime scenes and from samples taken from individuals in police custody can be held in the National DNA database.

DNA testing A DNA test takes place when a person provides a bodily sample that includes DNA material (e.g. mouth swab, hair follicle, etc.) for the purposes of comparison with other DNA material, e.g. found at the scene of a crime. Scientific tests can be carried out to ascertain the probability of two sets of DNA being from the same person. There are two purposes for which a sample might be taken. First, in order to confirm or disprove involvement in an offence being investigated, and secondly, to add to the national DNA database. In respect of the former, a DNA non-intimate sample (*q.v.*) can be taken without consent from a person in police detention for any recordable offence if a senior officer has reasonable belief that such a sample would confirm or disprove the suspect's involvement (Police and Criminal Evidence Act 1984 ss.62–63). In respect of the latter, any person who has been charged or informed that she or he is to be reported for any recordable offence may be required to give a non-intimate sample not for the purposes of the current investigation but for addition to the DNA database and for a "speculative search" against a database of known offenders or against samples held in connection with other offences (PACE 1984 as amended). See INTIMATE SAMPLE; SKIN IMPRESSION.

DNA testing may be used in some circumstances to establish paternity of a child.

DPP The Director of Public Prosecutions (*q.v.*).

damage, criminal See CRIMINAL DAMAGE.

damage-feasant [Doing damage] See DISTRESS DAMAGE-FEASANT.

damage, malicious See CRIMINAL DAMAGE.

damages Compensation or indemnity for a loss suffered by a person following a tort, breach of contract or breach of some statutory duty. See GENERAL DAMAGES; REMOTENESS OF DAMAGE; SPECIAL DAMAGE; AGGRAVATED DAMAGES; EXEMPLARY DAMAGES

damnosa hereditas [Roman Law] An inheritance which was a source of loss rather than of profit.

damnum absque injuria [Loss without wrong] Loss or damage for which there is no legal remedy. For a modern example see *Smith v Scott* [1973] Ch. 314.

damnum sentit dominus [The lord suffers the damage] The loss falls on him who is in law the owner.

damnum sine injuria esse potest There may be damage or loss inflicted without any act being done which the law deems an injury. For instance, harm may be caused by a person exercising his own rights of property (*Mayor of Bradford v Pickles* [1895] A.C. 587) or by trade competition (*Mogul Steamship Co v McGregor Gow & Co* [1892] A.C. 25).

Danegeld A tax on land levied to meet the expenses of the Danish invasions.

Danelage The laws of the Danish part of the kingdom in the 10th century.

danger, alternative The principle of law that where a person is suddenly put in a position of imminent danger by the wrongful act of another then, provided he acts reasonably, what is done by that person in the agony of the moment cannot fairly be treated as contributory negligence; e.g. jumping from a runaway coach and sustaining injury (*Jones v Boyce* (1816) 1 Starkie 493; *The Bywell Castle* (1879) 4 P.D. 219). A lady locked in a public lavatory is entitled to make reasonable efforts to escape (*Sayers v Harlow UDC* [1958] 1 W.L.R. 623).

dangerous animals Under the Animals Act 1971 the keeper is strictly liable for any damage which is caused by an animal which belongs to a dangerous species, i.e. those not commonly domesticated in the British Isles and which, when fully grown, are likely to cause severe damage unless restrained.

dangerous chattels See DANGEROUS THINGS.

dangerous cycling A person who rides a cycle on a road dangerously is guilty of an offence (s.28 Road Traffic Act 1988 (as amended)). A person is to be regarded as riding dangerously if (and only if) the way he rides falls far below what would be expected of a competent and careful cyclist, and it would be obvious to a competent and careful cyclist that riding in that way would be dangerous.

dangerous driving Offences relating to driving dangerously have been revised by the Road Traffic Act 1991, which substituted sections in the Road Traffic Act 1988. The old offences of causing death by reckless driving and reckless driving have been replaced by the offences of causing death by dangerous driving (s.1) and careless, or inconsiderate driving (*q.v*) (s.2). Section 2A of the 1988 Act provides that for the purposes of ss.1 and 2, a person is to be regarded as driving dangerously where they drive so as to fall far below what would be expected of a competent and careful driver and it would be obvious to a competent and careful driver that this would be dangerous. See CARELESS OR INCONSIDERATE DRIVING; MANSLAUGHTER; PENALTY POINTS.

dangerous premises The liability to compensate persons injured on premises owing to their dangerous state is in general upon the occupier and not the owner. By the Occupiers' Liability Act 1957, the occupier owes the same "common duty of care" to all lawful visitors (ibid. s.2) except in so far as the duty is modified by agreement.

Under the Occupiers' Liability Act 1984, a statutory duty is also owed by the occupier to persons other than his visitors, e.g. to trespassers. See TRESPASSER.

dangerous things (1) The occupier of land who keeps upon it anything likely to do damage if it escapes is liable for all direct damage so caused (*Rylands v Fletcher* (1868) L.R. 3 H.L. 330). Foreseeability of harm of the relevant type by the defendant is a prerequisite of the recovery of damages under the rule in *Rylands v Fletcher*. Defences include: the consent of the claimant; act of a third party; or act of God.

(2) Dangerous things are those which are especially likely to cause injury to those persons into whose possession they may come; i.e. ultimate transferees. The case of dangerous thing is a special instance of negligence where the law exacts a degree of diligence so stringent as to amount practically to a guarantee of safety (per Lord MacMillan, *Donoghue v Stevenson* [1932] A.C. 562 at 611–612). A manufacturer of products, which he sells in such a form as to show that he intends them to reach the ultimate consumer in the form in which they left him with no reasonable possibility of intermediate examination and with the knowledge that the absence of reasonable care in the preparation or putting up of the products will result in an injury to the consumer's life or property, owes a duty to the consumer to take that reasonable care (per Lord Atkin, ibid. at 599). See PRODUCT LIABILITY.

dangerous wild animals No person may keep any dangerous wild animal (as enumerated in Dangerous Wild Animals Act 1976) without a licence granted by the local authority.

data Defined in s.1(1) of the Data Protection Act 1998 as information which is: (a) being processed by equipment operating automatically in response to instructions given for that purpose (i.e. a computer); (b) is recorded with the intention that it should be processed by means of such equipment; (c) is recorded as part of a relevant filing system (or with the intention that it should form part of a relevant filing system (*q.v.*); (d) forms part of an accessible record (*q.v.*); or (e) information recorded by a public authority which does not fall within (a) to (d) above. The processing of data is regulated by the Data Protection Act 1998 as amended by the Freedom of Information Act 2000. The Information Commissioner's Office (*q.v.*) is the regulatory body.

data controller The person who, either alone or jointly with others, determines the purpose and manner in which the data (*q.v.*) is processed (see Data Protection Act 1998 s.1). The definition covers all legal persons so will include any organisation with a legal identity as well as individuals.

data processor Any person (other than an employee of a Data Controller (*q.v.*)) who processes the personal data (*q.v.*) on behalf of the data controller. This means that a data processor will be a third party individual or organisation who has been appointed by a data controller to carry out the processing on its behalf. (See Data Protection Act 1998 s.1).

data protection The legal provisions which establish a framework to prevent the misuse of information about individuals. The use of personal information is governed by The Data Protection Act 1998. See DATABASES; COMPUTER PROGRAM; HACKING.

data subject The individual who is the subject of personal data (*q.v.*) (see Data Protection Act 1998 s.1). The individual must be living; the Data Protection Act 1998 does not cover information relating to someone who has died or to information relating to a business or limited company.

databases Defined under the Copyright, Designs and Patents Act 1988 as a collection of independent works, data or other materials which are: (a) arranged in a systematic or methodical way; and (b) individually accessible by electronic or other means. A database may be regarded as a literary work (*q.v.*) and attract copyright protection if it is original and if by reason of the selection or arrangement of the contents of the database, it constitutes the author's own intellectual creation. Databases which fail to meet the requirements for copyright protection may still be commercially valuable and have involved substantial investment. These are protected by the database right in the Copyright and Rights in Databases Regulations 1997 implementing EC Directive 96/9.

days of grace Days allowed for making a payment or doing some other act after the time limited for that purpose has expired. Three days of grace were allowed for the payment of a bill of exchange but this was abolished by the Banking and Financial Dealings Act 1971 s.3. In relation to insurance policies, the payment of renewal premiums may expressly or by custom be subject to a period of grace, thus allowing additional time to pay.

de bonis asportatsis [Of goods carried away] See TRESPASS.

de bonis non (administratis) [Of goods not administered] A grant to an administrator appointed to succeed a deceased administrator to complete the administration of an intestate's estate.

de die in diem [From day to day]

De Donis (Conditionalibus) The Statute of Westminister II. See ESTATE.

de ejectione firmae The writ which originated the old action of ejectment (*q.v.*).

de executione facienda Writs of execution

de facto [In fact] (As opposed to de jure (*q.v.*).)

de homine replegiando A writ which formerly lay to bail out one wrongfully imprisoned.

de ingressu A writ of entry.

de injuria An averment in pleading that the defendant of his own wrong and without the alleged cause had done the acts alleged as a defence.

de jure [By right]

de medietate linguae A jury, one half of which consisted of aliens, before which aliens were formerly tried.

de minimis non curat lex [The law does not concern itself with trifles]

de non apparentibus, et non existentibus, eadem est ratio [Of things which do not appear and things which do not exist, the rule in legal proceedings is the same]

de novo [Anew]

de odio et atia [Of malice and ill-will] A writ which lay for a man committed to prison upon suspicion of murder, which commanded the sheriff to inquire whether the committal was upon just cause or suspicion or only upon malice and ill-will. If the latter, then another writ issued commanding the sheriff to bail him.

de recte A writ of right (*q.v.*).

de seisina habenda [For having seisin] The writ by which the King anciently enforced his right to year, day and waste (*q.v.*).

de son tort [Of his own wrong] See EXECUTOR DE SON TORT.

De Tallagio non Concedendo The statute (25 Edw. I) which enacts that no tallage or aid shall be levied without the assent of the realm.

de ventre inspiciendo Where the widow of an owner of land was suspected of pretending to be pregnant with a child heir to the estate, the heir presumptive could have a writ *de ventre inspiciendo*, to examine whether she was with child or not; and if so, to keep her under proper restraint until delivered (obsolete).

dead freight Amount payable by a charterer in respect of a ship's cargo space he has contracted to use, but does not fully use. Can only be charged insofar as the carrier could not fill the space and earn the same freight with other cargo.

dead rent The minimum or fixed rent payable under a mining lease, irrespective of whether minerals are worked or not. The purpose of such rent is to ensure that a mine is worked.

death, presumption of See PRESUMPTION OF DEATH.

death duties formerly death estate duty, succession duty and legacy duty, payable on property passing at death. Succession duty and legacy duty were abolished by the Finance Act 1949 s.27. Estate duty was superseded from March 13, 1975 by capital transfer tax (*q.v.*) and, in turn, from July 25, 1986 the latter tax was superseded by inheritance tax (*q.v.*).

debenture (1) A certificate of right to drawback (*q.v.*). (2) A document evidencing a loan to a company usually secured on its assets. "Debenture" includes debenture stock (*q.v.*), bonds and any other securities of a company whether constituting a charge on the assets of a company or not (Companies Act 1985).

debenture stock A company may raise money by issuing debenture stock (loan capital) (cf. issuing equity (share capital)) to the public which receives interest on it as a creditor rather than as a member of the company.

debit card Or Electronic Funds at Transfer Point of Sale (EFTPOS) card. Where the cost of the goods is debited from the purchaser's account and credited to the retailer instantaneously by electronic transfer.

debitor [Roman law] One against whom another possesses a personal right; one that can be compelled to perform an obligation.

debitor non praesumitur donare [A debtor is not presumed to give]

debitum connexum A debt giving rise to a lien.

debitum in praesenti, solvendum in future [Owed at the present time, payable (or to be performed) in the future]

debt A sum of money due from one person to another. Debts are: (1) of record, e.g. recognisances and judgment debts; (2) specialty debts, created by deed; (3) simple contract debts; (4) Crown debts (*q.v.*); (5) secured debts, those for which security has been taken; (6) preferential debts (*q.v.*) (Insolvency Act 1986 s.386). See IMPRISONMENT FOR DEBT.

debt administration debt administration is the taking of steps either to perform duties under a consumer credit agreement or a consumer hire agreement on behalf of the creditor or owner, or to exercise or to enforce rights under such an agreement on behalf of the creditor or owner so far as the taking of such steps is not debt-collecting. See Consumer Credit Act 1974 ss.145-160 as amended by the Consumer Credit Act 2006.

debt counselling Under the Consumer Credit Act 1974 s.145 the giving of advice to debtors or hirers about the liquidation of debts due under consumer credit agreements or consumer hire agreements constitutes the ancillary credit business of debt counselling and is subject to the relevant licensing and other provisions. See also DEBT ADMINISTRATION.

debt-collecting A type of ancillary credit business. See the Consumer Credit Act 1974 ss.145–160.

debtor–creditor agreement A class of credit agreement regulated by the Consumer Credit Act 1974 s.13.

debtor–creditor–supplier agreement A class of credit agreement regulated by the Consumer Credit Act 1974 s.12.

deceit A tort which arises where a defendant makes a false statement of fact knowing that it is false and intending the claimant to act on it and the claimant does act on it to his detriment.

deception The Theft Act 1968 ss.15-16 created the offences of obtaining property, money transfers or a pecuniary advantage by deception. These provisions were repealed by the Fraud Act 2006 which creates a number of offences including fraud by false representation (s.2), fraud by abuse of position (s.3) and obtaining services dishonestly (s.11). See FRAUD.

decision A decision taken by the Council (*q.v.*) or the Commission of the European Union (*q.v.*) "shall be binding in its entirety upon those to whom it is addressed" (art.249 EC Treaty). Such decisions may be addressed to any or all Member States, or to one or more legal or natural persons. It has the force of law. See also COMMUNITY LEGISLATION.

declaration (1) A formal statement intended to create, preserve, assert or testify to a right.
(2) The decision of a court or judge on a question of law or rights. It is a discretionary remedy and in administrative law it can be granted against the crown. See JUDICIAL REVIEW.

declaration of incompatibility A declaration made by the High Court or above under s.4 of the Human Rights Act 1998 that a piece of primary legislation is incompatible with a Convention right (*q.v.*). It has no effect on the proceedings in which it is made but may give rise to a remedial order under the Human Rights Act 1998 s.10, if the Government decides to change the law through a fast track procedure by Statutory Instrument, to make it compatible. See CONVENTION COMPLIANT; EUROPEAN CONVENTION ON HUMAN RIGHTS; HUMAN RIGHTS.

declaration of solvency Where it is proposed to wind up a company voluntarily, a statutory declaration may be made by the directors of a company that they are of opinion that the company will be able to pay its debts in full, within such period, not exceeding 12 months from the commencement of the winding-up, as may be specified in the declaration. It is a condition precedent of a members' voluntary winding-up, Insolvency Act 1986 s.89. Such a declaration is to be delivered to the Registrar of Companies. See VOLUNTARY WINDING UP.

declaration of use or trust The ordinary mode of creating a trust when the trust property is already vested in the intended trustee. A statement or admission that property is to be held to the use of or upon trust for a certain person. For example, if O, the owner of the property, decides to create a trust for the benefit of B, without transferring the property to another, O may declare that he holds the property on trust for B.

declaration, statutory See STATUTORY DECLARATION.

declaratory judgment A judgment which conclusively declares the legal relationship of the parties without the appendage of any coercive decree. Such a declaration may be made whether or not any consequential relief is or could be claimed. So a declaratory judgment may be made along with other relief, e.g. damages or injunctions.

declaratory statute One which declares or formally states what the existing law is on a given subject, so as to remove doubts. The law is stated without amendment.

decree An order of a court pronounced on the hearing of a suit.

decree absolute A final and conclusive decree, which finally dissolves the marriage. See DECREE NISI.

decree nisi Every decree of dissolution of marriage, whether for divorce or nullity, is in the first instance a decree nisi (nisi means unless) not to be made absolute until six weeks after the date of pronouncement unless the court orders a shorter time (See the Matrimonial Causes Act 1973). See DECREE ABSOLUTE.

dedication Granting a right of way to the public over private property. Dedication is achieved by the owner of the land showing by words or actions an intention to give the public a right of passage. An intention to dedicate may be inferred at common law on the facts; there being no minimum length of use of the way by the public for the manifestation of such intention. However, by statute a way over land is deemed to have been dedicated as a highway where used by the public as of right and without interruption for 20 years. Highways Act 1980 ss.31, 32.

dedititii [Roman law] Certain manumitted slaves who, in consequence of grave misconduct committed while they were slaves, were subjected to certain perpetual disabilities.

deed Under the Law of Property (Miscellaneous Provisions) Act 1989 a deed must make clear on its face that it is intended to be a deed; it must be signed in the presence of a witness who attests the signature, or at his direction and in his presence and the presence of two witnesses who each attest the signature; and must be delivered as a deed by him or a person authorised to do so on his behalf. For a corporation to validly execute an instrument as a deed prior to April 6, 2008, see the Companies Act 1985 s.36A, inserted by the Companies Act 1989. For the execution of deeds by companies on or after April 6, 2008, see the Companies Act 2006 s.44. See SEAL.

deed of arrangement See ARRANGEMENTS, DEEDS OF.

deed of covenant A covenant by a separate deed; e.g. to produce title deeds.

deed of gift A deed transferring property from one person to another. No consideration is required of that other to render the transaction enforceable.

deed poll A deed which is "polled" or smooth; i.e. not indented. A unilateral deed, e.g. for publishing a change of name.

deemed To be treated as.

defamation The tort consisting in the publication of a statement which tends to lower the claimant in the estimation of right thinking people generally, or which tends to make such people shun or avoid him. It may constitute libel (*q.v.*) if the statement is made in writing or some permanent form, or slander (*q.v.*) if made orally. There are a number of defences including justification and privilege. Legal aid has not been available to defendants in libel cases but the European Court of Human Rights has recently ruled that two impecunious individuals sued by McDonalds were denied a fair trial through being unrepresented. The House of Lords has ruled that a company having a trading reputation in England and Wales was entitled to pursue a remedy in a defamation action without being required to allege or prove that the publication complained of had caused it actual damage (*Jameel v Wall Street Journal Europe SPRL (No.3)* [2006] UKHL 44).

default To make default is to fail in some duty; e.g. to pay a sum due.

default judgment Under CPR 12 a judgment (*q.v.*) without trial in favour of a claimant where a defendant has either failed to file an acknowledgement stating an intention to defend the claim or failed to file a defence. The claimant may apply for default judgment for the amount claimed if the amount is specified or for judgment on liability if it is unspecified. In a number of cases it is not possible to obtain a default judgment. See CIVIL PROCEDURE RULES.

default summons An old summary means of recovering a debt or liquidated demand in the County Court. Now replaced by claim form (*q.v.*), CPR Pt 7.

defeasance Condition of termination of an estate (*q.v.*), the estate automatically coming to an end if the condition is satisfied.

defeasible An estate or interest in property, which is liable to be defeated or terminated by the operation of a condition subsequent or conditional limitation.

defective A person suffering from a state of arrested or incomplete development of mind, which includes severe impairment of intelligence and social functioning. Under the Sexual Offences Act 1956, it was an offence for a man to have unlawful sexual intercourse with a woman who is defective. Repealed by the Sexual Offences Act 2003 which provides for a number of offences involving sexual activity with a person with a mental disorder impeding choice. See SEXUAL OFFENCES.

defective product. Under and for the purposes of the Consumer Protection Act 1987 there is a defect in a product if the safety of the product is not such as persons generally are entitled to expect; and for those purposes "safety", in relation to a product, includes safety with respect to products comprised in that product and safety in the context of risks of damage to property, as well as in the context of risks of death or personal injury (ibid. s.3).

defence A defendant who wishes to defend a claim must file a defence. Failure to do so may result in a claimant obtaining a default judgment (*q.v.*).

Defence Regulations The regulations made by Her Majesty by Order in Council under the emergency legislation (*q.v.*).

defendant A person against whom an action or other civil proceeding (other than a petition) is brought; also a person charged with an offence.

defendant's costs order A court may order a defendant's costs to be paid out of central funds, e.g. where a defendant is acquitted, Prosecution of Offences Act 1985 s.16. The order will be for such amount as the court considers is reasonably sufficient to compensate the defendant for any expenses improperly incurred by him in the proceedings. A court should give reasons for declining to make a defendant's cost order.

defensor [Roman law] An unauthorised defender; one who without a mandate undertook the defence of another person who had failed to appear in his own defence.

defensores [Roman law] An inferior class of magistrates in provincial towns.

deferment of sentence The Crown Court or magistrates' court may defer passing sentence on an offender for up to six months so that the court, in determining sentence, may have regard to the offender's conduct after a conviction or to any change in his circumstances. The court must be satisfied that in the circumstances it would be in the interests of justice to defer sentencing; such deferral may only occur with the offender's consent and the offender must undertake to comply with any requirements as to his conduct during the period of the deferment that the court considers it appropriate to impose (Powers of Criminal Courts Act (Sentencing) Act 2000 as amended by Sch.23 to the Criminal Justice Act 2003).

deferred shares Deferred or founders' shares in a company (comparatively rare now, but were often taken up by the promoters of a company to show their faith in the business) are usually of small nominal value but with a right to take the whole or a proportion of the profits after a fixed dividend has been paid on the ordinary shares. The rights of the holders depend on the articles or the terms of issue but such shares sometimes carry high voting rights. See SHARES.

deforcement The wrongful holding of lands of another.

defraud, conspiracy to A common law offence. A person who, in agreement with one or more other persons, dishonestly seeks to deprive another of something which was either that other's or to which but for the fraud (*q.v.*) that other would have been entitled, is guilty of offence (see *Scott v Commissioner of Police for the Metropolis* [1975] A.C. 819).

degree A step in the line of descent or consanguinity (*q.v.*).

dehors [Without] Outside the scope of; irrelevant.

del credere agent An agent (*q.v.*) for the sale of goods who, in consideration of a higher reward than is usually given, guarantees to his principal, the due payment of the price of all goods sold by him to a third party buyer.

delegated legislation Legislation made by some person or body to whom Parliament has delegated its law making power. Such an Act is termed an enabling or parent Act. Types of delegated legislation include: Orders in Council, statutory instruments and byelaws. Delegated or subordinate legislation may be controlled by Parliament in that the Orders or instruments are printed and laid before Parliament which may then debate them. Such control depends upon provision being made in the parent Act. If the parent Act states that the power is exercisable by way of statutory instrument then the Statutory Instruments Act 1946 applies. This provides, inter alia, that statutory instruments are to be published and where a laying requirement is specified by the parent Act such procedures, are to some extent, regulated by the Act.

delegatus non potest delegare [A delegate cannot delegate] A person to whom powers have been delegated cannot delegate them to another.

delivery of a deed The formal act of handing over which gives effect to a deed (*q.v.*) previously executed. See EXECUTE; ESCROW.

delivery order An order by the owner of goods to a person holding them on his behalf, to deliver them to a person named.

delivery, writ of A writ of execution (*q.v.*) to enforce a judgment for the recovery of property other than land or money. It may be either for the return of chattels with the option of paying the assessed value, or for the return without such option (Ord. 45 r.4). See also Torts (Interference with Goods) Act 1977 s.3.

demandant The person bringing a "real" action. See ACTION.

dematerialisation A term used to describe the transfer of company securities by electronic means, i.e. a paperless system. See CREST.

demesne [Own] The part of the manor occupied by the Lord.

demise (1) Anciently, any transfer of a succession to a right.
(2) The grant of a lease.
(3) The term of years granted by a lease.

demise of the Crown The transfer of royal dignity which takes place when one King or Queen succeeds to another; not the death of the King or Queen.

demolition order A local authority previously had powers under the Housing Act 1985 to serve a demolition order requiring the demolition of a house unfit for human habitation. The power to serve a demolition order remains in s.265 of that Act but is amended by the Housing Act 2004 which provides a new system for assessing the condition of residential premises by reference to category 1 or category 2 hazards. A demolition order may be served on residential premises (*q.v.*) and will require that the premises be vacated within a specified period and demolished within six weeks after that period.

demur, to In pleading, to raise an objection by demurrer (*q.v.*).

demurrage (1) The detention of a ship beyond the number of days specified in the charterparty (*q.v.*), called lay days, allowed for loading and unloading.
(2) The sum contractually fixed by way of damages by the contract of affreightment (the charterparty) as payable to the shipowner for such detention. The term demurrage, in a popular but not a strict sense, also applies to unliquidated damages (*q.v.*) payable where no lay days are specified but the ship is unreasonably delayed due to the loading or unloading of the ship.

demurrer A pleading by which one of the parties alleged that the preceding pleadings of the other party showed no good cause of action or defence. Abolished in 1883. If a statement of case discloses no reasonable grounds for bringing or defending the claim it may be struck out (CPR r.3).
Demurrer in criminal cases is virtually obsolete but it is still theoretically possible to demur to the indictment; i.e. allege some substantial defect in it. A defendant may plead not guilty in addition to any demurrer (Criminal Law Act 1967).

denial of service attack (DoS attack). An attack on a commercial website intended to disrupt the operation of the site by flooding it with multiple requests. There was some uncertainty as to whether this constituted an offence under s.3 Computer Misuse Act 1990. However in *DPP v Lennon* [2006] EWHC 1201 (Admin) the High Court held that, whilst the owner of a computer which is able to receive emails is ordinarily to be taken as consenting to the sending of emails to the computer, this consent does not cover emails which are not sent for the purpose of communication with the owner, but are sent for the purpose of interrupting the proper operation and use of his system.

denizen Originally a natural-born subject of a country; then a person who was an alien born, but who had obtained from the Crown letters patent, called letters of denization, to make him an English subject. Denization was a prerogative power of the Crown. The law on naturalisation is now contained in the British Nationality Act 1981. It is unclear to what extent the prerogative power of denization remains.

denoting stamp A Revenue stamp on a document showing or "denoting" the amount of stamp duty paid and stamped on another document in respect of the same matter; e.g. on a counterpart of a lease in respect of the lease itself.

deodand [*Deo*, to God, and *dandam*, to be given] Formerly if a personal chattel was the immediate and accidental cause of the death of any reasonable creature, it was forfeited to the Crown under the name of a deodand. Abolished by the statute 9 & 10 Vict. c.62.

Department of Constitutional Affairs (DCA) Set up unexpectedly in 2003 to replace the Lord Chancellor's Department within Government. It was responsible for upholding justice, rights and democracy. In May 2007 the responsibilities of the DCA were transferred to the newly created Ministry of Justice (*q.v.*). See CHANCELLOR, LORD HIGH.

dependant See FAMILY PROVISION; FATAL ACCIDENTS.

dependency Territory which has not been formally annexed to the British Crown, but which is in practice governed and represented in relation to other foreign countries by the United Kingdom.

deponent A person who makes a written statement or deposition (*q.v.*).

deportatio in insulam [Roman law] Confinement for life within specified bounds. The person so punished was regarded as civilly dead: a *peregrinus*, no longer a *civis* He might be recalled and pardoned by the emperor.

deportation Expulsion from the United Kingdom (*q.v.*). Powers of deportation are contained in the Immigration Act 1971 ss.3–8 as amended by the Asylum and Immigration Act 1999. A person who is not a British citizen is liable to deportation from the United Kingdom if the Secretary of State deems his deportation to be conducive to the public good; or another person to whose family he belongs is or has been ordered to be deported. A person who is not a British citizen shall also be liable to deportation from the United Kingdom if, after he has attained the age of 17, he is convicted of an offence for which he is punishable with imprisonment and on his conviction is recommended for deportation by a court empowered by this Act to do so.

deposit (1) In a contract for the sale of land the deposit is a payment made demonstrating a willingness to complete the contract. The court has a general power to order the return of a deposit (Law of Property Act 1925 s.49(2)).

(2) A sum payable by a hirer or debtor as a down payment, e.g. under a hire purchase agreement (*q.v.*).

deposit of title deeds Delivery of the title deeds to land into the hands of a creditor as security for a debt, to hold until the debt is repaid. Such deposit is sufficient notice of any associated mortgage of the land to protect the creditor/ mortgagee against any subsequent purchaser of any interest in the land. However, following *United Bank of Kuwait v Sahib* [1997] Ch. 107, it appears that for an equitable mortgage to exist, writing signed by both parties is required by s.2 of the Law of Property (Miscellaneous Provisions) Act 1989.

deposition A statement on oath of a witness in a judicial proceeding. Exceptionally, a witness, instead of giving evidence orally in person, may do so by means of a deposition or written statement which is read before the court. For example, the deposition of a child victim may be admissible in criminal proceedings under the Children and Young Persons Act 1933 s.43. See also Criminal Justice Act 1967 s.9 and Magistrates' Court Act 1980.

In civil proceedings a party may apply for an order for a person to be examined before the hearing takes place. The examination will take place on oath before a judge, an examiner of the court or such other person as the court appoints. Such deposition may be used as evidence at a hearing unless the court orders otherwise (CPR 1998 r.34).

depositor A person who deposits money on investment.

depravity Formerly no petition for divorce might be presented to the court before the expiration of three years from the date of the marriage unless a judge so allowed on the ground that the case was one of exceptional hardship suffered by the petitioner or of exceptional depravity on the part of the respondent (Matrimonial Causes Act 1973 s.3). This provision is now repealed (Matrimonial and Family Proceedings Act 1984 s.1) and is substituted by an absolute prohibition on petitioning for divorce before the expiration of one year from the date of the marriage.

deprivation of liberty code of practice. Passed under the Mental Capacity Act 2005 to ensure that those lacking the capacity to consent do not lose their liberty unless absolutely necessary.

derelict A ship or cargo which has been abandoned at sea by those in charge of it, with no intention of returning to it, and with no hope of recovering it. See WRECK.

dereliction (1) The act of abandoning a chattel or movable.
(2) The gradual encroachment of water onto land thereby reducing the surface area of the foreshore.

derivative action In the context of an abuse or misuse of power by the directors or majority shareholders of a company (a fraud on the minority (*q.v.*)), an action brought in the name of a member was permissible subject to various conditions being satisfied. Under the Companies Act 2006 s.260, such actions may only be brought in future as statutory derivative actions (*q.v.*).

derogate To destroy, prejudice or evade a right or obligation. No one can derogate from his own grant. See, for example, *Wheeldon v Burrows* (1879) 12 Ch.D. 31.

derogating control order A control order (*q.v.*) which involves derogating from the European Convention on Human Rights (*q.v.*). It will be made by a court on application from the Secretary of State (see Prevention of Terrorism Act 2005 s.2). See *Secretary of State for the Home Department v JJ and Others* [2007] UKHL 45. See NON-DEROGATING CONTROL ORDER.

derogation The power given by art.15 of the European Convention on Human Rights for a country which is party to the Convention to take measures in time of war or other public emergency threatening the life of the nation, contrary to the country's obligations under the Convention. The measures must be limited to those that are strictly required by the exigencies of the situation, provided that such measures are not inconsistent with its other obligations under international law.

descent Before 1926 a distinction was made in the rules of succession between realty (*q.v.*) and personalty (*q.v.*) on an intestacy (*q.v.*). The rules relating to the descent of land were set out in the Inheritance Act 1833 and centred around the doctrine of male primogeniture (*q.v.*), in which male heirs were always preferred to female. The rules still apply in part to succession to the Crown and hereditary titles. The Administration of Estates Act 1925 as amended set up a unified scheme of intestate succession giving priority to the rights of surviving spouses.

descent case The doctrine that where a person who had acquired land by disseisin, abatement or intrusion, died seised of the land, the descent of it to his heir took away the real owner's right of entry, so that he could only recover the land by an action.

desertion (1) Desertion is where a husband or wife voluntarily and without reasonable cause leaves the other spouse against his or her will and with the intention of permanently ending the cohabitation. It is not essential that one or other party should actually depart from the matrimonial home if there is a complete abandonment of all matrimonial duties; desertion is not from a place but from a state of things. Where one party's conduct is such as to drive the other party away from the matrimonial home, such conduct may be called "constructive desertion", although it would probably also amount to what is now known as unreasonable behaviour (Matrimonial Causes Act 1973 s.1(2)(b)). See UNREASONABLE BEHAVIOUR.

Desertion for a continuous period of two years is a ground for showing that the marriage has irretrievably broken down (Matrimonial Causes Act 1973 s.1(2)(c)). See DIVORCE.

Magistrates may make a matrimonial order on the ground of desertion (Domestic Proceedings and Magistrates Courts Act 1978).

(2) To desert the armed forces is an offence under s.8 of the Armed Forces Act 2006.

design right There are two types of design right. The first is the design right registered under the Registered Designs Act 1949 as amended by the Registered Designs Regulations 2001. The second is a property right which exists in an original design and is analogous to copyright. Copyright, Designs and Patents Act 1988 s.213. Design is defined as any aspect of the shape or configuration (whether internal or external) of the whole or part of an article. Unlike a registered design right (*q.v.*), there is no requirement for eye appeal.

detailed assessment When a court makes a cost order it may make a detailed assessment (formerly taxation of costs). Generally this is conducted at the conclusion of proceedings by a costs officer (*q.v.*). Contrast SUMMARY ASSESSMENT; SEE SUPREME COURTS COST OFFICE.

detainer, writ of A writ authorising the detention of a man (already in custody for debt, etc.) upon a cause of action other than that upon which he had been arrested originally.

detention A person liable to examination on entry into the UK under the provisions of the Immigration Act 1971 (as amended) may be detained under the authority of an immigration officer pending his examination and pending a decision to give or refuse him leave to enter the United Kingdom. A person whose leave to enter has been suspended may be detained under the authority of an immigration officer pending completion of his examination, and a decision on whether to cancel his leave to enter. In certain circumstances the Secretary of State has the same power as immigration officers to detain a person. See REMOVAL CENTRE.

detention and training order An order which can be made for offenders under the age of 18 years. The sentence is half detention and training and half supervision. The order is available where the offender is convicted of a serious imprisonable offence. See YOUNG OFFENDER.

detention by police On arrest by a constable a suspect may be detained for 24 hours (Police and Criminal Evidence Act 1984 s.41). Continued detention may be authorised by a superintendent of police (ibid. s.42). A warrant of further detention may be issued by a magistrates' court (ibid. s.43). Under the Terrorism Act 2000 (as amended) a suspected terrorist (*q.v.*) may be detained for up to 28 days without charge.

detention centre (1) Replaced by young offender institution (*q.v.*) (Criminal Justice Act 1988). Where a custodial order is made against a young offender he may be detained at a young offender institution. See YOUNG OFFENDER.

(2) A person detained under the Immigration Act 1971 may be detained at a detention centre. Now known as removal centres (*q.v.*) and governed by the Nationality, Immigration and Asylum Act 2002 s.66.

detention in hospital By reason of the provisions of the Mental Health Act 1983 (as amended by the Mental Health Act 2007) a person may be detained in hospital for assessment or treatment of their mental disorder. The detention may occur as a consequence of an application made to the hospital managers by an approved mental health professional (*q.v.*) or by the nearest relative of the patient. In addition, detention may be directed by: (a) a court, either under the provisions of the Mental Health Act 1983 (as amended) or under the provisions of the Criminal Procedure (Insanity) Act 1964 (as amended by the Criminal Procedure (Insanity and Unfitness to Plead) Act 1991 and the Domestic Violence, Crime and Victims Act 2004); or (b) the Secretary of State for Justice as a consequence of a direction for transfer from prison to hospital under the provisions of the Mental Health Act 1983 (as amended).

determine (1) To come to an end; (2) To decide an issue or appeal.

detinue Formerly the action by which a person claimed the specific return of goods wrongfully retained or their value. Abolished by the Torts (Interference with Goods) Act 1977 s.2(1). The tort of conversion has been extended to cover what used to be dealt with by an action in detinue under a generic heading of wrongful interference with goods (ibid. s.1).

Deus solus haeredem facere potest non homo [God alone, and not man, can make an heir]

devastavit [He has wasted.] The personal representatives (*q.v.*) of a deceased person may be liable for the loss of assets of the estate caused by a breach of duty. Under the Trustee Act 2000 a statutory duty of care is imposed on personal representatives and trustees.

development The key definition in the system of town and country planning. Any development carried out without planning permission is unlawful and may be the subject of enforcement action by the local planning authority. Development means the carrying out of building, engineering, mining or other operations in, on, over or under land, or the making of any material change in the use of buildings or other land; Town and Country Planning Act 1990 s.55.

development plans Structure, local or unitary development plans which local planning authorities were obliged to prepare and which form the basis for development control decision making under the Town and Country Planning Act 1990, Pt II and s.54A. As from the September 28, 2004 local planning authorities have had to replace these development plans with a portfolio of development plan documents under the Planning and Compulsory Purchase Act 2004, which must be in compliance with the relevant Regional Spatial Strategy set by central government. See DEVELOPMENT.

development risks defence The Consumer Protection Act 1987 imposes strict liability (*q.v.*) on the producer, etc. in respect of damage caused by the supply of a defective product. It is a defence for the producer to prove that the state of scientific and technical knowledge at the relevant time was not such that a producer of products of the same description as the product in question might be expected to have discovered the defect if it had existed in his products while they were under his control, ibid. s.4.

deviation The intentional departure from instructions or the due course of a voyage. In shipping, a deviation may discharge the underwriters of a voyage policy of marine insurance, on the ground of the alteration of the risk. In certain cases a deviation is justifiable and a carrier of goods by sea is not liable for damage resulting from deviation to save life or property.

devilling (1) Where one counsel hands over a brief to another counsel to represent the former in court and conduct the case as if the latter had been briefed in person.

(2) Where pleadings, opinions, etc. are drafted by one counsel by way of assistance to the counsel who has been instructed, who subsequently approves and signs them.

Devil's Own, The The Inns of Court Regiment of the Territorial Army recruited primarily from members of the legal profession. It obtained its nickname from George III at a review in Hyde Park in 1803. By 1584 the Benchers and members of the Inns of Court had formed armed associations to serve and protect Queen Elizabeth I.

devise A gift of land or other realty by will, either specific, general or residuary; to make such a gift. The recipient is a devisee.

devolution The passing of title to property; particularly on the death of an owner to the personal representative or heir.

devolution of government power The decentralisation of government power. The most recent examples are the powers granted to the Scottish Parliament by the Scotland Act 1998 and to the Welsh Assembly by the Government of Wales Act 1998. See FIRST MINISTER.

diem clausit extremum [He has died] A special writ of *extendi facias*, or extent in chief, issuing after the death of the King's debtor, against his lands and chattels. It was abolished by the Crown Proceedings Act 1947 s.33. See EXTENT.

dies fasti [Roman law] Days on which the Praetor could lawfully exercise his general powers.

dies nefasti [Roman law] Days on which the Praetor could not pronounce any of the words *Do, Dico, Addico*; days on which the court did not sit.

dies non (juridicus) Non-business days. (1) Days on which no legal business could be transacted, e.g. Sunday, Good Friday, Christmas Day, a bank holiday. (2) Days on which the courts do not sit.

dies utiles [Roman law] Days not *nefasti* after the applicant knew of his right and was not unavoidably prevented from going on with his case.

digest A collection of rules of law on concrete cases, as opposed to a code (*q.v.*). The Digest of Justinian was a compilation of the Roman law from the writings of the jurists (AD 533).

digital signature See ELECTRONIC SIGNATURE.

dignity A title of honour; in land law a dignity is an incorporeal hereditament (*q.v.*).

dilapidations The extent of disrepair for which an occupier of land who is not owner in fee simple is liable to the reversioner.

dilatory plea A plea based on a fact other than the merits of a case, e.g. as to the jurisdiction of the court or the capacity of a party (obsolete).

diligentia [Roman law] Diligence; care. There were two grades: (1) *Excata*, all possible diligence; such care as would be taken by a good or most thoughtful *paterfamilias*; (2) *Quantum in suis rebus adhibere solitus est*, the diligence or care a man usually employs in his own affairs.

diminished responsibility A defence to a charge of murder that a person was suffering from such abnormality of mind as substantially impaired his mental responsibility for his acts and omissions in killing, or being a party to the killing of another; he is not to be convicted of murder, but of manslaughter. The burden of proof is on the defence. The standard of proof is not so high as that on the prosecution of having to prove guilt beyond reasonable doubt, being proof on the balance of probabilities (Homicide Act 1957 s.2). See also the Criminal Procedure (Insanity) Act 1964 s.6.

Diocesan Synod The body which provides representation of the clergy within the Anglican church and advice and consent for the Bishop who governs the diocese.

diplomatic asylum Sanctuary given in embassies and legations to persons seeking refuge from the State in which they are situated in cases of actual (not apprehended) danger. It is doubtful if it exists in international law. See ASYLUM, RIGHT OF.

diplomatic privilege (immunity) The exemption or immunity of an accredited diplomatic agent of a foreign State or Sovereign. An ambassador or other public minister exercising diplomatic functions and accredited to the Queen by a foreign State or Sovereign is not within the jurisdiction of the English courts during his term of office. The issue was raised in the case of General Pinochet in 1999.

The International Organisations Acts 1968 and 2005 confer analogous privileges upon certain international organisations and persons connected therewith. See also the European Communities Act 1972 s.4 Sch.3. See EXTRATERRITORIALITY

direct effect A general principle of European Community law established by the European Court of Justice in *Van Gend en Loos v Nederlandse Administratie der Belastingen* (Case 26/62). A directly effective provision of Community law is one which is sufficiently clear and precise and unconditional so as to confer a legally enforceable right upon an individual which must be upheld by a national court. The European Court has determined that Treaty articles are capable of both vertical direct effect (as against the state or an emanation of the state (*q.v.*)) and also horizontal direct effect as against another natural or legal person. Directives (*q.v.*) are however only capable of direct effect after the date for implementation has expired and also more controversially they are only capable of vertical direct effect (see *Marshall v Southampton Area Health Authority* (Case 152/84)). Regulations are also capable of direct effect. See INDIRECT EFFECT.

directions Case management directions by the court giving a timetable for pre-trial procedures. For example, in cases allocated to the small claims track (*q.v.*) the court may often give standard directions, whereas multi-track (*q.v.*) cases may require several directions hearings.

directive A form of European legislation. Article 249 EC Treaty provides that the institutions of the European Union may issue directives in order to carry out the tasks of the European Union. A directive is binding as to the results to be achieved, upon each Member State (*q.v.*) to which it is addressed. However Member States can determine the form and methods by which they achieve the directive's objectives providing that implementation into national law is in a legally certain manner (i.e. by statute or statutory instrument) and within the deadline prescribed within the directive. Failure on the part of a Member State to implement a directive at all or within the deadline constitutes a breach of Community law on the part of the Member State, which could result in enforcement proceedings against the Member State or potentially a claim for damages under the principle of state liability (*q.v.*). See DIRECT EFFECT.

directive waste The European Community wide definition of waste as provided for in Directive 2006/12/EC (which codifies the provisions of Directives 75/442 and 91/156). The definition of waste has been incorporated into s.75 of the Environmental Protection Act 1990. The EC aims to ensure a uniform system of waste management by securing a uniform definition of waste. Waste is directive waste if it is a substance or object set out in Annex I of the Directive and which the holder discards or intends or is required to discard. The European Court of Justice has held that a decision as to whether something is waste should be taken on a case by case basis having regard to all the circumstances of the case.

director A person charged with the management of a company, being in some respects an agent of the company, a trustee of the company's money and property, and having a fiduciary position. Appointment, powers, etc. are governed by the articles of association. The Companies Act 2006 Pt 10 codifies the common law and equitable duties relating to directors. These duties are owed to the company (ibid. s.170) and include a duty to promote the success of the company for the benefit of its members as a whole (ibid. s.172), a formulation that has not been without controversy in the debate prompted by the developments in corporate governance (*q.v.*). A public company (*q.v.*) must have at least two directors; private companies (*q.v.*), one (Companies Act 2006 s.154).

Director General of Fair Trading Established by the Fair Trading Act 1973 to review the carrying on of commercial activities in the United Kingdom relating to the provision of goods and services to consumers in order to eliminate or control unfair consumer trade practices. Under the Enterprise Act 2002 the office of Director General was abolished and his functions transferred to the Office of Fair Trading (*q.v.*).

Director of Public Prosecutions The head of the national independent Crown Prosecution Service established under the Prosecution of Offenders Act 1985 to oversee the prosecution of criminal offences. Consent of the Director is necessary before prosecution for designated serious offences can be instituted by the local prosecutor.

Directorates-General The bureaucracy of the European Commission (*q.v.*) is organised into directorates-general by subject-matter; e.g. DG competition (*q.v.*) deals with competition issues.

directory Of a statute or rule, one which is not mandatory or imperative, but specifies the way in which a thing should be done. A thing done otherwise is not invalid.

disablement benefit Payable to those who have suffered a loss of physical or mental faculty as a result of an industrial accident.

disability Legal incapacity, either general or special.
   A person with a "disability" is defined under the Disability Discrimination Act 1995 s.1(1), as someone who has: "a physical or mental impairment which has a substantial and long-term adverse effect on his ability to carry out normal day-to-day activities." See DISCRIMINATION; EQUALITY AND HUMAN RIGHTS COMMISSION.

Disability Appeal Tribunal Established in 1991 and modelled on social security appeal tribunals (*q.v.*), these bodies consisted of a legally qualified chairman and two lay persons, one drawn from a panel of medical practitioners and the other from persons who were non-practitioners but who were experienced in dealing with the needs of disabled persons (see Social Security Act 1998). These tribunals heard appeals from decisions of adjudication officers on the care or mobility elements of claims for disability living allowance or on an attendance allowance. Under the Tribunals, Courts and Enforcement Act 2007 their jurisdiction has transferred to the Social Security and Child Support Chamber of the First-tier Tribunal (*q.v.*). See TRIBUNALS SERVICE; UPPER TRIBUNAL.

disability discrimination The Disability Discrimination Act 1995, as originally enacted, contained provisions making it unlawful to discriminate against a disabled person in relation to employment, the provision of goods, facilities and services, and the disposal and management of premises. It also contained some provisions relating to education; and enabled the Secretary of State for Transport to make regulations with a view to facilitating the accessibility of taxis, public service vehicles and rail vehicles for disabled people. The Disability Discrimination Act 2005 introduces changes in relation to a range of areas including public authorities and transport. See DISCRIMINATION; EQUALITY AND HUMAN RIGHTS COMMISSION.

disability living allowance A non-contributory benefit introduced in 1992. The benefit has two elements: a care component and a mobility component. A person who works may be eligible for this benefit; if they work more than 16 hours a week on a low wage they additionally may be entitled to a working tax credit (*q.v.*).

Disability Living Allowance Advisory Board Formed in 1991 to assume the advisory functions of the now abolished Attendance Allowance Board. It is an advisory non-departmental public body whose purpose is to provide for a standing body of people who can develop expertise in questions relating to the care and mobility needs of people with disabilities. Its formal composition and functions are subject to regulations drawn up by the Secretary of State. See the Social Security Administration Act 1992.

Disability Rights Commission (DRC) The Disability Rights Commission Act 1999 replaced the National Disability Council with the Disability Rights Commission. In September 2007 this too ceased to exist and its functions and responsibilities were transferred to the newly established Equality and Human Rights Commission (*q.v.*) (see Equality Act 2006).

disability working allowance See now WORKING TAX CREDIT.

disabled person's tax credit This replaced disability working allowance in 1999 and was itself replaced by the working tax credit (*q*.v.) under the Tax Credits Act 2002.

disabling statute One which restricts a pre-existing right.

disaffection Loss of loyalty or allegiance. The offence of seducing any member of Her Majesty's forces from his duty or allegiance is punishable under the Incitement to Disaffection Act 1934.

disbar To expel a barrister from his Inn. A barrister may be disbarred on his own application, if, for instance, he desires to become a solicitor. See SENATE OF THE INNS OF COURT AND THE BAR.

discharge To deprive a right or obligation of its binding force; to release a person from an obligation or prison. Thus payment discharges a debt; rescission, release, accord and satisfaction, performance, judgment, composition with creditors and merger are all varieties of discharge. For discharge from bankruptcy, see BANKRUPTCY.

disciplinary procedures An employer should have contractual disciplinary procedures in place and should follow these procedures when disciplining employees otherwise there may be a breach of contract. There is also a Code of Practice issued by ACAS (*q.v.*) which gives guidance on fair procedures to adopt when disciplining or dismissing an employee. The Code is not legally binding, but an employment tribunal (*q.v.*) may make a finding of unfair dismissal (*q.v.*) if the employer does not have regard to it. In October 2004 a compulsory statutory dismissal and disciplinary procedure was introduced such that, if an employer failed to follow the requisite standard before dismissing, there would automatically be a finding of unfair dismissal (see Employment Act 2002 and Employment Act 2002 (Dispute Resolution) Regulations 2004). Under the Employment Act 2008, this statutory procedure has been abolished and replaced by granting employment tribunals (*q.v.*) a discretionary power to amend an award of compensation if the parties have not complied with the relevant statutory code. See GRIEVANCE PROCEDURES.

disclaimer Refusal to accept or to undertake; renunciation: e.g. a refusal, usually by deed, of a proposed trust; of a trustee in bankruptcy or liquidator of a company to accept onerous property and leaseholds.

disclosure Introduced by the Civil Procedure Rules 1998 (*q.v.*) it replaces the previous process of discovery. Documents which are to be relied upon to support a case, as well as adverse documents to such, are to be disclosed.

discontinuance Where a claimant voluntarily puts an end to his claim wholly or in part. A claimant may at any time discontinue his action by filing a notice of discontinuance and serving copies of it on the other parties to the proceedings. In certain instances the permission of the court is required to discontinue. The effect of discontinuance is that a claimant has to pay a defendant's costs unless the court orders otherwise (CPR 38).

discovery of documents A process whereby the parties to an action disclosed to each other all documents in their possession, custody or power relating to matters in question in the action. Now replaced by disclosure (*q.v.*).

discrimination The singling out of a person or group for special favour or disfavour. Doing so on grounds of sex, colour, race, nationality, ethnic or national origin, disability (*q.v.*), sexual orientation (*q.v.*), religious belief or age (*q.v.*) may be unlawful under the Sex Discrimination Act 1975, the Race Relations Act 1976 (as amended), the Disability Discrimination Act 1995, the Employment Equality (Sexual Orientation) Regulations 2003, the Employment Equality (Religious Belief) Regulations 2003 or the Employment Equality (Age) Regulations 2006. Discrimination may be direct, indirect or by victimisation. As a result of EU Directives harassment is now specifically held to be a form of discrimination on all grounds except sex. See also DISABILITY DISCRIMINATION; RELIGIOUS DISCRIMINATION; SEX DISCRIMINATION; SEXUAL ORIENTATION DISCRIMINATION; AGE DISCRIMINATION; RACIAL HARASSMENT; SEXUAL HARASSMENT.

disentailing assurance A deed by which a tenant in tail (*q.v.*) bars the entail (*q.v.*) so as to convert it into an estate in fee, either absolute or base. Enrolment of such a deed was necessary before 1926.

disgavel To cause land to cease to be of gavelkind tenure (*q.v.*).

dishonestly According to the Court of Appeal in *R. v Ghosh* [1982] 2 All E.R. 689, a jury should decide whether a person is dishonest by a two stage test: first, whether, according to the ordinary standards of reasonable and honest people what was done was dishonest; and secondly, whether the defendant must have realised that what he was doing was, by those standards, dishonest. See also s.2 of the Theft Act 1968 which gives examples of when conduct is not to be regarded as dishonest.

dishonour A bill of exchange is dishonoured if the drawee refuses to accept it, or having accepted it fails to pay it (see Bills of Exchange Act 1882 s.47). A banker who without justification dishonours his customer's cheque is liable to him for damages for injury to his credit; but damages may be only nominal in the case of non-traders.

dismissal [Of a claim] Striking out (*q.v.*) by the court for delay in procedural steps or for lack of evidence.

dismissal of employee An employee shall be treated as dismissed if, and only if: (a) his contract of employment is terminated by the employer, with or without notice; (b) where a contract for a limited term terminates without being renewed; or (c) the employee terminates the contract, with or without notice, in circumstances such that he is entitled to terminate it without notice by reason of the employer's conduct (Employment Rights Act 1996 ss.95 and 136 as amended). See also UNFAIR DISMISSAL; WRONGFUL DISMISSAL.

disorderly house Keeping a disorderly house is an indictable offence at common law. For a house to be disorderly there must be some element of keeping open house; it must be unchaste or of bad repute and it must violate law and good order (*R v Tan* [1983] Q.B. 1053).

disparagement The bestowing by a lord of an heir in an unsuitable marriage below the heir's rank or to someone of mental or bodily infirmity.

dispensing power The power claimed by the Tudors and Stuarts to give exemption in individual cases from the operation of Act of Parliament. See BILL OF RIGHTS.

disposal of uncollected goods See UNCOLLECTED GOODS.

disqualification from driving Under s.146 of the Powers of Criminal Courts (Sentencing) Act 2000 a court before whom a person is convicted may order him to be disqualified from driving for such period as the court thinks fit.

disqualification of directors Under the Company Directors Disqualification Act 1986 directors (or shadow directors (*q.v.*)) of a company may be disqualified from holding office on various grounds including fraudulent trading (*q.v.*), wrongful trading (*q.v.*) and persistent breaches of companies legislation.

disqualification order (1) Certain persons, e.g. undischarged bankrupts, are disqualified from acting as the director (*q.v.*) of a company (Company Directors Disqualification Act 1986). In other cases directors may be subject to a disqualification order if they have, e.g. persistently breached companies legislation or been convicted of breaching competition law.
(2) Under the Criminal Justice and Court Services Act 2000 a person who has committed an offence against a child may be subject to a disqualification order preventing him from working with children.

disseisin The wrongful putting out of him that is actually seised of a freehold (Coke). See SEISIN.

distance contract Under the Consumer Protection (Distance Selling) Regulations 2000 (as amended), a distance contract means any contract concerning goods or services between a supplier and a consumer made under an organised distance sales or provision scheme run by the supplier who makes exclusive use of one or more means of distance communication up to and including the moment at which the contract is concluded. The regulations provide an indicative list of means of distance communication such as email, mail order, telephone selling, cable television, or the internet and require certain information to be given to the consumer who is also entitled to a cooling-off period (*q.v.*) during which he can cancel the contract.

distrain To seize goods by way of distress (*q.v.*).

distraint See DISTRESS.

distress (1) The legal seizure of movable property of a wrongdoer, to satisfy a debt or claim; e.g. levying distress (distraining) for rent due under a lease.
(2) Goods so distrained upon.
At common law the right was to retain the thing seized until compensation was made, and included no right of sale; the landlord's power of sale of distress for rent is statutory. "Walking distress" is a seizure of goods which are then left in the possession of the wrongdoer subject to conditions.

distress damage-feasant Seizure of a chattel causing damage on land. This common law remedy was abolished as regards trespassing livestock by the Animals Act 1971, and replaced by a right to detain and sell them. It does not apply to the parking of unauthorised vehicles. See *Arthur v Anker* [1996] 2 W.L.R. 602.

distribution The division of trust property among the beneficiaries, particularly amongst the next-of-kin of a deceased. See INTESTATE SUCCESSION.

district auditor The officer of the Government whose duty was to disallow any expenditure by a local authority not authorised by law. Now the accounts of public bodies must be audited annually by the Audit Commission (Audit Commission Act 1998).

district council Urban and rural district councils were created by the Local Government Act 1894. They ceased to exist on April 1, 1974. Counties are divided into local government areas known as districts (Local Government Act 1972 ss.1, 20, Schs 1, 4). See also BOROUGH.

district judge A local county or High Court official having an administrative and judicial role. A person who has a five-year general qualification may be appointed as a district judge by Her Majesty on the recommendation of the Lord Chancellor. Formerly known as a district registrar (Courts and Legal Services Act 1990 s.74). See REGISTRAR.

district judge (magistrates' court) This office replaces stipendiary magistrates (*q.v.*) and metropolitan stipendiary magistrates. A person who has a five-year general qualification may be appointed as a district judge (magistrates' court) by Her Majesty on the recommendation of the Lord Chancellor. By virtue of his office, a district judge is a justice of the peace. A district judge (magistrates' court) has the power to do any act and exercise alone any jurisdiction which can be done or exercised by two justices. Some district judges are nominated to hear public law children applications under the Children Act 1989. See the Courts Act 2003.

district registrar See DISTRICT JUDGE.

district registry A branch office in the provinces of the Supreme Court of Judicature, in which proceedings may be instituted. If a defendant resides or carries on business within the district, he must enter an acknowledgment of service there, otherwise in London.

distringas [That you distrain] A writ so called from its commanding the sheriff to distrain on a person's goods for a certain purpose; e.g. to enforce appearance to an indictment, information or inquisition in the King's Bench. Abolished by the Common Law Procedure Act 1852.

distringas notice See STOP ORDER.

disturbance (1) Infringement of a right to an incorporeal hereditament; e.g. obstructing an ancient light (*q.v.*) or a right of way.
(2) Displacement of a person's home or business because of compulsory acquisition of land or because a landlord shows a ground for possession against a tenant. Compensation may be payable to the displaced person.

divest To take away an estate or interest which has already vested.

divi fratres [Roman law] The Emperors Marcus Aurelius Antoninus and Lucius Aurelius Verus, who reigned together AD 161–169.

dividend (1) A payment made out of profits after tax by a company (*q.v.*) to the shareholders of that company.
(2) The amount payable upon each pound of a bankrupt's liabilities.

divine service The tenure of an ecclesiastical corporation which is subject to the duty of saying prayers on a certain day, etc.

Divisional Court Two or more judges of the High Court sitting together to hear appeals. Each Division of the High Court has a Divisional Court and various statutes provide for appeal in civil and criminal cases.

divorce Dissolution of marriage. Before a petition for divorce can be presented the marriage must have subsisted for at least one year. The sole ground for divorce is that the marriage has broken down irretrievably (*q.v.*), but a marriage is not to be held to have broken down unless: (a) the respondent has committed adultery and the petitioner finds it intolerable to live with the respondent (see adultery); or (b) the respondent has behaved in such a way that the petitioner cannot reasonably be expected to live with the respondent (see unreasonable behaviour); or (c) the respondent has deserted the petitioner for a continuous period of two years immediately preceding the presentation of the petition (see desertion); or (d) the parties have lived apart for a continuous period of two years immediately preceding the presentation of the petition and the respondent consents to a decree being granted; or (e) the parties have lived apart for a continuous period of five years immediately preceding the presentation of the petition (Matrimonial Causes Act 1973 s.1). A petition for divorce may be filed in the Divorce Registry (in London) or in a Divorce County Court (elsewhere). See COUNTY COURTS; SPECIAL PROCEDURE; FINANCIAL PROVISION.

dock brief The direct instruction of counsel without the intervention of a solicitor by a prisoner in the dock. Previously a method of ensuring representation of impecunious defendants. Now abolished.

dock warrant A document of title issued by a dock warehouse to the owner of goods in the warehouse. Transfer of the document transfers ownership of the goods.

docket An epitome or abstract of a judgment, decree, order, etc.

document Something on which things are written, printed or inscribed, and which gives information: any written thing capable of being evidence. See the statutory definitions in the Civil Evidence Act 1995 s.13 and Criminal Justice Act 2003 s.140.

document of title A document proving ownership or a document which enables the possessor to deal with the property described in it as if he were the owner; e.g. a bill of lading (*q.v.*).

documentary credit A credit facility arranged with a bank by which the bank undertakes to make payment against presentation of certain specified documents. Most often used in international sales. Documentary credits are usually issued under the terms of the ICC (*q.v.*) Uniform Customs and Practice for Documentary Credits. See LETTER OF CREDIT.

documents: discovery of, list of See DISCOVERY OF DOCUMENTS.

Doe, John In early law a plaintiff had to find persons to act as security for the prosecution of his suit, but this subsequently became a formality and fictitious names were used, which often rhymed; e.g. John Doe and Richard Roe. Later these two "brothers in law" were used to play the fictitious parts of plaintiff and casual ejector, respectively, in the old action for ejectment (*q.v.*).

dole A share.

doli capax Capable of crime. See DOLI INCAPAX.

doli incapax Incapable of crime. There is a conclusive presumption that no child under the age of 10 years can be guilty of an offence. Until 1998 there was a rebuttable presumption that children between the ages of 10 and 14 were *doli incapax* that was abolished by the Crime and Disorder Act 1998.

dolus [Roman law] Fraud, wilful injury.

dom. proc. Domus Procerum (*q.v.*).

domain name A domain name is part of the unique website address of an individual, business or other organisation which is trading or providing information on the internet (*q.v.*), e.g. *www.sweetandmaxwell.co.uk* A domain name may be protected by, e.g. a passing-off action (*q.v.*) or action for trade mark (*q.v.*) infringement. Following a report by the World Intellectual Property Organisation (WIPO), the Uniform Domain Name Dispute Resolution Procedure (UDRP) was established to deal with the abusive registration of trade marks as domain names. *Nominet.uk* is the registry for .uk domain names and operates a dispute resolution service. See, for example, *C.S Lewis (PTE) Ltd v Richard Saville-Smith* (D2008-0821). See CYBERSQUATTERS.

Domesday Book The record of the survey of the kingdom, compiled by order of William the Conqueror and completed in 1086. Dome (or Doom) (*q.v.*) seemingly meaning what is within the jurisdiction—as in "kingdom".

domestic abuse/violence See OCCUPATION ORDERS; NON-MOLESTATION ORDERS.

domestic court Specially constituted magistrates' court comprised of magistrates from the domestic panel. See FAMILY PROCEEDINGS.

domestic proceedings Now known as family proceedings (*q.v.*).

domicile, or domicil The country in which a person is, or is presumed to be permanently resident; the place of a person's permanent home. It depends on the physical fact of residence plus the intention of remaining. The civil status of a person, or his legal rights and duties, including capacity to marry, are determined by the law of his domicile. His political status, or nationality, is independent of domicile.

Domicile may be (1) of origin or birth; (2) of choice. To acquire a domicile of choice a person must have an intention to establish a permanent residence in (and actually take up residence in) a new domicile. If a domicile of choice is abandoned the domicile of origin revives until a new domicile of choice is acquired. The burden of proof lies on the person asserting he has acquired a domicile of choice. Formerly a woman took the domicile of her husband but under the Domicile and Matrimonial Proceedings Act 1973, the domicile of a married woman is ascertained as in the case of any other person having an independent domicile (s.1). The domicile of a legitimate minor normally follows that of his father (s.3). Where the parents are living apart and the child lives with the mother the child's domicile is that of the mother (s.4).

dominant position Under EC law this relates to a position of economic strength enjoyed by an undertaking which enables it to prevent effective competition being maintained on the relevant market by giving it the power to behave to an appreciable extent independently of its competitors, customers and ultimately of its consumers (*United Brands Co v EC Commission* [1978] E.C.R. 207). Abuse of a dominant position in the market is prohibited by Art.82 EC Treaty. In the United Kingdom the Competition Act 1998 is closely modelled on the EC provisions and similarly prohibits abuse of a dominant position in the UK market under the Chapter II prohibition. See ANTI-COMPETITIVE PRACTICES

dominant tenement See EASEMENT.

Dominions Autonomous communities within the British Empire, equal in status and not subordinate one to another in any aspect of their domestic or internal affairs, though united by a common allegiance to the Crown. Now many are members of the British Commonwealth of Nations. See COMMONWEALTH.

dominium [Roman law] Ownership; lordship.

dominus litis [Roman law] The principal in a suit; as opposed to his procurator.

domitae naturae Of tame disposition. See ANIMALS.

Domus Procerum The House of the Nobles; the House of Lords.

domus sua cuique est tutissimum refugium

domus sua cuique est tutissimum refugium [To every one his house is his surest refuge] Every man's house is his castle. See *Semayne's Case* (1604) 5 Coke 91.

dona clandestina sunt semper suspiciosa [Clandestine gifts are always to be regarded with suspicion]

donatio [Roman law] [Gift] A *donatio inter vivos* (a gift between living persons) when completed was irrevocable except, e.g. for ingratitude of the donee. Under Justinian, a *donatio* was completed as soon as the donor manifested his intention, whether in writing or not.

donatio mortis causa A gift made in contemplation of death. It is a hybrid between a gift inter vivos and a testamentary gift. It must be made in anticipation of the donor's imminent death; be intended to take effect on the death, and be completed by delivery (in the case of real property, some symbolic act is required) to the donee before the death.

donatio propter nuptias [Roman law] A gift on account of marriage. A gift to a bride by the bridegroom, often returned to the groom as *dos* (*q.v.*).

donee A gratuitous recipient.

donor A giver.

doom; dome A judgment.

dormant funds Unclaimed funds in court.

dos [Roman law] The property contributed by a bride, or on her behalf to her groom; towards the upkeep of the matrimonial household. Also known as dower (*q.v.*).

double jeopardy The ancient principle that a person cannot be tried twice for the same offence has been removed by the Criminal Justice Act 2003 so that retrials may be permitted for serious offences such as manslaughter (*q.v.*) and murder (*q.v.*) where new and compelling evidence has come to light.

double plea See DUPLICITY.

double possibility The rule that a remainder limited to the child of an unborn person, after a life estate to the unborn parent, was void; also known as the old rule against perpetuities. It was abolished by Law of Property Act 1925 s.161, and an equitable interest in land may be given to an unborn person for life with remainder to any issue of that unborn person, provided the perpetuity rule is not infringed.

dower (1) [Roman law] The property which a bride brings to her groom in marriage. Also known as dowry or dowery.
(2) Under the mediaeval rules a widow had no right of succession to her deceased husband's property. However, it became customary, and then automatic, for a widow to be entitled to a life interest in one third of her husband's freeholds after his death. It was effectively abolished in 1925.

dower, writ of Proceedings whereby a widow who had no dower (*q.v.*, sense (2)) assigned to her within the proper time, claimed a remedy by "writ of dower *unde nihil habet*". If she had only part other dower assigned to her, she had a remedy by "writ of right of dower". Both writs were abolished by the Common Law Procedure Act 1880.

draft (1) An order for the payment of money, e.g. a cheque.
(2) A first attempt at a legal document yet to be approved and engrossed. See ENGROSSING.

dramatic work There can be copyright (*q.v.*) in an original dramatic work, which includes a work of dance or mime, but only when it is recorded, which may be in writing or otherwise. See Copyright, Designs and Patents Act 1988 s.3.

154

drawback The refund of duty or tax already paid when goods are exported.

drawee The person to whom a bill of exchange (*q.v.*) is addressed; on whom the bill is drawn.

drawer One who signs a bill of exchange (*q.v.*) as the maker; who draws the bill.

driftway A way affording a right of passage for cattle.

drink and driving Various offences are defined under the Road Traffic Act 1988 as amended by the Road Traffic Act 1991, an element of which is driving whilst unfit to do so through drink or drugs or with an amount of alcohol in the breath, blood or urine above prescribed limits (ibid. ss.3A, 4, 5). See BREATH TEST.

droit Right or law.

droit administratif [Administrative law] That part of the law of France administered by the Conseil d'Etat by which officials were tried for acts done in an official capacity. See RULE OF LAW.

droits of Admiralty See ADMIRALTY, DROITS OF

drug treatment and testing order Under the Powers of the Criminal Courts (Sentencing) Act 2000 s.52, where a person is found guilty of an offence then the court may make a drug treatment and testing order. This provision was repealed by the Criminal Justice Act 2003 but the courts may continue to make such orders in respect of 16 and 17-year-old offenders until April 2009. Such an order is to last between six months and three years and is to include the requirements and provisions of ss.53 and 54 of the Act. The order is not to be made unless the court is satisfied that the offender is dependent on or has the propensity to misuse drugs and this requires and may be susceptible to treatment. An order may not be made unless an offender expresses a willingness to comply with its requirements.

drugs, controlled Any substance or product specified as a "controlled drug" under the Misuse of Drugs Act 1971 e.g. cocaine, LSD, opium, cannabis. Possession of a controlled drug is an offence (s.5(1)). The maximum penalty depends on the classification of the drug. See POSSESSION OF DRUGS.

dubitante [Doubting] Used in law reports to signify that a judge cannot make up his mind as to the decision which he should give.

duces tecum Now replaced by witness summons (*q.v.*) See SUBPOENA.

Duchy Court of Lancaster A court formerly held before the Chancellor of the Duchy, concerning all matters of equity and revenue relating to lands holden of the King in right of the Duchy of Lancaster. It was distinct from the Chancery Court of the County Palatine.

due care and attention The standard of care which is implied in relation to the offences of causing death by careless or inconsiderate driving or careless or inconsiderate driving. Section 3ZA of the 1988 Act (inserted by s.30, Road Safety Act 2006) provides that a person is to be regarded as driving without due care and attention if (and only if) the way he drives falls below what would be expected of a competent and careful driver. In determining for the purposes of subs.(2) what would be expected of a careful and competent driver in a particular case, regard shall be had not only to the circumstances of which he could be expected to be aware but also to any circumstances shown to have been within the knowledge of the accused. A person is to be regarded as driving without reasonable consideration for other persons only if those persons are inconvenienced by his driving.

duke The highest rank in the peerage.

dum bene se gesserit [During good conduct] e.g. A judge of the High Court holds office during good behaviour, subject to removal by the Crown on the address of both Houses of Parliament.

dum casta vixerit [While she lives chastely]

dum fuit infra aetatem [While he was within age]

dum fuit non compos mentis [While he was not of sound mind]

dum sola [While single or unmarried]

duplicate A copy or transcript of a written document.

duplicity An indictment must not be double; i.e. no one count should charge the prisoner (except in the alternative) with having committed more than one offence unless part of one act and one entire transaction.

durante absentia [During absence]

durante bene placito [During the pleasure of the Crown]

durante minore aetate [During minority]

durante viduitate [During widowhood]

durante vita [During life]

duress (1) In civil law the unlawful pressure to perform an act. It may render the act void or voidable. (2) In criminal law, the defence of duress is available where a person has been compelled to commit a criminal offence because of threats of death or physical violence made by another. The defence of duress of circumstances is available where a person is compelled to commit a criminal offence because of the circumstances in which the defendant finds himself. This is sometimes referred to as the defence of necessity (*q.v.*). The defence of duress (either by threats or of circumstances) is not available on a charge of murder (*Howe* [1987] 1 A.C. 417) or attempted murder (*Gotts* [1992] 2 W.L.R. 284). Where duress is established, it results in a complete acquittal. See NECESSITY; ECONOMIC DURESS; NULLITY OF MARRIAGE.

duty of care As a term of art the concept of duty serves to define the interests that are protected by the tort of negligence (*q.v.*). It determines whether the type of loss suffered by the plaintiff in the particular way in which it occurred can, as a matter of law, be actionable.

dwelling Commonly used to mean a place where a person lives, treating it as a home, together with any yard, garden or appurtenance belonging to that building. Includes any part of a building where that is occupied separately as a dwelling.

dwelling house A building or part of a building which is used as a single private dwelling house and for no other purpose: Town and Country Planning (Fees for Applications and Deemed Applications) Regulations 1989 reg.2(1).

dying declaration A statement formerly admissible in evidence contrary to the hearsay rule (*q.v.*) because the dying declarant having abandoned hope of recovery would have no self-interest other than in telling the truth. Abolished as an exception to the hearsay rule by the Criminal Justice Act 2003.

E

E. & O. E [Errors and omissions excepted] A declaration on commercial documents intended to protect the maker from liability for mistakes.

EC European Community (*q.v.*).

ECB European Central Bank.

ECOSOC Economic and Social Council. United Nations organ facilitating international cooperation on standards-making and problem-solving in economic and social issues.

ECSC European Coal and Steel Community (*q.v.*).

EEA European Economic Area (*q.v.*).

EEA National A national of a State which is a Contracting Party to the Agreement on the European Economic Area signed in May 1992.

EEC European Economic Community (*q.v.*).

EEIG European Economic Interest Grouping (*q.v.*).

EESC European Economic and Social Committee (*q.v*)

EFTA European Free Trade Association.

EGM Extra-ordinary General Meeting.

EIA Environmental Impact Assessment (*q.v.*).

EIB European Investment Bank.

EMAS Eco-Management and Audit Scheme (*q.v.*)

EMU Economic Monetary Union (*q.v.*).

EU European Union (*q.v.*).

e-commerce The use of an electronic network to conduct business activities with associated technical data that are conducted electronically. See INTERNET; ELECTRONIC SIGNATURE; EMAIL.

e converso [Conversely]

earl The title third in the peerage. The wife of an earl is styled countess.

Earl Marshall An officer of the English peerage who formerly was one of the two chief officers of the feudal forces under the Norman kings. He jointly presided over the Court of Chivalry (*q.v.*) with the Lord High Constable (*q.v.*). Now the office is permanently held by the Dukes of Norfolk who preside over the College of Heralds and without whose warrant no new heraldic arms can be granted.

earmark An identity or ownership mark. Property is said to be earmarked when it can be identified or distinguished from other property of the same nature. It can then be followed and recovered. Money could only be treated as identifiable at common law if it had not become mixed with other property, but equity developed its own remedy of tracing (*q.v.*).

earnest A token sum given by one party to another to indicate commitment to an agreement.

easement A servitude; a right enjoyed by an owner of land over land of another such as a right of way, of light, of support, or to a flow of air or water. An easement must exist for the accommodation and better enjoyment of land to which it is annexed; otherwise only a mere licence can exist. An easement is acquired by grant or prescription (*q.v.*). The land owned by the possessor of the easement is called the dominant tenement, and the servient tenement is the land over which the right is enjoyed.

A positive easement consists of a right to do something on the land of another; a negative easement restricts the use the owner of the servient tenement may make of his land. An easement may be lost by abandonment, of which continued non-user may be evidence.

An easement may exist as a legal interest (Law of Property Act 1925 s.1(2)(a)). See QUASI-EASEMENT.

Easter offerings Payments originally due by statute 2 & 3 Edw. 6 c.13, s.10 from parishioners to the parish clergy at Easter. They are now mostly voluntarily paid to the clergy by their congregations. The amounts so paid are earnings and assessable to income tax.

eat inde sine die [Let him go without a day] The dismissal of a defendant from a suit.

Ecclesiastical Commissioners Established by the Ecclesiastical Commissioners Act 1836 to administer Church property and revenue. See now CHURCH COMMISSIONERS.

Ecclesiastical courts Courts having jurisdiction over the ecclesiastical law of the Church of England. They are the Arches Court of Canterbury and the Chancery Court of York, the Consistory Courts of the dioceses, the Commissary Court of the diocese of Canterbury, and the Court of Ecclesiastical Causes Reserved. The Judicial Committee of the Privy Council has appellate jurisdiction (Ecclesiastical Jurisdiction Measure 1963 ss.1, 8, 11).

Eco-Management and Audit Scheme (EMAS) A voluntary initiative designed to improve companies' environmental performance. It was initially established by European Regulation 1836/93, although this has been replaced by Council Regulation 76/2001. EMAS requires organisations to produce a public statement about their performance against targets and objectives, and incorporates the international standard ISO 14001.

Economic and Monetary Union (EMU) The Treaty on European Union 1992 laid down the foundations for the introduction of economic and monetary union. On December 31, 1998 the conversion rates between the common currency, now called the Euro (*q.v.*) and the currencies of Member States taking part in EMU were irrevocably fixed. Since January 1, 1999 the Euro has been the currency of the participating Member States.

Economic and Social Council United Nations organ facilitating international cooperation on standards-making and problem-solving in economic and social issues.

economic duress The coercion of a person's will, by means of exertion of economic pressure, which causes that person to enter into a contract. To vitiate the contract such pressure must be illegitimate, e.g. a threat to break a contract or to commit a tort; mere commercial pressure is not sufficient. It seems that the illegitimate threat must be a significant cause which induces the other to enter into a contract, e.g. leave the coerced party with no real alternative course of action. Economic duress makes a contract voidable.

Where such duress exists the wrongdoer is not entitled to the immunity from action conferred in respect of a trade dispute (*Universe Tankships Inc of Monrovia v International Transport Workers Federation* [1982] W.L.R. 803, HL).

economic loss See FINANCIAL LOSS.

effet utile Having full force and effect. A term commonly used in relation to European Community law. Article 10 of the EC Treaty requires Member States and the judiciaries of the Member States to ensure the full effectiveness (effet utile) of Community law. See, for example, Case 41/74 *Yvonne van Duyn v Home Office* [1974] E.C.R. 01337

ei incumbit probatio qui dicit, non qui negat [The burden of proof is on him who alleges, and not on him who denies]

ei qui affirmat, non ei qui negat, incumbit probatio [The burden of proof lies on him who affirms a fact, not on him who denies it]

Eire The gaelic name for the Republic of Ireland (Southern Ireland). The Ireland Act 1949 recognised and declared the independence of the Republic of Ireland. Eire ceased to be part of HM Dominions, or the Commonwealth, but it is not a foreign country.

ejectment Originally the action of ejectment was a remedy applicable to a leaseholder wrongfully dispossessed, but owing to the cumbrousness of the old real actions for trying the right to the freehold it was extended to freeholds by means of legal fictions. There was an imaginary lease by the person claiming the freehold to an imaginary "John Doe" who was assumed to be ejected by an imaginary "Richard Doe" (the casual ejector). The claimant, to substantiate the lease, endeavoured to prove his title and the person in possession was allowed to defend on admitting the fictions, and thus the freehold title was put in issue. An action was entitled, e.g. *Doe d. Rigge v Bell* (*Doe, on the demise or lease of Rigge v Bell*). It was abolished by the Common Law Procedure Act 1852. See RECOVERY.

ejusdem generis [Of the same kind or nature] A rule of interpretation that where particular words are followed by general words, the general words are limited to the same kind as the particular words. Thus, where the Sunday Observance Act 1677 s.1 provided that:

"no tradesman, artificer, workman, labourer or other person whatsoever shall do or exercise any worldly labour, business, or work of their ordinary callings upon the Lord's Day (works of necessity and charity only excepted)"

the words "or other person whatsoever" were to be construed ejusdem generis with those which preceded them, so that an estate agency was not within the section (*Gregory v Fearn* [1953] 1 W.L.R. 974).

Elder Brethren The Masters of the Trinity House (*q.v.*).

election Choice. The equitable doctrine of election is to the effect that he who wishes to take a benefit under an instrument must accept or reject the instrument as a whole; he cannot approbate and reprobate. Thus if the will of X makes a gift of A's property to B, and a gift to A, A can only take his gift by giving his own willed property or its value to B. Alternatively he can elect to keep his own property and reject the gift.

election court A court set up to try petitions challenging the validity of the election of a Member of Parliament or a Member of the European Parliament or of a local government councillor: Representation of the People Act 1983 ss.123, 130.

election petition A petition to an election court (*q.v.*) for inquiry into the validity of the election of a Member of Parliament or a Member of the European Parliament or local councillor when it is alleged that the election is invalid: Representation of the People Act 1983 ss.120–157.

elections, Parliamentary The process of choosing Members of Parliament by votes of the electorate. Parliamentary elections are governed by the Representation of the People Act 1983 as amended by the Representation of the People Act 2000, which deals with the franchise, the conduct of elections and election campaigns, and legal proceedings. See CORRUPT PRACTICES.

elective resolution See RESOLUTION.

Electoral Commission Established by Parliament as an independent body with a UK-wide brief and directly responsible to Parliament. Its functions are set out in the Political Parties, Elections and Referendums Act 2000 (as amended). It acts as the regulator of UK party and electoral finance, overseeing donations for campaign spending by political parties and others. It also has a remit to keep

Electoral Commission

under review electoral law and practice and to promote public awareness of the electoral process.

electronic signature A file attached to an email (*q.v.*) that confirms the identity of the sender. By virtue of the Electronic Communications Act 2000 s.7, an electronic signature incorporated into or logically associated with a particular electronic communication has the same legal status as a normal handwritten signature and is admissible in evidence in relation to the authenticity of the communication or data.

eleemosynary corporation A corporation established for the perpetual distribution of free alms or bounty of the founder. The Local Government Act 1933 (repealed) precluded a local authority from acting as a trustee of such a charity (defined in the Act to include all charities for the relief of individual distress), but the charity in question does not fail for want of a trustee.

elegit [He has chosen] A writ of execution by which a judgment debtor might obtain possession of the debtor's land and hold it until the debt was satisfied out of the rents and profits or otherwise. The issue of writs of elegit was ended by the Administration of Justice Act 1956 s.34 and the writ was finally abolished by the Supreme Court Act 1981 s.141. The modern equivalent remedy is a charging order (*q.v.*).

elisor A person appointed to return a jury for the trial of an action when the jury returned by the sheriff and that returned by the coroner has been successfully challenged. See CHALLENGE OF JURORS.

email Electronic mail. Correspondence transmitted via an electronic network, usually the internet (*q.v.*). See E-COMMERCE.

emanation of the state In European Community law an individual may invoke directly effective provisions of the EC Treaty and secondary legislation against a Member State or an emanation of the state. The ECJ (*q.v.*) has placed a broad interpretation on the meaning of the "state" to include organisations or bodies, whatever their legal form, which have been made responsible, pursuant to a measure adopted by the State, for providing a public service under the control of the State and has for that purpose special powers beyond those which result from the normal rules applicable in relations between individuals. Accordingly local and municipal authorities, health authorities, police authorities have been held to be emanations of the state. See *Foster v British Gas* Case (C-188/89) E.C.R. I-3313. See DIRECT EFFECT; HORIZONTAL EFFECT; VERTICAL EFFECT.

emancipatio [Roman law] An act by which freedom from his power was given by a *paterfamilias* (*q.v.*) to a *filius familias* (*q.v.*).

embargo A restraint or prohibition particularly one by a state on the arrival or departure of a ship. If applied by a state only to its own ships by virtue of municipal law, it is termed a civil embargo; if not, it is hostile embargo, which is a method of international redress short of war.

embezzlement The felony which consisted of the conversion to his own use by a clerk or servant of property received by him on behalf of his master (Larceny Act 1916 s.17(1)). It now falls within the definition of theft. See THEFT.

emblements Those growing crops which are the annual result of agricultural labour. At common law a tenant of land for life or at will or for other uncertain duration, whose right determined (other than by his own act) after the crops were sown but before they were reaped, was entitled to re-enter the land and take the emblements.

The right generally has been replaced by the provision of the Agricultural Holdings Act 1986 s.21, that a tenant at a rack-rent whose term ceases may

160

continue in occupation until a notice to quit of at least 12 months is given, expiring at the end of a year of the tenancy.

embracery The common law misdemeanour committed by a person who by any means whatsoever, except the production of evidence and argument in open court, attempts to corrupt, influence or instruct any juryman. The Criminal Law Act 1967 s.13 which abolished maintenance and champerty (*q.v.*) excepted embracery. The offence of embracery is now obsolete. Such conduct is now likely to result in a charge of perverting the course of justice. (*q.v.*).

embryo Under s.1 of the Human Fertilisation and Embryology Act 1990 an embryo is a live human embryo where fertilisation is complete, and references to an embryo include an egg in the process of fertilisation. For this purpose, fertilisation is not complete until the appearance of a two cell zygote. An embryo includes an organism created by cell nuclear replacement: *R. (on the application of Quintavalle (On behalf of ProLife Alliance) v Secretary of State for Health* [2003] UKHL 13.

emergency legislation The laws made in consequence of the outbreak of war in 1939, mainly in the form of Defence Regulations pursuant to the Emergency Powers (Defence) Acts 1939 and 1940. Certain provisions were made permanent by the Emergency Laws (Miscellaneous Provisions) Acts 1947 and 1953. See the Emergency Laws (Repeal) Act 1959 and the Emergency Laws (Re-enactments and Repeals) Act 1964. See also Civil Contingencies Act 2004.

emergency powers The Civil Contingencies Act 2004 Pt 2, confers powers on Ministers to make emergency regulations if an emergency has occurred, is occurring or is about to occur. The emergency event or situation may occur or be inside or outside the United Kingdom. An emergency event is an event or situation which threatens serious damage to human welfare or the environment in a place in the United Kingdom or war or terrorism which threatens serious damage to the security of the United Kingdom. Emergency regulations must be made by statutory instrument and treated for the purposes of the Human Rights Act 1998 as subordinate legislation and not primary legislation.

emergency protection order An order, which replaces a place of safety order, designed to protect a child who may be in danger of significant harm, Children Act 1989 ss.44 et seq. Such an order may include an exclusion requirement (*q.v.*). See also the Children Act 1989, Pt IV. See CHILD ASSESSMENT ORDER.

eminent domain A doctrine (originating in the United States of America) giving the government the right to take private property for public purposes. In international law the state is regarded as not only having a power of disposition over the whole of the national territory, but also as being the representative owner of both the national territory and all other property found within its limits.

emission The direct or indirect release of substances, vibrations, heat or noise into the air, water or land. See ENVIRONMENTAL PERMIT, ENVIRONMENTAL POLLUTION.

emphyteusis [Roman law] A grant of land for ever, or for a long period, on condition that an annual rent (*canon*) be paid to the grantor and his successors, otherwise the grant would be forfeited.

employer and employee The relationship of employer and employee exists where a worker is employed under a contract of employment, i.e. a contract of service (Employment Rights Act 1996 s.230). This relationship is distinguished from that of employer and independent contractor (*q.v.*) where the worker is employed under a contract for services. The distinction between the two types of relationship is to be found in the "tests" established by the courts over a long period. No one test provides a complete answer to the question of employment status and the courts have held that this issue is at best one of mixed law and fact and not one of law alone.

The distinction between different classes of worker is important for several purposes, e.g. (1) statutory employment protection is often afforded only to employees and not to the self-employed; (2) liability for tax and National Insurance contributions varies according to status; (3) an employer generally owes a greater duty of care to his employees than to the self-employed worker. See DISCRIMINATION; REDUNDANCY; UNFAIR DISMISSAL.

employers' liability See COMMON EMPLOYMENT; EMPLOYER AND EMPLOYEE.

employment See employer and employee.

employment agency Anyone who for profit or not provides services for the purposes of finding employment for workers or supplying employers with workers. (See Trade Union and Labour Relations (Consolidation) Act 1992 s.143).

employment and support allowance A new benefit to be paid to new claimants who have been assessed as having "limited capability for work" because of a health condition or disability (see Welfare Reform Act 2007 s.1). This allowance replaces contributory incapacity benefit and income support on the basis of incapacity but these benefits will continue to be paid to existing claimants.

Employment Appeal Tribunal A superior court of record to which appeal lies on a question of law only arising from any decision of an employment tribunal (*q.v.*) on a range of individual employment issues (e.g. discrimination, equal pay, unfair dismissal and redundancy) (see Employment Rights Act 1996). It may also hear appeals on both fact and law from certain decisions of the certification officer (*q.v.*). The Tribunal normally consists of a judge and two lay members. Further appeal lies, with leave, to the Court of Appeal. Although subject to administration by the Tribunals Service (*q.v.*) the EAT remains apart from the Upper Tribunal (*q.v.*).

employment tribunals Formerly called industrial tribunals. Established originally under the Industrial Training Act 1964 and now governed by the Employment Tribunals Act 1996, their jurisdiction has been gradually increased to deal with many areas of dispute between employer and employee, e.g. claims relating to redundancy, unfair dismissal, equal pay or terms of employment. The chairman of each tribunal (now referred to as an employment tribunal judge) is a barrister or solicitor who sits with two other persons. Appeal lies to the Employment Appeal Tribunal (*q.v.*). Employment tribunals are not part of the First-tier Tribunal (*q.v.*) but are subject to administration by the Tribunals Service (*q.v.*).

en autre droit [In the right of another]

en ventre sa mere [In the womb of its mother] A child not yet born.

enabling Act A statute legalising that which was previously illegal or ultra vires (*q.v.*).

enactment An Act of Parliament, or part of an Act of Parliament.

enclosure See INCLOSURE.

encroachment The unauthorised extension of the boundaries of land.

encumbrance A charge or liability, e.g. a mortgage.

endorsement See INDORSEMENT; ENDORSEMENT OF DRIVING LICENCE.

endorsement of driving licence Noting on a driving licence of a conviction under the Road Traffic Act 1988, as amended by the Road Traffic Act 1991, with particulars of the offence together with the number of penalty points (*q.v.*) attributable to the offence. See also Road Traffic Offenders Act 1988. See PENALTY POINTS; TOTTING UP.

endowment (1) The giving to a woman of her dower (*q.v.*).
(2) Property given in permanent provision, e.g. for charity or educational purposes.

endowment policy A policy (contract) of insurance on the life of a person to be paid on expiration of a period or earlier death of the person.

enduring power of attorney An enduring power of attorney was a power of attorney (*q.v.*) made under the Enduring Powers of Attorney Act 1985. The Act was repealed by the Mental Capacity Act 2005 and no new enduring power of attorney could be created after October 1, 2007. Replaced by lasting power of attorney (*q.v.*), Mental Capacity Act 2005 s.9.

enemy See ALIEN ENEMY.

enfeoff To invest a person with land by means of a feoffment (*q.v.*).

enforcement In civil proceedings, where a court judgment is not complied with, further proceedings to enforce that judgment may be necessary. For example, where damages ordered to be paid by a defendant to a claimant are not paid, the claimant will begin enforcement action against the defendant as a result of which a court may order further action to be taken such as the seizure of the defendant's property for sale. See the Civil Procedure Rules 1998, Schs 1 and 2. See WRIT OF EXECUTION.

enforcement notice An enforcement notice is a notice requiring the person on whom it is served to cease his breach of a permission or consent granted by a public body. For example, a local planning authority may serve an enforcement notice specifying a breach of planning control, the steps required to remedy it and the time for compliance (see Town and Country Planning Act 1990 ss.172–182). It may be registered as a Local Land Charge (*q.v.*) (Local Land Charges Act 1975 s.1). Similarly enforcement notices may also be served by the Environment Agency (*q.v.*) to enforce conditions laid down in various licences or permits, for example, under s.90B of the Water Resources Act 1991.
See STOP NOTICE; PROHIBITION NOTICE.

enfranchise To make free or to confer a liberty; to enlarge, e.g. to confer the right to vote; to enlarge copyhold land to freehold.

enfranchisement The right of a tenant of a house to acquire the freehold or an extended lease provided certain conditions as to the length of the tenancy, the rent and occupation are satisfied (see Leasehold Reform Act 1967 as amended). In the case of flats, long lessees have the right, subject to satisfying certain qualifying conditions, to collectively purchase the freehold and all intermediate interests, and an individual right to a new long lease (see Leasehold Reform, Housing and Urban Development Act 1993) (as amended).

engagement to marry Betrothal; agreement to marry. See BREACH OF PROMISE.

English information See INFORMATION.

engrossing (1) Preparing the final version of a deed in writing or print for execution.
(2) Buying in quantity corn, etc. to sell again at a high price; an offence abolished by (7 & 8 Vict. c.24).

engrossment A document prepared for signing particularly as a deed.

enjoyment The exercise of a right.

163

enlargement (1) Increasing an estate, e.g. when a base fee became united with the reversion or remainder in fee, the base fee was enlarged to the fee simple.

(2) The enlargement of the membership of the European Union (*q.v.*) from its original membership of 6 to 27 following the admission of Bulgaria and Romania in 2007.

enrol To enter (or copy) a document on an official record. The Enrolment Office was in the Court of Chancery; later transferred to the Central Office of the Supreme Court.

ens legis A legal being or entity such as a company.

entail Estate tail: a right inheritable only by a lineal descendant. The interest in real property created prior to 1926 by a grant "to A and the heirs of his body" (called a general tail), or "to A and the heirs of his body by his wife J" (called a special entail). A tail male or female occurs where property can descend only to males or females respectively. The owner of an entail was called the tenant in tail, and might bar the entail, converting it into a fee simple (see RECOVERY). Where, however, the entail was not an estate in possession, as where it was consecutive to an interest for life in possession, the tenant in tail could not completely bar the entail without the consent of the protector of the settlement (*q.v.*). Without such consent the tenant in tail could only bar his own issue, and not the estates in remainder or reversion. He thereby created a base fee (*q.v.*).

Since 1925 an entail in land can only subsist in equity under a trust. See ESTATE.

enter See ENTRY.

entering short Noting by a banker to whom a postdated bill of exchange (*q.v.*) has been presented that the bill has been received for collection in due course, and that it will be credited when it is paid.

enterprise zone An area designated as such under Sch.32 to the Local Government, Planning and Land Act 1980. The effect of designation is to grant permission for specific development (*q.v.*) or for particular classes of development. There are also fiscal advantages for development in such areas which are designed to revitalise the local economy. See also SIMPLIFIED PLANNING ZONE.

enticement The action in tort for damages for inducing by persuasion one spouse to leave the other, or to remain away from that other, without justification. Abolished by the Law Reform (Miscellaneous Provisions) Act 1970 s.5.

entire (1) A contract or claim of which each part is so connected with the rest that it cannot be separated into several distinct contracts or claims; as opposed to a severable or apportionate contract.

(2) Of a male animal, that it has not been castrated.

entireties Where an estate was conveyed or devised to a man and his wife during coverture (*q.v.*) they were tenants by entireties: each was seised of the whole and not separate parts; i.e. *per tout* and not *per my et per tout* After the Married Women's Property Act 1882 the husband and wife took as joint tenants. Tenancies by entireties were abolished by the Law of Property Act 1925 Sch.I, Pt VI, and under s.39(6) any tenancy by entireties which existed before the commencement of the Law of Property Act 1925 was converted into a joint tenancy.

entrapment Enticing a person into committing a crime in order to prosecute him. Generally not a defence to criminal proceedings, but see AGENT PROVOCATEUR.

entry (1) The act of going on land with the intention of asserting a right in it. (2) A key element in the offence of burglary (*q.v.*) See FORCIBLE ENTRY.

entry, writs of A real action which lay where land was wrongfully withheld. The writ was said to be *in the quibus* when it was against the person who had actually committed the wrong; *in the per and cui* when it was against the heir or grantee of such person; *in the per* where there had been two descents, two alienations or a descent and an alienation since the original commission of the wrong; and *in the post* when the original wrong was still more remote. It was abolished by the Real Property Limitation Act 1833, s.36.

enure To operate or take effect; to continue.

environment Under the Environmental Protection Act 1990 s.1(2), the environment was defined as consisting of all or any of the following media, namely, the air, water (*q.v.*) and land; and the medium of air includes the air within buildings and the air within other natural or man made structures above or below ground. This has been repealed by the Pollution Prevention Act 1999 which retains the same definition in the context of environmental pollution (*q.v.*). The Environmental Information Regulations 2004 contain a more expansive definition of what is included in the elements of the environment, including air and atmosphere, water, soil, land, landscape and natural sites including wetlands, coastal and marine areas, biological diversity and its components, including genetically modified organisms, and the interaction among these elements. See ENVIRONMENT AGENCY; ENVIRONMENTAL PERMIT; ENVIRONMENTAL INFORMATION.

Environment Agency The Environment Agency was established by the Environment Act 1995 (s.1) as a body corporate. The Agency subsumed the responsibilities of the National Rivers Authority; Her Majesty's Inspectorate of Pollution and the waste regulation authorities. The principal aim of the Agency is to protect or enhance the environment, taken as a whole, in order to achieve the objective of sustainable development (*q.v.*). The Agency is responsible, inter alia, for granting environmental permits (*q.v.*), consents and licences to pollute and for enforcing compliance with such permits including the right to prosecute. The Agency also has responsibility for flood defence, land drainage, navigation and fisheries. See ENVIRONMENT; POLLUTION.

Environmental Impact Assessment (EIA) An EIA involves the systematic collection, assessment and presentation of information on the environmental effects of a project as a mandatory requirement in the decision making process in relation to certain development proposals. Directive 85/337 (as amended) requires that for certain projects an EIA is mandatory. An EIA is required for a project falling within Sch.1 of the Regulations and also for a Sch.2 project which is likely to have significant effects on the environment. Where an EIA is required the developer must submit an Environmental Statement (*q.v.*) and the public has a right to inspect this in order to make informed representations to the planning authority. See the Town and Country Planning (Environmental Impact Assessment) (England and Wales) Regulations 1999 as amended. See also ENVIRONMENTAL INFORMATION; ENVIRONMENTAL STATEMENT; SCREENING AND SCOPING See STRATEGIC ENVIRONMENTAL ASSESSMENT.

Environmental Impact Assessment Development A development (*q.v.*) within the meaning of the Town and Country Planning legislation, which is subject to the requirements of the Town and Country (Environmental Impact Assessment) Regulations 1999 by virtue of the fact that the development falls within Sch.1 to the said regulations or Sch.2 and is likely to have significant effects on the environment by virtue of factors such as its nature, size or location.

environmental information (1) Where a planning application is made in respect of an EIA development (*q.v.*) the local planning authority, Secretary of State or planning inspector is prohibited from granting planning permission in respect of the development unless they have first taken the environmental information into consideration (s.3 of the Town and Country Planning (Environmental Impact Assessment) (England and Wales) Regulations 1999. Environmental information in this context includes the Environmental Statement (*q.v.*) submitted by the developer, along with any further information or representations made by the various bodies required to be consulted or any member of the public.

(2) The Environmental Information Regulations (EIR) 2004 (reg.2) provide a specific and lengthy definition of what information is to be classed as environmental information within the scope of the Regulations. Such information should be disclosed or withheld under the EIR as environmental information is exempt under the Freedom of Information Act 2000 s.39. The definition has the same meaning as that in EC Council Directive 2003/4. It includes any information in written, visual, aural, electronic or any other material form on, inter alia, the state of the elements of the environment; factors (such as emissions (*q.v.*) and discharges) affecting or likely to affect one of the elements of the environment; and measures (such as policies) affecting or likely to affect the elements or factors.

environmental permit Replaces a waste management licence (*q.v.*) in a simplified regime for the regulation of certain activities (e.g. combustion of waste oil, processing of metal or activities relating to asbestos) or of waste operation (see Environmental Permitting (England and Wales) Regulations 2007). Permits are issued by the Environment Agency (*q.v.*) or the relevant local authority in whose area the regulated facility (*q.v.*) is located. Section 33 of the Environmental Protection Act 1990 creates various offences in relation to deposit, treatment, keeping or disposal of controlled waste (*q.v.*) unless such activity is in accordance with an environmental permit. The environmental permitting programme aims to provide a single permitting and compliance system for waste operations and polluting activities subject to the Pollution and Prevention Control Act 1999.

environmental pollution Pollution of the air, water or land which may give rise to any harm. Pollution includes pollution caused by noise, heat or vibrations or any other kind of release of energy. Harm includes harm to the health of human beings or other living organisms; to the quality of the environment taken as a whole or to specific environmental media. Harm also includes the impairment of, or interference with, the ecological systems of which any living organisms form part; offence to the senses of human beings; damage to property; or impairment of, or interference with, amenities or other legitimate uses of the environment (s.1, Pollution Prevention and Control Act 1999; see also Council Directive 96/61/EC).

Environmental Statement In respect of any development which is regarded as an Environmental Impact Assessment development (*q.v.*) the developer must submit to the planning authority an environmental statement. The statement must include such information as is reasonably required to assess the environmental effects of the proposed development and at least the information prescribed in Pt II of Sch.4 of the 1999 Regulations. Failure to comply with this essential procedural requirement could result in a court quashing a decision to grant permission for an EIA development where no environmental statement has been submitted. See *Berkley v Secretary of State for the Environment and others* [2000] All E.R. (D) 933.

eo instanti [At that instant]

eo nomine [In that name]

eodem modo quo oritur, eodem modo dissolvitur [What has been effected by agreement can be undone by agreement]

eodem modo quo quid constituitur, eodem modo destruitur [A thing is made and is destroyed by one and the same means]

epitome of title Schedule of documents going back to the root of title (*q.v.*) to land. Copy documents are attached to it, performing the same function as an abstract of title (*q.v.*).

Equal Opportunities Commission A body which was set up under the Sex Discrimination Act 1975 s.53 to work towards the elimination of discrimination and promotion of equality of opportunity between men and women. It had both advisory and enforcement functions. The role of the Equal Opportunities Commission, along with that of the Commission for Racial Equality (*q.v.*) and the Disability Rights Commission (*q.v.*) was transferred to the Equality and Human Rights Commission (*q.v.*) by the Equality Act 2006. See DISCRIMINATION; COMMISSION FOR EQUALITY AND HUMAN RIGHTS.

equality One of the general principles of law followed by the European Court of Justice (*q.v.*) requiring equality of treatment so as to eliminate discriminatory practices. See also PROPORTIONALITY; LEGAL CERTAINTY.

Equality and Human Rights Commission (EHRC) Established as an independent, public body under the Equality Act 2006, the EHRC has taken over the roles of the separate discrimination bodies the Equal Opportunities Commission (*q.v.*), the Commission for Racial Equality (*q.v.*) and the Disability Rights Commission (*q.v.*). In addition the EHRC is responsible for more recent areas of equality: age, sexual orientation and religion or belief. It is also charged with the promotion of both the practice and the understanding of human rights.

equality clause Under the Equal Pay Act 1970 every woman's contract of employment is deemed to include such a clause. Its effect is to provide that any less favourable term in the woman's contract is to be modified to be no less favourable than that of a man in the same employment and any beneficial term in the man's contract which hers does not include is to be added. The equality clause will only operate where a woman (or man) can establish that she (he) is employed on like work (*q.v.*), worked rated as equivalent or work of equal value (*q.v.*) as a man (woman) in the same employment. Enforcement of an equality clause is by way of a claim to an employment tribunal (*q.v.*). See JOB EVALUATION STUDY.

Equality Commission for Northern Ireland Established under the Northern Ireland Act 1998, the Commission's duties include working towards the elimination of discrimination, promoting equality of opportunity, promoting good relations between people of different racial groups and keeping the relevant legislation under review. It took over the functions previously exercised by the Commission for Racial Equality for Northern Ireland, the Equal Opportunities Commission for Northern Ireland, the Fair Employment Commission and the Northern Ireland Disability Council.

equitable (1) That which is fair.
(2) That which arises from the liberal construction or application of a legal rule or remedy.
(3) In particular, that which is in accordance with, or regulated, recognised, or enforced by the rules of equity (*q.v.*), as opposed to those of the common law.

equitable assets Property available for payment of debts only in a court of equity and not of law. See ASSETS.

equitable assignment A transfer of property taking effect only in equity. No particular form is necessary; it need not even be in writing. An equitable assignee of a legal chose in action can enforce the right assigned by action, joining the assignor as a co-claimant, if he consents; or as a co-defendant if he does not. See ASSIGNMENT OF CHOSES IN ACTION.

equitable charge A security for a debt taking effect only in equity, because either the chargor has only an equitable interest, or the charge is made informally (without a deed). The remedy of an equitable chargee is to apply to the court for the enforcement of the charge by the sale of the property, or the appointment of a receiver, etc., as an equitable chargee cannot himself exercise a power of sale or appoint a receiver in the absence of a deed. See CHARGE; MORTGAGE.

equitable defence A defence available in equity although not at law. By the Judicature Act 1873, when law and equity were fused, it was provided that equitable defences should be available in all courts.

equitable easement An easement (*q.v.*) taking effect only in equity because created informally, or not for a full fee simple or term of years absolute. It is registrable as a land charge, Class D (iii) (Land Charges Act 1972 s.2).

equitable estate A right to exclusive use of land but recognised only in equity; since 1925 referred to as an equitable interest (*q.v.*); e.g. entails, life interests and all future interests in freehold.

equitable estoppel See ESTOPPEL.

equitable execution A means of enforcing the rights of a judgment creditor by the appointment of a receiver and, if necessary, an injunction to restrain dealings with the judgment debtor's equitable interests.

equitable interest A right recognised and enforceable only according to the rules of equity (*q.v.*). Strictly such a right is in personam (i.e. as against the person and not against the property) but for certain purposes is tantamount to a real right, particularly in following trust funds, which the beneficiary can recover subject to the doctrine of notice (*q.v.*). See TRACING.

equitable lien A type of security for a debt which exists independently of possession, but cannot be set up against a purchaser of the legal estate for value without notice of the lien; e.g. vendor's lien for his purchase-money, and the purchaser's lien for his deposit. See LIEN.

equitable mortgage A form of security for a debt which lacks the formality required by law or which relates only to equitable property. See MORTGAGE.

equitable waste See WASTE.

equity (1) Fairness or natural justice.

(2) That body of rules formulated and administered by the Court of Chancery to supplement the rules and procedure of the common law.

By the Judicature Act 1873 the Court of Chancery was amalgamated with the Common Law Courts to form the Supreme Court, and rules of equity are administered alongside the common law rules in all courts. Where there is any conflict between the rules of law and equity, equity is to prevail (see the Judicature Act 1925 ss.36–44).

(3) A right to an equitable remedy, e.g. for fraud, mistake or where an estoppel arises. An equity is weaker than an equitable interest (*q.v.*).

equity of redemption (1) The equitable right of a mortgagor to redeem the mortgaged property after the legal right to redeem has been lost by default in repayment of the mortgage money at the due date.

(2) The equitable estate or interest of a mortgagor in his mortgaged land in respect of which an equitable right to redeem subsists.

equity, maxims of Basic principles around which the rules of equity have been developed. There is no definitive expression of them but the following are commonly expounded:

(1) Equity acts in personam.

(2) Equity will not suffer a wrong without a remedy.

(3) Equity follows the law.

(4) Equity looks to the intent rather than the form.

(5) Equity looks on that as done which ought to be done.

(6) Equity imputes an intent to fulfil an obligation.

(7) Delay defeats equity.

(8) He who comes to equity must come with clean hands.

(9) He who seeks equity must do equity.
(10) Where there is equal equity, the law prevails.
(11) Where there are equal equities, the first in time prevails.
(12) Equality is equity.

equity's darling A bona fide purchaser for value of a legal estate in land without notice of an existing equitable interest in the land. See NOTICE.

error Some mistake in the foundation, proceeding, judgment or execution of an action in a court of record, requiring correction either by the court in which it occurred (in case of error of fact), or by a superior court (in case of error in law). To "bring error" was to apply for the rectification required. Abolished by Judicature Act 1973. See APPEAL; MISTAKE.

error of procedure Where there has been an error of procedure. An error of procedure such as a failure to comply with the Civil Procedure Rules or Practice Directions does not invalidate any steps taken in the proceedings unless the court orders. A court may make an order to remedy the error.

escape The misdemeanour committed by a person who permits any person in his lawful custody to regain his liberty otherwise than in due course of law. It is an indictable offence to aid a prisoner to escape (Prison Act 1952 s.39), and this offence can also be committed by bringing, throwing or otherwise conveying anything into a prison, or by causing someone else to bring, throw or otherwise convey anything into a prison or by giving anything to a prisoner or leaving anything anywhere inside or outside a prison with intent to facilitate an escape. Harbouring an escaped prisoner is an offence punishable summarily or on indictment (Criminal Justice Act 1961 s.22(2)).

escheat The reversion of land to the lord of the fee or the Crown on failure of heirs of the owner or on his outlawry. It is derived from the feudal rule that, where an estate in fee simple comes to an end, the land reverts to the lord by whose ancestors or predecessors the estate was originally created. Escheat was abolished by the Administration of Estates Act 1925 s.45, and the right of the Crown to take as bona vacantia was substituted (ibid. s.46).

escheator The officer anciently appointed to enforce the right of escheat on behalf of the Crown.

escrow A writing executed but to be held undelivered until certain conditions be performed, e.g. payment of money, and then to take effect as a deed. See DELIVERY OF DEED.

escuage A variety of tenure by knight's service. It imposed on the tenant the duty of accompanying the King to war for 40 days, or of sending a substitute, or of paying a sum of money which was assessed by Parliament after the expedition.

esquire The degree next below that of knight. A judge, a magistrate and a barrister-at-law are all esquires by virtue of their offices.

essence of the contract An essential condition or stipulation in a contract, without which the contract would not have been entered into, a breach of which entitles the innocent party to rescind. Unless a different intention appears from the terms of the contract, time of payment is not of the essence of a contract of sale of goods (Sale of Goods Act 1979 s.10).

essential facilities doctrine In EC competition law, the notion that in certain circumstances a dominant firm owning a facility that is essential to other users may be required to licence its use by them, in order to avoid a finding that it has abused its position.

established use certificate See CERTIFICATE OF LAWFUL USE OR DEVELOPMENT.

Establishment, right of See FREEDOM OF ESTABLISHMENT; FREEDOM TO PROVIDE SERVICES.

estate A right to the exclusive use of land for a period of time. An absolute estate is one granted without condition or liability to premature termination. A conditional estate is one liable to divest on fulfilment of a condition. A contingent estate is one the right to the enjoyment of which will accrue on the happening of some event. A determinable estate is one that is liable to determine on the happening of some event. An estate on expectancy is one which cannot be enjoyed until some future time. Estates other than absolute are now referred to as interests and can exist only in equity: See Law of Property Act 1925 s.1.

An estate in possession is one which gives the right of present enjoyment, and a vested estate is one the right to the enjoyment of which has accrued. An estate in severalty is one held by a person singly, and an estate in common is one held by several persons in undivided shares. A customary estate was one that existed in manors and boroughs by virtue of local custom (abolished by the Law of Property Act 1922).

An estate in fee simple absolute is the greatest estate a subject of the Crown can possess and endures until the current owner dies without an heir. An estate in freehold was originally one held by a freeman and subject to free services, and of uncertain duration; e.g. for life, or for the life of another. An estate of inheritance is one capable of descending to a person's heir, i.e. an estate in fee simple, fee tail or in frankalmoign (*q.v.*).

estate agent A person instructed by someone wishing to dispose of or acquire land, to find another person willing to acquire or dispose of such land. The Estate Agents Act 1979 and orders made under it (inter alia) empower the Office of Fair Trading to bar unfit persons from such work (s.3) and make provisions to protect clients' money (ss.12, 13, 14, 15).

estate clause The clause describing the right being conveyed and inserted in a conveyance after the parcels (*q.v.*). Rendered unnecessary by the Conveyancing Act 1881 s.63, now replaced by the Law of Property Act 1925 s.63, if the whole right of the conveyor is to pass.

estate contract A contract by an estate owner to convey or create a legal estate or interest in land including a right of pre-emption (Land Charges Act 1972 s.2(4)(iv)).

estate duty The tax imposed by the Finance Act 1894 s.1, upon the principal value of property, whether real or personal, settled or not, which passed on the death of any person dying after August 1, 1894. Estate duty was abolished in respect of deaths on or after March 13, 1975 (Finance Act 1975 s.49). It was replaced by capital transfer tax (*q.v.*) which itself has been replaced by inheritance tax (*q.v.*).

estate, legal An estate recognised at common law and valid against the whole world. By the Law of Property Act 1925 s.1. the only legal estates capable of subsisting are: (1) an estate in fee simple absolute in possession; (2) a term of years absolute. See INTEREST.

estate owner The owner of an estate (*q.v.*).

estate tail Entail. An estate (*q.v.*) enduring so long as the original owner had a lineal descendant on his death. Created by the grant of land to "a man and the heirs of his body" or to a man and specified heirs of his body; e.g. the issue of his first wife. The estate tail is derived from the Statute of Westminster II, De Donis Conditionalibus, before which a gift of land to a man and the heirs of his body created an estate in fee conditional on his having issue; as soon as the condition was performed the estate became absolute. The statute enacted that in such cases the terms of the gift should be carried out and the land should go to the issue of the donee, and on failure of such issue should revert to the donor. The Fines and Recoveries Act 1833 instituted a disentailing deed for barring the entail, which since the Law of Property Act 1925, need not be enrolled (s.133). Since 1925, the estate tail can be barred by will (ibid. s.176), and is an equitable interest (ibid. s.130).

estop To deny the assertion of a right.

estoppel A rule of evidence which precludes a person from denying the truth of some statement made by him of the existence of facts whether existing or not which he has by words or conduct led another to believe in. If a person by a representation induces another to change his position on the faith of it, he cannot afterwards deny the truth of his representation.

(1) Estoppel by record: a person is not permitted to dispute the facts upon which a judgment against him is based.

(2) Estoppel by deed: a person cannot dispute his own deed; he cannot deny the truth of the recitals contained in it.

(3) Estoppel in pais, or equitable estoppel or estoppel by representation: estoppel by conduct. Anciently estoppel in pais arose from some formal act which established relations between parties.

(4) Promissory estoppel: one arising from a promise as to future conduct.

estovers, common of Bote (*q.v.*). That which is necessary. A common of estovers is a right to take from woods or waste lands of another a reasonable portion of timber or underwood for use as fuel, for building or for repairs on the land of the commoner.

estrays Valuable animals found straying in any manor or lordship without an owner. After proclamation and a year and a day they belong to the Crown; or by special grant to the lord of the manor.

estreat Extract. (1) A copy of a record of a court.

(2) To forfeit a recognisance (*q.v.*).

et seq.; et sequentes And those following.

euro The European single currency (*q.v.*). Since January 1, 1999 the Euro has been the currency of the Member States participating in the Euro although Euro coins and notes were not issued to participating Member States until 2002. See ECONOMIC AND MONETARY UNION.

Eurojust A body of the European Union, established in 2002 and comprising 27 National Members, one seconded from each Member State (*q.v.*). Members are either senior prosecutors, judges or police officers. The task of Eurojust is to reinforce the fight against serious crime. Based in the Hague. See EUROPOL.

European Coal and Steel Community Established in 1951 by the Treaty of Paris. The Community came to an end on July 23, 2002.

European Commission The European Commission (formerly the Commission of the European Communities) is one of the institutions of the European Union (*q.v.*). The Commission is made up of 27 Commissioners selected by the Member States (*q.v.*) of the European Union on the grounds of their general competence and whose independence is beyond doubt (art.213 EC Treaty). The Commission is responsible for ensuring the proper functioning and development of the common market (*q.v.*). Its powers and functions are defined in arts 211–219 EC Treaty. The Commission is regarded as the Guardian of the EC Treaty because it can bring infringement actions (under art.226 EC Treaty) against any Member State for breaches of Community law.

European Community (EC) Formerly the European Economic Community (EEC 1992) (*q.v.*) but renamed by the Maastricht Treaty (formerly the Treaty on European Union) (*q.v.*). The European Community is the central pillar of the

European Community (EC)

European Union (*q.v.*). Following enlargement of the Community there are now 27 Member States.

European Convention on Human Rights and Fundamental Freedoms A 1950 Convention formulating the protection of human rights (*q.v.*) within the Member States (*q.v.*) of the Council of Europe (*q.v.*). The rights are often simply referred to as "Convention Rights" (*q.v.*). See CONVENTION COMPLIANT.

European Council Formally established as an EC institution by the Single European Act 1986. The composition and function of the European Council is now set out in art.D of the Treaty on European Union. The European Council is charged with the task of providing the Union with the necessary impetus for its development and defining the general political guidelines of the Union. It is made up of the Heads of State or of Government of the Member States and the President of the European Commission (*q.v.*), assisted by the Ministers of Foreign Affairs of the Member states and a member of the European Commission. See EUROPEAN UNION; COUNCIL OF THE EUROPEAN COMMUNITIES.

European Court of Human Rights Based in Strasbourg the Court can hear applications from any person, non governmental organisation or group of individuals claiming to be the victim of a violation of human rights by a state which is a signatory to the European Convention on Human Rights and Fundamental Freedoms (*q.v.*). This right only exists where the state has granted the right of individual petition. The United Kingdom granted this right in 1966. Subject to very narrowly defined exceptions an application can only be made when domestic remedies have been exhausted and the application must be made within six months of the exhaustion of domestic remedies. The Court's decision is binding on the government concerned but does not have any legal effect in that it does not automatically overturn domestic legislation or decisions but the government must take steps to implement the judgment. The Human Rights Act 1998 s.2, requires that when a court or tribunal is determining an issue which has arisen in connection with a Convention right in domestic law, it must take into account, among other matters, any judgement, decision, declaration or advisory opinion of the European Court of Human Rights.

The Court may also hear applications concerning breach of Convention rights by one Convention signatory country against another.

European Court of Justice See COURT OF JUSTICE OF THE EUROPEAN COMMUNITIES.

European Economic and Social Committee A consultative body established by art.257 of the EC Treaty. The Committee consists of representatives of the various economic and social components of organised civil society, and in particular representatives of producers, farmers, carriers, workers, dealers, craftsmen, professional occupations, consumers and the general interest.

European Economic Area (EEA) It came into existence on January 1, 1994 and consists of the Member States (*q.v.*) of the European Union (*q.v.*) plus Iceland, Liechtenstein and Norway. Many of the basic principles of the European Union operate within the EEA, e.g. free movement of goods, services, persons, capital. See internal market.

European Economic Community (EEC) Commonly referred to as the Common Market (*q.v.*) the EEC was established by the Treaty of Rome 1957. The EEC became the EC as a result of amendments made to the Treaty of Rome 1957 by the Treaty on European Union 1992. The United Kingdom signed the Treaty of Accession in 1972. See EUROPEAN UNION.

European Economic Interest Groupings (EEIG) Set up under European Community Law, the purpose of an EEIG is to encourage cross-frontier co-operation between businesses in different Member States, and its object must be to facilitate or develop the economic activities of its members and to improve or increase the results of those activities. An EEIG could be used, for example, for joint marketing or joint tendering between, say, a British and a French company. Once registered anywhere within the EU, an EEIG has a separate legal identity. The members of an EEIG have unlimited liability for its debts, if the EEIG itself is unable to pay them, both during membership and for five years after publication of withdrawal from membership. The United Kingdom's domestic legislation is the European Economic Interest Grouping Regulations 1989. An EEIG is formed by contract and registered in the United Kingdom at Companies House.

European Monetary Union (EMU) See SINGLE CURRENCY.

European Parliament One of the institutions of the European Union (*q.v.*). A body of directly elected representatives, known as Members of the European Parliament (MEPs). The number of members will reduce from 785 to 751 in 2009. The powers and functions of the European Parliament are laid down in arts 137-144 of the EC Treaty. The European Parliament participates in the various procedures leading up to the adoption of Community legislation (*q.v.*). Its powers vary depending upon the particular legislative procedure that is to be used. The European Parliament plays a supervisory role in relation to the other EU institutions and has its own Ombudsman empowered to receive complaints concerning instances of maladministration in the activities of the other Community institutions. See CO-DECISION

European Union (EU) The European Union was established by the Treaty on European Union 1992 (*q.v.*), often referred to as the Maastricht Treaty. Following the most recent enlargement in 2007 the Union now comprises 27 Member States (*q.v.*). The EU is founded on the European Communities and supplemented by the policies and forms of co-operation established by the EU Treaty. This is often described as a three pillar structure with the European Communities as the central pillar flanked by the two intergovernmental pillars of Common Foreign and Security Policy and Police and Judicial Co-operation in Criminal Matters. In relation to these twin pillars the Member States of the Union have agreed to co-operate at the intergovernmental level in order to achieve the objectives of the Union. See EUROPEAN COMMUNITY.

Europol The European Police Office, established in 1995 by the Europol Convention. Its remit requires it to improve police co-operation between Member States in preventing serious international criminal activity such as terrorism, drug trafficking, illegal immigrant smuggling and illegal money-laundering. See EUROPEAN UNION.

euthanasia Used generally to mean the bringing about the painless death of someone suffering from an incurable disease. Euthanasia by means of positive steps to end a patient's life, such as administering a drug to bring about death, is unlawful. See *Airdale NHS Trust v Bland* [1993] 1 All E.R. 821.
In medical practice, an issue is the deliberate withholding of medical treatment with intent that the patient should die. It may be voluntary or involuntary, active or passive. Active voluntary euthanasia is illegal in English law.

eviction Dispossession or recovery of land without due process of law. It may be an offence. See the Protection from Eviction Act 1977.

evidence The means, exclusive of mere argument, which tend to prove or disprove any matter of fact (See proof) the truth of which is submitted to judicial investigation. It may be:
(1) Oral: statements made by witnesses in court.
(2) Documentary: any writing including public and private documents, and statements of relevant facts made by persons in writing (see below).
(3) Conclusive: that which a court must take as full proof and which excludes all evidence to disprove it.

(4) Direct: that of a fact actually in issue; that of a fact actually perceived by a witness with his own sense.

(5) Circumstantial: that of a fact not actually in issue, but legally relevant to a fact in issue. An inference of fact may be drawn from this type of evidence although it does not prove the relevant fact directly.

(6) Real: that supplied by material objects produced for the inspection of the court.

(7) Extrinsic: that as to the meaning of a document not contained in the document itself.

(8) Hearsay (*q.v.*).

(9) Indirect: that of a fact which then implies the fact at issue. Also hearsay (*q.v.*).

(10) Original: that which has an independent probative force of its own.

(11) Derivative: that evidence which derives its force from some other source.

(12) Parol: oral.

(13) Prima facie: that which a court must take as proof of such fact, unless disproved by further evidence.

(14) Primary: original documentary.

(15) Secondary: that other than the original; e.g. oral evidence of the contents of a lost document or a copy of a document.

The rules of evidence are contained in CPR Pts 32 and 33.

evidence in chief The evidence given by a witness for the party who called him.

ex abundanti cautela [From excess of caution]

ex aequo et bono [In justice and good faith]

ex cathedra [From the chair] With official authority.

ex contractu [Arising out of contract]

ex curia [Out of court]

ex debito justitiae A remedy which the applicant gets as of right, e.g. a writ of habeus corpus.

ex delicto [Arising out of wrongs] Actions in tort.

ex diuturnitate temporis omnia praesumuntur esse rite et solennitur acta [From lapse of time, all things are presumed to have been done rightly and regularly]

ex dolo malo non oritur actio [No right of action can have its origin in fraud]

ex gratia [As a favour]

ex maleficio non oritur contractus [A contract cannot arise out of an illegal act]

ex mero motu [Of one's own free will]

ex nudo pacto non oritur actio [No action arises from a nude contract] A contract entered into without consideration cannot be enforced.

ex officio [By virtue of his office]

ex parte An application in a judicial proceeding made: (1) by an interested person who is not a party; (2) by one party in the absence of the other. Now called a "without notice" application under Civil Procedure Rules 1998.

ex post facto [By a subsequent act] Retrospectively.

ex proprio motu [Of his own accord]

ex provisione viri (obsolete) An estate tail of a wife in lands of her husband or his ancestors.

ex relatione; ex rel [From a narrative or information] (1) A report of proceedings not from first hand knowledge; (2) proceedings at the relation or information of a person.

ex turpi causa non oritur actio [An action does not arise from a base cause] e.g. an illegal contract is void. See ILLEGAL.

exaction The taking, by an officer of the law, of any fee or reward where none was due.

examination The interrogation of a person on oath. In court, in general, the evidence of a witness is obtained by oral examination, called the examination-in-chief; the witness is then examined by the opposite party in order to diminish the effect of his evidence (cross-examination). He is again examined by the party calling him (the re-examination) in order to give him an opportunity of explaining or contradicting any false impression produced by the cross examination.

examination, public The process by which a bankrupt is examined in open court by the Official Receiver as to events leading to his bankruptcy.

examined copy A copy of a document marked as a true copy by the person who has compared it with, examined it against, the original. Also called a marked copy.

examiner A person appointed by the Lord Chancellor under CPR 34.15 to record the examination of a witness in an action. A special examiner may be appointed by the High Court under CPR 34.13 to examine a witness in a foreign country.

exception (1) A saving clause in a deed so that the thing excepted does not pass by the grant.
(2) In procedure, an objection or challenge to an alleged fact.

exchange (1) Mutual transfer or conveyance of property.
(2) A place where merchants, dealers or brokers have by custom met to transact business, e.g. the Stock Exchange (q.v.).

exchange control A statutory restriction on the transfer of funds out of the United Kingdom (see Exchange Control Act 1947). No restrictions currently exist.

exchange of contracts The process where a buyer and seller of land swap an original and a copy (traditionally a carbon copy) of the contract, each having signed one or the other, to create a binding contract.

Exchequer (1) A public office, formerly consisting of two divisions, the Exchequer of Receipt and the Court of Exchequer (q.v.). The former managed the royal revenues, receiving and keeping money due to the Crown, and seeing that payments out were made on proper authority of the Treasury.
(2) The account with the Bank of England into which are paid all government receipts and revenues. The fund so formed is called the Consolidated Fund, out of which are paid the sums necessary for the public service, as authorised by Parliament, subject to the control of the Comptroller and Auditor General (q.v.). See the Government Resources and Accounts Act 2000 s.8. See CHANCELLOR OF THE EXCHEQUER.

Exchequer Chamber, Court of A former Court of Appeal originally divided into four divisions: Court of Error for the Exchequer; the Court of Equity for the Exchequer; the Court of Errors in the King's Bench; and the Court of Exchequer Chamber (an assembly of all the exchequer judges for considering questions of law).

excise An inland duty or tax chargeable on the manufacture or use of products or on a licence to deal in certain products.

excise warehouse A secure place approved by the Commissioners for Her Majesty's Revenue and Customs (*q.v.*) for the deposit of dutiable goods upon which a duty has not been paid. See Customs and Excise Management Act 1979.

exclusion clause See EXEMPTION CLAUSE.

exclusion order An order of a court barring a person from a place, e.g. under the Powers of Criminal Courts (Sentencing) Act 2000 s.40A prohibiting a convicted person aged under 16 years from entering a specified place for a period of not more than 3 months; under the Licensed Premises (Exclusion of Certain Persons) Act 1980 s.1 prohibiting a person convicted of an offence on licensed premises who resorted to violence or offered or threatened to do so, from entering those premises or other specified premises without the express consent of the licensee.

exclusion requirement (1) A requirement attached to an interim care order under the Children Act 1989 s.38A, excluding a person from a property with the consent of another person living there.

(2) A provision attached to certain criminal orders which prevents an offender from entering a place specified in the order for a specified period (Criminal Justice Act 2003 s.205).

exclusive jurisdiction of the Court of Chancery Its jurisdiction in cases where no relief was obtainable at law. The jurisdiction comprises trusts, administration of assets and the like.

exclusive rights The rights of an owner of a design, patent, trade mark or copyright to decide whether anyone else may use that item. Note that the extent of the monopoly varies depending on the right involved. For example, patent owners have the right to prevent the unauthorised use of their inventions, whether copied or independently devised; copyright owners can only prevent copying, not independent creation. See PATENT; DESIGN; TRADE MARK; COPYRIGHT.

exeat [Let him go] A permission from a Church of England Bishop allowing a priest to leave a diocese.

execute Of a deed, to formally sign and deliver. At common law both signing and sealing were required; now only signing as a deed in the presence of a witness who also signs: Law of Property (Miscellaneous Provisions) Act 1989 s.1.

executed Done. Of a document, one which is formally signed. See CONSIDERATION; EXECUTORY.

execution The act of completing or carrying into effect. (1) Of a judgment, compelling the defendant to do or to pay what has been adjudged. Writs of execution (*q.v.*) are enforced by High Court Enforcement Officers. See ATTACHMENT; CHARGING ORDER; COMMITTAL; DELIVERY; FIERI FACIAS; HIGH COURT ENFORCEMENT OFFICER; POSSESSION; SEQUESTRATION.

(2) Of a deed, the formal signing and delivery. See EXECUTE; WILLS.

Executive The Crown in its administrative aspect; the Government Departments and their officials or officers under the Ministers of the Crown. The principal executive body in the Constitution is the Cabinet (*q.v.*).

In principle, the Executive is charged with putting into effect the laws enacted by the Legislature, subject to the judgments and orders of the judiciary. In practice, the Legislature largely functions at the initiative of the Executive, and the Judiciary cannot interfere in purely administrative matters.

executor Person named in a will whom the testator wishes to administer the estate. The duties of an executor are to prove the will; to bury the deceased; to collect in the estate; to pay the debts in their proper order; to pay the legacies; and distribute the residue among the persons entitled. The executor may bring actions against persons who are indebted to the testator, or are in possession of property belonging to the estate. When several executors are appointed, and only some of them prove the will, these are called the proving or acting executors; the others are said to renounce probate. An executor is allowed a year to realise the testator's estate (Administration of Estates Act 1925 s.44). See ADMINISTRATOR; PERSONAL REPRESENTATIVE; RETAINER.

executor de son tort [Of his own wrong] One who, being neither executor nor administrator, intermeddles with the goods of the deceased as if he were, renders himself liable, not only to an action by the rightful executor or administrator, but also to be sued by a creditor or legatee of the deceased. He has all the liabilities, though none of the privileges, of an executor (see Administration of Estates Act 1925 s.28).

executory Remaining to be carried into effect. An executory contract is one which takes the form of promises to be performed in the future.

executory interest A right arising under a will or a use (*q.v.*) to enjoy property in the future should a particular event occur. If created by will it is known as an executory devise; if created by deed, under the Statute of Uses, as either a springing use, i.e. one that comes into being after the happening of some event; or a shifting use, i.e. one that shifts from one person to another on the happening of some event. See USE; CONTINGENT INTEREST.

exemplary damages Damages (*q.v.*) awarded in relation to certain tortious acts (defamation, intimidation and trespass) but not for breach of contract (*q.v.*). In contrast to aggravated damages (*q.v.*) which are still compensatory in nature, such damages carry a punitive element aimed at both retribution and deterrence for the wrongdoer and others who might be considering the same or a similar conduct.

According to the Court of Appeal in *AB v South West Water Services Ltd* [1993] Q.B. 507 to maintain a claim for exemplary damages the cause of action must be one in which such damages had been awarded before 1964 and the case of *Rookes v Barnard* [1964] A.C. 1129. In that case Lord Devlin identified three categories where exemplary damages might be awarded, namely: (a) oppressive, arbitrary or unconstitutional action by servants of the government; (b) wrongful conduct which was calculated by the defendant to make a profit for himself which might well exceed the compensation payable to the claimant; and (c) where such an award was expressly authorised by statute.

exemplification Proof of the contents of a public or judicial record by means of a copy of the record made under the Great Seal (*q.v.*) or the seal of the court where the document was kept which was admissible in evidence to prove the contents of the original record. Judicial records are now proved by office copies or certified copies.

exemption clause A clause in a contract excluding or limiting the liability of one or other of the parties. Such a clause must be expressly incorporated in the relationship between the parties from the outset (*Thornton v Shoe Lane Parking Ltd* [1971] 2 Q.B. 163, CA). See also *Photo Production Ltd v Securicor Transport Ltd* [1980] 2 W.L.R. 283, HL. See UNFAIR CONTRACT TERMS.

exequatur Permission by a government to the consul of another state to carry out his functions.

exhibit (1) A document or thing produced for the inspection of the court; or shown to a witness when giving evidence or referred to in a deposition: or a document referred to in, but not annexed to, an affidavit.

(2) To so produce such a document or thing or to refer to such in an affidavit.

exitus (1) Issue or offspring.
  (2) The yearly rents and profits of land.
  (3) The final step in pleadings: joinder of issue.

exoneration (1) Relief from liability.
  (2) The relieving of one part of the estate of a testator of a liability, by throwing it on another part, either by direction of the testator or by operation of law.

exor Executor (abbreviation) (*q.v.*).

expatriation Loss of nationality by renunciation of allegiance, and the acquisition of a foreign nationality.

expectant heir A person having either a vested or a contingent remainder in property, or who has the hope of succession to the property of an ancestor, either because heir-apparent (*q.v.*) or heir-presumptive (*q.v.*), or merely because of the expection of a devise or bequest on account of the supposed or presumed affection of the ancestor or relation. See CATCHING BARGAIN.

expectation loss Damages for breach of contract seek to compensate this loss by putting a claimant monetarily into the position he would have occupied had the contract been performed in accordance with its terms (*Robinson v Harman* (1848) 1 Ex. 850). See DAMAGES; RELIANCE LOSS.

expectation of life See LIFE, EXPECTATION OF.

expedit reipublicae ut finis sit litium [It is in the public interest that the decision of cases should be final]

expensae litis [Expenses of the cause] Costs.

expensilatio See LITERARUM OBLIGATIO.

expert witness A person with special skill, technical knowledge or professional qualification whose opinion on any matter within his cognisance is admitted in evidence, contrary to the general rule that mere opinions are irrelevant; e.g. a doctor or surgeon, a handwriting expert, a foreign lawyer. It is for the court to decide whether the witness is so qualified as to be considered an expert.
  In any case to be tried without a jury, the court may appoint an independent expert, called the "court expert", to inquire and report.

Expiring Laws Continuance Acts Acts passed to continue, generally until the end of the following year, a number of Acts which otherwise would expire.

exposure The intentional exposure of a person's genitals with the intent that someone will see them and be caused alarm or distress is an offence (Sexual Offences Act 2003 s.66). See INDECENCY; SEXUAL OFFENCES.

express Directly discoverable by word or act.

expressio unius personae vel rei, est exclusio alterius [The express mention of one person or thing is the exclusion of another] (A rule of interpretation).

expropriation Compulsorily depriving a person of his property by the state (perhaps without compensation).

extended sentence A determinate sentence served in custody to the half way point (e.g. for a 4 year custodial term automatic release will take place at the 2 year point) with additional extended supervision periods of up to five years for violent offenders and eight years for sexual offenders. Extended sentences imposed on or after 14 July 2008 must have a minimum custodial term of 4 years.

extendi facias (writ of) [That you cause to be extended] The Writ of Extent. See EXTENT.

extent (Writ of) The writ to recover debts of record due to the Crown, directed to the Sheriff, who proceeded to make a valuation of the property of the debtor by means of a statement on oath. An extent in chief was a proceeding by the Crown for the recovery of a debt due to it. An extent in aid was one sued out at the instance of a debtor of the Crown for the recovery of a debt owed to him, the Crown being merely the nominal plaintiff. An immediate extent was one which issued in urgent cases without the usual preliminary of a *scire facias* on proof that the debt was in danger of being lost. Proceedings for the determination of any issue upon a writ of extent have been abolished by the Crown Proceedings Act 1947.

extinguishment The cesser of a right or obligation, particularly by the consolidation or merger of it with another right: e.g. an easement is extinguished when ownership of the dominant and servient tenements becomes united in the same person.

extortion A misdemeanour committed by a public officer, who, under colour of his office, wrongfully takes from any person any money or valuable thing. It was abolished by the Theft Act 1968. See BLACKMAIL.

extortionate Excessive. For example, a credit bargain may be reopened by the court if the debtor or a relative of the debtor is required to make grossly extortionate payments (Consumer Credit Act 1974 ss.137–140).

extradition The delivery up by one state to another of a person who is accused of committing a crime in the other. No such proceedings can be taken unless an extradition treaty has been concluded with the foreign state concerned. No person may be extradited for a "political" offence. See the Extradition Act 2003.

extrajudicial Outside the scope of legal procedure: e.g. distress.

extraterritoriality The legal fiction by which certain persons and things are deemed for the purpose of jurisdiction and control to be outside the territory of the state in which they really are, and within that of some other state. Its principal applications are:
(1) Sovereigns, whilst travelling or resident in foreign countries.
(2) Ambassadors and other diplomatic agents while in the country to which they are accredited.
(3) Public vessels whilst in foreign ports of territorial waters.
(4) The armed forces of a state when passing through foreign territory. See DIPLOMATIC PRIVILEGE.

F

f.o.b. Free on board. A contract is f.o.b. when the price quoted includes the cost of placing the goods on board ship. Risk in the goods does not pass to the buyer, nor does the property, until the goods are actually on board.

FCS Free of capture and seizure. A term exempting marine underwriters from liability for the acts of the enemies of the Queen.

FSA Financial Services Authority (*q.v.*).

fabric land Timber land. Land given to provide materials or income for the repair of (to maintain the fabric or structure of) a church.

factor A mercantile agent (*q.v.*). A person who, in the usual course of his business has possession of goods, or the documents of title to goods, of another, with authority to sell, pledge, or raise money on the security of them (Factors Act

1889 s.1(1)). The principal is bound by such sale or pledge even though he has forbidden it, unless the buyer has notice of such prohibition.

factum Made. An act or deed.

factum probanda Facts which require to be proved.

factum probantia Facts which are given in evidence to prove other facts in issue.

faculty A licence to do an otherwise unlawful act. In ecclesiastical law the term is used in relation to the authorisation of works involving alterations to the fabric and content of churches and churchyards.

failure of record The unsuccessful plea of a defendant who alleged matter of record in defence.

fair comment Impartial observation or criticism. That a statement is fair comment is a defence to an action for defamation (*q.v.*) if the matter is of public interest, or has been submitted to public criticism. Such defence may be defeated by proof of malice on the part of the defendant.

fair dealing A copyright will not be infringed by unauthorised copying which amounts to fair dealing for the purposes of, e.g. research or private study (Copyright Designs and Patents Act 1988 ss.29–30).

fair rent Various Rent Acts have provided for the fixing by a Rent Officer (*q.v.*) of "fair rents" for certain types of residential tenancy: now governed by the Rent Act 1977 Pt IV. The rent fixed becomes the maximum which can be charged for the premises under a protected tenancy (*q.v.*).

fair trading The Fair Trading Act 1973 set up the Office of Fair Trading and laid down a framework of law to eliminate or control unfair consumer trading practices and to keep under review monopoly situations. The Fair Trading Act 1973 has largely been repealed by the Enterprise Act 2002.

fait Done. A deed.

falsa demonstratio non nocet [A false description does not vitiate] If a document contains a description, part of which is true and part false, but the true part describes the subject with sufficient certainty, the false part will be rejected or ignored.

false accounting See ACCOUNTING, FALSE.

false imprisonment The confinement of a person without just cause or excuse. There must be a total restraint of the person. An intention to frighten a person so they can not move or escape may constitute false imprisonment, *R. v James (Anthony David), The Times*, October 2, 1997.

false pretence An offence under the Larceny Act 1916 (now repealed) of obtaining money by false pretences. For the present position see s.15 of the Theft Act 1968, obtaining property by deception. See also the Proceeds of Crime Act 2002.

false representation See MISREPRESENTATION.

false return (To a writ). A reply to a court which is known to be untrue.

false statement Proceedings for contempt of court may be brought against a person if he makes, or cause to be made, a false statement in a document verified by a statement of truth without an honest belief in its truth. Proceedings are dealt with in the same way as other proceedings for contempt (*q.v.*), CPR 32.14.

falsification of accounts See ACCOUNTS, FALSIFICATION OF.

falsify Point out an error. Where a court has ordered an account to be taken and a party shows that an item of payment or discharge contained in it is false or erroneous, he is said to falsify it.

familia [Roman law] [Family] It may include:
(1) All those persons who were subject to the *potestas* of the same individual, whether his children, grandchildren, etc. or unconnected in blood, e.g. slaves.
(2) All descendants of the same ancestors.
(3) All persons agnate (*q.v.*).
(4) The slaves of a *paterfamilias* (*q.v.*).
(5) The property of a *paterfamilias.*

family assistance order An order under the Children Act 1989 s.16, whereby a local authority officer, CAFCASS officer or Welsh family proceedings officer is directed to advise, assist and befriend the person named in the order. See CAFCASS.

Family Division A division of the High Court created by the Administration of Justice Act 1970 s.1, by renaming the Probate, Divorce and Admiralty Division and redistributing the work of that court. See now Supreme Court Act 1981 s.5(1)(c). The President of the Family Division is the Head of Family Justice. There is a Deputy Head of Family Justice who is also Head of International Family Law. See Constitutional Reform Act 2005 s.9.

family proceedings [Formerly known as domestic proceedings] (1) Proceedings (which are not open to the public) before Magistrates under their domestic jurisdiction as set out in the Magistrates' Courts Act 1980 s.65; including proceedings under the Civil Partnership Act 2004 Sch.2 paras 69–72 of Sch.5 and Sch.6; the Adoption Act 2002; the Family Law Act 1996; the Children Act 1989 including family provision orders under Sch.1; and the Domestic Proceedings and Magistrates' Courts Act 1978 Pt 1.
(2) For the purposes of the Children Act 1989 s.8(3) defines certain types of proceedings as family proceedings. In these proceedings the court may exercise any of its powers to make orders under the Children Act 1989 in relation to a child, notwithstanding that an application has not been made in relation to such other orders (s.8(5) of the Children Act 1989).

family provision Benefit ordered by the court under the Inheritance (Provision for Family and Dependants) Act 1975 out of the estate of a deceased person on application by family or dependents who have not been adequately provided for by either the deceased under his will or by the rules of intestacy.
Application for such provision must generally be made within six months of representation being taken out. Those who may apply for provision are the deceased's spouse, child, former spouse who has not remarried, any person (not being a child of the deceased) who was treated by the deceased as a child of the family in relation to any marriage to which the deceased was a party; any person who during the whole of the two year period ending in the death of the deceased lived in the same household as the deceased as their husband or wife; and any other person who immediately before the death of the deceased was being maintained, either wholly or partly, by the deceased (1975 Act, s.1). The Civil Partnership Act 2004 amends s.1 and civil partners (*q.v.*) and former civil partners will also be entitled to claim under this Act.

famosus libellus [A scandalous libel (*q.v.*)]

farm business tenancy A tenancy granted after September 1, 1995 where since the start of the tenancy all or part of the land comprised in the tenancy has been farmed as part of a trade or business, the character of the tenancy is primarily or wholly agricultural, and certain notice conditions have been complied with. A tenancy of an agricultural holding cannot be a farm business tenancy. See Agricultural Tenancies Act 1995 s.1.

farm loss payment The Land Compensation Act 1973 provided for the payment of compensation to those displaced from an agricultural unit by compulsory purchase (*q.v.*) and who subsequently farmed another unit. Abolished by the Planning and Compulsory Purchase Act 2004 and replaced by Basic Loss Payments (*q.v.*) and Occupiers Loss Payments (*q.v.*).

fast day A day of abstinence from food declared by Royal Proclamation. Such a day was not a business day (*q.v.*).

fast track In civil proceedings there are three tracks and the selection of the appropriate track is generally governed by the financial value of the claim (CPR Pt 26). The fast track is the usual track in civil claims for any claim with a value of more than £5,000 but less than £15,000 provided the court considers that the trial is likely to last for no more than one day and any oral expert evidence will be limited to one expert per party in any expert area and expert evidence is used in no more than two expert areas. See TRACK ALLOCATION.

fatal accident An accident from which death unintentionally results. Under the Fatal Accidents Act 1976 s.1 where death is caused by any wrongful act, neglect or default which (if death had not ensued) would have entitled the person injured to maintain an action and recover damages, the person who would have been liable if death had not ensued shall be liable to an action for damages for the benefit of the dependents of the deceased. Dependents are the deceased's husband, wife, any person who immediately before and for the two years prior to the deceased's death was living with the deceased in the same household, children, grandchildren, stepchildren, parents, step-parents and grandparents and any person who is the issue of a brother, sister, uncle or aunt of the deceased. The Civil Partnership Act 2004 amends s.1 and civil partners (*q.v.*) and former civil partners will also be entitled to claim under this Act.

fatal accident claim In a fatal accident (*q.v.*) the claimant (*q.v.*) must state in his particulars of claim (*q.v.*) that the claim is brought under the Fatal Accidents Act 1976 (CPR PD 5.1). A fatal accident claim may include a claim for damages for bereavement (CPR PD 5.3).

fauces terrae A narrow inlet of the sea; a gulf.

fealty A service which every free tenant (except a tenant in frankalmoign (*q.v.*)) is in theory bound to perform to his feudal lord. It consisted of the tenant taking an oath of fidelity to the Lord.

federal state A state which apportions power between a central government and several regional governments in such a way that each is sovereign within its prescribed sphere.

fee Inheritable. Anciently land granted to a man and his heirs in return for services to be rendered to the feudal lord.

fee-farm rent A perpetual rent issuing out of land held in fee simple, reserved when the land was granted, and payable by the freeholder. A fee-farm rent is included in the term "rent-charge" (Law of Property Act 1925 s.205(1) (xxiii)) and is now subject to the provisions for extinguishment in the Rentcharges Act 1977 s.3. See RENTCHARGE.

fee simple Inheritable by any type of heir. A freehold right in land. An estate being the most extensive that a person can have under the Monarch; inheritance is clear of any condition, limitation or restriction to particular heirs.

fee tail See ENTAIL; ESTATE.

felo de se A person who commits suicide (*q.v.*).

felony At common law all felonies (except petty larceny) resulted in the offender forfeiting goods and land to the Crown and being sentenced to death. Statute also created numerous felonies. Forfeiture was abolished by the 1870 Forfeiture Act but the distinction between felony and misdemeanour remained until the Criminal Law Act 1967. The distinction between felonies and misdemeanours still exists in the United States of America.

female circumcision The excision, infibulation or mutilation of the whole or any part of the labia minora, labia majora or clitoris of another person is an offence under the Female Genital Mutilation Act 2003.

feodum A fee (*q.v.*).

feoffee to uses A person to whom a feoffment was made to the use of a *cestui que use* This vested the legal estate in the feoffee, who held on behalf of the beneficial owner, the *cestui que use* The Statute of Uses 1535 turned the use into the legal estate, and the *cestui que use* therefore became the legal owner. The feoffee to uses henceforth served merely as a conduit pipe, diverting the flow of the legal estate. The Statute of Uses was repealed by the Law of Property Act 1925.

feoffment Originally the grant of land in fee simple (*q.v.*) made by a feoffor to a feoffee was carried out by a ceremony known as livery of seisin. Once it became practice for the delivery to be recorded in writing the document was called a charter or deed of feoffment, and under the Real Property Act 1845 a feoffment had to be made by deed. Feoffments were abolished by the Law of Property Act 1925.

ferae naturae [Of a wild nature] See ANIMALS.

ferry A public highway across water connecting places where the public have rights of way. It can be granted by Royal charter or by statute or acquired by prescription (*q.v.*).

feu A perpetual lease at fixed rent.

feud (1) A fee (*q.v.*).
(2) An enmity or a quarrel.

feudal system The economic basis of society at the time of the Norman Conquest and beyond. After the Conquest all land was considered to be held of the king, who granted tenancies in chief by subinfeudation. The tenants in chief likewise granted land in return for services. All land holdings had a fixed quota of services and the tenant held the land as long as he performed them. In return he was entitled to protection from his lord. Services ranged from knight service owed by the chief tenants to the king, to villeinage where the agricultural services were not fixed and the villain (*q.v.*) was unfree. Prior to the Conquest the manor, comprising a vill or hamlet, had been the economic and social unit. In feudal legal theory, tenants holding of the same lord owed suit to the manor court, which controlled both agricultural activities and many other aspects of daily life. Feudalism was expounded as a system of tenures by Littleton in the 15th century, but by then the system had already changed drastically from its pristine purity, if that had ever existed.

fi. fa Abbreviation for fieri facias (*q.v.*).

fiat [Let it be done] A decree; a short order or warrant of a judge or public officer that certain steps should be taken. Many statutes provide that the *fiat* (consent) of the Attorney-General is necessary before proceedings are instituted.

fiat justitia [Let justice be done]

fiat justitia, ruat coelum [Let justice be done, though the heavens fall]

fictio legis non operatur damnum vel injuriam [A legal fiction does not work loss or injustice]

fiction, legal Maine used the term:
"to signify any assumption which conceals, or affects to conceal, the fact that a rule of law has undergone alteration, its letter remaining unchanged, its operation being modified."
Such fictions still exist in the form of, e.g. conclusive presumptions. The more extreme fictions were designed to give jurisdiction to courts and to extend substantive remedies by a false averment of a fact which could not be traversed, and were necessary in an era of formal pleading. An example was the collusive common recovery (*q.v.*).

fidei-commissarius [Roman law] The cestui que trust, the person to whom, by way of trust, the heir is required to give up the whole inheritance, or a share of it.

fidei-commissum [Roman law] A trust imposed upon the legal heir for the execution of the last wishes of a deceased person.

fide-jussor [Roman law] A surety.

fiduciary (1) A person who holds a position of trust in relation to another and who must therefore act for that person's benefit.
(2) A fiduciary relationship exists where someone is in a position of trust such as solicitors and their clients.

fieri facias [Cause to be made] A writ of execution addressed to a High Court Enforcement Officer and requiring him to seize property of the debtor in order to obtain payment of a judgment debt, interest and costs. Will be renamed a writ of control when the Tribunal, Courts and Enforcement Act 2007 s.62 comes into force.

fieri feci The return to a writ of fieri facias that the stated sum has been levied.

filacers Officers of the court who filed original writs.

filing In relation to a document, means delivering it, by post or otherwise, to the court office. The date on which a document was filed is recorded on the document by a seal or receipt stamp.

filius nullius [Son of nobody] A bastard.

filiusfamilias; filiafamilias [Roman law] Son; daughter. Any persons under the *patria potestas* of another.

film A recording on any medium from which a moving image may by any means be produced and including any accompanying soundtrack (Copyright, Designs and Patents Act 1988 s.5B).

final judgment The final order that ends civil proceedings, usually made by the trial court. A final judgment may be appealed. Compare an interlocutory order (*q.v.*).

final process A writ of execution on a judgment or decree.

Finance Bill A Parliamentary Bill dealing with taxation. The annual budget proposals are contained in the Finance Bill. A Finance Bill cannot be delayed by the House of Lords.

Finance Houses Association A company limited by guarantee established in 1945 to promote the interests of its members, the finance houses. It merged in 1992 with the Equipment Leasing Association to form the Finance & Leasing Association (*q.v.*).

Finance & Leasing Association The major UK representative body for the asset finance, consumer finance and motor finance sectors. It was formed in January

1992, by a merger of the Finance Houses Association and the Equipment Leasing Association.

finance lease In commercial usage a lease (or bailment (*q.v.*)) of equipment usually to one lessor for substantially the whole of the useful life of the equipment. In contrast, an operating lease is where equipment is leased for short end on contracts to a series of lessors, e.g. car hire. See Supply of Goods and Services Act 1982.

financial assistance It is unlawful for a public company or any of its subsidiaries to give financial assistance to a person for the purchase of the company's own shares, Companies Act 2006 s.678. This prohibition no longer applies to private companies.

financial loss A plaintiff may claim against a defendant for financial loss incurred as a consequence of the defendant's negligence. The development of the concept in *Junior Books Ltd v The Veitchi Co Ltd* [1982] 3 W.L.R. 477 has been discouraged in *Simaan General Contracting Co v Pilkington Glass Ltd (No.2)* [1988] 2 W.L.R. 761.

financial provision orders Orders made by the courts when granting decrees of divorce, nullity or judicial separation (see s.23 of the Matrimonial Causes Act 1973, orders for maintenance and lump sum provision).

financial relief Any or all of the following: orders for maintenance pending suit (*q.v.*), financial provision orders (*q.v.*), property adjustment orders (*q.v.*) and orders for maintenance during marriage. Financial relief provisions for children are consolidated in the Children Act 1989, but see also child support.

Financial Services and Markets The Financial Services and Markets Act 2000 (*q.v.*) provides a statutory framework which regulates the carrying on of investment business. The Act established a new, single financial regulator, the Financial Services Authority (FSA) (*q.v.*). It provides disciplinary sanctions in respect of behaviour defined as market abuse.

Financial Services and Markets Tribunal It considers appeals against decisions of the Financial Services Authority (*q.v.*), Financial Services and Markets Act 2000, s.132.

Financial Services Authority (FSA) The Financial Services and Markets Act 2000 provides a single legal framework for the regulation of the financial services industry under the Financial Services Authority, formerly the Securities and Investments Board. The FSA is a company limited by guarantee with four statutory objectives, market confidence, public awareness, consumer protection and the reduction of financial crime. It replaced various self regulating organisations and its powers include: making arrangement for regulation and authorisation of firms and individuals operating in insurance; investment business; and banking. It has powers to impose financial penalties for abuse of investment markets.

The FSA also operates as the United Kingdom Listing Authority (UKLA) (*q.v.*) having replaced the Stock Exchange in this role. As such it is responsible for the maintenance and the admission of company securities to the Official List (*q.v.*).

Financial Services Ombudsman (FSO) Set up under the Financial Services and Markets Act 2000, it is the single financial services ombudsman. The services covers banking, endowment policies, investment and insurance.

financial year Financial Year when used in any Act of Parliament passed after 1889, unless the contrary intention appears, the 12 calendar months ending on March 31. A company pays corporation tax on its chargeable profits calculated by reference to its accounting period. Corporation tax is charged on the financial year, which runs from April 1 to March 31. The year of assessment, or tax year (*q.v.*) for income tax purposes runs from April 6 to the following April 5. Annual public accounts are made up for the 12 calendar months ending on March 31.

finding (1) A conclusion upon an inquiry of fact.

(2) Under the Theft Act 1968 s.2(1)(c) the finding and keeping of lost things may constitute theft if the finder believes that the owner could be discovered on taking reasonable steps.

fine (1) A sum of money ordered to be paid to the Crown on conviction for an offence.

(2) A premium paid for the grant or renewal of a lease.

(3) A money payment made from a feudal tenant to his lord.

(4) A judicial proceeding used for conveying land. A fictitious suit was instituted and compromised with the consent of the court, and an agreement entered into between the parties as to the disposal of the land in question. A note of the proceedings was drawn up by an officer called the chirographer, and a document, called the chirograph or foot of the fine, which recited the whole proceedings was enrolled in the records of the court and delivered to the purchaser as a deed of title. A fine was one of the methods of barring an estate tail. It could be used by a person not in possession of the land, but it resulted in the creation of a base fee only. Fines were abolished by the Fines and Recoveries Act 1833.

fingerprints By s.65 of the Police and Criminal Evidence Act 1984 fingerprints, in relation to any person, means a record (in any form and produced by any method) of the skin pattern and other physical characteristics or features of any fingers or the palm.

finis finem litibus imponit [A fine puts an end to legal proceedings]

fire damage An occupier of land is liable for damage caused by a fire started negligently or by a non-natural use of the land, but not for a fire begun by accident, Fires Prevention (Metropolis) Act 1774.

firearms The Firearms Act 1968 contains detailed provisions defining firearms (s.57(1)) and regulating their use and possession, in particular making it an offence to possess or acquire a firearm or a shot-gun without holding a firearms or shot-gun certificate. Various exemptions are specified in the Act. The Firearms Act 1982 extends the provisions to imitation firearms that can be easily converted into firearms, the Firearms (Amendment) Act 1988, introduced after the Hungerford incident, strengthened some of the controls on the more dangerous types of shot-guns, etc. and the Firearms (Amendment) Act 1997 places restrictions on the transfer of firearms.

firm A business organisation, usually a partnership (*q.v.*) governed by the Partnership Act 1890. The firm name is the name under which the partners carry on business and an action by or against the firm, unless it is inappropriate to do so, must be brought in or against the firm name under CPR PD7 para.5A.

firma Victuals, rent, or a farm.

first fruits Annates (*q.v.*).

first impression A case which presents to a court of law for its decision a question of law for which there is no precedent.

First Minister The Scottish equivalent of Prime Minister. He is appointed under the Scotland Act 1998 s.45 and must be a member of the Scottish parliament. He is keeper of the Scottish Seal. See DEVOLUTION.

first registration A person in whom an unregistered legal estate is vested or who is entitled to have such an estate invested in him may apply to the Chief Land Registrar to be registered as the first proprietor of that unregistered legal estate (see s.3, Land Registration Act 2002). See LAND REGISTRATION, CAUTION.

First-tier Tribunal The Tribunals, Courts and Enforcement Act 2007 establishes as part of a new unified tribunal system a Tribunal with original jurisdiction to hear cases previously heard by the diverse range of tribunals across the judicial system. It retains a degree of specialism in that it is divided into three chambers: Social Entitlement; War Pensions and Armed Forces Compensation; and Health, Education and Social Care. The first of these hears appeals on a range of matters including asylum support cases, criminal injuries compensation, social security benefits and industrial accidents. The third chamber hears appeals related to, for example, children with special educational needs, the provision of health or social care and the registration of social workers. Appeals from the First-tier Tribunal go to the Upper Tribunal (*q.v.*). See ADMINISTRATIVE JUSTICE & TRIBUNALS COUNCIL; SENIOR PRESIDENT OF TRIBUNALS.

fish royal Whale, porpoise and sturgeon which, when caught near the coast or thrown ashore, are the property of the sovereign. The prerogative rights of the Crown with regard to wild animals were abolished by the Wild Creatures and Forest Laws Act 1971 but it contained a saving for royal fish.

fishery or piscary (1) A Royal fishery is the exclusive right of the Crown of fishing in a public river.

(2) A public or common fishery is the right of the public to fish in the sea and in public navigable rivers as far as the tide flows.

(3) A several fishery is an exclusive right of fishing in a particular water, and vested either in the owner of the soil or in someone claiming under him.

(4) Common of fishery is the right of fishing in another man's waters (e.g. the lord of the manor) in common with him. It is a profit a prendre.

(5) A free fishery is either a Royal fishery granted to a subject, or a common of fishery.

fit for habitation A statutory implied covenant relating to certain tenancies at low rent. Premises that are defective in, e.g. repair, natural lighting, drainage and sanitary conveniences, will not be fit for habitation.

fitness for purpose (sale of goods) See IMPLIED TERMS.

fitness to plead See UNFITNESS TO PLEAD; INSANITY.

fixed charge A charge on specific property of, e.g. a company. Compare a floating charge (*q.v.*).

fixed costs Costs in civil claims which are set at a certain level and can be claimed by one party from the other in specified circumstances. For example, where a claim is begun but no acknowledgement is received from the defendant, a claimant can obtain judgment and an order for fixed costs to be paid to be put towards the expense of beginning the claim. See CPR Pt 45.

fixed penalty notice A notice offering the opportunity of the discharge of any liability to conviction of the offence to which it relates by payment of a fixed penalty. See for example Pt III of the Road Traffic Offenders Act 1988 s.52(1).

fixed sum credit Credit for a specific amount which is fixed at the outset of a consumer credit agreement, e.g. hire purchase, personal loan. Contrast running account credit such as a bank overdraft. See the Consumer Credit Act 1974 s.10.

fixed term A tenancy or lease for a fixed period. The date of commencement and the length of the term must be agreed before there can be a legally binding lease.

fixed-date summons The term used, prior to the implementation of the Civil Procedure Rules 1998, for a summons form in the County Courts used to initiate a claim for a remedy other than money. Such actions are now begun using a standard claim form.

fixtures Any chattel that has been annexed to land or a building so as to become part of it. As a general rule anything so annexed becomes part of the realty (*q.v.*) and belongs to the owner of the soil. Some chattels such as articles of ornamental or domestic convenience (tenant's fixtures) or those erected to carry out a business (trade fixtures) may be removable. Whether a chattel has become a fixture which the tenant has no right to remove depends primarily upon the object and purposes of the annexation of the chattel to the property.

flagrante delicto [In the commission of the offence]

floating charge or security A type of equitable charge on a class of assets, such as stock in trade, or even the company's entire undertaking, which floats over those assets until it "crystallises" and then attaches to the relevant assets. In the meantime the company is able to deal with the assets in the ordinary course of business. It is often used as security for debentures (*q.v.*) issued by the company. The Enterprise Act 2002 modified the rights of floating charge holders with the effect that 50 per cent of the first £10,000 in respect of the proceeds of sale of the charged assets and 20 per cent of the rest up to a maximum of £600,000 is to be available for unsecured creditors.

floor of the court The part of the court between the judge's bench and the first row of counsels' seats.

flotation A term referring to the process when a company's securities are admitted to trading on the Stock Exchange (*q.v.*) and offered for sale to the public.

flotsam Floating wreckage which if unclaimed belong to the Crown. Under the Merchant Shipping Acts they are wreck (*q.v.*). See JETSAM.

flying freehold A freehold flat that is above ground level, an upper storey.

foenus nauticum [Roman law] The interest charged for money secured by what corresponded to out bottomry bond (*q.v.*).

foldage The right of the lord of the manor of having his tenant's sheep to feed on his fields, so as to manure the land, in return for which the lord provides a fold for the sheep.

foldcourse The right of the lord of the manor of feeding a certain number of sheep on the lands of the tenant during certain times of the year.

following trust property See TRACING.

food Under the Food Safety Act 1990 food has the same meaning as that provided in EC Regulation 2002/178, which lays down general principles and requirements of food law. Food, or foodstuff, means any substance or product, whether processed, partially processed or unprocessed, intended to be, or reasonably expected to be ingested by humans. It includes drink, chewing gum and any substance, including water, intentionally incorporated into the food during its manufacture, preparation or treatment. The Act regulates the sale of food and creates numerous offences for those who fail to comply.

football match The Sporting Events (Control of Alcohol, etc.) Act 1985 created offences relating to the possession of alcohol, being drunk and causing or permitting the carriage of alcohol on trains and coaches at or en route to designated sporting events.
　　The Football (Disorder) Act 2000 allows the imposition of banning orders preventing attendance at specified football matches. It also empowers the police to stop persons travelling to specified matches, to seize passports and require the suspect to appear before a magistrate within 24 hours.
　　Under the Football Spectators Act 1989, admission to a designated football match is controlled and under the Football (Offences) Act 1991, the Football (Offences and Disorder) Act 1999 and the Football (Disorder) Act 2000

disorderly conduct there is also controlled. Offences by spectators include throwing missiles and racist chanting.

footpath A highway (*q.v.*), other than a footway, over which the public have a right of way on foot only. See Highways Act 1980 s.329.

footway A way over which the public have a right of way on foot only and which is part of a highway (*q.v.*) over which there is also a right of way for vehicles.

forbearance A deliberate failure to exercise a legal right such as a right to sue for a debt. Such forbearance, if made at the debtor's request, may constitute consideration (*q.v.*) for a fresh promise by the debtor.

force majeure Coercion or irresistible compulsion. It is used in commercial contracts to describe events that might happen which would prevent a party from performing the contract by circumstances that are entirely outside the control of the parties to the contract, e.g. Act of God, fire, flood, riot.

forced marriage One where a person 'A' is forced into a marriage without A's free and full consent by the conduct of another person 'B'. The coercion used may be threats or other psychological means against A, B or another person (Family Law Act 1996 s.63A, as amended).

forcible detainer The misdemeanour committed by a person who, having wrongfully entered upon any land or tenements, detained them with violence or threats. It was abolished by the Criminal Law Act 1977 and replaced by new offences of entering and remaining on property.

forcible entry Entering land in a violent manner in order to take possession of it was a misdemeanour abolished by the Criminal Law Act 1977. The Act substituted the offence of using or threatening violence against people or property in order to secure entry into premises. There is a defence for entry secured by a displaced residential occupier (*q.v.*) or a protected intending occupier.

foreclosure When a mortgagor has failed to pay off the mortgage debt within the proper time, the mortgagee is entitled to bring an action in the Chancery Division by Part 8 claim form asking that a day be fixed on which the mortgagor is to pay off the debt and that in default of payment on that day the mortgagor may be foreclosed of his equity of redemption (*q.v.*), i.e. he will lose the mortgaged property. This order is a foreclosure order nisi. If it is not complied with the court may make the foreclosure order nisi absolute and the mortgaged property will then belong to the mortgagee, Law of Property Act 1925 s.88(2).

foreign Outside the jurisdiction of the court. For example a "foreign plea" was a plea contesting the jurisdiction of the court.

foreign agreement An agreement the proper law of which is not that of the United Kingdom.

foreign bill Any bill of exchange (*q.v.*) other than an inland bill.

foreign corporations Under the Foreign Corporations Act 1991, foreign corporations incorporated under the law of territories which the United Kingdom does not recognise as states may be treated as having legal personality.

foreign currency Any currency other than sterling.

Foreign Enlistment Act 1870 It is an offence under the Act (without the licence of the Crown) to enlist in the military or naval service of any foreign state which is at war with any state with which the United Kingdom is at peace.

foreign judgments The judgment of a foreign court may be enforced in an English court provided that certain conditions are met. See Foreign Judgments (Reciprocal Enforcement) Act 1933 and the Civil Jurisdiction and Judgments

Act 1982, as amended, which implement the provisions of the Brussels (1968) and Lugano (1989) Conventions on the jurisdiction and enforcement of judgments in civil and commercial matters.

foreign jurisdiction The jurisdiction of a state with regard to its subjects when they are, or the acts done by them are, outside its boundaries. See the Foreign Jurisdiction Acts 1890 and 1913.

foreign law Any legal system other than that of England. When a question of foreign law arises in a dispute in an English court it is usually treated as a matter of fact on which expert evidence is required, but it is determinable by the judge and not by a jury.

foreign revenue United Kingdom courts will not enforce the revenue laws of other sovereign states.

foreign travel order A civil order which may be applied for by the police under the Sexual Offences Act 2003 s.114. It prohibits those who have been convicted of offences against children under 16 and sentenced to 12 months or more from travelling abroad. The court making the order must be satisfied that it is necessary to protect children outside the UK.

foreman The spokesperson of a jury panel.

forensic medicine Medical jurisprudence: "that science which teaches the application of every branch of medical knowledge to the purposes of the law" (Taylor).

foreseeability The test of reasonable foreseeability is applied in determining liability in tort, contract and criminal law. In criminal cases, foreseeability may be relevant to both the actus reus (*q.v.*) and the mens rea (*q.v.*) of an offence. In offences, such as homicide, which require as part of the actus reus that the defendant's actions caused a certain consequence to occur, the defendant may not be liable if the required consequence was not a reasonably foreseeable consequence of his actions; see, for example, *Pagett* (1983) 76 Cr. App. R. 279. With regard to mens rea, the judge is required to direct the jury that, in determining whether a person has committed an offence, they are not bound to infer that he intended or foresaw a result of his actions merely because it was a natural and probable consequence of those actions but shall decide whether he did intend or foresee that result by reference to all the evidence (Criminal Justice Act 1967 s.8). Foresight is not the same as intention. However, in murder (*q.v.*), the mens rea for which is intention to cause death or grievous bodily harm, the jury may find that the defendant intended to cause death or do grievous bodily harm if death or grievous bodily harm was a virtual certain consequence of the defendant's actions and the defendant himself foresaw death or grievous bodily harm as being virtually certain to occur (*R. v Woollin* [1999] A.C. 82). In tort, the concept of what is reasonably foreseeable has been developed from *Donoghue v Stevenson* [1932] A.C. 532, where Lord Atkin said:
"You must take reasonable care to avoid acts or omissions which you can reasonably foresee would injure your neighbour—persons who are so closely and directly affected by my act that I ought reasonably to have had them in contemplation as being so affected when I am directing my mind to the acts or omissions which are called in question."
In contract the concept is particularly important in deciding on whether damages are too remote, see *Hadley v Baxendale* (1854) 9 Ex. 341; and *Koufos v Czarnikow Ltd* [1969] 1 A.C. 350. See RECKLESSNESS.

foreshore That part of the land adjacent to the sea and which is alternately covered and left dry by the ordinary flow of the tides. The property in the foreshore is prima facie vested in the Crown. Management of the foreshore is in the hands of the Crown Estate Commissioners. See TIDAL WATERS.

forest Formerly the exclusive right of keeping and hunting wild beasts and fowls of forest, chase, park and warren in a certain territory, with laws and officers of its own for the protection of the game. Now, primarily, forests are where timber is grown. National forests are maintained by the Forestry Commission. See the Forestry Act 1967 as amended.

forestall (1) To obstruct a person's way with force and arms.
(2) To raise the price of certain goods by holding up supplies, etc.

forfeiture A landlord may forfeit a lease, that is re-enter the demised property if the tenant breaches a covenant in the lease. The Law of Property Act 1925 requires the landlord to serve notice of intended forfeiture, specifying the alleged breach and requiring its remedy. Tenants may seek relief against forfeiture from the court. See LANDLORD AND TENANT.

forgavel A quit rent.

forgery The Forgery and Counterfeiting Act 1981 largely regulates these offences. The Act is based on the recommendations of the Law Commission and is a codifying statute. A person is guilty of forgery if he makes a false instrument, with the intention that he or another shall use it to induce somebody to accept it as genuine, and by reason of so accepting it to do or not do some act to his own or any other person's prejudice. The principal offences created are forgery contrary to s.1; copying a false instrument contrary to s.2; using a false instrument contrary to s.3; and possession of certain forged documents and machines for making forgeries.

forinsecus [Outside]

forjudge To deprive a person of a thing or right by a judgment.

forma pauperis See IN FORMA PAUPERIS.

forms of action See ACTION.

formulae [Roman law] The Praetorian procedure which superseded the *legis actiones*, under which the Praetor allowed the parties to a dispute to put in writing the issue to be decided by the arbitrators, and then, if the resulting *formula* met with his approval, he authorised the arbitrators to condemn or acquit the defendant according to his direction. A *formula* was a hypothetical command to a *judex*, to condemn the defendant to pay a sum of money to the plaintiff, if the latter established a right or proved an allegation of fact.

fornication Voluntary sexual intercourse between man and woman outside the bounds of matrimony. As such, it is not an offence. See ADULTERY.

forthwith As soon as reasonably can be (*Hillingdon LBC v Cutler* [1968] 1 Q.B. 124).

fortuna Treasure trove (*q.v.*).

forum [A place] A place where disputes may be tried. The court in which a case is brought. See LEX FORI.

forum rei The court of the country in which the subject of the dispute is situated.

fostering Looking after a child that is not your own, nor a relative, nor one for whom you have parental responsibility, for more than 28 days. Private fostering is now regulated by the Children Act 1989 Pt IX.

foster parent A local authority carrying out its duty to provide accommodation for a child whom it is looking after may place a child with a family, relative or other suitable person. Any such person with whom the child is placed is referred to in the Children Act 1989 as a local authority foster parent (s.23(2) and (3), ibid.) A local authority must pay regard to Fostering Service Regulations 2002 in deciding

191

whether or not to place a child with a local authority foster parent. A foster parent is defined by the regulations to mean a person with whom a child is placed, or may be placed under the regulations (a person who has not been duly approved and who, in an emergency situation, cares for a child for less than six weeks being excluded from this definition), see reg.2, ibid.

founders' shares See DEFERRED SHARES.

four corners Within the four corners of a document, etc. means contained exclusively within the document, etc. itself.

four seas Within the four seas, meaning within the United Kingdom.

Four-day Order Previously an order under RSC Ord. 42, r.2 which was replaced by the implementation of the Civil Procedure Rules 1998 (see CPR Pt 3).

fourteen day costs Formerly a form of fixed costs (*q.v.*) paid when a defendant admitted a claim for money in the High Court. Now governed by the CPR Pt 45.3.

fractionem diei non recipit lex [The law does not recognise any fraction of a day]

franchise (1) A special right conferred on a subject by the Crown, an example is the right to hold a market. It is an incorporeal hereditament.
(2) The right to vote at an election. Women over 21 were enfranchised in 1929. Under the Representation of the People Act 2000 the age at which those not otherwise incapacitated become eligible to vote is 18 years.

frankalmoign [Free alms] The free tenures originating in Saxon times, by which church lands were sometimes held, but ecclesiastics often held by military service. It involved no services except praying for the soul of the donor. It is now in effect, socage tenure.

franked investment income Dividends and other distributions received by a company as shareholder of another UK company together with the relevant tax credit. As a result the distribution is not therefore generally subject to corporation tax as far as the recipient company is concerned.

frank-fee Freehold land.

frank tenement Freehold.

frankmarriage A dowry or gift free from services to a woman about to marry. Land given in frankmarriage created an estate in tail special if it was given to a husband and wife by some blood relation of the wife. It was held by the husband and wife to them and their issue to the fourth degree free of services to the donor.

frankpledge The system of preserving the peace in force at the time of the Conquest by the compulsory association of men into groups of 10, each of whom was a surety for the others. The "view of frankpledge" was the duty of seeing that these associations were kept in perfect order and number, and was vested in the local courts, especially the Courts Leet.

fraud The obtaining of a material advantage by unfair or wrongful means; it involves obliquity. It involves the making of a false representation knowingly, or without belief in its truth, or recklessly. If the fraud causes injury the deceived party may claim damages for the tort of deceit. A contract obtained by fraud is voidable at the option of the injured party. Conspiracy to defraud remains a common law offence the *mens rea* of which has been defined as:
"to cause the victim economic loss by depriving him of some property or right corporeal or incorporeal, to which he is or would or might become entitled" (per Lord Diplock in *Scott v Metropolitan Police Commissioner* [1974] 3 All E.R. 1032).

Certain other frauds are likewise criminal offences.

The Fraud Act 2006 s.1, introduces a new general offence of fraud with three ways of committing it: fraud by representation; fraud by failing to disclose information; and fraud by abuse of position. The Act also creates the offences of: possessing, making or supplying an article for use in frauds; participating in fraudulent trading (*q.v.*) other than as a corporate trader; and obtaining services dishonestly.

fraud on a power The failure to exercise a special power of appointment bona fide to the end appointed by the donor, such as when the appointor intends to defeat what the donor of the power intended. Where an appointment is made in favour of a person of at least 25 years of age, who is entitled to a share in default of appointment, a purchaser for value without notice of fraud is protected to the extent of that share.

fraud on the minority One of the exceptions to the rule in *Foss v Harbottle* (1843) 2 Hare 461. The rule provides that, where a wrong has been done to a company, it is the company which has the right to decide whether to sue. Under this exception a shareholder was previously able to bring a derivative action (*q.v.*) but had to show fraud which was used in this context in a wide commercial sense, covering an abuse or misuse of power. The shareholder bringing the action also had to show that the wrongdoer had control of the company. Such proceedings are now only permitted as statutory derivative actions (*q.v.*).

Frauds, Statute of See STATUTE OF FRAUDS.

fraudulent conversion This is now included in the definition of theft in the Theft Act 1968.

fraudulent conveyance A disposition of land made without consideration and with intent to defraud a subsequent purchaser. Under the Law of Property Act 1925 it is voidable by the purchaser.

fraudulent misrepresentation See MISREPRESENTATION.

fraudulent preference See PREFERENCE.

fraudulent trading If in the course of the winding up of a company it appears that any business of the company has been carried on with intent to defraud creditors or for any fraudulent purpose then the court may order that any persons who were knowingly party to this conduct are liable to contribute such amount to the company's assets as the court thinks proper, Insolvency Act 1986 s.213. Fraudulent trading is also a criminal offence, Companies Act 2006 s.993. See WRONGFUL TRADING.

A director of a company who has been involved in fraudulent trading may be disqualified from acting as a director, Company Directors Disqualification Act 1986.

fraus omnia vitiat [Fraud vitiates everything]

free entry A customs entry for free (i.e. non-dutiable) goods.

free movement In order to achieve the Internal Market (*q.v.*) the EC Treaty makes specific Treaty provision, substantiated by EC secondary legislation to secure the free movement of goods, persons, services and capital. These are regarded as the fundamental freedoms (*q.v.*) in EC Law. See INTERNAL MARKET; FUNDAMENTAL FREEDOMS.

free movement of goods The cornerstone of Community law; one of the fundamental freedoms (*q.v.*) of Community law. Articles 23–31 of the EC Treaty provide for the creation of a customs union (*q.v.*) and the prohibition of quantitative restrictions on goods between Member States. See COMMON CUSTOMS TARIFF; CUSTOMS UNION; QUANTITATIVE RESTRICTION.

free movement of persons One of the fundamental freedoms (*q.v.*) of European Community law. The EC Treaty provides for the freedom of movement of citizens of the European Union, subject to conditions and limitations laid down by the Treaty. The free movement of workers and the self employed is provided for by arts 39 and 43 of the Treaty and various directives provide for the free movement of other persons, including students, who have sufficient financial resources not to become a burden on the host Member State. See CITIZENSHIP OF EUROPEAN UNION; INTERNAL MARKET.

freebench An estate analogous to dower (*q.v.*) which, by custom of most manors, the widow of a copyholder had in the land of which her husband had been tenant. It was abolished by the Law of Property Act 1922 and the Administration of Estates Act 1925.

freedom from encumbrance Property free of any binding rights of parties other than the owner. In contracts for the sale of goods (unless the contrary is specifically agreed) the seller impliedly warrants the goods to be free of encumbrances, Sale of Goods Act 1979 s.12.

freedom of establishment One of the fundamental freedoms (*q.v.*) of Community law. Under art.43 of the EC Treaty restrictions on the freedom of establishment of nationals of the Member States in the territory of another Member State is prohibited. Freedom of establishment includes the right to take up and pursue activities as self employed persons and to set up and manage undertakings, in particular companies or firms. See INTERNAL MARKET.

freedom of information The Freedom of Information Act 2000 provides that any person making a request for information to a public authority is entitled to be informed in writing by the public authority whether it holds information of the description specified in the request (the duty to confirm or deny) and, if that is the case, to have that information communicated to him. There are numerous exceptions to these rights. Schedule I lists what is covered by public authorities.

freedom of testation The right of a testator to divide his estate in whatever manner he chooses. It is subject to the courts' power to set aside wills made when the testator was of unsound mind and to provide reasonable maintenance for dependants under the Inheritance (Provision for Family and Dependants) Act 1975.

freedom to provide services One of the fundamental freedoms (*q.v.*) of Community law. Article 49 of the EC Treaty provides that restrictions on freedom to provide services within the Community shall be prohibited in respect of nationals of Member States who are established in a State of the Community other than that of the person for whom the services are intended. Services in this context are normally provided for remuneration and include services of an industrial, commercial, professional character and services of craftsmen.

freehold A legal estate in fee simple in possession. The most complete form of ownership of land.

freehold tenure Under the feudal system, land was held by military or socage tenure, both of which were freehold tenures. After the English Revolution, military tenure was abolished. There were three freehold estates: fee simple; fee tail; and life estate. Contrast freehold with leasehold (*q.v.*).

freeing for adoption The process by which consent to the adoption of one's child in general terms rather than by specific adopters, or the making of a court order on statutory grounds was made. Once an order was made parental rights and duties were vested in the adoption agency. The process of freeing for adoption was abolished by the Adoption and Children Act 2002, which makes provision for children to be placed for adoption by virtue of a placement order, or upon parental consent. See ADOPTION.

freeman One who possesses the freedom of a borough or city and the accompanying rights and privileges, such as a right to graze cattle on corporation land. The rights of freemen of a borough were preserved by the Local Government Act 1972.

freezing injunctions Defined in CPR, r.25.(1)(f) as an order which restrains a party from removing assets from the court's jurisdiction, or from dealing with any assets located inside or outside the court's jurisdiction. Such an order was commonly referred to as a "Mareva" injunction prior to the implementation of the Civil Procedure Rules 1998.

freezing orders The courts can make an order under the Matrimonial Causes Act 1973 s.37, preventing and setting aside dispositions of property made with the intention of defeating a claim for financial relief.

freight (1) The amount payable under a contract for the carriage of goods by sea. The shipowner has a lien on the goods carried for unpaid freight.
(2) The profit of a shipowner for the use of his ship.

fresh disseisin That disseisin (*q.v.*) which formerly a person might seek to defeat himself by his own power, as where it was not above, e.g. 15 days old.

fresh suit The following of a thing or person at once with the intention of reclamation. See CPR Pt 8.

friendly societies Unincorporated mutual insurance associations, registered under the Friendly Societies Acts 1974 and 1992, established to provide by the voluntary subscriptions of their members for the relief or maintenance of the members and their families during sickness or old age, and their widows and orphan children. Under the Consumer Credit Act 1974, mortgage lending by friendly societies was exempted, but the legislation has been amended by, e.g. the Building Societies Act 1986.

friendly suit [Pursuit] A suit brought between parties by mutual arrangement in order to obtain a decision upon some point in which both are interested.

frith The peace; a tract of common land.

frithsoken The right to take the view of frankpledge (*q.v.*).

from Subject to the context, it ordinarily excludes the day from which time is to be reckoned.

frontager A person owning or occupying land which abuts on a highway, river or seashore.

fructus industriales [Fruits of industry] Crops or produce of the soil that are the result of labour in sowing the seed or cultivation. In a sale of *fructus industriales*, on the terms that the owner of the soil is to cut or sever them from the land before delivery, the purchaser acquires no interest in the land, which is like a mere warehouse. See EMBLEMENTS.

fructus naturales [Fruits of nature] Crops or produce of the soil which grow naturally, such as grass, timber, etc.

frustra legis auxilium quaerit qui in legem committit [He who offends against the law vainly seeks the help of the law]

frustration Under the doctrine of frustration a contract may be discharged if, after its formation, events occur making its performance impossible, illegal or radically different from that which was contemplated at the time it was entered into.

FTSE indices Indices, e.g. the FTSE 100 index, which monitor the movements in securities on stock markets.

fugam fecit [He has made flight]

fugitive criminal A person accused or convicted of committing an extradition (*q.v.*) crime within the jurisdiction of any foreign state, who is in or is suspected of being in some part of her Majesty's dominions. Such person is liable to be surrendered to that country under the Extradition Act 2003.

full age Eighteen years of age. A person attains full age on reaching the age of 18.

full title guarantee The guarantee of title normally given by a seller of property who owns both the legal and equitable interests in the property. The covenants implied on a disposition of property by the use of such a guarantee are set out in Pt I of the Law of Property (Miscellaneous) Provisions Act 1994.

functus officio [Having discharged his duty] Once a magistrate has convicted a person charged with an offence before him, he is *functus officio*, and cannot rescind the sentence and retry the case.

fundamental freedoms The four freedoms that form the cornerstone of the European Community, viz. free movement (*q.v.*) of goods, persons, services and capital, see art.14 of the EC Treaty. The internal market (*q.v.*) shall comprise an area without internal frontiers in which the free movement of goods, persons, services and capital is ensured in accordance with the provisions of the EC Treaty.

fundus cum instrumento [Roman law] A farm with its stock and implements of culture including everything on a farm placed there for the purpose of its cultivation and necessary for cultivation.

fundus instructus [Roman law] A farm with furnishings, as well as stock and implements.

funeral expenses The reasonable costs of burial of the deceased. It is the first priority for payment from his estate.

furnished tenancy See ASSURED TENANCY; PROTECTED TENANCY.

further assurance See COVENANTS FOR TITLE.

further information A request for further information may be made under CPR Pt 18 by a party in civil proceedings in order to clarify any matter in dispute, or to give additional information in relation to any such matter, even though the matter may not be contained in a statement of case. The court also has a power to request further information from a party to the proceedings. Further information now generally covers the procedures formerly referred to as requests for further and better particulars and interrogatories.

furtum conceptum [Roman law] Where in a man's house before witnesses, something that has been stolen is sought and found. An *actio concepti* lies against the occupier.

furtum oblatum [Roman law] Where something that has been stolen is brought to a man's house with the intention that it shall be found there, and is so found on formal search in his house. The occupier has an *actio oblati* against the bringer.

future estates Estates limited to come into existence at some future time, such as contingent remainders (*q.v.*). They now exist only as equitable interests.

future goods Goods to be manufactured or acquired by a seller after the contract for sale has been made, Sale of Goods Act 1979 s.61. Where by a contract of sale the seller agrees to effect a present sale of future goods, the contract operates as an agreement to sell the goods, ibid. s.5(3).

future interest See FUTURE ESTATES.

future lease A lease that gives the tenant the right to possession on a future date.

future property Property which will be caught by, or subject to, a covenant presently made when it comes into possession at some future date, e.g. a covenant to settle after-acquired property on the trusts of a marriage settlement.

futures contract A contract to buy or sell at a future date.

G

GATT General Agreement on Tariffs and Trade (*q.v.*).

gage A pledge or pawn. See MORTGAGE.

gager de deliverance To give surety for the delivery of the goods which were in dispute in the action of replevin (*q.v.*).

gale Gavel (*q.v.*).

gambling Under the Gambling Act 2005 s.3, gambling means gaming (s.6), betting (s.9) and participating in a lottery (s.14). See GAMING; BETTING; LOTTERY.

Gambling Appeals Tribunal Set up to hear appeals from decisions of the Gambling Commission relating to the terms of gambling operating licences or the refusal to grant such licences.

Gambling Commission Established as a non-departmental government body by the Gambling Act 2005, it acts as a single regulator for gaming in Great Britain, taking over the role of the Gaming Board in regulating casinos, bingo, gaming machines and lotteries (except the National Lottery). It also has responsibility for overseeing betting and remote gambling and for preventing children and vulnerable people from being exploited by gambling.

gambling policies A person who effects a contract of marine insurance without having a bona fide interest therein commits an offence. Such a contract is deemed to be a contract by way of gambling on loss by maritime perils and the person effecting the contract is guilty of an offence under the Marine Insurance (Gambling Policies) Act 1909.

game Wild animals and birds hunted for sport. Under the Game Act 1831, game consists of: hares, pheasants, partridges, grouse, heath or moor game, and black-game. The right to kill game upon land is vested in the occupier unless the lease reserves it to the landlord.

game of chance Includes a game that involves both an element of chance and skill, a game that involves an element of chance that can be eliminated by superlative skill and a game that is presented as involving an element of chance. It does not include a sport. See Gambling Act 2005 s.6.

gaming Under the Gambling Act 2005 s.6, gaming means the playing of a game of chance for a prize. Gaming is regulated by the Gambling Act 2005. See LOTTERY; BETTING; GAMBLING.

gaming house Keeping a common gaming house was a common law misdemeanour. Premises used for gaming are now regulated under the Gambling Act 2005.

gaol delivery One of the commissions given to the judges or commissioners of assize. It authorised them to try, and (if acquitted) to deliver from custody, every prisoner who should be in gaol for some alleged crime when they arrived at the circuit town. Under the Courts Act 1971 references to a court of gaol delivery are to be construed as references to the Crown Court.

garden leave A clause in a contract of employment (*q.v.*) which provides for a long period of notice during which the employee will not be required to work yet will still be paid in full. Increasingly used by employers instead of a restraint of trade (*q.v.*) clause as a way of protecting the employer's business connections and confidential information from the post-termination actions of employees wishing to work for rival businesses. More usually found in the contracts of senior managers and executives.

garnish (1) To warn.
(2) To extract money from prisoners.

garnishee A person who has been warned not to pay a debt to anyone other than the third party who has obtained judgment against the debtor's own creditor.

garnishee proceedings A procedure by which a judgment creditor may obtain a court order against a third party who owes money to, or holds money for, the judgment debtor. It is usually obtained against a bank requiring the bank to pay money held in the account of the debtor to the creditor.

garrotting Choking, in order to rob, etc. There was a "moral panic" over the prevalence of garrotting in London in the 1840s.

Garter, Order of The most distinguished order of Knighthood (KG).

garth An enclosure; a yard; a weir or dam.

gavel Payment of tribute to a superior; rent (*q.v.*).

gavelkind The term used in Kent for the form of customary land tenure usually referred to as partible inheritance. Its principal incidents were: (a) the land descended on intestacy to all the sons of the tenant equally; (b) the widow or widower of the dead tenant took half the land as dower or curtesy until remarriage or death; (c) an infant tenant could alienate the land by feoffment at the age of 15; (d) a tenant was not liable to forfeit land on conviction for murder. Gavelkind was abolished by the Law of Property Act 1922 and Administration of Estates Act 1925.

Gazette The *London Gazette* is the official organ of the Government. It notifies appointments to public office; statutory rules and orders; proceedings in bankruptcy (*q.v.*) and insolvency (*q.v.*), etc. It is admissible in evidence for many purposes.

gazumping The withdrawal by a vendor from a proposed sale of land after agreeing a price with the purchaser but before a binding contract has been entered into, in the hope that he will receive a higher price from another purchaser. It became common during the property boom in the 1980s.

gazundering. The withdrawal at the last minute by a purchaser from a proposed purchase of land after agreeing a price with the vendor but before a binding contract has been entered into, in the hope that the vendor will accept a reduced price.

gearing The relationship of debt to equity in a company's capital structure. The more long-term the debt, the higher the gearing.

geld A tax, payment, tribute or a pecuniary penalty.

gemote; moot [Anglo-Saxon] A meeting or assembly.

gender reassignment For certain purposes, notably in the context of employment and vocational training, it is unlawful to discriminate against a person on the grounds that they intend to undergo, are undergoing or have undergone gender

reassignment (s.2A of the Sex Discrimination Act 1975, inserted by the Sex Discrimination (Gender Reassignment) Regulations 1999). Gender reassignment is defined as:
"a process which is undertaken under medical supervision for the purpose of reassigning a person's sex by changing physiological or other characteristics of sex, and includes any part of such a process" (Sex Discrimination Act s.82(1) as amended by the Regulations).

gender recognition certificate A certificate issued under the Gender Recognition Act 2004 following an application by a person of either gender who is at least 18 years old on the basis of living in the other gender, or having changed gender under the law of another country. Where a certificate is issued the applicant's gender becomes the acquired gender for all purposes.

gender recognition panel A panel appointed by the Lord Chancellor under the Gender Recognition Act 2004 to consider applications for gender recognition certificates (*q.v.*). A panel must comprise of at least one legally qualified person and one medically qualified person.

General Agreement on Tariffs and Trade (GATT) A multilateral, global agreement, concluded in 1947, which aims to "liberalise" world trade. It has been revised over the years and the most recent version is the GATT 1994 agreement, which can be found annexed to the World Trade Agreement 1994. See WORLD TRADE ORGANISATION.

general average See AVERAGE.

General Commissioners of Income Tax Appointed by the Lord Chancellor their function is to hear appeals against decisions made by HM Revenue & Customs on a variety of different tax related matters.

General Council of the Bar of England and Wales The governing body of the Bar. Known as the Bar Council. Founded in 1894 to represent the interests of barristers. It co-operates with the Inns of Courts (*q.v.*) through the Council of the Inns of Court (*q.v.*). See BAR STANDARDS BOARD.

general damages The kind of damage which the law presumes to follow from the wrong complained of and which therefore need not be set out in the claimant's pleadings (contrast special damages (*q.v.*) which always need to be specially pleaded). General damages also mean damages given for a loss that is incapable of precise estimation such as pain and suffering. See DAMAGES.

general equitable charge A class of land registrable under the Land Charges Act 1925 that affects a legal estate in land but that neither arises under a trust nor is secured by depositing the title deeds.

general improvement area A primarily residential area designated by the local authority for the improvement of houses or amenities. Replaced by renewal area (*q.v.*).

general issue See ISSUE.

General Medical Council The statutory body which registers doctors, and exercises professional discipline over them. Its most draconian penalty is the removal of the doctor's name from the register.

general meeting One of the principal decision making bodies of a company (*q.v.*) at which members can attend and vote. See RESOLUTION.

general safety requirement Under the Consumer Protection Act 1987 consumer goods are required to be reasonably safe having regard to all the circumstances. It is an offence for a supplier of consumer goods to fail to meet the requirement.

general sessions The court of record held by two or more justices of the peace for the trial of offenders.

general ship A ship which carries the goods of merchants generally under bills of lading (*q.v.*), as opposed to a chartered ship which is let to particular persons only under a charterparty (*q.v.*).

general verdict (1) In a civil case, a verdict wholly in favour of one party. (2) In a criminal case, a verdict of guilty or not guilty. Compare special verdict (*q.v.*).

general warrant A warrant issued for the arrest of unnamed persons or for the search of unspecified premises or for unspecified property. In 1765, in *Wilkes' Case*, they were held to be invalid, Camden L.J. saying that "public policy is not an argument in a court of law".

general words Descriptive words added to the parcels clause in a conveyance (*q.v.*), to transfer all the rights in the property of the grantor. They were rendered unnecessary by the Conveyancing Act 1881, re-enacted with a variation by the Law of Property Act 1925.

generale tantum valet in generalibus quantum singulare in singulis [When words are general they are to be taken in a general sense, just as words relating to a particular thing are to be taken as referring only to that thing]

generalia specialibus non derogant [General things do not derogate from special things]

generalibus specialia derogant [Special things derogate from general things]

Geneva Conventions A series of international conventions on the laws of war (*q.v.*) the first of which was formulated at Geneva in 1864. That and the convention of 1906 protect sick and wounded soldiers. The Geneva Protocol of 1925 prohibits the use of gas and bacteriological methods of warfare and was observed by the Germans during World War II, though subsequently it has been breached by other states. The 1949 Conventions deal with in turn: (i) wounded and sick in armed forces in the field; (ii) wounded, sick and shipwrecked in armed forces at sea; (iii) prisoners of war; (iv) civilians. The Geneva Convention Act 1957 gives direct effect to the 1949 Convention; grave breaches committed anywhere are triable in the United Kingdom and punishable with up to life imprisonment. The Conventions are supplemented by two protocols of 1977 the first of which relates to the protection of victims of international armed conflicts, and imposes an obligation to distinguish between the civilian population and combatants and thus prohibits indiscriminate attacks. The Geneva Conventions (Amendment) Act 1995 prospectively incorporates certain provisions of these protocols into UK law. See INTERNATIONAL LAW; WAR; WAR CRIMES.

genocide Genocide is defined in the International Criminal Court Act 2001 to mean any of the following committed with intent to destroy, in whole or in part, a national, ethnical, racial or religious group, as such: (a) killing members of the group; (b) causing serious bodily or mental harm to members of the group; (c) deliberately inflicting on the group conditions of life calculated to bring about its physical destruction in whole or in part; (d) imposing measures intended to prevent births within the group; (e) forcibly transferring children of the group to another group. The penalty is life imprisonment for murder and up to 30 years' imprisonment for any other case.

gestation The time which elapses between the conception and birth of a child. It is usually about nine months of 30 days each. The time is added, where necessary, to the period allowed under the rule against perpetuities.

get A Jewish religious divorce, executable only by the husband delivering a bill of divorce to the wife in the presence of two witnesses.

gift A grant or transfer of property not made for monetary consideration. For a gift to be valid there must be an intention to give and acts to give effect to the intention such as a physical handing over. A gift may be made by deed. Gifts are liable to capital gains tax (*q.v.*) and to inheritance tax (*q.v.*).

gilda mercatoria A guild merchant. The association of merchants of a town with the royal grant of the exclusive right of trading and levying tolls on "foreign" traders.

gilds Voluntary associations in towns in medieval England for religious and benevolent, or economic purposes. The chief were the Craft and Merchant Gilds. Survivors today are the City Companies.

Gillick competence Sufficient maturity and understanding to appreciate what is involved in the particular decision in question, e.g. regarding a particular medical treatment or procedure, or in relation to court proceedings. See *Gillick v West Norfolk and Wisbech Area Health Authority* [1986] A.C. 112.

gipsy The word derives from "Egyptian" and previously strangers calling themselves or consorting with Egyptians were liable for felony without benefit of clergy (*q.v.*). The Housing Act 2004 requires local authorities to include gipsies in their local housing needs assessments.

glebae ascriptitii Villeins (*q.v.*) who could not be removed from their holdings, provided they performed the prescribed service.

glebe Land attached to a benefice as part of its endowment. By the Endowments and Glebe Measure 1976 s.15 glebe land has vested in the Diocesan Boards of Finance.

glue sniffing During the 1970s the sniffing of glue as a means of becoming intoxicated received much publicity, and the sale of intoxicating substances to persons under the age of 18 years was made an offence under the Intoxicating Substances (Supply) Act 1985.

go-slow A go-slow, like a strike (*q.v.*) or working to contract, can amount to a breach of contract by an employee.

God's penny Earnest (*q.v.*).

going public When a private company re-registers as a public one or when a new public company (*q.v.*) registers, it is said to go public.

going through the Bar The old practice of the judge of asking, in order of seniority, each barrister who was in court whether he had anything to move.

golden formula, the See IN CONTEMPLATION OR FURTHERANCE OF A TRADE DISPUTE.

golden rule One of the rules of interpretation of statutes. See STATUTORY INTERPRETATION.

golden share In some of the privatisations of nationalised industries the government retained a "golden share" to prevent more than 15 per cent of a company being owned by one person, or to prevent a privatised industry from becoming foreign-owned.

good faith An act carried out honestly. See BONA FIDE.

good leasehold title Under the Land Registration Act 2002 a good leasehold title may be given if the Registrar considers that the title is such as a willing buyer could properly be advised by a competent professional advisor to accept. Registration with good leasehold title has the same effect as registration with absolute title, except that it does not affect the enforcement of any estate, right or interest affecting, or in derogation of, the title of the landlord to grant the lease. It usually occurs when the deeds showing the title of the landlord or superior landlord have not been registered. See LANDLORD.

goods Personal chattels and items of property but not land. The definition in the Sale of Goods Act 1979 s.61 also excludes choses in action (*q.v.*) and money.

goodwill The benefit a business has from its reputation and trade connections. It is an asset of a business and may be dealt with separately from the other assets on a transfer.

The tort of passing off (*q.v.*) relates to the protection of goodwill attached to a business, for example, by a defendant using a confusingly similar trade mark (*q.v.*) to a claimant.

government circulars Documents circulated by government departments which may provide administrative guidelines.

government department An organ of central government responsible for a particular area of activity such as Education. Staffed by civil servants, it is headed by a Minister who takes political responsibility for it. See CABINET; MINISTER.

Governor, Colonial The head of the executive of a British colony. He is the representative of the Crown and cannot be held liable for acts of state done within the scope of his authority.

Governor-General The representative of the Crown who heads the government of a Commonwealth country, he is appointed by the Sovereign on the advice of the country concerned, e.g. Australia.

grace See ACT OF GRACE; DAYS OF GRACE.

Grand Committees There are three grand committees in the House of Commons, a Scottish Grand Committee, a Welsh Grand Committee and a Northern Ireland Grand Committee. Each Grand Committee consists of all the MPs who represent the constituencies within that country together with up to 5 other members in the Welsh Grand Committee and not more than 25 other members in the Northern Ireland Grand Committee. They meet either at Westminster or in the country they cover. The business of each Grand Committee includes questions to ministers, short debates, ministerial statements, the consideration of bills before second or third readings, and other legislative proposals. In the House of Lords if a public bill is not committed to a committee of the whole house, it will usually be committed to a Grand Committee in which any member of the House of Lords may take part in.

Grand Coustumier du Pays et Duche de Normandie A collection of the ancient laws and customs of Normandy, the basis of the laws of the Channel Islands.

grand jury The role of the grand jury (consisting of an uneven number of men) was recognised by the Assize of Clarendon in 1166, and was to make presentments of criminal offences, originally from its own knowledge, later by considering a previously drafted bill of indictment. If found "true" a defendant then faced trial by a petty jury of 12 men. If not found guilty, the bill was marked "ignoramus" and the bill was not proceeded with. Grand juries were abolished in all cases by the Criminal Justice Act 1948. They remain a feature of the American trial system.

grand serjeanty A civil variety of land tenure whereby the tenant in chief was obliged to perform personal services for the king such as looking after his wine. The incidents were preserved under the Law of Property Act 1922, which has now been repealed as obsolete, however the honorary services remain. See PETTY SERJEANTY.

grant (1) The creation or transfer of ownership of property by a written instrument, e.g. a conveyance. Since the Law of Property Act 1925 it is no longer possible to convey land by delivery.

(2) The allocation of rights, money, etc. by the Crown or Parliament to particular persons or for particular purposes.

grant of representation The authority of the court to administer the estate of a dead person granted to named persons or a trust corporation. If the person dies intestate or named no executors (*q.v.*) or the named executors will not prove the will the grant is of letters of administration. If the person left a will the grant is of probate (*q.v.*) to the named executors.

grants in aid Central government grants to local authorities for specific services.

gratis dictum [Mere assertion]

Gray's Inn One of the Inns of Court (*q.v.*).

Great Council The Magnum Concilium. The assembly of the lords of the kingdom after the Conquest, in place of the Anglo-Saxon Witenagemot, from which developed the House of Lords.

Great Seal In the custody of the Lord Chancellor and used to seal writs for elections and treaties with foreign states.

Greater London Authority Established by the Greater London Authority Act 1999. It comprises a directly elected Mayor of London and a separately elected London Assembly. It has responsibility in London for transport, policing, fire and emergency planning, economic development, planning, culture, environment and health.

Greater London Council Established in 1972 to act as a unitary authority for the 12 inner and 20 outer London boroughs, the City of London and the Inner and Middle Temples. It was abolished in 1985 and its powers devolved to the boroughs and its property vested in a residuary authority, which sold off most of it.

green form This was the common name for the form on which application was made for legal advice and assistance. It has now been replaced by the Legal Help and Help at Court form. See LEGAL AID; LEGAL SERVICES COMMISSION.

green paper See COMMAND PAPERS.

Gretna Green Between 1753 (Lord Hardwicke's Act) and 1856 (Marriage (Scotland) Act) a marriage in England required either a licence or the calling of banns, whereas a marriage in Scotland required only the consent of the parties expressed in the presence of witnesses. Accordingly elopements to Gretna Green became a means of avoiding the requirements of the English law.

grievance procedures An employer should have a contractual procedure in place for handling grievances in the workplace. Since October 2004 there have been statutory grievance procedures (both standard and modified) which the employee should normally follow prior to presenting a claim on a range of matters (e.g. unlawful deductions, unlawful discrimination, breach of working time and unfair dismissal) to an employment tribunal (*q.v.*). See Employment Act 2002 and Employment Act 2002 (Dispute Resolution) Regulations 2004. The Employment Act 2008 has repealed these provisions. See DISCIPLINARY PROCEDURES.

grievous bodily harm Serious harm (to be understood in its natural meaning).

gross negligence A high degree of negligence (*q.v.*).

grossing up Both income and inheritances are subject to grossing up for purposes of calculating tax due.

ground rent See RENT; RENTCHARGE.

groundage Harbour dues.

group accounts Group accounts are required to be prepared by a company that has subsidiaries and to show the collective financial position of the companies. See Companies Act 2006 ss.398–408.

guarantee A secondary agreement in which one person (the guarantor) will become liable for the debt of the principal debtor if the principal debtor defaults. By the Statute of Frauds 1677 s.4 a guarantee must be evidenced in writing. It also requires independent consideration (*q.v.*).

guarantee company A company whose liability is limited by the guarantees of its members to pay a specified sum in the event of a winding up. Such companies are usually formed not for profit but to incorporate clubs or associations. See COMPANY; LIMITED COMPANY; PRIVATE COMPANY.

guarantee payments Under the Employment Rights Act 1996 s.28, an employee continuously employed for one month is entitled to a guarantee payment in respect of any whole day in which the employee is not provided with work because of lack of work or any other occurrence affecting the employer's business for a maximum of five days in any three-month period.

guarantor The person who binds himself by guarantee (*q.v.*).

guard dog Under the Guard Dogs Act 1975 it is a summary offence to use a guard dog (to protect people or property) unless it is either secured or is controlled by a handler.

guardian A person having the right and duty of protecting the persons, property or rights of one who is without full legal capacity or otherwise incapable of managing his own affairs. Under the Children Act 1989 the guardianship of children has been simplified and clarified. A guardian can only be appointed by the court in family proceedings with or without an application by a parent with parental responsibility (*q.v.*) or by an existing guardian. An appointment must be made by a signed and dated written document, though it does not need to be by deed or will (*q.v.*). The guardian obtains parental responsibility for the child. See WARD OF COURT.

guardian ad litem (1) This was the term used prior to the introduction of the Civil Procedure Rules 1998 (*q.v.*) for a person appointed to defend an action or other proceeding on behalf of a minor (*q.v.*) or person under a disability. Such a person is now called a litigation friend (*q.v.*).

(2) A guardian *ad litem*, now called a children's guardian, is a person appointed by the court to represent a child in certain proceedings under the Children Act 1989.

guardians of the poor The authority previously charged with the administration of the Poor Laws. Boards of Guardians were abolished by the Local Government Act 1929.

guardianship A patient who suffers from mental illness, mental impairment, severe mental impairment or psychopathic disorder, and who is aged 16 years or over, may be received into the guardianship of the local social services authority or of any other person, by reason of the provisions of the Mental Health Act 1983 s.7. The Magistrates' Court and the Crown Court may direct that a defendant be placed under guardianship (Mental Health Act 1983 s.37; Crown Court only, the Criminal Procedure (Insanity) Act 1964 s.5.

guardianship order An order made under the Mental Health Act 1983 or by a court in care proceedings, placing a person suffering from certain types of mental illness, under the guardianship of a local authority or approved person.

A guardianship order may be made under the Children Act 1989 s.5 allowing parents or guardians to appoint a guardian for a child to take their place after death.

guillotine A procedure to speed up the passage of legislation. The government specifies the time to be allotted to the committee and report stages and on the expiry of the specified times the guillotine falls and votes are taken immediately. See CLOSURE.

guilty The plea offered by a person who admits that he has committed the crime (*q.v.*) with which he is charged, or the verdict of a court after a trial on a not guilty plea that he has committed the crime charged.

H

habeas corpora juratorum A writ upon which trial of causes at *nisi prius* was held in the Court of Common Pleas. It commanded the sheriff to have before the court at Westminster, or before the judges of assize and nisi prius (*q.v.*), the bodies of the jurors named in the panel to the writ as having been summoned to make a jury for the trial. It was abolished by the Common Law Procedure Act 1852.

habeas corpus A prerogative writ used to challenge the detention of a person either in official custody or in private hands. Under CPR Sch.1, RSC Ord.54, application for the writ is made to the Divisional Court of the Queen's Bench, or during vacation to any High Court judge. If the court is satisfied that the detention is prima facie unlawful the custodian is ordered to appear to justify it and if he cannot do so the person is released.

habendum The clause in a conveyance which indicates the estate to be taken by the grantee. Formerly it commenced "To have [*habendum*] and to hold [*teneaum*]."

habere facias possessionem [That you cause to have possession] The writ by which the claimant in the old action of ejectment obtained possession of land.

habere facias seisinam [That you cause to have seisin] A writ which was formerly addressed to the sheriff requiring him to give seisin of a freehold estate recovered in an action.

habere facias visum [That you cause to have the view] A writ which formerly issued in real actions where it was necessary that a view should be had for lands.

habitual residence The place where a person has his home. It is necessary to establish domicile (*q.v.*).

hacking Unauthorised access to computer material. Such activity is an offence (Computer Misuse Act 1990 s.1). There is also an aggravated offence where there is intention to commit or facilitate the commission of other offences (e.g. theft, by diverting funds to one's own account) (ibid. s.2). The Act was passed following the House of Lords' decision confirming the convictions of two defendants in *R. v Gold; R. v Schifren* [1988] A.C. 1063 for unauthorised use of commercial databases. See INTERCEPTION OF COMMUNICATIONS.

haeres legitimus est quem nuptiae demonstrant [The lawful heir is he whom wedlock shows so to be]

Hague Convention Came into effect in 1969 and deals, inter alia, with the service of process from other states.

Hague Conventions A series of agreements signed in 1899 and 1907 regulating the laws of war. They include the "Martens Clause", which provides that circumstances not specifically dealt with in the regulations would be governed by customary law.

Hague Rules The rules which govern the international shipment of goods. The Hague-Visby Rules of 1968/79 are incorporated into UK law by the Carriage of Goods at Sea Act 1971. See also BILLS OF LADING.

half blood See BLOOD.

half secret trust A trust whose existence is disclosed in a will or other document which creates it but where the beneficiaries are undisclosed. See also SECRET TRUST.

Hallamshire The Sheffield Division of the County of York was created a separate county by the name of Hallamshire by the Criminal Justice Administration Act 1962.

hallimote; hallmote The Anglo-Saxon court equivalent to the Court Baron.

handling stolen goods An indictable offence under the Theft Act 1968 s.22. It consists in the receiving or assisting in the retention or realisation of goods the defendant knows or believes to be stolen.

handsale A sale of chattels concluded by the shaking of hands.

handsel Earnest (*q.v.*) money.

Hansard The term commonly used to describe the Official Report of Parliamentary Debates after the printers of the reports in the 19th century. Hansard may now be used as an aid to the construction of statutes in the courts in certain circumstances. See *Pepper v Hart* [1992] 3 W.L.R. 1032, HL.

Hanseatic Laws of the Sea The maritime law of the Hanse towns collected and published as a code by the Hanseatic League in 1591, and accepted as authoritative throughout northern Europe.

harassment (1) Of debtors. It is an offence to harass a debtor with demands for payments which are calculated to subject him or members of his family or household to alarm distress and humiliation.

(2) Of occupiers. Under the Protection from Eviction Act 1977 it is an offence for a landlord of residential property or his agent to use or threaten violence to obtain possession of his property.

(3) Racial harassment is specifically unlawful under the Race Relations Act 1976 (as amended) and sexual harassment effectively prohibited as less favourable treatment under the Sex Discrimination Act 1975. See RACIAL HARASSMENT; SEXUAL HARASSMENT.

(4) The Protection from Harassment Act 1997 creates a criminal offence of harassment and a civil remedy in the form of a restraining order and damages if relevant. The Act has been amended by the Serious Organised Crime and Police Act 2005 s.125 which introduces a new offence aimed at countering the activities of, for example, animal rights activists where their activities involve harassing two or more persons with the intention of persuading a person not to do something that he is entitled to do.

harbouring spies It is an offence knowingly to hide a person who has committed an offence under the Official Secrets Act 1911.

hard labour An additional punishment to imprisonment, introduced by statute in 1706, and unknown to the common law. It was abolished by the Criminal Justice Act 1948.

hardship See DEPRAVITY; SPECIFIC PERFORMANCE.

harm Under the Environmental Protection Act 1990 s.1, harm means harm to the health of living organisms or other interference with the ecological systems of which they form part and, in the case of man, includes offence caused to any of his senses or harm to his property; and "harmless" has a corresponding meaning. See also s.1 of the Pollution Prevention and Control Act 1999 in which harm also includes impairment of, or interference with, amenities or other legitimate uses of the environment. See ENVIRONMENT.

Under the Family Law Act 1996 the issue of whether a child or adult has suffered harm, that is ill treatment or impairment of health, is relevant to the court's decision on making an occupation order (*q.v.*).

harmless See HARM.

harmonisation In order to secure a common market (*q.v.*) in which goods, persons, services and capital can move freely within the European Community (*q.v.*), the Community has adopted harmonisation legislation in order to facilitate the common market. By setting harmonised standards EC law enables goods, persons, services and capital to move freely. Specifically art.95 of the EC Treaty confers on the institutions of the Community power to adopt measures (*q.v.*) for the approximation of the laws and practices of the Member States.

hawker A travelling seller of goods (Hawkers Act 1888 s.1 (repealed)).

headings The words that prefix sections of a statute and that may be used to resolve ambiguities.

headnote A summary of the points decided in a case which is not a part of the judgment. See LAW REPORT.

Head of Family Justice Under the Constitutional Reform Act 2005 s.9, this position will be held by the President of the Family Division (*q.v.*). There will also be a Deputy Head of Family Justice.

Health and Safety Commission The supervisory and advisory body established by the Health and Safety at Work Act 1974 which has powers to promote occupational health and safety by encouraging research and training. It consists of a chairman, up to nine members and a secretariat.

Health and Safety Executive The operational and enforcement arm of the Health and Safety Commission (*q.v.*) which shares with local authorities responsibility for the enforcement of the Health and Safety at Work Act 1974.

health in pregnancy grant A lump sum payment made to a woman who satisfies prescribed conditions in relation to a pregnancy of hers (see Social Security Contributions and Benefits Act 1992 Pt 8A, as introduced by the Health and Social Care Act 2008). It is a non-contributory, non-income related benefit. It is only payable where a pregnant woman has received advice on maternal health from a health professional.

Health Service Commissioner Appointed under the Health Service Commissioners Act 1993, and investigates complaints of unsatisfactory treatment or service by the National Health Service.

Health Service Ombudsman See HEALTH SERVICE COMMISSIONER.

Hearing Officer An independent officer appointed by the European Commission (*q.v.*) to ensure that the case of a firm being investigated by the Commission in relation to breaches of EC competition law is understood.

hearing The trial of a case before a court or tribunal. It is usually held in public but some hearings are in camera (*q.v.*).

hearsay The general rule at common law was that hearsay evidence (oral statements of a person other than one testifying or statements contained in documents offered to prove the truth of the contents) was not admissible. However, the Civil Evidence Act 1995 abolished the common law restriction on hearsay evidence in civil proceedings provided certain procedural requirements are fulfilled. The admissibility of hearsay evidence in criminal proceedings is governed by the provisions of the Criminal Justice Act 2003 which retains the general common law rule that hearsay evidence is inadmissible in criminal proceedings but provides four circumstances in which hearsay evidence may be admissible, these being: through a statutory exception to the hearsay rule, through a preserved common law exception to the hearsay rule, by agreement of all parties in the proceedings or if the court deems the admission of the evidence to be in the "interests of justice".

heavy applications In the Commercial Court, an application expected to involve an oral hearing of more than half a day.

heir apparent A person who will be heir to his ancestor if he survives him (e.g. an eldest son). Properly, he is not heir until after the death of his ancestor, for *"nemo est haeres viventis"* [nobody is the heir of a living person].

heir or heir at law Prior to the Administration of Estates Act 1925 the person who, under the common law or statutory rules, inherited the real property of his intestate ancestor. Heirs could be (1) customary or special inheriting by virtue of a custom such as gavelkind (*q.v.*) or borough English (*q.v.*); (2) general inheriting by descent as fixed by law; or (3) special or in tail inheriting according to the nature of the entailed interest.

heir presumptive A person who would be an heir if the ancestor died immediately (e.g. an only daughter); but who is liable to be displaced by the birth of a nearer heir such as a son.

heirlooms Goods or chattels that, contrary to the nature of chattels, go by special custom to the heir of the owner (together with the house or land) rather than to his personal representatives.

Herald's College The College of Arms, incorporated by Richard III in 1483. It is under the jurisdiction of the Earl Marshall and has jurisdiction on armorial bearings and matters of pedigree.

hereditament (1) Historically real property (*q.v.*) which on intestacy could have passed to an heir (*q.v.*). Corporeal hereditaments are visible and tangible objects such as houses and land; incorporeal hereditaments are intangible objects such as tithes (*q.v.*), easements (*q.v.*) and profits a prendre (*q.v.*).
(2) A unit of land that was separately assessed for rating purposes.

heres [Roman law] The universal successor of a deceased person by virtue of his rights under the civil law. He might be appointed by will or take on intestacy.

heres fiduciarius [Roman law] An heir that has *fidei commissum* (*q.v.*) entrusted to him to carry out.

heresy An ecclesiastical offence, consisting in the holding of a false opinion repugnant to some point of doctrine essential to the Christian faith. It was formerly punishable by death, but the writ *de haeretico comburendo* was abolished by the statute (29 Car. 2 c.9). The power of the Archbishop of Canterbury to cite any person for heresy was abolished by the Ecclesiastical Jurisdiction Measure 1963.

heriditas [Roman law] Inheritance; the succession by virtue of civil law rights to the whole legal position of a deceased person.

heriot The custom of heriot in feudal landholding entitled the lord of the manor to seize the best beast or chattel of a deceased tenant (*q.v.*). The custom more commonly affected unfree than free tenures. Heriots survived chiefly as an incident of copyhold tenure (*q.v.*), but were abolished as a manorial incident subject to compensation by the Law of Property Act 1922.

High Commission The Court of High Commission was set up in 1583 to exercise the supreme personal jurisdiction of the Head of the Anglican Church, particularly in criminal matters. It was hated especially for its administration of the *ex officio* oath, which obliged a person to answer questions. It was abolished, along with the other prerogative court of Star Chamber (*q.v.*), during the English Revolution.

High Commissioner The chief representative in the United Kingdom of a Commonwealth country and vice versa.

High Court enforcement officers Authorised by the Lord Chancellor (*q.v.*) or his delegate to carry out enforcement duties in relation to judgment debts and judgments for the possession of land (Courts Act 2003 s.99 and Sch.7). They are assigned to enforcement districts across England and Wales and have the same powers and duties as sheriffs (*q.v.*) whom they replace. They are entitled to be assisted by constables in carrying out their role. See BAILIFF.

High Court of Justice The High Court of Justice was created as part of the Supreme Court by the Judicature Acts 1873–1875. It consists of the Lord Chancellor, Lord Chief Justice, President of the Family Division, Vice Chancellor, Senior Presiding Judge, Vice President of the QBD and not more than 108 puisne judges. It has three divisions: the Queen's Bench Division (which includes the Admiralty Court, the Administrative Court, the Technology and Construction Court and the Commercial Court); the Chancery Division (which includes the Patents Court, the Bankruptcy Court and the Companies Court); and the Family Division. It is a superior court of record.

high seas The seas or open salt water not part of the territorial waters of a state. Under the 1982 Convention on the Law of the Sea (UNCLOS) the territorial sea cannot exceed 12 nautical miles. The English courts have jurisdiction to try offences committed anywhere on the high seas in a British ship.

high security hospital Hospitals for persons detained under the Mental Health Act 1983 who, in the Secretary of State's opinion, require treatment under conditions of special security on account of their dangerous, violent or criminal propensities (National Health Service Act 1977 s.4). There are presently three such hospitals: Ashworth, Broadmoor and Rampton.

high treason See TREASON.

highway A road or way open to the public as of right for the purpose of passing and repassing. It may be created by prescription (*q.v.*); statute; or dedication to the public by the owner. The duty to repair a highway now vests in the Secretary of State or the local authority. Where the Secretary of State is considering building a highway he must now carry out an Environmental Impact Assessment (*q.v.*). Obstruction of the highway is an offence under the Highways Act 1980.

Highway Code The Code compiled by the Secretary of State comprising such directions as appear to him proper for the guidance of persons using roads. Failure to observe it is not of itself an offence, but may be relied upon in any proceedings to establish or negative liability.

hijacking Under the Aviation Security Act 1982 it is an offence to unlawfully seize an aircraft in flight by the use of force and threats. Jurisdiction is given to the British courts regardless of the nationality of the perpetrator or whether the aircraft is in the United Kingdom. It is an offence under the Aviation and Maritime Security Act 1990 to seize control of a ship or fixed platforms.

Hil. Hilary sittings, or Hilary term, which is from January 11 to the Wednesday before Easter Sunday.

hire A contract for the temporary use of another's goods, or the temporary provision of his services or labour in return for payment.

hire-purchase agreement An agreement for the hire (bailment (*q.v.*)) of goods under which the hirer may buy the goods at the end of the hire period. It differs from a conditional sale agreement inasmuch as the debtor does not agree to buy, but merely has an option to do so. Most hire purchase agreements are now regulated by the Consumer Credit Act 1974 under which goods are bailed in return for periodical payments by the hirer (bailee). See CONSUMER CREDIT AGREEMENT If the hirer complies with the conditions of the agreement and exercises his option to purchase, ownership will pass to him. Terms as to quality, etc. are implied into hire-purchase agreements by the Supply of Goods (Implied Terms) Act 1973.

historic buildings The Historic Buildings and Monuments Commission ("English Heritage") has extensive powers relating to the preservation and upkeep of historic buildings under the National Heritage Act 1983.

historic cost accounting Companies are required to prepare balance sheets that present a "true and fair view" of the state of the company's finances. The accounts may be prepared on either a historic cost accounting basis or a current cost accounting basis.

hiving down A means of preparing the viable parts of a business for sale as a going concern while leaving the debts and other liabilities with the parent company.

HMO grant A grant towards the cost of improvement of a house in multiple occupation.

holder of bill Under the Bills of Exchange Act 1882 there are three different classes of holders of bills of exchange (*q.v.*) who are able to enforce the bill either by presenting it for payment or taking enforcement proceedings if it is dishonoured. They are holders, holders for value and holders in due course. The holder in due course has the most rights and is defined as a person who takes a bill of exchange which is complete and regular on its face, before it is overdue and without notice of dishonour, in good faith and for value and without notice of any defect of title of the transferor. He holds free from any defect of title of prior parties and may enforce payment against all parties liable on the bill, Bills of Exchange Act 1882 s.29.

holding company A company that controls a subsidiary company (*q.v.*); a parent company of a group of companies. See the Companies Act 2006.

holding defence A defence such as "the debt is denied—details to follow" does not comply with the Civil Procedure Rules (*q.v.*) and may be struck out.

holding out A person who "holds himself out" as, or purports to be, of a certain capacity (e.g. a partner in a firm), and who is accepted by others as such. When others act on the assumption that he is what he allows himself to be represented to be, he is estopped from denying the truth of such representation. See ESTOPPEL.

holding over A tenant (*q.v.*) who continues in occupation after the determination of his tenancy is holding over. If the landlord (*q.v.*) accepts rent from such a tenant, a new tenancy is created. If the holding over is without the landlord's consent, the tenant may be liable for damages to the landlord.

holograph A deed or will hand-written by the grantor or testator himself.

homage A free tenant for an estate in fee simple (*q.v.*) or fee tail (*q.v.*) was bound to perform homage to his lord (by kneeling and saying "I become your man of life and limb"). Homage created an obligation of assistance by the tenant to his lord and of protection by the lord to his tenant. It was abolished as an incident of tenure by 12 Car. 2 c.24.

Home Condition Report From 2007 a home condition report is an optional addition to Home Information Packs provided by sellers of owner-occupier residential property when marketing their property. The reports provide buyers with details of the condition of the property, and are prepared following an inspection of the property.

Home Information Pack Introduced in December 2007, by the Housing Act 2004, to tackle problems associated with the buying and selling of owner-occupier residential property. Home Information Packs (HIPs) are required to be produced for potential buyers whenever a home is marketed for sale. HIPs must include an index, energy performance certificate, sustainability information, sale statement, evidence of title and standard searches. It may also contain optional information such as a home condition report *(q.v.)*.

Home Secretary The Minister in charge of the Home Office. The Home Secretary is responsible throughout England and Wales for law and order (including the administration of the criminal law, the police and the prisons, and advising the sovereign on the exercise of the prerogative of mercy) and for other matters such as nationality, immigration and extradition.

home-loss payment Where a person is displaced, by a public authority, from a dwelling, e.g. by reason of compulsory purchase *(q.v.)*, subject to conditions as to the period and nature of occupation, a payment may be claimed in addition to other compensation *(q.v.)* (Land Compensation Act 1973 s.29 as amended by the Planning & Compensation Act 1991 s.68). This sum is intended to ameliorate the somewhat nebulous but personal value represented by the loss of a "home" rather than a "house".

homeless person Under the Housing Act 1996 a person is homeless if he has no accommodation available for his occupation or if he has accommodation but is unable to secure access to it. Where a local authority is satisfied that a person is homeless (but not intentionally so) they are under an obligation to secure accommodation for him.

Homes and Communities Agency. Established under the Housing and Regeneration Act 2008 as a statutory corporation with the aim of: improving the supply and quality of housing; securing the regeneration or development of land or infrastructure; supporting in other ways the creation, regeneration or development of communities or their continued well-being; and contributing to the achievement of sustainable development and good design. The Agency's overall remit is to meet the needs of people living in England. It has been given relevant powers to achieve these objects.

homicide Coke C.J. defined homicide as:
"when a man of sound memory and of the age of discretion, unlawfully killeth within any county of the realm any reasonable creature *in rerum naturae* under the king's peace with malice aforethought, either expressed by the party or implied by law so as the party wounded or hurt, etc., die of the wound or hurt, etc., within a year and a day after the same."
That definition remains valid for murder today, save that the Law Reform (Year and a Day Rule) Act 1996 abolished the requirement for the death to occur within that period. If it occurs more than three years later, the consent of the Attorney-General is necessary for a prosecution. Murder is punishable with a mandatory sentence of life imprisonment. The new homicide offence of causing or allowing the death of a child or vulnerable adult was introduced by the Domestic Violence Crime and Victims Act 2004. Manslaughter has two categories: voluntary manslaughter is murder reduced to manslaughter by reason of some extenuating circumstances such as provocation; involuntary manslaughter is an unlawful killing without malice aforethought. Manslaughter is punishable by a maximum sentence of life imprisonment. See MANSLAUGHTER.

homosexual acts The Sexual Offences Act 1967 s.1 made legal homosexual acts between consenting parties over 21 years carried out in private. Under the Criminal Justice and Public Order Act 1994 the age was reduced to 18 and under the Sexual Offences Amendment Act 1999, to 16. The Sexual Offences Act 1967 s.1 has been repealed (Sexual Offences Act 2003 Sch.6, para.15).

hon The Honourable. The title of the younger sons of earls; all children of viscounts and barons; justices of the High Court; members of governments and of legislative councils in the colonies; and certain ladies. Right Honourable is the title of Privy Councillors. See PRIVY COUNCIL.

honorarium A payment for services given voluntarily.

honorary services The services incident to tenure in grand serjeanty (*q.v.*) or petty serjeanty (*q.v.*).

honour (1) A seignory *in capite* on which several inferior lordships or manors depend; and the land or district included therein. Since the statute of Quia Emptores, an honour cannot be created, save by Act of Parliament.
(2) To honour a bill of exchange (*q.v.*) is to pay it or accept it as may be due.

honour clause A clause in an agreement stating that it is binding in honour only. The courts will usually therefore not enforce the agreement.

honours The Queen is the "fountain of honour" but the creation of peers and the conferment of most honours are done on the advice of the Prime Minister (*q.v.*), subject to scrutiny by the Political Honours Scrutiny Committee.

horizontal agreements Agreements between parties operating at the same level of a trade as opposed to vertical agreements between parties operating at different levels of a trade. Both fall within the scope of the competition policies of the European Community and the United Kingdom.

horizontal effect In EC law a provision of Community law is capable of direct effect (*q.v.*), if it meets certain conditions laid down by the European Court of Justice. Provisions of Community law are capable of both vertical direct effect (*q.v.*) and horizontal direct effect. Where a provision of Community law is horizontally directly effective it is capable of conferring legally enforceable rights on an individual as against another individual as well as against the state (see Case 43/75 *Defrenne v Sabena* [1976] E.C.R 455). EC Directives are not capable of horizontal direct effect. See also VERTICAL DIRECT EFFECT; INDIRECT EFFECT.
(2) In relation to the Human Rights Act 1998, the idea that the Act can have an effect not only in respect of relations between the state and the citizen—vertical effect, but also in respect of relations between private individuals or organisations—horizontal effect. It seems clear that there is some horizontal effect by virtue of the status of the courts and tribunals as public authorities: s.6(3)(a) of the Act. They are obliged to make their decisions in a way that is compatible with Convention rights even in litigation between private parties. They must also interpret all legislation in a way that is compatible with Convention rights (*q.v.*). The extent of horizontal effect has been a matter of controversy and there is no consensus as to how far the courts will develop human rights jurisprudence in the purely private sphere.

hors de la loi Outlawed.

hospital, detention in See DETENTION IN HOSPITAL.

hospital order By reason of the provisions of the Mental Health Act 1983 s.37, the Magistrates Court and the Crown Court are empowered to order the detention of an offender in hospital if satisfied that she or he is suffering from mental illness, mental impairment, severe mental impairment or psychopathic disorder and that other statutory criteria are met.

hospital records protocol A request for the hospital records of a patient in contemplation of proceedings should follow the pre-action protocol for the resolution of clinical disputes.

Hospitia Cancellariae [Inns of Chancery]

Hospitia Curiae [Inns of Court]

hospitium The relation between host and guest; the shelter of an inn. It includes the inn buildings and stables, and may also include a yard or car park.

hostages The Taking of Hostages Act 1982 creates an offence of detaining another, intending to compel a state to do or refrain from doing anything. Proceedings need the consent of the Attorney-General (*q.v.*).

hostile witness A witness who gives evidence adverse to the interest of the party calling him. With the leave of the court, a hostile witness may be cross-examined by the party calling him and a previous inconsistent statement may be put to him.

hotchpot Bringing into account on an intestacy benefits received by one beneficiary prior to the death of the intestate. Under the Administration of Estates Act 1925, unless a contrary intention is expressed, all advances made to children before death are to be brought into account. The Law Reform (Succession) Act 1995 has repealed the provision in relation to persons dying intestate after January 1, 1996.

House of Commons The Lower House of Parliament, consisting of 659 members elected on a first past the post system. The following are, inter alia, disqualified from membership: aliens, minors, the mentally ill, peers (other than Irish peers), bankrupts, members of the armed forces, clergymen of the Church of England and Ireland; and the holders of certain offices such as the Steward of the Chiltern Hundreds (*q.v.*). The House is presided over by a Speaker elected from among the members at the start of each Parliament.

House of Lords The Upper House of Parliament, consisting of the Lords Temporal (hereditary peers and peeresses, life peers and peeresses and the Lords of Appeal in Ordinary) and the Lords Spiritual (the Archbishops of Canterbury and York, the Bishops of London, Winchester and Durham and 21 other Anglican bishops). Under the House of Lords Act 1999 the right to sit in the House of all save 92 hereditary peers was removed. A decision on the proposals of the Royal Commission on reform of the House of Lords, which put forward three alternatives in all of which the majority of members of the House of Lords are unelected and which only minimally alter the powers of the Lords, has been postponed. Under the Peerage Act 1963, any person who succeeds to an hereditary peerage may disclaim it for life. The House is presided over by the Lord Chancellor (*q.v.*). The House of Lords is the final court of appeal in both criminal and civil cases. As a court of appeal it adopts decisions of its appellate committee in which, by convention, only the Lord Chancellor, the Lords of Appeal in Ordinary (*q.v.*) and other peers who have held high judicial office participate. Once the Constitutional Reform Act 2005 comes into force the House of Lords' judicial role will be transferred to the Supreme Court (*q.v.*).

housebreaking See BURGLARY.

housing authority For the purposes of the Housing Act 1985, a local housing authority is a district council, London borough council, the Common Council of the City of London, a Welsh county council or county borough council, or the Council of the Isles of Scilly.

housing action area The Housing Act 1985 provided that a housing authority (*q.v.*) might designate an area a housing action area with a view to improving the standards of living accommodation for the residents within it. Since the Local Government and Housing Act 1989 the local authority no longer has that power but can declare a renewal area (*q.v.*).

housing action trust The Housing Act 1988 allows central government to remove housing from local authority control by handing it over to a housing action trust which is intended to improve conditions for tenants.

housing association A non-profit society to improve housing accommodation.

housing association tenancy A tenancy in which the landlord is a housing association (*q.v.*), a housing trust (*q.v.*) or the Housing Corporation. A tenancy entered into on or after January 15, 1989 cannot be a housing association tenancy except in certain transitional situations.

housing benefit Claimable by those on a low income who pay rent for their home whether or not they are in work (Social Security Contributions and Benefits Act 1992).

Housing Corporation A body corporate which maintains a register of and supervises social landlords (*q.v.*).

housing grant Under the Housing Grants Construction and Regeneration Act 1996 grants are available towards the cost of work required for the provision of facilities for disabled persons.

housing revenue account subsidy An annual contribution payable by central government towards the provision of housing by local authorities.

housing trust A corporation required to use its funds to provide accommodation.

hovercraft Under the Hovercraft Act 1968 the Admiralty Court (*q.v.*) has jurisdiction in relation to hovercraft.

Howe v Earl of Dartmouth The rule in *Howe v Earl of Dartmouth* (1802) 7 Ves. 137, establishes that, subject to a contrary provision in the will, there is a duty to convert where residuary personalty (*q.v.*) is settled in favour of persons who are to enjoy it in succession.

hue and cry The old common law process for apprehending criminals by local pursuit.

Human Fertilisation and Embryology Authority This was established by the Human Fertilisation and Embryology Act 1990 to review information about embryos, to licence the provision of treatment and research into embryology, and to maintain a register about treatments. See ABORTION; ARTIFICIAL INSEMINATION.

human organs Under the Human Tissue Act 2004 commercial dealings with human organs are prohibited.

human rights Rights and freedoms which every person is entitled to enjoy, possibly deriving from natural law but more likely to be enforced in international law if founded on e.g. the United Nations Universal Declaration of Human Rights of 1948. They can be divided into political rights and economic rights, and the latter are even less likely than the former to be enforceable. The European Convention on Human Rights and Fundamental Freedoms 1950 (*q.v.*) established a Commission, to investigate and conciliate, and a Court of Human Rights (*q.v.*), to hear cases. In 1998 the Court and Commission were merged. The rights protected under the Convention include the right to life and the right to respect for private and family life. The Human Rights Act 1998 requires public authorities (*q.v.*) to act in a way that is compatible with the Convention rights (*q.v.*) and requires the courts, so far as it is possible to do so, to read and give effect to primary legislation in a way that is compatible with the Convention rights (*q.v.*). See CONVENTION COMPLIANT.

hundred A district forming part of a county, originally so called because each consisted of a hundred freeholders, or ten tithings. Each hundred formerly had its court, and was governed by a high constable or bailiff. In the north of England the organisation was into wapentakes, not hundreds. See also CHILTERN HUNDREDS.

hundred court The court of the hundred. It was similar to the old county court in jurisdiction and procedure. Judgment was given by the suitors.

hundredor One of the inhabitants of a hundred (*q.v.*) who was liable to serve on a jury trying an issue regarding land situated there.

husband and wife At common law, husband and wife were one person and, as Blackstone wrote, "the husband is that one". A woman's property passed to her husband at marriage and she could own no goods: even wages earned by working women were in law the property of her husband. Equity slightly ameliorated the position for those women wealthy enough to have trustees of real property. Not until the Married Women's Property Act of 1882 was a woman's property her own. One spouse cannot be compelled to testify against the other for the prosecution in criminal proceedings.

husbandry Farming.

hush money Money paid to persuade a person not to prosecute or to give evidence or information.

hybrid bill A mixed public and private bill. See BILL.

hybrid company Prior to 1980 it was possible to register a company limited by guarantee with a share capital, but under subsequent Companies Acts no new hybrid companies may be registered.

hypnotism The Hypnotism Act 1952 as amended regulates the demonstration of hypnotic phenomena for public performance. See MEDIUMS.

hypothecation (1) A charge on a ship or her freight or cargo to secure moneys borrowed by the master for necessities required during the voyage. If on the ship with or without cargo, it is bottomry (*q.v.*); if on the cargo alone, *respondentia*.
(2) A charge on property as security for the payment of a sum of money where the property remains in the possession of the debtor.

I

ICC International Chamber of Commerce (*q.v.*).

ICE contract The Institution of Civil Engineers Conditions of Contract being a leading standard form of contract in use in the United Kingdom for works of civil engineering construction.

IPC Integrated Pollution Control (*q.v.*)

IPPC Integrated Pollution Prevention Control (*q.v.*).

IOU [I owe you] A written acknowledgement of a debt. It is not a negotiable instrument (*q.v.*).

ibid. (ibidem). [In the same place]

id certum est quod certum reddi potest [That is certain which can be made certain]

idem [The same]

identification To identify a thing or person is to prove that the thing or person produced or shown is the one in question in the proceedings.

identification parade A person suspected of a crime may take part in an identification parade and evidence of his identification would be admissible provided that the Code of Practice under the Police and Criminal Evidence Act 1984 is followed. In practice most identification procedures take place as video parades referred to as VIPER parades (video identification parades electronic recording).

identity cards A card showing a person's identity, and required to be carried in many countries but not, so far, in the United Kingdom.

ignorantia eorum quae quis scire tenetur non excusat [Ignorance of those things which everyone is bound to know does not constitute an excuse]

ignorantia facti excusat; ignorantia juris non excusat [Ignorance of the fact excuses; ignorance of the law does not excuse]

ignorantia juris quod quisque scire tenetur non excusat [Ignorance of the law which everybody is supposed to know does not afford excuse]

illegal An act which the law forbids. It can be contrasted with acts which the law will disregard, such as a void (*q.v.*) contract.

illegal contract A contract that is prohibited by statute (e.g. under the Gaming Act 1845) or at common law as being contrary to public policy (such as agreements in restraint of marriage). It is void (*q.v.*) and neither party can recover money paid under it.

illegitimacy See LEGITIMACY.

immemorial Beyond legal memory, that is, prior to 1189. Immemorial usage is a practice that has existed since time out of mind. See PRESCRIPTION.

immigration Entry to a country other than one's own with the intention of living there permanently. Successive Immigration Acts have imposed greater controls on immigration into the United Kingdom.

Immigration Services Commissioner Is appointed by the Secretary of State. An independent public body which ensures that immigration advisors are fit and competent and act in the best interests of their clients. It does not regulate members of professional bodies, such as the Law Society, who give immigration advice.

Immigration Services Tribunal Deals with appeals under the Immigration and Asylum Act 1999. It can order an organisation to stop giving immigration advice. The members of the Tribunal are appointed by the Lord Chancellor.

immorality A contract founded on sexual immorality, such as an agreement for future illicit co-habitation, is void (*q.v.*), but the courts will now recognise, e.g. rights in the "matrimonial home" of a cohabitee. See COHABITATION.

immovables Tangible things that cannot be physically moved, such as buildings.

immunity Exemption from legal proceedings. For example, Members of Parliament have immunity in respect of words spoken in debate. See also DIPLOMATIC PRIVILEGE.

immunity from suit Expert witnesses are currently immune from suit in respect of anything said at trial but in *Hall v Simmons* T.L.R. July 2, 2000 the House of Lords removed the immunity of advocates.

impanel To enter the names of a jury in the panel (*q.v.*).

impeachment A procedure by which a minister of the Crown may be tried in front of his peers in Parliament. Last used in the United Kingdom in 1805.

impeachment of waste An action that may be brought against a tenant (*q.v.*) for damage caused by him.

impeding apprehension Under the Criminal Law Act 1967 s.4 it is an offence, knowing a person has committed an offence, to impede his apprehension or prosecution.

imperfect trust A trust which is not enforceable by the cestui que trust (*q.v.*).

imperitia culpae adnumeratur [Inexperience is accounted a fault]

impersonation: personation Pretending to be another person. It is an offence to impersonate a police officer, for example.

implication The inference from acts done or facts ascertained of the existence of an intention or state of things that may or may not exist in fact, but which is presumed by the law to exist.

implied condition See IMPLIED TERM.

implied malice The *mens rea* (*q.v.*) that the law considers necessary for a crime even where there is no intention to commit the crime. The doctrine of implied malice in murder (*q.v.*) has been severely attenuated in recent years.

implied repeal Where a later Parliamentary statute is at odds with an earlier one the judges will deem the earlier one to be impliedly repealed. But see e.g. Statute of Westminster or European Communities Act 1972.

implied term A term in a contract which has not been expressly stated but which the courts are willing, or required by statute, to imply. See SATISFACTORY QUALITY.

implied trust A trust implied by law as founded upon the unexpressed but presumed intention of the party. It includes resulting trusts (*q.v.*) and constructive trusts (*q.v.*).

import quotas Restrictions placed by government on the import of certain items often in order to protect a domestic market.

importune Under the Sexual Offences Act 1956 it was an offence for a man persistently to importune in a public place for an immoral purpose. This offence has now been abolished by the Sexual Offences Act 2003 and replaced with an offence of engaging in sexual activities in a public lavatory (s.71).

impossibility In incitement (*q.v.*) and common law conspiracy (*q.v.*) the impossibility of the act incited, etc. is a defence. In a statutory conspiracy, and in attempt (*q.v.*), a person may be guilty of the offence even though the facts are such that its commission would be impossible if he would have had the necessary mens rea had the facts been as he believed them to be. In contract law impossibility of performance may arise before or after the contract is made. In the former case the contract is void (*q.v.*) for mistake; in the latter will be discharged by virtue of the doctrine of frustration (*q.v.*).

impossibilium nulla obligato est [Impossibility is an excuse for the non-performance of an obligation] See IMPOSSIBILITY.

impotence The inability to have normal sexual intercourse. If it is permanent, a marriage may be voidable for nullity. It should be distinguished from a wilful refusal to consummate. See NULLITY OF MARRIAGE.

impotentia excusat legem [Impotency excuses law] To an obligation imposed by law, impossibility of performance is a good excuse.

impound To seize goods; to put distrained cattle or other goods in a pound (*q.v.*) or to keep them as security.

impounded documents Documents which the court has taken charge of under CPR r.39.7.

impressment

impressment A power possessed by the Crown of compulsorily taking persons or property to aid in the defence of the country. It was usually used until 1815 to obtain seamen for the navy.

imprest Money advanced by the Crown for its use.

imprimatur [Let it be printed]

imprisonment As a punishment for criminal offences it consists of the detention of the offender in a prison. It includes any restraint of a person's liberty by another. See also FALSE IMPRISONMENT.

imprisonment for debt Prior to the Debtors Act 1869 it was common for those who could not pay debts to be imprisoned. Imprisonment still exists for debt in certain circumstances.

improperly-executed agreement A term of art used by the Consumer Credit Act 1974 s.65 to refer to agreements regulated by that Act but which are to be treated as unenforceable by the creditor or owner (as the case may be) against the debtor or hirer by reason of some failure to comply with the requirements of the Act. The court has power to order enforcement.

impropriation The transfer of the property of an ecclesiastical benefice into the hands of a layman, and the possession by a layman of the property so transferred.

impropriator A lay rector. See TITHE.

improvement notice A notice issued by an inspector from the Health and Safety Executive (*q.v.*) served upon a person who, in the opinion of the inspector, is responsible for the breach of any health and safety enactment. The notice requires its recipient to remedy the contravention within a stated period (Health and Safety at Work, etc. Act 1974). An appeal against a notice lies to an employment tribunal (*q.v.*). See PROHIBITION NOTICE.

impubes [Roman law] A person below the legal age of puberty. A male under 14 or a female under 12.

imputation An allegation of misconduct or bad faith made by an accused against the prosecutor or one of his witnesses.

in aequali jure melior est conditio possidentis [Where the rights of the parties are equal, the claim of the actual possessor is the stronger]

in ambiguis orationibus maxime sententia spectanda est ejus qui eas protelisset [In dealing with ambiguous words the intention of him who used them should especially be regarded]

in Anglia non est interregnum [In England there is no interregnum] The doctrine that the king never dies, for immediately upon the decease of the reigning prince his kingship vests by act of law in his heir.

in articulo mortis [At the point of death]

in autre droit [In the right of another] An executor holds property in the right of his testator.

in banc Sittings of the judges of the Queen's Bench, Common Pleas and Exchequer at Westminster for determination of questions of law, prior to the Judicature Acts 1873–1875. See NISI PRIUS.

in bonis [In the goods of]

in camera The hearing of a case in private, either by excluding the public from the court or by conducting the hearing in the judge's private rooms. Although criminal cases must be heard in public, where national security is invoked by the prosecution, the public may be excluded. Cases in the Family and Chancery Divisions are often heard in private.

in capite See CAPITE, TENURE IN.

in casu extremae necessitatis omnia sunt communia [In cases of extreme necessity, everything is in common]

in commendam [In trust]

in conjuctivis oportet utrumque, in disjunctivis sufficit alteram partem esse veram [In conjunctives both must be true; in disjunctives it is sufficient if one of them be true]

in consimili casu [In a like case] The Statute of Westminister II, 1288 (13 Edw. 1 c.24), enacted that when a writ was found in Chancery, but in a similar case falling under the same right and requiring the same remedy no writ was to be found, the clerks should make a new writ, or refer the matter to Parliament. See also ACTION ON THE CASE.

in contemplation or furtherance of a trade dispute Under trade union legislation workers, trade unions and their officers, officials and members do not have positive rights to take particular action but are granted immunities from certain tortious liability where their actions are taken in contemplation or furtherance of a trade dispute (*q.v.*) (the so-called "golden formula"), Trade Union and Labour Relations (Consolidation) Act 1992 ss.219–220. Whether a person acts in contemplation or furtherance of a trade dispute is a subjective question to be determined in the light of the intentions and beliefs of the person taking the action (*Express Newspapers Ltd v McShane* [1980] I.C.R. 42, HL).

in contractis tacite insunt quae sunt moris et consuetudinis [The clauses which are in accordance with custom and usage are an implied part of every contract]

in conventionibus contrahentium voluntas potius quam verba spectari placuit [In construing agreements the intention of the parties, rather than the words actually used, should be considered]

in curia [In open court]

in custodia legis [In the custody of the law]

in esse [In being] Actually existing.

in extenso [At full length]

in forma pauperis [In the character of a pauper]

in futuro [In the future]

in gremio legis [In the bosom of the law]

in gross A right that is not appendant, appurtenant, or otherwise annexed to land.

in house litigation A form of alternative dispute resolution in which the lawyers for the parties present their case before executives from each side and an independent chair.

in invitum [Against a reluctant person]

in jure non remota causa, sed proxima spectatur [In law the proximate, and not the remote, cause is to be regarded]

in limine [On the threshold] See POSTLIMINIUM.

in loco parentis [In the place of a parent] One who assumes the liability for providing for a minor in the way a parent would do.

in medias res [In the midst of the matter]

in misericordia [At mercy] See AMERCIAMENT.

in nomine [In the name of]

in pais [In the country] Without legal proceedings or documents. Trial *per pais* means trial by the country, i.e. trial by jury.

in pari causa potior est conditio possidentis [Where there are equal claims (to property), that of the possessor is preferred] Everyone may keep what he has got, unless and until someone else can prove a better title.

in pari delicto, potior est conditio possidentis [Where parties are equally in fault, the condition of the possessor is preferred]

in pari materia [In an analogous case]

in perpetuum [For ever]

in personam Historically equitable interests were rights in personam only, that is they were enforced only against the person originally bound. They became enforceable against all save a purchaser without notice and thus developed into proprietary rights or rights in rem (*q.v.*).

in pleno [In full]

in posse A thing which does not actually exist, but which may exist.

in praesenti [At the present time]

in propria persona [In his own proper person]

in re [In the matter of]

in rem An act, proceeding or right available against the world at large, as opposed to *in personam* (*q.v.*). A right of property is a right in rem. An Admiralty action is a proceeding *in rem* when the ship itself is arrested and adjudicated upon.

in situ [In its original situation]

in specie In its own form and essence, and not in its equivalent. In coin as opposed to paper money.

in statu quo [In the former position]

in terrorem Intended to frighten or intimidate: a condition in a will or gift which is in terrorem may be void.

in totidem verbis [In so many words]

in toto [Entirely; wholly]

in transitu [In course of transit] See STOPPAGE IN TRANSITU.

in vitro fertilisation Fertilisation of a human egg outside the body. See HUMAN FERTILISATION AND EMBRYOLOGY ACT 1990.

inadequate professional services Under the Solicitors Act 1974 the Council of the Law Society may, inter alia, require a solicitor to compensate a client for inadequate professional services.

inalienable Not transferable. There is a general rule of law that land must not be rendered inalienable.

incapacity Certain persons, such as minors and the mentally disordered, are considered incapable of entering into contracts.

incapacity benefit Introduced by the Social Security (Incapacity for Work) Act 1994, it is available to people unable to work because of illness or disability.

incendiarism Arson (*q.v.*).

incerta persona [Roman law] An indeterminate person, not a specific living individual. A legatee was held to be indeterminate when a testator added him with an indeterminate notion in his mind, as, e.g. the man who comes first to my funeral.

incest Sexual penetration by a person aged 16 or over of a relative aged 18 or over is an offence under the Sexual Offences Act 2003 s.64. A person aged 16 or over commits an offence if they consent to sexual penetration by a relative aged 18 or over (ibid. s.65). Sexual penetration occurs when a person penetrates another person's vagina or anus with a part of his or her body or anything else, or penetrates the other person's mouth with his penis, and "relative" means his or her parent, grandparent, child, grandchild, brother, sister, half-brother, half-sister, uncle, aunt, nephew or niece.

inchoate offence A crime which has just started—an attempt, conspiracy or incitement to crime, which may be punishable even if uncompleted.

incident A thing appertaining to or following another. Thus a rent may be incident to a reversion, though it may be separated from it; that is, the one may be conveyed without the other.

incidental horizontal effect A concept emerging in European Union Law as result of the absence of the horizontal direct effect of directives. The term has been used to describe the situation where an individual has sought to exploit the principle of direct effect (*q.v.*) not to enforce rights but rather to establish the illegality of a national law and thereby prevent its application to them. This has arisen in situations where an individual seeks to use a directive in effect horizontally in a defence against another individual, where that latter individual was relying on national law that did not comply with the directive. See e.g. Case C-194/94 *CIA Security International SA v Signalson SA* [1996] ECR 1–2201. See DIRECT EFFECT, DIRECTIVE.

incidents of tenure Under the feudal system the following were incidents of tenure: military service; homage, fealty and suit of court; wardship and marriage; relief and primer seisin; aids; and escheat and forfeiture. With the abolition of particular tenures by the Statute Quia Emptores, the Tenures Abolition Act 1660, and the Property Acts 1922 and 1925, the incidents of tenure disappeared with them, except that the honourable incidents of grand serjeanty (*q.v.*) and petty serjeanty (*q.v.*) were expressly preserved (Law of Property Act 1922 s.136).

incitement Encouragement or persuasion to commit a crime is the common law offence of incitement, even though the crime is not committed. Once the Racial and Religious Hatred Act 2006 comes into force it will be an offence to incite hatred against persons on racial or religious grounds.

incitement to disaffection Endeavouring to seduce members of the armed forces from their allegiance is an offence under the Incitement to Disaffection Act 1934.

inclosure Extinguishing common rights in land in favour of vesting it in some person as absolute owner. Inclosure could be effected by the lord of the manor, or the tenants by special custom, by prescription (*q.v.*), by agreement, or by Act of Parliament.

inclusio unius est exclusio alterius [The inclusion of one is the exclusion of another]

income support A means-tested ("income-related") benefit available to those not required to be available for work. Since 1996 income-based job seeker's allowance (*q.v.*) has replaced income support for claimants who are required to register for work. Income support has been phased out for new claimants since October 2008 by Employment and Support Allowance (*q.v.*).

221

income tax A duty or tax on income or profits. The Income and Corporation Taxes Act 1988 consolidated all the substantive law of income tax and corporation tax. The Taxes Management Act 1970 consolidated the administrative provisions. The tax is imposed each year by the annual Finance Act. Income tax has historically been levied in respect of income from the sources classified in six Schedules as follows, each Schedule having its own set of rules:

    (1) Schedule A (property income);

    (2) Schedule B (occupation of commercial woodlands—abolished from April 6, 1988);

    (3) Schedule C (profits arising from public revenue dividends—abolished from 1996);

    (4) Schedule D (trade or professional profits or gains; also income not chargeable under the other Schedules);

    (5) Schedule E (emoluments of offices and employment—see the Income Tax (Earnings and Pensions) Act 2003);

    (6) Schedule F (company dividends and distributions—with the abolition of advance corporation tax (*q.v.*) from 1999 the tax credit was set at one ninth).

The tax system has been significantly altered in recent years (most recently in 2005, see below) and there is now a personal allowance set against income, but many of the other allowances such as the married couple's allowance have been abolished and replaced by, e.g. the children's tax credit.

The income tax year of assessment runs from April 6 to April 5. The tax is managed by the Commissioners for Her Majesty's Revenue and Customs (*q.v.*), Inspectors of Taxes being their subordinate local officers. A person who is aggrieved by the amount of the assessment upon him may appeal to the local General Commissioners (*q.v.*) or, in certain cases, to the Special Commissioners (*q.v.*). A person who is dissatisfied with the decision of the General or Special Commissioners may, in general, appeal by case stated to the High Court on a question of law.

An updated classification of income for tax purposes is to be introduced from April 2006 by the Income Tax (Trading and Other Income) Act 2005. The Act rewrites income tax legislation relating to trading, property and investment income. This Act repeals, for income tax purposes, the remaining Schedules A, D and F.

incorporation Merging together to form a single whole; conferring legal personality upon an association of individuals, or the holder of a certain office, pursuant to Royal Charter or Act of Parliament. See COMPANY.

incorporeal hereditaments See HEREDITAMENT.

incorrigible rogue A person deemed to be an incorrigible rogue under the 1824 Vagrancy Act may be imprisoned.

INCOTERMS A set of internationally agreed commercial trade terms for contracts of sale of goods which define the duties of the parties in relation, to carriage of goods, risk, insurance, etc., e.g. f.o.b; c.i.f. Published by the International Chamber of Commerce (ICC) (*q.v.*) the current version is INCOTERMS 2000. Under English law the terms must be expressly incorporated into the contract in order to have legal effect.

incriminate To involve oneself or another in responsibility for a criminal offence. Generally a person cannot be compelled to answer a question which might incriminate him. There are statutory exceptions, e.g. Civil Evidence Act 1968 s.14(1); Criminal Damage Act 1971 s.9. See also CHARACTER, EVIDENCE OF.

incumbent A rector with cure of souls, vicar, perpetual curate, curate in charge or minister of a benefice.

indebitatus assumpsit See ASSUMPSIT.

indecency That which is offensive to public decency and morality: outraging public decency is a common law offence. See EXPOSURE.

indecent assault Formerly an assault or battery accompanied by circumstances of indecency and punishable under the Sexual Offences Act 1956. Now covered by the offences of sexual assault (*q.v.*) (s.3) and assault by penetration (*q.v.*) (s.2) under the Sexual Offences Act 2003.

indemnify To make good a loss which one person has suffered in consequence of the act or default of another. See Mercantile Law Amendment Act 1856 s.5.

indemnity A collateral contract or security to prevent a person from being damnified by an act or forbearance done at the request of another. See ACT OF INDEMNITY. For indemnity by way of contribution, see JOINT TORTFEASORS.

indemnity principle In general where a party to an action is ordered to pay the other side's costs it is on an indemnity basis.

indenture A document written in duplicate on the same parchment or paper, and divided into two by cutting through in a wavy line. The two parts could be fitted together to prove their genuineness, and were known as counterparts. A deed between parties to effect its objects has the effect of an indenture though not indented or expressed to be an indenture, and any deed, whether or not being an indenture, may be described as a deed simply (Law of Property Act 1925 ss.56(2), 57). See COUNTERPART.

independent contractor Term used to distinguish from an employee a person who contracts to perform a particular task for another and is not under the other's control as to the manner in which he performs the task. An employer is not normally liable for the torts of an independent contractor and the distinction is also significant in employment and social security law. See EMPLOYER AND EMPLOYEE.

Independent Police Complaints Commission Established by the Police Reform Act 2002. It is a body corporate consisting of a chairman and 10 other members. Its functions include dealing with complaints made about the conduct of persons serving with the police.

index map The map maintained at the Land Registry.

indictable offence An offence which, if committed by an adult, is triable on indictment in the Crown Court whether it is exclusively so triable or triable either by Crown Court or the Magistrates' Court (Criminal Law Act 1977). Under the Crime and Disorder Act 1998 an adult charged with an indictable only offence is sent forthwith to the Crown Court.

indictment A formal document setting out the charges against the accused. A written accusation of one or more persons of a crime, at the suit of the Queen formerly presented on oath by a grand jury. Indictments were highly technical in form but the Indictments Act 1915 provided that particulars should be set out in ordinary language in which the use of technical terms should not be necessary. An indictment consists of three parts: (1) the introduction indicating the venue and defendant; (2) the statement of offence; (3) particulars of the offence.

indirect effect The doctrine developed by the European Court of Justice which places an obligation on a national court (as part of the state) to interpret national law (as far as is possible) in the light of the relevant Community provisions so as to give effect to the provisions of Community law. The doctrine was developed in Case 14/83 *Von Colson & Kamann v Land Nordrhein-Westfalen* [1984] E.C.R. 1891 and is also referred to as the duty of sympathetic interpretation.

individual voluntary arrangement Under the Insolvency Act 1986, as amended by the Insolvency Act 2000, a proposal by an individual to his creditors for a composition (*q.v.*) in satisfaction of his debts or a scheme of arrangement (*q.v.*) of his affairs providing for some person ("the nominee") to act as his trustee. The nominee must be an insolvency practitioner (*q.v.*) and the court is involved only to a limited extent. For procedure, see generally Insolvency Rules 1986. See also VOLUNTARY ARRANGEMENT; INSOLVENCY; BANKRUPTCY.

indivisum That which is held by two persons in common without partition.

indorsement A writing on the back of an instrument. Indorsement is a mode of transference of bills of exchange (*q.v.*), bills of lading (*q.v.*), etc. consisting of the signature of the person to whom the instrument is payable on the back of the instrument and delivery to the transferee (called an indorsement in blank). A special indorsement specifies the name of the transferee.

inducement, matters of Introductory statements in a pleading (obsolete).

industrial action Action taken by workers (*q.v.*) and/or their trade union (*q.v.*) in pursuance of a trade dispute (*q.v.*). It may take a number of forms, e.g. a strike (*q.v.*), a ban on overtime, a go-slow, the blacking of goods of a particular supplier or customer. Such action will almost invariably involve a breach of contract by the workers and may also lead to an economic tort, e.g. intimidation (*q.v.*) or conspiracy (*q.v.*).

industrial and provident societies A society for carrying on any industry, businesses, or trades specified in or authorised by its rules, whether wholesale or retail, including dealings with land, and banking business. When registered such a society becomes a body corporate with limited liability (Industrial and Provident Societies Acts 1965, 1975, 1978 and 2002).

industrial assurance company One that grants life assurances for small sums at less periodical intervals than two months.

Industrial Councils See WAGES COUNCIL.

industrial injuries Injuries in accidents arising out of and in the course of employment. Under the Social Security Contributions and Benefits Act 1992 those suffering such an injury may qualify for disablement benefit, reduced earnings allowance or retirement allowance.

industrial injuries disablement benefit Paid to compensate those who have suffered disablement from a loss of physical or mental faculty caused by an industrial accident or prescribed disease, e.g. pneumoconiosis or mesothelioma (see Social Security Contributions and Benefits Act 1992 ss.103 and 108).

industrial tribunals See EMPLOYMENT TRIBUNALS.

inevitable accident An accident which cannot be avoided by the exercise of ordinary care, caution and skill.

infamous conduct The term previously used in respect of disgraceful or dishonourable behaviour by medical men. The position is now covered by the Medical Act 1983 s.36 which gives the General Medical Council the power to deal with cases of "serious professional misconduct".

infamy Loss of public standing or character: at one time a disability which debarred a person from giving evidence. It was incurred at common law by a person on conviction of forgery, perjury, etc. but no longer operates to disqualify a witness.

infans [Roman law] A child not yet able to speak. Later, a child under the age of seven.

infant See now MINOR.

infanti proximus [Roman law] A child that can speak but not with understanding (*intellectus*). A child that has not yet passed his seventh year.

infanticide The killing of a newly born child. The Infanticide Act 1938 provides that where a woman by any wilful act or omission causes the death of her child, being a child under the age of 12 months, but at the time the balance of her mind was disturbed by reason of her not having fully recovered from the effect of giving birth to the child, or by reason of the effect of lactation consequent upon the birth of the child, then she shall be guilty of infanticide and punishable as for manslaughter, if but for the Act she might have been convicted of murder.

inferior court Any court other than the Supreme Court, notably county courts and magistrates' courts. The inferior courts are amenable to quashing orders (*q.v.*) (formerly *certiorari*), mandatory orders (*q.v.*) (formerly *mandamus*) and prohibiting orders (*q.v.*) (formerly prohibition).

information A step by which certain civil and criminal proceedings are commenced.

An information is the normal method of instituting criminal proceedings before justices of the peace and amounts to a statement of the facts of the case by the prosecutor to enable appropriate steps to be taken to secure the appearance of the alleged offender before the court.

In criminal procedure, informations were brought to enforce a penalty or forfeiture under a penal statute. They were abolished by the Criminal Law Act 1967.

In Chancery proceedings on behalf of the Crown the information was the statement of facts offered by the Attorney General to the court. In the Exchequer Division there was a proceeding under the equitable jurisdiction of the court to recover damages or money due to the Crown and known as the English Information. The more usual form of proceeding by the Crown to recover a debt was by way of Latin Information of the Revenue side of the King's Bench Division. Latin Informations and English Informations were abolished by the Crown Proceedings Act 1947.

Information Commissioner Oversees and enforces compliance with the Data Protection Act 1998 and the Freedom of Information Act 2000. An independent supervisory authority which reports directly to Parliament.

information meeting Under the Family Law Act 1996 a meeting to discuss, inter alia, the possibility of marriage counselling and the welfare of the children.

information notice A written notice by the Information Commissioner (*q.v.*) to a data controller (*q.v.*) asking for information which he needs in order to carry out his functions. Failure to comply with a notice is an offence.

information padlock A symbol designed by the Information Commissioner (*q.v.*) and the National Consumer Council which warns a data subject (*q.v.*) that their personal data is being collected and processed. Also known as an information signpost.

information sheet The information required to be supplied as part of the case management system in e.g. the Commercial Court.

Information Tribunal Hears appeals by data controllers (*q.v.*) against notices issued by the Information Commissioner (*q.v.*) under the Data Protection Act 1998 and appeals by public authorities against enforcement notices and information notices under the Freedom of Information Act 2000.

informed consent See CONSENT.

informer A person who brought an action or some other proceeding for the recovery of a penalty of which the whole or part went to him. The Common Informers Act 1951 abolished common informer procedure and provided that any offence formerly only punishable by common informer proceedings was to be punishable on summary conviction by fine. The identity of a police informer is generally protected as a matter of public policy.

infortunium, per [By misadventure] See HOMICIDE.

infra [Below]

infringement Interference with, or the violation of, the right of another, particularly the right to a patent (*q.v.*) or copyright (*q.v.*). The remedy is an injunction to restrain future infringements, and an action for the recovery of the damage caused or profits made by the past infringements.

ingenuus [Roman law] A free-born man; a man free from the moment of his birth; being born in wedlock the son of parents either freeborn or made free.

inheritance That which descends from a man to his heirs. See WILL.

inheritance tax Previously known as capital transfer tax and renamed by the Finance Act 1986. Subject to exceptions and reliefs, inheritance tax is charged on chargeable transfers made during the taxpayer's lifetime as well as on death. However, lifetime gifts may be potentially exempt transfers which escape tax unless death occurs within seven years; for deaths between three and seven years a "sliding scale" applies.

inhibition (1) A prohibition from proceeding in a cause or matter.
(2) An entry under the Land Registration Act 1925 on the register forbidding for a given time, or until further order, any dealing with the lands or charges registered. Under the Land Registration Act 2002 inhibitions are subsumed into restrictions (*q.v.*) and no new inhibitions may be created. See LAND REGISTRATION.
(3) An ecclesiastical censure (Ecclesiastical Jurisdiction Measure 1963 s.49).

inhuman or degrading treatment Prohibited under the European Convention on Human Rights (*q.v.*).

injunction An order or decree by which a party to an action is required to do, or refrain from doing, a particular thing. Injunctions are either positive or negative, interim or permanent. The jurisdiction of the High Court to grant an injunction is discretionary.

injuria [A legal wrong]

injuria non excusat injuriam [One wrong does not justify another]

injurious falsehood Sometimes called malicious falsehood or trade libel. A tort consisting of the malicious publication of written or oral falsehoods calculated to produce and resulting in actual damage to a person's business reputation. Injurious falsehood can be distinguished from defamation (*q.v.*) though the distinction is blurred and a party may choose which to sue for.

injury (1) [From the Latin *injuria*] A violation of another's legal rights.
(2) Any disease or impairment of a person's physical or mental condition.

Inner Temple One of the Inns of Court (*q.v.*).

innkeeper One who holds himself out as being prepared to receive and entertain travellers, and who is bound to receive those who are ready to pay his expenses, provided there is sufficient room in the inn. He has a lien for his charges on all property brought by his guest to the inn, even though it is stolen property. The liability of an innkeeper for the loss, or damage, of guests' property is subject to the Hotel Proprietors Act 1956.

innominate term Or intermediate term. A contractual term (*q.v.*), which is neither a condition (*q.v.*) nor a warranty (*q.v.*). The remedy for breach of the term is thus only ascertainable after it has occurred. Serious consequences will entitle a party to the remedies appropriate to a breach of condition and less serious consequences to those appropriate to a breach of warranty.

Inns of Chancery These were legal seminaries attached to the greater bodies, the Inns of Court, to whom their senior students migrated, and from whom they received Readers, or instructors in law. From about 1650 they were entirely in the hands of the attorneys, who did not maintain them for educational purposes, and during the 19th century the Inns of Chancery ceased to exist as such.

Inns of Court The four Inns of Court: Inner Temple, Middle Temple, Lincoln's Inn, and Gray's Inn. They are unincorporated voluntary associations with the exclusive right of call to the Bar. They were established in the 14th century as hostels and schools of law, outside the walls of the City of London. They are not subject to the jurisdiction of the courts, but the judges act as a domestic forum, or as visitors. There are three classes of member: the benchers, senior lawyers and judges who are the governors of the Inn; the barristers who are called by the benchers; and students. See GENERAL COUNCIL OF THE BAR OF ENGLAND AND WALES.

innuendo In proceedings for defamation (*q.v.*), the part of the statement of claim which connects the alleged libel with its subject, or states the latent meaning of words which are not on the face of them libellous. It usually commences with the words "meaning thereby". It must be expressly pleaded. An innuendo should not be left to the jury unless it is supported by extrinsic fact.

inofficious testament [Roman law] A will which wholly passes over, without assigning sufficient reason, those having strong and natural claims on the testator.

inops consilii [Without advice]

inquest An inquisition. An inquiry held by a coroner as to the death of a person who has been slain, or has died suddenly, or in prison, or under suspicious circumstances. See CORONER.

inquiry (1) Under the Court of Protection Rules 2001 the court may make inquiries before deciding whether to appoint a receiver for a patient.
(2) Under the Inquiries Act 2005 s.1 a Minister may set up an inquiry where it appears to him that: (a) particular events have caused or are capable of causing public concern; or (b) there is public concern that particular events may have occurred.

inquisitio [Roman law] Inquiry; made in certain cases by the *Praetor* (or *Praeses*) as preliminary to the confirmation of persons appointed tutors or curators.

inquisition (1) An inquiry by a jury, held before an officer or commissioner of the Crown (inquisitor).
(2) A formal document recording the result of the inquiry.

inquisitorial procedure The system of law in countries whose legal systems originate in Roman or Civil Law under which the judge initiates all necessary investigations and summons and examines witnesses and in which a trial is an inquiry by the court. The only common example of such procedure in English Law is a Coroner's Inquest. See CORONERS; CONTRAST ACCUSATORIAL PROCEDURE.

insanity Unsoundness of mind; mental disease giving rise to a defect of reason which renders a person not responsible in law for his actions.
Every man is presumed sane until the contrary is proved. To establish a defence on the ground of insanity it must be proved that at the time the offence was allegedly committed the party accused was labouring under such a defect of reason from disease of the mind as not to know the nature or quality of the act

he was doing, or if he did know it, that he did not know he was doing wrong (*M'Naghten's Case*, 10 Cl. & Fin. 200). In the Crown Court when the jury find that the accused did the act but was insane, they must return a special verdict (*q.v.*) that the accused is not guilty by reason of insanity. In a case of murder the court must then commit the defendant to hospital without limit of time. For other offences a range of orders are available. A defence of insanity in the magistrates' court can result in a complete acquittal (Criminal Procedure (Insanity) Act 1964). See also diminished responsibility (*q.v.*) which is not to be confused with unfitness to plead (*q.v.*), which refers to the state of mind of the accused at the time of trial.

A contract entered into by an insane person is valid unless the other party was aware that he was incapable of understanding its nature.

insider dealing Under the Criminal Justice Act 1993 insider dealing is an offence triable either way. It consists of an insider, that is an individual who as a director or employee has inside information, that is information that is price sensitive and is not public, dealing himself or encouraging others to deal in or to disclose the information.

insolvency The inability to pay debts in full. The law as to insolvency of an individual is contained in the Insolvency Act 1986 as amended by the Insolvency Act 2000 (and the Insolvency Rules 1986), and may be dealt with by means of individual voluntary arrangement (*q.v.*) or by bankruptcy (*q.v.*). The law as to insolvent companies is also contained in the Insolvency Act 1986 as amended and the Enterprise Act 2002 but reference must also be made to the Company Directors Disqualification Act 1986 as amended by the Insolvency Act 2000. Insolvency of a company may be dealt with by company voluntary arrangements (*q.v.*), administration procedure (*q.v.*) or administrative receivership (*q.v.*), or winding up (*q.v.*). See also DISQUALIFICATION OF DIRECTORS.

insolvency offences Under the Insolvency Act 1986 and the Insolvency Rules 1986 there are a number of offences in relation to the winding-up of a company or bankruptcy of an individual, e.g. transactions in fraud of creditors.

insolvency practitioner A person qualified to act as a liquidator, administrator, administrative receiver or as supervisor of a voluntary arrangement (*q.v.*), or trustee in bankruptcy (*q.v.*). Provisions as to qualifications, e.g. membership of an approved professional body, are contained in the Insolvency Act 1986: it is a criminal offence to act as an insolvency practitioner when not qualified to do so (ibid. ss.388–389).

insolvent A person who is unable to pay his debts as they become due. As to companies, See WINDING UP.

inspection of documents Under the Civil Procedure Rules (*q.v.*) a party to an action is required after the first case management hearing to disclose documentation in his possession and the other party is entitled to inspect it.

inspection of property See SEARCH ORDER.

installation. One of more than 20,000 facilities carrying out the activities listed in Sch.1 of the Environmental Permitting Regulations 2007. These include activities in the energy, metals, minerals, chemicals and waste sectors. Such installations, along with various waste operations and waste mobile plant are regulated facilities (*q.v.*) under the 2007 Regulations. See INTEGRATED POLLUTION PREVENTION CONTROL; ENVIRONMENTAL PERMIT.

instalment A part or portion of the total sum or quantity due, arranged to be taken on account of the total sum or quantity due. See HIRE-PURCHASE AGREEMENT.

instance, court of first A court in which proceedings are commenced, as distinct from an appellate court.

instrument A formal legal document in writing; e.g. a deed of conveyance.

insurable interest The interest which the insured person must have in the subject matter of the insurance (*q.v.*) contract in order to be able to enforce the contract.

insurance A contract (*q.v.*) whereby a person called the insurer agrees in consideration of money paid to him, called the premium, by another person, called the insured, to indemnify the latter against loss resulting to him on the happening of certain events. The policy is the document in which is contained the terms of the contract. (Assurance, traditionally, is the word used in relation to an event which will definitely happen at some time, e.g. death, whereas insurance refers to events which may or may not happen, e.g. fire insurance.) Insurance is a contract uberrimae fidei (of the utmost good faith). It can be classified into two broad categories: indemnity, where the insured is indemnified against actual loss so that the amount paid is the amount of the loss, and contingency, where a specified sum is payable upon the occurrence of an event such as death. It is regulated by the Financial Services and Markets Act 2000.

intangible property Things not physical in nature but capable of being owned, e.g. shares in a company or intellectual property rights.

Integrated Pollution Prevention Control (IPPC) The system of pollution control established by the Pollution Prevention Control Act 1991, which gives effect to the Integrated Pollution Prevention Control Directive 96/61. Certain industrial activities must be authorised by means of a PPC permit in order to achieve an integrated prevention and control of pollution to all environmental media. The system of IPPC is wider in scope than the system of integrated pollution control which it replaced from 2007. The aim of the IPPC Directive is to prevent, reduce and eliminate pollution at source and also to secure the prudent use of natural resources. See ENVIRONMENTAL PERMIT; BATNEEC.

intellectual property An all-embracing term covering copyright (*q.v.*), patents (*q.v.*), trade marks (*q.v.*) and analogous rights founded on confidence and passing off (*q.v.*). The term describes those rights which protect the product of one person's work by hand or brain against unauthorised use or exploitation by another. Intellectual property rights are mainly created by statute and often only give protection if duly registered. The large exception to the need for registration is copyright. The United Nations provides an international focus through the World Intellectual Property Organisation (WIPO) (*q.v.*). In the United Kingdom cases are dealt with by the Patents Court.

intendment of the law A legal presumption.

intention The purpose, aim or desire with which an act is done. Many serious criminal offences require proof of intention (or recklessness) on the part of a defendant and in criminal proceedings the court or jury must decide whether or not the accused did intend or foresee the result of his actions by reference to all the circumstances of the case. They are not bound in law to infer intention merely because the result is the natural and probable result of the action taken (Criminal Justice Act 1967). See also *R. v Hancock & Shankland* [1986] A.C. 455; *R. v Moloney* [1985] A.C. 905; and *R. v Woollin* [1999] A.C. 82. See MALICE; MENS REA.

inter alia [Among others]

inter arma leges silent [Between armies the law is silent] As between the state and its external enemies the laws are silent, and as regards subjects of the state, laws may be silenced by necessity in time of war or disturbance.

inter partes [Between the parties]

inter vivos [During life: between living persons]

interception of communications Under the Regulation of Investigatory Powers Act 2000 it is a criminal offence for a person to intercept, intentionally and without authority, at any place in the United Kingdom, any communication in the course of its transmission by means of a public postal service, or a public or private telecommunication system. Interception takes place if a person modifies or interferes with the system or its operation or monitors transmissions made by means of the system.

There are some permitted interceptions under the Telecommunications (Lawful Business Practice) (Interception of Communications) Regulations 2000. These include: to prevent or detect crime; to investigate or detect the unauthorised use, or to ensure the effective operation of, a telecommunication system; to ascertain compliance with regulatory or self regulatory practices applicable to a system.

Where there is permissible interception, all reasonable efforts must be made to inform any person who might use the system that communications may be intercepted. See INTERCEPTION OF COMMUNICATIONS TRIBUNAL.

Interception of Communications Tribunal Established under the Interception of Communications Act 1985 to decide whether there is proper authorisation for the interception of communications (*q.v.*).

interdicta [Roman law] The procedure by which the *Praetor* (*q.v.*) ordered or forbade something to be done, chiefly in disputes about possession or quasi-possession.

interesse termini [Interest of a term] The interest which a lessee under a lease at common law had before he entered or took possession of the land demised. By the Law of Property Act 1925 s.149 the doctrine of *interesse termini* was abolished, and leases take effect from the date fixed for the commencement of the term without actual entry.

interest A person is said to have an interest in a thing when he has rights, titles, advantages, duties, liabilities connected with it, whether present or future, ascertained or potential, provided they are not too remote.

Any direct interest in the subject-matter of legal proceedings disqualifies anyone from acting in a judicial capacity and will invalidate the proceedings if such person so acts, unless such interest is announced to or known by the parties and they waive the right to object. Formerly, the parties to a case, their spouses, and persons with any pecuniary interest in a case, were incompetent witnesses. But now, in general, all persons are competent witnesses and considerations of interest merely affect the weight of their evidence. See HUSBAND AND WIFE.

Interest also signifies a sum payable in respect of the use of another sum of money, called the principal. For the power to award interest on debts and damages, see Supreme Court Act 1981 s.35A.

interest reipublicae ne maleficia remaneant impunita [It is a matter of public concern that wrongdoings are not left unpunished]

interest reipublicae ne sua re quis male utatur [It concerns the State that no one should make a wrongful use of his property]

interest reipublicae ut sit finis litium [It concerns the State that lawsuits be not protracted]

interference with goods See CONVERSION.

interim authority notice A notice given to a licensing authority following the lapse of a premises licence (*q.v.*) due to the death, incapacity or insolvency of the licence holder. Its effect is to reinstate the licence for a short period of time to allow an application for transfer to be made (see Licensing Act 2003 ss.47–49).

interim order An order made in the course of proceedings, not being a final order, e.g. an order for financial relief (*q.v.*), made in the course of matrimonial proceedings, intended to last for a limited period only.

interim payment May be ordered by the court where, inter alia, a defendant has admitted liability or where judgment has been entered for a sum to be assessed: CPR Pt 25.

interim remedies Are dealt with by CPR Pt 25. They take various forms including an interim injunction; a freezing order (*q.v.*) (formerly a Mareva order) and a search order (*q.v.*) (formerly an Anton Piller order). The list given in the rule is not exhaustive and the court retains its inherent jurisdiction. Application is usually made by an application notice, with or without notice being given to the other side.

interlocutory order While a final order determined the rights of the parties an interlocutory order left something further to be done to determine those rights. See now INTERIM ORDER.

interlocutory proceeding One taken during the course of an action and incidental to the principal object of the action, namely, the judgment. Thus, interlocutory applications in an action include all steps taken for the purpose of assisting either party in the prosecution of his case; or of protecting or otherwise dealing with the subject-matter of the action, or of executing the judgment when obtained.

intermeddling Taking steps in the administration of a deceased person's estate (other than arranging the funeral) which an executor (*q.v.*) should do. An executor who intermeddles before taking a grant will be unable to renounce probate (*q.v.*). A third party who intermeddles is liable as an executor *de son tort* (*q.v.*).

internal market The principal aim of the European Community (*q.v.*) as laid down in art.14 of the EC Treaty (*q.v.*). The internal market is an area without internal frontiers in which the free movement of goods (*q.v.*), persons, services and capital is ensured in accordance with the EC Treaty. See FUNDAMENTAL FREEDOMS; HARMONISATION

International Chamber of Commerce (ICC) A non-governmental organisation which represents the international trade community, promoting and developing international trade. It provides a number of services, e.g. an arbitration service, and has published several documents designed to produce harmonisation and uniformity in commercial practice, e.g. INCOTERMS (*q.v.*) and the Uniform Customs and Practice for Documentary Credits (UCP).

International Court of Justice Established by the United Nations Charter and based in The Hague. It sits in judgement on disputes between states which have accepted its jurisdiction.

International Criminal Court A permanent court situated in The Hague to try individuals for genocide, crimes against humanity and war crimes. Established under the Rome Statute of the International Criminal Court, which was ratified by the United Kingdom in the International Criminal Court Act 2001.

International Labour Organisation (ILO) Established in 1919 by the Treaty of Versailles as an organ of the League of Nations, its mission is to promote fair working conditions in all countries.

international law The rules accepted by civilised states as determining their conduct towards each other, and towards each other's subjects. It is a law of imperfect obligation inasmuch as there is no sovereign superior to enforce it, but the United Nations set up tribunals to try enemy persons accused of offences against, inter alia international law, committed during the Second World War.

In order to prove an alleged rule of international law it must be shown either to have received the express sanction of international agreement or it must have grown to be part of international law by the frequent practical recognition of states in their dealings with each other. International law is only binding on the courts of this country insofar as it has been adopted and made part of municipal law. See GENEVA CONVENTION; PRIVATE INTERNATIONAL LAW; WAR; WAR CRIMES; EUROPEAN CONVENTION ON HUMAN RIGHTS; FUNDAMENTAL FREEDOMS.

international supply contract The provisions of the Unfair Contract Terms Act 1977 do not apply to international supply contracts, as defined in s.26 of that Act.

internet A vast network of computers which stores and transmits information around the world. This term is often used interchangeably with the term WORLD WIDE WEB (WWW) (*q.v.*).

interpleader The process by which a person from whom two or more persons claim the same property can protect himself from legal proceedings by requiring the parties to interplead so that title can be determined by the court.

interpretatio chartarum benigne facienda est ut res magis valeat quam pereat [The construction of deeds is to be made liberally, that the thing may rather avail than perish]

interpretation See the Interpretation Act 1978. See also STATUTORY INTERPRETATION.

interpretation clause A section in an Act of Parliament or clause in a deed setting out the meaning which is to be attached to particular expressions.

interrogatories The old distinction between interrogatories and further and better particulars has been abolished, and CPR Pt 18 now sets out the procedure for obtaining further information (*q.v.*).

intervener A person who voluntarily interposed in an action or other proceeding with the leave of the court under old Ord. 15, r.6; Ord. 16.
A person against whom adultery is alleged may be allowed to intervene in a suit for divorce or judicial separation (Matrimonial Causes Act 1973 s.49(5)). As to intervention after decree nisi, see ss.9 and 15 of that Act.

intestacy Dying intestate, i.e. without leaving a will (*q.v.*). Partial intestacy is the leaving of a will which validly disposes of part only of the property, so that the rest goes as on an intestacy.

intestate succession Intestacy (*q.v.*) is governed by the Administration of Estates Act 1925 as amended by various statutes. The statutory rules governing the distribution of an intestate's estate are based upon the principle that those who die intestate would, had they made a will, have made provision for certain classes of near relations, e.g. children, and would have preferred some relations to others.

intestatus [Roman law] A person who died intestate, i.e. if he had not made a will at all, or if he had made it wrongly, or if the will he had made had been broken, or become null, or if no one was heir under it.

intimate sample A sample of blood, semen or any other tissue fluid, urine or pubic hair; a dental impression; a swab taken from any part of a person's genitals (including pubic hair) or from a person's body orifice other than the mouth (Police and Criminal Evidence Act 1984 s.65(1) as amended). They may be required even from persons not in police custody. See DNA TESTING; NON-INTIMATE SAMPLE.

intimidation The use of violence or threats to compel a person to do or abstain from doing any act which he has a legal right to do or abstain from doing. The tort of intimidation requires the use of unlawful threats to harm the plaintiff's business, see *Rookes v Barnard* [1964] A.C. 1129; and the Trade Union and Labour Relations (Consolidation) Act 1992.

intra vires [Within the power of] See ULTRA VIRES.

introductory tenancy Under the Housing Act 1996 local housing authorities may operate an introductory tenancy regime under which a tenant will have no security of tenure for the first 12 months and the landlord can recover possession for unsatisfactory conduct by the tenant.

intrusion Where the tenant for life of an estate dies, and before the heir of the reversioner or remainderman enters, a stranger enters or "ntrudes" on land. The heir's remedies are entry or an action for recovery of the land. See REVERSION; REMAINDER.

invalid care allowance See now CARER'S ALLOWANCE.

investiture In the legal sense, the delivery of corporeal possession of land granted by a lord to his tenant; livery of seisin (*q.v.*).

investment business Controlled by the Financial Services and Markets Act 2000. See REGULATED ACTIVITY.

invitation to purchase. A commercial communication indicating characteristics of the product and the price in a way appropriate to the means of that commercial communication and thereby enabling the consumer to make a purchase (Consumer Protection from Unfair Trading Regulations 2008 reg.2).

invitation to treat An invitation to others to make an offer (*q.v.*) such as an advertisement, a circular, a request for tenders or the display of goods in a shop window.

invitee A person invited to enter the property of another. An invitee is a person who comes on the occupier's premises with his consent, on business in which the occupier and he have a common interest. At common law, an invitee, using reasonable care on his own part for his own safety, is entitled to expect that the occupier shall on his part use reasonable care to prevent damage from unusual danger which he knows or ought to know. By the Occupiers' Liability Act 1957 s.2 the occupier must take reasonable care to see that a visitor will be reasonably safe in using the premises. An occupier's liability for non-invitees is governed by the Occupier's Liability Act 1984.

invito beneficium non datur [Roman law] A benefit is not conferred upon anyone against his consent.

ipsissima verba [The identical words]

ipso facto [By the mere fact]

Ireland By the Ireland Act 1949 Eire became the independent Republic of Ireland, but Northern Ireland's constitutional position was declared and affirmed.

irrebuttable presumption See PRESUMPTION.

irregularity The departure from, or neglect of, the proper formalities in a legal proceeding. They may be waived or consented to by the other party, or rectified by the court on payment of costs occasioned.

irretrievable breakdown The ground on which a decree of divorce is granted under the Matrimonial Causes Act 1973. See DIVORCE.

irrevocable Not capable of being revoked.

233

Isle of Man A British possession. Has powers of self-government and its own system of courts and law. The UK Government remains responsible for its international relations and defence.

issuable (A pleading) raising a substantial question of fact or law, a judgment or verdict which would determine the action on its merits.

issue (1) The issue of a person consists of his children, grandchildren, and all other lineal descendants. At common law, a gift "to A and his issue" conferred a life estate only because of the failure to use the appropriate word "heirs". The Wills Act 1837 s.29 provided that in a will the words "die without issue" are to be construed as meaning a want or failure of issue in the lifetime, or at the death of, the party, and not an indefinite failure of issue, unless a contrary intention appears by the will. Since 1925, "issue" has been construed as a word of purchase (*q.v.*). See MALE ISSUE.

(2) "Issues" is the technical name for the profits of land taken in execution under a writ of distringas (*q.v.*).

(3) When the parties to an action have answered one another's pleadings in such a manner that they have arrived at some material point or matter affirmed on one side and denied on the other, the parties are said to be "at issue".

A "general issue" was a plea used where the defendant wished to deny all the allegations in the declaration or the principal fact on which it was founded: such is a plea of not guilty to an indictment.

issued share capital See SHARE CAPITAL.

itemised pay statement The Employment Rights Act 1996 s.8 provides that employees are entitled to receive a written pay statement on, or before, the day they are paid, detailing the gross and net amount of pay and any fixed or variable deductions.

J

jactitation of marriage Where a person boasted that he or she was married to someone, so that a common reputation of their marriage might have ensued, the person aggrieved was able to present a petition praying a decree of perpetual silence against the jactitator (abolished by the Family Law Act 1986).

jeopardy, in In danger of being convicted on a criminal charge. See AUTREFOIS ACQUIT.

jetsam Goods which are cast into the sea and there sink and remain under water. See FLOTSAM; WRECK.

jettison The throwing overboard of goods from necessity to lighten the vessel in a storm, or to prevent capture.

job evaluation study Under the Equal Pay Act 1970 s.1(5) a woman is to be regarded as employed on work rated as equivalent with that of a man in the same employment where her work and his have been given an equal value, in terms of various factors, e.g. effort, skill and decision, on a study carried to evaluate the jobs. An employer is under no obligation to undertake a job evaluation study and thus, in practice, claims on this basis are rare and a woman is more likely to pursue an action under the heading of work of equal value (*q.v.*). See EQUALITY CLAUSE; LIKE WORK.

Jobseeker's allowance Introduced by the Jobseekers Act 1995 to replace unemployment benefit. It provides for 26 weeks of benefit, in contrast with unemployment benefit which provided 52 weeks of non-means-tested benefit.

joinder of causes of action The Supreme Court Act 1981 requires the court to try to avoid a multiplicity of cases and this may be done by joining several causes of action, subject to the power of the court to separate part of a claim, to consolidate claims and to try two or more claims on the same occasion under the court's case management powers in CPR Pt 3.

joinder of parties The joining of additional persons in one action as claimants or defendants where the claim is in respect of the same transaction or series of transactions and common questions of law or fact arise under CPR Pt 19.

joint account Where two or more persons advance money and take the security to themselves jointly, each is in equity deemed to be separately entitled to his proportion of the money, so that on his death it passes to his personal representatives and not to his surviving co-lenders. The Law of Property Act 1925 s.111 made it sufficient to say that the money is advanced by the lenders out of money belonging to them on a joint account. This is simply conveyancing machinery, however, and does not conclude the question whether the survivor is entitled beneficially to the whole of the money, or must hold part as trustee for the representatives of the deceased mortgagee.

A joint account in business is one that can be operated by any or all of the persons concerned, either singly or collectively as may be arranged and agreed, e.g. a joint banking account.

joint and several obligation An obligation entered into by two or more persons, so that each is liable severally, and all liable jointly, and a creditor or obligee may sue one or more severally, or all jointly, at his option.

joint liability Parties who are jointly liable share a single liability and each party can be held liable for the whole of it.

joint obligation A bond or covenant or other liability entered into by two or more persons jointly, so that all must sue or be sued upon it together. A judgment against one joint contractor, even though unsatisfied, is generally a bar to any action against the others; a release given to one joint contractor releases all. But one joint obligor who pays a joint debt is entitled to contribution from the others.

joint stock company See COMPANY.

joint tenancy A form of co-ownership in which two or more persons are each regarded as being wholly entitled to the whole property. On the death of one of the joint owners (or tenants) the property remains vested in the survivors by right of survivorship (*jus accrescendi*). A joint tenancy only exists if the four unities are present. These are the unities of:

(1) time—each co-owner must acquire the right at the same time;

(2) title—each must acquire by virtue of the same act or document;

(3) interest—each must acquire the same interest;

(4) possession—each must be entitled to possession of the whole property.

Lack of any of these unities will mean that co-owners are tenants in common (to which the right of survivorship does not attach). Equity "leans against a joint tenancy", i.e. it will find co-ownership to be in common, if possible, but a legal ownership in common cannot now exist in land (Law of Property Act 1925 s.1(6)). See TENANCY IN COMMON.

joint tortfeasors [Joint wrongdoers] Persons who are jointly and severally responsible for the whole damage caused by their wrongdoing. At common law a judgment obtained against one joint wrongdoer released all the others, even if it was unsatisfied and one joint tortfeasor had no right of contribution or indemnity from another joint tortfeasor. These rules were abolished by the Law Reform (Married Women and Tortfeasors) Act 1935 and the position is now governed by the Civil Liability (Contribution) Act 1978. Any person liable in respect of damage suffered by another person may recover contribution in respect of the same damage from any other person liable having regard to each party's responsibility for the damage.

joint venture In criminal law a party to a joint venture may be charged as an accessory to the crime committed. In business a joint venture involves the setting up of a company by two or more parents. In EC law it may be co-operative or concentrative.

jointress A woman entitled to a jointure (*q.v.*).

jointure A provision made by a husband for the support of his wife after his death: originally an estate in joint tenancy of a husband and wife, granted to them before marriage, as provision for the wife.

journals of Parliament The records made in the House of Lords from 1509 and the House of Commons from 1547 of business done, but not of speeches made. The journals of the House of Lords, but not those of the House of Commons, are public records.

joy riding The term commonly applied to the offence of taking a motor vehicle or other conveyance for one's own or another's use without the consent of the owner or other lawful authority, or driving a vehicle or allowing oneself to be carried in it knowing it to have been taken without authority (Theft Act 1968 s.12). See AGGRAVATED VEHICLE TAKING.

judge An officer of the crown who sits to administer justice according to law. Judges are Lords of Appeal in Ordinary (House of Lords), Lords Justices of Appeal (Court of Appeal), puisne judges (High Court), circuit judges (Crown Court and county court), recorders (Crown Court and county court) and district judges (county court and magistrates' court). See now SUPREME COURT.

The Courts and Legal Services Act 1990 specifies minimum eligibility qualifications for each judicial office. Judges of the High Court and above may only be removed from office by both Houses of Parliament.

judge advocate The Judge Advocate-General advises the Secretary of State for Defence in reference to courts-martial (*q.v.*) and other matters of military law. The Judge Advocate of the Fleet holds an analogous post in regard to the Navy. Both these offices are provided for by the Courts-Martial (Appeals) Act 1951. A judge advocate is appointed by or on behalf of the Judge Advocate-General or the Judge Advocate of the Fleet to be a member of every court martial and his rulings on law are binding on the court.

judge's order An order made by a judge in chambers in the Chancery Division so called to distinguish it from a Master's order.

Judges' Rules A set of administrative directions formerly used for the guidance of the police in questioning persons suspected of an offence. Now superseded by the provisions regarding detention, treatment and questioning of persons in custody by the police contained in the Police and Criminal Evidence Act 1984 Pt V and the relevant Codes of Practice.

judgment The decision or sentence of a court in a legal proceeding. Also the reasoning of the judge which leads him to his decision, which may be reported and cited as an authority, if the matter is of importance, or can be treated as a precedent (*q.v.*). The drawing up and filing of judgments is dealt with in CPR Pt 40.

judgment creditor One in whose favour a judgment for a sum of money is given against a judgment debtor.

judgment debtor One against whom judgment is given for a sum of money, and for which the property is liable to be taken in execution at the instance of the judgment creditor.

judgment summons The process used to procure the committal (*q.v.*) of a judgment debtor.

judgments, enforcement of foreign The process by which judgments obtained in the courts of one country may be enforced, by registration, in the courts of another country. See the Administration of Justice Act 1920, the Foreign Judgments (Reciprocal Enforcement) Act 1933 and the Civil Jurisdiction and Judgments Act 1982. For procedure see CPR 1998 Sch.1.

judicatum solvi stipulatio [Roman law] A stipulation whereby a plaintiff took security at the beginning of a suit for satisfaction of the judgment.
(1) Before Justinian. In a real action commenced by *formula petitoria* the defendant was required to give the *cautio judicatum solvi*—a security with sureties. In a personal action, the defendant sued in his own name did not give security.
(2) Under Justinian. The defendant, if sued in his own name, was required to give security that he would appear personally and remain in court to the end of the trial.

Judicature Acts The Judicature Act 1873, which took effect in 1875, amalgamated the then existing superior courts into the Supreme Court of Judicature (*q.v.*) consisting of the Court of Appeal and the High Court of Justice. It also provided for the fusion of law and equity, with the supremacy of equity in case of conflict (s.25).
The Judicature Acts were re-consolidated by the Supreme Court of Judicature (Consolidation) Act 1925 (usually referred to as the Judicature Act 1925). See now Supreme Court Act 1981.

judici officium suum excedenti non paretur [Effect is not given to the decision of a judge delivered in excess of his jurisdiction]

judicia publica [Roman law] Public prosecutions: so called, because generally it was open to any citizen to institute them and carry them through.

Judicial Appointments and Conduct Ombudsman The Judicial Appointments and Conduct Ombudsman investigates complaints about the judicial appointments process and the handling of matters involving judicial discipline or conduct. There are two distinct aspects to the ombudsman's role: to seek redress in the event of maladministration (including delay, rudeness, bias, faulty procedures, offering misleading advice, refusal to answer questions and unfair treatment); and, through recommendations and constructive feedback, in the form of an annual report, to improve standards and practices in the authorities or departments concerned.

Judicial Appointments Commission A body established under the Constitutional Reform Act 2005 s.61, to remove from the Lord Chancellor (*q.v.*) sole responsibility for the selection and appointment of the judiciary. Its remit is to ensure that candidates for judicial office are chosen on merit through fair and open competition from as wide a range as possible. Its membership includes lay, professional and judicial persons.

Judicial Committee The Committee of the Privy Council constituted by the Judicial Committee Act 1833. It has power to entertain an appeal from any Dominion or Dependency of the Crown in any matter, civil or criminal, except where its jurisdiction has been excluded. Appeals may require special leave. It is the final court of appeal from the Ecclesiastical Courts and Prize Courts. The Judicial Committee also hears appeals against striking off from e.g. the General Medical Council.
It is composed of the Lord President, Lord Chancellor, former Lord Presidents, the Lords of Appeal in Ordinary, and members of the Privy Council (*q.v.*) who hold or have held high judicial office in the United Kingdom and Commonwealth.

The Judicial Committee does not formally deliver judgment, but the Queen is given its advice. An order in Council is then issued to give effect to the advice. Formerly dissenting opinions were not disclosed but this is no longer the case.

Once the Constitutional Reform Act 2005 comes into force the Privy Council's judicial role in devolution will be transferred to the Supreme Court (*q.v.*). Membership of the Judicial Committee will also be amended to consist of any member of the Privy Council who holds, or has held, high judicial office or who is a member of the Committee by virtue of any other enactment.

judicial notice The courts take cognisance or notice of matters which are so notorious or clearly established that formal evidence of their exercise is unnecessary: and matters of common knowledge and everyday life; e.g. that there is a period of gestation of approximately nine months before the birth of a child.

judicial precedent See PRECEDENT.

judicial review A uniform system for the exercise by the High Court of its supervisory jurisdiction over inferior courts, tribunals and public bodies and persons. Upon application to the High Court for judicial review the remedies available are orders for a mandatory order (*q.v.*), prohibitory order (*q.v.*) or quashing order (*q.v.*); or for a declaration or injunction (Supreme Court Act 1981 s.31; CPR 1998 Sch.1). The remedy of judicial review is concerned not with the decision of which review is sought but with the decision-making process.

judicial separation Under the Matrimonial Causes Act 1973 a petition for judicial separation may be presented to the court by either party to a marriage on the same grounds as those required for a divorce (*q.v.*) except that there is no requirement that the marriage has broken down irretrievably. After the decree the petitioner is not bound to cohabit with the respondent, although the decree does not end the marriage.

judicial trustee A trustee appointed by the court under the Judicial Trustees Act 1896 and regulated by the Judicial Trustee Rules 1983.

judicium Dei [The judgment of God] Trial by ordeal.

junior barrister A barrister who is not a Queen's Counsel.

jura eodem modo destituuntur quo constituuntur [Laws are abrogated by the same means by which they were made]

jura publica anteferenda privatis [Public rights are to be preferred to private]

jura regalia [Sovereign rights] Such rights were exercised under royal grant by the Lords Marchers (*q.v.*).

jurat A memorandum at the end of an affidavit stating where and when the affidavit was sworn, followed by the signature and description of the person before whom it was sworn.

juratores sunt judices facti [Juries are the judges of fact]

juris praecepta sunt haec: honeste vivere, alterum non laedere, suum cuique tribuere [These are the precepts of the law: to live honestly, to hurt no one, and to give to every man his own] (Justinian)

juris utrum A writ or action by an incumbent to recover possession of land held by him in right of the church.

jurisdiction (1) The power of a court or judge to entertain an action, petition or other proceeding.

(2) The district or limits within which the judgments or orders of a court can be enforced or executed. The territorial jurisdiction of the High Court of Justice is over England and Wales.

In general, the court may take cognisance of acts committed or matters arising abroad, but in practice the defendant must be within the jurisdiction at the time the writ was served, except in cases where leave is given for service out of the jurisdiction, CPR 1998 Sch.1.

jurisprudence The science or theory of law. The study of the principles of law. The philosophical aspect of the knowledge of law (Cicero). The knowledge of things human and divine, the science of the just and unjust (Ulpian). Jurisprudence as a formal science was developed in England by Hobbes, Bentham and Austin. Sir Henry Maine fostered the study of the historical development of law and comparative jurisprudence, the purpose being "to aim at discovering the principles regulating the development of legal systems, with a view to explain the origin of institutions and to study the conditions of their life" (Vinogradoff).

jurisprudentia [Roman law] Law learning, the learning of the *Jurisprudentes* (men skilled in the law).

juror A person is liable to serve as a juror if he is on the electoral register, aged between 18 and 70 and has lived in the United Kingdom for at least five years since the age of 13. Certain classes of persons, for example, the mentally disordered, are ineligible. In addition, those who have served certain prison or community service sentences or who are on bail in criminal proceedings are disqualified.

jury [*jurare*, to swear] A body of sworn persons summoned to decide questions of fact in a judicial proceeding. The jury in origin was a body of neighbours summoned by some public officer to give, upon oath, a true answer to some question (Maitland). They originally testified to and decided issues of fact of their own knowledge. With the introduction of sworn witnesses the jury became exclusively the judges of fact. The statute law relating to juries, jurors and jury service is to be found in the Juries Act 1974 (as amended by the Criminal Justice Act 2003).

There is a right to trial by jury in criminal matters which are triable only on indictment or those which are triable either on indictment or summarily. However, s.43(2) of the Criminal Justice Act 2003 makes provision in cases involving complex or lengthy fraud trials for the prosecution to apply to a Crown Court judge to have the trial conducted in the absence of a jury. In civil cases, a qualified right to jury trial is given in some cases (notably defamation) and in other cases there is a discretion to order jury trial (Supreme Court Act 1981). See CHALLENGE OF JURORS; JURY VETTING.

jury vetting Under the Juries Act 1974 s.5, the prosecution and the defence have a right to inspect the panel from which jurors will be or have been drawn to try their case. They may make enquiries about the potential jurors in order to see if they might object to any of them sitting on the jury (*q.v.*). See CHALLENGE OF JURORS; JURY.

jus [Roman law] In its widest sense, includes moral as well as legal obligations. It means: (1) "law" as opposed to *lex* (a statute); (2) a right; (3) relationship; and (4) the court of a magistrate.

jus accrescendi [Roman law] The right of accrual.

jus accrescendi inter mercatores pro beneficio commercii locum non habet [The right of survivorship among merchants, for the benefit of commerce, does not exist] See JOINT TENANCY.

jus aedilicium [Roman law] The rules of law as stated in the edicts published by the curule aediles and administered by them. It was included in the *jus honorarium* (*q.v.*).

jus canonicum Canon law.

jus civile [Roman law] (1) The law peculiar to a particular state, e.g. Rome. (2) The old law of Rome, as opposed to the later *jus praetorium.*

jus disponendi [Roman law] The right of disposing; the right of alienation.

jus ex injuria non oritur [A right does not arise out of a wrong]

jus gentium [Roman law] The law of nations. The law common to all peoples. The rules of private law, recognised generally by different nations.

jus honorarium [Roman law] Magisterial law, *jus praetorium* (*q.v.*) and *jus aedilicium* (*q.v.*).

jus in personam A right against a specific person.

jus liberorum [Roman law] The special rights granted to the mother of three or four children; or to the father.

jus mariti [The right of a husband] See HUSBAND AND WIFE; INTESTATE SUCCESSION.

jus naturale [Roman law] The law that nature has taught all living things (Justinian). The law supposed to be constituted by right reason, common to nature and to man; the principles deducible from the *jus gentium.*

jus non scriptum [Roman law] The unwritten law. The law that use has approved (Justinian).

jus postliminii See POSTLIMINIUM.

jus potestatis See PATRIA POTESTAS.

jus praetorium [Roman law] The rules of law as stated in the *Praetor's* edict and administered by the *Praetor* Part of the *jus honorarium* (*q.v.*).

jus privatum [Roman law] That part of the law which related to causes between private individuals; divided into three parts, according as it related to persons, things, or actions.

jus publicum [Roman law] That part of the law concerning public affairs; that which dealt with causes between the State and private individuals. It comprised ecclesiastical law, constitutional law, and criminal law.

jus publicum privatorum pactis mutari non potest [Public law is not to be superseded by private agreements]

jus quaesitum tertio [Rights on account of third parties] A contract cannot confer rights on a third party and only a party to a contract can sue on it. The position with regard to third parties is now governed by the Contracts (Rights of Third Parties) Act 1999. See PRIVITY OF CONTRACT.

jus scriptum [Roman law] The written part of the law consisting of statutes, decrees of the plebs and of the senate, decisions of emperors, edicts of magistrates and answers of jurisprudents.

jus spatiandi et manendi [The right to stray and remain] *Jus spatiandi* is the right to wander at will over a servient tenement, and can constitute an easement (*Re Ellenborough Park* [1956] Ch. 131).

jus tertii [The right of a third person] A defendant cannot plead that the claimant (*q.v.*) is not entitled to possession as against him because a third party is the true owner, except where the defendant is acting with the authority of the true owner.

jus tripertitum [Roman law] The threefold law, e.g. *jus privatum* was *tripertitum*, as composed of the *jus naturale, jus gentium* and the *jus civile.*

just satisfaction This is a phrase arising from the European Convention on Human Rights (*q.v.*) and represents the remedy that must be given for established breaches of human rights. The phrase has become important for UK lawyers as the courts may only grant damages for breach of Convention rights under s.8 of the Human Rights Act 1998 if it is necessary to afford just satisfaction and must take into account the principles applied by the European Court of Human Rights (*q.v.*) in doing so.

justice The upholding of rights, and the punishment of wrongs, by the law. See also JUSTITIA.

justices of the peace [Magistrates] Persons formerly appointed by the Crown to be justices within a certain area for the conservation of the peace, and for the execution of other duties. Under the Courts Act 2003 they are assigned to a local justice area (*q.v.*) but have national jurisdiction. They initiate the proceedings for indictable offences and commit defendants to the Crown Court for trial. They act judicially in all cases where they have summary jurisdiction, whether criminal or civil. On the hearing of appeals from magistrates' courts and on proceedings on committal for sentence, justices sit with a Crown Court judge (*q.v.*). See MAGISTRATES.

Justices of the Supreme Court See SUPREME COURT.

justiciability The courts have declined to review matters such as the exercise of the prerogative power or the validity of an Act of Parliament (except to declare it incompatible with EU law or the Convention for the Protection of Human Rights and Fundamental Freedoms) on the ground that they are not suitable for such review; they are non-justiciable.

justiciar The chief political and legal officer of the Norman and Plantagenet kings. He was *ex officio* regent when the King went overseas, and presided over the *Curia Regis* (*q.v.*). The office ceased to exist during the reign of Henry III.

justicias facere To hold pleas; to exercise judicial functions.

justification (1) The plea in defence of an action which admits the allegations of the claimant but pleads that they were justifiable or lawful. For example, in libel a plea of justification admits the publication of the defamatory words, but pleads that they are true in substance and in fact.

(2) In criminal law, a justification provides a defence for the accused's conduct as it renders such conduct lawful.

justitia [Roman law] Justice. The constant and perpetual wish to give each man his due (Justinian).

juvenile Children, i.e. those under 14 years, and young persons, i.e. those aged over 14 and under 17 years are dealt with summarily by a youth court (*q.v.*). See COMMUNITY HOMES; DETENTION CENTRE; REMAND; YOUNG OFFENDERS.

juvenile courts See YOUTH COURTS.

K

K.C King's Counsel. See QUEEN'S COUNSEL.

kerb crawling The term used to describe the offence under s.1 of the Sexual Offences Act 1985 (as amended by the Sexual Offences Act 2003) where a person persistently solicits a person or persons for the purpose of prostitution from a motor vehicle in a street or public place in such a manner or circumstances as to annoy the person or persons solicited or be a nuisance to other persons in the neighbourhood.

Keys, House of The Legislative Assembly of the Isle of Man (*q.v.*).

Khanna hearing A hearing to determine whether a witness should produce the documents requested in the witness summons.

kidnapping A common law offence involving the carrying away of a person by another by force or fraud without their consent or lawful excuse.

King's (Queen's) Bench See COURT OF KING'S (QUEEN'S) BENCH.

King's (Queen's) Chambers Those portions of the British territorial waters which are inclosed within headlands so as to be cut off from the open sea by imaginary straight lines drawn from one promontory to another.

King's (Queen's) Coroner and Attorney Originally this officer was concerned with deaths in the King's Bench Prison (now abolished). In 1892 the office was merged in that of Master of the Crown Office. See CROWN OFFICE; CLERK OF THE CROWN.

kitemark A mark displayed on a product which complies with the standards of the British Standards Institution.

knight The lowest title of dignity. It is not hereditary. Knights are of the following orders: Garter, Thistle, St Patrick, Bath, St Michael and St George, Star of India, Indian Empire, Royal Victorian, British Empire, and last, Knights Bachelor.

knight's service, tenure by Where a man held land of another or of the Crown by military service, of which the principal varieties were escuage, grand serjeanty, castleward and cornage. It had five incidents, namely, aids, relief, wardship, marriage and escheat; the King's tenants *in capite ut de corona* were further liable to primer seisin and fines for alienation. Tenure by knight's service was converted into common socage by the statute 1660 (12 Car. 2 c.24).

know-how In the Income and Corporation Taxes Act 1988 (as amended), this is defined as any industrial information and techniques likely to assist in the manufacture or processing of goods or materials. The owner of secret know-how may often make it available for others to use by way of a know-how licence in return for payment.

L

LLB [Bachelor of laws from Latin *legum baccalaureus*] Undergraduate degree in law.

LLM [Master of laws from Latin *legum magister*] Postgraduate degree in law.

LPC See LEGAL PRACTICE COURSE.

L.S. *locus sigilli* (*q.v.*).

Labourers, Statute of The statute (23 Edw. c.3), passed in 1349 after about half the population had died of the Black Death. It enacted that everyone under 60, except traders, craftsmen, those with private means and land owners, should work for anyone willing to employ them at the wages paid from 1340 to 1346.

laches Negligence or unreasonable delay in asserting or enforcing a right. A delay sufficient to prevent a party from obtaining an equitable remedy under the maxim that equity aids the vigilant and not the indolent. The maxim does not apply to cases to which the Limitation Acts apply.

laesae majestatis, crimen [The crime of injured majesty] Treason (*q.v.*).

lagan Goods cast into the sea from a ship that perishes that are heavier than water and are buoyed so that they will not sink. See WRECK.

Lammas August 1.

Lammas lands Lands held by a number of holders in severalty during a portion of the year. After the severalty crop has been removed they are commonable also to other classes of commoners. The date of opening them is now August 12.

Lancaster, County Palatine of See PALATINE COURT.

land According to the Law of Property Act 1925:
"land includes land of any tenure, and mines and minerals, whether or not held apart from the surface, buildings or parts of buildings (whether the division is horizontal, vertical or made in any other way) and other corporeal hereditaments; also a manor, an advowson, and a rent and other incorporeal hereditaments, and an easement, right, privilege or benefit in, or over, or derived from land".

In respect of Acts of Parliament passed after 1978, "land" includes buildings and other structures, land covered with water and any estate, interest, easement, servitude or right in or over land (see Interpretation Act 1978).

land certificate A certificate issued by the Land Registry to the registered proprietor of land. See LAND REGISTRATION.

land charges Under the Land Charges Act 1972 (as amended by the Local Land Charges Act 1975) registers are maintained at the Land Charges Registry. There are six classes of land charge which can be registered:
Class A: statutory land charges such as a rent or annuity;
Class B: similar charges not made on the application of any person, if created or conveyed after 1925 and not being local land charges (*q.v.*) such as a charge on land recovered for a legally assisted person under the Legal Aid Act 1984;
Class C: (not being a local land charge) (i) puisne mortgages, (ii) limited owner's charges, (iii) general equitable charges, (iv) estate contracts, if created after 1925, or acquired after that date;
Class D: (not being a local land charge) (i) Inland Revenue charges for inheritance tax under the Inheritance Tax Act 1984, (ii) restrictive covenants created after 1925, except covenants in leases, (iii) equitable easements, rights and privileges created after 1925;
Class E: annuities created before 1926; and
Class F: charges affecting any land by virtue of the Family Law Act 1996.
Registration is normally deemed to constitute notice of the matter and will bind a purchaser.
See LOCAL LAND CHARGE.

land, compulsory acquisition Land may be acquired compulsorily by statute for public purposes, e.g. for planning (*q.v.*). The Land Compensation Act 1961 consolidates the law relating to the assessment of compensation on compulsory acquisition, and the Acquisition of Land Act 1981 lays down a standardised procedure.

land registration The system whereby transactions in land in England and Wales are subject to registration at the Land Registry. Under the Land Registration Act 1925, only two kinds of estate were recognised as registrable: the freehold and the long lease. The Land Registration Act 2002 extended the categories of rights which can be registered as independent registered estates to include freehold estates, leasehold estates with more than seven years unexpired, leases for discontinuous periods, leases taking effect in possession more than three months from the date of their grant, some leases to which the Housing Act 1985 applies, rentcharges (*q.v.*), franchises and profits a prendre (*q.v.*) in gross.

243

Details of title are placed on the Land Register, which is intended to be a complete record of the property, providing a description of it, of who owns it and of any matters affecting it, for example, a mortgage. See LAND CHARGES.

Land Registry A statutory body first established in 1862 but now operating under the Land Registration Act 2002 and dealing with registration under that Act.

land tax A tax formerly payable annually in respect of the beneficial ownership of land. The tax was originally levied in 1692 under the statute (4 Will. & Mary c.1), and was made redeemable by the Land Tax Perpetuation Act 1798. The Finance Act 1949 Pt V provided for the stabilisation and compulsory redemption of land tax. Land tax was finally abolished by the Finance Act 1963.

landfill tax Under the Finance Act 1996, charged on the disposal of waste at a landfill site after October 1, 1996.

landlord and tenant The relation of landlord and tenant (*q.v.*) depends upon contract and is created by the landlord allowing the tenant to occupy the landlord's property for a consideration termed rent, recoverable by distress. Exclusive possession of the premises must be granted, for a defined term. The contract is embodied in a lease (*q.v.*) or in a tenancy agreement. Private residential tenancies are mostly now governed by the Housing Act 1996; business tenancies by the Landlord and Tenant Act 1954.

The security of tenure of tenants, previously statutorily protected, has been lessened under more recent legislation. See SECURITY OF TENURE HARASSMENT.

Lands Tribunal The tribunal established by the Lands Tribunal Act 1949 (in place of official arbitrators and others) to determine questions relating to compensation for the compulsory acquisition of land and other matters, including the discharge or modifications of restrictive covenants under Law of Property Act 1925 s.84 (as amended by Law of Property Act 1969 s.28), and appeals from the local valuation courts. Appeal is by way of case stated to the Court of Appeal.

lapse As a general rule, when a person to whom property has been devised or bequeathed dies before the testator (*q.v.*), the devise (*q.v.*) or bequest (*q.v.*) fails or lapses, and the property falls into residue, except that a lapsed share of residue does not fall into residue, but devolves as upon an intestacy (*q.v.*). But if land is given to a person in tail who dies before the testator, leaving issue capable of taking under the entail, the land goes as if the devisee had died immediately after the testator (Wills Act 1837 s.32). And if the testator bequeaths (or devises) property to his child or other issue of himself and such issue dies leaving issue who survive the testator, the legacy (or devise) does not lapse but takes effect as a gift to the issue and if more than one, in agreed shares *per stirpes* (*q.v.*) (s.33). This rule is subject to contrary intention in the will. It applies to illegitimate children or other issue (Family Law Reform Act 1969 s.16).

Proceedings lapse in the event of the death of a defendant in criminal proceedings, or where no step is taken in an action within the appropriate time.

larceny The offence of larceny and related offences, largely contained in the Larceny Act 1916, was abolished and replaced by theft and related offences under the Theft Act 1968. See THEFT.

lasting power of attorney See POWER OF ATTORNEY.

lata culpa dolo aequiparatur [Roman law] Gross negligence is equivalent to fraud.

late payment of commercial debts Interest on sums due under a commercial contract may be payable under the terms of the contract or under the Late Payment of Commercial Debts (Interest) Act 1998. This Act provides that, where both parties to a contract for the supply of goods or services and for connected purposes are acting in the course of a business, then it is an implied term that simple interest may be charged on outstanding payments. Where a party enters as purchaser into a contract on written standard terms, the contract being one to which the 1998 Act applies and any of those written standard terms would be void under the Act, the court can, on an application by a representative body, grant an injunction restraining the purchaser from relying on the term (Late Payment of Commerical Debts (Interest) Regulations 2002).

latitat See BILL OF MIDDLESEX.

law A law is an obligatory rule of conduct. The commands of him or them that have coercive power (Hobbes). A law is a rule of conduct imposed and enforced by the Sovereign (Austin). But the law is the body of principles recognised and applied by the State in the administration of justice (Salmond). Blackstone, however, maintained that a rule of law made on a pre-existing custom exists as positive law apart from the legislator or judge.

Law Commission The Law Commission is a body set up to promote the systematic development, simplification and modernisation of the law (Law Commissions Act 1965).

Law Lords The Lord Chancellor, the Lords of Appeal in Ordinary (*q.v.*), ex-Lord Chancellors, and other peers who have held high judicial office. They sit in the Appellate Committee of the House of Lords to hear appeals. Under the Constitutional Reform Act 2005 the Lords of Appeal in Ordinary will become the initial Justices of the Supreme Court (*q.v.*). See also JUDICIAL COMMITTEE; SUPREME COURT.

law merchant The custom of merchants as settled by judicial decisions. It had its origin in the international usages of merchants, and some part of it was borrowed from Roman law. It was administered in special courts, such as courts of the markets and fairs; e.g. courts of pie poudre. Before the time of Lord Mansfield, all the evidence in mercantile cases was left to the jury, the custom of merchants being treated as a question of fact. When so proved a mercantile custom became part of the general law. Lord Mansfield separated the law from the facts in his charges to the jury, and henceforward the law merchant became assimilated to the common law. See COMMERCIAL CAUSE.

law of nations International law (*q.v.*) or public international law.

law of nature The *jus naturale* (*q.v.*). The Roman conception of a hypothetical law of a bygone state of nature or golden age, and believed to exist in part in all then existing bodies of law; to be ascertained by segregating the principles common to many or all of them, i.e the *jus gentium* (*q.v.*). The *jus naturale* or law of nature is simply the *jus gentium* or law of nations seen in the light of a particular theory—stoic philosophy (Maine).

Law of Property Acts The name given to the following group of Acts (and the Acts amending them): Law of Property Act 1925; Administration of Estates Act 1925; Land Charges Act 1925; Land Registration Act 1925; Settled Land Act 1925; Trustee Act 1925; Universities and College Estates Act 1925. The Law of Property Act 1922 was drafted by a committee set up by Lord Birkenhead, when Lord Chancellor, to reform the law and rid it of the traces of the feudal system, and is consequently known as Lord Birkenhead's Act. It was due to come into operation on January 1, 1925, but was postponed, and finally only came into effect as amended by the Law of Property (Amendment) Act 1924, with regard to the abolition of copyhold tenure, as from January 1, 1926. The rest of the Act was split up into Acts dealing with particular subjects, as above, with effect from January 1, 1926.

Law Officers of the Crown The Attorney General (*q.v.*) and the Solicitor-General (*q.v.*), see the Law Officers Act 1944 (as amended).

law reform See LAW COMMISSION.

law report A published account of a legal proceeding, giving a statement of the facts, and the reasons the court gave for its judgment. The Law Reports (see below) give an account of the arguments of counsel. There is a "headnote" or "short points" to law reports for the convenience of users, but they may be misleading. Reports by barristers are cited in arguments as precedents. Regular law reporting appears to have commenced in the 13th century with the Year Books (*q.v.*). In 1865 the Council of Law Reporting commenced a series of reports covering all the superior courts, known as the Law Reports. Reports in *The Times* and in professional journals may be cited if a case is not officially reported. The Stationary Office "Tax Cases" give revised shorthand reports of the judgments. The official Weekly Law Reports give promptly published reports of decided cases, some only of which will appear in the Law Reports. See citation. See also appendix: law reports, journals, and their abbreviations.

Law Society The Law Society is the representative body for solicitors in England and Wales. It was previously entrusted with the control and regulation of the solicitors' profession, a role now undertaken by the Solicitors Regulation Authority (SRA) (*q.v.*) which is an independent regulatory body of the Law Society. Formed in 1825, incorporated in 1831, and entrusted with the custody of the roll of solicitors in 1888, since when no person can be admitted as a solicitor unless he has obtained from the Society a certificate that he has passed certain examinations (Solicitors Act 1974).

lawful A statute is normally permissive, but may confer legal rights, the resistance to which, or the infringement of which by others would be wrongful.

lay days The days which are allowed by a charterparty for loading and unloading the ship. If the vessel is detained beyond the period allowed, demurrage (*q.v.*) becomes payable.

lay justice a justice of the peace (*q.v.*) who is not a District Judge (Magistrates' Courts). See MAGISTRATE.

lay-fee Lands held in fee of a lay lord, as distinguished from lands held in frankalmoign (*q.v.*).

Le Roy (or La Reine) le veult [The King (or the Queen) wishes it] The form of the royal assent to Bills in Parliament.

Leader, or leading counsel Queen's Counsel (*q.v.*).

leading case A judicial decision or precedent (*q.v.*) settling the principles of a branch of law.

leading questions Questions which directly or indirectly suggest to a witness the answer he is to give, or which put disputed matters to the witness in a form admitting of the answer "Yes" or "No". The general rule is that leading questions are allowed in cross-examination, but not in examination-in-chief.

League of Nations The society or association of states established by Pt I of the Treaty of Peace between the Allied and Associated Powers, and Germany, signed at Versailles, June 28, 1919. The League was superseded by the United Nations (*q.v.*) following the Second World War.

leapfrog An appeal from the High Court or Divisional Court direct to the House of Lords, thereby "leapfrogging" the Court of Appeal. A certificate must be granted by the trial judge, all parties must agree and the House of Lords must give leave (Administration of Justice Act 1969 ss.12–15). See SUPREME COURT.

lease A grant of the exclusive possession of property to last for a term of years or periodic tenancy, usually with the reservation of a rent. It is essential that a lease shall specify the period during which the lease is to endure, and the beginning and end of the term. The person who grants the lease is called the landlord or lessor, and the person to whom it is granted the tenant or lessee. A lease must be for a smaller estate than the tenant has in the property, for if it comprises his whole interest it is an assignment of that interest. Where a person, who is himself a tenant, grants a lease of the same property to another person for a shorter term, it is called a sublease. A lease is a legal estate in land, if correctly created (Law of Property Act 1925 ss.52 and 54). For the purposes of creating a legal estate all leases are to be by deed, except leases taking effect in possession for a term not exceeding three years at the best rent obtainable without taking a fine (or premium), which may be made orally or in writing. A lease void because not made by deed may be enforceable in equity, provided that there is a valid contract under s.2 of the Law of Property (Miscellaneous Provisions) Act 1989 (*Walsh v Lonsdale* (1882) 21 Ch.D. 9). Leases come to an end by expiry, notice, forfeiture, surrender, merger, or by becoming a satisfied term, by being enlarged into a fee simple or by disclaimer or by frustration. See ESTATE; FORFEITURE; LEASEHOLD; REVERSION; TENANT; TERM OF YEARS.

lease and release A mode of conveying freehold land which was in common use from 1536 to 1841. It was used to evade the Statute of Enrolments (27 Hen. 8 c.16), passed to prevent land from being conveyed secretly by bargain and sale (*q.v.*). The Act required only bargains and sales of estates of inheritance or freehold to be enrolled, and therefore it soon became the practice on a sale of land for the vendor to execute a lease to the purchaser for a year by way of bargain and sale, which under the Statute of Uses (27 Hen. 8 c.10), gave him seisin (*q.v.*) of the land without entry or enrolment, and then the vendor released his reversion to the purchaser by a deed known as a release, thus vesting in him the fee simple in possession without entry or livery of seisin (*q.v.*). The lease and the release were executed on the same day, the release being dated for the following day and being executed after the lease. The consideration for the lease was a nominal sum of five or ten shillings, which was never paid, the real consideration being stated in the release. In 1841 the statute (4 Vict. c.21) made a release effectual without the preliminary lease for a year, and in 1845 the Real Property Amendment Act 1845 made a deed of grant sufficient for the conveyance of all corporeal hereditaments. Conveyance by bargain and sale was finally abolished by the Law of Property Act 1925 s.51(1).

lease by estoppel If a person makes a lease of land in which he has no interest, and he afterwards acquires the land, he is estopped or precluded from denying the existence of the lease.

leasehold A term of years absolute (see TERM OF YEARS). One of the two legal estates in land.

Leasehold Valuation Tribunal A tribunal which handles disputes between leaseholders and freeholders of property concerning service charges, the quality of services provided, the purchase of the freehold and extension of a lease.

leave and licence Permission. In an action for trespass it is a good defence to plead that the act complained of was done with the "leave and licence", i.e the permission, of the claimant.

legacy A gift of personal property by will. The person to whom the property is given is called the legatee, and the gift of property is called a bequest. The legatee's title to the legacy is not complete until the executor has assented to it. (1) A specific legacy is a bequest of a specific part of the testator's personal estate. (2) A demonstrative legacy is a gift of a certain sum directed to be paid out of a specific fund. (3) A general legacy is one payable only out of the general assets of the testator. See ABATEMENT OF LEGACIES.

legacy duty An ad valorem duty on all legacies of personal property other than leaseholds. It was abolished by the Finance Act 1949 s.27.

legal advice privilege See LEGAL PROFESSIONAL PRIVILEGE.

legal aid The scheme which publically funds advice, assistance and/or representation in legal proceedings. It is administered by the Legal Services Commission (*q.v.*). In criminal proceedings, the Criminal Defence Service (*q.v.*) authorises and monitors firms conducting criminal work. It does not make decisions about individual funding of proceedings; this is the responsibility of the court. The magistrates' court makes its decision based on an interests of justice test together with a means test. The Crown Court makes its decision solely on an interests of justice test but this may be extended to also include a means test in due course. In civil and family proceedings, legal aid is the responsibility of the Community Legal Service (*q.v.*). In order to qualify, an applicant must satisfy a merits test and the case must fall within one of the limited categories of types of case which the scheme funds.

legal certainty One of the general principles of law followed by the European Court of Justice (*q.v.*) embracing, inter alia, "respect for vested rights" and "recognition of legitimate expectations". See also PROPORTIONALITY; EQUALITY.

legal estate; legal fiction; legal memory See ESTATE; FICTION; MEMORY.

legal executive Solicitors' non-admitted staff, previously known as managing clerks. The Institute of Legal Executives prescribes examinations, regulations, etc. Fellows of the Institute may practise in both contentious and non-contentious areas, carrying out the work of a qualified solicitor. The rights of audience of Legal Executives are governed by the Courts and Legal Services Act 1990 as amended by the Legal Services Act 2007.

legal personality A legal person (human or corporate) is a person who enjoys, and is subject to, rights and duties at law. See PERSON; CORPORATION.

Legal Practice Course The vocational stage of training for a solicitor. The Solicitors Regulation Authority validates and monitors the delivery of these courses nationally.

legal professional privilege The privilege which attaches to two types of confidential communications: (i) communications between the client and his legal adviser for the purpose of giving and receiving legal advice (*Three Rivers DC v Bank of England (Disclosure) (No.4)* [2004] UKHL 48; [2004] 3 W.L.R. 1274, HL). This is also known as legal advice privilege; (ii) communications between legal adviser and a third party or the client and a third party where the sole or dominant purpose of the communication was its use by the legal adviser in advising the client in relation to litigation which has already commenced or which is contemplated (*Wheeler v Le Marchant* (1881) 17 Ch. D. 675). This is also known as LITIGATION PRIVILEGE

Legal Services Board Established as an independent body under the Legal Services Act 2007 as part of the overall reform to the provision and regulation of legal services in England and Wales. The Board is sponsored by the Ministry of Justice but otherwise is independent of both government and legal professions. Once it is fully operational (expected to be in 2010), it will establish a new regulatory framework for the provision of legal services. Amongst its other duties is a requirement to establish a Consumer Panel (*q.v.*). See REGULATORY OBJECTIVES.

Legal Services Commission An executive non-departmental public body established under the Access to Justice Act 1999. It replaced the Legal Aid Board and exercises functions relating to the Criminal Defence Service (*q.v.*) and the Community Legal Service (*q.v.*). See LEGAL AID.

Legal Services Consultative Panel Established by the Access to Justice Act 1999, the panel has a duty to assist in the maintenance and development of standards in the education, training and conduct of persons offering legal services and provide the Secretary of State, at his request, with advice regarding the provision of legal services.

Legal Services Ombudsman Appointed under the Courts and Legal Services Act 1990, in the event of a complaint against a lawyer the Ombudsman investigates the manner in which that complaint was handled by the lawyer's professional body to ensure that any complaint has been handled fairly, thoroughly and efficiently. See OFFICE FOR LEGAL COMPLAINTS.

legal tender Tender or offer of payment in a form which a creditor is obliged to accept. Bank of England notes and gold coins are legal tender for the payment of any amount. Cupro-nickel and bronze coins are legal tender for relatively small amounts (Coinage Act 1971 s.2 as amended by the Currency Act 1983). A creditor is not obliged to give change; the exact sum due must be tendered.

legatarius partiarius [Roman law] A legatee to whom the testator had in his will instructed his heir to give a definite share of his universal succession (*hereditas*), called a legacy of partition (*legatum partitionis*) because the legatee divided the inheritance with the heir.

legatum [Roman law] A legacy (*q.v.*); any gift from a deceased person.

legatum generis [Roman law] A legacy of a thing in general terms as belonging to a class; e.g. a slave.

legatum nominis [Roman law] A legacy of a debt.

legatum optionis [Roman law] A legacy of choice, where the testator directs the legatee to choose from among his slaves or other property.

legatum partitionis [Roman law] A legacy where the legatee divided the inheritance with the heir.

legatum poenae nomine [Roman law] A legacy by way of penalty, to constrain their heir to do or not to do something.

leges posteriores priores contrarias abrogant [Later laws abrogate prior contrary laws.]

legislation See ACT OF PARLIAMENT; DELEGATED LEGISLATION.

legitimacy The condition of being born in lawful wedlock. Every child born of a married woman during the subsistence of the marriage is presumed to be legitimate but this presumption may be rebutted. An illegitimate child is legitimated by the marriage of its parents and is thereafter in the same position as if it had been legitimate when born. The Family Law Reform Act 1987 reduced the legal significance of illegitimacy by providing that references in a statute to any relationship between two persons shall, unless the contrary intention appears, be construed without regard to whether or not the father and mother of either of them, or the father and mother of any person through whom the relationship is deduced, have or had been married to each other at any time.

legitimatio [Roman law] Children of concubinage could be legitimated:
(1) *per subsequens matrimonium;* by the subsequent marriage of the parents;
(2) by offering to the *curio (per oblationem curiae)*, i.e. by making a son a *decurio*, a member of the magisterial class;
(3) by rescript of the emperor (Justinian).

lessee One to whom a lease is granted.

lessor One who grants a lease.

letter of credit An authority by one person to another to draw cheques (*q.v.*) or bills of exchange (*q.v.*) (with or without a limit as to amount) upon him, with an undertaking to honour the drafts on presentation. An ordinary letter of credit contains the name of the person by whom the drafts are to be negotiated or cashed: when it does not do so, it is called an open letter of credit.

letter of request Where a party to proceedings wishes to obtain a deposition from someone outside the jurisdiction, the country not being a Regulation State (as defined in Council Regulation 1206/2001), he may apply to the court for an order to issue a letter of request. The letter is a request to the judicial authorities in which the deponent is to take his evidence or arrange for it to be taken. Letters of request are issued at the office of the Master's Secretary (CPR Sch.1).

letters of administration Where a person dies without making a valid will, administrators will apply for a grant of letters of administration which confers on the administrators the right to administer the estate. If the deceased made a will but no executors were appointed or those who were appointed are not able or willing to act, administrators will apply for a grant of letters of administration with the will annexed. This also confers the right to administer the estate.

letters of marque (or mart) Extraordinary commissions issued, either in time of war or peace, by the Lords of the Admiralty, or the vice-admirals of a distant province, to the commanders of merchant ships, authorising reprisals for reparation of the damages sustained by them through enemies at sea. They were either "special", to make reparation to individuals, or "general", when issued by the government of one state against all the subjects of another. Letters of countermarque were issued as a reprisal for the issue of letters of marque.

letters patent Grants by the Crown of lands, franchises, etc., contained in charters or intruments not sealed up but exposed to open view with the Great Seal pendent at the bottom, and usually addressed to all the subjects of the realm. See PATENT.

levant and couchant [Risen and laid down] Refers to cattle which have been on another's field and have been able to feed and lie down on the land. When land to which a right of common pasture is annexed can maintain during the winter by its produce, or requires, to plough and manure it, a certain number of cattle, those cattle are said to be levant and couchant on the land.

levy To raise money compulsorily, e.g. by means of a distress, or by taxes.

lex Angliae sine Parliamento mutari non potest [The law of England cannot be changed except by Parliament]

lex domicilii The law of the place of person's domicile (*q.v.*).

lex fori The law of the forum or court in which a case is tried. More particularly the law relating to procedure or the formalities in force (adjective law) in a given place.

Lex Hortensia (187 B.C.) [Roman law] It provided that *plebiscita* (measures passed in the common people's assembly) should bind the whole people equally with *leges*

lex hostilia [Roman law] It permitted an action of theft to be brought on account of persons who were among the enemy or away in the service of the commonwealth or who were in the *tutela* of some person bringing the action.

lex loci celebrationis [The law of the place of celebration (of marriage)]

lex loci contractus [The law of a place where a contract is made]

lex loci solutionis [The law of the place of performance]

lex mercatoria [The law merchant] (*q.v.*).

lex non cogit ad impossibilia [The law does not compel the impossible]

lex non requirit verificari quod apparet curiae [The law does not require that which is apparent to the court to be verified]

lex non scripta [The unwritten law] The common law.

lex posterior derogat priori [A later Act overrules an earlier one]

Lex Regia [Roman law] The statute by which the people vested the supreme power in the emperor.

lex rei situs [The law of the situation of the thing]

lex scripta [The written law] Statute law.

lex situs [The law of the place where property is situated] The general rule is that lands and other immovables are governed by the *lex situs*.

lex spectat naturae ordinem [The law has regard to the order of nature]

lex talionis The primitive law embodied in the phrase "an eye for an eye, a tooth for a tooth."

liability Subjection to a legal obligation; or the obligation itself. The person who commits a wrong or breaks a contract or trust is said to be liable or responsible for it. Liability is civil or criminal according to whether it is enforced by the civil or criminal courts. A contingent liability is a future unascertained obligation. See VICARIOUS LIABILITY.

liable Subject to or incurring legal liability.

libel Defamation (*q.v.*) by means of writing, print, or some other permanent form. The publication of words in the course of television or sound broadcasts or other telecommunication systems is treated as publication in permanent form (Broadcasting Act 1990 s.166). The publication of false defamatory words, etc. is a tort actionable without proof of special damage. To establish the tort, the claimant must prove that the material was defamatory, that it referred to the claimant and that it was published to a third person. It is a defence to an action for libel that the words used were true or that the publication was privileged, either absolute or qualified, or that it was a fair comment on a matter of public interest. The Defamation Act 1996 provides that certain communications will be privileged. It also creates a defence of innocent dissemination and provides for an offer of amends to be made in such circumstances. See SLANDER.

libertas [Roman law] Freedom; the capacity to possess the rights and to fulfil the duties of a free person.

libertas directa [Roman law] The setting free of his own slave by a master, as when he appointed his slave as a tutor. Either the testator accompanied the appointment with express enfranchisement or the law implied his intention to do so.

libertas fideicommissaria [Roman law] Where the testator appointed as a tutor another man's slave, entrusting his heir to purchase and enfranchise the slave.

libertinus [Roman law] A freedman; a man who had been set free from lawful slavery by manumission. They fell originally into three classes: (1) full Roman citizens; (2) *Latini Juniani*; (3) *Dedititii.*

liberty An authority to do something which would otherwise be wrongful or illegal. Formerly used in the sense of franchise (*q.v.*) denoting both a right or rights, and the place where they were exercisable.

The right to personal liberty is protected by art.5 of the Convention for the Protection of Human Rights and Fundamental Freedoms which was incorporated into English law by the Human Rights Act 1998.

251

liberum tenementum A freehold or frank tenement.

libripens [Roman law] A scalesman.

licence An authority to do something which would otherwise be inoperative, wrongful or illegal, e.g. to enter on land which would otherwise be a trespass. A licence to occupy land passes no interest in the land, in contrast with a lease (*q.v.*).

The presence or absence of exclusive possession will be decisive in determining whether an agreement is a licence or a lease (*Street v Mountford* [1985] A.C. 809).

Licences do not receive the statutory protection of security of tenure granted to leases. A mere licence is not assignable and is always revocable. A contractual licence is one which has been created by a contract. Whether it is revocable and/or assignable depends upon the terms of the contract between the parties. See BARE LICENSEE.

licence, marriage As a preliminary to a valid marriage, the law requires for an Anglican ceremony either the calling of banns or the obtaining of a licence. A common licence may be obtained from the Church authorities; a special licence may be issued on behalf of the Archbishop of Canterbury. For civil or non-Anglican religious ceremonies these formalities may be satisfied by obtaining a superintendent registrar's certificate. See MARRIAGE.

licensable activity An activity on premises regulated by the Licensing Act 2003 involving the retail sale of alcohol, supply of alcohol by or on behalf of a club (*q.v.*) to one of its members, the provision of registered entertainment and late night refreshment.

licensed conveyancer A person who holds a licence to provide conveyancing services.

licensee One to whom a licence (*q.v.*) is given.

licensing authority Under the Licensing Act 2003 the authority with the power to grant premises licences or club premises certificates (*q.v.*) permitting licensable activities (*q.v.*) to be carried on premises. Normally the local authority (*q.v.*) for the area in which the premises are situated or in which the applicant for the licence resides.

licet dispositio de interesse futuro sit inutilis, tamen fieri potest declaratio praecedens quae sortiartur effectum, interveniente novo actu [Although the grant of a future interest is inoperative, yet it may become a declaration precedent, which will take effect on the intervention of some new act] See LEASE BY ESTOPPEL.

lie (1) An action "lies" if, on the facts of the case, it is competent in law, and can properly be instituted or maintained.

(2) Under the rules of evidence, the jury may be entitled to draw an inference of the guilt of the accused from lies told by him either out of court or in court, provided they are satisfied beyond a reasonable doubt that the accused did lie and that he did so because he was guilty, and not for some other reason (*R. v Burge* [1996] 1 Cr. App. R. 163).

lien The right to hold the property of another as security for the performance of an obligation. A common law lien lasts only so long as possession is retained, but while it lasts can be asserted against the whole world. An equitable lien exists independently of possession; i.e. it may bind property not in possession at the time the obligation is incurred, but it cannot avail against the purchaser of a legal estate for value without notice of the lien.

A possessory lien is the right of the creditor to retain possession of his debtor's property until his debt has been satisfied. A particular lien exists only as a security for the particular debt incurred, while a general lien is available as a security for all debts arising out of similar transactions between the parties. Thus a solicitor has a lien on his client's papers to secure his costs. A charging lien is the right to charge property in another's possession with the payment of a debt or the performance of a duty. A maritime lien is a lien on a ship or freight, either possessory, arising out of contracts of carriage, or charging, arising out of collision or other damage. A vendor's lien is the right of a seller to retain the property till payment of the purchase price, e.g. under the Sale of Goods Act 1979 s.41, an unpaid seller (*q.v.*) of goods who is in possession of the goods may retain possession until payment or tender of the price.

lieu, in In the place of.

life estate A "mere" freehold, as not being an estate of inheritance. It arises by grant or operation of law for the benefit of a person for the rest of his own life. Since 1925 it can exist in freeholds only in equity, under a trust, as a "life interest." See ESTATE; FREEHOLD; TENANT FOR LIFE.

life, expectation of At common law a person who was injured by another's negligence could recover as an independent head of damage, compensation for the loss of his normal expectation of life (*Flint v Lovell* [1935] 1 K.B. 354). However, by virtue of the Administration of Justice Act 1982 s.1(1) no damages are recoverable as a separate head in respect of any loss of life caused by the injuries, but a court in assessing damages for pain and suffering caused by the injuries, must take into account any suffering due to awareness that the expectation of life has been reduced. On the other hand, an injured person may recover, as a separate head of damage, damages for the loss of earnings during the "lost years" (*Pickett v British Rail Engineering Ltd* [1980] A.C. 136). But it is not possible for the personal representatives of a person killed to recover damages either for the deceased's loss of expectation of life or for the loss of earnings during the "lost years" (Administration of Justice Act 1982 s.4).

life in being See PERPETUITY.

life peer A person who is entitled to sit and vote in the House of Lords. The peerage expires on the person's death. The majority of peers are now life peers.

life, presumption of Once the fact of life on a given date has been established, the law will presume its continuance unless there is evidence, or a presumption of fact recognised by the law, to the contrary effect.

lifting the veil See VEIL OF INCORPORATION.

ligan See LAGAN.

light There is no right at common law to the unobstructed access of light to one's windows, but such a right might be acquired by grant of an easement (*q.v.*) or by prescription (*q.v.*) (Prescription Act 1832). The 1832 Act stipulated uninterrupted enjoyment of the access of light for 20 years. The Rights of Light Act 1959 provided that an owner of land may prevent the acquisition of a right to light over his land by registration of a notice in the local land charges register.

like work The basis on which, under the Equal Pay Act 1970, a woman (or man) may bring a claim that her (his) work and that of a man (woman) in the same employment (the comparator) are:
"of the same or a broadly similar nature, and the differences (if any) between the things she does and the things they do are not of practical importance in relation to terms and conditions of employment", s.1(4).
    Claims are brought before an employment tribunal (*q.v.*) which may make an award of arrears of remuneration (according to *Levez v T H Jennings Ltd (No. 2)* [1999] I.R.L.R. 764 the limitation in s.2(5) of the Act on arrears to two years is in breach of the principle of equivalence in EC law and the normal six year time

limit under the Limitation Act 1980 applies). In addition, the applicant's contract of employment will be modified such that any less favourable term in her (his) contract is replaced with that in the man's (woman's) and any beneficial terms in the man's (woman's) contract which hers (his) does not include will be added. See EQUALITY CLAUSE.

limitation To limit an estate is to mark out the extreme period during which it is to continue, and the clause by which this is done in a conveyance is called a limitation. See WORDS OF LIMITATION.

limitation of liability The imposition of a maximum amount of liability for loss or damage of, e.g. a carrier, by contract, or more particularly, by statute. See also LIMITED COMPANY.

limitation, statute of The statute which prescribes the periods within which proceedings to enforce a right must be taken or the action barred is the Limitation Act 1980 which is a Consolidating Act. The time limits prescribed in respect of actions founded on the following matters are as indicated: tort (other than one causing personal injuries, libel or slander): six years (s.2); simple contract: six years (s.5); speciality: 12 years (s.8(1)); contribution: two years from date of right to recover (s.10); action for libel or slander: one year (s.5 of the Defamation Act 1996); action for personal injuries: three years from either the cause of action arising or, if later, the date of knowledge of the injured person (s.11); for defective products: ten years from date of supply unless the product causes personal injury or loss or damage to property, in which case the limit is three years (s.11A). If the injured person dies before the expiration of the limitation period, the period is three years from the date of death or from the date of knowledge of the personal representative (s.11(5)).

Additional time limits are: for actions under the Fatal Accidents Act 1976: three years from the date of death or from the date of knowledge of the person for whose benefit the action is being brought (s.12(2)); recovery of land: 12 years (s.15); redemption actions: 12 years (s.16); mortgagee's actions: 12 years from the date of accrual of the right to receive the money (s.20). The date from which time begins to run may be postponed for disability, fraudulent concealment or mistake (see Pt II of the Act). There is also discretion to exclude the time limits in certain cases involving personal injury and death (see s.33) and for libel and slander. In cases involving the equitable jurisdiction of the court the time limits do not normally apply (s.36). The defendant must plead the statutes if he intends to rely on them; the court will not of its own motion take notice that an action is out of time.

In *Pirelli General Cable Works Ltd v Oscar Faber & Partners* [1983] 2 A.C. 1 it was held that a cause of action for defective building work accrues from the date the damage occurs, not the date of discovery. The harshness of this rule is mitigated under the Latent Damage Act 1986 in respect of actions for damages other than those for personal injury. Under the Act an action may be brought after the expiration of either six years from the date on which the cause of action accrued, or three years from the earliest date on which the claimant (or any person in whom the cause of action was vested before him) first had both the knowledge required for bringing an action for damages and a right to bring such an action, whichever is the later.

limited company A company where the liability of its members is limited. Liability may be limited by shares or by guarantee. In a company limited by shares, the liability of its members is limited by its constitution to the amount, if any, unpaid on their shares. In a company limited by guarantee, the liability of its members is limited by its constitution to the amount the members have agreed to contribute to the company's assets in the event of its being wound up. See Companies Act 2006 s.3.

A public company (plc) is a limited company. A private company may be a limited or an unlimited company. In an unlimited company there is no limit on the liability of the company's members. See COMPANY; PUBLIC COMPANY; PRIVATE COMPANY.

limited liability partnership A new form of business entity (abbreviated as LLP or llp) introduced by the Limited Liability Partnership Act 2000. It is a body corporate with legal personality separate from that of its members of which there must be at least two. It has unlimited legal capacity and the liability of its members to contribute to its assets in the event of its being wound up is limited to the extent provided for in the Act. The LLP does not pay tax but the members are liable for tax on its income and capital profits in the same way as in an ordinary partnership. See partnership.

limited owner The owner of an interest in property less than the full fee simple; e.g. tenant for life (*q.v.*).

limited owner's charge An equitable charge in favour of a tenant for life or statutory owner (*q.v.*) who has discharged any inheritance tax or other liabilities (Land Charges Act 1972 s.2(1), Class C (ii)).

limited partnership See PARTNERSHIP.

limited title guarantee Limited title guarantee provides the same covenants as full title guarantee, which include, inter alia, that the transferor warrants to transfer the right to dispose of property in the way he purports to do so and to dispose of the whole interest/lease, but differs from full title guarantee in that the transferor does not warrant that the property is free from all charges (*q.v.*) and encumbrances (*q.v.*) and from all other rights which the transferor does not and could not reasonably be expected to know about. Instead, the transferor warrants that he has not charged or encumbered the property by a charge or encumbrance which still exists, he has not granted any third party rights and is not aware that anyone has done so since the last disposition for value. Limited title guarantee will usually be given where the transferor is a personal representative (*q.v.*) or a trustee (*q.v.*) who holds the property on trust for persons other than himself.

Lincoln's Inn One of the Inns of Court (*q.v.*).

linea recta semper praefertur transversali [The direct line is always preferred to the collateral]

linked transaction A transaction identified by the Consumer Credit Act 1974 as so closely related to the principal regulated consumer credit or consumer hire agreement as requiring special treatment, e.g. if the principal agreement is cancelled then the linked transaction is treated as never having been entered into (s.19).

liquid assets Cash in hand or at bank, and readily realisable property.

liquidated Fixed or ascertained. A debt is liquidated when paid, and a company when wound up.

liquidated damages A genuine covenanted pre-estimate of damages for an anticipated breach of contract, as contrasted with a penalty (*q.v.*). The sum fixed as liquidated damages is recoverable; a penalty is not, but only the damages actually incurred.

liquidation committee A committee which may be appointed when a company is in liquidation to assist and supervise the work of the liquidator (*q.v.*), Insolvency Act 1986 ss.101, 141. See CREDITORS' COMMITTEE; WINDING UP.

liquidator A person appointed to carry out the winding-up (*q.v.*) of a company. In a members' voluntary winding-up, the liquidator is appointed by the members.

In a creditors' voluntary winding-up, the creditors and the members may nominate a liquidator but the creditors' nomination will prevail. Where there is a compulsory winding-up of the company by a court order, the court may appoint a provisional liquidator as soon as the winding-up petition is presented. Once a winding-up order is made, the official receiver (*q.v.*) becomes the liquidator of the company. The company's creditors and contributories may then nominate an individual as the liquidator of the company. The creditors' nomination will prevail. If there is no such appointment then the official receiver will continue as liquidator.

The functions of a liquidator are to gather in and realise the property of the company, to pay its debts and to distribute the surplus, if any, to the members entitled to it. The powers and duties of a liquidator are specified in the Insolvency Act 1986 (as amended by the Insolvency Act 2000) ss.165–170, Sch.4. Certain powers may be exercised without sanction; others require either the approval of the court, or a liquidation committee, or a meeting of the company's creditors or an extraordinary resolution of the company. See RESOLUTION.

To act as a liquidator, a person must be a qualified insolvency practitioner (*q.v.*) in relation to the company concerned (Insolvency Act 1986 Pt XIII as amended by the Insolvency Act 2000).

lis A suit or action, where there is an issue between parties in dispute.

lis alibi pendens [A suit pending elsewhere] Actions may be stayed on this ground.

lis mota Existing or anticipated litigation. See ANTE LITEM MOTAM.

lis pendens or lite pendente A pending suit, action, petition or matter, particularly one relating to land. A *lis pendens* may be registered under the Land Charges Act 1972 s.5.

listed company A public company (*q.v.*) whose securities are admitted by the United Kingdom Listing Authority (*q.v.*) to the Official List (*q.v.*) as suitable for trading on a Stock Exchange (*q.v.*).

listing Under the CPR, the term "listing for trial" replaced "setting down for trial".

listing rules The rules made by the Financial Services Authority (*q.v.*), as the UK Listing Authority, in relation to the admission of securities to the Official List (*q.v.*).

literal rule An approach to statutory interpretation which attributes the ordinary dictionary meaning to a word.

literarum obligatio (or expensilatio) [Roman law] Created by an entry in the account books (*codex*) of the creditor, with the consent of the debtor, charging the debtor as owing a certain sum.

literary work Any work, other than a dramatic or musical work which is written, printed, spoken or sung. Under the Copyright, Designs and Patents Act 1988, literary copyright subsists in such a work provided it is recorded, in writing or otherwise. See copyright.

litigant in person One who sues or defends without legal representation. Every litigant in person is entitled to be accompanied by another person who may assist or quietly advise the litigant but who has no right to address the court. See MCKENZIE FRIEND.

litigation The pursuance or defence of contested civil or criminal proceedings.

litigation friend This term, introduced by the Civil Procedure Rules 1998, replaces the old terms of "guardian *ad litem*" (*q.v.*) and "next friend". A person who conducts legal proceedings on behalf of a child (*q.v.*) or a person suffering from mental incapacity, i.e. a patient (*q.v.*), CPR Pt 21.

litigation privilege See LEGAL PROFESSIONAL PRIVILEGE.

livery Formerly when an infant heir of land held *in capite ut de corona*, he was obliged on attaining 21 to sue livery, that is, to obtain delivery of the possession of the land, for which he paid half-a-year's profit of the land.

livery of seisin An "overt ceremony", which was formerly necessary to convey an immediate estate of freehold in lands or tenements. It was the transfer of the feudal possession of the land. The Real Property Act 1845 required a feoffment (*q.v.*) to be evidenced by deed, unless made by an infant under a custom. The Law of Property Act 1925 s.51(1) provided that since 1925 all lands and all interests therein lie in grant, and are incapable of being conveyed by livery of seisin. See GRANT.

livestock See ANIMALS.

Lloyd's An association of underwriters and insurance brokers in the City of London, incorporated and regulated by the Lloyd's Acts 1871 to 1982.

local authority A body charged with the administration of local government (*q.v.*), for example a county council, a district council, a London borough council or a parish council. The meetings of such bodies are open to the public.

Local Better Regulation Office A statutory corporation charged with ensuring that local authorities exercise their functions effectively, in a way that does not give rise to unnecessary burdens and in a way which conforms to the (now disbanded) Better Regulation Commission's Principles of Good Regulation, namely that regulatory activities should be carried out in a way which is transparent, accountable, proportionate and consistent and should be targeted only at cases in which action is needed. See Regulatory Enforcement and Sanctions Act 2008.

local development order An order which allows a local planning authority to extend permitted development rights within its area.

local government The system under which the administration of the local affairs of the whole of England and Wales is in the hands of parish meetings, parish district and county councils and the Common Council of the City of London, called local authorities (*q.v.*). They exercise important functions in regard to public health, education, highways, council tax, town planning, housing, licensing, etc. Under the Local Government Act 1985, the metropolitan county councils were abolished and their functions re-allocated to the metropolitan district councils. The Greater London Authority Act 1999 established the Greater London Authority and introduced the Mayor of London and the London Assembly. The Local Government (Wales) Act 1994 created 11 new counties and 11 new county boroughs in Wales to replace the Welsh counties and abolished the system of districts and their councils. Under the Regional Assemblies (Preparations) Act 2003, the Secretary of State could cause referenda to be held about the establishment of elected assemblies for the regions of England (except London). Plans to carry out such elections have since been abandoned.

local housing authority The body which exercises a local authority's statutory powers and duties in relation to housing the homeless.

local justice area An area established by order of the Lord Chancellor to replace former magistrates' courts committees which are abolished (see Courts Act 2003 s.8). Magistrates (*q.v.*) are assigned to a particular area but now have national jurisdiction.

local land charge A charge binding on land registrable in the local land charges registers kept by local authorities (Local Land Charges Act 1975).

loco citato [At the passage quoted]

locus in quo [The place in which]

locus poenitentiae [A place (or opportunity) of repentance] The interval between the time money is paid or goods are delivered for an illegal purpose and the time the illegal purpose is carried out. During this interval the person who has so paid the money or delivered the goods may recover them back.

locus regit actum [The place governs the act] The validity of an act depends on the law of the place where it is done; e.g. marriage.

locus sigilli [The place of the seal]

locus standi [A place of standing] The right to be heard in court or other proceeding.

lodger A person who occupies rooms in a house of which the general possession remains in the landlord, as shown by the fact that he retains control over the street or outer door.

log or log-book Under the Merchant Shipping Act 1995, an official log book must be kept of every UK ship, recording the happenings in, and to, the ship, including its speed and progress. In the case of aircraft registered in the United Kingdom, the Air Navigation Order 2000 requires that a log book be kept recording times of take off and landing and any known defects.

loiter To idle in the street for an unlawful purpose. Loitering contrary to the Vagrancy Act 1824 is no longer an offence, but loitering for purposes of prostitution (*q.v.*) is an offence (Street Offences Act 1959 s.1).

London Gazette The official journal of government. Certain notices, e.g. petitions for winding up a limited company, must be advertised in it.

long title This usually gives a general summary of the purpose of an Act of Parliament. See SHORT TITLE.

Long Vacation The period usually during August and September when the Supreme Court (*q.v.*) does not transact business. A Vacation Court usually sits to deal with urgent business.

lord (1) A person of whom land is held by another as his tenant. The relation between the lord and the tenant is called tenure (*q.v.*), and the right or interest which the lord has in the services of his tenant is called a lordship or seignory (*q.v.*).
(2) A peer of the realm.

Lord Advocate The chief law officer of the Crown in Scotland.

Lord Campbell's Act The Fatal Accidents Act 1846.

Lord Chamberlain See CHAMBERLAIN, LORD.

Lord Chancellor See CHANCELLOR, LORD HIGH.

Lord Chief Justice of England The head of the judiciary in England and Wales. This role was previously held by the Lord Chancellor (*q.v.*) before the Constitutional Reform Act 2005 came into force on April 3, 2006. The Lord Chief Justice of England has around 400 statutory responsibilities which include being the President of the Courts of England and Wales.

Lord High Admiral See ADMIRAL.

Lord High Constable An office abolished in 1521. See EARL MARSHALL.

Lord High Steward Formerly, when a person was impeached, or when a peer was tried on indictment for treason or felony before the House of Lords, one of the lords was appointed Lord High Steward, who presided *pro tempore*, or, in the absence of such an appointment, the Lord Chancellor presided. If the House of Lords was not sitting, the Court of the Lord High Steward was instituted by commission from the Crown, to which were summoned all the peers of Parliament. The Lord High Steward was the sole judge.

Lord Keeper of the Great Seal Now the Lord Chancellor.

Lord Lieutenant The Crown's representative in the County. His main duties are arranging visits by, and escorting, members of the Royal Family, encouraging voluntary activities, working with local units of the Forces, presenting awards on the monarch's behalf, leadership of the local magistracy, liaison with the Lord Chancellor and duties as keeper of the Rolls.

Lord President of the Council The President of the Privy Council. The office is held by such person, being a member of one House of Parliament or the other, as the Queen in Council, from time to time, orally declares to be the Lord President of the Council. It is of Cabinet rank. See CABINET.

Lord Privy Seal The officer who affixed the Privy Seal to documents, especially letters patent, which were to pass the Great Seal. The Great Seal Act 1884 s.3 abolished the use of the Privy Seal and the Lord Privy Seal has now no official duties. The office carries Cabinet rank. See CABINET.

Lord Steward of the Queen's Household He originally presided over the court of the Lord Steward of the King's Household. He supervises the servants and the arrangements of the Royal Household.

Lord Treasurer or Lord High Treasurer and Treasurer of the Exchequer The office dates from the earliest Norman period. After 1612 it was sometimes put in commission, and since 1714 it has always been in commission. The Commissioners constitute the Treasury Board, which now never meets. See TREASURY.

Lords Justices of Appeal The designation of the ordinary judges of the Court of Appeal (*q.v.*).

Lords Marchers Until the conquest of Wales in 1282 the English kings permitted their nobles to conquer and hold such parts of Wales as they could. Each noble, known as a Lord Marcher, was given *jura regalia*, or sovereign rights, within the area held by him.

Lords of Appeal in Ordinary Law Lords appointed for the purpose of hearing appeals; they must have held some high judicial office for two years, or have had a right of audience in relation to all proceedings in the Supreme Court for at least 15 years (see Courts and Legal Services Act 1990 Sch.10). Due to be replaced under the Constitutional Reform Act 2005 by Justices of the Supreme Court (the relevant provisions are not yet in force), although initially existing Law Lords will fill this position. See SUPREME COURT.

loss See TOTAL LOSS.

lost or not lost Words inserted in a maritime policy of insurance to prevent the operation of the rule that if a ship is lost at the time of insurance, the policy is void, although the assured did not know of the loss. See the Marine Insurance Act 1906 s.6(1).

lost years See FATAL ACCIDENTS; LIFE, EXPECTATION OF.

lottery A distribution of prizes by chance where the persons taking part in the operation, or a substantial number of them, make a payment or consideration in return for obtaining their chance of a prize (*Reader's Digest Association Ltd v Williams* [1976] 3 All E.R. 737, per Lord Widgery C.J.). The National Lottery Act 1993 authorised the promotion of lotteries as part of the National Lottery.

The Gambling Act 2005 repealed the existing legislation (but not the National Lottery Act 1993) on gaming, betting and participating in lotteries (except the National Lottery) and replaced it with a new unified framework. Under the 2005 Act, s.14 lottery means an arrangement under which (a) persons are required to pay in order to participate in the arrangement; (b) in the course of the arrangement one or more prizes are allocated to one or more members of a class; and (c) the prizes are allocated by a process which relies wholly on chance (Gambling Act 2005 s.14). The Act terms the former a "simple lottery". In the case of a "complex lottery" the allocation of prizes is by a series of processes, the first of which relies wholly on chance. Participating in the National Lottery is not gambling (*q.v.*) under the 2005 Act. See BETTING; GAMING.

low cost home ownership accommodation A form of social housing (*q.v.*) which must satisfy certain statutory conditions, namely that the accommodation must be occupied in accordance with shared ownership arrangements (*q.v.*), equity percentage arrangements (*q.v.*) or shared ownership trusts (*q.v.*); it must also comply with rules that ensure that such accommodation is available to those whose needs are not adequately served by the commercial housing market (see Housing and Regeneration Act 2008 s.70). See OFFICE FOR TENANTS AND SOCIAL LANDLORDS.

low cost rental accommodation A form of social housing (*q.v.*) which is made available for rent at below the market rate and which complies with rules that ensure that such accommodation is available to those whose needs are not adequately served by the commercial housing market (see Housing and Regeneration Act 2008 s.69). See OFFICE FOR TENANTS AND SOCIAL LANDLORDS.

Low Pay Commission The body set up, initially on a non-statutory basis and subsequently under the National Minimum Wage Act 1998, to monitor and evaluate the operation of the Act and to advise the Government accordingly. See NATIONAL MINIMUM WAGE.

lump sum Payment of a specified sum of money. A lump sum payment may be ordered for a party to a marriage (*q.v.*) or a child of the family (*q.v.*) on or after the grant of a decree of divorce, judicial separation or nullity of marriage (Matrimonial Causes Act 1973 s.23(1)(c)). The essence of a lump sum is that it is a capital sum (as opposed to periodical payments of maintenance). Only one lump sum order may be made, although the order may specify payment of more than one sum on different dates. Magistrates' courts have jurisdiction to order limited lump sums in the exercise of their domestic jurisdiction (Domestic Proceedings and Magistrates' Courts Act 1978, s.2(1)(b)). See FINANCIAL PROVISION ORDERS; DOMESTIC PROCEEDINGS.

lunatic This term is no longer used. The Mental Health Act 1983 uses the term "patient". See MENTAL DISORDER.

Lyndhurst's Act (Lord) The Marriage Act 1835 which provided that any marriage after 1835 between persons within the prohibited degrees of affinity should be null and void.

M

M.R Master of the Rolls (*q.v.*).

MEQR Measure having equivalent effect to a quantitative restriction.

Maastricht, Treaty of See TREATY OF EUROPEAN UNION.

McKenzie friend The name derives from *McKenzie v McKenzie* [1971] P. 33. It refers to someone who attends court with a litigant in person to assist the litigant in presenting his case but is not legally qualified. See LITIGANT IN PERSON.

magistrate A judicial officer having a summary jurisdiction in matters of a criminal or quasi-criminal nature; a justice of the peace. Under the Courts Act 2003 they are assigned to a local justice area (*q.v.*) but have national jurisdiction. District Judges (Magistrates' Courts) are appointed to act in particularly complex or sensitive cases with wider powers than ordinary justices and, unlike justices, receive a salary. See JUSTICES OF THE PEACE.

magistrates' court Any justice or justices of the peace (*q.v.*) acting under any enactment or by virtue of his or their commission or under the common law (Magistrates' Courts Act 1980 s.148(1) as amended). Magistrates' courts are the inferior criminal courts which try those offences only triable summarily and those offences "triable either way" which are found to be suitable for summary trial following mode of trial proceedings. Magistrates' courts also act as examining justices in committal proceedings. Courts normally consist of two or more lay justices but a district judge (magistrates' courts), a legally qualified justice of the peace (*q.v.*), will normally sit alone. Magistrates' courts are a key part of the criminal justice system and the great majority of cases are completed there. In addition magistrates' courts deal with many civil cases, e.g. family matters, betting and gaming.

Magna Carta The charter originally granted by King John, and afterwards re-enacted and confirmed by Parliament more than 30 times. The charter now in force is the statute (9 Hen. c.3), with which our statute book commences. It contained provisions to protect the subject from abuse of the Royal prerogative in the matter of arbitrary arrest and imprisonment, and from amercements, purveyance and other extortions (See McKechnie, *Magna Carta*).

Magnum Concilium The Great Council (*q.v.*).

mail preference service A free service funded by the direct mail industry to allow consumers to have their names and addresses removed or added to lists used by the industry.

mainprize Taking into hand; the process of delivering a person to sureties or pledges (mainpernors) who undertook to produce him again at a future time. Bail applied only to cases where a man was arrested or imprisoned, while a man could be mainperned not only in such cases, but also, e.g. in an appeal of felony. Mainpernors were not bound by recognisances to the Crown, and they could not relieve themselves of responsibility by seizing and remitting to custody the man for whom they had gone security.

maintenance The supply of the necessaries of life for a person. A maintenance clause in a deed of settlement is the provision of income for such a purpose.
　Applications to the High Court, County Court or the Magistrates' Court may be made by either party to a marriage on the ground that the other party has failed to provide reasonable maintenance for the applicant (Matrimonial Causes Act 1973 s.27 and Domestic Proceedings and Magistrates' Courts Act 1978 s.1). The courts' powers to make maintenance orders in respect of children were restricted by the Child Support Act 1991. Under the Act, the calculation of child maintenance is primarily the responsibility of the Child Support Agency. See CHILD SUPPORT.
　On a petition for divorce, nullity of marriage or judicial separation either party to the marriage may be ordered to make periodical payments for the maintenance of the other from the presentation of the petition to the determination of the suit (Matrimonial Causes Act 1973 s.22). See MAINTENANCE

PENDING SUIT. After a decree nisi (*q.v.*), permanent financial provision may be ordered to be made (ss.23–33, 37–40).

Under the Maintenance Enforcement Act 1991 as amended, the High Court, county courts and magistrates' courts have the power, when making, varying or enforcing a maintenance order requiring periodical payment, to impose a method of payment order or make an attachment of earnings order (*q.v.*). Maintenance agreements are subject to the jurisdiction of the court. Maintenance may be obtained from the estate of a deceased spouse under the Inheritance (Provision for Family and Dependants) Act 1975. See also Children Act 1989 Sch.1.

See PERIODICAL PAYMENTS; FINANCIAL PROVISION ORDERS; DOMESTIC PROCEEDINGS.

maintenance and champerty The offence of maintenance was abolished by the Criminal Law Act 1967 s.13. That Act provides that no person shall be liable in tort for maintenance or champerty (s.14). Agreements involving maintenance and champerty (*q.v.*) are void and illegal.

maintenance pending suit After a petition for divorce, judicial separation or nullity of marriage has been filed one party may apply for an order that the other make payments for his or her maintenance (Matrimonial Causes Act 1973 s.22). Such an order will expire on decree nisi (*q.v.*) in the case of judicial separation or decree absolute (*q.v.*) otherwise.

majority, age of The age of majority is 18 years.

majority rule The principle in company law under which decisions by the majority of the company members are binding on the company. There are statutory and common law protections for minority shareholders, See RESOLUTION; VOTING; UNFAIR PREJUDICE.

making off without payment A person who, knowing that payment on the spot for any goods supplied or service done is required or expected of him, dishonestly makes off without having paid with intent to avoid payment commits an offence (Theft Act 1978 s.3).

mala fides [Bad faith] See BONA FIDE.

mala grammatica non vitiat chartam [Bad grammar does not vitiate a deed]

mala in se; mala prohibita *Mala in se* are acts which are wrong in themselves, such as murder, as opposed to *mala prohibita*, acts which are merely prohibited by law, e.g. smuggling. A distinction not now of great importance.

mala praxis Where a medical practitioner injures his patient by neglect or want of skill, giving rise to a right of action for damages.

maladministration The task of the Parliamentary Commissioner for Administration (*q.v.*) is to investigate complaints of "injustice in consequence of maladministration". The term maladministration is not defined, but the late Richard Crossman introducing the Parliamentary Act 1967 suggested that maladministration "might include such things as bias, neglect, inattention, delay, incompetence, perversity, turpitude, arbitrariness ...". See also COMMISSIONS FOR LOCAL ADMINISTRATION.

male issue This is a term of art, meaning male descendants claiming exclusively through the male line, although it will yield to a contrary indication in the context. "Male descendants" is a term of ordinary speech, though it may mean "male issue" in its context (*Re Du Cros' Settlement Trusts* [1961] 1 W.L.R 1252).

maledicta expositio quae corrumpit textum [It is a bad exposition which corrupts the text]

malfeasance The doing of an unlawful act, e.g. a trespass (*q.v.*).

malice Ill-will or evil motive: personal spite or ill-will is sometimes called malice. In criminal law, the mens rea of certain non-fatal offences against the person, namely those under the Offences Against The Person Act 1861 ss.18 and 20, is to act maliciously (although s.18 also requires an intention to do grievous bodily harm or resist arrest). The term has been interpreted as being an intention to do, or recklessness as to doing, some physical harm (*Mowatt* [1968] 1 Q.B. 421). See UNLAWFUL WOUNDING.

Malice in the law of tort is a constituent of malicious prosecution (*q.v.*), defamation (*q.v.*), malicious falsehood and conspiracy (*q.v.*).

malice aforethought The element of mens rea in the crime of murder. It is satisfied by an intention to kill or an intention to commit grievous bodily harm (*Moloney* [1985] 1 A.C. 905).

malicious falsehood See INJURIOUS FALSEHOOD.

malicious injury to the person See MALICE.

malicious injury to property The Malicious Damage Act 1861, which dealt with this, has been repealed and replaced by the Criminal Damage Act 1971. See CRIMINAL DAMAGE.

malicious prosecution The tort consisting of an abuse of the process of the court by wrongfully instituting criminal proceedings against another. It must have been without reasonable and probable cause, have been instituted or carried on maliciously, terminated in the claimant's favour and resulted in damage to the claimant's name, person or property.

malitia supplet aetatem [Malice supplements age] See DOLI INCAPAX.

mandamus [We command] A high prerogative writ which issued in the King's name from the High Court of Justice on application to the King's Bench Division to some person or body to compel the performance of a public duty. It was replaced by an order of mandamus, now a mandatory order (*q.v.*), which is now comprised in the procedure known as judicial review (*q.v.*).

mandatarius terminos sibi positos transgredi non potest [A mandatory cannot exceed the limits imposed upon him]

mandatary The receiver of a mandate (*q.v.*).

mandate (1) A direction, request, or authoritative command. Thus a cheque is a mandate by the drawer to his banker to pay the amount to the transferee or holder of the cheque.

(2) The authority which was conferred on "advanced nations" by the Covenant of the League of Nations (*q.v.*), Art.22, to administer, as Mandatories on behalf of the League, former enemy colonies and territories which were inhabited by peoples not yet able to stand by themselves under the strenuous conditions of the modern world, applying the principle that the well-being and development of such peoples formed a sacred trust of civilisation. See TRUST TERRITORIES.

mandatory See INJUNCTION.

mandatory order Formerly mandamus. A remedy available on application for judicial review ordering an inferior court, public authority or tribunal to perform its duties. The remedy does not lie against the Crown.

mandatory sentence A minimum sentence for an offence as prescribed by law. There is a mandatory life sentence for murder and for persons convicted of a second "serious offence", e.g. manslaughter, rape, unless there are exceptional circumstances. Unless unjust, there is a minimum seven year sentence for a third Class A drug trafficking offence, or three years for a third domestic burglary.

mandatum See BAILMENTS.

mandavi ballivo [I have commanded the bailiff] Where a sheriff received a writ which had to be executed within a place which was a liberty, he would command the bailiff of the liberty to execute the writ.

manor A district of land of which the freehold was vested in the lord of the manor, of whom two or more persons, called freeholders of the manor, hold land in respect of which they owed him certain free services, rents or other duties. Hence every manor must have been a least as old as the Statute of Quia Emptores and consisted of demesne lands, the right to hold a court baron, and the right to services of free tenants in fee, who were liable to escheat and owed attendance at the court baron. With the enfranchisement of copyholds since 1925, effected by the Law of Property Act 1922, and the extinguishment of manorial incidents, manors have ceased to exist.

manorial incidents Incidents of land held on copyhold tenure in respect of which the tenants were liable to the lord of the manor.

The following manorial incidents were temporarily saved from the effect of the general enfranchisement of copyhold lands effected by the Law of Property Act 1922:

(1) quit rents, chief rents, etc.;

(2) fines, reliefs, heriots and dues;

(3) forfeitures other than those for the conveyance of an estate of freehold in the land, and for alienation without licence;

(4) rights of timber.

Certain incidents, such as rights to mines and minerals, and rights of common, were preserved indefinitely. See the Law of Property Act 1922 Pt VI.

manslaughter A crime of unlawful homicide. Manslaughter may be divided into two categories:

(1)Voluntary manslaughter where the defendant killed with malice afore-thought but the presence of a mitigating factor at the time of the killing, namely provocation (*q.v.*), diminished responsibility (*q.v.*) or killing in pursuance of a suicide pact (*q.v.*) reduced the defendant's liability to manslaughter.

(2) Involuntary manslaughter where the defendant killed without malice aforethought but with a certain required fault element. The fault element required is that the defendant caused the death whilst committing an unlawful and dangerous act or that his act or omission which caused the death was grossly negligent or reckless.

mansuetae naturae [Tame by nature] Animals such as a dog, cow, or horse. See ANIMALS.

manual data. A relevant filing system (*q.v.*) can include manual data such as hard copy papers and anything which is not processed automatically using equipment. See DATA.

manumissio [Roman law] The giving of his freedom to a slave; setting him free from the "hand" or *potestas* of his master.

manus [Roman law] Hand: marital power. A woman was subjected to the *manus* of her husband by:

(1) *Confarreatio* (a religious ceremony);

(2) *Coemptio* (fictitious sale);

(3) *Usus* (cohabitation).

marches The boundary between England and Wales and that between England and Scotland. See LORDS MARCHERS.

marchet; marcheta; merchetum A fine which some tenants had to pay to their lord for liberty to give away their daughters in marriage.

Mareva injunction See FREEZING INJUNCTION.

marginal notes The notes printed at the side of sections of an Act of Parliament. In interpreting an Act, such cannot alter the meaning of clear words (*Chandler v DPP* [1964] A.C. 763) but consideration of them is not absolutely ruled out (*DPP v Schildkamp* [1971] A.C. 1).

marine insurance A contract of marine insurance is a contract whereby the insurer undertakes to indemnify the assured in a manner and to an extent agreed against marine losses, that is losses incident to marine adventure. Marine Insurance Act 1906 s.1.

A contract of marine insurance may be extended by its express terms or by trade usage so as to protect the assured against losses on inland waters or on any land risk of which may be incidental to any sea voyage.

maritagium The power which the lord had of disposing of his infant ward in marriage. Also land given as a marriage portion: a dowry.

marital breakdown See IRRETRIEVAL BREAKDOWN.

marital rights Formerly the right of a husband to property of his wife during marriage, *jus mariti* (*q.v.*). It is now used as synonymous with conjugal rights.

maritime lien See LIEN.

marked copy See EXAMINED COPY.

market abuse Behaviour based on information which is not generally available but behaviour which would be likely to be regarded as a failure to observe the standard of behaviour reasonably expected of a person in his position in the market. The behaviour must (inter alia) be likely to give the regular user a false or misleading impression about an investment and be viewed by that user to be likely to distort the market (Financial Services and Markets Act 2000 s.118).

market maker (Formerly known as a stockjobber) A member of the Stock Exchange who buys or sells certain company securities. A member must be registered in respect of a particular company security before he can act as a market maker in that security and registration requires the market maker to provide quotations as to the buying and selling prices of those securities. See STOCK EXCHANGE.

market overt [Open market] The doctrine of market overt was that all sales of goods made therein, except horses, were not only binding on the parties, but also on all other persons: so that if stolen goods were sold in market overt, the purchaser, if acting in good faith, acquired a valid title to them against the true owner (Sale of Goods Act 1979 s.22(1)). This doctrine was abolished by the Sale of Goods (Amendment) Act 1994.

markets and fairs At common law a market or a fair is a franchise or privilege to establish meetings of persons to buy and sell, derived either from Royal grant or from prescription implying such grant.

marque See LETTERS OF MARQUE.

marquis; marquess The rank in the peerage next below that of duke, dating from 1386. The wife of a marquis is styled marchioness.

marriage Marriage is essentially the voluntary union for life of one man and one woman to the exclusion of all others, subject to the rules as to consanguinity (*q.v.*) or affinity and capacity to perform the duties of matrimony prevailing in the place of domicile of the parties and subject to the formalities required either by the law of England or the place where the marriage takes place. An agreement to marry is a contract, but failure to complete it does not give rise to an action. See BREACH OF PROMISE.

The formalities which must be complied with to constitute a valid marriage are contained in the Marriage Acts 1949 to 1983. A void marriage is one where the parties went through a marriage ceremony but there was lacking some necessary ingredient of a valid marriage: it is void from the beginning and is regarded as never having taken place. A voidable marriage is a valid subsisting marriage until a decree of nullity is pronounced. See AFFINITY; NULLITY; LICENCE, MARRIAGE; REGISTRATION OF MARRIAGE.

Under the Civil Partnership Act 2004 two persons of the same sex, aged 16 or over, may register as civil partners of each other. See CIVIL PARTNERSHIP.

marriage settlement A conveyance of property for the benefit of the parties to, and the prospective issue of, a marriage. A marriage settlement is made by means of a vesting deed and a trust instrument.

marriage-brocage A contract to procure a marriage between two persons for reward. Such a contract is void (see *Hermann v Charlesworth* [1905] 2 K.B. 123).

married woman See HUSBAND AND WIFE.

marshal In the Queen's Bench Division of the High Court, a marshal is an officer who attends each judge on circuit in a personal capacity. The Marshal of the Admiralty Court is entrusted with execution of warrants and orders of the court.

marshalling (1) As between creditors. Where there are two creditors of the same debtor, and one creditor has a right to resort to two funds of the debtor for payment of his debt, and the other creditor has the right to resort only to one fund, the court will order the first creditor to be paid out of the fund against which the second creditor has no claim, so far as that fund will extend, so as to leave as much as possible of the second fund for payment of the second creditor. If the first creditor has already paid himself out of the second fund, the court will allow the second creditor to stand in his shoes and resort to the first fund to the extent to which the second fund has been exhausted by the first creditor.

(2) As between beneficiaries. If any beneficiary is disappointed of his benefit under the will through a creditor being paid out of the property intended for that beneficiary, he may recoup himself by going against any property which ought to have been used to pay debts before his property was resorted to.

(3) As between legatees, where certain legacies are charged on real estate and others not, a case for marshalling arises where the realty is specifically devised.

(4) The term used to describe the time spent when a person sits on the bench with a judge and observes legal proceedings.

martial law Originally the law administered in the court of the Constable and Marshal. Now it means the suppression of ordinary law and the temporary government of a country or parts of it by military tribunals (Dicey). Martial law is the assumption by officers of the Crown of absolute power, exercised by military force for the suppression of an invasion and the restoration of order and lawful authority. Where actual war is raging, acts done by the military authorities are not justiciable by the ordinary tribunals (*Ex parte Marais* [1902] A.C. 109).

There is usually a proclamation made that a state of martial law exists, but the courts will determine whether there exists such a state of war as renders martial law necessary. Acts of Indemnity are always passed to legalise the acts done during war or while martial law prevails.

Master A master of the Supreme Court or Court of Protection. The jurisdiction of a master is, with some exceptions, that of a judge in chambers.

master and servant See EMPLOYER and EMPLOYEE.

Master in Lunacy Now the Master of the Court of Protection (*q.v.*).

Master of the Crown Office A Master of the Supreme Court who files criminal informations in the Court of Queen's Bench upon the relation or complaint of private persons. The role has been combined with that of the Registrar of Criminal Appeals and the Queen's Coroner and Attorney.

Master of the Mint The Chancellor of the Exchequer (Coinage Act 1971 s.4).

Master of the Rolls (M.R.) The President of the Civil Division of the Court of Appeal (*q.v.*) (Supreme Court Act 1981 s.3(2)). Originally keeper of the records and assistant to the Lord Chancellor. In the reign of Edward I he acquired judicial authority. By the Judicature Act 1881 he became a judge of the Court of Appeal. Today he is the senior member of the Court of Appeal (Civil Division) and is second in judicial importance to the Lord Chief Justice. See PRESIDENT OF THE COURTS OF ENGLAND AND WALES.

Masters in Chancery They were assistants of the Lord Chancellor, and of the Master of the Rolls. They sat in chambers for the discharge of functions which were partly ministerial and partly judicial. The Court of Chancery Act 1852 abolished the Masters and provided for the appointment of eight Chief Clerks (*q.v.*). However, since 1987, by an order of the Lord Chancellor, they have been entitled to be called Masters of the Supreme Court and this term has been used in subsequent legislation.

material change of use Under the Town and Country Planning Act 1990 planning permission (*q.v.*) is needed for any development (*q.v.*) of land. The making of a material change in the use of any building or land is a development for planning purposes, ibid. s.55(1). Whether a change of use is material is largely a question of fact and degree, to be determined by the local planning authority. The matter to be considered is the character of the use and not the particular purpose of the applicant.

material consideration When dealing with an application for planning permission (*q.v.*), a local planning authority must have regard to the development plan (*q.v.*) in so far as it is material to the application, and any other material considerations, Town and Country Planning Act 1990 s.70(2). Material considerations include ministerial policy, availability of alternate sites, noise and nuisance levels, and fear of setting a precedent. See PLANNING; PLANNING OBLIGATION.

maternity allowance. A benefit payable to working pregnant women who do not qualify for statutory maternity pay (*q.v.*). A claimant must have been employed or been working as a registered self-employed person for at least 26 weeks out of the 66 weeks before the expected week of childbirth and have been earning on average £30 per week.

maternity leave The term covers a range of rights afforded a pregnant woman under the Maternity and Parental Leave etc. Regulations 1999 (as amended by the Employment Act 2002 and the Work and Families Act 2006), for example, the right to take time off work for ante-natal care, the right to be absent from work for a stipulated period over the time of the birth and the right to statutory maternity pay. See Employment Rights Act 1996 Pt VIII. See also PATERNITY LEAVE.

maternity pay See STATUTORY MATERNITY PAY.

mate's receipt The receipt given by the mate for goods shipped on board, which is later given to the master of the ship so that he may sign the bills of lading for the goods.

matricide The crime of murdering your own mother.

matrimonial causes Petitions for divorce, nullity of marriage, judicial separation.

matrimonial home The place where husband and wife have lived together. A spouse who has no right by virtue of any estate, interest, contract or enactment to occupy the matrimonial home is given protection from eviction or exclusion by the Family Law Act 1996 s.30.

matrimonium [Roman law] Matrimony, the marriage-tie. See NUPTIAE.

mayhem Violently depriving another of the use of a member proper for his defence in fight, such as an arm, a leg, an eye, etc. It was both a civil injury and a criminal offence.

Mayor's and City of London Court A new court formed in 1921 by the amalgamation of the Mayor's Court of London and the City of London Court (Mayor's and City of London Court Act 1920). The court was abolished but, in effect, revived with normal county court jurisdiction (Courts Act 1971 s.42 Sch.5).

me judice [In my opinion]

measure of damages See DAMAGES; REMOTENESS OF DAMAGE.

measures By the Church of England Assembly (Powers) Act 1919 every measure prepared by the Church Assembly with the assistance of the Legislative Committee of the Church Assembly is submitted to the Ecclesiastical Committee, consisting of 15 members of each House of Parliament, who consider the measure and report on it, especially with relation to the constitutional rights of all Her Majesty's subjects. The report, after communication to the Legislative Committee, and with its concurrence, is made to Parliament, and the measure is laid before Parliament, which has no power to amend it. On a resolution passed by both Houses it is presented for the Royal Assent and has the effect of a statute.

The Church Assembly was renamed the General Synod of the Church of England and reconstituted (Synodical Government Measure 1969).

The Ecclesiastical Jurisdiction Measure 1963 reformed and reconstructed the system of ecclesiastical courts (*q.v.*) of the Church of England, and replaced the existing enactments relating to ecclesiastical discipline.

measures having equivalent effect to a quantitative restriction Member States (*q.v.*) are prohibited by art.28 EC Treaty from introducing any quantitative restrictions on imports and also any measures having equivalent effect. (Similar provision exists in relation to exports under art.29 EC Treaty). The European Court of Justice (*q.v.*) has defined MEQRs as all trading rules enacted by Member States which are capable of hindering, directly or indirectly, actually or potentially, intra-Community trade. Known as the *Dassonville* formula from Case 8/74 *Procureur du Roi v Dassonville* [1974] E.C.R. 837. See FREE MOVEMENT OF GOODS.

mechanical right In the music industry, the exclusive right of a copyright owner to determine who can first record and manufacture his work.

mediation A form of non-adversarial alternative dispute resolution (*q.v.*). Sometimes this term is used interchangeably with conciliation (*q.v.*). The parties in dispute employ a neutral third party as a mediator who will seek to promote communication between the parties. Ultimately, it is hoped that the mediator's exploration of the case privately with each side will lead to common ground emerging between the parties upon which a settlement of the dispute may be based. However, this process does not guarantee a resolution of a dispute as such depends upon the agreement of the parties, the mediator having no power to decide the dispute. It is encouraged as a process in civil and family proceedings.

medical inspection May be required in cases of nullity of marriage (*q.v.*) where it is alleged that the marriage has not been consummated. See Family Proceedings Rules 1991.

medical jurisprudence This term has been replaced by forensic medicine (*q.v.*).

mediums Any person who for reward (and not solely for entertainment) with intent to deceive, purports to act as a spiritualistic medium, or to exercise any powers of telepathy or clairvoyance or other similar powers, or uses any fraudulent device in so doing, commits an offence (Fraudulent Mediums Act 1951).

meetings, public See PUBLIC MEETING.

melior est conditio possidentis et rei quam actoris [The position of the possessor is the better; and that of the defendant is better than that of the claimant]

member of a company The Companies Act 2006 s.112, provides that a member of a company includes the subscribers to a company's memorandum who are deemed to have agreed to become members of the company and, on its registration become members and, as such, are entered on the register of members. In addition the term includes every other person who agrees to become a member of a company and whose name is entered on the register of members. See ASSOCIATION, MEMORANDUM OF; COMPANY.

Member of Parliament (M.P.) A person elected on the 'first past the post' system to represent a constituency in the House of Commons (*q.v.*).

Member State Those states that are members of the European Union (*q.v.*). There are currently 27 Member States.

memorandum A note of the particulars of any transaction or matter. A clause inserted in a policy of marine insurance to prevent the underwriters from being liable for injury to goods of a peculiarly perishable nature and for minor damages. See also ASSOCIATION, MEMORANDUM OF.

memorial An abstract of the material parts of a deed, with the parcels at full length, and concluding with a statement that the party desires the deed to be registered, which is left at the Land Registry for registration. See LAND REGISTRATION.

memory "Living memory" is time whereof the memory of man runneth not to the contrary, i.e. the period for which evidence can be given by the oldest living available witnesses.
"Legal memory" runs from the accession of Richard I, in 1189, because the Statute of Westminster 1 (3 Edw. 1 c.39) fixed that period as the time of limitation for bringing certain real actions.

menaces Threats of injury to persons or property, including third persons, to induce the person menaced to part with money or valuable property, e.g. threats to accuse of immorality or misconduct. An unwarranted demand with menaces made with a view to gain or to cause loss to another constitutes blackmail (*q.v.*), contrary to Theft Act 1968 s.21.

mens rea The state of mind expressly or impliedly required by the definition of the offence charged. There is a presumption that it is an essential ingredient in every criminal offence, liable to be displaced either by the words of the statute or by the subject-matter with which it deals. Many minor statutory offences, however, are punishable irrespective of the existence of mens rea; the mere intent to do the act forbidden by the statute is sufficient. If a particular intent or state of mind is an ingredient of a specific offence, that must be proved by the prosecution; but the absence of mens rea generally is a matter of defence. See INTENTION; MALICE AFORETHOUGHT; RECKLESSNESS.

mental disorder Any disorder or disability of the mind (Mental Health Act 1983 as amended by the Mental Health Act 2007).

Mental Health Review Tribunal A statutory body consisting of legal, medical and other members which considers applications and references for discharge by and in respect of patients who are subject to detention under the Mental Health Act

1983 or who are subject to guardianship (*q.v.*) or after-care under supervision ibid. s.65. See MENTAL DISORDER; MENTAL IMPAIRMENT.

mental impairment Previously defined in s.1 of the Mental Health Act 1983 as a state of arrested or incomplete development of mind not amounting to severe mental impairment which includes significant impairment of intelligence and social functioning and which is associated with abnormally aggressive or seriously irresponsible conduct on the part of the person concerned. However, this definition has now been repealed by the Mental Health Act 2007 with effect from November 3, 2008.

mercantile agent A person having authority, in the customary course of his business, as such agent, either to sell or to buy goods, or to consign goods for the purpose of sale, or to raise money on the security of goods including pledging them (Factors Act 1889 s.1).

mercantile law The branch of English law which has succeeded to the "Law Merchant." It usually comprises partnership, companies, agency, bills of exchange, carriers, carriage by sea, insurance, sale, bottomry (*q.v.*) and respondentia (*q.v.*), debt, guarantee, stoppage in transit, lien (*q.v.*) and bankruptcy (*q.v.*).

merchandise marks See TRADE DESCRIPTION.

merchantable quality Now replaced by satisfactory quality (*q.v.*). A condition (*q.v.*) which was implied into contracts for the sale of goods and other analogous contracts under which goods were supplied in the course of a business. Goods were defined as being of merchantable quality when they were as fit for the purpose or purposes for which goods of that kind are commonly bought as it was reasonable to expect, having regard to any description applied to them, the price (if relevant) and all the other relevant circumstances.

merger That operation of law which extinguishes a right by reason of its coinciding with another and greater right in the same person, e.g. a life estate is merged in or swallowed by the reversion when the two interests come into the hands of the same person. A right of action on a simple contract debt is merged in the right of suing on a bond for the same debt, and a right of action is merged in a judgment in the sense that no further action may be brought on the debt, but only on the judgment. A special characteristic of the debt, however, such as being a preferential claim in bankruptcy, is not lost merely because judgment is obtained in respect of the debt.

In equity, merger is a question of intention. If the benefit of a charge on property, and the property subject to the charge, vest in the same person, then equity will treat the charge as kept alive or merged according to whether it be of advantage or not to the person entitled. The Law of Property Act 1925 s.185 provided that there is no merger at law if there would have been none in equity.

As mergers between companies may have a considerable impact upon competition, they are strictly regulated by European Community legislation. See ANTI-COMPETITIVE PRACTICES.

The proprietor of two or more registrations of a trade mark may ask the Registrar of Trade Marks to merge them into a single registration (Trade Mark Rules 2000).

In evidence, where a party to litigation brings a successful action, his cause of action merges into the judgment and, thereafter, ceases to exist.

merits The real matters in question as opposed to technicalities. An affidavit of merits is an affidavit showing that a defendant has a substantial ground of defence to an action.

Merton, Statute of The statute (20 Hen. 3 cc.1–11), enacting that children born before the marriage of their parents were illegitimate, in connection with which the Barons declared "Nolumus leges Angliae mutari" [We will not have the laws of England changed]. That is, the barons refused to agree to the adoption of the canon law rule of legitimation by subsequent marriage. See LEGITIMACY

mesher order An order in matrimonial proceedings which preserves the interests of both parties in the matrimonial home but postponing sale of the property until a certain specified event, e.g. the youngest child reaches 18 years of age, see *Mesher v Mesher & Hall* [1980] 1 All E.R. 126.

mesne Middle, intervening or intermediate. See PROCESS.
A mesne lord was one who held of a superior lord.

mesne profits The damages payable to a landlord for losses incurred because his tenant stayed in possession of the property after the tenancy came to an end.

messuage A house, including gardens, courtyard, orchard and outbuildings.

metes and bounds By measurement and boundaries.

Middle Temple One of the Inns of Court (*q.v.*).

military law The law to which persons in the military service of the Crown are subject.

militia The force raised after the Restoration of 1660 as a substitute for those which had been raised under the commissions of array and lieutenancy. It was superseded by the Territorial Forces after 1907. See the Reserve Forces Acts 1980 and 1982.

mind The state of a man's mind is as much a fact as the state of his digestion (per Bowen L.J., *Edgington v Fitzmaurice* (1885) 29 Ch. D. 459 at 483). See MENS REA; REPRESENTATION.

mineral planning authority In respect of a site in a non-metropolitan county, this is the county planning authority and, in respect of a site in a metropolitan district, a London borough or in Wales (Local Government (Wales) Act 1994), the local planning authority. This designated body has responsibility for planning applications relating to the development of minerals.

minimum wage See NATIONAL MINIMUM WAGE.

minister A "Servant of the King"; a member of the Cabinet (*q.v.*); or a holder of high office under the Crown who vacates it on a change of Government. Every act of the Crown must be done through Ministers, who can be personally sued in law for their own acts. The constitutional doctrine of Ministerial responsibility is that every member of the Cabinet who does not resign is absolutely responsible for all that is done at Cabinet meetings; that is, Ministers are collectively responsible to Parliament. But the individual Minister is responsible for all the acts of his own Department.
The functions, styles, and titles of ministers may be altered under the Ministers of the Crown Act 1975. The number of ministers entitled to sit in the House of Commons is 95 (House of Commons (Disqualification) Act 1975 s.2, Sch.2).

ministerial act An act or duty which involves the exercise of administrative powers or the carrying out of instructions (e.g. the arrest of a person), as opposed to a judicial or discretionary act.

Ministry of Justice Replacing the Department of Constitutional Affairs, it has responsibility for the courts and tribunals, prisons and probation in addition to criminal, civil, family and administrative law. It also oversees constitutional affairs such as electoral reform and the Judicial Appointments Commission (*q.v.*).

minor A person under the age of 18 years. He becomes of full age from the first moment of the 18th anniversary of his birth (Family Law Reform Act 1969 ss.1,

9). An infant may be described as a minor (s.12). A minor does not have full legal capacity. For the purposes of the criminal law, a child aged ten or over is fully liable for his actions (Crime and Disorder Act 1998 s.34). See CAPACITY; NECESSARIES.

minor interests Interests not capable of being disposed of or created by registered dispositions, and capable of being overriden by the proprietors, unless protected as provided by the Land Registration Act 2002, and all rights and interests which are not registered or protected on the register, and are not overriding interests (Land Registration Act 1925 s.3(xv), as amended by the Land Registration Act 2002). See LAND REGISTRATION

minutes (1) Notes or records of business transacted at a meeting.

(2) Copies of a draft order or decree before being embodied in a formal judgment of the court.

misadventure An accident or mischance, unexpected and undesigned, arising out of a lawful act. See HOMICIDE.

miscarriage of justice In its legal sense means a failure of justice.

mischief of the statute The wrongs intended to be redressed by a statute; the gist or real purpose and object of it. The mischief of the statute is often to be found from the preamble and sometimes from the marginal notes (*Stephens v Cuckfidd RDC* [1960] 2 Q.B. 373). See STATUTORY INTERPRETATION.

misdemeanour At common law all crimes were classified as either misdemeanours or felonies. The distinction between the two was abolished by the Criminal Law Act 1967 s.1.

misdescription An error, mistake, or misstatement in the description of property. A misdescription affecting the title, value or character of land in a contract of sale may be: (1) substantial, so that the property purchased is not that which it was intended to purchase; or (2) slight, so that compensation in money would be proper. In (1) the misdescription is a defence to an action for specific performance (*q.v.*), and a ground for rescission (*q.v.*); the purchaser cannot be compelled to take the property. The purchaser may, however, at his option, generally compel specific performance of the contract with an abatement of the purchase price. The vendor cannot enforce the contract where he has been guilty of fraud (*q.v.*) or misrepresentation (*q.v.*).

misdirection When the judge improperly or erroneously directs or informs the jury as to the law or the evidence they have to consider in arriving at their verdict. The withdrawal of evidence, or of a question, from the jury which might have influenced their decision is misdirection. A judge sitting alone can misdirect himself, as where, e.g. he puts the wrong questions to himself to answer.

Misdirection is a ground of appeal for a new trial in a civil action if some substantial wrong or miscarriage of justice is thereby occasioned.

misericordia [Mercy] See AMERCIAMENT.

misfeasance Misfeasance is the improper performance of a lawful act, e.g. where there is negligence (*q.v.*) or trespass (*q.v.*). A misfeasor is a person who is guilty of a misfeasance.

misjoinder Where persons are wrongly joined as claimants or defendants in an action, i.e. where persons are made parties who ought not to be. No action can now be defeated by a misjoinder or non-joinder of parties, and the court may of its own motion, or on application, order a party to cease to be a party (CPR 19.1).

misleading actions Under the Consumer Protection from Unfair Trading Regulations 2008 reg.3, misleading actions are unfair commercial practices and are prohibited. A commercial practice (*q.v*) will be a misleading action

272

under reg.5 if it causes the average consumer to take a transactional decision he would not have done otherwise and contains false information in relation to the existence or nature of the product, the main characteristics of the product, the extent of the trader's commitments, the motives for the commercial practice, the nature of the sales process, any statement relating to sponsorship or approval of the trader or the product, price, price advantage, the need for service, part, replacement or repair, or in relation to the consumer's rights or risks faced. In addition, a commercial practice will be a misleading action if it causes the average consumer to take a transactional decision he would not have done otherwise and concerns marketing of a product which creates confusion with a competitor or a failure by a trader to comply with a commitment in a code of conduct by which the trader has firmly indicated he is bound.

misleading omissions Under the Consumer Protection from Unfair Trading Regulations 2008, reg.3, misleading omissions are unfair commercial practices and are prohibited. A commercial practice (*q.v*) will be a misleading omission under reg.6 where it causes the average consumer to take a transactional decision he would not have otherwise taken and which omits material information, hides material information, provides material information in an unclear manner or fails to identify its commercial intent. In this context material information means the information a consumer needs to take an informed transactional decision and any information required as a result of a community obligation.

misnomer A misnaming. An amendment in consequence can be made in either civil or criminal causes.

misprision (1) Misprision of treason is where a person who knows that some other person has committed high treason (*q.v.*) does not within a reasonable time give information thereof to a justice of the peace or other authority. At common law the punishment is a fine and imprisonment at the discretion of the court.
   (2) Misprision of felony was the concealment of knowledge of the commission of a felony. It was a common law misdemeanour. The offence has lapsed with the abolition of the distinction between felony and misdemeanour. See FELONY; MISDEMEANOUR.

misrepresentation A representation (*q.v.*) that is untrue; a statement or conduct which conveys a false or wrong impression. Where a person is induced to enter into a contract because of a false statement of fact made by the other, the contract is voidable. The innocent party may elect to rescind or affirm the contract. A false or fraudulent misrepresentation is one made by someone who does not honestly believe it to be true. A negligent misrepresentation is one made with no reasonable grounds for believing it to be true. An innocent misrepresentation is one made with reasonable grounds for believing it to be true, as where an honest mistake is made.
   A misrepresentation may amount to the tort of deceit if fraudulently made or the tort of negligent misstatement if made carelessly. See FRAUD; NEGLIGENCE.

mistake In contract law a mistake may nullify consent, e.g. the parties contract on a fundamental mistaken basis or negative consent, e.g. the parties never reach agreement because of the mistake. Mistake may negative consent if as to: (1) the identity of the person contracted with, where this is material (*Cundy v Lindsay* (1878) 3 App. Cas. 459); (2) the subject-matter of the contract, or the identity of the thing contracted for (*Raffles v Wichelhaus* (1864) 2 H. & C. 906; *Bell v Lever Bros* [1932] A.C. 161); (3) the intention or promise of one party known to the other party (*Webster v Cecil* (1861) 30 Beav. 61). At common law, mistake makes a contract void. See NON EST FACTUM.

Money paid under mistake of fact may be recovered, as money had and received to the use of the person paying it (*Jones v Waring and Gillow* [1926] A.C. 670). Money paid under a mistake of law previously was not recoverable, but this rule was overruled in *Kleinwort Benson Ltd v Lincoln CC* [1999] 2 A.C. 349.

Mistake is usually no defence in an action of tort. In criminal law, a mistake of law is no excuse, but where, because of an honest mistake of fact, the accused lacks the mens rea (*q.v.*) for an offence, he cannot be convicted of that offence, whether or not the mistake was a reasonable one to have made (*DPP v Morgan* [1976] A.C. 182).

misuse of drugs The Misuse of Drugs Act 1971 sets out a number of offences in relation to the production, supply and possession of controlled drugs.

mitigation Where a defendant or prisoner whose responsibility or guilt is not in dispute proves facts tending to reduce the damages or punishment to be awarded against him, he is said to show facts in mitigation of damages, or of sentence, as the case may be.

In general, it is the duty of the party whose legal rights have been infringed to act reasonably in mitigation of damages.

mittimus [We send]

mixed fund A fund consisting of the proceeds of both real and personal property.

M'Naghten Rules The rules which set out the requirements for the defence of insanity (*q.v.*) in criminal proceedings.

mobilia sequuntur personam [Movables follow the person] Thus the law of a man's domicile governs the descent of his personal property.

mobility allowance Benefit payable to a person suffering from a physical disablement so that he was unable or virtually unable to walk (Social Security Act 1975). This benefit was abolished by the Disability Living Allowance and Disability Working Allowance Act 1991 s.2(3). It has been replaced by the mobility component of disability living allowance (*q.v.*).

mock auction One not conducted in good faith. The Mock Auctions Act 1961 prescribes penalties for their promotion or conduct.

mode of address For the correct way to address judges, recorders, etc. see *Lord Chief Justice's Practice Direction* [1982] 1 All E.R. 320.

modo et forma A denial that the thing alleged in the pleading of the other side had been done *modo et forma* [in the manner and form] alleged. This put the opposite party upon strict proof of every averment.

modus The payment of tithes otherwise than by a tenth of the yearly increase of land, e.g. by a payment of twopence per acre.

modus et conventio vincunt legem [Custom and agreement overrule law] Within ever decreasing limits, the parties to a contract can make their own rules.

modus legem dat donationi [Agreement gives law to the gift] e.g. the agreement for the transfer of land settles the conditions upon which the land is to be held.

molest To pester or interfere with someone. For remedies against molestation see injunction.

money The medium of exchange, and measure of value. "Money" is construed widely when used in wills, as including cash in hand or at a bank, and it may be investments.

money bill A bill which in the opinion of the Speaker of the House of Commons contains only provisions dealing with finance and taxation.

A money bill can only originate in the House of Commons, and any bill certified by the Speaker to be a money bill must be presented for the Royal Assent at the end of the session in which it passes the Commons, whether it is or is not passed by the Lords (Parliament Act 1911).

money claim A civil claim whereby the claimant seeks a monetary award, whether for a specified sum or not.

money had and received Money which is paid to one person which rightfully belongs to another, as where money is paid by A to B on a consideration which has wholly failed, is said to be money had and received by B to the use of A, and is recoverable by action by A. See QUASI-CONTRACT.

money laundering The phrase covers a number of offences contrary to the Proceeds of Crime Act 2002 (as amended by the Serious Organised Crime and Police Act 2005) involving criminal property. For example, it is an offence contrary to s.327 to conceal, disguise, convert, transfer or remove criminal property from the United Kingdom. The 2002 Act is supported by the Money Laundering Regulations 2007 which implement the Third Directive on the Prevention of Money Laundering and Terrorist Financing (2005/60/EC).

moneylender A moneylender was defined for the purpose of the Moneylenders Acts 1900 and 1927 (repealed by the Consumer Credit Act 1974) as any person whose business was that of moneylending, or who advertised or announced himself or held himself out in any way as carrying on that business; but not including pawnbrokers, friendly societies, bodies authorised by law to lend money, bankers, or bodies exempted by the Department of Trade (Moneylenders Act 1900 s.6). The business of most moneylenders is now regulated by the Consumer Credit Act 1974.

monopoly A commercial monopoly arises where the supply of a certain commodity is controlled by one manufacturer, trader or group. In European Community law and the Competition Act 1998, a monopoly is defined as an undertaking with a dominant position. The concern behind legislation regulating monopolies is that the monopolist will exploit its power over the market and act anti-competitively. Investigations into alleged monopolies are carried out by the Competition Commission. See ANTICOMPETITIVE PRACTICES

monstrans de droit [Manifestation of right] A remedy which a subject had when the Crown (*q.v.*) was in possession of property belonging to him, and the title of the Crown appeared from facts set forth upon record. In such a case the claimant might present a *monstrans de droit*, either showing that upon the facts as recorded he was entitled to the property, or setting forth new facts showing that he was entitled. It was superseded by the Petition of Right, and abolished by the Crown Proceedings Act 1947 Sch.1.

month A month is either a lunar month of 28 days, or a calendar month. A month at common law meant a lunar month, but in ecclesiastical and mercantile law, a month meant a calendar month. Now, unless a contrary intention appears, "month" means calendar month (Interpretation Act 1978 ss.5, 22 and 23; Law of Property Act 1925 s.61; CPR 2.10).

In calculating the period of a month or months that have elapsed after a certain event, e.g. a notice, the period ends on the corresponding date in the appropriate subsequent month irrespective of whether some months are longer than others (*Dodds v Walker* [1981] 1 W.L.R. 1027, HL).

moot A meeting of the members of an Inn of Court (*q.v.*) in Hall at which points of law arising in a given case were argued by selected barristers before the benchers who in turn gave their opinions thereon. Moots were an essential part of professional legal education until about the end of the seventeenth century.

They still survive on a voluntary basis at Gray's Inn, where one of the benchers is appointed "Master of the Moots", and amongst law students elsewhere.

moral defectives See MENTAL DISORDER.

moral rights Intellectual property rights (*q.v.*). Moral rights are granted to authors (*q.v.*), etc. of copyright (*q.v.*) works and relate to the protection of reputation rather than of economic interests.

morally wrong This is distinguishable from legally wrong (*Sofaer v Sofaer* [1960] 1 W.L.R. 1173). See also IMMORALITY.

moratorium The general postponement of payment of debts authorised by statute, e.g. as on the outbreak of war in 1914.

moratur in lege [He tarries in the law] A demurrer.

morganatic marriage Marriage between a royal or noble person and one of lower rank in which the children do not inherit the royal or noble rank.

mortgage More correctly termed a charge by way of legal mortgage. It provides security over land for a debt. If the debt is not repaid, it can be recovered from a sale of the land subject to the charge. The person who borrows money against the property is known as the mortgagor and he retains ownership of the property during the term of the loan. The lender is known as the mortgagee.
A legal mortgage must be created by deed. Where the land is registered, the mortgage is effected by registration at the Land Registry. Until registration, the mortgagee receives only an equitable mortgage over the property. Where the land is unregistered, any first legal mortgage of the freehold or of a leasehold with more than seven years remaining now triggers first registration of the freehold or leasehold at the Land Registry. See EQUITY OF REDEMPTION; CLOG ON EQUITY OF REDEMPTION; OPTION MORTGAGE; LAND REGISTRATION.

mortgagee The person to whom property is mortgaged; the lender of the mortgage debt.

mortgagor The person who mortgages his property as security for the mortgage debt; the borrower.

mortmain The alienation of land to corporations, whereby the benefit of the incidents of tenure was lost, because "a corporation never dies". Land could not be conveyed to corporations except by statutory authority or by licence of the Crown ((7 Edw. 1, stat. 2 c.13) and (15 Ric. 2 c.5), replaced by the Mortmain and the Charitable Uses Act 1888). An assurance or conveyance to a corporation not authorised to hold land rendered the land liable to forfeiture to the Crown. The law of mortmain was abolished by the Charities Act 1960 s.38.

mortuary A place for the reception of dead bodies before interment.

mortuum vadium [A mortgage] (*q.v.*)

mote A meeting or assembly.

motion An application to a court or judge for an order directing something to be done in the applicant's favour. Ordinarily a motion is to be made only after a notice has been given to the parties affected, but in certain cases it may be made ex parte. The process of commencement in the High Court by originating motion was abolished by the introduction of the Civil Procedure Rules (CPR) (*q.v.*) and replaced by the "claim form" (*q.v.*). In Chancery proceedings, "motion" has been replaced by the CPR with the term "judge's application".

motive The reason why the defendant committed a criminal offence.

Motor Insurers' Bureau A company formed by motor insurers in 1946 operating within the terms of an agreement between the MIB and the government. The agreement makes provision to meet the claims both of victims of uninsured drivers and of victims of drivers who cannot be traced.

movables Personal property, e.g. goods.

mulier [*mulier*, a wife] A woman, virgin, wife, or a legitimate child.

multifariousness A demurrer to a bill in Chancery that attempted to embrace too many objects or causes of suit. See joinder of causes of actions.

multi-track The case management track to which civil claims in excess of £15,000 are normally allocated by the courts under CPR Pt 26. See CASE MANAGEMENT; FAST TRACK; SMALL CLAIMS TRACK; TRACK ALLOCATION.

municipal corporation Formerly the local government authority of a borough, consisting of a mayor, aldermen and councillors, which had been incorporated by royal charter. Municipal corporations were regulated by the Municipal Corporations Acts 1835 and 1882 and the Local Government Act 1933. Outside London, they ceased to exist on April 1, 1974 (Local Government Act 1972 s.1(11)). See DISTRICT COUNCIL.

municipal law The law of a state or country, as opposed to international law; internal law.

muniments [*Munio*, to defend or fortify] Title deeds and other documents relating to the title to land.

murder The crime of unlawful killing during the Queen's Peace with malice aforethought (*q.v.*); as where the accused causes death by an unlawful act with the intention to cause death or grievous bodily harm (*R. v Moloney* [1985] A.C. 905). The burden of proving malice aforethought rests upon the prosecution (*Woolmington v DPP* [1935] A.C. 462). Where a person kills another in the course or furtherance of some other offence, the killing does not amount to murder unless done with the same malice aforethought as is required for a killing to amount to murder when not done in the course or furtherance of another offence (Homicide Act 1957 s.1(1)).

The partial defences of provocation (*q.v.*), diminished responsibility (*q.v.*) and killing in pursuance of a suicide pact (*q.v.*) reduce murder liability to voluntary manslaughter. A person who killed but lacked the mens rea for murder when he did so may be found guilty of manslaughter, provided he killed as part of an unlawful and dangerous act or with gross negligence or recklessness. See MANSLAUGHTER.

musical work Any work which consists of music, exclusive of any words or action intended to be sung, spoken or performed with the music. Under the Copyright, Designs and Patents Act 1988, copyright (*q.v.*) subsists in such a work provided it is recorded.

mutatis mutandis [The necessary changes being made]

mute An accused, who being arraigned (*q.v.*), either makes no answer at all, or with such matter as is not allowable. In the first case, a jury must be sworn to try whether the prisoner stands mute of malice (i.e. obstinately) or by visitation of God (e.g. being deaf or dumb). If he is found mute of malice, or if he will not answer directly to the indictment, it formerly exposed him to the *peine forte et dure* (*q.v.*); now the court, under the Criminal Law Act 1967 s.6(1)(c), orders a plea of not guilty to be entered, and the trial proceeds accordingly. If he is found by the jury to be mute by visitation of God, the issue of whether the defendant is fit to be tried must be heard. Should a defendant be found unfit then the trial cannot proceed.

A witness in a criminal trial who is mute and incapable of communicating through an interpreter is incompetent to testify (*R. v Whitehead* (1866) L.R. 1 C.C.R. 33).

Mutiny Act The Bill of Rights (1 Will. & M., sess. 2 c.2) declares that the raising or keeping, a standing army within the kingdom in time of peace, unless it be with the consent of Parliament, is illegal. Consequently, an Act of Parliament called the Mutiny Act was passed annually to legalise the Army for the year. The Mutiny Act was replaced by an annual Army Act from 1881 onwards. The Army Act 1955 changed the position by conferring a power to continue the Army Act 1955 by Order in Council for periods of five years. The same applies to the Air Force Act 1955 and the Naval Discipline Act 1957. All the armed forces Acts are now continued in force by the Armed Forces Act 2006. See ARMED FORCES.

mutual credits Where there have been mutual credits, mutual debts or other mutual dealings between a debtor and a creditor, only the balance is to be claimed or paid in the debtor's bankruptcy proceedings (Insolvency Act 1986 s.323).

mutual trust and respect (or confidence), implied duty of A term to be implied into a contract of employment imposing on an employer an obligation not to act in a way likely to destroy the or seriously damage the employment relationship (see *Malik v BCCI SA* [1997] I.C.R. 606, HL). Failure to observe this duty may lead to a claim of constructive dismissal (*q.v.*) by an employee. See DISMISSAL OF EMPLOYEE; UNFAIR DISMISSAL.

mutuum A bailment (*q.v.*) consisting of the loan of personal chattels to be consumed by the borrower and to be returned to the lender by way of replacements that are similar in kind and quantity.

N

N.P Nisi prius (*q.v.*).

nam; namium The taking or distraining of the goods of another.

name and arms clause The clause, sometimes inserted in a will (*q.v.*) or settlement (*q.v.*), by which property is given to a person, for the purpose of imposing on him the condition that he shall assume the surname and arms of the testator or settlor, with a direction that if he neglects to assume or discontinues the use of them, the estate shall devolve on the next person in remainder. A name and arms clause which is sufficiently certain is valid. See, e.g. *Re Neeld* [1969] 1 W.L.R. 998.

name, change of Other than in relation to aliens, there are no rules limiting an individual's freedom to change his Christian name. A person may change his surname (e.g. by deed poll). A deed poll for change of name by a British subject whose permanent place of residence is in the United Kingdom may be enrolled (Supreme Court Act 1981 s.133; Enrolment of Deeds (Change of Name) Regulations 1994).

A company may change its name by special resolution (Companies Act 2006 s.77) but its choice of name is subject to certain restrictions (e.g. a name may not be chosen if it is the same as a name appearing in the index of names kept by the Registrar of Companies (ibid. s.66). In certain circumstances the Secretary of State may direct a company to change its name (ibid. s.76).

National Crime Squad This has now been abolished and replaced by the Serious Organised Crime Agency (*q.v.*).

National Criminal Intelligence Service This has now been abolished and replaced by the Serious Organised Crime Agency (*q.v*).

National Health Service The Service was established by the National Health Service Act 1946, which was subsequently amended on a number of occasions and eventually largely repealed and replaced by the National Health Service Act 1977. Under the National Health Service and Community Care Act 1990 the Secretary of State may establish National Health Service trusts to own and manage hospitals and other facilities previously managed by health authorities, thereby enabling such hospitals to be self-governing.

National Health Service Trust A body corporate having a board of directors, consisting of a chairman appointed by the Secretary of State and executive and non-executive members. Such trusts assumed responsibility for the ownership and management of hospitals or other establishments or facilities which were previously managed or provided by regional, district or special health authorities. The function of the National Health Service Trusts is to provide goods and services for the purposes of the health service.

national insurance Social security under the National Insurance Acts and the National Insurance (Industrial Injuries) Acts was replaced by the scheme under the Social Security Act 1975, as subsequently amended. Claimants for the various benefits may appeal from the decision of an adjudication officer to a social security appeal tribunal (*q.v.*) or a disability appeal tribunal (*q.v.*). Further appeal on a point of law lies to a Social Security Commissioner (*q.v.*).

National Minimum Wage The right of workers to receive minimum rates of pay was introduced by an Act of the same name in 1998. The Act did not originally apply to those under the age of 18 and there are reduced rates for those under the age of 22 and for those aged 16 to 17. There is also the possibility of exclusions for apprentice workers under the age of 26. There is no automatic indexing of wages and uprating is at the discretion of the Secretary of State for Business Enterprise and Regulatory Reform who may consult the Low Pay Commission (*q.v.*). The Act and the Regulations passed under it provide a complex formula for establishing a worker's entitlement.

national parks See CONSERVATION.

National River Authority This was replaced by the Environment Agency (*q.v.*).

National Trust A trust for the preservation of places of historic interest or natural beauty was incorporated by the National Trust Act 1907. It is a charity (*q.v.*).

nationality The character or quality arising from membership of a particular nation or state, which determines the political status and allegiance of a person. See british citizen; british subject; citizenship.

nations, law of International law (*q.v.*).

natural child (1) The child of one's own body.
(2) In certain circumstances the term could include illegitimate children (see *Bentley v Blizard*, 4 Jur. N.S. 652). Under the Family Law Reform Act 1987 the policy has been to eliminate the discrimination between children born to married parents and those born to unmarried parents.

natural justice The courts in the interest of fairness impose certain obligations upon those with power to take decisions affecting other people. These obligations arise from the rules of natural justice which, although "sadly lacking in precision" have generally been subsumed under two heads: the *audi alteram partem* (*q.v.*) rule; and the *nemo judex in re sua* (*q.v.*) rule. By virtue of these rules, decision makers must act fairly, in good faith and without bias and must afford each party the opportunity to adequately state his case. The principles of natural justice do not apply to certain acts of the Executive. See EXECUTIVE.

natural law The law of nature; law as the emanation of the Divine Providence, rooted in the nature and reason of man. It is both anterior and superior to positive law.

natural persons Human beings, as distinguished from artificial persons or corporations recognised by the law, e.g. companies. See PERSON.

natural rights Fundamental rights common to the law of all civilised peoples, e.g. right of personal liberty, of ownership and possession of property, freedom of speech, etc. See LIBERTY.

naturales liberi [Roman law] Natural children.
　　(1) Children not born in lawful wedlock, as opposed to *legitimi.*
　　(2) Children born as opposed to adopted. See NATURAL CHILD.

naturalisation When a person becomes the subject of a state to which he was before an alien. Certificates of naturalisation as a British citizen (*q.v.*) may be granted to persons of full age and capacity who fulfil certain requirements set out in the British Nationality Act 1981 Sch.1; where, on making the citizenship oath and pledge, such persons become British Citizens (Act of 1981 ss.6 and 42; Sch.5).
　　The qualification required for naturalisation as a British citizen set out in Sch.1 to the Act of 1981 may be summarised as relating to residence, character, language, sufficient knowledge of life in the UK and intentions. A person may also acquire British Overseas Territories citizenship (*q.v.*) by naturalisation (Act of 1981 s.18; Sch.1, as amended).

Navy The discipline of the Navy is regulated by the Naval Discipline Act 1957.

ne exeat regno A writ which issues from the High Court of Justice (in the Chancery Division) to restrain a person from going out of the kingdom without licence of the Crown or leave of the court. It is a high prerogative writ, which was originally applicable to purposes of state only, but was afterwards extended and confined to absconding debtors. For the modern practice see *Felton v Callis* [1969] 1 Q.B. 200.

nearest relative The term should not be confused with the term "next-of-kin". The term "nearest relative" derives from, and is peculiar to, mental health legislation. Under the Mental Health Act 1983, as amended, the nearest relative has certain powers and rights. The identifying of the nearest relative of a patient (*q.v.*) is made by the application of the provisions of ss.26–28 of the Act. It should be noted that: (a) the County Court may displace the nearest relative and appoint another person to act as the nearest relative; and (b) the role can be delegated to another person.

nec tempus nec locus occurrit regi [Neither time nor place affects the King]

nec vi, nec clam, nec precario [Not by violence, stealth, or entreaty] User as of right, in order to found a title by prescription (*q.v.*) to an easement (*q.v.*), must be *longus usus nec per vim, nec clam, nec precario* [long use not by violence, stealth or entreaty].

necessaries Minors (*q.v.*) (and mental patients) normally incapable of making a binding contract, can contract to buy necessaries, i.e. goods suitable to the condition in life of such minor and to his actual requirements at the time of the sale and delivery (Sale of Goods Act 1979 s.3). See CAPACITY.
　　For ships, the term "necessaries" means such things as are fit and proper for the service in which the ship is engaged, and such as the owner, being a prudent man, would have ordered if present. The master may hypothecate the ship for necessaries supplied abroad so as to bind the owner. See HYPOTHECATION.

necessitas inducit privilegium quoad jura privata [Necessity gives a privilege as to private rights] See NECESSITY.

necessitas non habet legem [Necessity knows no law]

necessitas publica major est quam privata [Public necessity is greater than private] A maxim favoured by the Executive (*q.v.*).

necessity The invasion of the private rights of others may possibly be justified and defended on the grounds of necessity. Thus to destroy property in the path of a conflagration to halt it, or to enter on property and damage it in time of war, may be justified as for the common good. Similarly, acts injurious to others may be done in the defence of a man's own property which is in imminent danger. Thus, at common law, a farmer may shoot a savage dog which is attacking his sheep. The test is whether there was reasonable necessity for the act in the circumstances existing at the time (*Cresswell v Sirl* [1948] 1 K.B. 241). However, the rule in *Cresswell v Sirl* has been replaced, so far as the protection of livestock against dogs is concerned, by the Animals Act 1971 s.9. This provides a defence given the fulfilment of certain conditions. See ANIMALS; RIGHT OF WAY.

Necessity may be an excuse for committing what would otherwise be a criminal offence if the act or omission which is in question was necessary to prevent the execution of an illegal purpose. But mere personal necessity is no justification for a crime, e.g. hunger (*R. v Dudley and Stephens* (1884) 14 Q.B.D. 273). In certain statutory offences allowance is made for situations where the accused has acted under the stress of necessity (e.g. the driver of a fire engine failing to observe the speed limit, see Road Traffic Regulation Act 1984 s.87). It has been held that a defence of duress of circumstances may provide a limited general defence of necessity (see *R. v Willer* (1986) 83 Cr.App.R. 225; and *R. v Martin* [1989] 1 All E.R. 652). A person raising this defence must have reasonably perceived the threat of death or serious injury (see *R. v Cairns* [1999] 2 Cr.App.R. 137). See DURESS.

neck verse The words *Miserere mei Deus*, with which the 51st Psalm begins. A prisoner was entitled to benefit of clergy (*q.v.*) if he could read or recite these words.

negative clearance The European Commission (*q.v.*) may certify that, on the basis of facts in its possession, there are no grounds under arts 81 or 82 of the Treaty of Rome (as consolidated) for action on its part in respect of an agreement, decision or practice. See BLOCK EXEMPTION.

negative pregnant A literal denial in pleading which does not go to the substance of the allegation. Where a traverse is of a negative averment so that it is clear that it is intended to set up an affirmative case, particulars of the affirmative case ought to be delivered (*IRC v Jackson* [1960] 1 W.L.R. 873).

negligence As a tort (*q.v.*), negligence is the breach by the defendant of a legal duty to take care, which results in damage to the claimant. See DUTY OF CARE; BREACH.

Alternatively, negligence may signify a state of mind, i.e. either a person's inadvertence to the consequences of his conduct or the deliberate taking of a risk without necessarily intending the consequences attendant upon that risk.

negotiable instrument An instrument the transfer of which to a transferee who takes in good faith and for value passes a good title, free from any defects or equities affecting the title of the transferor. The most important kinds of negotiable instruments are bills of exchange (*q.v.*), cheques (*q.v.*) and promissory notes (*q.v.*). Bills and cheques must order the payment of money whereas notes must contain a promise to pay. Negotiability may be conferred by custom or statute, and restricted or destroyed by the holder of the instrument. Negotiability is also used popularly as equivalent to transferability.

negotiate To transfer for value by delivery or indorsement (*q.v.*).

negotiorum gestio Interference of one in the affairs of another merely from benevolence and without authority. In English law a man so interfering: (1) has no claim on the other in respect of what he may do; (2) is liable for the wages of anyone whom he may employ; (3) must have skill and knowledge necessary for whatever he takes it on himself to do.

nem con.: nemine contradicente [No one saying otherwise]

nem. dis.: nemine dissentiente [No one dissenting]

neminem oportet legibus esse sapientiorem [It is not permitted to be wiser than the laws]

nemo admittendus est inhabilitare seipsum [Nobody is to be permitted to incapacitate himself]

nemo agit in seipsum [No one can take proceedings against himself]

nemo contra factum suum proprium venire potest [No one can go against his own deed]

nemo dat quod non habet [No one gives who possesses not]

nemo debet bis puniri pro uno delicto [No one should be punished twice for one fault]

nemo debet esse judex in propria causa [No one can be judge in his own cause] A judge may not have any pecuniary or personal interest in a case which he tries. If he has some interest he must declare it, e.g. shares in a company which is party to an action or an interest in the promotion of a cause related to a party in a case (see *R. v Bow Street Metropolitan Magistrate and others Ex p. Pinochet Ugarte (No. 2)* [1999] 1 All E.R. 577).

nemo est haeres viventis [No one is the heir of anyone who is alive]

nemo ex proprio dolo consequitur actionem [No one obtains a cause of action by his own fraud]

nemo ex suo delicto meliorem suam conditionem facere potest [No one can improve his position by his own wrongdoing]

nemo judex in re sua [No man a judge in his own cause] See natural justice.

nemo plus juris ad alium transferre potest, quam ipse haberet [The title of an assignee can be no better than that of his assignor]

nemo potest esse simul actor et judex [No one can be at once suitor and judge]

nemo potest facere per alium, quod per se non potest [No one can do through another what he cannot do himself]

nemo potest plus juris ad alium transferre quam ipse habet [No one can transfer a greater right to another than he himself has]

nemo prohibetur pluribus defensionibus uti [No one is forbidden to use several defences]

nemo tenetur ad impossibile [No one is required to do what is impossible]

nemo tenetur se ipsum accusare [No one is bound to incriminate himself]

nervous shock Injury to health due to nervous shock is a form of bodily harm for which damages may be claimed (*Hambrook v Stokes* [1925] 1 K.B. 141). But for the defendant to be liable he must owe a duty to the claimant to take care with respect to him, and the fact that the claimant would suffer injury from nervous shock as a result of the defendant's act must have been reasonably foreseeable by him, i.e. the claimant must have been within the area of potential danger

(*Bourhill v Young* [1943] A.C. 92). However, in *McLoughlin v O'Brien* [1983] 1 A.C. 410 it was held that a claimant who had not been at the scene of an accident might recover damages for nervous shock brought on by injury caused not to herself but to a near relative, or by fear of such injury. In *Alcock v Chief Constable of the South Yorkshire Police Force* [1991] 4 All E.R. 907, HL, it was stated that the class of persons to whom a duty may be owed is not limited by reference to particular relationships such as husband and wife, or parent and child. But, whatever the relationship, to recover damages in such circumstances a claimant must be sufficiently proximate to the accident in both time and space and must see or hear the accident or its immediate aftermath. Persons viewing disasters on television or hearing radio broadcasts are not sufficiently proximate (ibid.).

The claimant must suffer a genuine psychiatric illness or disorder, emotional distress or grief is not enough. However, in the case of a "primary victim" (*q.v.*) if some personal injury is foreseeable, damages for psychiatric damage may be recovered even if such damage is not foreseeable (see *Page v Smith* [1995] 2 All E.R. 736, HL). For a "secondary victim" (*q.v.*) there is an expectation of reasonable fortitude and recovery for psychiatric damage will only be possible if such loss is foreseeable. Serving police officers attending a disaster were viewed by a majority of the House of Lords in *White v Chief Constable of South Yorkshire* [1999] 1 All E.R. 1 as rescuers who were in no physical danger and hence were treated as secondary victims. (See also *Liability for Psychiatric Illness* (1998) Law Com. No. 249.)

new towns The New Towns Act 1946 provided for the creation of new towns by means of development corporations. Various measures enacted since that time have been consolidated in the New Towns Act 1981. See PLANNING.

new trial Under the Access to Justice Act 1999 s.54, the rules of court may provide that any right of appeal to a county court, the High Court or the Court of Appeal may be exercised only with such permission as those rules determine. A right of appeal includes the right to make an application for a new trial (ibid. subs.(6)). Grounds for a new trial include: (a) misdirection of the jury or himself by the judge, or improper admission or rejection of evidence by the judge, provided substantial injustice was caused; (b) verdict against weight of evidence; (c) discovery of fresh evidence; (d) excessive or inadequate damages. In the case of (d) the court may be empowered by rules of court to substitute such sums as it considers proper (Courts and Legal Services Act 1990 s.8). Section 54 of the Access to Justice Act 1999 does not apply to criminal proceedings. As to criminal proceedings see VENIRE DE NOVO.

next friend Now referred to as a litigation friend (*q.v.*) under the Civil Procedure Rules 1998 r.21.2. A minor (*q.v.*) or patient (*q.v.*) who desires to bring an action must, as a rule, do so through the intervention of a person called a litigation friend; in the case of a child this will generally be a relation with no interest adverse to the child.

next-of-kin The nearest blood relatives. Strictly, those who are next in degree of kindred to a deceased person. The degrees of kindred are according to the Roman law, both upwards to the ancestor and downwards to the issue, each generation counting for a degree. Thus, from father to son is one degree and from brother to brother is two degrees, namely, one upwards to the father and one downwards to the other son. By this means husband and wife did not rank as next-of-kin. However, the old rule whereby a husband or wife did not take as statutory next-of-kin was abolished by the Administration of Estates Act 1925.

nihil: nil [Nothing] No goods.

nihil facit error nominis cum de corpore constat [A mistake as to the name has no effect when there is no mistake as to who is the person meant]

nisi A decree, order, rule, declaration, or other adjudication of a court is said to be made nisi when it is not to take effect unless the person affected by it fails to show cause against it within a certain time, that is, unless he appears before the court, and gives some reason why it should not take effect. See ABSOLUTE; DECREE NISI.

Nisi Prius A trial at Nisi Prius was a trial by a jury before a single judge, either at the sittings held for that purpose in London and Middlesex, or at the assizes. Formerly all common law actions were tried at the bar, that is before the full court, consisting of several judges; and, therefore, the writ for summoning the jury commanded the sheriff to bring the jurors from the county where the cause of action arose to the court at Westminster. But when the statute (13 Edw. 1) directed the justices of assize to try issues in the county where they arose, the sheriff was thenceforth commanded to bring the jurors to Westminster on a certain day, "unless before that day" (nisi prius) the justices of assize came into the county.

noise Noise includes vibration (Environmental Protection Act 1990 s.79). Where a local authority is satisfied that noise amounts to a statutory nuisance (*q.v.*), the local authority shall serve an abatement notice (*q.v.*) on the creator of the noise. Contravention of the notice without reasonable excuse is a criminal offence (see Pt III of the EPA 1990). The Noise Act 1996 requires authorities to investigate complaints of excessive night-time noise (between 11pm and 7am) and serve a warning notice and a fixed penalty notice. Under the Control of Pollution Act 1974 local authorities have power to deal with construction noise (ss.60–61) and to create Noise Abatement Zones (s.63). Compensation for noise from the use of public works may be claimed under the Land Compensation Act 1973.

nolle prosequi Historically, an acknowledgment or undertaking entered on record by the plaintiff in an action, to forbear to proceed in the action, either wholly or partially; superseded by the modern practice of discontinuance. In criminal prosecutions by indictment or information, a *nolle prosequi* to stay proceedings may be entered by leave of the Attorney General at any time before judgment; it is not equivalent to an acquittal and is no bar to a new indictment for the same offence. The powers of the Attorney General are not subject to control by the court (*R. v Comptroller of Patents* [1899] 1 Q.B. 909 at 914).

nolumus leges Angliae mutari [We will not have the laws of England changed] See MERTON, STATUTE OF.

nominis umbra [The shadow of a name] e.g. a one-man company.

non aliter a significatione verborum recedi oportet quam cum manifestum est aliud sensisse testatorem [There should be no departure from the ordinary meaning of words except in so far as it appears that the testator meant something different]

non assumpsit [He did not promise] The plea to an action of assumpsit (*q.v.*).

non cepit modo et forma [He did not take in the manner and form (alleged)] The plea to the action of replevin (*q.v.*).

non compos mentis [Not sound in mind] See MENTAL DISORDER; PATIENT.

non constat [It does not follow]

non culpabilis [Not guilty]

non debet, cui plus licet, quod minus est non licere [It is lawful for a man to do a less thing if he is entitled to do a greater thing]

non-derogating control order A control order (*q.v.*) made by the Secretary of State which does not involve derogating from the European Convention on Human Rights (*q.v.*). It is made after seeking permission from the court or if made

non potest rex gratiam facere cum injuria et damno aliorum

without the court's permission, in a case of urgency, by immediate referral to the court for confirmation (see Prevention of Terrorism Act 2005 s.2). See DEROGATING CONTROL ORDER.

non est factum [It is not his deed] The old common law defence which permitted a person who had executed a written document in ignorance of its character to plead that notwithstanding the execution "it is not his deed". See, e.g. *Saunders (Executrix in the Estate of Rose Maud Gallie) v Anglia Building Society* [1971] A.C. 1004.

non est inventus [He has not been found] The return which a sheriff has to make upon a writ commanding him to arrest a person who is not within his bailiwick (*q.v.*).

non-intimate sample. A sample of hair other than pubic hair; a sample taken from a nail or from under a nail; a swab taken from any part of a person's body other than a part from which a swab would be an intimate sample (*q.v.*); saliva; a skin impression (*q.v.*) (Police and Criminal Evidence Act 1984 s.65(1) as amended). See DNA TESTING.

non-joinder The omission of a person who ought to be made party to an action. The court, however, has a discretion in the matter, and an action cannot be defeated merely by reason of non-joinder (CPR 19).

non justiciable Not appropriate for decision by the courts. For example, even where there are grounds to judicially review a decision, the courts have chosen not to intervene in certain cases involving issues of national security, stating that the matters in question should more appropriately be left to the decision of a democratically elected government.

non liquet [It is not clear]

non-molestation order An order which may contain a provision prohibiting the respondent from molesting another person who is associated with that respondent and/or a provision prohibiting the respondent from molesting a relevant child, Family Law Act 1996 s.42. Associated persons include: persons who are or have been married to each other; present or former cohabitants; parents of the same child; and relatives (e.g. father, mother, brother, aunt, niece). The Domestic Violence, Crime and Victims Act 2004 s.1 adds to the protection given by the 1996 Act by providing that a breach of a non-molestation order is a criminal offence.

non observata forma infertus adnullatio actus [Non-observance of the prescribed formalities involves the invalidity of the proceeding]

non obstante (veredicto) [Notwithstanding the verdict] Upon an application for a new trial the Court of Appeal may set aside the judgment of the court below and enter judgment notwithstanding the verdict (Supreme Court Act 1981 s.17; CPR 1998 Sch.1, Ord. 59, rr.2, 11).

non omittas propter libertatem [Omit not on account of a liberty] A clause formerly inserted in a writ of execution directing the sheriff "not to omit" to execute the writ by reason of any liberty (in a privileged district). This clause authorised the execution despite the liberty. See NON-INTROMITTANT CLAUSE.

non omne quod licet honestum est [All things that are lawful are not honourable]

non placet [It is not approved]

non possessori incumbit necessitas probandi possessiones ad se pertinere [A person in possession is not bound to prove that what he possesses belongs to him]

non potest rex gratiam facere cum injuria et damno aliorum [The king cannot confer a favour on one man to the injury and damage of others]

non pros.; non prosequitur [He does not follow up] Judgment non pros. was available for the defendant in an action when the plaintiff failed to take the proper steps within the prescribed time.

non quod voluit testator, sed quod dixit, in testamento inspicitur [Not what the testator wished, but what he said, is considered in construing a will]

non refert an quis assensum suum praefert verbis, an rebus ipsis et factis [It matters not whether a man gives his assent by his words, or by his acts and deeds]

non refert quid notum sit judici, si notum non sit in forma judicii [It matters not what is known to the judge, if it be not known judicially]

non sequitur [It does not follow]

non solent quae abundant vitiare scripturas [Surplusage does not vitiate writings]

non videntur qui errant consentire [Those who are mistaken are not deemed to consent] See MISTAKE.

non videtur consensum retinuisse si quis ex praescripto minantis aliquid immutavit [He is not deemed to have consented who has altered anything at the command of anyone using threats]

nonagium; nonage The ninth part of the movables of a deceased which was anciently paid for pious uses to the clergy of his parish.

nonfeasance The neglect or failure to do some act which ought to be done, e.g. failing to keep in repair the highway (*q.v.*). The exemption from civil liability enjoyed by the highway authority was abrogated by the Highways (Miscellaneous Provisions) Act 1961 s.1(1), but the absence of negligence is a defence; see now Highways Act 1980 s.58.

nonsuit Formerly, the abandonment of a case at the trial, before the jury had given its verdict, whereupon judgment of nonsuit was given against the plaintiff. The modern equivalent in the High Court is where the judge withdraws the case from the jury and directs a verdict for the defendant. Nonsuit still applied in the county court but in *Gilham v Browning* [1998] 2 All E.R. 68 the Court of Appeal held that the introduction into county court rules of provisions for discontinuance had made the preservation of a general common law right to be nonsuited unnecessary.

noscitur a sociis [The meaning of a word can be gathered from the context]

not guilty (1) The appropriate plea to an indictment where the prisoner wishes to raise the general issue, i.e. when he wishes to deny everything and to let the prosecution prove what it can. It was also a plea formerly used in common law actions of tort, when the defendant simply denied that he had committed the wrong complained of. Under the present system of pleading, a defendant must deal with all allegations made by the claimant which he does not admit.

(2) A verdict finding that an accused person has not committed the offence with which he was charged.

not negotiable When these words are endorsed on, for example, a cheque the meaning is that the holder can acquire no better right to the cheque than a previous owner. See NEGOTIABLE INSTRUMENT.

not proven A verdict returnable in Scotland only, not in England or Wales, meaning that the charge has not been proved.

Notary Public A legal practitioner, usually a solicitor, who attests deeds or other documents or makes certified copies of them in order to render the deeds or copies authentic, especially for use abroad.

notation Making a memorandum of some special circumstance on a probate or letters of administration.

note of a fine See FINE.

notice Knowledge or cognisance. In land, the doctrine of notice is that a person who acquires a legal estate (*q.v.*) in land will do so subject to any existing equitable interest in the land of which he knows (actual notice), ought to know (constructive notice) or of which an agent acting for him in that transaction knows or ought to know (imputed notice). A person has constructive notice if the fact would have come to light had proper searches and enquiries been made before acquiring the estate. This equitable doctrine of notice is greatly modified by the systems of registration of charges under the Land Charges Act 1972 and registration of title to land under the Land Registration Act 2002. See LAND REGISTRATION.

Under the rule in *Dearle v Hall* (1823) 3 Russ. 1, assignees of a chose in action (*q.v.*) rank according to the order in which each gave notice of the particular assignment to the person against whom the chose could be enforced and by ss.136–137 of the Law of Property Act 1925 this rule was extended to equitable interests (*q.v.*) in a trust of land, the trustees being the persons to whom the notice ought to be given.

notice (employment) For the minimum periods of notice to be given as between employer and employee see Employment Rights Act 1996 s.86.

notice of intended prosecution A written notice issued to a person charged with any of certain specified driving offences stating that prosecution will be undertaken. See the Road Traffic Offenders Act 1988 s.1 and Sch.1 (as amended).

notice of trial At one time a party to an action who set it down for trial had within 24 hours after doing so, to notify the other parties that he had done so. Such notice is no longer necessary.

Under the Civil Procedure Rules case management principles provide timetables for the handling of cases dependent on track allocation (*q.v.*). See SMALL CLAIM; FAST TRACK; MULTI TRACK.

notice to admit facts A party may serve notice, at least 21 days before the trial, on another party requiring him to admit the facts specified in the notice. Any admission (*q.v.*) made by the other party may only be used against him in those specific proceedings. See CPR 1998 Pt 32.18.

notice to admit or produce documents A party will be deemed to admit the authenticity of documents disclosed to him unless he serves notice that he wishes the document to be proved at trial, CPR 1998 (*q.v.*) Pt 32.19.

notice to quit A method by which a tenancy may be determined. The length of notice to be given depends upon the type of tenancy and such notice may be subject to statutory control. A periodic tenancy (*q.v.*) will continue to run indefinitely unless either the landlord or the tenant serves a notice to quit on the other so as to prevent a new period. The notice must specify the correct date for the termination of the tenancy which must be an anniversary date; it must be unconditional and must relate to the whole premises. A notice to quit must comply with s.5 of the Protection from Eviction Act 1977 (see Notices to Quit, etc. (Prescribed Information) Regulations 1988). A notice to quit is of no effect in relation to a periodic assured tenancy under the Housing Act 1988.

notice to treat The notice which a public body having compulsory powers for the purchase of land gives to any person interested in land it desires to purchase. See COMPULSORY PURCHASE; VESTING DECLARATION.

notification for exemption The procedure under reg.17/62 whereby an undertaking may notify an agreement that is likely to breach art.81(1) of the EC Treaty with a view to obtaining exemption for it from the Commission under art.81(3).

noting A minute or memorandum made by a notary on a bill of exchange (*q.v.*) which he has presented, and which has been dishonoured. It consists of his initials and charges and the date, and, in the case of foreign bills, is preparatory to a formal protest.

nova constitutio futuris formam imponere debet, non praeteritis [A new law ought to regulate what is to follow, not the past]

Nova Statuta The statutes from the year 1327 to 1483.

novatio [Roman law] (1) The renewal or re-making of an existing obligation.
(2) The transmutation of an obligation so that it ceases to exist and is renewed as a new obligation.

novation A tripartite agreement whereby a contract between two parties is rescinded in consideration of a new contract being entered into on the same terms between one of the parties and a third party. A common instance is where a creditor at the request of the debtor agrees to take another person as his debtor in the place of the original debtor. It involves the substitution of one party to a contract by another person, and its effect is to release the obligations of the former party and to impose them on the new party, as in the case of a change in the membership of a partnership firm. The creditors of the old firm will usually be deemed to have accepted the new firm as their debtor by continuing to trade with a new firm as if it were identical with the old.

novel disseisin See ASSIZE OF NOVEL DISSEISIN.

novellae See CORPUS JURIS CIVILIS.

novus actus interveniens [A new intervening act] The intervention of human activity between the defendant's act and its consequences. The doctrine that A is not liable for damage done to B if the chain of causation between A's act and B's damage is broken by the intervention of the act of a third person. B's damage is then said to be too remote. If, however, the intervening act is a direct or foreseeable consequence of the defendant's act, then the doctrine does not apply, nor does it apply where the intervening actor is not fully responsible, or if his act is intentionally procured by the defendant.

nudum pactum [A nude contract] An agreement made without consideration and upon which, unless it be under seal, no action will lie, e.g. *Four Oaks Estate Ltd v Hadley* (1986) *The Times*, July 2, CA.

nuisance "An inconvenience materially interfering with the ordinary comfort physically of human existence, not merely according to elegant or dainty modes and habits of living, but according to plain and sober, simple notions among the English people." (per Knight-Bruce V.C. in *Walter v Selfe* (1851) 4 De G. & Sm. 332.)
A public or common nuisance is an act which interferes with the enjoyment of a right which all members of the community are entitled to, such as the right to fresh air, to travel on the highways, etc. The remedy for a public nuisance (which is a crime) is by indictment, information, or injunction at the suit of the Att Gen, and in certain cases by summary process, or abatement (*q.v.*). If special damage is caused to an individual, he has an action for damages or injunction against the wrongdoer. A claim in respect of "nuisance" arising from the use of public works may be made under the Land Compensation Act 1973 ss.1–19. Recurring public nuisance may be restrained by an abatement notice (*q.v.*) served by the local authority, on which, if necessary, a prosecution may be founded (Environmental Protection Act 1990 s.80). See ABATEMENT OF NUISANCE.

A private nuisance is a tort (*q.v.*) consisting of (1) any wrongful disturbance or interference with a person's use or enjoyment of land or of an easement or other servitude appurtenant to land; (2) the act of wrongfully causing or allowing the escape of deleterious things into another person's land, e.g. water, smoke, smell, fumes, gas, noise, heat, vibrations, electricity, disease-germs, animals, and vegetation. Nuisance is commonly a continuing injury, and is actionable only at the suit of the person in possession of land injuriously affected by it; there must be actual damage to the claimant. The remedy for a private nuisance is either by abatement (*q.v.*) or by an action for damages or an injunction.

nul tiel record The plea or defence that "no such record" as that alleged by the plaintiff exists.

nulla bona [No goods] The return made by a sheriff to a writ or warrant authorising him to seize the chattels of a person, when he has been unable to find any to seize.

nulla pactione effici potest ut dolus praestetur [By no contract can it be arranged that a man shall be indemnified against responsibility for his own fraud]

nulla poena sine lege [No punishment except in accordance with the law]

nullity of marriage A marriage affected by certain irregularities may be void *ab initio* or voidable; if voidable a decree of nullity must be obtained if the marriage is not to remain valid and, if void, may be obtained (although theoretically unnecessary as the marriage will never have had valid existence).

The present grounds on which a marriage is void are set out in the Matrimonial Causes Act 1973 s.11, and those on which a marriage is voidable in s.12. A petition for nullity of a voidable marriage may be refused if one of the bars set out in s.13 operates. A voidable marriage which is annulled is now treated as if it existed up to the date of the decree (s.16).

On a decree of nullity (of a void or voidable marriage) being granted, the court has the same powers in respect of financial provision (*q.v.*) as on divorce. Children of voidable marriages are legitimate and those of void marriages will be treated as legitimate if, at the time of intercourse resulting in birth (or the marriage, if later) both or either party reasonably believed the marriage to be valid (Legitimacy Act 1976 s.1). See LEGITIMACY.

nullius filius A bastard (*q.v.*).

nullum crimen nulla poena sine lege [There is no crime nor punishment except in accordance with law]

nullum simile est idem [Nothing similar is the same]

nullum tempus aut locus occurrit regi [Time never runs against the Crown] But see the Crown Proceedings Act 1947 and the Limitation Act 1980 s.37.

nullus videtur dolo facere qui suo jure utitur [A malicious or improper motive cannot make wrongful in law an act which would be rightful apart from such motive] i.e. he who avails himself of his legal rights is not to be deemed a wrongdoer. See MALICE.

nunc pro tunc [Now for then] As when the court directs a proceeding to be dated as of an earlier date than that on which it was actually taken.

nuncupative will Oral directions as to the disposal of the testator's property which are made in front of witnesses and not immediately put in writing. See WILL.

nuptiae [Roman law] Marriage, the ceremonies with which the legal tie was formed; the union of a man and a woman involving unbroken harmony in the habits of life.

nuptiae, justiae [Roman law] Legal marriage. That union of the sexes which gave the father *potestas* over the children born to him by his wife. Conditions of *justiae nuptiae:*
   (1) consent of the parties duly expressed;
   (2) puberty;
   (3) *connubium* (the legal power of contracting marriage).

nuptias non concubitus sed consensus facit [It is consent, not consummation which makes a marriage]

O

oath A solemn appeal by which the party calls his God to witness that what he says is the truth, or that what he promises to do he will do. Evidence is given on oath "for the law presumeth that no man will forswear himself for any wordly thing". An affirmation may be made instead of an oath; see AFFIRM See generally Oaths Act 1978. See also PERJURY.

obiter dictum [A saying by the way] An observation by a judge on a legal question suggested by a case before him, but not arising in such a manner as to require decision. It is therefore not binding as a precedent (*q.v.*).

obligatio civilis [Roman law] A statutory obligation, or one recognised by the *jus civile.*

obligatio literarum See LITERARUM OBLIGATIO.

obligatio praetoria, or honoraria [Roman law] An obligation established by the *Praetor* in the exercise of his jurisdiction.

obligatio verborum See VERBORUM OBLIGATIO.

obligation A duty: the bond of legal necessity which binds together two or more individuals. It is limited to legal duties arising out of a special personal relationship existing between them, whether by reason of a contract or a tort, or otherwise, e.g. debtor and creditor. See LIABILITY.

obligee One to whom a bond is made.

obligor One who binds himself by bond.

obscene A publication, the tendency of which is to deprave and corrupt those whose minds are open to immoral influences, and into whose hands it is likely to fall (per Cockburn C.J. in *R. v Hicklin* (1868) L.R. 3 Q.B. 360 at 371). Obscene publications or libels were punishable with fine or imprisonment, being misdemeanours (*q.v.*) at common law.
   By the Obscene Publications Act 1959 (as amended by the Obscene Publications Act 1964 and the Criminal Justice Act 1967 s.25), an article is deemed to be obscene if its effect (or if composite, the effect of any one of its items) is, if taken as a whole, such as to deprave or corrupt persons likely to read, see, or hear the contents of it (Obscene Publications Act 1959 s.1). Section 4 provides that a person should not be convicted if it is proved that the publication of the article in question is justified as being for the public good on the ground that it is in the interests of science, literature, art, or learning; the opinion of experts may be admitted. Premises may be searched and obscene articles seized and forfeited (Obscene Publications Act 1964 s.3) but a warrant is to be issued only on any information laid down by the Director of Public Prosecutions or by a constable (Criminal Justice Act 1967 s.25).

Sending obscene articles through the post is an offence under the Postal Services Act 2000 s.85(3). For restrictions on the use of obscene cinematograph material see the Criminal Law Act 1977 s.53 and the Cinemas Act 1985.

Under the Protection of Children Act 1978 (as amended by the Sexual Offences Act 2003) it is an offence to take and distribute indecent photographs of children. A photograph includes data stored on a computer disk or by other electronic means (ibid. s.7). Downloading indecent photographs from the internet and either printing them out or storing them on a computer is thus an offence under the Act (see *R. v Bowden* [2000] 2 All E.R. 418).

obtaining credit See DECEPTION; BANKRUPTCY.

occupancy The taking possession of a *res nullius* or ownerless thing.

occupant See TENANT PUR AUTRE VIE.

occupatio [Roman law] The taking possession of a thing belonging to nobody (*res nullius*) but capable of being owned.

occupation (1) The exercise of physical control or possession of land; having the actual use of land.
(2) Taking possession of enemy territory by the armed forces.

occupation order An occupation order may be applied for under various provisions of the Family Law Act 1996 depending, e.g. upon whether the parties are married or cohabitants or property owners. An occupation order may contain a range of provisions in relation to a dwelling house, e.g. enforcing the applicant's right to remain in occupation as against the respondent, requiring the respondent to leave the dwelling house, requiring the respondent to allow the applicant to enter and remain in the dwelling house.

occupiers' liability See DANGEROUS PREMISES; TRESPASSER.

of course A writ or a step in an action or proceeding which the court had no discretion to refuse, provided the proper formalities had been observed. An order of course was one made on an ex parte application to which a party was entitled as of right on his own statement, and at his own risk.

offence Generally synonomous with crime (*q.v.*).

offensive weapon Under the Prevention of Crime Act 1953 s.1(4) (amended by the Public Order Act 1986) offensive weapon means any article made or adapted for use for causing injury to the person or intended by the person having it with him for such use by him or by some other person. See also the Restriction of Offensive Weapons Acts 1959 and 1961; and see the Firearms Act 1982 and the Criminal Justice Act 1988.

offer A promise which, when accepted, constitutes an agreement. An offer (made by an offeror) consists of an expression of a willingness to be bound by certain terms should the other (the offeree) accept. The formula of a true offer is "I promise, if you will in return make a certain promise or do a certain act." It must be distinguished from an invitation to treat—an invitation to make an offer, e.g. as by an auctioneer.
An offer may be withdrawn or revoked at any time before it has been unconditionally accepted, it may be rejected, or it may lapse because of the death of the offeror, or non-acceptance within a reasonable time.
An acceptance of an offer "subject to contract" does not constitute a binding contract, because it is not unconditional.

office (1) Offices are either public or private, a public office being one which entitles a man to act in the affairs of others without their appointment or permission.

(2) Office premises means a building, or part, used for office purposes, including administration, clerical work, handling money, and telephone and telegraph operating (Offices, Shops, and Railway Premises Act 1963 s.1(2)). The main object of that Act is to set standards of health, welfare and safety for employees in such premises. The Act was amended by the Health and Safety at Work, etc. Act 1974.

office copy A copy made by an officer appointed for that purpose, and sealed with the seal of his office.

Office for Legal Complaints. An independent body, subject to the regulation of the Legal Services Board (*q.v.*) to which it must report, which will take over the handling of complaints against lawyers. Under the terms of the Legal Services Act 2007 it is required to establish a new ombudsman scheme (ibid. s.122). It is not expected to commence work until 2010 when it will take over from the Legal Services Ombudsman (*q.v.*).

Office for Tenants and Social Landlords Also referred to as the Regulator of Social Housing, this statutory corporation has been established under the Housing and Regeneration Act 2008 as the regulator of social housing (*q.v.*) and is required to perform its functions in a way that meets a series of fundamental objectives laid down by the Act (see s.86). These objectives include: encouraging and supporting a supply of well-managed social housing, of appropriate quality, sufficient to meet reasonable demands, so that actual or potential tenants have both choice and protection; ensuring that registered providers of social housing perform their functions efficiently, effectively and economically, with proper management and financial viability; and encouraging investment in social housing.

Office of Public Guardian. See PUBLIC GUARDIAN, OFFICE OF.

official list The list of all securities officially listed by the UK Listing Authority (*q.v.*). The Financial Services Authority (*q.v.*) is the UK Listing Authority with responsibility for admission of securities to the Official List as suitable for trading on a stock exchange (*q.v.*).

official receiver An officer appointed by the Secretary of State for Trade and Industry who acts as an officer of the court in bankruptcy (*q.v.*), winding up (*q.v.*) or individual voluntary arrangements (*q.v.*). His functions include the investigation of the causes of insolvency (*q.v.*). See the Insolvency Act 1986 ss.399–401.

official referee See REFEREE.

official secret The Official Secrets Acts, 1911, 1920, 1939, and now 1989, seek to prevent breaches of official confidence (for which there was no penalty at common law), and also to counter espionage and sabotage (*Chandler v DPP* [1964] A.C. 763). See also the European Communities Act 1972 s.11 (Euratom information). See WHISTLEBLOWER.

Official Solicitor The Official Solicitor is an Officer of the Supreme Court appointed by the Lord Chancellor under the Supreme Court Act 1981 s.90. Much of the work of this Office arises in general litigation, where it becomes clear to the court that one of the parties is under a legal disability, e.g. a minor (*q.v.*) or a person with a mental disorder (*q.v.*). The court will then invite the Official Solicitor to act as "litigation friend" (*q.v.*) for an incapable claimant or for an incapable defendant. Other areas where the Official Solicitor may be called upon to act include medical consent cases, divorce and liberty of the subject. One area of work formerly undertaken by the Official Solicitor, namely cases concerning wardship, adoption and the Children Act, has now been transferred to CAFCASS (*q.v.*). Since April 2001 the trust work of the Official Solicitor's office and that of the Public Trustee have been merged, although the two positions retain separate corporate functions.

Official Trustee of Charity Lands; Official Trustee of Charitable Funds The Charities Act 1960 s.3, provided for the appointment of an Official Custodian of Charities, who takes the place of these Trustees. Now governed by the Charities Act 1993 s.2.

Old Bailey Now the Central Criminal Court (*q.v.*).

ombudsman Originally the popular name (derived from Scandinavia) of the Parliamentary Commissioner for Administration. The Parliamentary Commissioner was appointed under the Parliamentary Commissioner Act 1967 to investigate complaints by members of the public who claim to have suffered injustice in consequence of maladministration (*q.v*) connected to administrative action.

Ombudsmen have also been appointed in other public and private areas, e.g. in the health service (see Health Service Commissioners Act 1993). Under the Government of Wales Act 1998 the office of Welsh Administration Ombudsman was established to perform similar duties with respect to bodies such as the National Assembly of Wales but that office is now subsumed under the office of the Public Services Ombudsman for Wales (see Public Services Ombudsman (Wales) Act 2005). See WELSH ASSEMBLY; COMMISSIONS FOR LOCAL ADMINISTRATION.

omne quod inaedificatur solo cedit [Everything which is built into the soil is merged therein]

omne testamentum morte consummatum est [Every will is completed by death] A will is ambulatory until death.

omnes licentiam habent his, quae pro se indulta sunt, renunciare [Everyone has liberty to renounce those things which are granted for his benefit]

omnia praesumuntur contra spoliatorem [All things are presumed against a wrongdoer] As in *Armory v Delamirie* (1722) 1 Strange 504, where jewels were presumed, as against a wrongful possessor, to be of the finest quality.

omnia praesumuntur legitime facta donec probetur in contrarium [All things are presumed to have been legitimately done, until the contrary is proved]

omnia praesumuntur rite et solemniter esse acta [All acts are presumed to have been done rightly and regularly]

onerous Where the obligations attaching to ownership counterbalance or exceed the advantages.

onus probandi [The onus of proof] (*q.v.*)

op. cit. [*opere citato*] The work previously cited.

open contract A contract for the sale of land which merely specifies the names of the parties, a description of the property, and a statement of the price leaving the common law and statute to imply other necessary terms.

operating licence A form of licence which may be granted under the Gaming Act 2005. It may authorise a licensee inter alia to operate a casino (*q.v.*), to provide facilities to play bingo, to make gaming machines available or to operate a lottery (*q.v.*).

operative part The part of an instrument which carries out the main object; as opposed to recitals (*q.v.*).

opinion See BARRISTER'S OPINION/ADVICE.

oppression A common law indictable offence committed by any public officer who, under colour of his office, wrongfully inflicts upon any person any bodily harm, imprisonment or injury.

optima est lex minimum relinquit arbitrio judicis; optimus judex qui minimum sibi [That system of law is best which confides as little as possible to the discretion of a judge; that judge is best who trusts as little as possible to himself]

optima legum interpres est consuetudo [Custom is the best interpreter of the law]

optimus interpres rerum usus [The best interpreter of things is usage]

option A right of choice; a financial instrument which conveys a right (but not an obligation) to engage in a future transaction; the right to convey a piece of property within a certain time scale. An option, exercisable by notice in writing, is not validly exercised by the mere posting of a letter; it must be actually communicated (*Holwell Securities v Hughes* [1974] 1 W.L.R. 155).

oratio [Roman law] An address by the emperor to the senate, stating what he wished them to embody in a senates consultum.

Orcinus [Roman law] Pertaining to Orcus (Pluto), the nether world, or death; a freedman who had received freedom directly from the will of his master, having been the slave of the testator at the date of the will as well as the time of his death.

ordeal The most ancient mode of trial; it involved an appeal to the supernatural, or the *judicium Dei* The ordeal by fire consisted of taking up in the hand a piece of red-hot iron, or of walking barefoot and blindfolded over red-hot plough-shares. If the party was unhurt he was innocent; if otherwise, he was guilty. Ordeal by hot water was performed by plunging the arm in boiling water, with similar consequences. The cold water ordeal consisted of throwing the offender in a pond or river; if he sank he was innocent, and if he floated he was guilty. The ordeal was abolished in the reign of Henry III, and was ultimately replaced by the trial by jury.

order For example, the Rules of the Supreme Court and the County Court Rules which supplement the CPR (*q.v.*) consist of Orders subdivided into rules.

order and disposition See REPUTED OWNERSHIP.

Order in Council An Order made by the Queen "by and with the advice of Her Majesty's Privy Council", for the purposes of government, either in virtue of the royal prerogative, as e.g. declarations of war and peace, the Queen's Regulations for the Army and Navy, and legislation for Crown Colonies and Protectorates; or under statutory authority. The latter may be termed subordinate legislation and is much used in modern times for giving the force of law to the administrative regulations and provisions drawn up by Government Departments. See DELEGATED LEGISLATION; STATUTORY INSTRUMENTS

ordinance (1) Formerly an Act of Parliament which lacked the consent of one of the three elements: Crown, Lords, and Commons.
(2) A declaration of the Crown lacking the authority of Parliament.

ordinary The bishop of a diocese when exercising the ecclesiastical jurisdiction annexed to his office, he being *judex ordinarius* (ecclesiastical Judge) within his diocese.

Organization for Security and Co-operation in Europe (OSCE) Previously known as the Conference on Security and Co-operation in Europe (CSCE). The OSCE consists of 55 Member States and is active in conflict prevention, crisis management, human rights, democracy building and post-conflict rehabilitation throughout the Euro-Atlantic region, extending to the Caucasus and Central Asia. Although the OSCE has similar structures and working methods to an international organisation it is not considered to have international legal personality (*q.v.*) separate from its participating States. It is, therefore, not currently an "organisation" for the purposes of the International Organisations Act 1968. The International Organisations Act 2005 brings the OSCE within the scope of the 1968 Act.

original writ See WRIT.

originating summons Proceedings could be begun by originating summons, as well as by writ, motion, or petition. Proceedings suitable for commencement by originating summons were those where the principal question was the construction of an Act, statutory instrument, deed, will, contract or other document, or some other question of law, and where there was unlikely to be any substantial dispute of fact. Under the CPR (*q.v.*) the originating summons has been replaced by the Pt 8 claim (*q.v.*).

ouster The deprivation of a person of his freehold.

ouster clause A provision in an Act of Parliament seeking to restrict or eliminate judicial review (*q.v.*).

ousterlemain A writ directing the possession of land to be delivered out of the hands of the Crown into those of a person entitled to it. It was the mode by which an heir in ward of land held of the Crown *ut de honore* obtained possession of it on attaining majority. It also meant a judgment on a *monstrans de droit*, deciding that the Crown had no title to a thing which it had seized.

outgoings Necessary expenses and charges; e.g. a receiver appointed under a mortgage must apply moneys received by him, in the first place, in discharge of all rents, taxes, rates and outgoings affecting the mortgaged property (Law of Property Act 1925 s.109(8)(i)).

outlaw A person put outside the protection of the law by a judgment of outlawry (*q.v.*).

outlawry A judgment declaring a person an outlaw. In effect it was a conviction; there was attainder (*q.v.*), forfeiture of chattels, and an escheat (*q.v.*) of realty after the King's "year, day, and waste". Where an indictment had been found against a person and summary process proved ineffectual to compel him to appear, process of outlawry might be issued. Outlawry was subsequently extended to civil proceedings, e.g. trespass. Outlawry proceedings, having long been obsolete, were finally abolished by the Administration of Justice (Miscellaneous Provisions) Act 1938. See PROCESS.

outstanding Yet to be collected in: e.g. a legal estate in land was said to be outstanding when it had been conveyed to a mortgagee, and had not been reconveyed to the mortgagor when the mortgage debt had been cleared off; similarly, when a term of years had not been brought to an end although the purpose for which it was created had been realised.

over In conveyancing, a gift or limitation "over" is intended to take effect on the cessation or failure of a prior estate.

overdue A bill of exchange (*q.v.*) is said to be overdue when the time for its payment has passed or, if it is a bill payable on demand, when it appears to have been in circulation for an unreasonable length of time (Bills of Exchange Act 1882 s.36(3)). Anyone taking an overdue bill takes it subject to the equities of prior holders (ibid. s.36(2)).

overreaching clause A clause in a settlement which saved the powers of sale or leasing given to the tenant for life by the original settlement, when the same powers were intended under the resettlement; so called because it provided that the resettlement be overreached by the exercise of the old powers.

295

overreaching conveyance A conveyance (*q.v.*) which enables the owner of an estate which is subject to equitable interests and charges, to convey it to another free from such interests or charges, which are thereby shifted from the land to the purchase money. See CURTAIN PROVISIONS.

overriding interests The encumbrances, interests, rights, and powers not entered on the register, but subject to which registered dispositions took effect under the Land Registration Act 1925. This Act was repealed in its entirety by the Land Registration Act 2002 and the law relating to overriding interests was amended. The 2002 Act does not use the term overriding interests but instead specifies those unregistered interests which override first registration, and those which override registered dispositions. Some of the interests will be abolished at the end of a ten year period which commenced on October 13, 2003. See LAND REGISTRATION.

overriding objective The fundamental principle of the Civil Procedure Rules 1998 (*q.v.*) is that the overriding objective of the civil justice system is to deal with cases justly. This includes ensuring that the parties are on a equal footing, saving expense and dealing with a case proportionate to its complexity, importance, the value of the claim and the financial position of each of the parties. Under the Criminal Procedure Rules 2005 (*q.v.*), the overriding objective is to deal with criminal cases justly. The courts must give effect to this objective when interpreting and applying the rules.

overriding trust A trust which takes precedence over other trusts previously declared.

overseas company A company incorporated outside the UK, see Companies Act 2006 s.1044. Such companies are required to register as such under Pt 34 of that Act.

overt act An open act; in criminal law, an open act is an act capable of being observed, and from which a criminal intention may be deduced. See TREASON.

ownership The right to the exclusive enjoyment of a thing (Austin). Strictly, it denotes the relation between a person and any right that is vested in him (Salmond). Ownership is absolute or restricted. Absolute ownership involves the right of free as well as exclusive enjoyment, including the right of using, altering, disposing of or destroying the thing owned. Absolute ownership is of indeterminate duration (Land is in strictness not subject to absolute ownership because it cannot be destroyed, and because of the theory that all land is ultimately held by the Crown). Restricted ownership is ownership limited to some extent; as, for example, where there are several joint owners, or a life tenancy, or where the property is charged with the payment of a sum of money, or subject to an easement. Beneficial ownership is the right to the enjoyment of a thing as contrasted with the legal or nominal ownership. Ownership is always subject to the rule that a man must so use his own property as not to injure his neighbour. See REPUTED OWNERSHIP.

oyer and terminer [To hear and determine] A commission to the judges to try offences committed in a certain area. References to a court of oyer and terminer are to be construed as references to the Crown Court (Courts Act 1971 Sch.8).

P

PACE Acronym for the Police and Criminal Evidence Act 1984.

PAYE [Pay as you earn] The system of collection of income tax by deductions made by the employer from emoluments assessable to tax under Sch.E to the

Income and Corporation Taxes Act 1988. An employer deducts from taxable emoluments paid to an employee the relevant amount of tax as indicated by tax tables supplied by the Inland Revenue such that the deductions keep pace so far as possible with the accruing tax liability of the employee. The employer then accounts to the Inland Revenue on a monthly basis for deductions so made.

PC Privy Council.

PFI See PRIVATE FINANCE INITIATIVE.

PLC See COMPANY.

PPI [Policy proof of interest] A policy of marine insurance where the assured has no insurable interest is void (Marine Insurance Act 1906 s.4). An insurance policy by way of gaming or wagering, made without proof of interest beyond the policy itself (rules contained in the Gambling Act 2005).

pace [By permission of]

package As in package holiday, means a pre-arranged combination of at least two specified components, e.g. transport, accommodation, other tourist services, when sold or offered for sale at an inclusive price and when the service covers a period of time of more than 24 hours or includes overnight accommodation. See the Package Travel, Package Holidays and Package Tours Regulations 1992.

pacta dant legem contractui [Agreements constitute the law of contract]

pacta quae contra leges constitutionesque vel contra bonos mores fiunt, nullam vim habere, indubitati juris est [It is undoubted law that agreements which are contrary to the laws and constitutions, or contrary to good morals, have no force]

pacta sunt servanda [Agreements should be performed]

pains and penalties See BILL OF PAINS AND PENALTIES.

pais See IN PAIS.

Palatine Court A court of a County Palatine (*q.v.*) (the jurisdiction of which is now vested in the High Court).

panel The list of the persons who have been summoned to serve as jurors for a trial

paper office An office of records. (1) In Whitehall. (2) In the Old Court of King's Bench.

paper, special A list kept in the Queen's Bench Division of matters set down for argument on points of law, awards in the form of a special case and other matters. See Directions given by the Lord Chief Justice on December 9, 1958, art.1(2)(g).

parage; paragium Equality of blood, name or dignity.

parallel exemption Under the Competition Act 1998, an agreement that benefits from an exemption in EC law, either through individual exemption or under a block exemption, is granted parallel exemption from the UK competition provisions.

paraphernalia Such apparel and personal ornaments given to a married woman by her husband as were suitable to her condition in life; they remained the property of the husband unless the wife survived the husband, when she kept them for herself. The husband might dispose of them during his life, and they were liable for his debts, on his death, after other assets had been exhausted. The continued existence of the doctrine of paraphernalia is doubtful.

parcels Parts or portions of land detailed in the part of an instrument following the operative words and containing a description of the property dealt with.

parcener; parcenary The equivalents of coparcener (*q.v.*) and coparcenary.

pardon The release by the Crown of a person from punishment incurred for an offence. Some offences, however, cannot be pardoned: e.g. a common nuisance while it remains unredressed: and a pardon cannot be pleaded to a parliamentary impeachment. Pardons may be given posthumously.

parent Father or mother of a child.

parental leave The right of a parent who has been continuously employed for at least one year and who has, or expects to have, parental responsibility (*q.v.*) for a child is entitled to a statutory period of parental leave for the purpose of caring for that child. Leave must normally be taken before a child's fifth birthday. (See Employment Rights Act 1996 Pt VIII and the Maternity and Parental Leave, etc. Regulations 1999.)

parental responsibility All the rights, duties, powers, responsibilities and authority which by law a parent of a child has in relation to the child and his property, Children Act 1989 s.3, as amended by the Adoption and Children Act 2002.

pares Peers, equals.

pari passu [With equal step] Equally, without preference.

parish The unit of local government in England, formerly coincident with the ecclesiastical parish. Parish meetings and councils were created by the Local Government Act 1894. Rural parishes, boroughs and urban districts became parishes as a result of the Local Government Act 1972 s.1, Sch.1. Every parish in England has a parish meeting and in most cases a parish council (s.9). It acts as a local authority (*q.v.*). A parish may by resolution take on itself the status of a town with a town mayor and town council. The parish meeting will thereupon become the town meeting (s.245). Former boroughs may regain the status of boroughs. See BOROUGH; COMMUNITIES.

park Strictly an enclosed chase (*q.v.*). See also the National Parks and Access to the Countryside Act 1949. Franchises of park were abolished by the Wild Creatures and Forest Laws Act 1971.

Parliament The sovereign legislative authority in the Constitution consisting of the Queen, the House of Lords, and the House of Commons. Originally all legislation required the assent of both Houses of Parliament. Bills, other than a money (or finance) Bill, may be introduced into either House. With regard to money Bills (which are introduced in the House of Commons), it was a convention that the House of Lords might reject, but could not amend, them. The Parliament Act 1911 was enacted to enable, exceptionally, legislation to be effected by the King and Commons alone. Thus if the House of Lords fail within one month to pass a Bill which, having passed the Commons, is sent up endorsed by the Speaker as a money Bill before the end of the session, it may be presented for the Royal assent without the consent of the House of Lords. With regard to non-money Bills, the Act provided in effect for a suspensory veto for the House of Lords.

The Parliament Act 1911 was amended by the Parliament Act 1949 which reduced the "suspensory period" from three to two successive sessions; the 1949 Act itself was passed under the 1911 Act provisions without the consent of the House of Lords. The duration of Parliament is for five years, but it has the power of prolonging its own life by Act of Parliament. See HOUSE OF LORDS.

parliamentary agents Persons (usually solicitors) who transact the technical business involved in passing private Bills through the Houses of Parliament.

Parliamentary Commissioner See OMBUDSMAN.

parliamentary committees A committee of the whole House, whether in the Lords or the Commons, is really the House of Lords or the House of Commons, as the case may be, presided over by a chairman instead of by the Lord Chancellor or the Speaker. The standing or sessional committees and the select committees consist in each House of a certain number of Members who perform various functions in connection with Bills. Joint committees consist of equal numbers of Members of each House.

parliamentary franchise The right to vote at elections of Members of Parliament. The persons entitled to vote in any constituency are those resident there on the qualifying date who are Commonwealth citizens or citizens of the Republic of Ireland of full age and not subject to any legal incapacity to vote, and registered there in the register of parliamentary electors. Such persons may vote in only one constituency (Parliamentary Constituencies Act 1986 s.1). Persons disqualified from voting include: aliens, minors, persons of unsound mind, peers, and persons convicted of electoral offences.

The Representation of the People Act 1949 consolidated the law relating to the parliamentary franchise, see now the Representation of the People Act 1983 as amended by the Representation of the People Act 2000. See ELECTIONS, PARLIAMENTARY.

parochial church council A body corporate to which has been transferred the functions of vestries in matters relating to the affairs of the church, e.g. consultations with the minister, consideration of matters of religious and public interest and dealing with the diocesan synod (*q.v.*): Parochial Church Councils (Powers) Measure 1956, amended by the Synodical Government Measure 1969 s.6. See also the Pastoral Measures 1968 and 1983.

parol Oral; but often used of a document in writing but not under seal.

parole The release on licence of a prisoner serving his sentence. Such licence may be revoked.

parricide The killing of a parent or near relative. See PATRICIDE.

parson The ecclesiastical officer in charge of a parish church. He is a corporation sole. His house is called the parsonage.

Part 8 claims Under CPR (*q.v.*) these replace the originating summons (*q.v.*). The Part 8 procedure is used where the claimant seeks the court's decision on a question which is unlikely to involve a substantial dispute of fact (Pt 8.1(2)).

Part 20 claims Part 20 claims under CPR (*q.v.*), r.20.2, cover counterclaims, claims made by a defendant against a co-defendant for a contribution or indemnity or a claim against a third party and also include claims made by a third party against a person who is already a party to the action or a fourth party. A Pt 20 claim is issued on a Pt 20 claim form which is similar to an ordinary claim form (*q.v.*). A Pt 20 claim is procedurally related to the main claim but does exist to an extent independently of that claim.

part performance The equitable doctrine that a contract required to be evidenced in writing would still be enforceable even if it was not so evidenced provided one of the parties to the contract did certain acts by which the contract was partly performed. A sufficient act of part performance had to be unequivocally referable to the alleged contract (e.g. entry into possession of the relevant land) and had to be such that it would amount to a fraud in the defendant to take advantage of the lack of writing.

The doctrine applied primarily to contracts for the sale of land. However, such contracts entered into on or after September 27, 1989 are now required to be in writing (not merely evidenced in writing) if they are to be valid: Law of Property (Miscellaneous Provisions) Act 1989 s.2. Acts of part performance will not, as such, validate an unwritten contract for the sale of land.

partial surrogacy Achieved by artificial insemination of the carrying mother with sperm from the commissioning father. The genetic and legal mother of the child is the carrying mother, Human Fertilisation and Embryology Act 1990 s.27. See SURROGACY.

particeps criminis One who has a share in a crime: an accessory.

particular average See AVERAGE.

particular estate An estate which preceded a reversion (*q.v.*) or remainder (*q.v.*): thus a grant to A for life with remainder to B and his heirs gave A a particular estate and B a reversionary estate.

particulars of claim Formerly referred to as particulars or statements of claim. Particulars of claim must be contained in a claim form (*q.v.*) or served with or after the claim form. They must include a concise statement of the facts on which the claimant relies, CPR, r.16.4(1) A, together with various other details as relevant.

parties Persons involved in legal proceedings. See CLAIMANT; DEFENDANT.

partition The physical division of land owned by persons jointly among the owners in severalty. Partition was either voluntary by deed or compulsorily by order of the court. Until the Partition Act 1868, the court had no power to order a sale and division of the proceeds instead of a partition of the land itself. By the operation of the Law of Property Act 1925 land belonging to joint owners is vested in trustees on trust for sale, with power to postpone the sale, and the Partition Acts are repealed.

partnership The relation which subsists between persons carrying on a business in common with a view to profit (Partnership Act 1890 s.1). The rights of the partners between themselves are governed by the partnership agreement. A partnership firm (except for a limited liability partnership (*q.v.*) under the Limited Liability Partnership Act 2000) is not a separate legal entity in English law but it may sue and be sued in the firm's name.

In general, every partner is entitled and bound to take part in the conduct of the firm's business, unless it is otherwise agreed between them. Every partner is liable for the debts of the partnership to the whole extent of his property. As between the partners, each partner is bound to contribute to the debts in proportion to his share of the profits, unless otherwise agreed. As regards third persons, the act of every partner, within the ordinary scope of the business, binds his co-partners, whether they have sanctioned it or not. The relationship between the partners being personal, no one of them can substitute a stranger in his place without the consent of the others. Where no time for the duration of the partnership is fixed, it is called a partnership at will, and may be dissolved at the pleasure of any partner. Dissolution takes place ordinarily by bankruptcy (*q.v.*), or by the death of a partner, or on an order of dissolution being made by the court on the ground of, incapacity, misconduct of a partner, or of the hopeless state of the business (Partnership Act 1890 ss.32–35).

A limited partnership is one which, although there must be one or more partners responsible for all the liabilities of the partnership, there may be one or more partners who are under no liability other than an agreed sum for partnership purposes, provided that they take no part in the management, and that the partnership is registered as a limited partnership (see the Limited Partnership Act 1907). See LIMITED LIABILITY PARTNERSHIP.

part-owners Persons who are entitled to a property in common, e.g. a ship.

party A person who takes part in a transaction or legal proceeding.

party and party See COSTS.

party fence wall In effect a garden wall which stands astride a boundary. Defined under the Party Wall, etc. Act 1996 s.20:

"a wall (not being part of a building) which stands on lands of different owners and is used or constructed to be used for separating such adjoining lands, but does not include a wall constructed on the land of one owner the artificially formed support of which projects into the land of another owner". See PARTY WALL.

party wall A wall belonging to different owners. In the absence of evidence to the contrary, tenancy in common of the wall was presumed. By the Law of Property Act 1925 s.38(1), however, a party wall or structure is deemed to be severed vertically between the respective owners, each of whom has the requisite rights of support and user over the rest of the structure.

The Party Wall, etc. Act 1996 provides a statutory framework to assist adjoining owners in reaching agreement on matters relating to party walls and other structures and laying down procedures to be followed to deal with disputes where agreement cannot be reached. In s.20 of the Act, a party wall is defined as: "(a) a wall which forms part of a building and stands on lands of different owners to a greater extent than the projection of any artificially formed support on which the wall rests; and (b) so much of a wall not being a wall referred to in paragraph (a) .... as separates buildings belonging to different owners".

Pasch [The Passover] Easter.

passage An easement of way over private water.

passim In various places or everywhere in the reference book. Used to indicate that something appears frequently in a cited work.

passing off The pretence by one person that his goods or business are those of another. Where a person sells goods, or carries on business under a name, mark, description, or otherwise in such a manner as to mislead the public into believing that the goods or business, etc. are those of another person, the latter person has a right of action in damages or for an account, and for an injunction to restrain the defendant in the future. See the House of Lords' restatement of the necessary elements of passing off in *Reckitt & Colman Products Ltd v Borden Inc* [1990] 1 All E.R. 873 at 880.

passport The document (in book form) issued by the Government to a person who contemplates travelling abroad, containing particulars enabling the bearer to be identified, and a request to all concerned to allow the bearer to pass without let or hindrance and to afford all necessary assistance and protection.

It is an offence to forge or make false statements for procuring a passport (Criminal Justice Act 1925 s.36 as amended by the Criminal Law Act 1977 and the Forgery and Counterfeiting Act 1981). The offence is triable either way (Magistrates' Courts Act 1980 s.17, Sch.1).

In international law, it means primarily the document issued by a belligerent to a diplomatic representative of an enemy state after the outbreak of war, to enable that person to return to the country represented, by virtue of the immunity of diplomatic representatives.

pasture, common of The right of feeding beasts on the land of another. Common of pasture appendant was the right which every freehold tenant of a manor possessed to feed his cattle used in agriculture (i.e. horses, cattle and sheep) upon the lord's waste, provided they were levant and couchant on the tenant's freehold land.

Common of pasture appurtenant is a right annexed to certain land, by virtue of which the owner of those lands feeds cattle on the soil of another person.

Common because of vicinage is where the tenants of two adjoining places, or the owners of two contiguous pieces of land, have from time immemorial "intercommoned", i.e. allowed each other's cattle to stray and pasture on each other's land, or on a waste or open field lying between their lands.

301

Common of pasture in gross differs from the foregoing varieties of common in being unconnected in any way with the tenure of occupation of land.

patent (1) Letters patent from the Crown, e.g. conferring a peerage. (2) The right conferred by letters patent of the exclusive use and benefit of a new invention capable of industrial application. See generally the Patents Act 1977, as amended and supplemented by the Copyright, Designs and Patents Act 1988 and the Patents Act 2004, and the Patents (Compulsory Licensing and Supplementary Protection Certificates) Regulations 2007. A patent is obtained by making application accompanied by specifications to the Patents Office. The normal duration of a patent is 20 years and this may not be extended (1977 Act s.25). A patent once granted may be revoked (s.72(1)). For the system of European Patents now incorporated into English Law see 1977 Act Pt II, ss.77–95.

The 1977 Act established a Patents Court as part of the Chancery Division to deal with such proceedings relating to patents and other matters as may be prescribed by rules of court (see now the Supreme Court Act 1981 s.6). The court took over the jurisdiction of the former Patents Appeal Tribunal. Infringement of a Patent is actionable; for the definition of infringement, see s.60. Under the 1988 Act the Lord Chancellor was given powers to designate a county court (see, e.g. the Central London County Court) as a patents county court to hear cases involving patents.

pater est quem nuptiae demonstrant [He is the father whom marriage indicates]

paterfamilias [Roman law] One invested with *patria potestas* over another; a man sui juris or not under the authority of another.

paternity The state of parenthood. Any presumption of law as to legitimacy or illegitimacy may in civil proceedings be rebutted on a balance of probabilities, rather than by proof beyond reasonable doubt (Family Reform Act 1969 s.26) and a scientific test may be ordered to establish paternity (ibid. ss.20–25). As to parentage of children conceived by artificial insemination see the Human Fertilisation and Embryology Act 1990.

paternity leave An employee, who is (a) the father of a child; or (b) is married to or the partner of the mother of a child (including same sex couples) but not the child's father; or (c) one member of a couple who have jointly adopted a child may choose to take one weeks' leave or two consecutive weeks' leave in respect of the child. The leave is to be taken within a period of time set by statute. Entitlement to such leave is dependent upon the employee being continuously employed for a period of not less than 26 weeks ending with the week immediately preceding the 14th week before the expected week of the child's birth and having responsibility for the child's upbringing. In the case of adoptive parents the period of 26 weeks must end no later than the week in which a match is made with a child. See Employment Rights Act 1996 (as amended) and the Paternity and Adoption Leave Regulations 2002.

patient A person who by reason of mental disorder (*q.v.*) is incapable of managing his own affairs. It is the term used since the passing of the Mental Health Act 1959, in lieu of lunatic, or person of unsound mind (see now the Mental Health Act 1983 s.145). A patient must have a litigation friend (*q.v.*) to conduct proceedings on his behalf, CPR Pt 21.2(1).

patria A jury of neighbours. See JURY.

patria potestas [Roman law] The rights enjoyed by the head of a Roman family (*paterfamilias*) over his legitimate children. It was acquired by: (1) birth; (2) legitimation; (3) adoption. It was lost (1) by death of the *paterfamilias*; (2) by loss of status of parent or child; (3) by promotion of the son to the patriciate; (4) by emancipation.

patrial The term formerly used in the Immigration Act 1971 s.2 to denote a person with a right of abode in the United Kingdom. The term is now replaced by the term "British citizen" (*q.v.*) (British Nationality Act 1981 s.39 and Sch.4 as amended by the Immigration Act 1988 s.3).

patriciatus [Roman law] The patriciate; from the time of Constantine, the highest rank at court.

patricide The killing of a father. See PARRICIDE.

patrimonium [Roman law] Things *in nostro patrimonio* are things belonging to individuals. Things *extra nostrum patrimonium* are things belonging not to individuals but to all men (*communes*), to the state (*publicae*), to corporate bodies (*universitatis*), or to no one (*nullius*).

patronage The right of presenting to a benefice (*q.v.*).

Patronage Secretary The Chief Government Whip. See WHIPS.

pauper (1) A person in receipt of relief under, formerly, the poor laws.
(2) A person suing or defending an action *in forma pauperis* (*q.v.*). See LEGAL AID.

pauperies [Roman law] Mischief occasioned by an animal; damage done without injuria, or wrong intent, on the part of the doer. See ACTIO NOXALIS.

pawn To pledge a chattel as security for debt, i.e. to part with its possession to the lender. A special property is conferred on the pawnee, who has the power of sale in default of redemption. The surplus, after satisfying the debt, belongs to the pawnor. It is a tort for the pawnee to retain the goods after payment or tender of the debt. Under the Consumer Credit Act 1974, pawn means any article subject to a pledge. See BAILMENTS; PLEDGE; LIEN.

pawnbroker A person who carries on the business of taking chattels in pawn (*q.v.*). The Pawnbrokers Acts 1872 to 1960 were repealed by the Consumer Credit Act 1974, and replaced by ss.114–122 which relate to what the Act treats as "regulated agreements" (*q.v.*), which cover a wider range of transactions than are traditionally associated with the business of pawn-broking.

payee The person to whom a bill of exchange (*q.v.*) is payable.

Paymaster-General The officer who makes the payments out of public money required for the Government Departments, by issuing drafts on the Bank of England. The person holding this office is usually a minister without portfolio. See MINISTER.

payment into court The CPR encourage parties to settle proceedings by offers and payments into court, CPR Pt 36. Offers to settle which are not accepted may result in increased costs or interest payments. Part 36 does not apply to cases on the small claims track (*q.v.*), Pt 27.2(1).

peace In early times criminal matters and offences against public order were within the jurisdiction of local lords and local courts, and the King's Court exercised jurisdiction over offences committed within the vicinity of the King himself: committed "*contra pacem Domini,*" or "against the peace of our Lord the King." By a fiction that the King's peace extended to the highways and ultimately over the whole realm, the King's Court acquired its comprehensive jurisdiction. See BREACH OF THE PEACE.

pecuniary advantage See DECEPTION.

peer (1) An equal; trial by peers was the solemn trial of a vassal by his fellow vassals in the court of their lord.

(2) A Member of the House of Lords. The privilege of peerage, i.e. the right of a peer to be tried on a charge of felony by the House of Lords, was abolished by the Criminal Justice Act 1948 s.30.

Peers, in order of precedence, are dukes, marquesses, earls, viscounts and barons. See Peerage Act 1963. See also LIFE PEER; HOUSE OF LORDS.

peine forte et dure The torture inflicted upon a prisoner indicted for felony who refused to plead and submit to the jurisdiction of the court. Heavy weights were applied to his body until he consented to be tried by pleading "guilty" or "not guilty", or until he died.

After the procedure of appeal of felony (*q.v.*), ordeal (*q.v.*), and compurgation (*q.v.*) became obsolete there was no suitable mode of proof for the graver crimes. Consequently the judges sought to persuade the alleged criminal to "put himself on his country", i.e. to abide the decision of a jury of his neighbours. The alternative was the *peine forte et dure* A prisoner who refused to plead escaped the attainder (*q.v.*) and forfeiture of property which resulted from conviction of felony.

In 1772 the statute (12 Geo. 3 c.20) abolished the *peine forte et dure* and made refusal to plead to a charge of felony equivalent to a plea of guilty; subsequently by (7 & 8 Geo. 4) a plea of not guilty was to be entered.

penal action An action (now abolished) for a penalty imposed by statute as a punishment, recoverable by any person who sued for it. See QUI TAM, etc.

penal servitude The punishment substituted for transportation by the Penal Servitude Acts 1853 and 1857. It might be for life or any period not less than three years. It was abolished by the Criminal Justice Act 1948 s.1, which substituted imprisonment for it.

penalty (1) A punishment, particularly a fine or money payment.

(2) A sum payable: (a) by an obligor on breach of the condition in a bond; (b) on breach of a term in a contract. Should the sum payable be larger than, for example, the debt owed then only the sum representing the actual loss can be recovered, as equity will relieve against a penalty.

Whether a sum specified in a contract as being payable on breach thereof is a penalty or an agreed sum for damages is a question of construction of the contract judged as at the time of the making of it. The use of the term "penalty" or "liquidated damages" (*q.v.*) is not conclusive.

penalty points When a person's driving licence is endorsed with particulars of a road traffic offence the endorsement includes details of the number of penalty points attributable to that offence (Road Traffic Offenders Act 1988 s.44).

Under the penalty points system for road traffic offences, offenders acquire points which are endorsed on their licence and these are "totted up" so that once there are 12 points on their licence, they are automatically disqualified from driving for at least six months. The courts are required to impose penalty points for certain offences, e.g. dangerous driving (*q.v.*), but in other cases it is discretionary. Some offences carry a fixed number of points, e.g. disobeying traffic lights carries three points. The court will only take into account the points which have been endorsed for the offence under consideration and those endorsements for offences committed within the previous three years. See Road Traffic Offenders Act 1988.

See also TOTTING UP.

pendente lite [While litigation is pending] After an action has been commenced, and before it has been disposed of.

pending action An action which has not been tried. A pending action relating to land, or any interest or charge on land, may be registered as a Land Charge (*q.v.*) in the register of pending actions (Land Charges Act 1972 s.17(1)).

pension-sharing order Matrimonial Causes Act 1973 as amended by the Welfare Reform and Pensions Act 1999 enables the court to make pension sharing orders on divorce under which the pension arrangement of the transferor will be debited with a specified amount, which amount will then be credited to the transferee. Pension attachment orders, formerly earmarking orders, remain as an alternative option in certain situations.

peppercorn See RENT.

per [As stated by]

per, actions in the See ENTRY, WRITS OF.

per annum [By the year]

per autre vie [For the life of another] See TENANT PUR AUTRE VIE.

per capita [By heads] Individually. Distribution of property is per capita if it is divided amongst all entitled to it in equal shares. See PER STIRPES.

per cur.: per curiam [By the court]

per incuriam [Through want of care] A decision of the court that is mistaken. A decision of the court is not a binding precedent if given *per incuriam*; i.e. without the court's attention having been drawn to the relevant authority, or statute.

per infortunium [By mischance] See HOMICIDE.

per mensem [By the month]

per minas [By menaces] (*q.v.*)

per my et per tout [By the half and by the whole] See JOINT TENANCY.

per pro.: per procurationem [As an agent] On behalf of another.

per quod [Whereby]

per quod consortium et servitium amisit [Whereby he lost her society and services] An action for damages by a husband lay against any person who committed a tortious act or breach of contract against his wife, whereby he was deprived for any period of her society or services. In so far as the action lay for enticement of a spouse or a child, it was abolished by the Law Reform (Miscellaneous Provisions) Act 1970 s.5. See CONSORTIUM.

per se [By itself] Taken alone.

per stirpes [By stock (or branches)] Distribution of property is *per stirpes* if amongst those entitled to it according to the number of stocks of descent: e.g. where grandchildren of a donor take amongst themselves the share which their parent would have taken if that parent were alive (rather than sharing *per capita* (*q.v.*) with siblings of that parent).

per totem curiam [By the whole court]

perambulation The act of walking over the boundaries of a district or piece of land, either for the purposes of determining them or of preserving evidence of them.

peremptory An order or writ which permits no excuse for non-compliance.

performance The doing of that which is required by a contract or condition. A contract is discharged by performance. Where a person covenants to do an act, and he does some other act of a kind to be available for the performance of his covenant, he is presumed to have had the intention of performing the covenant, because "Equity imputes an intention to fulfil an obligation." This doctrine applies (1) where there is a covenant to purchase and settle lands, and a purchase is in fact made (see *Lechmere v Earl of Carlisle* (1733) 3 P. Wms. 211); (2) where there is a covenant to leave personalty to A and the covenantor dies intestate, and property thereby comes in fact to A (see *Blandy v Widmore* (1716) 1 P. Wms. 323). See SPECIFIC PERFORMANCE.

performance bond A bond agreed with a creditworthy third party, e.g. a bank, to ensure completion of contract works. It is common in construction projects. The bondholder undertakes to pay an employer a sum of money on default in completion of work by a contractor.

Performing Right Tribunal This tribunal was constituted by the Copyright Act 1956 to adjudicate in certain disputes about licences for the public performance, including broadcasts, of literary, dramatic or musical works. It was placed under the supervision of the Council on Tribunals (*q.v.*). It was renamed the Copyright Tribunal (*q.v.*) under the Copyright, Designs and Patents Act 1988.

periculum rei venditae, nondum traditae, est emptoris [Roman law] A thing sold but not yet delivered, is at the risk of the purchaser.

perils of the seas A term in marine insurance which refers only to fortuitous accidents or casualties of the seas, and does not include the ordinary action of the winds and waves (Marine Insurance Act 1906 s.30(2), Sch.1, r.7). Examples of perils of the seas include, foundering of a ship at sea, collisions and unintentional stranding.

periodic tenancy In land, a right to occupy exclusively for a period (generally weekly, monthly or yearly) which automatically repeats itself as each period terminates unless either party serves a notice to quit (*q.v.*) on the other.

periodical payments Payments ordered to be made, e.g. weekly or monthly by one person for the maintenance of another. See FINANCIAL PROVISION ORDERS.

perjury False swearing. The making on oath by a witness or interpreter in a judicial proceeding of a statement material in that proceeding, which he knows to be false or which he does not believe to be true. Perjury is an indictable criminal offence which is punishable with imprisonment. See s.1 of the Perjury Act 1911.

permitted development The Town and Country Planning (General Permitted Development) Order 1994 (as amended) grants planning permission for certain types of development for which it will not be necessary to obtain planning permission.

perpetua lex est, nullam legem humanam ac positivam perpetuam esse, et clausula quae abrogationem excludit, ab initio non valet [It is an everlasting law, that no positive and human law shall be perpetual, and a clause which excludes abrogation is invalid from its commencement]

perpetuity Endless years. A disposition of property in perpetuity is contrary to the policy of the law, because it "ties up" the property and prevents its free alienation. The "rule against perpetuities" forbids any disposition by which the absolute vesting of property is or may be postponed beyond the period of the life or lives of any number of persons living at the time of the disposition and the further period of 21 years after the death of the survivor (with the possible addition of a period of gestation) (*Cadell v Palmer* (1831) 1 Cl. & Fin. 372). The "lives in being" must be those referred to in the disposition and must be ascertainable. If there is no reference to lives in being, the period is 21 years.

   Under the Perpetuities and Accumulations Act 1964, a settlor or testator may specify a period not exceeding 80 years as the perpetuity period (s.1). Sections 2–12 of the 1964 Act remove a number of technical difficulties arising out of the rule against perpetuities. See Morris and Leach, *Rule Against Perpetuities*.

persistent offenders See EXTENDED SENTENCE.

person The object of rights and duties; capable of having rights and of being liable to duties. Persons are of two kinds, natural and artificial. A natural person is a human being; an artificial person is a collection or succession of natural persons forming a corporation. "Individual" generally denotes a human being but, e.g. under the Consumer Credit Act 2006 s.1, individual "includes a partnership consisting of two or three persons not all of whom are bodies corporate; and (b) an unincorporated body of persons which does not consist entirely of bodies corporate and is not a partnership".

persona [Roman law] (1) A human being.
(2) A being or entity capable of enjoying legal rights, or subject to legal duties: a natural person or a corporation.
(3) A person's political and social rights collectively; a person's legal capacity.

persona designata A person pointed out or described as an individual, as opposed to a person ascertained as a member of a class, or as filling a particular character.

persona extranea [Roman law] A person outside one's family.

persona incerta See INCERTA PERSONA.

persona non grata A person who is not welcome.

persona publica [Roman law] A public officer; a notary.

personal action An action in personam, as opposed to an action in rem. See ACTION.

personal data. The Data Protection Act 1998 imposes obligations on data controllers (*q.v.*) in respect of the processing of personal data and at the same time confers rights of access on data subjects in relation to their personal data. If data is not personal then it does not fall within the provisions of the Act. Section 1(1) defines personal data as data which relates to a living individual who can be identified from this data, or from this data and other information which is in the possession of, or is likely to come into the possession of, the data controller. Personal data also includes any expression of opinion about the individual and any indication of the intentions of the data controller or any other person in respect of the individual. See SENSITIVE PERSONAL DATA; PROCESSING (DATA).

personal injuries Damage to the physical person rather than to a person's property. See DAMAGES; NERVOUS SHOCK; LIMITATIONS, STATUTE OF.

personal property Movable property; goods and chattels. Movable property, if lost or taken, could not as of right be recovered from the wrongful possessor; the latter had the option of paying its value as damages in lieu. The action against the wrongdoer was called a personal action, and the property in question personal property. Leasehold interests in land are personal property.

personal representative An executor (*q.v.*) or administrator. By s.55(1)(xi) of the Administration of Estates Act 1925, "personal representative" means the executor, original or by representation, or administrator for the time being of a deceased person.
By the Administration of Estates Act 1925 s.1:
(1) real estate to which a deceased person was entitled for an interest not ceasing on his death, (notwithstanding any testamentary disposition thereof) devolves on the personal representative of the deceased in like manner as, before 1926, chattels real (*q.v.*) devolved on the personal representative of the deceased;
(2) the personal representative for the time being of a deceased person is deemed in law his heir and assignee within the meaning of all trusts and powers;

(3) the personal representative shall be the representative of the deceased in regard to both real and personal estate.

personalty Used particularly in regard to the estate of a deceased. "Pure personalty" is personal property other than leasehold estates. see PERSONAL PROPERTY.

personation The act of representing oneself to be someone else, whether living or dead, real or fictitious and in such character doing something to his prejudice or to prejudice another without consent (criminal law)

perverting the course of justice It is an indictable only offence at common law to act in a way which has a tendency and is intended to pervert the administration of justice, e.g. producing fabricated evidence (*R. v Vreones* [1891] 1 Q.B. 360); making a false allegation to the police of criminal conduct by another (*R. v Rowell* [1978] 1 W.L.R. 132); improperly interfering with a witness (*R. v Kellett* [1976] Q.B. 372).

petition Under the CPR (*q.v.*) the principal method of commencing an action is the claim form. However, certain actions are still commenced by petition, including proceedings for bankruptcy (*q.v.*), insolvency (*q.v.*) or an application for relief from unfair prejudice (*q.v.*).

The right of the subject to petition the Crown or Parliament was affirmed by the court in the case of the Seven Bishops (12 St.Tr. 183), and in the Bill of Rights (*q.v.*).

petition of right (1) The mode by which a subject could claim relief from the Crown for certain kinds of injury arising from the acts of the Crown or its servants, e.g. an illegal seizure of goods, or a claim for breach of contract. The petition could be presented in any of the divisions of the High Court on the Home Secretary granting his fiat for that purpose (Petition of Right Act 1860 s.1); proceedings by way of Petition of Right were abolished by the Crown Proceedings Act 1947. See CROWN PROCEEDINGS.

Petty Bag Office The principal office on the common law side of the Court of Chancery, under the management of the Clerk of the Petty Bag (*q.v.*). Out of it issued all original writs.

petty jury See JURY.

petty serjeanty A form of tenure (*q.v.*), which consisted in the rendering of some minor personal service to the lord, such as yielding him yearly a sword or pair of gilt spurs. The Act 1660, (12 Car. 2 c.24), did not affect its incidents, which were expressly preserved by the Law of Property Act 1922 s.136. This Act has since been repealed but the honorary services remain. See GRAND SERJEANTY.

petty sessional court or petty sessions Now known as magistrates' court (*q.v.*). A court of summary jurisdiction consisting of two or more justices when sitting in a petty sessional court-house, and including the Lord Mayor or any alderman of the City of London; or any salaried magistrate when sitting in any place where he is authorised by law to do alone any act for which two justices are required.

picketing The posting of persons in the vicinity of a place of work during a trade dispute in order to persuade others not to work, to communicate information about the trade dispute or to obstruct them from working. There is no "right to picket" as such. The law only authorises those who act in contemplation or furtherance of a trade dispute (*q.v.*) to attend at or near their own place of work in order to peacefully picket, i.e. to peacefully obtain or communicate information or to peacefully persuade any person to work or abstain from working (Trade Union and Labour Relations (Consolidation) Act 1992 s.220). Those who exceed these limits may incur civil or criminal liabilities (ibid. s.219(3) and see, e.g. *Broom v DPP* [1974] 1 All E.R. 314, HL and Public Order Act 1986). See SECONDARY PICKETING.

Piller, Anton See SEARCH ORDERS.

pin money An allowance made by a husband to a wife for her dress and personal expenses. It may be secured by settlement, or it may be given voluntarily.

pipe A "roll" in the Exchequer, also known as the Great Roll. It consisted of the accounts relating to the hereditary revenues of the Crown.

piracy (1) In international law, piracy *jure gentium* is governed by the United Nations Convention on the Law of the Sea (New York 1982) and before a UK court is treated as part of the law of nations by virtue of the Merchant Shipping and Maritime Security Act 1997 s.26. Schedule 5 of the Act adopts the definition in the Convention, according to which piracy includes:
"(a) any illegal acts of violence or detention, or any act of depredation, committed for private ends by the crew or the passengers of a private ship or aircraft and directed—(i) on the high seas, against another ship or aircraft, or against persons or property on board such ship or aircraft, (ii) against a ship, aircraft, persons or property in a place outside the jurisdiction of any State; (b) any act of voluntary participation in the operation of a ship or of an aircraft with knowledge of facts making it a pirate ship or aircraft" or (iii) any act of inciting or intentionally facilitating an act described in head (i) or (ii) above".
(See also Aviation Security Act 1982 and Aviation and Maritime Security Act 1990.) See HIJACKING.
(2) The Infringement of Copyright (*q.v.*).

piscary Fishery (*q.v.*).

place of safety A place to which a child (*q.v.*), or a young person, or a person who appears to be suffering from a mental disorder (*q.v.*), may be taken in accordance with statutory powers in certain statutorily defined circumstances (primarily emergency situations). Definitions of a place of safety can be found in the Children and Young Persons Act 1933 s.107(1) and in the Mental Health Act 1983 s.55.

placita [Pleas]

plaint The cause for which the plaintiff complained against the defendant and for which he obtained a writ or summons.

plaintiff One who brings an action at law, now called a claimant (*q.v.*).

planning blight Land the value of which is adversely affected by a proposal contained in a development plan (*q.v.*) by a public authority. Owner-occupiers who suffer hardship by being unable to sell their land at a reasonable price may serve a blight notice on the local authority requiring the authority to purchase the land.

planning contravention notice A notice under the Town and Country Planning Act 1990 s.171C, which may be served by a local planning authority where it appears that there may have been a breach of planning control, requiring owners or occupiers or others interested in land to provide specified information relating to any operations or other activities on the land. The notice is used to secure information with a view to the serving of an enforcement notice (*q.v.*).

planning contribution The planning obligation (*q.v.*) is replaced by the planning contribution. Under the Planning and Compulsory Purchase Act 2004 ss.46–48 the Secretary of State may by regulations make provision for the making of a planning contribution in relation to the development or use of land in a local planning authority's area. The regulations may require the local planning authority to include in, for example, a development plan document, the following: for which developments and uses of land a contribution will be required; the circumstances in which a contribution will not be sought; the purposes to which receipts from contributions will be put; and the criteria for determining the value of the contribution. The contribution may be in the form of a sum of money or a benefit in kind or a combination of both.

planning inspectorate Responsible for the processing of planning and enforcement appeals and holding inquiries into local development plans. Also deals with a wide variety of other planning related casework including listed building consent appeals, advertisement appeals, and reporting on planning applications called in for decision by the Office of the Deputy Prime Minister or, in Wales, the Welsh Assembly Government.

planning obligation The term planning obligation replaced that of planning agreement and such obligations could be either agreements with the local planning authority or unilateral undertakings by the developer. The usual object of such obligations was to render more likely the granting of planning permission (*q.v.*) for the development (*q.v.*) of land where such development might otherwise be refused. The obligations could take the form of undertakings which were conditional on the granting of a related planning permission. A planning obligation was a local land charge (*q.v.*) for the purposes of the Local Land Charges Act 1975. Replaced by the planning contribution (*q.v.*).

planning permission At common law a landowner can develop his land as he likes. Since, however, the Housing, Town Planning, etc. Act 1919 local authorities have had increasing powers of control over the use and development of land. The modern scheme of development control was instituted by the Town and Country Planning Act 1947 and is now contained in consolidating legislation, the Town and Country Planning Act 1990 as amended by the Planning and Compensation Act 1991. Development (*q.v.*) is controlled by the need for planning permission first being obtained by application to the local planning authority (the appropriate council), subject to appeal to the Secretary of State. Planning permission is allowed for minor development, without application, under the terms of the Town and Country Planning (General Permitted Development) Order 1995 which replaced and re-enacted the General Development Order 1988.

If development is carried out without planning permission, an enforcement notice (*q.v.*) may be served by the planning authority, subject to appeal to the Secretary of State. See MATERIAL CHANGE OF USE.

planning policy guidance notes (PPG's) and planning policy statements (PPS's) A series of documents issued by the Office of the Deputy Prime Minister setting out government policy and advice on planning issues such as sustainable development (*q.v.*), housing and transport.

plantations The early name for British colonial possessions in America, e.g. in the West Indies.

plea The reply to a "plaint" (*q.v.*); a mode of defence in an action at law. In a criminal prosecution the prisoner has to plead to the indictment, which he may do (1) by pleading to the jurisdiction, that is, alleging the court has no jurisdiction to try him; (2) by a demurrer (*q.v.*); or (3) by some plea in bar, either a general plea, "guilty", or "not guilty", or a special plea, such as "autrefois acquit." The accused may plead not guilty in addition to any demurrer or special plea. He may plead not guilty of the offence charged but guilty of another offence of which he might be found guilty on the indictment (Criminal Law Act 1967 s.6).

Formerly in a civil action, pleas were of two kinds, dilatory and peremptory (*q.v.*). The former included pleas to the jurisdiction, pleas in suspension, e.g. an allegation of infancy, and pleas in abatement; the latter consisted of pleas in bar which showed a substantial defence to the action, either by traverse or by confession and avoidance (*q.v.*). Under the CPR a defendant must submit a statement of case (*q.v.*).

plea bargain An arrangement by which a defendant to criminal proceedings may agree to plead guilty knowing he will receive a lighter sentence. A judge was not to indicate what sentence he had in mind to induce a defendant to change his plea, as the law considered that a defendant must have a free choice of plea. However, the Criminal Justice Act 2003 Sch.3 para.6, dealing with allocation of offences triable either way, allows a court, at the request of a defendant, to indicate whether a sentence will be custodial or non-custodial should a case be dealt with summarily and the defendant plead guilty. Following *R. v Goodyear* [2005] All E.R. (D) 266 the Crown Court may, at the request of a defendant, indicate the maximum sentence to be imposed should a defendant plead guilty.

plead To make a plea (*q.v.*).

pleader (1) An advocate.
(2) One who draws pleadings.

pleadings See STATEMENT OF CASE.

pleas in abatement A plea which showed that in criminal proceedings, the prosecutor, or in civil proceedings, the plaintiff, had committed some defect in formality which prevented him from succeeding. Now obsolete owing to the powers of amending pleadings.

pleas of the Crown Offences averred to have been committed *contra pacem Domini Regis, coronam et dignitatem suam* [against the peace of our Lord the King, his crown and dignity], which were triable only in the King's Courts, as distinguished from offences which could be tried in the local courts; e.g. the county court. A general term for criminal prosecutions. See PEACE.

pledge The transfer of the possession (but not ownership) of a chattel as security for the payment of a debt or performance of an obligation. On default being made the chattel may be sold. By the Consumer Credit Act 1974 pledge means the pawnee's rights over an article taken in pawn. See PAWN; LIEN.

plene administravit The defence set up by an executor or administrator when sued upon a debt of his testator, that he has fully administered the deceased's estate and that he has no assets to satisfy the claim.

plenipotentiary Having full powers.

poaching The offence of unlawfully taking or destroying game on another person's land. See the Night Poaching Act 1828; Poaching Prevention Act 1862; Game Laws (Amendment) Act 1960; Criminal Law Act 1977 ss.15, 30, 65(4), Sch.1, Sch.12, as amended by the Magistrates' Courts Act 1980 Sch.9.

poena [Roman law] A penalty as punishment for an offence: generally inflicted for delicts. It is not confined to a money payment, as is multa, a fine, but may extend to the *caput* (*q.v.*) of the offender, and is not left to the discretion of the judge, but is attached to or appointed for each particular delict.

Police Authorities Independent bodies responsible for overseeing and monitoring local policing. Membership consists of magistrates, local councillors and independent members. Police Authorities have a statutory duty to consult with local people in the relevant area and form a link between the police and the public. They must prepare a policing plan (*q.v.*) setting out local priorities and targets and have a duty to ensure that the local community gets best value from its policing service in accordance with the policing plan. The Chief Constable of that area will account for the delivery of the policing service.

Police Complaints Authority An independent body which oversees the investigation of complaints made by the public or referred directly by police services against police officers in England and Wales. Now replaced by the Independent Police Complaints Commission (*q.v.*). See Police Reform Act 2002.

311

police court A petty sessional court (*q.v.*), held in London and in other cities by a magistrate; now called a magistrates' court.

police, obstruction of It is an offence to wilfully obstruct a constable in the execution of his duty (Police Act 1996 s.89). The prosecution must prove that there was an obstruction of the constable, that the constable was acting in the execution of his duty, and that the person obstructing did so wilfully (*Rice v Connolly* [1966] 2 All E.R. 651).

policing plan Drawn up by a police authority (*q.v.*) on both an annual and three yearly basis to inform the local community in that authority what the policing priorities are, based on the views of the community.

policy of assurance An instrument containing a contract of insurance (*q.v.*). An undervalued policy is where the value of the thing insured is not stated; a valued policy is where the value is stated (Marine Insurance Act 1906 ss.27, 28).

political asylum Under the Immigration Act 1971 anyone who is not a British citizen (*q.v.*), or a national of a Member State of the European Union exercising their European free movement rights, needs to be granted leave to enter or leave to remain (permission to stay) in order lawfully to enter into, or remain in, the United Kingdom. The Immigration and Asylum Act 1999 introduced new powers enabling the Secretary of State by order to make additional provision about the giving, refusing, or varying of leave to enter the United Kingdom. See ASYLUM; ASYLUM SEEKER.

political offence There is no statutory definition of this term, nor of the phrase "an offence of a political character", and the courts have also refused to provide any exhaustive determination. However, the offence must be in some way connected with organised political upheaval or opposition to the established political control in the country requesting extradition (*q.v.*) of any person. A person seeking political asylum in the United Kingdom is protected from extradition. Under the Extradition Act 1989 Pt III a person may not be returned under the extradition procedures if it appears that the offence of which that person is accused is an offence of a political character or that the request for his return is made to punish him for his race, religion, nationality or political opinions. Genocide is not an offence of a political character (Extradition Act 1989 s.23). See also Suppression of Terrorism Act 1978 Sch.1, for offences, e.g. murder and rape, which are not to be regarded as political offences. See EXTRADITION; HUMAN RIGHTS.

poll Taking a vote on election, or on a motion. At a general meeting of members of a company, for example, questions are decided in the first place by a show of hands, but there is a right of members to demand a poll, unless expressly excluded, and, if demanded, it must be taken. The usual method is to require the persons present in person (or, normally, by proxy) to sign a paper headed "for" or "against" the motion. The poll is taken by counting these votes. See RESOLUTION.

Poll tax A tax upon every poll or head, that is to say upon every person. The common term used to refer to the "community charge" which was introduced by the Local Government Finance Act 1988 upon its abolition of domestic rates. The poll tax was in turn replaced by council tax (*q.v.*). See RATE.

pollution (of the environment) Under the Environmental Protection Act 1990 s.1(3), this involves pollution due to the release (into any environmental medium) from any process of substances which are capable of causing harm (*q.v.*) to man or any other living organisms supported by the environment. See also in respect of pollution from waste on land the Environmental Protection Act 1990 s.29(3). See ENVIRONMENT; HARM.

polygamy Marriage to more than one person at a time. A polygamous marriage may be recognised by the English courts in some circumstances (Matrimonial Causes Act 1973 s.47).

poor law The law which related to the public (compulsory) relief of the indigent poor. By the Poor Relief Act 1601 overseers of the poor were appointed in every parish to provide for the relief of paupers settled there, and to levy a rate (*q.v.*) on property therein. The system of overseers being unsatisfactory, the statute (22 Geo. 3 c.83), authorised any parish to appoint guardians in lieu of overseers, and also to enter into a voluntary union with other parishes (*q.v.*).

A highly complex system was eventually consolidated by the Poor Law Act 1930 and terminated by the National Assistance Act 1948.

poor person See LEGAL AID.

poor rate The rate formerly levied by the overseers for the relief of the poor. See POOR LAW.

port (1) A city or town (Anglo-Saxon).

(2) A harbour or other stretch of water available for the loading and unloading of goods on ships. The Commissioners of Customs and Excise may by order appoint and name as a port for the purposes of customs and excise any specified area in the United Kingdom (Customs and Excise Management Act 1979 s.19), and approve fit places for the loading and unloading of goods therein: referred to as "approved wharves" (ibid. s.20 and s.20(A)).

portion (1) The provision made for a child by a parent or one *in loco parentis.*

(2) The gross sums of money provided in a strict settlement for the children, other than the eldest son, on their attaining 21, or, if female, marrying before that age. See SATISFACTION.

portreeve The chief magistrate of a town.

positions of trust A term used in relation to the Sexual Offences Act 2003 which includes those looking after (involved in caring for, training, supervising or being in sole charge of) persons under the age of 18 in hospitals, care homes, children's homes, detention centres and educational institutions, ibid. ss.21–22. See SEXUAL OFFENCES; ABUSE OF POSITION OF TRUST.

positive law (1) That part of law which consists of rules imposed by the sovereign on his subjects.

(2) Law proper as opposed to moral law (Austin). See LAW.

posse comitatus [The power of the county] An assemblage of the able-bodied male inhabitants of a county, except peers and clergymen. The sheriff of the county could summon it either to defend the county against the King's enemies or to enforce the King's writ.

possessio [Roman law] Legal possession. The detention or physical apprehension of a thing with the intention of holding it as one's own (detention, together with *animus possidendi*). It was protected by interdicts.

possessio civilis [Roman law] Civil possession; possession capable of ripening into ownership by *usucapio,* i.e. if it was free from *vitium* and held *ex justa causa* and bona fide.

possessio naturalis [Roman law] Natural possession; where a person possessed a thing not *ex justa causa* and bona fide. It was not protected by interdicts.

possession Physical detention coupled with the intention to hold the thing detained as one's own (Maine). The continuing exercise of a claim to exclusive use of a material object (Salmond). Possession has two elements: (1) the physical

313

possession of the thing; (2) the *animus possidendi*, the intention to appropriate to oneself the exclusive use of the thing possessed.

Immediate possession is possession retained personally; mediate possession or custody is possession retained for or on account of another. Incorporeal possession is the possession not of a material thing, but of a legal right. Constructive possession is possession in contemplation of law as opposed to de facto possession or actual possession in fact.

Possession is prima facie evidence of ownership. "Possession is nine-tenths of the law" means that possession is good against all the world except a person with a better right (e.g. the true owner). Possession can ripen into ownership by effluxion of time. Adverse possession (*q.v.*) of land (i.e. not by agreement with the owner) for 12 years may destroy the title of the owner.

possession money The fee to which a sheriff's officer is entitled for keeping possession of property under a writ of execution.

possession of drugs It is an offence to have in one's possession a controlled drug (Misuse of Drugs Act 1971 s.5(1)). For the drug to be in a person's possession that person must have physical control or custody of the drug and have the knowledge that it is in his custody or control (*Warner v Metropolitan Police Commissioner* [1969] A.C. 256). The quantity of drug must be such as to amount to something, and this is a question of fact for the jury; however, it does not have to be useable. The question is not usability but possession (*R. v Boyeson* [1982] 2 All E.R. 161, HL). See DRUGS, CONTROLLED.

possession, writ of The writ which commands the sheriff to enter the land and give possession of it to the person entitled under a judgment for possession (Ord. 45, r.3).

possessory action A real action to recover the possession of land.

possessory title Title by reason of long possession without documentary right. See SQUATTER'S TITLE.

possibility A future event the happening of which is uncertain; an interest in land which depends on the happening of such an event. A possibility is said to be either bare, or coupled with an interest. Thus, the expectation of an eldest son of succeeding to his father's land was a bare possibility, which was not capable of transfer. If land was conveyed to A for life, and if C should be living at his death, then to B in fee, B's contingent remainder was a possibility coupled with an interest, which might be transferred. See DOUBLE POSSIBILITY.

possidere pro herede [Roman law] To possess in the belief that one is heir.

possidere pro possessore [Roman law] To possess the part of the whole of an inheritance without any right, and with the knowledge that one is not the owner.

post litem motam After litigation has been in contemplation. See LIS MOTA.

postea A formal statement, indorsed on the nisi prius record, which gave an account of the proceedings at the trial of the action.

postliminium [Beyond the threshold] The doctrine of the Roman law that persons captured by the enemy were, on their return, deemed to revert to their original status, on the fiction that no capture had occurred. The doctrine has been adopted by international law as the rule by which persons, property and territory tend to revert to their former condition on the withdrawal of enemy control.

post-mortem examination A medical examination of a corpse in order to discover the cause of death. It may be ordered by a coroner and may be made without an inquest (Coroners Act 1988 s.19).

post-obit A money bond conditioned for payment at or after the death of some person.

post traumatic stress disorder See NERVOUS SHOCK.

postumus [Roman law] (1) A child of a testator, born after his death, who, if born in his lifetime, would have been under his *potestas*, and entitled to succeed him if he died intestate.

(2) A child of a testator conceived before the date of the will, but born *a suus heres* after the date of the will, and before the testators's death. This was called a *postumus Vellaeanus*, from *lex Junia Vellaea*, which provided that the testator might institute or exclude such a child.

postumus alienus [Roman law] A posthumous stranger; a posthumous child that would not have been under the testator's power if born in his lifetime.

potior est conditio defendentis [The condition of a defendant is the better] i.e. the onus of proof is on the plaintiff.

potior est conditio possidentis [The condition of a possessor is the better] i.e. the onus is on a claimant to prove a superior title in himself to that of the possessor.

pound A place where goods which have been seized as distress (*q.v.*) are placed by the distrainor, and which goods are in the custody of the law. A pound is either overt (open overhead) or covert (closed in).

poundage (1) A fee of so much in the pound.

(2) Formerly a customs duty on the value of imports other than wine. See TONNAGE.

pound-breach (1) The offence of taking goods out of a pound (*q.v.*) before the distrainor's claim has been satisfied. Once goods are impounded, they are *in custodia legis*, and a pound must be respected by all persons; ignorance that goods are impounded is no defence. See DISTRAIN; RESCUE; CONVERSION.

(2) Forcible release of cattle or other animals lawfully placed in a pound.

power The ability conferred on a person by law to determine, by his own will directed to that end, the legal relations of himself or others (Salmond). A power is the converse of disability. It differs from a right (*q.v.*) in that there are no accompanying duties. Powers are public, i.e. when vested by the state in its agent or employee; or private, when conferred by one person on another.

power of appointment See APPOINTMENT, POWER OF.

power of attorney A deed by which one person empowers another to represent him, or act in his stead either generally or for specified purposes. The donor of the power is called the principal or constituent; the donee is called the attorney.

A lasting power of attorney is a power of attorney under which the donor ("P") confers on the donee (or donees) authority to make decisions about all or any of the following: (a) P's personal welfare or specified matters concerning P's personal welfare; and (b) P's property and affairs or specified matters concerning P's property and affairs, and which includes authority to make such decisions in circumstances where P no longer has capacity (*q.v.*) (see Mental Capacity Act 2005 s.9). The 2005 Act repealed the Enduring Powers of Attorney Act 1985.

practice Procedure (*q.v.*). That which pertains to the actual conduct of legal proceedings and is governed by the CPR (*q.v.*) for civil proceedings and the CrPR (q.v.) for criminal proceedings.

practice court The Bail Court (*q.v.*).

practice directions General guidance from the court regarding the procedure to be followed in certain circumstances or cases. Most of the Civil Procedure Rules (*q.v.*) are followed by a practice direction referring to and giving further guidance on the application of the rule. See the Civil Procedure Rules 1998.

While a source of civil procedural law, such directions are made under the inherent jurisdiction of the court to regulate its own process and not by statutory instrument.

practising certificate The certificate taken out annually by a solicitor (*q.v.*) from the Law Society (*q.v.*) which entitles him to practise as a solicitor.

praecipe (1) A species of original writ, which required the sheriff to command the defendant either to do a certain thing or show cause why he had not done it.

(2) A slip of paper on which a party to a proceeding writes the particulars of a document which he wishes to have prepared or issued; he then hands it to the officer of the court whose duty it is to prepare or issue the document.

praedia stipendiaria [Roman law] Provincial lands belonging peculiarly to the Roman people.

praedium dominans [Roman law] The land in favour of which a servitude existed over the land of another.

praedium serviens Land subject to a servitude in favour of the owner of adjoining land.

praefectus urbi [Roman law] The city prefect or governor. His civil jurisdiction extended to 100 miles around Rome, and his criminal jurisdiction throughout Italy. An appeal lay to him from the Praetor (*q.v.*).

praemunire The offence of directly or indirectly asserting the supremacy of the Pope over the Crown of England, as by procuring excommunication or bulls from Rome, contrary to the Statute of Praemunire (16 Ric. 2 c.5). The writ employed commenced with the words *praemunire facias* [that you cause to be forewarned].

praepositus [One put in front] A person in authority.

praeses [Roman law] The president or governor of a province; a *legatus Caesaris* being the governor of a province reserved by the emperor.

praesumptio See PRESUMPTION.

praetor [Roman law.] The consul whose special function was to administer justice in the city (*Praetor Urbanus*). A second Praetor was appointed to deal with cases between citizens and aliens, or between aliens alone (*Praetor Peregrinus*). Although theoretically the Praetor merely administered the law, his powers of interpretation and amendment developed the law. He applied, as far as possible, the rules of natural justice (*naturalis aequitas*). On taking office he issued an edict stating the rules by which he would be guided.

The Praetors achieved:

(1) admission of aliens to Roman law;

(2) the supersession of formulism by rules giving effect to the intention of the parties;

(3) change of the law on intestate succession from the basis of *potestas* to blood.

pre-action protocols See PROTOCOLS.

preamble The recitals set out in the beginning of a statute showing the reason for the Act.

precatory words Words of wish, hope, desire or entreaty accompanying a gift, that the donee will dispose of the property in some particular way. The modern tendency is against construing precatory words as imposing a trust on the donee. See *Re Adams and Kensington Vestry* (1884) 27 Ch.D. 394.

Precedence, Patent of Letters patent whereby the Crown assigns to some person a rank higher than that to which he would otherwise be entitled.

316

precedent A judgment or decision of a court of law cited as an authority for deciding a similar set of facts; a case which serves as an authority for the legal principle embodied in its decision. The common law has developed by broadening down from precedent to precedent.

A case is only an authority for what it actually decides:

"The only use of authorities or decided cases is the establishment of some principle which the judge can follow out in deciding the case before him" (per Sir George Jessel M.R.; *Re Hallett* (1880) 13 Ch.D. 712).

An original precedent is one which creates and applies a new rule; a declaratory precedent is one which is merely the application of an already existing rule of law. An authoritative precedent is one which is binding and must be followed; a persuasive precedent is one which need not be followed, but which is worthy of consideration. Decisions of the House of Lords or the Court of Appeal are authoritative precedents. The High Court, however, will usually follow its own decisions (unless they are distinguishable). American or Commonwealth judgments, etc. are persuasive precedents. See RATIO DECIDENDI; STARE DECISIS.

In conveyancing or drafting, a precedent is a copy of an instrument used as a guide in preparing another similar instrument.

precept An order or direction given by one official person or body to another, requiring some act to be done, e.g. the payment of a sum of money.

pre-emption (1) A right of first refusal; a right to purchase property before or in preference to other persons should the owner wish to sell.

(2) In international law, the right of a government to purchase, for its own use, the property of subjects of another power in *transitu*, instead of allowing it to reach its destination.

preference An individual gives a preference to a creditor etc. when he does anything or allows anything to be done which has the effect of putting that creditor into a better position than he would otherwise have had on the occasion of the individual's bankruptcy. The trustee in bankruptcy of the bankrupt's estate may make application to the court for an order re-opening a transaction entered by the bankrupt, within the "relevant time", where there has been a "preference" within the scope of the Insolvency Act 1986 (ss.340–342). There are similar provisions in respect of companies in administration or winding up (*q.v.*) (Insolvency Act 1986 ss.239–241).

preference shares Shares (*q.v.*) in a joint stock company which are entitled to a fixed rate of dividend payable in preference to the dividend on the ordinary shares. Unless preference shares are made preferential as to capital they rank pari passu with the ordinary shares on a winding-up. They are presumed to be cumulative. See SURPLUS ASSETS.

preferential debts Those debts paid in priority to others in distributing an estate, as in the distribution of a bankrupt's estate; of a deceased insolvent's estate; in the winding-up of a company; and out of any assets coming to the hands of a receiver taking possession under a floating charge (Insolvency Act 1986 ss.40, 175, 328, 386 and Sch.6.)

Since the Enterprise Act 2002 they are limited to such debts as four months' wages or salaries of employees and pension contributions. These debts rank equally amongst themselves, and if the assets are insufficient to pay them in full, they abate in equal proportions.

pre-incorporation contract Where it is claimed that a contract is made by or on behalf of a company before that company is incorporated (i.e. before the company exists legally), then such a contract takes effect, subject to agreement to the contrary, as one made with the person claiming to act on the company's behalf and that person is personally liable on the contract, Companies Act 2006 s.51.

prejudice Pre-judgment. Injury. A statement which is made "without prejudice" for the purpose of settling a dispute cannot be construed as an admission of liability or given in evidence.

preliminary act In marine law, a sealed document giving particulars of a collision between vessels, which must be filed by the solicitor for each party in an Admiralty action for damages for collision. One particular feature of a collision action is that the parties must prepare and file a collision statement of case. This is now covered by CPR 1998 Pt 61. A collision statement of case used to be called a Preliminary Act and the law relating to preliminary acts still applies to collision statements of case.

preliminary ruling The reference of a "question of Community law" by a court of a Member State to the European Court of Justice. Any court may refer such a question arising in any case relating to the interpretation of the EC Treaty. A court against whose decision there is no further judicial appeal must refer such a question to the European Court of Justice art.234 (ex art.177) Treaty Establishing the European Community. See ACTE CLAIR.

premises (1) In pleadings, that which has been stated before.
(2) In a conveyance (*q.v.*), when the property has been fully described, it is commonly referred to in the subsequent parts of the deed as "the premises hereinbefore described." From this, "premises" has acquired the sense of land or land or buildings.
(3) That part of a deed which describes the property and precedes the *habendum* (*q.v.*).

premises licence Means a licence granted under Pt 3 of the Licensing Act 2003 in respect of any premises, which authorises the premises to be used for one or more licensable activities, e.g sale and supply of alcohol, provision of regulated entertainment, provision of late night refreshment (see s.1 of the Licensing Act 2003).
The Licensing Act 2003 provides a new system of regulation of such activities and it completely replaces the licensing system put in place by the Licensing Act 1964. Licences can now be issued in a number of forms including a premises licence. The applicant for a premises licence is able to choose the days and hours during which he wants to be authorised to carry on any licensable activity, at the premises for which a licence is sought. Usually for the sale of alcohol a premises licence and a personal licence is required. A premises licence can also be issued under the Gambling Act 2005 in connection with the provision of gambling activities. See CLUB PREMISES CERTIFICATES; LICENSABLE ACTIVITY; QUALIFYING CLUB ACTIVITY.

premium (1) A sum payable in advance of or over and above the consideration for an agreement.
(2) The consideration for a contract of assurance (*q.v.*).
(3) A lump sum payable upon the grant of a lease which forms a capitalised part of the rent for the property.
See SHARE PREMIUM.

prender The power of taking a thing without its being offered.

prerogative, royal The exceptional powers and privileges of the Sovereign, e.g. the command of the Army, or the treaty-making power. The prerogative appears to be historically and as a matter of actual fact simply the residue of arbitrary authority which at any given time is legally left in the hands of the Crown (Dicey, *Law of the Constitution*).

prerogative writs Writs which are issued from the superior courts for the purpose of preventing inferior courts, or officials, from exceeding the limits of their legitimate sphere of action, or of compelling them to exercise their functions in

accordance with the law, to assure the full measure of justice to the Queen's subjects. These writs were: (1) Habeas Corpus; (2) Quashing Order; (3) Prohibitory Order; (4) Mandatory Order; (5) Quo Warranto; (6) Ne Exeat Regno; (7) Procedendo. They were within the jurisdiction of the Queen's Bench Division.
See JUDICIAL REVIEW.

prescribe (1) To claim a right by prescription.
(2) To lay down authoritatively.

prescription The acquisition of a right by reason of lapse of time. Now only relevant to acquisition of an easement or profit over land. Negative prescription is the loss of a right by the same process. In Roman law the *praescriptio* was a clause placed at the head of the formula or pleadings (*prae*, before and *scribere*, to write). *Praescriptio* was also a variety of *usucapio*, i.e. a mode of acquiring property by undisturbed possession for a certain length of time.
At common law, title by prescription can be acquired by the enjoyment (user) of a use from time immemorial (or time out of mind) from which an original grant was implied. Such title is presumed from the evidence of long actual user, but the presumption might be rebutted by proof that the enjoyment has in fact commenced within legal memory (now since 1189). The doctrine of the lost modern grant overcomes this difficulty by presuming from long user that an actual grant of the use was made at some time subsequent to 1189, and that unfortunately this grant has been lost.
The Prescription Act 1832 enacts that in the case of a profit à prendre (*q.v.*), the period of enjoyment (user) as of right required to establish title is 30 years unless consent was given to the use, however, enjoyment for 60 years establishes an absolute right unless written consent was given. In the case of an easement the terms are 20 and 40 years respectively but for light, when enjoyment for 20 years gives an absolute right unless with written consent. Where a person claiming a right by prescription proves that it has been enjoyed by him and his predecessors in title by virtue of ownership of land, he is said to prescribe in a que estate. Prescription in gross arises where a person claims that he and his ancestors have exercised a right to a profit à prendre over the land of another but unrelated to ownership of any land. See MEMORY; SQUATTER'S TITLE; LIMITATION.

present To tender or offer, e.g. to present a bill of exchange for acceptance or payment to the acceptor.

presentment The presenting of a person or item. For example, bills of exchange (*q.v.*) must generally be presented for payment.
Formerly, the presentment of an accusation by a grand jury (*q.v.*) (abolished by the Administration of Justice (Miscellaneous Provisions) Act 1933 s.1) was a condition precedent to the putting of any person on trial before a petty jury (*q.v.*).

President of the Courts of England and Wales An office held by the Lord Chief Justice (*q.v.*) whose duties include representing the views of the judiciary to Parliament, maintaining appropriate arrangements for the welfare, training and guidance of the judiciary, and allocating work within courts. By virtue of this office the President is entitled to sit in the Court of Appeal, the High Court, the Crown Court, the county courts, and the magistrates' courts. See Constitutional Reform Act 2005 s.7.

President of the Supreme Court One of the 12 Justices of the Supreme Court (*q.v.*) may be appointed its President (see Constitutional Reform Act 2005 s.23).

presumption A conclusion or inference as to the truth of some fact in question, drawn from other facts proved or admitted to be true.

319

(1) Irrebutable or conclusive presumptions (*praesumptiones juris*) are absolute inferences established by law; evidence is not admissible to contradict them: they are rules of law. See, e.g. DOLI INCAPAX.

(2) Rebuttable presumptions of law (*praesumptiones juristantum*) are inferences which the law requires to be drawn from given facts, and which are conclusive until disproved by evidence to the contrary, e.g. the presumption of the innocence of an accused person.

(3) Presumptions of fact (*praesumptiones hominis vel facti*) are inferences which may be drawn from the facts, but not conclusively. See PROOF.

presumption of death Any married person who alleges that reasonable grounds exist for supposing the other party to the marriage to be dead may petition to have it presumed that the other party is dead and to have the marriage dissolved (Matrimonial Causes Act 1973 s.19(1)). Absence of seven years where the petitioner has no reason to believe the other party has been living within that period shall be evidence that the other party is dead unless the contrary be proved (1973 Act s.19(3)).

pre-trial review In higher value and more complex civil cases (referred to as multi-track cases), the court may fix a case management conference or a pre-trial review at any time after the case has been allocated to the multi-track (*q.v.*). See CPR 1998, Pt 29.3. See TRACK ALLOCATION Further, in criminal cases, a pre-trial review hearing can be held to ensure that all legal and other matters are complete in preparation for trial.

previous convictions Under ss.98 and 112 of the Criminal Justice Act 2003, previous convictions are a form of bad character evidence (*q.v.*). Generally a defendant cannot be asked about previous convictions while being tried for an offence except where the conditions contained within s.101 of the Criminal Justice Act 2003 apply. Previous convictions of a person other than the defendant to the proceedings in a criminal trial may be introduced in evidence if the conditions in s.100 of the Criminal Justice Act 2003 are satisfied.

When sentencing, a court must treat previous convictions as an aggravating factor in determining the seriousness of the offence which the Court is sentencing. The court should have regard to the nature of the previous conviction and time which has lapsed since the previous offence was committed, Criminal Justice Act 2003 s.143.

pricking the sheriffs The formal ceremony of the Sovereign selecting for appointment sheriffs by pricking their names with a bodkin. The ceremony is a survival from the days when their selection was by chance. A sheriff must be selected annually for each county in England and Wales. Also known as Pricking the Lites.

prima facie case [Of first appearance] A case in which there is evidence which will suffice to support the allegation made in it, and which will stand unless there is evidence to rebut the allegation. When a case is being heard in court, the party on whom the burden of proof rests must make out a prima facie case, otherwise the other party will be able to submit that there is no case to answer, and if he is successful, the case will be dismissed.

primage A payment made by the owner of goods to the master of the ship in which they are carried in return for taking care of the goods. It is recoverable from the consignee. In practice, the master forgoes primage in return for a regular salary, so that the primage belongs to the ship owner.

primary market See STOCK EXCHANGE.

primary victim A person who is involved "either mediately or immediately, as a participant" in an accident and who suffers recoverable personal injury as a consequence whether physical or psychiatric (see per Lord Oliver in *Alcock v Chief Constable of South Yorkshire* [1991] 4 All E.R. 907 at 923, HL). See NERVOUS SHOCK.

Prime Minister In theory the office holder is chosen by the Sovereign, but in practice the Sovereign invites the leader of the political party which commands a majority in the House of Commons to form a government. The Prime Minister also holds offices of First Lord of the Treasury and Minister for Civil Service. As chairman of the Cabinet, the Prime Minister is executive head of the government. The Prime Minister also advises the Sovereign on appointments such as Lords of Appeal, Lords Justices of Appeal, peerages, Privy Councillors, bishops and deans of the Church of England, and certain honours.

primo loco [In the first place]

primogeniture The rule whereby the eldest male in a given group of relatives inherited property to the exclusion of all others, e.g. the rule whereby real property, on a death intestate before 1926, generally descended to the eldest son.

Prince of Wales The eldest son of the reigning Sovereign is always created Prince of Wales and Earl of Chester by patent (*q.v.*). He is Duke of Cornwall by inheritance during the life of the Sovereign. Since the accession of James I, the heir apparent has been by inheritance Duke of Rothesay, Earl of Carrick, and Baron Renfrew, Lord of the Isles and Great Steward of Scotland.

principal (1) The principal to a criminal offence is the actual perpetrator: the person who, with the required mens rea (*q.v.*), commits the actus reus (*q.v.*) of the offence. Formerly a distinction was made between principals in the first degree and principals in the second degree, but now the proper terminology is simply principal and secondary party. See SECONDARY LIABILITY.

(2) A principal is one who authorises another (an agent) to create legal relations between the principal and third parties.

Contracts made by the agent bind the principal and the third party. If an agent purports to act on his own behalf, without disclosing that he is an agent, his principal is called an undisclosed principal (*q.v.*). In general the third party can sue the undisclosed principal when he discovers his existence and the principal can sue the third party, with certain exceptions. See COMMERCIAL AGENT.

(3) A principal debtor is one whose debt is guaranteed by a surety (*q.v.*), and so is primarily liable to pay the debt.

(4) A sum of money lent out at interest.

principum placita [Roman law] The enactments of constitutions of the emperors, e.g. edicts, decrees, instructions to officials. "What the emperor determines has the force of a statute."

priority Precedence; the right to enforce a claim in preference to others.

(1) Mortgages. If there is more than one mortgage (*q.v.*) over land and the value of the land when sold is not enough to pay them all, the order in which they are paid will depend on their priority. If the mortgage affects a legal estate in land with unregistered title and is made after 1925, the priority of the first mortgagee is protected by entitlement to the title deeds (Law of Property Act 1925 s.85(1)). Priority of other legal mortgages of land with unregistered title is governed by the order of their registration as land charges (Law of Property Act 1925 s.97). Further, s.4(5) of the Land Charges Act 1972 provides that an unregistered land charge of this type is void against a purchaser (including a later mortgagee), but it is unclear which of these conflicting rules has precedence. If one mortgage is protected by deposit of the title deeds and the other is not, and the title to the land is not registered, the first in time prevails except where the first mortgagee is guilty of gross negligence with the title deeds or the first mortgagee is equitable and the second legal and the doctrine of

notice (*q.v.*) applies. Mortgages of land with registered title rank between themselves in the order shown on the register (Land Registration Act 2002 s.48). See LAND REGISTRATION.

(2) Where there are successive assignments of a chose in action (*q.v.*) (e.g. a debt) or dealings with an equitable interest in land, priority is governed by the order in which written notice is given by the assignee to the other party to the action or the trustees, as appropriate (Law of Property Act 1925 s.136; the rule in *Dearle v Hall*).

(3) The priority of payments from a deceased person's insolvent estate, or on bankruptcy or the winding up of a company or receivership. See PREFERENTIAL PAYMENTS.

(4) Certain rights may be claimed from a priority date. For example a patent granted for an invention is valid from the date of application known as the priority date.

priority notice A person in whose favour an interest which is registrable as a land charge is about to be created can enter a priority notice at the Land Charges Registry. This has the effect that, if the interest is duly registered in time, the registration is effective from the date the interest was created (Land Charges Act 1972 s.11).

prisons Places to intern individuals as punishment for the commission of a criminal offence and where the individual will be deprived of their liberty and other personal freedoms. Most of the law relating to prisons can be found in the Prison Act 1952. This Act describes the prison authorities and their general duties. It also contains details relating to the administration of the system and the way in which prisoners are held.

The Home Secretary has general control over prisons and is empowered to make further rules regulating them under the Prison Act 1952.

prison breach The offence of escaping lawful custody by force. See also ESCAPE.

prison mutiny An offence under s.1 of the Prison Security Act 1992, where two or more prisoners, while on the premises of any prison engage in conduct which is intended to further a common purpose of overthrowing lawful authority in that prison.

privacy The European Convention on Human Rights, given effect in domestic law by the Human Rights Act 1998, contains, in art.8, provision for the protection of personal privacy. See, e.g. *Douglas and others v Hello! Ltd* [2003] 3 All E.R. 996. A limited right to privacy in photographs and films is contained in the Copyright, Designs and Patents Act 1988 s.85 and to privacy in data in the Data Protection Act 1998. See DATA PROTECTION; DATABASES.

private company A registered company under the Companies Acts which is not a public company (*q.v.*). It may be registered as a limited or unlimited liability company. There is no minimum share capital requirement and a private company may have only one member and one director. It is an offence for a private company to offer its shares to the public. See COMPANY.

private defence A person may use such force as is necessary in the circumstances in protection of himself, another or property. Also known as the defence of self-defence.

private finance initiative (PFI) PFI contracts are essentially contracts for the provision of services not assets. The private sector funds the construction of the asset and is not paid until the asset is completed. It then recovers its costs and a profit element via the provision of services to the public sector body, e.g. building maintenance, car parking, catering, security, etc.

Public bodies seek "value for money" and in assessing whether to proceed with a PFI option rather than seek public funding, the private sector option must offer better value than the public sector comparator and be affordable. To improve the value for money element of proceeding with a private sector scheme, the scheme must demonstrate that risk is transferred to the private sector, so that the public body carries less risk than if it were to provide the asset itself. The idea is to encourage innovative, efficient solutions. Examples of PFI used to provide public sector services include, new schools, hospitals, prisons and social housing.

private international law [Commonly referred to as conflict of laws] The body of rules for determining questions of jurisdiction, and questions as to the selection of the appropriate law in civil cases which come to court and contain a foreign element (e.g. where the cause of action arose abroad or a party to a contract resides abroad). Its objects are to prescribe the conditions under which the court is competent to hear the case; to determine for each class of case the internal system of law by reference to which the rights of the parties must be ascertained; to specify the circumstances in which a foreign judgment can be recognised as finally deciding a case, and the enforcement of foreign judgments through the English courts.

privateers Vessels belonging to private owners which in times of war were furnished with a commission from the State, known as letters of marque (*q.v.*), empowering them to carry on war against the enemy, and to capture enemy vessels and property. Privateering is abolished (Declaration of Paris 1856).

privatorum conventio juri publico non derogat [An agreement between private persons does not derogate from the public right]

privatum commodum publico cedit [Private good yields to public good]

privatum incommodum publico bono pensatur [Private loss is compensated by public good]

privilege An exceptional right, immunity or exemption belonging to a person by virtue of status or office, e.g. the immunity from arrest of diplomats or Members of Parliament.

(1) In defamation, where a statement is shown to be privileged, this will be a defence. A statement which is defamatory is privileged as follows:
   (i) A statement is absolutely privileged, in that no action will succeed, even if the statement was made with malice (*q.v.*) if made in the course of judicial proceedings; in proceedings in Parliament; or in advising the Sovereign on affairs of state;
   (ii) A statement has the benefit of qualified privilege unless it was made with malice if made in the discharge of a public or private duty, or where there is a legitimate common interest in the subject matter of the statement shared between the defendant and the person or persons to whom the words were published.

(2) In the law of evidence, privilege can be used as reason not to give certain evidence. The following matters are generally protected from disclosure on the grounds of privilege:
   (i) communications between solicitor and client where the dominant purpose of their creation was for the litigation in question;
   (ii) title deeds, etc. of a stranger to the action, in criminal proceedings only ;
   (iii) matrimonial communications and whether intercourse has taken place, in criminal proceedings only;
   (iv) self-incriminating evidence;
   (v) official communications of state, if their disclosure is contrary to the public interest;
   (vi) details of what was said, who voted etc. in parliament (unless leave is granted by Parliament).

(3) Rights and immunities arising out of the law and custom of Parliament claimed by the Houses of Parliament and their members to enable their

functions to be carried out effectively and to safeguard them from outside interference, for example an MP's privilege of freedom of speech.

(4) In Law of Property Act 1925 s.1(2)(a) (legal interests in land), a profit à prendre (*q.v.*), and any other right in land known to law, other than a rentcharge (*q.v.*).

Privileges, Committee on Standards and A Parliamentary select committee (*q.v.*) which investigates complaints of breaches of Parliamentary privilege.

Privileges, Joint Committee on A joint committee of both Houses of Parliament set up to investigate matters of parliamentary privilege.

privilegium clericale [Benefit of clergy] (*q.v.*)

privilegium non valet contra rempublicam [A privilege avails not against the state]

privity (1) Privity of contract. The doctrine of privity of contract states that, a contract cannot usually give rights or impose obligations on anyone who is not a party to the contract. See now Contracts (Rights of Third Parties) Act 1999. See THIRD PARTY.

(2) Privity of estate is the relationship between a landlord and a tenant who holds directly from him (not, e.g. between a landlord and sub-tenant). It enables an action to be brought to enforce covenants between any landlord or tenant, whether or not they were parties to the lease, if the breach of covenant occurred while the party in question held his interest in the lease.

(3) With knowledge and consent. For example s.503 of the Merchant Shipping Act 1894 formerly limited the amounts that the owners of a ship may be liable to pay in compensation for loss of life or personal injury, or loss or damage to goods, occurring on board their ship without their actual fault or privity.

privy One who is party to, or had a share or interest in something.

Privy Council The principal council of the Crown. The members are not limited in number and are appointed by the Crown on the advice of the Prime Minister, and include distinguished politicians, peers, churchmen, British ambassadors and senior judges. Members hold the title "Right Honourable". The functions of the Council are far fewer than in the past, and the Council seldom meets as a whole. Its main function is to formally approve documents put to it by its own committees, ministers or government departments. The Queen makes Orders in Council (*q.v.*) on the advice of the Council, and the Council is present when new ministers accept office. There are various committees of the Privy Council, of which the most important is the Judicial Committee (*q.v.*). Once the Constitutional Reform Act 2005 comes into force the Privy Council's judicial role will be transferred to the Supreme Court (*q.v.*).

Privy Purse A sum of money for the use of the monarch and the royal family and household which is not part of the Civil List (*q.v.*). The money comes largely from the income of the Duchy of Lancaster and the Duchy of Cornwall when this is not held by the Prince of Wales.

Privy Seal A seal used by the Crown, mainly as authority to the Lord Chancellor to affix the Great Seal (*q.v.*) to documents. Its use was abolished in 1884; since when the office of Lord Privy Seal (*q.v.*) has been a purely honorary one.

prize Ships and goods captured from an enemy at sea, and aircraft captured from an enemy anywhere. In the case of ships and goods captured at sea, the prize belongs to the Crown. The Prize Act 1948 abolished the prerogative right to make grants of prize money to captors of prize, and to grant prize bounty (a share of the prize).

prize courts Courts specially constituted to decide questions of maritime capture in times of war according to international law. The jurisdiction of the British

Prize Court is set out in the Prize Acts 1864 to 1944. It is exercised by the Queen's Bench Division of the High Court (*q.v.*). Appeals from the Queen's Bench lie to the Judicial Committee of the Privy Council (*q.v.*) (Supreme Court Act 1981 s.27 and s.16(2)).

prize fight A fight between two contestants with ungloved fists until one of them can fight no more. The fight is illegal, and the contestants are guilty of assault (*R. v Coney* (1882) 8 Q.B.D. 534). If one of the contestants dies, the survivor is guilty of manslaughter (*q.v.*).

pro bono Free. Used to denote the giving of free legal advice and services.

pro confesso [As if conceded]

pro forma [As a matter of form] Often refers to a standard document which can be adapted to suit particular circumstances.

pro hac vice [For this occasion] An appointment which is for a particular occasion only.

pro indiviso [As undivided]

pro interesse suo [As to his interest]

pro rata [In proportion]

pro tanto [For so much; to that extent]

probabilities, balance of See PROOF.

probate The legal process of dealing with the estate of a deceased person and distributing property under a valid will. The grant of probate confirms the authority of the executor which derives from the will (*q.v.*).
It is a certificate granted by the Family Division of the High Court of Justice to the effect that the will of a certain person has been proved and registered in the court and that administration of that person's effects has been granted to the executor proving the will. A copy of the will, so far as it is valid, is bound up in the certificate.
Probate may be granted either in common form or solemn form. In the straightforward case, the executor applies for probate to the Probate Registry (*q.v.*). Probate in solemn form is only used when there is likely to be a dispute as to the validity of the will or the right to administer. The person seeking to establish the validity of the will commences an action against the person challenging its validity. The procedure is governed by the Civil Procedure Rules Pt 57 and Practice Direction 57.

Probate, Divorce and Admiralty Division The Division of the High Court of Justice which exercised jurisdiction in matters formerly within the exclusive domain of the Court of Probate (*q.v.*), the Court for Divorce and Matrimonial Causes and the Court of Admiralty (see Judicature Act 1925 s.4(3)). See ADMIRAL.
It has been renamed the Family Division. Admiralty and prize jurisdiction have been transferred to the Queen's Bench Division. Probate (other than non-contentious or common form probate business) has been transferred to the Chancery Division. Non-contentious probate has been transferred, together with family work, to the Family Division (Administration of Justice Act 1970 ss.1–2, as amended by the Supreme Court Act 1981).

probate duty Formerly a stamp duty on the grant of probate assessed on the value of the personal property (Customs and Inland Revenue Act 1881). Replaced initially by estate duty (*q.v.*) and now by inheritance tax (*q.v.*).

probate registry The office (the principal registry of the Family Division, which also has a number of district registries and sub-registries) which deals with the issue of grants of probate and letters of administration and the issue of caveats (*q.v.*) and citations (*q.v.*) and standing searches (*q.v.*).

probation orders Renamed initially as community rehabilitation orders and subsequently community orders (*q.v.*). See also COMMUNITY SENTENCE.

procedendo A writ which was formerly issued to move a case back to a lower court from the High Court or to restore an order of a lower court.

procedure The mode or form of conducting judicial proceedings, civil or criminal. For civil cases, see the Civil Procedure Rules 1998. In cases involving a foreign element, procedure is governed by the *lex fori* (*q.v.*) (see *Leroux v Brown* (1852) 12 C.B. 801). For criminal cases, see the Criminal Procedure Rules 2005 (*q.v.*).

process A form of proceeding taken in a court of justice for the purpose of giving compulsory effect to its jurisdiction. An originating process is the form used to begin proceedings. Under the Civil Procedure Rules 1998 these forms are referred to as claim forms.

processing (data) The Data Protection Act 1998 sets out certain key principles (the data protection principles) which apply to the processing of personal data (*q.v.*). For the purposes of the Act processing is defined as obtaining, recording or holding the information or data or carrying out any operation or set of operations on the information or data. This includes the organisation, adaption or alteration of the information or data; the retrieval, consultation or use of the information or data; the disclosure of the information or data by transmission, dissemination or otherwise making available; or the alignment, combination, blocking, erasure or destruction of the information or data. See PERSONAL DATA; SENSITIVE PERSONAL DATA.

proclamation A declaration under the authority of the Sovereign, with the advice of the Privy Council (*q.v.*), having the force of law. In modern times, Royal proclamation is used, e.g. to summon, dissolve or prorogue Parliament, to declare a state of emergency and to declare war or peace. The proclamation is generally authorised by Order in Council (*q.v.*). A copy or extract from the proclamation must be certified by the clerk to the Council or a councillor. No new offence can be created by proclamation, but the Sovereign can by proclamation warn the people against breaches of the law (Case of Proclamations (1610)).

proctors (1) In the Ecclesiastical, Admiralty, Probate, Divorce and Matrimonial Courts, proctors discharged duties similar to those of solicitors and attorneys in other courts. By the Judicature Acts 1873 and 1875, proctors were entitled to be treated as solicitors of the Supreme Court. The proctor was appointed by written proxy signed by the client.

(2) Elected representatives of the clergy and some universities to attend the Convocation of the Church of England.

procuration The action of taking care of or acting as agent e.g. signature by procuration. The abbreviations "per pro.", "per proc." or "p.p." following a signature on a bill of exchange (*q.v.*) indicate that the signatory signs only as an agent and has limited authority to bind his principal. The person taking the bill should therefore require proof of the agent's authority. The signature binds the principal only so far as the agent has authority and does not make the agent personally liable (Bills of Exchange Act 1882 ss.25, 26).

procurator [Roman law] An agent appointed by a mandate to act for another in a single, or in all, actions. Appointment was generally informal. He might be appointed under any conditions or arrangements; no special words were needed. The procurator superseded the cognitor (*q.v.*).

Procurator-General The Treasury Solicitor (*q.v.*).

procure (1) The procuring of something, e.g. where a person procures or induces another to breach a contract. This is a tort (*q.v.*) against the injured third party.

(2) Procuring an office. It is an offence under the Representation of the People Act 1983, to procure an office for a voter to induce the voter to vote in a certain way at a local or Parliamentary election (ibid. s.113).

prodigus [Roman law] A prodigal; a person who cannot be trusted to look after his own property. A curator (*q.v.*) would be appointed to look after the property.

product liability (1) The liability in tort of producers, own-brand retailers and importers in relation to defective goods (see the Consumer Protection Act 1987 implementing the EC Directive on Product Liability 85/374).

(2) The liability in contract of a seller or other supplier of goods in relation to defective goods (see the implied terms in contracts for the Sale of Goods Act 1979; Supply of Goods and Services Act 1982).

professional diligence The standard of special skill and care which a trader (*q.v.*) may reasonably be expected to exercise towards consumers which is commensurate with either (a) honest market practice in the trader's field of activity, or (b) the general principle of good faith in the trader's field of activity (Consumer Protection from Unfair Trading Regulations 2008 reg.2).

professional principles These are that persons authorised to act, for example, as solicitors, barristers, patent attorneys or law costs draftsmen should: act with independence and integrity; maintain proper standards of work; act in the best interests of their clients; when exercising rights of audience or conducting litigation, comply with their duty to the court to act with independence in the interests of justice; should keep the affairs of their clients confidential (Legal Services Act 2007 s.1(3)).

profit à prendre The right, which may attach to the ownership of the land or be in common, to take from the land of another some thing which is capable of ownership. Common rights include pasture; fishing (piscary); turf or peat; or wood (estovers). Profits attaching to ownership of land may include the above and, in addition, rights to mines and minerals, crops and sporting rights.

Profits attaching to the ownership of land are acquired in similar manner to easements (*q.v.*).

prohibited steps order An order that no step which could be taken by a parent in meeting his or her parental responsibility (*q.v.*) for a child, and which is of a kind specified in the order, shall be taken by any person without the consent of the court, Children Act 1989 s.8. Such orders, together with specific issues orders (*q.v.*), etc. are now used in practice instead of wardship (*q.v.*) proceedings.

prohibiting order An order issued by the High Court and directed at a lower Court, tribunal, public authority or body which is susceptible to judicial review, to forbid that Court, tribunal, authority or body from acting outside its jurisdiction or contrary to law. Such an order is concerned with future decisions of the Court, tribunal, authority or body, as a method of control. See JUDICIAL REVIEW.

prohibition A writ formerly issued out of the High Court to restrain an inferior court from exercising its powers. The writ of prohibition was replaced by the order of prohibition (Supreme Court Act 1981 s.29) to be used not only to restrain an inferior court or tribunal from exceeding its jurisdiction, or acting contrary to the rules of natural justice, but also to control a minister or public authority (*q.v.*) in the exercise of their judicial or quasi-judicial functions. For the modern procedure, see JUDICIAL REVIEW; PROHIBITING ORDER.

prohibition notice A notice is issued by an inspector from the Health and Safety Executive served upon a person who, in the opinion of the inspector, is responsible for any activity to which health and safety enactments apply and which, if carried on in contravention of such enactments, will involve a risk of serious personal injury. The notice, which may take effect immediately or after a specified period, must set out the prohibited activities (Health and Safety at Work, etc. Act 1974 ss.22, 23 and 53 as amended by the Consumer Protection Act 1987 s.3 Sch.3). An appeal against a notice lies to an employment tribunal (*q.v.*). See IMPROVEMENT NOTICE.

prolucutor A speaker.

promise The expression of an intention to do or forbear from some act. In order to have legal effect and thus take effect as a contract, it must be contained in a deed (*q.v.*) in which case it is described as a covenant, or be in consideration (*q.v.*) of an act to be done (normally the payment of money) by the party to whom the promise is made. See BREACH OF PROMISE.

promissory note An unconditional promise in writing made by one person to another, signed by the maker, engaging to pay on demand, or at a fixed or determinable future time, a sum of money certain to, or to the order of, a specified person or to bearer (Bills of Exchange Act 1882 s.83(1)).

promoter (1) Anciently, the persons who laid themselves out to bring, as common informers (*q.v.*), penal and popular actions.
(2) A person who introduces a private Act of Parliament.
(3) The person who is active in the setting up of a company. As such a promoter owes certain duties to that company.
(4) A person who arranges a sporting event.

proof (1) The evidence which satisfies the court as to the truth of a fact. Generally the burden of proof lies on the party who asserts the truth of the issue in dispute. If that party adduces sufficient evidence to raise a presumption (*q.v.*) that what is claimed is true, the burden passes to the other party, who will fail unless sufficient evidence is adduced to rebut the presumption. In civil cases, the court makes its decision on the "balance of probabilities". In criminal cases, a case must be proved "beyond reasonable doubt".
(2) To prove a debt is to establish that a debt is due from a bankrupt's estate.
(3) To prove a will is to obtain probate of it.
(4) Proof means the standard of strength of spirituous liquors (Alcoholic Liquors Duties Act 1979 ss.2, 4).

proper law of a contract The system of law by which a contract containing an international element is to be interpreted. See PRIVATE INTERNATIONAL LAW.

property (1) That which is capable of ownership, whether real or personal, tangible or intangible.
(2) A right of ownership, e.g. the property in goods (see Sale of Goods Act 1979 s.2(1)). Property may be general, i.e. that which every owner has, or special. Special property means that the subject-matter is incapable of absolute ownership (such as a wild animal) or that it can only be treated in a limited way (e.g. under a bailment (*q.v.*)).
(3) Intellectual property (*q.v.*).

property adjustment orders Orders made by the court when granting decrees of divorce, nullity or judicial separation. They may provide for transfer or settlement of property or variation of a settlement, Matrimonial Causes Act 1973 s.24. See FINANCIAL PROVISION ORDERS.

property misdescription See TRADE DESCRIPTION.

proportionality A principle which requires a reasonable relationship between the legitimate objective sought by law and the means used to achieve that objective.
(1) The principle of proportionality is a general principle of European Community (*q.v.*) law and the European Convention on Human Rights (*q.v.*). It means that interference with, for example, Convention rights (*q.v.*), must be no more than is necessary in order to achieve a legitimate end. If an interference is

disproportionate then it will not be necessary and will be unlawful. Proportionality is also a principle used to interpret alleged infringements of national written constitutions.

(2) In judicial review, exercises of discretionary powers where there is no reasonable relationship between the objective sought and the means used, or where punishments imposed by administrative bodies or inferior courts are wholly out of proportion to the relevant misconduct may be quashed. See also LEGAL CERTAINTY; EQUALITY.

(3) The concept of proportionality is contained in the Civil Procedure Rules 1998 which govern the conduct of civil litigation. Rule 1 states that the overriding objective (*q.v.*) is to deal with cases justly, and this includes dealing with cases in ways that are proportionate to the sums involved, the importance of the case, the complexity of the issues and the financial position of each party. See OVERRIDING OBJECTIVE.

propositus The person by reference to whom a relationship is ascertained, e.g. the children of A, A being the *propositus*.

propound a will To commence an action to obtain probate in solemn form. See PROBATE.

proprietary rights Rights in property; rights of ownership.

proprietas nuda; proprietas deducto usufructu [Roman law] Bare ownership; ownership without profit.

prorogation The ending of a session of Parliament by use of the royal prerogative (which is exercised on the advice of the Prime Minister). Most bills lapse on prorogation and must be re-introduced in the new session, but in certain circumstances bills may be carried over, as, e.g. the Financial Services and Markets Bill 1999/2000.

prosecution right to stand by The prosecution has the right to require a juror to "stand by" if they do not feel that he is sufficiently competent or impartial to secure a fair trial. It is only when the jurors on the relevant panel have been exhausted that it is necessary to challenge for cause. See CHALLENGE OF JURORS.

prosecutor A person who commences criminal proceedings on behalf of the Crown. It may be the Crown Prosecution Service (*q.v.*) or the victim or, in grave crimes, the Director of Public Prosecutions (*q.v.*).

prospectus A document setting out in the nature and objects of an issue of shares or debentures by a company (*q.v.*), and inviting the public to subscribe to the issue (the term includes any advertisement, notice circular or other invitation). A copy must be filed with the Registrar of Companies. Where such securities are offered to the public for the first time and there is no application for admission to the Official List (*q.v.*), then the prospectus must comply with the Prospectus Regulations 2005 which implement the Prospectus Directive (2003/71) and require each prospectus to be approved by the Financial Services Authority (or the equivalent competent authority from any other EU Member State) before any offer of securities is made to the public.

prostitution The act of a person (A) who offers or provides sexual services to another person in return for payment or a promise of payment to (A) or a third person (s.51(2) of the Sexual Offences Act 2003). For example it is an offence for a prostitute to loiter or solicit in a street or public place for prostitution (Street Offences Act 1959 s.1). It is an offence for a person to intentionally cause or incite another person to become a prostitute (Sexual Offences Act 2003 s.52), or intentionally control any of the activities of another person relating to that person's prostitution, in any part of the world for financial gain for him or herself or a third party (s.53). See KERB CRAWLING; SEXUAL OFFENCES.

protected shorthold tenancy A protected tenancy (*q.v.*) originally created by the Rent Act 1977 which was granted on or after November 28, 1980, and before January 15, 1989, for a specified term of not less than one year or more than five years and which satisfied certain conditions set out in the Housing Act 1980, now repealed. See ASSURED SHORTHOLD TENANCY.

protected tenancy A tenancy (*q.v.*) within the Rent Act 1977 under which the tenant had security of tenure (*q.v.*). A tenancy entered into on or after January 15, 1989 cannot generally be a protected tenancy as they have been replaced by assured tenancies (*q.v.*). See Housing Act 1988 s.34(5) and Housing Act 1996.

protection (1) See COURT OF PROTECTION.

(2) Emergency protection order. A court order made under s.44 of the Children Act 1989 which enables a child who is at risk of suffering significant harm to be taken to, or kept at, a place of safety.

(3) Protection order. An order under the Licensing Act 2003 granted to a person who proposes to apply for a transfer of a licence if the justices are satisfied that he is a person to whom it is proper to transfer the licence. The order gives the applicant authority equal to that under the last licence. Unless superseded by the transfer or removal of the licence or further protection order, it lasts until the conclusion of the second licensing session after the date of the order.

protective award An award made by an employment tribunal (*q.v.*) on the ground that an employer has failed to consult the appropriate representatives of any employee who is affected by a redundancy situation. Appropriate representatives include representatives of any trade union recognised by the employer with regard to those employees or, where there is no recognised trade union, any representatives elected for the purpose of consultation. By virtue of a protective award an employer is obliged to pay remuneration to the affected employees for a specified period (Trade Union and Labour Relations (Consolidation) Act 1992 ss.188–190 as amended). See REDUNDANCY; REDUNDANCY CONSULTATION.

protective trust A trust for the life, or lesser period, of a beneficiary (*q.v.*) which is determinable on bankruptcy (*q.v.*) or some other event, at which point a discretionary trust arises for the maintenance of the beneficiary and his family, Trustee Act 1925 s.33. A person may not make a settlement determinable on his own bankruptcy.

protector of a settlement A person whose consent is required to the barring of an entail (*q.v.*) of real or personal property. He is either the person appointed by the settlement or the person entitled to a prior interest in possession. If the protector's consent is not obtained, a base fee is created, Fines and Recoveries Act 1833 s.22. The protector's consent is also required to enlarge a base fee (*q.v.*) into a fee simple (*q.v.*).

protectorate, British An area of which the land does not belong to the Crown, but whose foreign relations are subject to its control. The arrangement is established by agreement by treaty, grant, capitulation, etc. No protectorates now remain.

protest (1) An express declaration by a person doing an act that the act is not to give rise to an implication which might otherwise arise, e.g. that payment of money implies that there existed a debt.

(2) A solemn declaration by a Notary Public (*q.v.*) stating that he has demanded acceptance or payment of a bill, and that it has been refused, with the reasons, if any, given by the drawee or acceptor for the dishonour. A protest is only required for a foreign bill, Bills of Exchange Act 1882 s.51. The purpose is to give satisfactory evidence of the dishonour to the drawer or other antecedent party.

(3) A written statement by the master of a ship, attested by a notary public or consul (*q.v.*), of the circumstances whereby an injury occurred to his ship or cargo.

(4) A payment under protest is where A makes a payment on demand, but denies that it is owed by him, intending to recover it later.

prothonotary A principal notary; a chief clerk, similar to the modern master. See MASTER OF THE SUPREME COURT.

protocols (1) The records of the proceedings of an international conference, or drafts, signed by the delegates to form a basis for the final document.

(2) Pre-action protocols. Steps required to be taken by litigants under the Civil Procedure Rules 1998 (*q.v.*) prior to the commencement of proceedings. The aim of these steps is to increase openness between the parties in order to encourage early settlement. Sanctions including costs orders can be made against any party who fails to comply with a pre-action protocol. Specific protocols apply to different kinds of case so that there are separate protocols for personal injury, clinical negligence, construction disputes, defamation, professional negligence, judicial review, disease claims, housing/disrepair claims and debt claims. Many cases are not governed by a specific protocol but it is considered good practice to follow the spirit of the protocols in all cases.

province A geographical area. A country may be divided into provinces. The Church of England divides England into the provinces of Canterbury and York under the jurisdiction of an Archbishop. Each province is subdivided into dioceses.

Provisional Orders Orders made by a Minister, under statutory powers, on the application of a local authority or statutory undertaking, in place of private bills taking effect when confirmed by Act of Parliament. Replaced by special procedure orders, see Statutory Orders (Special Procedure) Act 1945.

provisional statement Any individual or business who is engaged in the construction, extension or alteration of premises or is about to embark on such a project where the premises are to be used for a licensable activity such as the sale of alcohol or gambling, can make an application for a provisional statement under ss.29–32 of the Licensing Act 2003 or Gambling Act 2005 respectively. An application should be made to the relevant licensing authority (*q.v.*) on a prescribed form and a fee is payable. The application must also include certain documents and must be advertised. Those about to embark on construction work can get some assurances by the granting of a provisional statement as to their future potential trading conditions and the prospects of any application for a premises licence in the future.

See PREMISES LICENCE; LICENSABLE ACTIVITIES.

proviso A clause in a document qualifying an earlier provision. It customarily commences with the words, "provided always that".

provocation Words or conduct which are sufficient to prevent the exercise of reason and which would temporarily deprive a reasonable person of his self-control.

Provocation of violence is an offence under s.4 of the Public Order Act 1986. Provocation negates the existence of malice and so reduces the crime of murder to manslaughter (*q.v.*).

Where there is evidence of provocation, the question of whether the provocation was sufficient to cause the reasonable man to act as the defendant did is left to the jury (Homicide Act 1957 s.3). In *R. v Camplin* [1978] A.C. 705, it was held that the "reasonable man" to be considered is one of the same age and sex as the accused, but in other respects sharing such of the accused's characteristics as would affect the gravity of the provocation to him. In *AG for*

Jersey v Holley [2005] the Privy Council decided that *R. v Smith* [2001] 1 A.C. 146 had been wrongly decided and that the defendant's mental characteristics could not be taken into account when determining the defence of provocation.

Provost-Marshal An officer appointed by army, navy or air force officers to deal with offences committed by persons subject to military law, to arrest offenders and detain them for trial by court-martial (*q.v.*).

proxy A lawfully appointed agent; a person appointed to vote for another. A member of a company is entitled to appoint another person as his proxy to exercise all or any of his rights to attend, to speak and to vote at a meeting of the company, see the Companies Act 2006 s.324. See VOTING.

prudentium responsa [Roman law] The answers of the wise. The opinions of the jurisconsults, restricted by the Law of Citation (A.D. 426) to Papinian, Paul, Gaius, Ulpian and Modestinus.

pseudo-photograph An image which appears to be a photograph but is in fact made from a number of images modified by computer. An offence is committed where the impression created by such a photograph is that the subject is a child and the image is indecent. Protection of Children Act 1978 s.1 as amended by the Criminal Justice and Public Order Act 1994 s.84 and Sexual Offences Act 2003 s.139.

psychopathic disorder A persistent disorder or disability of mind (whether or not including significant impairment of intelligence) which results in abnormally aggressive or seriously irresponsible conduct on the part of the person concerned (Mental Health Act 1983 s.1(2) and s.145(1)). See MENTAL DISORDER; MENTAL IMPAIRMENT.

pubertas [Roman law] The legal age of puberty, 14 for males and 12 for females. *Plena pubertas* was reached at 18, when the body was regarded as fully developed.

pubertati proxime [Roman law] Children at the stage prior to puberty.

public assembly See PUBLIC MEETING.

public authorities (1) Bodies or persons exercising functions for public benefit rather than private profit, such as local authorities (*q.v.*).
   (2) In European law, the state and regional and local authorities (EC Directive 80/723, art.2, para.1).
   A public authority is a body that is bound to act compatibly with Convention rights (*q.v.*) by virtue of the Human Rights Act 1998 s.6(1). Section 6 provides that it is unlawful for a public authority to act in a way that is incompatible with Convention rights unless its primary legislation means that it could not have acted differently (s.6(2)(a)) or it was enforcing or giving effect to a provision of or made under primary legislation which cannot be read or given effect in a way that is compatible with the Convention rights (s.6(2)(b)). A public authority is not defined apart from the explicit inclusion of the courts and tribunals (s.6(3)(a)) and "any person certain of whose functions are functions of a public nature" (s.6(3)(b)). It is clear that there are two types of public authority, "pure" public authorities such as local government which must act compatibly with the Convention rights in respect of all of its functions and "hybrid" public authorities which have some public and some private functions. In respect of their private functions they are not caught by the duty in s.6(1). An example of a hybrid public authority given by the government in the passage of the Bill was Railtrack.

public benefit For the purposes of the Charities Act 2006, unlike the common law, there is no presumption that particular purposes are for the benefit of the public (ibid. s.3). The Charity Commission (*q.v.*) is charged under the Act with the duty to provide guidance on the requirement for a charitable purpose to have a public benefit.

public company A company limited by shares or limited by guarantee and having a share capital whose certificate of incorporation states that it is a public company. It must also comply with the legal requirements for registration as a public company, see Companies Act 2006 s.4. Some public companies are also listed companies (*q.v.*) whose shares have been admitted to the Official List (*q.v.*) and are traded on the Stock Exchange. See COMPANY; STOCK EXCHANGE.

public document A document made so that the public may make use of it, e.g. a register kept by a public officer or a judicial record. It is admissible in evidence if there was a judicial or quasi judicial duty to inquire, it was prepared by a public officer for public purposes and it was intended that the public should make reference to it. If admissible in evidence, the original or a copy is produced, or a certificate as proof of its contents.

public examination See EXAMINATION, PUBLIC.

Public Guardian An office established under the Mental Capacity Act 2005 s.57, with its holder appointed by the Lord Chancellor (*q.v.*). The officeholder's functions include establishing and maintaining a register of lasting powers of attorney (*q.v.*), directing a Court of Protection Visitor (*q.v.*) to visit a donee of a lasting power of attorney and reporting to the Court of Protection (*q.v.*) on such matters relating to proceedings under the Act as the Court requires (see ibid. s.58). The Public Guardian Board scrutinises the work of the Public Guardian and reports to the Lord Chancellor.

Public Guardian, Office of (OPG) An executive agency, part of the Ministry of Justice, it was established in 2007 and replaced the Public Guardianship Office (*q.v.*). Under the terms of the Mental Capacity Act 2005 the OPG works in conjunction with the Court of Protection (*q.v.*) and the judiciary to support those with capacity issues.

Public Guardianship Office (PGO) The PGO replaced the Public Trust Office (*q.v.*) in the area of mental health work. It oversaw the work of receivers appointed by the Court of Protection (*q.v.*) to deal with the financial affairs of those who lacked mental capacity. See now PUBLIC GUARDIAN, OFFICE OF.

public-house Premises licensed for the sale of intoxicating liquor for consumption on the premises. No one may insist that the publican serve them and this position should be contrasted with that of the innkeeper (*q.v.*).

public interest immunity This replaces the concept of Crown privilege (*q.v.*) and means that, in considering whether to allow evidence to be admitted, the court must balance the public interest which is served by maintaining confidentiality against the interests of justice in ensuring that the best evidence is available to the court.

public lending right A scheme whereby authors receive payments in respect of loans of their books from public libraries (Public Lending Right Act 1979 and Public Lending Right Scheme 1982 as amended).

public meeting There is no general definition of this term. An open air meeting in a public place attended by two or more people is a "public assembly" within the terms of s.16 of the Public Order Act 1986 (as amended by the Anti-social Behaviour Act 2003 s.57). No prior permission is required to hold such a meeting but the police may impose conditions as to the size, timing, etc. of such a meeting in order to prevent disorder, damage, disruption or intimidation (ibid. s.14).

There is no power to impose conditions on indoor public meetings although the police common law powers to take action to prevent a breach of the peace (*q.v.*), including their power to enter private premises, would allow them to take action in appropriate cases to limit the numbers, etc.

Public access to local authority meetings is regulated by the Public Bodies (Admission to Meetings) Act 1960 and the Local Government (Access to Information) Act 1985.

Newspaper reports of public meetings enjoy qualified privilege in the law of defamation (*q.v.*) (Defamation Act 1996 s.15). See VIOLENT DISORDER.

public mischief At common law, a misdemeanour (*q.v.*) committed by a person who wilfully interferes with the course of justice by an act or attempt which tends to prejudice the community. The offence no longer exists, since it was more recently regarded as part of the offence of conspiracy, which was abolished by the Criminal Law Act 1977. Now, such conduct may fall within the offence of wasting police time (Criminal Law Act 1967 s.5 as amended). See also PERVERTING THE COURSE OF JUSTICE.

public nuisance Causing damage, injury or inconvenience to the public.

An unlawful act or omission to perform a legal duty, which endangers the life, health, property, morals or comfort of the public constitutes an offence at common law.

Any person suffering damage over and above that suffered by the public at large may sue in tort for damages. See NUISANCE.

public officer (1) The holder of a public office under the Crown, or public agent who discharges any duty in which the public is interested.

(2) An officer of a company or corporation (*q.v.*), such as a director (*q.v.*).

public order The police have a prime duty to preserve the peace and have a range of common law and statutory powers to enable them to preserve public order. The major public order offences, contained in the Public Order Act 1986 ss.1–5 (as amended by the Criminal Justice and Public Order Act 1994), are riot (*q.v.*), violent disorder (*q.v.*), affray (*q.v.*), causing fear of or provocation of violence, or intentionally causing or causing harassment, alarm or distress. The Act does not, however, deal with every aspect of public order and the common law power of the police to take action to prevent a breach of the peace remains of prime importance (see, e.g. *Moss v McLachlan* [1988] I.R.L.R. 76). See also the Highways Act 1980 s.137 as amended and the common law offence of public nuisance (*q.v.*). See also HARASSMENT.

public policy In the interests of the public as a whole, so that something contrary to public policy would not be in the wider interests of society. For example certain laws may not be enforced by the court where to do so would be contrary to public policy. Certain contracts are void as being contrary to public policy, in particular those prejudicial to the married state, contracts which purport to oust the jurisdiction of the courts (although some arbitration (*q.v.*) agreements may legitimately restrict access to the courts), and contracts in restraint of trade (*q.v.*).

A court may refuse to grant a remedy on the ground that it is not in the public interest. See JUDICIAL REVIEW; PREROGATIVE WRIT.

Certain evidence may be excluded on the grounds of public policy, e.g. evidence of arbitrators of their reasoning in making an award, evidence of jurors as to their reasoning, evidence of advocates, illegally obtained evidence. See PUBLIC INTEREST IMMUNITY.

Public Prosecutor The Director of Public Prosecutions (*q.v.*). See also CROWN PROSECUTION SERVICE.

Public Records Documents deemed to be of such importance that they are placed in the custody of the Lord Chancellor and retained and preserved in the National Archives. Under the Freedom of Information Act 2000 the public have a right to access information stored as public records.

Public Trust Office Renamed the Public Guardianship Office (*q.v.*) which took over the mental health work of the Public Trust Office. The Trust functions transferred to the Official Solicitor's Office (*q.v.*). The Court Funds Office transferred to the Court Service.

publication (1) Copyright. The issue of any copyright protected work to the public (Copyright, Designs and Patents Act 1988). See COPYRIGHT.
(2) Libel or slander. The requirement that defamatory words should have been brought to the knowledge of some person other than the claimant. In criminal libel, publication to the victim is sufficient. See LIBEL; SLANDER.

publication right Any person who after the expiry of copyright protection publishes for the first time a previously unpublished work has a property right, known as publication right, equivalent to copyright (Copyright and Related Rights Regulations 1996).

publici juris [Of public right] For example, the right to light and air; flowing water.

publicity right The right of the individual to control the commercial use and exploitation of his image, voice, likeness and personality. The right is recognised in the United States of America but not in the law of England and Wales.

puis darrein continuance A plea in which the defendant pleaded some matter of defence which had arisen since the last continuance or adjournment.

puisne [Later born, or younger] A puisne judge is a High Court judge other than the Lord Chancellor, the Lord Chief Justice or the President of the Family Division (Supreme Court Act 1981 s.4(2)).

puisne mortgage A legal mortgage not protected by deposit of title deeds. It is a second or subsequent mortgage. In the case of registered land, it must be protected by an entry on the register in order to bind a registered transferee for value of the land (see Land Registration Act 2002). In the case of unregistered land, it must be registered as a Class C(i) Land Charge in order to bind a purchaser for value of the land (Land Charges Act 1972).

pupil master/mistress A barrister (*q.v.*) who is sufficiently experienced to train a student barrister as a pupil.

pupillage The period of training required in order to practise as a barrister. There are two stages of pupillage required: a first six (months), where the pupil will train under a barrister but have no rights of audience; and a second six where the pupil will still train under a barrister but will have rights of audience in all courts. It is now possible to link the two sixes together and have a 12-month pupillage. It is also possible to undertake other periods of training, e.g. working in a solicitor's office, completing a STAGE in the European Commission or undertaking some Marshalling (*q.v.*) which all count towards and result in time being taken off any pupillage requirements.

pupillus [Roman law] A person sui juris (*q.v.*), under the age of puberty, whose affairs are managed by a tutor (*q.v.*).

pur autre vie [For the life of another] See TENANT PUR AUTRE VIE.

purchase To buy something pursuant to a written or oral contract for sale.

purchase notice Where land has become incapable of reasonably beneficial use and cannot be rendered capable of such use by the carrying out of development (*q.v.*) then, in certain circumstances, the owner or a person entitled to an interest in the land may serve a purchase notice requiring the appropriate local authority to purchase his interest (Town and Country Planning Act 1990 Pt VI). See also PLANNING BLIGHT.

purchaser (1) A buyer. One who acquires something by purchase (*q.v.*).
(2) The opposite party, in a sale, to the vendor (*q.v.*) or seller.

(3) A purchaser may be further defined in statute (see, e.g. in the Law of Property Act 1925 s.205(1)(xxi)) as a purchaser in good faith for valuable consideration.

purgation The act of clearing one's name of an offence charged, either by wager of law (whereby the defendant and his supporters swear as to the truth on oath), or by combat *(q.v)* or by ordeal *(q.v).*

purpresture Inclosure *(q.v.)* or house.

purveyance The Crown's prerogative right, at an appraised price, to buy up provisions and other necessaries for the Royal Household, and of impressing horses and vehicles for the royal use.

purview The part of a statute which provides or enacts, as opposed to the preamble; the scope or policy of a statute. See ACT OF PARLIAMENT.

putative father The person alleged to be the father of an illegitimate child in proceedings for child support.

Q

Q.C. Queen's Counsel *(q.v.).*

q.v. [*Quod vide,* which see]

qua [In the capacity of; as]

quae non valeant singula, juncta juvant [Words which are of no effect alone are effective when combined]

quaelibet concessio fortissime contra donatorem interpretanda est [Every grant is to be construed as strongly as possible against the grantor]

qualified privilege See PRIVILEGE.

qualified property Rights in a chattel *(q.v.)* that do not amount to absolute ownership. See SPECIAL PROPERTY.

qualified title A title registered subject to an estate, right, or interest arising before a specified date or under a specified instrument, or otherwise particularly described in the register (see Land Registration Act 2002 s.9(4)). Qualified title will only be awarded if the registrar is of the opinion that the person's title to the estate has been established only for a limited period or is subject to certain reservations such as those mentioned above that cannot be disregarded.

qualifying club activity A qualifying club activity is a licensable activity that relates to the supply of alcohol by or on behalf of a club to a member of the club, the sale of alcohol to a guest of a member of the club and or the provision of regulated entertainment by or on behalf of a club member (Licensing Act 2003 s.1(2)). See LICENSABLE ACTIVITY; PREMISES LICENCE.

quality (1) The nature of an estate *(q.v.)* in terms of its duration.
(2) Property or attribute.
(3) Degree of excellence. For example, where a seller sells goods in the course of a business, there is an implied term that the goods will be of satisfactory quality *(q.v.)*. See Sale of Goods Act 1979 s.14(2), as amended by Sale and Supply of Goods Act 1994.

quamdiu se bene gesserit [During good behaviour]

quando acciderint [When it happens] A judgment to be levied when assets come into the hands of a personal representative in the future.

quando aliquid mandatur, mandatur et omne per quod pervenitur ad illud [When anything is authorised, everything by which it can be achieved is also authorised]

quando aliquid prohibetur fieri, prohibetur ex directo et per obliquum [Whenever anything is forbidden, it is forbidden to do it directly or indirectly]

quando duo jura in una persona concurrunt, aequum est ac si essent diversis [When two titles coincide in one person, it is the same as if they were in different persons]

quando jus domini regis et subditi concurrunt, jus regis praeferri debet [When the titles of the King and the subject coincide, the title of the King is to be preferred]

quando lex aliquid alicui concedit, concedere videtur id sine quo res ipsa esse non potest [When the law gives anything to anyone, it also gives those things without which the thing itself could not exist]

quando plus fit quam fieri debet, videtur etiam illud fieri quod faciendum est [When more is done than is required, then that which is required is considered to have been done]

quango Acronym for quasi-autonomous non-government organisation. Such an organisation is funded by the government but operates independently of it.

quantity (1) The nature of an estate (*q.v.*) in respect of its duration.
(2) See trade description.

quantum [How much] The amount of damages. See QUANTUM RAMIFACTUS.

quantum meruit [As much as he has earned] This is a remedy in quasi-contract (*q.v.*), which is available:
(1) Where one person has expressly or impliedly requested another to carry out a service without specifying remuneration, but where it is implied that a payment will be made of as much as the service is worth.
(2) If a person is committed by contract to carry out a piece of work for a lump sum, and he only carries out part of the work or carries out work different from the contract, he cannot claim under the contract, but may be able to claim on a quantum meruit (e.g. if he was unjustifiably prevented by the other party from completing the contract).
(3) When work was done and accepted under a void contract which was believed to be valid.

quantum ramifactus [The amount of damage suffered] In civil cases, reference is generally made to issues of "*quantum*" as opposed to "liability".

quantum valebant [As much as they were worth] An action analogous to quantum meruit (*q.v.*), but in relation to the value of goods supplied, without agreement as to price, under an implied promise to pay.

quarantine [40 days] (1) The period which persons coming from a country or ship in which an infectious disease is prevalent are required to wait before they are permitted to land. Animals to be exported from or imported into this country may also be subject to quarantine (see the Animal Health Act 1981).
(2) The period during which a widow was previously entitled to remain in her husband's dwelling house after his death.

quare impedit [Wherefore he hinders] An ancient writ which is brought by a person in possession of an advowson (*q.v.*) of a church and who was disturbed in his presentation of it. Abolished by the Common Law Procedure Act 1860.

quarta Antoninia or quarta d Pii [Roman law] The right of an adrogated son under puberty (adrogation being a type of adoption by agreement), if he was emancipated or disinherited (in either case without cause), or died, to receive back all the property he had brought to the adrogator or acquired for him, together with one quarter of the adrogator's property, as enacted by Antonius Pius.

quarter sessions A court comprised of a chairman, two or more justices of the peace and a jury. Such courts would convene at least four times per year to hear criminal and civil cases as well as to carry out certain administrative functions. The court was abolished in 1972 (Courts Act 1971 s.3). The legal jurisdiction of the court was transferred to the Crown Court (*q.v.*), and its administrative functions to the local authorities (*q.v.*) (ibid. ss.8, 56, Schs 1, 8–10).

quarter-days Christmas Day (December 25), Lady Day (March 25), Midsummer Day (June 24), Michaelmas Day (September 29). Different quarter days apply in Scotland.

quash To discharge or set aside, e.g. a wrongful conviction or an administrative act subject to judicial review (*q.v.*).

quashing order An order under the Civil Procedure Rules 1998 Pt 54 which may be obtained on an application for judicial review to quash a judgment, order or conviction. Such orders were previously referred to as orders of certiorari. See CERTIORARI; JUDICIAL REVIEW.

quasi [As if it were]

quasi-contract This comprehends an obligation not arising by, but similar to contract. The consent of the person bound is not required and it may be broadly said that the classes of claim recognised as quasi-contractual have little in common other than that they extend to:
"liability, not exclusively referable to any other head of law, imposed upon a particular person to pay money to another particular person on the ground of unjust benefit" (Winfield).
Examples of recognised claims include: (i) where the defendant has acquired a benefit from or by the act of the claimant; (ii) where the defendant has acquired from a third party a benefit for which he must account to the claimant; (iii) where the defendant has acquired a benefit by virtue of his own wrongful act.
See Goff and Jones, *The Law of Restitution*.

quasi-easement A right which would amount to an easement (*q.v.*) if the dominant and servient (benefited and burdened) lands were in separate ownership and occupation. Such a right may become an easement (*q.v.*) in favour of a purchaser on the sale or lease of the dominant land under the rule in *Wheeldon v Burrows* (1879) 12 Ch. D. 71, if the right was being actually exercised at the time of the transaction and was reasonably necessary to the enjoyment of the dominant land, or was continuous and apparent (visible on inspection of the land).

quasi-entail An entail (*q.v.*) created out of an estate *pur autre vie* (*q.v.*). It is not true entail, because it ends on the death of the measuring life.

quasi-estoppel Another name for equitable or promissory estoppel. See ESTOPPEL.

quasi-judicial Executive functions which involve the exercise of a discretion but require a part of the decision-making process to be conducted in a judicial manner; e.g. where a minister makes an order after considering the findings of a formal public local inquiry into a planning appeal then he is said to act quasi-judicially. See NATURAL JUSTICE.

quasi-trustee A person who, without authority, acts as a trustee (*q.v.*) and is held liable as though he were a trustee.

que estate A dominant tenement. See PRESCRIPTION.

Queen A Queen Regnant is a reigning Sovereign in her own right. A Queen Consort is the wife of the Sovereign. A Queen Dowager or Queen Mother is the widow of a deceased Sovereign.

Queen's Bench Division One of the three divisions of the High Court (*q.v.*), consisting of the Lord Chief Justice (*q.v.*) and puisne judges (*q.v.*). See Supreme Court Act 1981 s.5(l)(6), Sch.1(2).

Queen's Counsel (Q.C.) Barristers (*q.v.*) "learned in the law" who have been appointed Counsel to Her Majesty following approval by the Q.C Approval Selection Panel and recommendation by the Secretary of State for Justice. They wear silk gowns (and are sometimes referred to as "Silks"), sit within the bar and take precedence over junior barristers. A Q.C. is called a "leader" when retained to conduct a case in court with "juniors" also instructed to represent.

Queen's evidence A prisoner who, instead of being put on trial, is permitted to give evidence against others associated with him in crime, on the understanding that he will go free, is said to turn Queen's evidence. See ACCOMPLICE.

Queen's Proctor The Treasury Solicitor (*q.v.*) who represents the Crown in maritime and matrimonial cases. His main function is to intervene to show cause why a decree nisi (*q.v.*) should not be made absolute because material facts have not been disclosed (Matrimonial Causes Act 1973 ss.8, 9, 15 as amended by the Family Law Act 1996, see also s.39 of the Civil Partnership Act 2004). He shows cause by entering an appearance in the suit and filing a plea setting out his case. His assistance may be invoked by the court itself by investigating the circumstances of a case, or to argue a difficult point of law.

Queen's regulations Regulations issued by the Crown under the royal prerogative to govern discipline in the Army, Navy and Air Force.

Queen's Remembrancer An officer who performed duties connected with recovery of penalties and debts due to the Crown; kept the documents relating to the passing of lands to and from the Crown and had functions in connection with English Bills. The present duties include certain functions connected with selection of sheriffs (*q.v.*), the swearing in of the Lord Mayor of London, and proceedings by the Crown on the Revenue side of the Queen's Bench Division. Today the office is held by the Senior Master of the Supreme Court (*q.v.*) (Supreme Court Act 1981 s.89).

querela Any civil proceedings in any court. See AUDITA QUERELA.

qui facit per alium facit per se [He who acts through another is deemed to act in person] A principal is liable for the acts of his agents.

qui haeret in litera haeret in cortice [He who sticks in the letter sticks in the bark] Meaning a person who does not get to the substance or the meaning.

qui jure suo utitur neminem laedit [He who exercises his legal right harms no one]

qui jussu judicis aliquod fecerit non videtur dolo malo fecisse quia parere necesse est [He who does anything by command of a judge will not be supposed to have acted from an improper motive; because there an obligation to obey]

qui omne dicit nihil excludit [He who says everything excludes nothing]

qui per alium facit, per seipsum facere videtur [He who does anything by another is deemed to have done it himself]

qui prior est tempore potior est jure [He who is first in time has the strongest claim in law]

qui sentit commodum sentire debet et onus; et e contra [He who enjoys the benefit ought also to bear the burden; and vice versa]

qui tacet consentire videtur [He who is silent is deemed to consent] When people are speaking on even terms, and an accusation is made, the fact that the person charged does nothing to deny an accusation is some evidence that he admits its truth.

qui tam pro domino rege quam pro si ipso in hac parte sequitur [Who sues on behalf of our Lord the King as well as for himself] An action by an informer. See PENAL ACTION.

qui vult decipi decipiatur [If a man wants to be deceived, then let him be deceived]

quia emptores [Because purchasers] The Statute of 1290 which commences with these words. The effect was that every free man was at liberty to sell his lands, but that the purchaser would hold from his vendor's lord and not from his vendor, thus abolishing subinfeudation (*q.v.*).

quia timet [Because he fears] A *quia timet* action is one by which a person may obtain an injunction (*q.v.*) to prevent or restrain some threatened act being done which, if done, would cause him substantial damage, and for which money would be no adequate or sufficient remedy.

quicquid plantatur solo, solo cedit [Whatever is affixed to the soil belongs to the soil] See FIXTURES.

quicquid solvitur, solvitur secundum modum solventis; quicquid recipitur, recipitur secundum modum recipientis [Whatever is paid, is paid according to the intention or manner of the party paying; whatever is received, is received according to the intention or manner of the party receiving]

quid pro quo [Something for something] See CONSIDERATION.

quiet enjoyment The right of a grantee of property (and any person deriving title from him) to enter and remain in enjoyment free from lawful interruption by or on behalf of the grantor or anyone deriving title from him other than a purchaser for value. A covenant for quiet enjoyment was implied into every conveyance of freehold land made before July 1, 1995. A covenant for quiet enjoyment is implied into the demise of every lease. See COVENANTS FOR TITLE.

quiet possession There is an implied warranty (*q.v.*) in a sale of goods contract (*q.v.*) that a buyer will enjoy quiet possession of the goods except in so far as it may be disturbed by the owner of the goods or any other person entitled to the benefit of any charge or encumbrance disclosed to the buyer before the contract, Sale of Goods Act 1979 s.12(2)(b) as amended by the Sale and Supply of Goods Act 1994 Sch.2 paras 5(1) and (3).

quietare To quit, discharge or save harmless.

quietus A discharge granted by the Crown or its officer to a person indebted to the Crown, e.g. an accountant or sheriff who has given in his accounts.

quietus redditus [Quit rent] See RENT.

quilibet potest renunciare juri pro se introducto [Every man is entitled to renounce a right introduced in his favour]

quit rent See RENT.

quittance An acquittance (*q.v.*).

quo ligatur, eo dissolvitur [Whatever binds can also release]

quo minus [By which the less] The initial words of the writ whereby the Court of Exchequer obtained its extended jurisdiction. It permitted the claimant (formerly plaintiff) to plead that he was a debtor of the King, and by reason of the cause of action pleaded he had become less able to pay his fictitious debt to the King.

quo warranto [By what authority] A prerogative writ issued by the Crown against one who claimed or usurped any office, franchise or liberty, to inquire by what authority he supported his claim. The writ was supplanted by an "information in the nature of a writ quo warrants," which could be brought at the relation of an individual with leave of the court. These informations were abolished by s.9 of the Administration of Justice (Miscellaneous Provisions) Act 1938 and substituted by proceedings by way of an injunction (Supreme Court Act 1981 s.30). Applications for injunctions similar to *quo warranto* proceedings should now be brought as applications for judicial review (*q.v.*).

quoad hoc [Regarding this]

quod ab initio non valet, in tractu temporis non convalescit [That which is bad from the beginning does not improve by length of time]

quod aedificatur in area legata cedit legato [That which is built on ground which is devised or left by will passes to the devisee or beneficiary]

quod contra legem fit, pro infecto habetur [What is done contrary to law is deemed not to have been done at all]

quod fieri non debet, factum valet [A thing which ought not to have been done may be perfectly valid when it is done]

quod non apparet non est [That which does not appear does not exist]

quod nullius est, est domini regis [That which belongs to no one belongs to our Lord the King]

quod per me non possum, nec per alium [What I cannot do in person, I cannot do through another]

quod prius est verius; et quod prius est tempore potius est jure [What is first is truer; and what is first in time is better in law]

quod semel meum est amplius meum esse non potest [What is once mine cannot be more fully mine]

quod semel placuit in electione, amplius displicere non potest [Where election is once made it cannot be revoked]

quorum [of whom] The minimum number of persons which constitutes a formal meeting, e.g. the Companies Act 1985 s.370 provides that at a company meeting two members personally present are a quorum. Business transacted at an inquorate meeting is not binding and has no legal effect.

quoties in verbis nulla est ambiguitas ibi nulla expositio contra verba expressa fienda est [When there is no ambiguity in the words, no interpretation contrary to the words is to be adopted]

quousque [Until]

R

R *Regina*, the Queen; or *Rex*, the King.

race relations The Race Relations Act 1976 (RRA) makes racial discrimination (*q.v.*) unlawful in the fields of employment (ss.4–16), education (ss.17–19), the provision of goods, facilities, services or premises (ss.20–27). The RRA set up the Commission for Racial Equality (ss.43–52) which, before its replacement by the Equality and Human Rights Commission (*q.v.*) worked towards the elimination of discrimination, promoted equality of opportunity and monitored the working of the RRA. See also the Human Rights Act 1988 which may allow reliance on the European Convention right to freedom from discrimination on grounds of race in actions under the RRA. The Race Relations (Amendment) Act 2000 substitutes a new s.71 into the RRA which imposes a statutory duty on public authorities to eliminate unlawful discrimination when carrying out their functions. Public authorities are also under a duty to promote equality of opportunity and promote good relations between people of different racial groups. The EU Race Discrimination Directive (2000/43) was transposed into law by the Race Relations Act 1976 (Amendment) Regulations 2003. These Regulations provide for a statutory definition of racial harassment (*q.v.*), introduce changes to the burden of proof and provide a new definition of indirect discrimination.

A person commits an offence under Pt 3 of the Public Order Act 1986 if he publishes, distributes or uses in public words or written matter which is or are threatening, abusive or insulting, where hatred is likely to be stirred up against any racial group in Great Britain by the matter or words in question. See RACIAL HATRED OFFENCES.

racial aggravation An offence under ss.29–32 of the Crime and Disorder Act 1998 is racially aggravated if at the time of committing the offence, or immediately before or after doing so, the offender demonstrates hostility towards the victim based on the victim's membership (or presumed membership) of a racial group, or if the offence is motivated by hostility towards members of a particular racial group (ibid. s.28). See RACIALLY AGGRAVATED OFFENCES; RACIAL GROUP.

racial discrimination Direct racial discrimination is defined in Race Relations Act 1976 s.1 as treating a person less favourably, on racial grounds, than another would be treated. Acts which indirectly discriminate against a person of a particular racial group and which disproportionately impact upon that group without justification or without having a legitimate aim also amount to racial discrimination. The Act further covers victimisation and segregation.

racial grounds Under the Race Relations Act 1976 s.3 means colour, race, nationality or ethnic or national origins. The EU Race Discrimination Directive confines itself to discrimination on grounds of racial or ethnic origin.

racial group (1) Under the Race Relations Act 1976 s.3 means a group of persons defined by reference to colour, race, nationality or ethnic or national origins. The definition is given a wide meaning and can include, for example, Sikhs who are not a group defined by reference to colour or race or nationality, but are a group defined by their ethnic origins (*Mandla v Dowell Lee* [1983] 2 A.C. 548, HL).

(2) Under the Crime and Disorder Act 1998 s.28 means a group of persons defined by reference to race, colour, nationality (including citizenship) or ethnic or national origins.

racial harassment The Race Relations Act 1976 (Amendment) Regulations 2003 insert a new s.3A into the Race Relations Act 1976 which provides for a statutory definition of racial harassment. Previously a claim for racial harassment was only possible by interpretation of the Act through case law. The new statutory definition of racial harassment provides that a person subjects another to harassment where on grounds of race or ethnic or national origins, he engages in unwanted conduct which violates that other person's dignity or creates an intimidating, hostile, degrading, humiliating or offensive environment for him. Importantly the definition allows for the differences in reaction of victims to racial harassment.

There is also an offence of racially aggravated harassment under the Crime and Disorder Act 1998 s.32. The offence is committed if a person is guilty of an offence under s.2 or s.4 of the Protection from Harassment Act 1997 which is racially aggravated. See HARASSMENT; RACIAL AGGRAVATION; RACIALLY AGGRAVATED OFFENCES.

racial hatred Hatred against a group of persons defined by reference to colour, race, nationality (including citizenship), or ethnic or national origins (Public Order Act 1986 s.17). See RACIAL GROUP.

racial hatred offences The Public Order Act 1986 Pt III (ss.18–23) provides six offences relating to racial hatred (*q.v.*). Each of those offences requires that the defendant intends to stir up racial hatred or that given the circumstances racial hatred is likely to be stirred up.

racially aggravated offences Introduced by the Crime and Disorder Act 1998 these offences are based on aggravated versions of pre-existing offences and carry a higher maximum punishment. Section 29 provides that a person is guilty of an offence of malicious wounding, grievous bodily harm, actual bodily harm, or common assault, which is racially aggravated for the purposes of that section. There are also racially aggravated criminal damage and public order offences, see Crime and Disorder Act 1998 ss.30–31. See RACIAL AGGRAVATION.

rack-rent Rent of the full annual value of the property at the commencement of the lease (i.e. full market rent).

Railway and Canal Commission A court established by the Railway and Canal Traffic Act 1888, having jurisdiction in matters directly relating to railways and canals, and also as regards the construction of telegraphs and the water supply of London. It was abolished by the Railway and Canal Commission (Abolition) Act 1949, which transferred its functions to the High Court.

rank (1) A claim to a prescriptive payment, such as a *modus* (*q.v.*), which is excessive, and therefore void.

(2) Order in precedence, or priority.

rape A person (A) commits rape if he intentionally penetrates the vagina, anus or mouth of another person (B) with his penis, B does not consent to the penetration, and A does not reasonably believe that B consents (Sexual Offences Act 2003 s.1(1)). The maximum penalty for rape is life imprisonment. The longstanding marital exemption to rape which meant that a husband could not be convicted of the rape of his wife was abolished by *R. v R* [1991] 4 All E.R. 481. Under s.5 of the Act the actus reus (*q.v.*) of the offence of rape of a child under 13 is the same as for rape but consent is irrelevant. See SEXUAL OFFENCES.

rate A sum assessed by a local authority (*q.v.*) on the occupier of property according to its value. The Rating and Valuation Act 1925 consolidated various pre-existing rates into one general rate for a district. The Local Government Finance Act 1988 replaced the general rate with a community charge (colloquially known as the poll tax (*q.v.*)) levied on each person living in the district in respect of domestic premises, but retained a unified business rate in respect of commercial property. The community charge is replaced by the council tax (*q.v.*).

rate of exchange The amount of one currency which will be given in exchange for a different currency. If the consideration for a contract is expressed in a foreign currency, an English court must determine the currency of the contract and give judgment in that currency. If the judgment is to be enforced in the United Kingdom, the sum awarded must be converted to sterling at the commencement of enforcement proceedings (*The Despina R* [1979] 1 All E.R. 421).

ratification (1) The act of adopting a contract, or other transaction, by a person who was not bound by it originally because it was entered into by an unauthorised agent. The transaction must have been carried out on behalf of the principal (*q.v.*). The principal must have been in existence, capable and ascertainable, and ratification must take place in a reasonable time.

(2) Ratification of a treaty is a formal ceremony whereby some time after the treaty has been signed, the parties exchange solemn confirmations of it. Normally, a treaty must be ratified in order to be binding.

ratio decidendi [The legal reason (or ground) for a judicial decision] It is the ratio decidendi of a case which will be binding on later courts under the system of judicial precedent. See PRECEDENT.

ratione soli [By reason only]

ratione tenurae By reason or in respect of his tenure.

ravishment The tortious act of taking away a wife from her husband, or a ward from her guardian. Popularly, rape (*q.v.*).

re [In the matter of]

real property Land; things growing in or attached to land, minerals (also referred to as corporeal hereditaments); rights over land, such as easements (*q.v.*) and profits (also referred to as incorporeal hereditaments); but not leasehold (*q.v.*) land or beneficial interests under a trust for sale (*q.v.*). See HEREDITAMENTS.

real representative The person in whom the real property of a deceased person devolved on death, after the Land Transfer Act 1897. All property now devolves on the personal representative (*q.v.*) (executor or administrator) who is technically also the real representative. The Supreme Court Act 1981 s.113 provides for a grant to be made limited to real, personal or trust property, if separate executors are appointed for different parts of the estate.

real securities Securities charged on land.

realty Real property (*q.v.*).

rebut To disprove something, e.g. to rebut a presumption (*q.v.*) by producing evidence that it was not intended to apply.

rebutter Under the rules governing statements of case (*q.v.*), formerly known as pleadings, applying before the Supreme Court of Judicature Act 1873 in civil actions all statements of case were given particular names. The defence might be met with a reply, followed by a rejoinder from the defendant, then a surrejoinder, then a rebutter from the defendant, then a surrebutter. Under the Civil Procedure Rules 1998 (*q.v.*) there will rarely be anything beyond the claimant's reply to the defendant's defence or defence to the defendant's counterclaim (*q.v.*).

recaption A remedy available without recourse to the courts to a person deprived of his personal or real property or where another wrongfully detains a wife, child or servant. The injured party can lawfully retake them, as long as this is done without causing a breach of the peace (*q.v.*).

receditur a placitis juris potius quam injuriae et delicta maneant impunita [We dispense with the forms of law rather than allow wrongs and crimes to go unpunished]

receipt An acknowledgement of the receipt of money paid in exchange for goods or services, or for money paid in discharge of a debt. A receipt may be implied by conduct. In rent cases, an entry in a Rent Book or any document for notification or collection of rent will suffice. A receipt under seal is conclusive evidence of payment, as is a receipt in a document over 20 years old.

receiver A person appointed by the court or an individual for the collection or protection of property. If appointed by the court, a receiver is an officer of the court deriving authority from the court order. If appointed by an individual, the receiver derives powers and duties from the terms of the appointment.

A receiver is appointed by the court whenever it appears to the court to be just and equitable (Supreme Court Act 1981 s.37). The appointment may be unconditional or on such terms and conditions as the court thinks just. Examples:

(1) The Court of Protection may appoint a receiver to manage the affairs of a mental patient.

(2) When a landlord fails to collect rents and repair property in multiple occupation, a receiver may be appointed to fulfil the landlord's obligations (*Hart v Emelkirk* [1983] 3 All E.R. 15).

(3) The court can appoint a receiver of a company if the debenture holders have failed to do so and the appointment is for the benefit of the debenture holders.

(4) On the bankruptcy of an individual, an interim receiver may be appointed between the bankruptcy petition and the bankruptcy order. His powers come from the Insolvency Act 1986 s.287.

(5) A receiver by way of equitable execution is appointed to enable a judgment creditor to obtain payment of his debt when the debtor is in possession of property or has an interest in property which cannot be reached by normal process of execution.

Appointment of a receiver may also be made out of court:

(1) When a person defaults on a mortgage, the mortgagee has power to appoint a receiver under the Law of Property Act 1925 s.101. The receiver manages property which is let out to tenants on behalf of the mortgagor. The powers of the receiver are set out in ibid. s.109.

(2) Debenture holders can appoint a receiver once a relevant charge has crystallised. If appointed after 1986, the receiver is called an administrative receiver and he must give certain information under the Insolvency Act 1986 ss.46–49.

(3) Partners wishing to realise partnership assets may appoint a receiver. See OFFICIAL RECEIVER.

receiver of wreck An officer appointed by the Secretary of State for Transport under the Merchant Shipping Act 1995 s.248. His main function is to deal with reports of wrecks and to investigate ownership of the recovered property. Where such property remains unclaimed he must arrange disposal and ensure that the person who found the wreck is rewarded where appropriate.

receiving order Former name for the order made by the court, on presentation of a bankruptcy (*q.v.*) petition. Now a bankruptcy order (*q.v.*) (Insolvency Act 1986).

receiving stolen property See HANDLING STOLEN GOODS.

recipient liability Where a third party has knowingly received trust funds aware of the breach of trust, also referred to as knowing receipt. Unlike accessory liability (*q.v.*) dishonesty is not a necessary element of such a claim. It is sufficient to show that the defendant's knowledge was such that it would be unconscionable for him to retain the benefit of the funds that he has received. See *BCCI (Overseas) Ltd v Akindele* [2000] 4 All E.R. 221.

345

recitals Statements to introduce the operative part of an instrument (normally a conveyance (*q.v.*) of land or assignment of a lease). They give details of the relevant earlier deeds or events leading up to the present deed, and explain the background of the transaction (e.g. whether it is based on contract (*q.v.*) or gift (*q.v.*)).

In relation to statutory interpretation a recital will detail the existing law which the new law is intended to replace. Recitals commence with the word "whereas".

reckless driving See DANGEROUS DRIVING.

recklessness For certain criminal offences the mens rea may be satisfied by intention or recklessness. Recklessness is the taking of an unjustifiable risk accompanied by foresight of the risk. There were until 2003, two types of recklessness: (i) where the defendant himself recognised the risk that certain consequences might occur as a result of his actions or that certain circumstances existed and took it anyway ("Cunningham" recklessness); (ii) the defendant either recognised such a risk and took it anyway, or failed to give any thought to such a risk where the risk was one which would have been obvious to the reasonable man ("Caldwell" recklessness). "Caldwell" recklessness applies only to offences under the Criminal Damage Act 1971 and "Cunningham" recklessness to all other offences. "Caldwell" recklessness was overruled in 2003 by the House of Lords in *G and another* [2003] 4 All E.R. 765. The House of Lords held that "reckless" in the Criminal Damage Act 1971 should be assessed in the subjective sense as it had been before *Caldwell* There had to be a risk of foresight by the defendant of the risk of damage.

recognisance An obligation or bond, with or without sureties, acknowledged before a court or authorised officer, and enrolled in a court of record (*q.v.*). The purpose is to secure the performance of some act by the person bound, who may or may not be the person who entered into the bond, such as to appear in court, to keep the peace, or be of good behaviour. See BAIL; BINDING OVER.

reconversion The equitable doctrine whereby property converted (e.g. from land into personal property, by virtue of there being a direction in a will to executors to sell land) may be converted back into its original form, e.g. if the beneficiary wishes to take the property in its original form. The same applies if X covenants to expend a sum of money in the purchase of land for a settlement of which X turns out to be the sole beneficiary. See CONVERSION.

reconveyance When property was subject to a mortgage created prior to 1926, the property was conveyed to the mortgagee, who reconveyed the property to the mortgagor on repayment of the loan. Since 1925, a receipt endorsed on the mortgage deed has been sufficient to discharge the mortgage and later determine the lease or sub-lease or reconvey the property on which it is secured (Law of Property Act 1925 s.115).

record (1) An authentic memorial preserved by a court or the legislature. When an error appears on the record of an inferior tribunal which shows that the decision is wrong in law, an order of certiorari is available to quash it. See JUDICIAL REVIEW; PUBLIC RECORDS.

(2) Formerly the official statement of the writ (now the claim form) and pleadings (now the statements of case) for the use of the judge in a common law action.

(3) The relevant documents to be used in an appeal hearing for example before the Privy Council.

record, conveyances by Conveyances of land effected by judicial or legislative act, as evidenced by the record, e.g. fines or an Act of Parliament.

record, courts of See COURT OF RECORD.

record, trial by Where in an action one party alleged and the other denied the existence of a record, there was the issue known as *nul tiel record* (*q.v.*), and the court would thereupon order a trial by inspection and examination of the record. If the record was not proved, judgment was given for the party who denied its existence.

recordari facias loquelam Formerly a writ used to remove a suit from an inferior court not of record into one of the superior courts of common law.

recorded delivery The Recorded Delivery Service Act 1962 s.1 provides that any document or thing which by any enactment is required to be sent by registered post, may be sent either by registered post or by recorded delivery, when the recipient must sign a receipt. The Post Office is liable for any loss or damage.

recorder Prior to 1972, a barrister (*q.v.*) appointed to act as justice of the peace and judge in a court of quarter sessions (the court being abolished by the Courts Act 1971). The Courts Act 1971 s.21 permits a barrister or solicitor (*q.v.*) of 10 years' standing to be appointed a recorder to act as a part-time judge of the Crown Court.

recovery Proceedings for the recovery of land from a person wrongfully in possession may be taken in the High Court or the county court. A judgment is enforced by a writ of possession.

rectification The correction of an error in a register or instrument, e.g. conveyance, on the ground of mutual mistake, e.g. a clerical or drafting error, with the result that the instrument does not give effect to the agreement between the parties.

The Administration of Justice Act 1982 s.20 permits a court to order rectification of a will (*q.v.*) if it fails to give effect to the testator's intention because of clerical error or failure to understand his instructions.

recto de dote A writ for right of dower (*q.v.*) issued against her husband's heir by a widow who had only received part of her dower.

recto de dote unde nihil habet A writ for right of dower (*q.v.*) issued by a widow who had received none of her dower.

rector An officer of the church having a benefice (*q.v.*) with cure of souls and an exclusive right to the emoluments of the living. Since the Reformation, lay persons may take the emoluments, with vicars to perform the cure of souls. Such lay persons are called lay improprietors (*q.v.*).

reddendo singula singulis [Giving each to each] When interpreting a document, one of two provisions in one part is taken as referring to one of two provisions in another part. Thus, e.g. "I devise and bequeath all my real and personal property to A". The word "devise" is taken to refer to real property, and the word "bequeath" is taken to refer to personal property.

reddendum [That which is to be paid or rendered] The clause in a lease dealing with the payment of rent (*q.v.*).

redditus [Rents]

redemption The repayment of a mortgage debt, whereupon the lease securing the mortgage terminates on the mortgagee signing a receipt on the mortgage deed. See RECONVEYANCE.

If the mortgagee refuses to release the property from the mortgage on repayment of the loan, the mortgagor can bring a redemption action to force him to do so.

reduction into possession Exercising a right conferred by a chose in action (*q.v.*) so as to convert it into a chose in possession, e.g. bringing action to recover a debt. See CHOSE.

347

reduction of capital Any limited company having a share capital may reduce its share capital by special resolution confirmed by the court (see Companies Act 2006 s.641). A private company limited by shares may additionally reduce capital where all the directors make a solvency statement in the prescribed form and manner (ibid. s.642). See COMPANY.

redundancy The dismissal of an employee wholly or mainly on the ground that the employer has or intends to cease carrying on the business for which the employee was employed or to cease doing so in the place where the employee was employed or the requirements of that business for employees to do work of that kind have diminished or are expected to do so either completely or in the place where the employee was employed (Employment Rights Act 1996 s.139). Subject to minimum criteria regarding length of service, the employee dismissed as a result of redundancy is entitled to receive from his employer a redundancy payment.

redundancy consultation Under the Trade Union and Labour Relations (Consolidation) Act 1992 s.188 as amended an employer must consult about proposed redundancies involving 20 or more employees with appropriate representatives of any affected employees. Appropriate representatives include representatives of any trade union recognised by the employer with regard to those employees or, where there is no recognised trade union, any representatives elected for the purpose of consultation. Consultation must begin in good time and in any event at least 90 days before the first dismissal takes effect if the proposal is to dismiss 100 or more employees within 90 days or at least 30 days in any other case. Failure to comply may result in the making of a protective award (*q.v.*) by an employment tribunal. See PROTECTIVE AWARD.

re-entry See RIGHT OF ENTRY.

reeve An officer or steward, e.g. the shire-reeve or sheriff (*q.v.*).

re-examination See EXAMINATION.

re-exchange See RATE OF EXCHANGE.

re-extent A second execution by extent in respect of the same debt. See EXTENT.

referee (1) Official referee—formerly a judge appointed to hear complex cases known as "official referees" "business" involving prolonged examination of documents or accounts of a technical, scientific or legal nature. The Official Referees Court is now replaced by the Technology and Construction Court (TCC) which deals with technically complex cases and/or cases where trial by a TCC judge is desirable, such as construction disputes, environmental claims, trespass cases or cases involving complex accounts. Official Referees are now known as TCC judges and they have been nominated by the Lord Chancellor to deal with such cases, see Supreme Court Act 1981 s.68, as amended.

(2) Referees on Private Bills are members appointed by the House of Commons to report on questions of locus standi (*q.v.*).

reference (1) The decision or opinion of a referee (*q.v.*).

(2) A credit reference (an opinion as to credit worthiness) by a bank, say for a prospective tenant. An error may give rise to liability in negligence or breach of fiduciary duty.

reference in case of need A person whose name is indorsed on a bill of exchange (*q.v.*) and to whom the bill may be presented if it is dishonoured (Bills of Exchange Act 1882 s.15).

referendum The submission to the electorate for approval of a proposed legislative measure, e.g. the Referendums (Scotland and Wales) Act 1997 which provided for a vote on the establishment of the Welsh Assembly (*q.v.*).

referral order A sentence applicable to a young offender *(q.v)* who has pleaded guilty to his first offence in court where the case is neither so serious that it merits custody nor so minor that it merits a fine or absolute discharge. The youth will be referred to a youth offender panel and together they will agree on a programme of behaviour which aims to prevent re-offending. The programme can include terms such as unpaid work, reparation, mediation, curfew and complying with supervision. See Powers of Criminal Courts (Sentencing) Act 2000 Pt 3.

refresher A fee paid to counsel on the trial of an action in addition to the fee originally marked on the brief.

refreshing memory A witness in a civil or criminal case may refresh their memory, while giving evidence, by referring to a document or memorandum made by them or made by another and verified by them at the time of the events in question or while the events were fresh in their mind. Documents may be used to refresh memory even if they would not be admissible if tendered in evidence.

regalia (1) The royal prerogative, or rights.
(2) The Crown jewels. See JURA REGALIA.

Regency Acts The Regency Act 1937 provides for the powers of the Sovereign to be exercised by the next adult in line of succession if the Sovereign is under 18 or incapacitated by illness. If the Sovereign is absent or infirm, powers are delegated by letters patent to Counsellors of State, who are the spouse of the Sovereign and the next four adults in line of succession.

regional planning body A Regional Planning Body is a body recognised by the Secretary of State whether that body is incorporated or not, which satisfies certain prescribed criteria and which has responsibility for the planning in a particular region (Planning and Compulsory Purchase Act 2004 s.2). A region is defined in Sch.1 to the Regional Development Agencies Act 1998 and includes the East Midlands, Eastern, London, North East, North West, South East, South West, West Midlands, Yorkshire and Humber. Sixty per cent or more of the membership of a Regional Planning Body must be members of a district council, a county council, a metropolitan district council, a National Park Authority or the Broads Authority. The Regional Planning Body must keep under review the regional spatial strategy *(q.v.)* and monitor its implementation and consider whether it is achieving its purposes. The Regional Planning Body must also review any matters that might affect development in its region and give advice to any other person or body who may assist in the implementation of the regional spatial strategy.

regional spatial strategy (RSS) Section 1 of the Planning and Compulsory Purchase Act 2004 introduced the requirement for each region to have a regional spatial strategy, setting out the Secretary of State's policies in respect of the development and use of the land in the region. It should provide a broad development strategy for the region over a 15–20 year period. As from September 2004 the existing regional planning guidance (RPG) has become the RSS. See REGIONAL PLANNING BODY.

register of charities See CHARITIES, REGISTER OF.

register of writs The collection of, inter alia, various specialist writs and orders affecting land issued or made by any court for the purpose of enforcing a judgment, and which are kept at the Land Registry *(q.v.)*.

registered design A design, which is protected by entry on the Register of Designs which fulfils the criteria for registration set out in the Registered Designs Act 1949 (as amended by the Copyright, Designs and Patents Act 1988) one of which is compliance with the definition of design as features of shape, configuration, pattern or ornament applied to an article by any industrial process, being features which in the finished article appeal to and are judged by the eye. See DESIGN RIGHT (UNREGISTERED DESIGN).

registered office A company (*q.v.*) must have a registered office to which communications and notices may be addressed. Notice of the address and any change must be given to the Registrar of Companies (see Companies Act 2006 ss.86–87). Under s.1139 delivery of a document to a company's registered office constitutes effective service on the company.

registered proprietor The person who is registered as proprietor of registered land. See LAND REGISTRATION.

registered title A title registered at the Land Registry (*q.v.*) under the Land Registration Act 2002. The Land Registration Act 2002 makes provision for compulsory (ss.4–8) and voluntary registration (s.3). The freehold estate in land and a leasehold estate with more than seven years left to run are compulsorily registrable on the happening of certain events prescribed by the Act. Section 3 provides for voluntary registration of an unregistered legal estate of an estate in land, a rentcharge (*q.v.*), a franchise, and a profit à prendre in gross (*q.v.*). See LAND REGISTRATION.

registered trade mark A trade mark (*q.v.*) which is entered on the Trade Marks Register under the Trade Marks Act 1994 as opposed to an unregistered trade mark which may be protected under the law of passing off (*q.v.*). A registered trademark is personal property and the owner has all of the rights and remedies provided by the Trade Marks Act 1994.

registered trade mark agents Also known as trade mark attorneys, under the Trade Marks Act 1994 s.83 (as due to be amended by the Legal Services Act 2007), the Secretary of State for Business, Enterprise and Regulatory Reform is empowered to make rules as to the keeping of a register of persons who act as agents for others for the purpose of applying for or obtaining the registration of trade marks (*q.v.*). It is an offence for any person to use the title "registered trade mark agent (attorney)" when not entitled to do so (ibid. s.84). See TRADE MARK.

registrar (1) Originally an officer responsible for keeping a register, e.g. an officer of the Chancery Division responsible for keeping records and drawing up orders. Registrars of the Family Division, county court and district registrars of the High Court (now referred to as district judges, s.74 of the Courts and Legal Services Act 1990) perform a judicial function, hearing and determining interim applications (*q.v.*) and some final hearings, possessing all the powers of a judge, save of committal to prison.
   (2) Registrar of Companies. This officer is the chief executive of Companies House, the main functions of which are to incorporate and dissolve limited companies, to examine and store documents delivered to the Registrar under Companies legislation and to allow public inspection of such documents.

Registrar-General of Births, Marriages and Deaths The officer responsible for registration of all births, deaths and marriages (see Marriage Act 1983; Births and Deaths Registration Act 1953).

registration as British citizen A minor may become a British citizen (*q.v.*) by registration at the discretion of the Home Secretary, although certain minors born outside the United Kingdom may be registered as of right. Registration generally is dealt with in the British Nationality Act 1981 ss.3–5 as amended by the British Overseas Territories Act 2002. The organisation responsible for dealing with registration is the Home Office UK Border Agency.

registration of births, marriages and deaths There is a duty to register all births, marriages and deaths, generally at the local office of the registrar of Births,

Marriages and Deaths (Births and Deaths Registration Act 1953; Marriage Acts 1949 and 1983).

registration of business names See BUSINESS NAMES.

registration of land See LAND REGISTRATION.

registration of marriage Every marriage in England must be registered. If it is conducted in the presence of the registrar of Births, Marriages and Deaths, it is registered by that person, and in all other cases by the authorised person in whose presence the marriage was conducted (Marriage Acts 1949 and 1983).

registration of title See LAND REGISTRATION.

regnal years The years of the reign of a monarch. Statutes are sometimes arranged in regnal years, rather than calendar years. See Table of Regnal Years of the English Sovereigns, below.

Regulae Generales [General Rules] The Rules of the Supreme Court. Now largely superseded by the Civil Procedure Rules 1998 (*q.v.*).

regulated activity Under the Financial Services and Markets Act 2000 a specified activity carried out by someone in business dealing with the investment of an asset, right or interest (i.e. buying and selling investments or advising on the buying and selling of investments).

regulated agreement A consumer credit agreement (*q.v.*) or a consumer hire agreement (*q.v.*) which is not an exempt agreement under the Consumer Credit Act 1974 as amended by the Consumer Credit Act 2006.

regulated facility A facility regulated under the Environmental Permitting Regulations 2007. The Regulations aim to provide for a streamlined and single permitting system for various polluting activities, installations (*q.v.*) and waste operations, including waste mobile plant.

regulated tenancy A protected tenancy (*q.v.*) or statutory tenancy (*q.v.*), which is not a controlled tenancy (*q.v.*) (Rent Act 1977 s.18(1)). The distinction between controlled and regulated tenancies has been abolished by the Housing Act 1980, all tenancies under the Rent Act now being regulated. Residential tenancies created after January 15, 1989 are now assured tenancies under the Housing Act 1988. See ASSURED TENANCY.

Regulation See COMMUNITY LEGISLATION.

regulatory objectives. Under the Legal Services Act 2007 s.1, these include: protecting and promoting the public interest; supporting the constitutional principle of the rule of law; improving access to justice; encouraging an independent, strong, diverse and effective legal profession; increasing public understanding of the citizen's legal rights and duties; and promoting and maintaining adherence to the professional principles (*q.v.*). The Legal Services Board (*q.v.*) is charged with acting in compliance with these objectives (ibid. s.3).

rehabilitation of offenders See SPENT CONVICTION.

rehearing The re-arguing of a case which has already been adjudicated. All appeals to the Court of Appeal or Divisional Court are by way of rehearing. The rehearing is on the basis of the documents, including the judge's notes and any transcript of the evidence. New evidence may be introduced (see Civil Procedure Rules Pt 52).

reinstatement (1) When an Employment Tribunal finds that an employee was unfairly dismissed, it may order that the employer take the employee back as if he had not been dismissed (Employment Rights Act 1996 s.114).
    (2) The replacement of a building in the event of destruction.

reinsurance An insurer has an insurable interest in the risk he has insured. Reinsurance is thus the act of an insurer who insures with another insurer a risk which he himself insured. This is permitted, e.g. in respect of marine insurance (Marine Insurance Act 1906 s.9).

rejoinder Old term for the defendant's response to a claimant's reply in a civil case. Abolished by the Civil Procedure Rules 1998 (*q.v.*). See PLEADINGS.

relation back The doctrine by which an act is made to take effect as if it occurred at an earlier time. Thus on bankruptcy (*q.v.*), the trustee may by notice claim property acquired by or devolving on the bankrupt after the commencement of the bankruptcy or the death of an insolvent person (Insolvency Act 1986 s.307(1)).

If a person enters land with permission, and he later abuses the permission, he becomes a trespasser and his wrongful act relates back to the time of the entry.

relator The private person whose name was inserted in proceedings taken in an action by way of information (*q.v.*) in Chancery. See now CPR Pt 19, r.7.

release (1) The giving up of a claim, by deed (*q.v.*) or supported by consideration (*q.v.*) and with full knowledge of the relevant facts. It is generally used by trustees or executors who have wound up an estate and obtain a release from the beneficiaries before making final distribution.

(2) Where a number of persons have interests in the same land (e.g. as joint tenants), the transfer of an interest by one to the others.

(3) The release of an offender from custody. In certain situations an offender can be released after serving half of his sentence, either unconditionally or on licence, see Criminal Justice Act 1991 s.33 as amended by the Criminal Justice Act 2003 and s.26 Criminal Justice and Immigration Act 2008 (to be appointed).

relegatio [Roman Law] Banishment. A prohibition from entering a named place.

relegation Exile or banishment short of outlawry (*q.v.*).

relevant A fact so connected, directly or indirectly, with a fact in issue that it tends to prove or disprove the fact in issue. All facts are admissible in evidence which are relevant and not excluded.

relevant filing system Data which recorded as part of a relevant filing system (or be intended to be part of a relevant filing system) falls within the definition of data (*q.v.*) in the Data Protection Act 1998. A relevant filing system is defined in s.1(1) of the Act as "any set of information relating to individuals to the extent that, although the information is not processed by means of equipment operating automatically in response to instructions given for that purpose, the set is structured, either by reference to individuals or by reference to criteria relating to individuals, in such a way that specific information relating to a particular individual is readily accessible". The definition has been controversial with noticeable differences of interpretation put forward by the Information Commissioner (*q.v.*) and the Court of Appeal in *Durant v Financial Services Authority* [2003] EWCA Civ 1746.

relevant transfer The transfer of an undertaking situated immediately before the transfer in the United Kingdom to another person where there is a transfer of an economic entity which retains its identity. In such a situation any employees affected by the transfer are afforded statutory protection of their employment rights under TUPE (*q.v.*).

reliance loss Where a claimant incurs expense in reliance on a contract which is subsequently broken, thereby causing such expense to be wasted, that loss may be compensated by the award of damages. See DAMAGES; EXPECTATION LOSS.

relief (1) The right of the feudal lord to a payment, normally of one year's value of the land, when an heir of full age succeeded to land on the death of a tenant. See MANORIAL INCIDENTS.
(2) The remedy sought by a claimant, e.g. damages, injunction.
(3) The right of a tenant whose lease is being forfeited to be restored to the land. The right is extended to a sub-tenant on forfeiture of the head lease (Law of Property Act 1925 s.146(4)). See FORFEITURE.
(4) Allowances from an individual's total income or the profits of a company before computing the tax payable (see Income & Corporation Taxes Act 1988 as amended).

religion or belief Any religion, religious belief, or similar philosophical belief (see Employment Equality (Religion or Belief) Regulations). See RELIGIOUS DISCRIMINATION.

religious aggravation An offence under ss.29–32 of the Crime and Disorder Act 1998 (as amended by the Anti-Terrorism, Crime and Security Act 2001) is religiously aggravated if at the time of committing the offence, or immediately before or after doing so, the offender demonstrates hostility towards the victim based on the victim's membership (or presumed membership) of a religious group, or if the offence is motivated by hostility towards members of a particular religious group (ibid. s.28). See RELIGIOUSLY AGGRAVATED OFFENCES; RELIGIOUS GROUP.

religious discrimination Religious discrimination was not previously outlawed explicitly in the United Kingdom until the Employment Equality (Religion or Belief) Regulations 2003, although there had been legislation specifically to deal with the religious divide in Northern Ireland. The Regulations, implementing the European Framework Directive for equal treatment (Directive 2000/78), outlaw direct and indirect discrimination, victimisation and harassment on the grounds of religion or belief (*q.v.*) in employment and vocational training. All major religions will be covered by the Regulations but application to some fringe religious groups may be less certain and guidance may be drawn from case law on art.9 of the European Convention on Human Rights.

religious group A group of persons defined by reference to their religious belief or lack of religious belief (Crime and Disorder Act 1998 s.28(5)). There is no definition of 'religious belief' but it is clear from case-law that Sikhs, Muslims and Rastafarians are religious groups, although the last two are not racial groups. See RACIAL GROUP.

religious harassment The statutory definition of religious harassment provides that a person subjects another to harassment where on grounds of religion or belief (*q.v.*), he engages in unwanted conduct which violates that other person's dignity or creates an intimidating, hostile, degrading, humiliating or offensive environment for that person. Importantly the definition allows for the differences in reaction of victims to the harassment. See the Employment Equality (Religion or Belief) Regulations 2003.

religiously aggravated offences Introduced by the Anti-terrorism, Crime and Security Act 2001 as an extension to the Crime and Disorder Act 1998 these offences are based on aggravated versions of pre-existing offences and carry a higher maximum punishment. Section 29 of the Crime and Disorder Act 1998 provides that a person is guilty of an offence of malicious wounding, grievous bodily harm, actual bodily harm, or common assault, which is religiously aggravated for the purposes of that section. There are also religiously aggravated criminal damage and public order offences, see ibid. ss.30–31. See RELIGIOUS AGGRAVATION.

remainder An estate (*q.v.*) limited to take effect after an estate in possession, where both estates arise under the same disposition, e.g. "To A for life, remainder to B in fee simple." Since 1925, remainders can only take effect as equitable interests (*q.v.*) (Law of Property Act 1925 s.1). If the identity of a beneficiary who is to take a remainder or the size of his share may not be ascertained for some time the gift may fail by virtue of the Rule against Perpetuities. See PERPETUITIES.

remand An order from the court that the defendant either be admitted to bail (*q.v*) or kept in custody pending the next hearing. The Magistrates' Court Act 1980 s.128, as amended, provides that a remand in custody should not normally exceed eight days, but that in some cases, after the first remand, a remand in custody may be for up to 28 days at a time. The court may direct that time spent on remand be deducted from any period of imprisonment, see Criminal Justice Act 2003 s.240.

remanet A term formerly used for an action in the Queen's Bench Division which had been set down for trial at one sitting, but had not come on, so that it was delayed until the next sittings.

remedial order An order made under s.10 of and Sch.2 to the Human Rights Act 1998, which enables primary legislation to be altered to be made compatible with the Convention rights (*q.v.*) following a declaration of incompatibility (*q.v.*) or a decision of the European Court of Human Rights (*q.v.*) concerning the United Kingdom. The mechanism permits primary legislation to be changed without the need for the introduction of a new Bill into Parliament; this is sometimes known as a Henry VIII clause. See HUMAN RIGHTS; CONVENTION COMPLIANT.

remediation A term used in environmental law to denote the clean-up of land following a pollution incident. Under Pt IIA of the Environmental Protection Act 1990 (inserted by s.57 of the Environment Act 1995), remediation of contaminated land (*q.v.*) includes the doing of anything for the purpose of assessing the condition of the contaminated land; and also the doing of any works or operations in order to prevent, minimise, remedy or mitigate the effects of any significant harm which causes the land to be contaminated. The relevant local authority determines the level of remediation required following consultation with the appropriate persons (*q.v.*) and on a suitable for use basis, Pt IIA of the Environmental Protection Act 1990. See CONTAMINATED LAND; REMEDIATION NOTICE; SPECIAL SITE.

remediation notice When land has been identified as contaminated land (*q.v.*) or a special site (*q.v.*) the local authority or the Environment Agency (*q.v.*) (in the case of a special site) is under a duty to serve a remediation notice on each person who is an appropriate person (*q.v.*), Environmental Protection Act 1990 s.78E(1). The duty to serve the notice is qualified (ibid. s.78H(5)) and can only be served after a three month period of consultation (ibid. s.78H(1)). The purpose of the remediation notice is to specify what the recipient must do by way of remediation (*q.v.*) and the periods within which this must happen. It is a criminal offence to fail to comply, without reasonable excuse, with the notice.

remedy The means whereby breach of a right is prevented, or redress is given. The law has allowed remedies of four kinds:

(1) By act of the injured party, e.g. defence, recaption, distress, abatement and seizure.

(2) By operation of law, e.g. retainer and remitter.

(3) By agreement between the parties, e.g. accord and satisfaction, arbitration.

(4) By judicial process, e.g. damages, injunction.

remembrancers (1) The three officials of the Exchequer known as the Queen's Remembrancer (*q.v.*), the Lord Treasurer's Remembrancer, and the Remembrancer of the First Fruits.

(2) The Rembrancer of the City of London represents the Corporation before parliamentary committees; he accompanies the sheriffs when they wait on the Sovereign in connection with any address from the Corporation; and he is bound to attend all Courts of Aldermen and Common Council when required.

remise To release or surrender.

remission (1) The reference of a case by a higher to a lower court.
(2) The forgiveness of a debt.
(3) The reduction of a prison sentence. Reduction for good behaviour was abolished by the Criminal Justice Act 1991. See PAROLE; RELEASE.

remitter When a person has two titles to land, even if possession is taken by virtue of the later title, possession is deemed to have been taken under the earlier, because the older title is the stronger.

remoteness A disposition of property which does not vest within the period allowed by the rule against perpetuities fails for remoteness. See PERPETUITY.

remoteness of damage Loss which results from the defendant's wrongdoing but not sufficiently directly and so is irrecoverable by the claimant. In negligence (*q.v.*) the test is whether the consequences could have been foreseen by the reasonable man (*The Wagon Mound* [1961] A.C. 388). The same rule applies to nuisance (*q.v.*) claims (*Overseas Tankship (UK) Ltd v Miller Steamship Co* [1967] 1 A.C. 617). See NOVUS ACTUS INTERVENIENS.
In contract (*q.v.*), the test is whether the damage arose naturally, in the normal course of events, from the breach or the loss was reasonably contemplated by the parties at the time of the contract as the probable result of the breach (*Hadley v Baxendale* (1854) 23 L.J. Ex. 179). See DAMAGES.

removal centre For the purposes of immigration and asylum controls, a place which is used solely for the detention of detained persons but which is not a short-term facility, a prison or part of a prison (Immigration and Asylum Act 1999 s.147). See DETENTION CENTRE.

render To yield or pay.

rendition More generally referred to as extraordinary rendition which consists of the extra judicial handing over of a person from one jurisdiction to another, in particular where torture or other physical or psychological abuse may be involved with that person's detention. See EXTRADITION.

renewal area Part VII of the Local Government and Housing Act 1989 provides framework to facilitate the revitalisation of an area of poor private housing by declaring it to be a "renewal area". Under such a declaration the local housing authority has power to buy land and carry out or help carry out repairs or improvements.

rent (1) The periodical payment due from a tenant to a landlord as compensation for the right to possession of the property let, and which constitutes the legal acknowledgement of the landlord's title. It is generally, though not necessarily, a money payment. Sometimes, a nominal rent is reserved, normally a peppercorn, which in practice is not handed over. Other special terms relating to rent include rack-rent (*q.v.*), and dead rent (*q.v.*). The remedy of distress (*q.v.*) is available only for non-payment of rent.
(2) Rent service is a payment of rent payable by a tenant to a lord by virtue of the relationship between them. The statute Quia Emptores 1290 forbade the reservation of rent service in relation to freehold land. Thus the only rent service to be found is in the landlord and tenant relationship. See FEALTY.
(3) The quit rent arose when a feudal tenant who owed services to his lord had his services commuted to a monetary payment.

(4) **Ground rent** refers to rent due on a long lease for which the tenant pays an initial lump sum (called a fine or premium) followed by a lower rent.

Rent Assessment Committee The committee whose function it is to assess market rents and agree terms of the statutory periodic tenancy under the Housing Act 1988 and to hear appeals from the decision of the Rent Officer under the Rent Act 1977.

rent book The book which must be provided to every residential tenant whose rent is payable weekly, to record rent payments, and which must contain certain specified information. It is a criminal offence not to comply with the obligation to provide a rent book (Landlord and Tenant Act 1985 ss.4–7).

rentcharge A periodic sum charged on freehold land not as a result of tenure. New rentcharges may not be created, with certain exceptions (Rentcharges Act 1977). Existing rentcharges will be extinguished over 60 years, subject to certain exceptions and may be redeemed.

rent control Rent control originated in the Increase of Rent and Mortgage Interest (War Restrictions) Act 1915. The rent of private residential tenants whose tenancy was created prior to January 15, 1989 is restricted to a fair rent under the Rent Act 1977 s.70 and the rent of such tenants (which now includes tenants of Housing Associations) created after that date is restricted by Housing Act 1988 s.14, to a market rent.

rent officer The official whose function it is to determine a fair rent under the Rent Act 1977. See RENT CONTROL.

rent rebates Formerly allowances towards rent for tenants in needy circumstances under the Housing Finance Act 1972 ss.18–26; the Furnished Lettings (Rent Allowances) Act 1973 and the Rent Act 1974. See HOUSING BENEFIT.

rent tribunal A tribunal for adjudicating the rent level for restricted contracts under the Rent Act 1977 s.77 as amended.

renunciation The refusal to take out a grant of probate or letters of administration of a deceased person's estate by a person entitled to do so. Renunciation is effected by filing the appropriate document at the probate registry (*q.v.*). Intermeddling by an executor precludes renunciation. Renunciation may be retracted with leave of a registrar (Non-Contentious Probate Rules 1987 r.37).

renvoi A doctrine regarding choice of law in a case with a foreign element where the law of more than one jurisdiction may be applicable. The question raised by this doctrine is whether, in applying the law of a particular jurisdiction, the court must also apply the private international law (*q.v.*) of that jurisdiction (governing choice of law), even if this means that the rules applicable state that the case must be decided by reference to the law of some other country.

repair The making good of defects. For example in a property which has deteriorated from its original state. The work required may involve curing defects arising from the defective design or construction of the building, but it must fall short of effectively reconstructing the premises or improving them.

repatriation (1) The resumption of a nationality which has been lost.
(2) The sending back of an alien to his own country. See EXPATRIATION.

repeal Abrogation of statute. This occurs when a statute is no longer to have effect, either because a later statute expressly so declares or as a necessary result of a later statute which is inconsistent. If the later statute is repealed, the earlier statute is not revived (Interpretation Act 1978 ss.15, 17). See STATUTE LAW REVISION.

repeat offender See MANDATORY SENTENCE.

repleader A term formerly used for a judgment that pleadings (now statements of case (*q.v.*)) in an action be started again on the ground that the pleadings failed to raise a definite issue.

replegiare facias The writ of replevin (*q.v.*).

replevin The redelivery to their owner of chattels wrongfully seized and the action for such redelivery, e.g. where distress (*q.v.*) has been unlawfully levied. In order to succeed, the claimant whose goods have been seized must produce security for his rent and the costs of the case and undertake to pursue an action to determine the defendant's right to distrain. Power to grant this remedy vests solely in a district judge of the county court (County Courts Act 1984 Sch.1). For a more modern remedy, see CONVERSION.

replication See REPLY.

reply The claimant's answer to a defence. This may be combined with the claimant's defence to the defendant's counterclaim. Further statements of case (*q.v.*) cannot be served without the permission of the court. See Civil Procedure Rules 15.8 and 16.7.

reply, right of The right of counsel in a case to make the last speech to the jury, before the judge's summing-up.

report, pre-sentence An oral or written report prepared by either a probation officer or a social worker to assist the court in determining the most suitable sentence for an offender, see Criminal Justice Act 2003 s.158.

representation (1) One person represents another when he acts on that other's behalf, e.g. a solicitor or barrister acting on behalf of a client, an agent acting on behalf of a principal.
(2) A statement of fact or belief, expectation or present intention made by one party to another before or at the time of a contract, of some matter or circumstance relating to the contract (see *Edgington v Fitzmaurice* (1885) 29 Ch. D. 459). It does not include mere statements of opinion or a seller "puffing" his goods. If the statement is untrue, liability may result for breach of contract if the representation is a term of the contract. If the representation is not a term, liability may arise under the Misrepresentation Act 1967. See MISREPRESENTATION.

representative A person who takes the place of another. In many hearings parties must be heard through a legally qualified representative (see AUDIENCE, RIGHT OF). The executor or administrator of a deceased person is his personal representative because he represents him in respect of his estate, both real and personal. See REAL REPRESENTATIVE; PERSONAL REPRESENTATIVE.

representative action An action brought by one or more members of a class on behalf of the entire class. The names of those represented are attached as a schedule to the claim. See Civil Procedure Rules 19.3.

reprieve The suspension of the execution of a sentence. A judge may grant a reprieve of his own initiative by way of a suspended sentence (*q.v.*), or the Home Secretary may exercise the prerogative of mercy on behalf of the Crown.

reprisal (1) A recaption (*q.v.*).
(2) A remedy for breach of international law, which covers every means short of war (including embargo (*q.v.*) and retorsion (*q.v.*)), used by one state against another to obtain redress for an injury other than one committed in self-defence. The methods of reprisal permitted may be limited by treaty, e.g. the Geneva Convention.

republication (1) The doctrine whereby a codicil to a will has the effect of the will being reinterpreted as if it were written at the date of the codicil (*q.v.*). This may affect the identification of beneficiaries and property referred to in the will (*q.v.*).

(2) republication of a defamatory statement by a person to whom it was published may give rise to tortious liability

repudiation Words or conduct indicating that a person does not regard himself as being bound by an obligation, e.g. a party may repudiate a contract by refusing to perform according to its terms. Repudiation will give the innocent party the right to treat the contract as discharged and claim damages.

repugnant Contrary to, or inconsistent with.

reputation (1) Matters of public and general interest, such as the boundaries of parishes, rights of common, highways, fisheries, etc. may be proved in evidence by general reputation, e.g. by the statements of deceased persons made before the dispute arose or by old documents, etc. notwithstanding the general rule against secondary evidence.

(2) Evidence of reputation is admissible in civil cases (see Civil Evidence Act 1995 s.7).

(3) Damage to reputation may be compensated in libel or slander. See defamation.

reputed ownership If property was in a trader's possession, order or disposition, with the permission of the owner, in circumstances which would reasonably lead persons dealing with him to infer that he was the owner, the property was said to be in the reputed ownership of the trader and so was divisible among his creditors if he became bankrupt. This doctrine was abolished by the Insolvency Act 1986.

requisitions on title Queries raised by a buyer of land concerning the seller's title. They may relate to, e.g. outstanding mortgages, the identity of the property, the stamping and execution of deeds.

re-registration, company A company (*q.v.*) may change its registered status, e.g. a limited liability company may re-register as an unlimited company, and vice versa; a private company may re-register as a public company, and vice versa. See Companies Act 2006 ss.89–111.

res [Things]

res accessoria sequitur rem principalem [Accessory things follow principal things]

res extincta [Things have been destroyed] The doctrine that a contract will become void for mistake if the subject-matter is, without the knowledge of either party, no longer in existence.

res furtivae [Stolen goods]

res gestae Evidence which is said to "form part of the *res gestae*" may be admissible in criminal proceedings under any of a number of common law exceptions to the hearsay rule which are preserved by s.118 of the Criminal Justice Act 2003. Essentially, these exceptions apply where the statement was made by someone who was so emotionally overpowered by events that it is very unlikely that the statement is a fabrication, where the statement relates to a contemporaneous physical sensation or mental state or where the statement accompanied an act and can only be evaluated as evidence if the act and statement are considered together.

res integra A point, which is not governed by any earlier decision or rule of law, and so must be decided for the first time on general principle.

res inter alios acta alteri nocere non debet [A transaction between others does not prejudice a person who was not a party to it]

res ipsa loquitur [The thing speaks for itself] The doctrine applicable in cases where there is prima facie evidence of negligence, the precise cause of the incident cannot be shown, but it is more probable than not that an act or omission of the defendant caused it and the act or omission arose from a failure to take proper care for the claimant's safety.

res judicata pro veritate accipitur [A thing adjudicated is received as the truth] A judicial decision is conclusive as between the parties, although other parties may not be bound. A criminal conviction is admissible in evidence in a civil case and it is presumed that the convicted person committed the offence unless the contrary is proved (Civil Evidence Act 1968 s.11).

res nova [A matter not yet decided]

res nullius A thing which has no owner. See BONA VACANTIA; TREASURE TROVE.

res sic stantibus [Things standing so, or remaining the same] Agreements, treaties, etc. entered into on the basis that circumstances will remain unchanged. See FRUSTRATION.

res sua nemini servit [No one can have a right over his own property]
(1) A person cannot acquire an easement over land owned by himself.
(2) If a person enters a contract to buy property which he already owns, the contract is void for mistake.

resale, right of See RIGHT OF RESALE.

resale royalty right A legal right belonging to the creator, to a proportion of the proceeds of all subsequent sales of an aesthetic work. Originating in France in 1920, but not yet applied in the United Kingdom.

rescission Abrogation or revocation. Most typically, the termination of a contract, either by act of the parties or the court, whether for breach of contract, mistake or misrepresentation (*q.v.*). It is only possible if restitution is feasible. In equity, it means restoring the parties to the position they would have been in had there been no contract. At law, the effect is merely to relieve the parties of any further obligation to perform the contract.

rescous Rescue (*q.v.*).

rescue (1) Forcibly and knowingly freeing a person from imprisonment is an offence punishable on indictment by a fine and imprisonment at the discretion of the court.
(2) Forcibly taking back goods which have been distrained and are being taken to the pound. If the distress (*q.v.*) was unlawful, the rescue is lawful; if the distress was lawful, the rescuer is liable to an action by the distrainor. See POUND BREACH.

rescue cases Cases dealing with injury resulting from intervention to rescue others from danger where it may be alleged that there has been a voluntary assumption of risk, see, e.g. *Haynes v Harwood* [1935] 1 K.B. 146. See NERVOUS SHOCK.

reservation A clause in a deed whereby the grantor keeps back some right out of the estate which has been granted, e.g. the payment of rent in respect of the grant of a lease or the reservation of rights of way over land granted.

reservation of title See RETENTION OF TITLE.

reserved legal activities Under the Legal Services Act 2007 s.12, these are: the exercise of a right of audience in court; the conduct of litigation; reserved instrument activities; probate activities; notarial services; and the administration of oaths. It is an offence to pretend to be entitled, or to offer or to carry out such activities when not entitled to do so.

residence The place where a person lives or from which the affairs of a company are directed. The place of a person's residence governs their domicile and liability to taxation. A company is resident for tax purposes in the country where its central management and control are exercised.

residence order An order settling the arrangements to be made as to the person with whom a child is to live, Children Act 1989 s.8.

residential occupier A person occupying premises as a residence under a contract, statute or rule of law giving the right to remain. See Protection from Eviction Act 1977 s.1 as amended by the Housing Act 1988. Such a person is protected against harassment and unlawful eviction by his landlord and others.

residential premises. Under the Housing Act 2004 s.1, these are: (a) any building or part of a building occupied or intended to be occupied as a separate dwelling; (b) any house in multiple occupation; (c) any building or part of a building constructed or adapted for use as a house in multiple occupation but for the time being either unoccupied or only occupied by persons who form a single household; and (d) any common parts of a building containing one or more flats. The 2004 Act introduces a new system for assessing housing conditions as part of a policy of improving housing standards.

residuary devisee The beneficiary entitled under a will to all real property not included in specific gifts in the will or any codicil to it.

residuary legatee The beneficiary entitled under a will to all personal property not included in any other gift in the will or in any codicil and not taken for the payment of debts or expenses. In the appropriate context, the gift also includes real property.

residue The remainder of a deceased person's estate after all other legacies and the debts, funeral, testamentary, and administration expenses and inheritance tax (*q.v.*) have been paid. If it is not effectively disposed of by the will, it passes on a partial intestacy. Once the size of residue has been ascertained, it is said that the adminstration of the estate is complete and the personal representative (*q.v.*) holds henceforth as trustee, but probably an assent is required before the administration is complete.

resolution An opinion or decision arrived at by vote at a meeting. A private company can pass a resolution either as a written resolution (see Companies Act 2006 s.288) or at a members' meeting, whereas a public company may only pass a resolution at a general meeting. Resolutions passed at company meetings may be:
(1) ordinary, i.e. passed by simple majority of those voting (see Companies Act 2006 s.282);
(2) special, i.e. passed by a majority of not less than 75 per cent of the members (ibid. s.283);
(3) a resolution requiring special notice; such a resolution is not effective unless notice of the intention to move it has been given at least 28 days in advance (ibid. s.312).

resoluto jure concedentis resolvitur jus concessum [The grant of right comes to an end on the termination of the right of the grantor]

respite To discharge or dispense with.

respite care One of the services which a local authority (*q.v.*) may be under a duty to provide to safeguard and promote the welfare of children in need within its area.

respondeat ouster [Let him answer over] A judgment formerly given when a defendant failed to substantiate a plea, which ordered him to plead again. See PLEA.

respondeat superior [Let the principal answer] Where the relationship of employer and employee exists, the employer is liable for the acts of the employee committed in the course of his employment. See EMPLOYER AND EMPLOYEE; VICARIOUS LIABILITY; STRICT LIABILITY.

respondent The person against whom a petition is presented (e.g. for divorce), a summons issued, or an appeal brought.

responsible clinician For the purposes of the Mental Health Act 1983 (as amended by the Mental Health Act 2007 s.9) is the approved clinician (*q.v.*) responsible for a person who is a community patient (*q.v.*) or liable to be detained under the Act. It is a role that may be fulfilled not only by medical practitioners but also by other professions, such as nursing, psychology, occupational therapy and social work.

restitutio in integrum [Restoration to the original position] The restoration of the parties to their original position following rescission of a contract between them. This may be effected by court order. See RESCISSION.

restitution (1) The rules concerned with reversing a defendant's unjust enrichment at the claimant's expense, specifically recognised as a separate area of law by the House of Lords in *Lipkin Gorman (a firm) v Karpnale Ltd* [1991] 2 A.C. 548.
(2) In relation to contract where there is no performance by one party, a performing party may gain restitution for the benefit he has provided.

restitution order (1) A High Court order made on application by the Financial Services Authority (*q.v.*) if the court is satisfied that a person has contravened a requirement under the Financial Services and Markets Act 2000 s.382. Such an order may require the infringing party to pay a sum commensurate with any profit made to the FSA.
(2) Where goods have been stolen and a person is convicted of any offence with reference to the theft, the court may order anyone having possession or control of the stolen goods to restore them to any person entitled to recover them from him or to pay a sum not exceeding the value of the goods, Power of Criminal Courts (Sentencing) Act 2000 s.148.

restitutionary interest The interest of a performing party in recovering an unjust enrichment made by a non-performing party where, for example, the former has conferred a benefit on the latter without counter-performance. In exceptional circumstances the innocent party may be able to claim an account of profits from the party in breach (See *Att Gen v Blake* [2000] 3 W.L.R. 625, HL).

restraint of marriage A contract, or disposition, the object of which is to restrain a person from marrying at all, or not to marry anyone except a specific person, is void as against public policy.

restraint of trade Contractual interference with individual liberty of action in trading, which as a general rule is void as being contrary to public policy. Such a restriction will be valid, however, if it is reasonable in reference to the interests of the parties concerned, and of the public, and if it is so framed as to protect the party in whose favour it is imposed, without being injurious to the public (see, per Lord Macnaghten in *Maxim-Nordenfelt Gun Co v Nordenfelt* [1894] A.C. 535). Restraints of trade may be reasonable not only in protection of a purchaser of a business, but also in protection of an employer from improper use of trade secrets, confidential information, etc. by an employee when he leaves his employment. See GARDEN LEAVE. Since the Monopolies and Restrictive Practices (Inquiry and Control) Act 1948, the major developments in the area of restrictive trade practices (*q.v.*) have been through legislative action. Under art.81 EC Treaty (ex art.85):
"agreements between undertakings, decisions by associations of undertakings and concerted practices which may affect trade between Member States and

which have as their object or effect the prevention, restriction or distortion of competition within the common market (*q.v.*)" are void unless special exemption is granted.

restraint on anticipation; restraint on alienation A clause restraining anticipation was generally introduced into a settlement of property on a woman in order to protect her from the influence of her husband by preventing her from depriving herself of the benefit of future income. By the Law Reform (Married Women and Tortfeasors) Act 1935, however, a restraint upon anticipation of property of a married woman could not be imposed unless pursuant to an obligation incurred before 1936, or unless it was contained in a will executed before 1936 of a testator who died before 1946. Existing restraints continued in force. The Married Women (Restraint upon Anticipation) Act 1949 abolished any restraint upon anticipation or alienation attached to the enjoyment of property by a woman which could not have been attached to enjoyment by a man. Where property was given to a married woman to her separate use without power of disposing of it, by means of a restraint on anticipation, she had the power of a tenant for life under the Settled Land Act 1925 (see ss.1, 20, 25). See ANTICIPATION.

restricted patient A term which derives from the Mental Health Act 1983 to describe: (i) a patient who on being made subject to a hospital order by the Crown Court is also made subject to special restrictions; and (ii) a patient who on being transferred on the order of the Secretary of State from prison to hospital is made subject to special restrictions. The special restrictions are set out in s.41 of the Mental Health Act 1983 as amended and relate to various aspects of the detention of the patient to whom they apply.

restriction order An order made under the Mental Health Act 1983 s.41 as amended that an offender who is subject to a hospital order (*q.v.*) should be subject to special restrictions with or without time limit. An order may be made where, having regard to the nature of the offence, the antecedents of the offender and the risk of further offences being committed, the court views it to be necessary for the protection of the public.

restrictive covenant See COVENANT.

restrictive indorsement An indorsement on a bill of exchange which prohibits the further negotiation of the bill, or expresses that it is a mere authority to deal with the bill as thereby directed, and not a transfer of the ownership thereof, e.g. "Pay X only," or "Pay X, or order, for collection" (Bills of Exchange Act 1882 s.35(1)).

restrictive trade practices See ANTI-COMPETITIVE PRACTICES.

rests The period for which accounts are balanced and interest is ascertained and charged, and added to the principal sum, e.g. half-yearly.

result A thing is said to result when, after having been ineffectually or only partially disposed of, it comes back to its former owner or his representatives, e.g. property subject to a trust which fails returns to the author of the trust under a resulting trust. See RESULTING TRUST.

resulting trust An implied trust where the beneficial interest in property reverts (results) to the person who transferred the property upon trust or provided the means of obtaining it. The principal situations are:
  (1) the automatic resulting trust, where the express trust does not exhaust the whole of the trust fund;
  (2) the presumed resulting trust, where property is conveyed into the name of someone other than the provider of the consideration.

362

There is an overlap between the concept of the resulting trust and that of the constructive trust (*q.v.*).

resulting use Where property, prior to 1926, was conveyed to a person without any mention of a use, and without any consideration, the property was held to the use of the grantor, which use was "executed" by the Statute of Uses (*q.v.*) so that the legal estate immediately revested in and remained in the grantor, and the grantee took nothing.

resumption The taking again of lands by the owner.

retail The sale of goods in small quantities to the public, as in a shop.

retainer (1) The right of the executor or administrator of a deceased person to retain out of the assets sufficient to pay any debt due to him from the deceased in priority to the other creditors whose debts are of equal degree. The right was abolished by the Administration of Estates Act 1971 s.10.

(2) The engagement of a barrister or solicitor to take or defend proceedings, or to advise or otherwise act for the client.

retention of title (ROT) Sometimes referred to as a Romalpa clause; see *Aluminium Industrie Vaassen BV v Romalpa Aluminium Ltd* [1976] 1 W.L.R. 676. A clause in a contract for the sale of goods by which a seller seeks to retain ownership of the goods, despite delivery to the buyer, usually against payment in full. The clause may be drafted more widely, e.g. to retain ownership of goods until all sums owing by the buyer to the seller are paid, or to extend title to goods which have been manufactured from the product supplied or to the proceeds of a sub-sale of goods. The extended retention of title clauses have usually been unsuccessful when construed by the courts. (See *Re Peachdart* [1983] 3 All E.R. 204; *Clough Mill Ltd v Martin* [1984] 3 All E.R. 982).

The Sale of Goods Act 1979 s.19 provides that a seller may, by the terms of the contract etc., reserve the right of disposal of goods until certain conditions are fulfilled. In such a case, despite delivery to the buyer etc., ownership in the goods does not pass until the condition is fulfilled. See SALE OF GOODS.

retirement age The Employment Equality (Age) Regulations 2006 provide for a national default retirement age of 65 but all employees have the right to request that they be allowed to work beyond that age, or any other retirement age set by their employer. See AGE DISCRIMINATION.

retorsion A form of lawful retaliation, unfriendly, but not affording a cause of war, consisting of the adoption of measures directed against an offending nation analogous to those to which exception is taken, e.g. the imposition of a differential tariff.

retour sans protêt [Return without protest] A direction in case a bill of exchange is dishonoured, that it shall not be "protested". See PROTEST.

retractation An executor who has renounced probate may, in certain circumstances, be permitted to withdraw that renunciation (*q.v.*).

return A report. For example, a sheriff executing a writ of execution (*q.v.*) can be required by notice to indorse on the writ immediately after execution a statement of the manner in which he has executed it and to send a copy of that statement to the party serving such notice (see RSC Ord. 46, r.9, CPR Sch.1). See ANNUAL RETURN.

returning officer A person responsible for the conduct of an election. For parliamentary elections it is the sheriff or mayor or chairman of a district council (Representation of the People Act 1983 s.24). His duties are discharged by the registration officer (ibid. s.28).

returnus brevium [The Return of Writs] The manorial right of making returns to writs addressed to residents within the manor.

reus [Roman law] Any party to a case, including a stipulator. See ACTUS REUS.

reversal The setting aside of a judgment on appeal.

reversion Where land is granted by the owner for an estate or interest less than he himself has, his undisposed-of interest is termed the reversion; possession of the land will revert to the owner on the determination of the particular estate (*q.v.*), e.g. where the fee simple owner grants a lease. A reversion gives a right to possession of the land in the future and exists only in equity.

reversionary interest Any right in property the enjoyment of which is deferred; e.g. a reversion or remainder, or analogous interests in personal property. See REVERSION.

reverter A reversion (*q.v.*).

revesting The vesting of property again in its original owner, e.g. on a buyer's rejection of goods.

review of taxation Formerly, prior to the introduction of the Civil Procedure Rules (*q.v.*), the reconsideration of taxed costs on the application of a dissatisfied party. See DETAILED ASSESSMENT; TAXING OF COSTS.

review officer Detention of a person detained by a police officer whether charged or not must be reviewed by the custody officer (*q.v.*) (if the person has been arrested and charged) or an officer of at least the rank of inspector who has not been involved in the investigation (where the person has not been charged). Either officer is the review officer (Police and Criminal Evidence Act 1984 s.40).

revival The renewal of rights which were at an end or in abeyance by subsequent acts or events, e.g. a will once revoked may be revived by republication.

revocation Recalling, revoking, or cancelling.
 (1) Revocation by act of the party is an intentional or voluntary revocation, e.g. in the case of a will by a later inconsistent will or codicil (*q.v.*) (Wills Act 1837 s.20).
 (2) A revocation in law is produced by a rule of law, irrespective of the intention of the parties. Thus, a power of attorney, or the authority of an agent, is in general revoked by the death of the principal.
 (3) By an order of the court, e.g. when a grant of probate or letters of administration have been improperly obtained, it may be revoked by the court at the instance of a person interested.
 (4) In the law of contract, an offer may be revoked at any time before acceptance, but the revocation must be communicated to the offeree to be operative (*Byrne v Van Tienhoven* (1880) 5 C.P.D. 344).

reward (1) A sum of money paid to a person who has actively assisted in the apprehension of an offender. The sum may compensate him for the expenses, exertions and loss of time involved in the apprehension. The sum will be whatever the court deems reasonable and sufficient to afford compensation (Criminal Law Act 1826 as amended, Criminal Law Act 1967 s.10(1) and (2) and Sch.2 para.3(1) Pt 3, Courts Act 1971 s.56 (1) and Sch.8 para.2, Statute Law (Repeals) Act 1998, Serious Organised Crime and Police Act 2005 s.111 and Sch.7).
 (2) Advertising a reward for the return of stolen goods, "no questions asked" is an offence (Theft Act 1968 s.23).

rex non potest peccare [The King can do no wrong]

rex nunquam moritur [The King never dies]

rex quod injustum est facere non potest [The King cannot do what is unjust]

Rhodes, Law of A code of sea laws compiled at a very early date in the Island of Rhodes, and declared by the Roman emperors to be binding on the world at large.

rider (1) Anciently, a rider-roll meant an additional clause on a separate piece of parchment which was added to the parchment roll containing an Act of Parliament. Now, a rider is an addition in the form of a new clause added to a Bill, amendments, etc. by means of a separate sheet of paper to a legal document.

(2) A recommendation to mercy added by a jury to their verdict at the time that a court could order the death penalty.

right An interest recognised and protected by the law, respect for which is a duty and disregard of which is a wrong (Salmond). A capacity residing in one man of controlling, with the assent and assistance of the state, the actions of others (Holland).

right of action The right to bring an action. Thus a person who is wrongfully dispossessed of land has a right of action to recover it. It is used also as equivalent to *chose in action* (*q.v.*).

right of audience See AUDIENCE, RIGHT OF.

right of entry The right of taking or resuming possession of land by entering on it in a peaceable manner. A right of entry is usually reserved in a lease in respect of breaches of covenant. After 1925 all rights of entry affecting a legal estate may be made exercisable by any person and the person deriving title under him (Law of Property Act 1925 s.4(3)). See ENTRY.

right of establishment The right of persons who are nationals of a Member State of the European Community (*q.v.*) to take up and pursue activities as self-employed persons and to set up and manage companies and firms in any Member State (art.43, EC Treaty (ex art.52)). This right also extends to companies and firms formed according to the law of one of the Member States and which are based within the Community (art.48 EC Treaty (ex art.58). Restrictions on the freedom of establishment are prohibited and art.43 of the EC Treaty may be enforced at the suit of an individual by the national courts. This right is one of the four fundamental freedoms (*q.v.*) guaranteed by the EC Treaty (*q.v.*). The right to provide services (*q.v.*) (art.49 EC Treaty (ex art.59, EC Treaty) extends the free movement provisions in favour of those who are established in one Member State and wish to provide services in another. See FUNDAMENTAL FREEDOMS; DIRECT EFFECT; INTERNAL MARKET.

right of resale An unpaid seller of goods may exercise a right to sell the goods to another within the terms of the original agreement or as provided by the Sale of Goods Act 1979 Pt V.

right of silence See SILENCE.

right of way The right of passing over land of another. A right of way is either public or private. A public right is called a highway (*q.v.*). Rights of way are of various kinds and may be for limited purposes only, e.g. a footway, horseway, carriageway, way to church, agricultural way, etc. Any person who uses a highway for any purpose other than that of passage (including purposes ordinarily incidental thereto) becomes a trespasser (*q.v.*). See DEDICATION.

A private right of way is either an easement (*q.v.*) or a customary right. A way of necessity is a right of way which arises where a man having a close surrounded with his own land grants (or devises) the close to another; the grantee has a right of way to the close over the grantor's land, otherwise he cannot derive any benefit from the grant (or devise). Similarly, where the grantor keeps the close and grants the surrounding land, a way of necessity is implied in his favour.

right to begin The right of an advocate of first addressing a court or jury. It usually belongs to the party on whom the onus of proof rests. See PROOF.

right to light There is no common law right to light for owners of land. A right to light may constitute a negative easement. See LIGHT.

right to provide services The right to provide services is one of the four fundamental freedoms (*q.v.*) guaranteed by the EC Treaty. Article 49 (ex art.59) prohibits any restrictions on the freedom of a person or company that is established in one Member State to provide services within another Member State. Such services may be of an industrial, commercial, professional and craft character and are normally provided for remuneration. In order to facilitate this aim the Community institutions may adopt legislation relating, inter alia, to the mutual recognition of qualifications. The European Court of Justice (*q.v*) has held that the right to provide services in another Member State is directly effective and also includes the right to move freely around the Community to receive services of a private nature, such as private medical treatment and tourism (*Luisi and Carbone v Ministero del Tesoro* [1984] E.C.R. 377). See FUNDAMENTAL FREEDOMS; DIRECT EFFECT; INTERNAL MARKET.

right to roam The term used to describe those rights of the public to access to the countryside under the Countryside and Rights of Way Act 2000. By s.2, any person is entitled to enter and remain on any access land for the purpose of open air recreation, providing he does so without breaking or damaging any well, fence, hedge, stile or gate and he observes certain general restrictions.

rights in personam Rights that are enforceable against certain categories of persons.

rights in rem Rights in respect of a piece of land which are enforceable against any person who acquires an estate or interest in that land.

rights issue An issue of shares (*q.v.*) or other securities which is offered first to existing investors in a company (*q.v.*) when that company wants to raise additional finance.

riot An assembly of 12 or more persons present together who use or threaten unlawful violence for a common purpose and this conduct is such as would cause a person of reasonable firmness present at the scene to fear for his personal safety (Public Order Act 1986 s.1). A person is guilty of riot only if he intends to use violence or was aware that his conduct may be violent (s.6). The common law offence of riot was abolished by the Public Order Act 1986 s.9(1).

riparian Associated with a river or stream, e.g. land which abuts or is adjoining a river. Owners of land adjoining a watercourse are termed riparian owners and normally own the river bed, but not the water itself.

risk note A contract, signed by the consignor, which denotes the transfer of the goods to the consignee without any indication of liability on the part of the carrier.

risk of sexual harm orders A civil order which may be applied for by the police. Applications for orders are based on evidence that the offender has on at least two occasions engaged in certain acts including engaging in sexual activity in the presence of a child or communicating with a child, where any part of the communication is sexual (Sexual Offences Act 2003 s.123). An order, which the court must believe it is reasonably necessary to make because of the offender's acts, may be granted even though an offender has never been convicted of a sexual offence (*q.v.*). Orders, which will last for a minimum of two years, will specify the prohibitions which the court deems necessary for the protection of children generally or a particular child from harm from the defendant. Breach of the order constitutes a criminal offence.

road Under the Road Traffic Act 1988 s.192, a road includes any highway and any other road to which the public has access, including bridges over which a road passes. By s.34(1)(b), road includes footpaths, bridleways and restricted byways as being within the definition of a road.

roam, right to See RIGHT TO ROAM.

robbery A person is guilty of robbery if he steals, and immediately before or at the time of stealing, and in order to steal, he uses force on any person or puts or seeks to put any person in fear of being then and there subjected to force (Theft Act 1968 s.8).

Roe, Richard See DOE, JOHN.

rolls In ancient times, records were written on pieces of parchment stitched together so as to form a long continuous piece, which was rolled up when not in use. The Parliament Rolls are the records of the proceedings of Parliament, especially Acts of Parliament.

Romalpa clause See RETENTION OF TITLE.

Rome, Treaty of Treaty establishing the European Economic Community (EEC) (*q.v.*), renamed the European Community (EC) (*q.v.*) by the Treaty on European Union 1992 (TEU) (*q.v.*).

root of title Section 44(1) of the Law of Property Act 1925, (as amended by the Law of Property Act 1969) requires that a seller of unregistered freehold (*q.v.*) land must prove a good root of title to that land of at least 15 years from the date of the contract. To be a good root of title a document must deal with or prove ownership of the legal and equitable interest in the relevant, identified property and not raise any doubts about the seller's title. The best root of title is a conveyance for value of the relevant freehold estate. See LAND REGISTRATION.

rout An old common law offence which was abolished by the Public Order Act 1986 s.9(1). It was intermediate between an unlawful assembly (*q.v.*) and a riot (*q.v.*).

Royal Assent The assent of the Crown to a Bill in Parliament becoming law as an Act of Parliament.
An Act of Parliament (*q.v.*), unless otherwise provided, commences to operate from the beginning of the day on which the Act receives the Royal Assent, Interpretation Act 1978 s.4.

Royal Commission An independent standing body established to advise the Crown (*q.v.*) about the need for law reform in specific areas. The Commission will be made up of independent experts. Its primary role is to contribute to policy development and to give advice on law reform, mainly in the form of reports which are usually the outcomes of major studies. Commission members are appointed by the Queen on the advice of the Prime Minister.

royal title "Elizabeth the Second, by the Grace of God of the United Kingdom of Great Britain and Northern Ireland and of Her other Realms and Territories Queen, Head of the Commonwealth and Defender of the Faith" (Royal Titles Act 1953).

rule (1) A regulation made by a court of justice or a public office with reference to the conduct of business therein. Rules made under the authority of an Act of Parliament have statutory effect. Rules of court are made by the judges for the regulation of practice and procedure.

367

(2) An order or direction made by a court of justice in an action or other proceeding. A rule is either: (i) absolute in the first instance; or (ii) nisi, i.e. calling upon the opposite party to show cause why the rule applied for should not be granted. If no sufficient cause is shown, the rule is made absolute; otherwise it is discharged.

(3) A principle of law, e.g. the rule against perpetuities, or the rule in *Howe v Lord Dartmouth.*

rule of law The doctrine of English law expounded by Dicey, in *Law of the Constitution,* that all men are equal before the law, whether they be officials or not (except the Queen), so that the acts of officials in carrying out the behests of the executive government are cognisable by the ordinary courts and judged by the ordinary law, as including any special powers, privileges or exemptions attributed to the Crown by prerogative (*q.v.*) or statute. The Constitutional Reform Act 2005 s.1 specifically provides that the Act does not adversely affect (a) the existing constitutional principle of the rule of law; or (b) the Lord Chancellor's (*q.v.*) existing constitutional role in relation to that principle.

So far as offences are concerned, an offender will not be punished except for a breach of the ordinary law, and in the ordinary courts; there is here an absence of the exercise of arbitrary power. Further, the fundamental rights of the citizen; the freedom of the person; freedom of speech; and freedom of meeting or association, are rooted in the ordinary law, and not upon any special "constitutional guarantees". See now HUMAN RIGHTS; EUROPEAN COURT OF HUMAN RIGHTS.

running account credit See FIXED SUM CREDIT.

running days A charterparty (*q.v.*) includes all days, whether working or non-working, as well as Sundays and holidays. But custom may, as in the City of London, make either "running days" or "days" equivalent to working days.

running with the land See COVENANT.

ruptum [Roman law] Broken. In the *lex aquilia, ruptum* means *corruptum* or spoliation in any way.
"Not only breaking and burning, but also cutting and crushing and spilling, and in any way destroying or making worse are included under this term."

Rylands v Fletcher, rule in A rule of strict liability (*q.v.*). A person who brings onto and keeps dangerous things (*q.v.*) on his land, which, if they escape, are likely to do harm, will be liable for any harm which is a natural consequence of the escape, *Rylands v Fletcher* (1865) 3 H. & C. 774. See TORT.

S

S.C. Same case.

SEA Single European Act 1986 (*q.v.*).

SEAQ Stock Exchange Automated Quotations system for UK securities.

SEAQ International Stock Exchange Automated Quotations system for non-UK securities.

SETS Stock Exchange Electronic Trading System. See STOCK EXCHANGE.

SI Statutory instrument (*q.v.*).

SIB Securities and Investments Board Limited (*q.v.*). See THE FINANCIAL SERVICES AUTHORITY.

S.G. Solicitor-General.

S.R. & O. Statutory Rules and Orders (*q.v.*).

SRO Self-regulating organisation (*q.v.*). See THE FINANCIAL SERVICES AUTHORITY.

sac Jurisdiction.

safe conduct A pass issued to an enemy subject by a belligerent state.

safe system of work At common law an employer is under a duty to provide a safe system of work for employees (*Wilsons & Clyde Coal v English* [1938] A.C. 57). A statutory duty is imposed by the Health and Safety at Work Act 1974 s.2.

sale A transfer of a right of property in consideration of a sum of money.

sale of goods A contract for the sale of goods is a contract where the seller transfers or agrees to transfer the property (*q.v.*) in goods to the buyer for a money consideration (*q.v.*) called the price (Sale of Goods Act 1979 s.2(1).

Where the transfer of the property in the goods is to take place at a future time, or subject to some condition thereafter to be fulfilled, the contract is called an agreement to sell (ibid. s.2(5)).

sale or return A contract where the buyer has the right to return the goods to the seller within the terms of the agreement or within a reasonable time. Unless a different intention appears, the time at which property passes in goods which have been delivered to the buyer on approval or on sale or return is governed by the Sale of Goods Act 1979 s.18, r.4.

sale, power of The right of a person to sell the property of another and apply the proceeds in satisfaction of a debt or claim due to him from that other; usually conferred by statute. Thus a mortgagee has a power of sale of the mortgaged property, where the mortgage is made by deed, as soon as any of the mortgage money has become due (Law of Property Act 1925 s.101(1)(i), subject to the Commonhold and Leasehold Reform Act 2002 s.21).

saliva test Under s.6C of the Road Traffic Act 1988 (as substituted) a specimen of either saliva or sweat may be taken as a preliminary test for determining whether a person has "a drug in his body or is under the influence of a drug" in the context of some driving offences.

salus populi est suprema lex [The welfare of the people is the paramount law]

salvage (1) The High Court has jurisdiction to award salvage remuneration to persons (salvors) for services rendered in saving life from a ship or an aircraft or in preserving cargo, apparel or wreck (*q.v.*) from danger or loss at sea under the Merchant Shipping Act 1995 s.224 or the Civil Aviation Act 1982 s.87. The assistance must be voluntary and salvors have a retaining lien (*q.v.*) for their remuneration on the property rescued.

(2) The service rendered by a salvor, i.e. that which saves or contributes to the safety of a vessel, etc.

salvo jure [Without prejudice]

sanction The penalty or punishment provided as a means of enforcing obedience to law.

sanctuary Consecrated places in which neither the civil nor criminal process of the law could be executed: abolished by 21 Jac. 1 c.28, s.7.

sans frais [Without expense]

sans nombre A right of common of pasture where the number of beasts is not fixed but is not without limit.

sans recours [Without recourse] Where an agent so signs a bill of exchange, he is not personally liable on it (Bills of Exchange Act 1882 s.16).

satisfaction The extinguishment of an obligation by performance, e.g. the payment of a debt. A judgment may be satisfied by payment or execution. The equitable doctrine of satisfaction relates to the doing of an act in substitution for the performance of an obligation.

(1) Satisfaction of debts. If A, after contracting a debt, makes a will (*q.v.*) giving B a pecuniary legacy equal to or greater than the debt, the legacy is considered a satisfaction of the debt unless a contrary intention appears.

(2) Satisfaction of portions. When a father or a person in loco parentis has covenanted to provide a portion (*q.v.*) and subsequently by will provides a portion, or subsequently makes a gift in the nature of a portion, the second provision is presumed to be wholly or *pro tanto* in substitution for the first.

Equity leans against satisfaction of debts but favours satisfaction of portions. See ADEMPTION; ACCORD AND SATISFACTION.

satisfaction, certificate of When a registered county court judgment has been paid, the court may send a certificate of satisfaction to the Registry Trust which keeps a record of county court judgments.

satisfactory quality (formerly merchantable quality). A term implied into contracts for the sale of goods and other analogous contracts where the goods are supplied in the course of a business. Under the Sale of Goods Act 1979 s.14(2A) goods are of satisfactory quality if they meet the standard that a reasonable person would regard as satisfactory, taking account of any description of the goods, the price (if relevant) and all the other relevant circumstances. Section 14(2B) states that the quality of goods includes their state and condition and aspects of quality may include: (a) fitness for all the purposes for which goods of the kind in question are commonly supplied; (b) appearance and finish; (c) freedom from minor defects; (d) safety; and (e) durability.

satisfied term Where property is subject to a term of years and the purpose for which the term was created is fulfilled, the term is said to be "satisfied". See the Satisfied Terms Act 1845 (8 & 9 Vict. c.112), now superseded by the Law of Property Act 1925 s.5. See TERM OF YEARS.

scaccarium The Exchequer (*q.v.*).

scandalous Formerly grounds for striking out (*q.v.*) pleadings. A statement of case (*q.v.*) may be struck out if it is an abuse of the Courts' process or is otherwise likely to obstruct the just disposal of the proceedings (CPR r.3.4) if it is vexatious, scurrilous or obviously ill-founded.

scandalum magnatum The former offence of making defamatory statements regarding persons of high rank, such as peers, judges or great officers of state.

schedule An appendix to an Act of Parliament or an instrument.

scheme of arrangement A form of individual voluntary arrangement (*q.v.*) between a debtor and his creditors for the application of the debtor's assets or income in proportionate payment of his debts, see the Insolvency Act 1986 Pt VIII, as amended by the Insolvency Act 2000. A company can also enter into such a voluntary arrangement (*q.v.*) with its creditors, see the Insolvency Act 1986 Pt I as amended by the Insolvency Act 2000 and the Enterprise Act 2002.

For arrangements and reconstructions between a company and its creditors or a company and its members, see Companies Act 2006 ss.895-901.

Schengen Agreement An agreement between most of the Member States (*q.v.*) of the European Community (*q.v.*) plus Norway and Iceland with the main aim of abolishing internal border controls. The United Kingdom has opted-in to part of the Schengen Agreement primarily in respect of co-operation in cross-border criminal matters.

scienter Having knowledge; an allegation in a pleading that a thing has been done knowingly; the knowledge of the owner of an animal of its mischievous disposition. Liability for animals is now governed by the Animals Act 1971. See ANIMALS.

scilicet [That is to say; to wit]

scot and lot The rates formerly payable by the inhabitants of a borough.

scribere est agere [To write is to act]

scrip A certificate issued by a newly formed company or the issuers of a loan, acknowledging that the person named or the holder is entitled to certain shares, bonds, etc. Scrip certificates are negotiable instruments (*q.v.*). See RIGHTS ISSUE.

script A draft of a will (*q.v.*) or codicil (*q.v.*), or written instructions for the same. If the will is destroyed a copy of its contents becomes a script.

scrutiny A close and careful investigation; an inquiry into the validity of votes recorded at an election; the detailed examination "line by line, clause by clause" of Parliamentary bills at the committee stage.

scurrilous A court may strike out a statement of case (*q.v.*) if it is vexatious, scurrilous or obviously ill-founded (CPR r.3.4). See STATEMENT OF CASE; STRIKING OUT.

scutage Escuage (*q.v.*). A tax on a knight's fee.

scuttling The intentional casting of a ship away, for the sake of the insurance money, etc.

seal A method of expressing consent to a written instrument by attaching to it wax impressed with a device, or now, more commonly, a paper seal. A circle with the letters L.S. (*locus signilli*) may suffice. Sealing is no longer a requirement for the valid execution of an instrument as a deed (*q.v.*) by an individual (Law of Property (Miscellaneous Provisions) Act 1989 s.1). Where a company (*q.v.*) has a seal then a document may be executed by the company by the affixing of its common seal (Companies Act 2006 s.44). Whether the company has a seal or not, a deed may be executed by signature by a single director (if that signature is witnessed and attested), or by a director and secretary, or two directors, of the company. Corporations not registered under the Companies Acts remain subject to the common law requirement of sealing and delivery in the execution of deeds. See EXECUTION; SIGNATURE.

search of the person (1) The Police and Criminal Evidence Act 1984 permits, in the case of a person arrested at a place other than a police station, a police officer to search a person on arrest if he has reasonable grounds for believing that the person may present a danger to himself or others or that the person has anything which might be used for the purposes of escape or might be evidence of an offence (ibid. s.32). Under the Extradition Act 2003 s.163, similar powers apply where a person has been arrested under an extradition arrest power.

The custody officer will search an arrestee brought to a police station. PACE also permits strip and intimate searches, subject to certain conditions.

(2) Under the Education Act 1996 (as amended by the Violent Crime Reduction Act 2006) a school pupil or his possessions may be searched for a knife or other offensive weapon where it is reasonably suspected that he may have such on his person or in his possession.

search orders Formerly an Anton Piller order. A search order is an interim order which requires a person to admit another person to premises for the purposes of preserving evidence which might be destroyed or concealed by the respondent. See Civil Procedure Act 1997 s.7.

search warrant An order issued by a justice of the peace authorising a named person to enter specified premises and look for and seize certain specified material. Such material must not consist of or include items subject to legal privilege, excluded material or special procedure material. See the Police and Criminal Evidence Act 1984 s.8 as amended by the Serious Organised Crime and Police Act 2005 ss.113–114.

searches Examination of records and registers for the purposes of finding encumbrances (*q.v.*) affecting the title to property. Under the Land Charges Act 1972 s.10, an official search may be made and a certificate of the result issued. See land charges; local land charges; land registration.

seat belts Regulations governing the wearing of seat belts in motor vehicles have been made (see the Road Traffic Act 1988, as amended). The Motor Vehicles (Safety Equipment for Children) Act 1991 makes provision in relation to safety equipment for children in motor vehicles (see Road Traffic Act 1988 s.15A). A local education authority is not obliged to fit seatbelts in school minibuses (*R. v Gwent County Council Ex p. Harris* [1994] 2 F.L.R. 1021.) For offences relating to seat belts, see the Road Traffic Offenders Act 1988, as amended.

seaworthiness The fitness of a vessel in all respects to undertake a particular voyage which is a matter of concern to shipowners who contract for carriage of goods by sea, and marine insurance underwriters. Under the Marine Insurance Act 1906 s.39 a ship is deemed to be seaworthy when she is reasonably fit in all respects to encounter the ordinary perils of the seas of the adventure insured. If there is loss or damage to ship or cargo on a voyage, where the Carriage of Goods by Sea Act 1971 applies, there is an implied warranty that due diligence has been used to make the ship seaworthy, and to secure that the ship is properly manned, equipped and supplied, and to make the holds in which goods are carried fit and safe. The effect of a breach of the warranty of seaworthiness is not to displace the whole of the contract of carriage as in deviation (*q.v.*) but to nullify the exceptions from liability of the shipowner in so far as the loss results from unseaworthiness (*The Europa* [1908] P. 84).

seck Dry or bare rent. Where there is no tenure created and consequently no incidents such as the right of distress (*q.v.*) and escheat (*q.v.*). See RENTCHARGE.

secondary action In common usage, action taken during a trade dispute not against the employer in the dispute (the "primary employer") but against another employer in a business relationship with the primary employer. Under the Employment Act 1980 such action lost its immunity against liability in tort where it broke or interfered with that business relationship, unless it was "justified" within the terms of s.17 of that Act. After the Employment Act 1990 the only "justified" secondary action became that carried out in the course of lawful picketing (*q.v.*) (see Trade Union and Labour Relations (Consolidation) Act 1992 s.224).

secondary liability It is not only the actual perpetrator of an offence (known as the principal) who may be liable for its commission. A person who does not actually commit an offence may still be liable for participating in it on the basis that he was a secondary party or accessory to the offence. A secondary party is someone who aids, abets, counsels or procures the principal to commit the offence. Under the Accessories and Abettors Act 1861 s.8, and the Magistrates' Courts Act 1980 s.44, a secondary party is liable to be tried, indicted and punished as a principal offender. See ACCESSORY.

In trust law such liability as an accessory arises even though no trust property is handled by the accessory. See ACCESSORY LIABILITY.

secondary market See STOCK EXCHANGE.

secondary picketing Picketing (*q.v.*) which is not carried out at or near a person's own place of work or attendance on a picket line by persons not employed by the employer in dispute. The immunity provided by the Trade Union and Labour Relations (Consolidation) Act 1992 s.220 to lawful pickets does not apply to secondary pickets.

secondary victim A person who is a "passive and unwilling witness of injury caused to others" who must establish that any consequent psychiatric harm is foreseeable if it is to be recoverable in action for negligence (see per Lord Oliver in *Alcock v Chief Constable of South Yorkshire* [1991] 4 All E.R. 907 at 923, HL; and *White v Chief Constable of South Yorkshire* [1999] 1 All E.R. 1, HL). See NERVOUS SHOCK; PRIMARY VICTIM.

secret profits Profits made by persons acting in a fiduciary capacity, e.g. as a trustee, or as a company director, which are acquired by reason of and in the course of their duty and not disclosed to the person to whom that duty is owed. See *Regal (Hastings) v Gulliver* [1967] 2 A.C. 134 and Companies Act 2006 s.175.

secret trust A trust (*q.v.*) where the identity of the beneficiary is secret between the settlor and the trustees though the existence of the trust may be public. A secret trust is a personal obligation which binds the individual donee, unless he renounces or disclaims, or dies in the lifetime of the donor.

Secretary of State The expression means "one of Her Majesty's Principal Secretaries of State" (Interpretation Act 1978 s.5), e.g. the Home Secretary and Foreign Secretary. They may sit in the House of Commons. Each Secretary of State can do anything which any one of the others is empowered to do (see *R. (on the application of BAPIO Action Ltd) v Secretary of State for the Home Department* [2008] UKHL 27). He is assisted by one or more Ministers of State and one or more Under-Secretaries of State.

secta A following. (1) A service, due by custom or prescription, which obliged the inhabitants of a particular place to make use of a mill, kiln, etc.
(2) The followers or witnesses whom the plaintiff brought into court with him to prove his case.

secta curiae Suit and service done by tenants at the court of the lord.

secta regalis The obligation to attend twice a year at the Sheriff's Tourn.

section 8 orders Orders made under the Children Act 1989. These are contact (*q.v.*), prohibited steps (*q.v.*), specific issue (*q.v.*) and residence (*q.v.*) orders.

sectioned A term commonly used to describe the process by which a person has been detained in hospital following the application of the provisions of a section of the Mental Health Act 1983, e.g. "the patient has been sectioned".

secure children's home A facility run by a local authority for the most vulnerable young offenders who may often have been in care or have mental health problems. The focus of those running such centres is on the physical, emotional and behavioural needs of their residents. See SECURE TRAINING CENTRE; YOUNG OFFENDER INSTITUTION.

secure tenancy A tenancy (*q.v.*) under the Housing Act 1985 under which the tenant has security of tenure (*q.v.*).

secure training centre A facility for vulnerable young offenders below the age of 17 sentenced to custody or remanded to secure accommodation. Centres are run by private sector operators under contracts and are education-focused with the aim of rehabilitation and prevention of reoffending. See SECURE CHILDREN'S HOME; YOUNG OFFENDER INSTITUTION.

Securities and Investments Board Limited (SIB) The independent regulatory agency set up under the Financial Services Act 1986 with powers in respect of the regulation of financial services. The SIB formally changed its name to the Financial Services Authority (FSA) (*q.v.*) in 1997.

security A possession such that the grantee or holder of the security holds as against the grantor a right to resort to some property or some fund for the satisfaction of some demand, after which satisfaction the balance of the property or fund belongs to the grantor. There are thus two persons with an interest but the right of one has precedence over the other.

security for costs A defendant may apply for security of his costs to be given by a party acting as claimant on the grounds specified in CPR r.25.13. An application for security of costs should be made at the first case management conference.

security for good behaviour See SURETIES OF THE PEACE AND GOOD BEHAVIOUR.

security of tenure A statutory right of a tenant (*q.v.*) to continue in occupation of land after the contractual term has expired. See Landlord and Tenant Act 1954; Rent Act 1977; Agricultural Holdings Act 1986; Housing Act 1988.

secus [Otherwise]

sedition Sedition is any acts done or words spoken with the intention of exciting disaffection, hatred or contempt against the Sovereign, or the government and constitution of the United Kingdom, or either House of Parliament, or the administration of justice, or of exciting Her Majesty's subjects to attempt, otherwise than by lawful means, the alteration of any matter in Church or State, or of exciting feelings of ill-will and hostility between different classes of Her Majesty's subjects, or inciting persons to any crime in disturbance of the peace.

seditious libel The publication, in any form constituting a libel, of any words or matter which contain an incitement to disorder and violence.

seduction (1) An action for damages in tort could be brought by a parent (or employer) for loss of services of his daughter (or employee) owing to her seduction and consequent illness. The cause of action was abolished by the Law Reform (Miscellaneous Provisions) Act 1970 s.5.

(2) Anyone who maliciously and advisedly endeavours to seduce any member of Her Majesty's forces from his duty or allegiance to Her Majesty is guilty of an offence under the Incitement to Disaffection Act 1934 s.1.

seignory A lordship. The interest of one who has tenants holding of him in fee simple.

seised in demesne as of fee One in whom an immediate freehold in severalty was vested for an estate in fee simple.

seisin Feudal possession; the relation in which a person stands to land or other hereditaments, when he has in them an estate of freehold in possession. It is formal legal ownership as opposed to mere possession or beneficial interest. Seisin in deed is actual possession of land. Seisin in law is that which an heir had when his ancestor died intestate seised of land, and neither the heir nor any other person had taken actual possession of the land. See LIVERY OF SEISIN.

seisina facit stipitem [Seisin makes the stock of descent] The old rule was that when a person died intestate as to his land, it descended to the heir of the person who was last seised of it. See DESCENT.

self-defence See PRIVATE DEFENCE.

self-incrimination Where a witness answers questions which may incriminate him. Subject to statutory provisions, a person need not answer questions the answers to which would have a tendency to expose the witness to a criminal charge, a penalty or forfeiture. The rule does not apply to an accused who is called as a witness on his own behalf so far as the question relates to the offence with which he is charged. Protection against self-incrimination may not be invoked where the compulsion to answer questions created no material increase to an existing risk of incrimination such as when the defendant had already admitted the relevant facts (see *R. v Khan* [2007] EWCA Crim. 2331).The risk of exposure to civil proceedings is not protected by the privilege against self-incrimination.

Under the Serious Crime Act 2007 s.15, a statement made by a person in response to a requirement imposed by a serious crime prevention order (*q.v.*) may be used against a person in relation to the offence of failing to comply with the order or in other limited circumstances.

Self Regulating Organisation (SRO) A recognised legal body, financed and supervised by its own members, which was responsible for the regulation of a particular area of the investment market. The Financial Services Authority (*q.v.*) has taken over the functions of the SROs.

semble [It appears] Used in law reports and text books to introduce a proposition of law which is not intended to be stated too definitely, as there may be doubt about it.

semestria [Roman law] Half-yearly ordinances, the records of the half-yearly imperial council of senators.

semper in dubiis benigniora praeferenda [In doubtful matters the more liberal construction should always be preferred]

semper praesumitur pro legitimatione puerorum [It is always to be presumed that children are legitimate]

semper praesumitur pro negante [The presumption is always in favour of the negative]

Senate of the Inns of Court and the Bar Formerly the governing body of the Bar. See GENERAL COUNCIL OF THE BAR OF ENGLAND AND WALES.

Senior Courts of England and Wales See SUPREME COURT⁴OF JUDICATURE.

Senior President of Tribunals A new judicial office created under the Tribunals, Courts and Enforcement Act 2007, the holder of which office will be the leader of the tribunals system with various powers and duties related to the operation of the newly formed First-tier Tribunal (*q.v.*) and Upper Tribunal (*q.v.*).

sensitive personal data Under the Data Protection Act 1998 certain personal data (*q.v.*) is classified as sensitive personal data and as such cannot be processed without meeting certain specific conditions which are over and above those required for the processing of personal data. Sensitive personal data is personal data consisting of information about the racial or ethnic origin of the data subject; his political opinions; his religious beliefs or other beliefs of a similar nature; whether he is a member of a trade union; his physical or mental health or condition; his sexual life; the commission or alleged commission by him of any offence; or any proceedings for any offence committed or alleged to have been committed by him, the disposal of such proceedings or the sentence of any court in such proceedings. See DATA; PROCESSING (DATA).

sentence The judgment of a court, particularly in a criminal cause.

Sentencing Advisory Panel An independent body which originally provided advice to the Court of Appeal but subsequently advises the Sentencing Guidelines Council (*q.v.*) on sentencing guidelines (Criminal Justice Act 2003 s.169). Its work is informed by the consultation of prescribed consultees and the wider public.

Sentencing Guidelines Council Established as an independent body, its role is to issue sentencing guidelines based on informed and publically accepted principles (Criminal Justice Act 2003 s.167). It is supported by the work of the Sentencing Advisory Panel (*q.v.*).

separate estate Property given to a married woman to her separate use as if she were a *feme sole*. She was entitled to the income of it, and could charge it, or dispose of it by deed or will, unless she was restrained from anticipation or alienation, without the consent of her husband. The doctrine was invented in equity to overcome the common law rule, that a married woman was incapable of owning property apart from her husband, which was abolished by the Married Women's Property Act 1882 s.2. The Law Reform (Married Women and Tortfeasors) Act 1935 s.2 abolished the doctrine of separate estate of a married woman, and her property now belongs to her in all respects as if she were a *feme sole*. See also the Law Reform (Husband and Wife) Act 1962 s.3(2). Restraint on anticipation was abolished by the Married Women (Restraint upon Anticipation) Act 1949.

separation (divorce) See DIVORCE.

separation agreement An agreement which may provide for maintenance to or for a spouse or child, for the upbringing of any children and for the disposition of the matrimonial home. The essence of a separation agreement is that it also contains a clause which provides that the parties agree to separate. For interpretation and effect of separation agreements see *Edgar v Edgar* [1980] 3 All E.R. 887.

separation decree See JUDICIAL SEPARATION.

sequela villanorum The possessions of a villein, which were at the disposal of the lord.

sequestration Legal process consisting of the temporary deprivation of a person of his property. A writ of sequestration is a means of enforcing a court order, normally an injunction (*q.v.*). The original court order must make it clear that breach of the order will be contempt of court punishable by imprisonment or sequestration for a body corporate. If sequestration is ordered, four sequestrators are appointed to enter the contemner's land and seize the personal property until the contempt is purged.

serious crime prevention order A new kind of civil injunctive order which is aimed at preventing serious crime. A person breaching an order commits a criminal offence (Serious Crime Act 2007 s.1). An order may be made by the high court if it is satisfied that a person has been involved in serious crime and it has reasonable grounds to believe that the order would protect the public from further involvement by that person in such activity. An order could, for example, prohibit or restrict a person's travel plans or financial dealings. The Crown Court has power to make such an order where a person has been convicted of a serious offence (ibid. s.19).

Serious Organised Crime Agency (SOCA) Set up under the Serious Organised Crime and Police Act 2005 s.1, it is a corporate body which replaces the National Criminal Intelligence Service (*q.v.*) and the National Crime Squad (*q.v.*).

Serjeants-at-Law Barristers of superior degree of the Order of the Coif, to which they were called by writ under the Great Seal. They formed an Inn called Serjeants' Inn, with buildings in Fleet Street and Chancery Lane. Formerly they were supposed to serve the Crown (hence their name, serjeants or *servientes ad legem*); they had a right of exclusive audience in the Court of Common Pleas; and every judge of the Superior Courts of Common Law had to be a Serjeant. This rule was abolished by the Judicature Act 1873 s.8. The degree of Queen's

Counsel supplanted that of Serjeant, and the Old Serjeants' Inn (in Chancery Lane) was sold in 1877. See COIF.

serjeanty [Norman-French, *serjantie*, Latin, *serviens*, a servant] Service: a form of tenure. See GRAND SERJEANTY; PETTY SERJEANTY.

service (1) The duty due from a tenant to his lord. Services were: (i) spiritual, e.g. as in tenure by frankalmoign (*q.v.*); (ii) temporal, (a) free, (b) base or villein.
(2) The relationship of a servant to his master. See EMPLOYER AND EMPLOYEE.

service of claim A claim form must be served on each defendant within four months after the date of issue. CPR r.6.2.1 sets out five ways in which documents may be served and CPR r.6.5 the appropriate place of service for different types of party. The methods of service include personal service by leaving it with the person to be served (CPR r.6.4) unless the defendant's solicitor is authorised to accept service on behalf of the party; by first class post (or alternative service providing delivery on the next working day); by leaving the documents at a place specified in CPR r.6.5; through a document exchange or by fax or other means of electronic communication in accordance with the relevant practice directions. The documents to be served include the sealed claim form.

service of process A writ of summons and all other originating processes. Now replaced by a service of claim form (*q.v.*).

services, freedom to provide See RIGHT TO PROVIDE SERVICES.

servient tenement A tenement subject to a servitude or easement (*q.v.*).

servitium Services.

servitude An easement (*q.v.*) or profit a prendre (*q.v.*).

servitus [Roman law] Slavery. An institution of the *jus gentium* by which, contrary to nature, a man becomes the property of a master.

servus ordinarius [Roman law] A slave holding some special post in the establishment as cook, baker, etc.

servus poenae [Roman law] A penal slave: a convict, e.g. slaves sent to the mines, or condemned to fight with wild beasts. Abolished by Justinian.

servus vicarius [Roman law] An attendant or assistant of a *servus ordinarius*: often purchased by the latter out of his *peculium*.

session The period between the opening of Parliament and its prorogation (*q.v.*).

Session of the Peace Formerly a sitting of justices of the peace for the exercise of their powers. There were petty and special sessions. The magistrates' court and justices were organised on the basis of commission areas; petty session areas and petty sessional divisions. Each petty session area consisted of either the whole of a commission area or an area wholly included within a commission area. See Justices of the Peace Act 1997. Under the Courts Act 2003 s.8, England and Wales are divided into areas known as local justice areas (*q.v.*) although magistrates (*q.v.*) now have national jurisdiction.

set down A request in the proper form to the appropriate officer to list a case for hearing. See LISTING.

set-off Where a claim by a defendant to a sum of money (whether of an ascertained amount or not) is relied on as a defence to the whole or part of a claim made by the claimant, it may be included in the defence or counterclaim (*q.v.*) and set-off against the claimant's claim. The Court has power to give separate judgments when dealing with counterclaims or it may order a set-off between the two claimants and enter a judgment for the balance (CPR r.40.13(2)).
There can, in general, be no set-off against the Crown.

settle

settle (1) To draw up a document and decide upon its terms, e.g. a partnership deed may be settled by counsel.
(2) To compromise a case.
(3) To create a settlement (*q.v.*).

settled account See ACCOUNT, SETTLED.

settled land Land limited to several persons in succession or to an infant. Under the Settled Land Act 1925 s.1, settled land is land:
(1) Limited in trust for any person by way of succession.
(2) Limited in trust for any person in possession, (a) for an entailed interest; (b) for an estate subject to an executory limitation over; (c) for a base or determinable fee; (d) being a minor, for an estate in fee simple or for a term of years absolute.
(3) Limited in trust for a contingent estate.
(4) Limited to or in trust for a married woman with a restraint on anticipation (but see restraint on anticipation).
(5) Charged with any rentcharge for the life of any person. See TENANT FOR LIFE.

No new settlements can be created on or after January 1, 1997 (see ss.2(1) and 27(2) of the Trusts of Land and Appointment of Trustees Act 1996). Instead the land will be held on a trust of land (*q.v.*). Land which is settled land before that date will continue to be so until there is no longer any property subject to the settlement.

settlement The instrument or instruments by which land is settled. See SETTLED LAND.
A compound settlement is the description of a number of documents, e.g. deeds and wills, extending over a period, by means of which land is settled. No new settlements can be created on or after January 1, 1997 (see ss.2(1) and 27(2) Trusts of Land and Appointment of Trustees Act 1996). Instead the land will be held on a trust of land (*q.v.*). Land which is settled land before that date will continue to be so until there is no longer any property subject to the settlement.
A marriage or ante-nuptial settlement is an instrument executed before or at the time of a marriage, and wholly or partly in consideration of it.
A strict settlement is one which is designed to retain landed estates in the family.
A voluntary settlement is one not made for valuable consideration.

several Separate; as opposed to "joint".

severalty Property is said to belong to persons in severalty when the share of each is ascertained (so that he can exclude the others from it) as opposed to joint ownership, ownership in common, and coparcenary, where the owners hold in undivided shares.

severance Where a transaction is composed of several parts, and it is possible to divide it up so as to preserve part and disregard the other part, the contract is said to be severable. Thus if one of the promises is to do an act which is either in itself a criminal offence or *contra bonos mores* (*q.v.*), the whole contract is void, but if the objectionable part is only subsidiary, then it may be treated as struck out and the contract enforced without it. Severance is also the process by which a joint tenant is able to separate his notional share of the ownership of the land from that of other joint tenants so that he becomes a tenant in common. See s.36(2) of the Law of Property Act 1925 (as amended by the Trusts of Land and Appointment of Trustees Act 1996) for statutory procedure for severance.

sex discrimination Discrimination against a person on the grounds of their sex. Certain kinds of sex discrimination are unlawful and relate equally to discrimination against both men and women on the grounds of their sex. See

378

the Sex Discrimination Acts 1975–86 and art.141 of the EC Treaty (ex art.119) which is directly effective and may be enforced by the national courts. See DISCRIMINATION.

sex offender order See SEXUAL OFFENCES PREVENTION ORDER.

sexual assault An offence under the Sexual Offences Act 2003 s.3 which includes all non-consensual sexual touching but which unlike rape (*q.v.*) and assault by penetration (*q.v.*) does not involve penetration.

sexual grooming An offence under the Sexual Offences Act 2003 s.15 aimed at abuse of the internet and mobile telephone communications. Meeting or travelling to meet a child under 16, having met or communicated with the child on at least two earlier occasions, with the intent of committing an act which would constitute a sexual offence, is itself unlawful and subject to a maximum term of seven years' imprisonment on indictment. It is also an offence for an adult to meet a child where the child travels with the intention of meeting the adult after such communications (s.15 as amended by the Criminal Justice and Immigration Act 2008).

sexual harassment Under the Sex Discrimination Act 1975 s.4A, a person subjects a woman to harassment if he engages in unwanted conduct that is related to her sex or that of another person or he engages in any form of unwanted verbal, non-verbal or physical conduct of a sexual nature that has the purpose or effect of violating her dignity, or of creating an intimidating, hostile, degrading, humiliating or offensive environment for her. It is also harassment to treat a person less favourably because of her rejection of or submission to such unwanted conduct. This applies equally to treatment of a man. Conduct will only be regarded as having this unwanted effect if in all the circumstances, including the victim's perception, it should reasonably be regarded as having that effect. See DISCRIMINATION; HARASSMENT; RACIAL HARASSMENT.

sexual offences Substantially revised by the Sexual Offences Act 2003 which introduces various new or amended offences including: rape (*q.v.*), sexual assault (*q.v.*), incest (*q.v.*), exposure (*q.v.*), buggery (*q.v.*), abuse of a position of trust (*q.v.*), voyeurism (*q.v.*) and prostitution (*q.v.*). The Act pays particular attention to child sex offences (e.g. sexual grooming (*q.v.*)). Sexual activity with a child under 13 is a strict liability offence (*q.v.*). Part 2 of the Act establishes various methods of controlling sexual offenders including foreign travel orders (*q.v.*), sexual offences prevention orders (*q.v.*) and risk of sexual harm orders (*q.v.*).

sexual offences prevention order A civil order which may be applied for by the police, replacing the sex offender order under the Sex Offenders Act 1997. Applications for orders are based on evidence that the offender has behaved in a manner indicating that the public face serious sexual harm from that offender (Sexual Offences Act 2003 s.104). An order may be granted even though an offender has never been convicted of a sexual offence. Orders, which will last for a minimum of five years, will specify the prohibitions which the court deems necessary for the protection of the public.

sexual orientation For the purposes of the Employment Equality (Sexual Orientation) Regulations 2003 means a sexual orientation towards: (a) persons of the same sex; (b) persons of the opposite sex; or (c) persons of the same sex and the opposite sex.

sexual orientation discrimination The Employment Equality (Sexual Orientation) Regulations 2003 render it unlawful to discriminate against a person on the grounds of sexual orientation (*q.v.*). This protection is largely confined to the field of employment and vocational training and, unlike the Sex Discrimination Act 1975 and the Race Relations Act 1976, does not afford protection in the context of provision of services or education. However, further rights may be available under the EC Equal Treatment Framework Directive 2000/78 (see *Maruko v Versorgungsanstalt der Deutschen Buhnen* [2008] I.R.L.R. 450) and under the European Convention on Human Rights (see *EB v France* [2008] 1 F.C.R. 235. See DISCRIMINATION.

sexual orientation harassment The new statutory definition of sexual orientation harassment provides that a person subjects another to harassment where on grounds of sexual orientation, he engages in unwanted conduct which violates that other person's dignity or creates an intimidating, hostile, degrading, humiliating or offensive environment for that person. Importantly the definition allows for the differences in reaction of victims to the harassment. See the Employment Equality (Sexual Orientation) Regulations 2003; SEXUAL HARASS-MENT.

shadow director A person in accordance with whose directions or instructions the directors of a company are accustomed to act, Companies Act 2006 s.251. See DIRECTORS.

share A share represents a portion of a company's share capital and is a measure of the interest that a shareholder has in a company. It confers certain rights and liabilities on the shareholder, e.g. voting rights, dividend rights, liability to pay for the shares. The legal holder whose name is entered in the register of members is a member of the company. A share is a chose in action. Most shares are issued as ordinary shares but a company can create different classes of shares, e.g. preference shares, with different rights attached to that class of shares.

share capital A company's share capital is the amount in money or money's worth which shareholders contribute to the company as payment for shares. Formerly the authorised share capital figure was stated in a company's memorandum of association and represented the nominal value of the total number of shares which a company could issue. Under the Companies Act 2006 there is no longer any limit on a company's share capital. The issued capital is the amount of capital which has been issued to shareholders. The amount shareholders have been required to pay for shares at a particular time is referred to as the called up share capital. The amount still outstanding in respect of payment for shares but not as yet required to be paid is the uncalled share capital. The paid up share capital is the amount contributed to a company is respect of its issued share capital. For public companies (*q.v.*) the nominal value of the issued share capital must comply with the statutory minimum of £50,000, a quarter of which, plus any share premium, must be paid up.

share certificate A document executed by a company which states that the person named in it is registered as the holder of a stated number of shares and the extent to which those shares are paid up. The certificate is only prima facie evidence of title to the shares and is not a negotiable instrument.
  Share certificates are no longer required for Stock Exchange (*q.v.*) listed shares of companies participating in CREST (*q.v.*). See DEMATERIALISATION.

share premium The amount paid by shareholders to a company on the purchase of the company's shares which is in excess of the nominal value of the shares, reflecting the market value of the shares. It is paid into the company's share premium account.

share transfer The transfer of ownership of shares. The transfer procedure is usually set out in a company's (*q.v.*) articles of association. The Stock Transfer Act 1963 introduced a simplified procedure for the transfer of fully paid shares. The Companies Act 2006 s.770 requires that the transfer of shares for which share certificates have been issued must be made in writing using a proper instrument of transfer unless otherwise exempt or the transfer falls under ss.783-

790 (paperless holdings and transfers). Usually a stock transfer form is completed, stamped and forwarded to the company together with the relevant share certificate in order to effect a transfer of shares and the relevant entries on the company's register of members.

See CREST (*q.v.*) for a system of paperless transfer of shares (Uncertificated Securities Regulations 2001).

share transmission The automatic transfer of shares by operation of law on the death or bankruptcy of the shareholder. See SHARE.

sheriff The chief officer of the Crown in the county. He is appointed by the Crown every year and must hold some land within the county. The duties of sheriffs include the charge of parliamentary elections, the execution of process issuing from the High Court and the criminal courts, and the levying of forfeited recognisances. See PRICKING THE SHERIFFS.

shifting use See USE.

ship Includes every description of vessel used in navigation. For registration as a "British ship" see Merchant Shipping Act 1995 Pt II.

ship's husband The agent of the owners in regard to the management of all affairs of the ship in the home port.

ship's papers A ship's registry certificate, bill of health, charterparty and log, which show the character of the ship and cargo.

shire The county.

shire-reeve or shire clerk The sheriff.

shoplifting To steal goods from a shop. Not a distinct offence as it amounts to theft contrary to Theft Act 1968 s.1. In *R. v Page* it was held that a custodial sentence should be the last resort unless the offence involved the use of a child or was persistent.

shops Shop premises means a shop, or a building, or part, where retail or wholesale trading is carried on, or where goods are delivered by the public for repair or treatment, and also solid fuel sale depots (Offices, Shops and Railway Premises Act 1963 s.1(3)). The main object of that Act is to set standards of health, welfare and safety for the employees working in such premises.

short title The short title of an Act is the name by which the Act is commonly known in contrast to the long title which describes the scope of the Act.

shorthold tenancy A tenancy of a residence under which the landlord has the mandatory ground for obtaining possession that it is a shorthold tenancy. See ASSURED SHORTHOLD TENANCY; PROTECTED SHORTHOLD TENANCY.

show cause When an order, rule, decree or the like has been made nisi, the person who appears before the court and contends that it should not be allowed to take effect is said to show cause against it.

shrink wrap licence A commercial term to denote the means by which the person who owns software rights seeks to impose the terms of a licence for use of the software on the purchaser. The basis is that the terms of the licence are detailed on the outside packaging and visible through the transparent wrapping. The legal effect is uncertain.

sic utere tuo ut alienum non laedas [So use your own property as not to injure your neighbour's] See NUISANCE.

sickness benefit Payable to people who were not entitled to statutory sick pay (*q.v.*) for incapacity for work on account of illness or disablement. Sickness benefit was replaced by incapacity benefit by the Social Security (Incapacity for Work) Act

381

1994. See also Social Security Act 1998. This in turn has been replaced by employment and support allowance (*q.v.*) under the Welfare Reform Act 2007.

sign manual The signature or "royal hand" of the Queen, as distinguished from the signing of documents by the signet.

signature A document is signed when the relevant person writes or marks something on it in token of that person's intention to be bound by its contents. It is commonly done by the writing of a name but illiterate people may "make their mark" (a cross). Corporations may execute (*q.v.*) a document by affixing their common seal. Whether a company (*q.v.*) has a seal or not, a document signed by a single director (if that signature is witnessed and attested), or by a director and secretary, or by two directors of a company has the same effect as if executed under the common seal of the company. See SEAL.

signet A seal with which certain documents are sealed by a principal Secretary of State on behalf of the Queen. The signet is the principal of the three seals by the delivery of which a Secretary of State is appointed to his office.

silence, right to At common law there is generally no obligation on a suspect to answer questions either to assist the police with enquiries when investigating offences or to give evidence at his own trial and a court or jury may not draw an adverse inference from a defendant's refusal to answer questions.

The Criminal Justice and Public Order Act 1994 does not alter the position that a person has a right to silence but does provide that the court, in determining whether a defendant is guilty of the offence charged or whether there is a case to answer, may draw such inferences as appear proper from evidence that on being questioned under caution by the police about the offence, the defendant failed to mention any fact relied on in his defence, which, in the circumstances existing at the time, he could reasonably have been expected to mention, ibid. ss.34–37.

similiter [In like manner] Formerly a set form of words used by the plaintiff or defendant in an action by which he signified his acceptance of the issue tendered by his opponent.

simple contract A contract made orally or in writing but not by deed.

simplified planning zone (SPZ) An area in which a simplified planning zone scheme is in force. The effect of a scheme is to grant, in relation to the zone, planning permission for development (*q.v.*) specified in the scheme or for any class of development so specified. Planning permission granted in a SPZ may be unconditional or subject to such conditions as may be specified in the scheme. (See Town and Country Planning Act 1990 ss.82–87.) See also ENTERPRISE ZONE.

simony The selling of such things as are spiritual, by giving something of a temporal nature for the purchase thereof (Stephen). Selling the next presentation to a living was simony. The Simony Act 1713 was repealed by the Statute Law (Repeals) Act 1971. See ADVOWSON.

sine die [Without day] Indefinitely. See EAT INDE SINE DIE.

single currency The objective of the European Monetary Union (EMU) was to achieve a single currency in three stages. Stage one consisted of the completion of the internal market (*q.v.*), stage two which began on January 1, 1994 aims to ensure the convergence of the economies of the Member States (*q.v.*). Only those Member States that achieve the convergence criteria were able to join the single currency. The final stage involved the irrevocable locking of exchange rates of the currencies of the Member States and the introduction of a common, single currency, the euro. Euro coins and notes were not issued to participating Member States until 2002.

Single European Act (SEA) The Single European Act, despite its nomenclature, was a Treaty which amended the EEC Treaty of Rome. The SEA contained amendments designed to facilitate the passage of Community legislation (*q.v.*) for the completion of the internal market (*q.v.*).

single market A term commonly used to describe the internal market (*q.v.*) in the European Community.

single member company Since 1992 it has been possible to form a private company limited by shares or guarantee with one member. See now Companies Act 2006 s.7.

sittings There are four sittings of the Supreme Court in every year: the Hilary sittings, beginning on January 11 and ending on the Wednesday before Easter Sunday; the Easter sittings, beginning on the second Tuesday after Easter Sunday and ending on the Friday before the spring bank holiday at the end of May; the Trinity sittings, beginning on the second Tuesday after the spring bank holiday and ending on July 31; and the Michaelmas sittings, beginning on October 1 and ending on December 21 (Practice Direction 39B and Court of Appeal Practice Direction).

Sittings of the High Court may be held at any place in England and Wales (Supreme Court Act 1981 s.71).

skeleton argument A concise written resumé of an advocate's proposed arguments. The skeleton argument indicates to the parties and the court what points are, or are not, in issue and the nature of the arguments about the points. In the case of points of law, the skeleton argument should state, with citations, the principal authorities in support of the argument. A skeleton argument must be numbered in paragraphs and state the name of the advocate who prepared it. Skeleton arguments are often accompanied by a chronology. They are usually required for hearings in the High Court and are required for all High Court appeals and Court of Appeal cases.

skin impression In relation to any person, means any record (other than a fingerprint) which is a record (in any form and produced by any method) of the skin pattern and other physical characteristics or features of the whole or any part of his foot or of any other part of his body (Police and Criminal Evidence Act 1984 s.65(1) as amended). See DNA TESTING; INTIMATE SAMPLE; NON-INTIMATE SAMPLE.

slander Defamation (*q.v.*) by means of spoken words or gesture. It is a tort and not a crime and is not actionable without proof of special damage, except in four cases when the words are said to be actionable per se, i.e.:

(1) Imputing that a person has committed a crime punishable with imprisonment.

(2) Imputing that a person has a contagious or infectious disease which carries some moral opprobrium, such as a sexually transmitted disease.

(3) Disparaging a person in his office, profession, calling, trade or business, whether or not the words are spoken of him in the way of his office, etc. (Defamation Act 1952 s.2).

(4) Imputing unchastity or adultery to a woman (Slander of Women Act 1891). See: Defamation Act 1996; Broadcasting Act 1990. See also LIBEL.

The publication of words in the course of the performance of a play is, in general, treated as a publication in a permanent form (Theatres Act 1968 ss.4 and 7).

slander of title A false and malicious statement about a person, his property, or business which inflicts damage, not necessarily on his personal reputation, but on his title to property, or on his business, or generally on his material interests (Winfield). Examples are false allegations that a house is haunted; that a lady engaged to be married is married already; or that goods are liable to a lien or infringe a patent or copyright. It includes slander of goods: a false and malicious comment on the quality of the merchandise manufactured and sold by the plaintiff (*White v Mellin* [1895] A.C. 154).

sleeping partner A partner who does not take an active role in the business of the partnership (*q.v.*).

slip A memorandum containing the agreed terms of a proposed policy of marine insurance, and initialled by the underwriters. The insurance cover commences from the moment the slip is signed. See the Marine Insurance Act 1906 ss.21–22.

slip rule Clerical mistakes, accidental omissions, etc. in judgments and orders may be corrected by the court at any time on application by motion or summons.

small claims The term commonly and formerly applied to cases involving £1,000 or less dealt with in county courts under the arbitration procedure. See SMALL CLAIMS TRACK; TRACK ALLOCATION.

small claims track Under CPR r.26 every defended civil claim must be allocated to one of the three tracks by a procedural judge after the parties to the proceedings have completed an allocation questionnaire (*q.v.*). The small claims track (see CPR r.27) is intended to provide a proportionate procedure for the most straightforward types of cases such as consumer disputes, small accident claims, disputes about the ownership of goods and landlord and tenant cases other than claims for possession. This is the normal track for defended claims with a value of less than £5,000 although there are certain exceptions in respect of personal injuries cases where the value of the claim for pain, suffering and loss of amenity exceeds £1,000 (r.26.6(1)(a)and (2)); claims by tenants of residential premises seeking orders that their landlords should carry out repairs or other works to the premises where the value of the claim exceeds £1,000 (r.26.6.(1)(b)); claims by residential tenants seeking damages against their landlords for harassment or unlawful eviction (r.26.7(4)); and claims involving a disputed allegation of dishonesty (Practice Direction 26, 8.1(1)(d)). See TRACK ALLOCATION.

smuggling The offence of importing or exporting prohibited goods, or of importing or exporting goods and fraudulently evading the duties imposed on them. Anyone found guilty of a smuggling offence shall be liable to: (a) on summary conviction a penalty of the prescribed sum or of three times the value of the goods, whichever is the greater, or up to six months' imprisonment; or (b) on indictment to an unlimited penalty or up to seven years' imprisonment, or both (Customs and Excise Management Act 1979). In relation to import or export of certain prohibited weapons or ammunition the term of imprisonment may be up to 10 years.

socage A variety of tenure with fixed and certain services, as distinguished from frankalmoign and knight's service.

Social Fund Controlled and managed by the Secretary of State who may make payments out of it including those related to maternity, funeral or cold weather payments, crisis loans or community care grants (Social Security Contributions and Benefits Act 1992, as amended by the Welfare Reform Act 2007).

Social Fund Commissioner. Appointed by the Secretary of State to oversee the system of discretionary payments from the Social Fund, the Commissioner in turn appoints Social Fund inspectors, monitors their decisions and provides an annual report on their work.

Social Fund Inspectors Appointed by the Commissioner, they conduct independent reviews of the discretionary decisions of officers at a Jobcentre Plus to refuse a payment from the Social Fund (*q.v.*).

social housing Under the Housing and Regeneration Act 2008 such is low cost rental accommodation (*q.v.*) and low cost home ownership accommodation (*q.v.*). See OFFICE FOR TENANTS AND SOCIAL LANDLORDS.

social security appeal tribunal Formed by the merger of national insurance local tribunals and supplementary benefit appeal tribunals (Health and Social Services and Social Adjudications Act 1983). Tribunals which were organised regionally, consisted of a legally qualified chairman and two laypersons with "knowledge or experience of conditions in the area" who were "representative of persons living or working" there. (See Social Security Administration Act 1992 s.40.) Their primary function was to hear appeals against the refusal of a benefit, contributory or means-tested, by an adjudication officer. See TRIBUNALS.

social security and child support appeals tribunal An independent appeal tribunal dealing with disputes about social security benefits, housing benefits, tax credits and child support maintenance. The composition of a tribunal will depend on the type of case being heard but may include lawyers, medical practitioners or disability experts. Appeals from this tribunal go to a Social Security and Child Support Commissioner (*q.v.*).

Social Security and Child Support Commissioners Commissioners, who must be barristers or solicitors of 7 years' standing, exercise appellate jurisdiction from social security and child support appeals tribunals and decide appeals on points of law in social security, tax credit, child support, housing benefit, council tax benefit and compensation recovery cases. They also decide appeals from Pensions Appeal Tribunals relating to war pensions and the armed and reserve forces compensation scheme and cases which have been referred to them under the Forfeiture Act 1982. Leave to appeal must be obtained either from the tribunal chairman or the Commissioner. Commissioners' decisions are binding on tribunals and adjudication officers. In certain circumstances those decisions may be reported. An appeal lies from a Commissioner to the Court of Appeal with the leave either of the Commissioner or the Court.

soft law A term commonly used to describe certain documents or rules which do not have legally binding force in the sense that they have been enacted by parliament in the form of a statute (*q.v.*) or a statutory instrument (*q.v.*) but are important in many areas of regulation, e.g. Guidance issued by a Secretary of State, Government Circulars, Planning Policy Guidance Notes, Codes of Practice. The chief function of such documents and the rules they contain within them are to regulate the exercise of official discretion, e.g. by a local authority. There are also many other voluntary agreements on good standards and practice, e.g. codes of practice published by trade associations; safety standards for products, etc.

software See COMPUTER PROGRAM.

sole trader An individual who carries on a business on his own account. He is fully liable for any losses of the business and pays income tax on any taxable profits of the business. A sole trading business is an unincorporated business as is a partnership (*q.v.*). Contrast with a company (*q.v.*) which is an incorporated business.

solicitor Solicitor of the Supreme Court of England and Wales. A person employed to conduct legal proceedings or to advise on legal matters. To enable a person to practise as a solicitor, he must (a) be admitted as a solicitor; (b) have his name on the roll of solicitors; and (c) have in force a practising certificate (*q.v.*) issued by the Law Society (*q.v.*) (Solicitors Act 1974) (see SOLICITORS REGULATION AUTHORITY). Solicitors are not only bound to use reasonable care and skill in transacting the business of their clients, but they also occupy a fiduciary (*q.v.*) position towards their clients. Any person duly admitted as a solicitor is an officer of the Supreme Court.

A solicitor has a lien (*q.v.*) on documents of which he has possession in his capacity of solicitor, e.g. title deeds, until his proper costs are paid. Also any court in which a solicitor has been employed to prosecute or defend any suit, matter or proceeding may make a charging order on the property recovered or preserved through his instrumentality for his taxed costs. See TAXATION OF COSTS.

A solicitor should exercise reasonable skill and care in the performance of his instructions and where a solicitor has been negligent the client may bring a civil action against the solicitor. Where solicitors act as advocates they enjoy the same immunity as barristers (*q.v.*) (see s.62 of the Courts and Legal Services Act 1990). However, in *Arthur J.S. Hall & Co (a firm) v Simons* [2000] 3 All E.R. 673 the House of Lords held that advocates no longer enjoy immunity from suit in respect of their conduct of civil and criminal proceedings.

solicitor advocate A solicitor (*q.v.*) or a registered European lawyer providing advocacy services. See ADVOCATE.

solicitor, change of A person who sues or defends any cause or action by means of a solicitor may change that solicitor by filing a notice of change at the appropriate office and then serving copies of the notice on every other party and on the former solicitor (CPR r.42).

Solicitor-General The second of the law officers who acts as deputy to the Attorney-General (*q.v.*). One or the other is usually a member of the House of Commons.

Solicitors Regulation Authority (SRA) An independent body set up to replace the Law Society Regulation Board in anticipation of changes under the Legal Services Act 2007. It regulates the qualification of solicitors, monitors those providing legal training and draw ups the rules of professional conduct. It also administers the roll of solicitors and issues practising certificates. The SRA includes within its remit the promotion of choice, innovation and accessibility in the provision of legal services. See LAW SOCIETY.

solvency, declaration of See DECLARATION OF SOLVENCY; VOLUNTARY WINDING UP.

solvent In a position to pay debts as they become due.

solvit ad diem The plea by the defendant, in an action on a bond, bill, etc. that he had "paid on the day" the money which was due.

solvitur ambulando The question is resolved by action.

solvitur in modum solventis [Money paid is to be applied according to the wish of the person paying it]

sound recording A recording of sounds from which the sounds may be reproduced, or a recording of the whole or part of a literary, dramatic or musical work from which sounds reproducing the work or part may be reproduced: Copyright, Designs and Patents Act 1988 s.5A. Copyright is a property right which can exist in works such as sound recordings, films, broadcasts or cable programmes, ibid. s.1. These categories of recording works attract copyright in the recording itself even though they may be based on other work.

sounding in damages An action which is brought to recover damages, as opposed to an action for debt. For the claimant to succeed he must prove he suffered some damage.

sovereignty The supreme authority in an independent political society. It is essential, indivisible and illimitable (Austin). However, it is now considered both divisible and limitable. Sovereignty is limited externally by the possibility of a general resistance. Internal sovereignty is paramount power over all action within, and is limited by the nature of the power itself. In the British Constitution the Sovereign de jure is the Queen or Crown. The legislative sovereign is the Queen in Parliament, which can make or unmake any law whatever. The legal sovereign is the Queen and the Judiciary. The executive sovereign is the Queen and her Ministers. The de facto or political sovereign is the electorate: the Ministry resign on a defeat at a general election.

Speaker The Speaker of the House of Commons (*q.v.*) is the member of the House through whom it communicates with the Sovereign and who presides over the proceedings of the House and enforces obedience to its orders. The Speaker is elected by the Commons from their own numbers, subject to the approval of the Crown (*q.v.*), on the first day that a new Parliament assembles.

Special Commissioners of Income Tax Legally qualified persons who hear and determine appeals concerning decisions of the HM Revenue and Customs relating to income tax, corporation tax, capital gains tax and inheritance tax. The office of the Special Commissioners is part of the Tribunals Service (*q.v.*), an executive agency of the Ministry of Justice. See GENERAL COMMISSIONERS.

special damages Damage of a kind which is not presumed by law, but must be expressly pleaded and proved. Contrast with general damages (*q.v.*).

Slander (*q.v.*) is not (with some exceptions) actionable without proof of special damage. Also, in an action for slander of title (*q.v.*), or other malicious falsehood (*q.v.*), it shall not be necessary to allege or prove special damage if the words are calculated to cause pecuniary damage to the claimant and are published in writing or other permanent form; or are calculated to cause pecuniary damage to the claimant in respect of any office, profession, calling, trade or business held or carried on by him (Defamation Act 1952 s.2).

An action will lie for a public nuisance (*q.v.*) at the instance of a person who has suffered special damage (over and above that suffered as a member of the public) as a result of the nuisance.

special jury Where a trial by jury was ordered, either party could formerly insist upon a special jury drawn from a panel of persons with a higher property qualification than common jurors. Special juries have been abolished (Juries Act 1949 ss.18–19; Courts Act 1971 s.40).

special licence A licence to marry without the publication of bans may be granted by the Archbishop of Canterbury. See LICENCE, MARRIAGE.

special procedure list The name given to those divorce cases dealt with by the district judge reading the affidavit of the petitioner and certifying that the petitioner has proved the contents of the petition and is entitled to a decree. The procedure thus avoids either party appearing in court. All undefended divorces are now dealt with in this way so that the description is to some extent a misnomer. See Family Proceedings Rules 1991 r.2.24(3).

special resolution See RESOLUTION.

special site A local authority may designate an area of contaminated land (*q.v.*) as a special site if the land meets the criteria specified in regulations issued by the Secretary of State. Responsibility for determining the remediation (*q.v.*) of land which is designated a special site lies with the Environment Agency (*q.v.*) rather than the local authority in whose area the land is situated. See CONTAMINATED LAND.

special verdict See VERDICT.

specialia generalibus derogant [Special words derogate from general ones]

specialty A somewhat archaic term used to refer to a contract made by deed (*q.v.*). A specialty debt is one due under a deed.

specific disclosure After documents have been disclosed and inspected, a party may make an application to the court for specific disclosure of further information (Practice Direction 31). The court may grant a specific disclosure order under CPR 1998 r.31.12 which can order a party to disclose the documents specified in the order or to carry out a search for further documents located as a result of the search. See disclosure.

specific goods Defined in the Sale of Goods Act 1979 s.61 as goods identified and agreed on at the time the contract of sale is made and includes an undivided share, specified as a fraction or percentage, of goods identified and agreed on. See ASCERTAINED GOODS; UNASCERTAINED GOODS.

specific issue order An order giving directions for the purpose of determining a specific question (e.g. about medical treatment or education) which has arisen, or which may arise, in connection with any aspect of parental responsibility for a child, Children Act 1989 s.8. See also PROHIBITED STEPS ORDER; SECTION 8 ORDERS.

specific performance Where damages would be inadequate compensation for the breach of an agreement, the contractor may be compelled to perform what he has agreed to do by a decree of specific performance, e.g. in contracts for the sale, purchase or lease of land, or for the recovery of unique chattels (i.e. not obtainable in the market). Specific performance will not usually be decreed for contracts of personal service, but a defendant may be restrained by injunction from the breach of a negative stipulation in such a contract, e.g. a covenant not to give services elsewhere during the term of the contract. Specific performance is an equitable remedy and at the discretion of the court. Where a court has jurisdiction to award specific performance, it may award damages in addition to, or in substitution for, specific performance. Actions for the specific performance of contracts relating to real estate are assigned to the Chancery Division.

specificatio The making of a new article out of the chattel of one person by the labour of another.

specification The statement in writing describing the nature of an invention in an application for a patent (*q.v.*). See Patents Act 1977 and Copyright, Designs and Patents Act 1988.

spent conviction After a certain period of time a conviction may become spent and the convicted person may be considered rehabilitated (*q.v.*). Under the Rehabilitation of Offenders Act 1974 a sentence of imprisonment or corrective training for a term exceeding six months but no more than thirty months has a "rehabilitation period" of ten years from the date of the conviction. Spent convictions should not be referred to in an open court in criminal proceedings without leave of the judge. Some sentences such as life imprisonment can never be "spent".

spes successionis A mere hope of succeeding to property, e.g. on the part of the next-of-kin of a living person who will take his property if he happens to die intestate. See EXPECTANT HEIR.

sponsus [Roman law] Betrothed. The man who intended to marry a woman stipulated with the person that was to give her in marriage that he would so give, and on his part promised to marry her. *Sponsa* was the woman thus promised; *sponsus* the man who promised to marry her. *Sponsalia* denoted the proposal and promise of marriage.

spouse A husband or wife. See HUSBAND AND WIFE.

springboard doctrine A concept used in intellectual property litigation to prevent a defendant gaining a head start in commercial activity as a result of an infringing act. Where, for example, confidential information has been used illegally, that use has been stopped by court action and the information then later comes into the public domain, the defendant may be prevented from using the information immediately and delayed by court order. The delay will be equivalent to the time that it might have been reasonably expected to take to develop the information towards commercial use had no infringement occurred. (See *Terrapin Ltd v Builders' Supply Co (Hayes) Ltd* [1960] R.P.C. 128 CA.)

springing use See USE.

spurii [Roman law] Bastards: persons born out of lawful marriage.

squatter A person who occupies land (not being a tenant or tenant holding over after the termination of a tenancy) who has entered into or who remains in occupation of the land without a licence or the consent of the person entitled to occupation. For summary proceedings for claiming possession of land as against squatters, see CPR Pt 55. For criminal liability, see FORCIBLE ENTRY.

squatter's title The title acquired by one who, having wrongfully entered upon land, occupies it without paying rent or otherwise acknowledging any superior title. A squatter in possession has a good title against all but the true owner whose right may be barred by lapse of time. See LIMITATION, STATUTE OF.

stabit praesumptio donec probetur in contrarium [A presumption will stand good until the contrary is proved]

stakeholder (1) A person with whom money or property (in which he himself claims no interest) is deposited to abide an event, e.g. pending the decision of a bet or wager. The term is commonly used in relation to a contract for the sale of land where deposit monies are held by the purchaser's solicitor. (2) In the context of corporate governance (*q.v.*) used to denote members of a company, its employees, suppliers or creditors, or the public at large.

stallage A payment for the exclusive occupation of a portion of the soil within a market.

stamp duty A tax charged on documents where certain types of property are transferred, e.g. share transfers, conveyances, leases. Since 2003 land transactions have instead been subject to a stamp duty land tax (*q.v.*). Stamp duties are either fixed in amount, or ad valorem (*q.v.*), that is, proportionate to the value of the property dealt with by the instrument. Ad valorem duty is charged only on sales not on gifts. The purchaser submits the documents for stamping to the relevant Revenue Stamp Office with the requisite payment. The document is impressed with the official stamp as proof of payment and returned. Documents should be presented for stamping within 30 days of execution. There are fines for late stamping. See the Stamp Act 1891 and the Stamp Duties Management Act 1891, as amended by various Finance Acts.

stamp duty land tax. A modern self-assessed tax on land transactions involving any estate, interest, right or power in or over land in the United Kingdom. It was introduced by the Finance Act 2003.

standard of proof In all legal proceedings it is necessary for the party bringing the action to establish the facts upon which the case is reliant. This is the burden of proof. Therefore if A claims that B has been negligent, A must prove the facts upon which he relies to the satisfaction of the court. The level of proof required, or the standard of proof, differs according to the proceedings. In criminal cases the prosecution must establish the defendant's guilt beyond reasonable doubt. In civil proceedings, the standard of proof is on the balance of probabilities. See PROOF.

standing See LOCUS STANDI.

Standing Orders Rules and forms regulating the procedure of each House of Parliament.

standing search A search at the probate registry for grants made within the previous twelve or following six months from the date of the search, Non-Contentious Probate Rules 1987 r.43(3) amended by Non-Contentious Probate (Amendment) Rules 1991 and 1998.

stannaries Parts of Devon and Cornwall where any tin works are in operation. Civil actions in respect of mining matters might formerly be brought in the Stannary Court, which was abolished in 1896. See the Stannaries Acts 1869 and 1887.

staple towns The seaports from which wool, leather, tin and lead (collectively termed the staple) were exported, and which were regulated by the Statute of the Staple. The merchants of those towns, the Staplers, had, from the reign of Edward I, a monopoly in the staple. In each staple town the mayor of the staple held Staple Courts.

Star Chamber The *Aula Regis* sitting in the Star Chamber at Westminster, with a residuary jurisdiction after the severance of the Courts of Common Law and Chancery. It acted as a "court of equity" in criminal matters. By the statute 1487, (3 Hen. 7 c.1), a court was constituted to consist of the chief officers of state and the two chief justices, with jurisdiction over unlawful combinations, riots and assemblies, and offences of sheriffs and jurors; later extended to offences against Royal Proclamations. This court appears to have become assimilated in the Court of Star Chamber. The Star Chamber was abolished by the Statute 1640 (16 Car. 1 c.10).

stare decisis The "sacred principle" of English law by which precedents are authoritative and binding, and must be followed. See PRECEDENT; RATIO DECIDENDI.

State The organised community: the central political authority.
In international law, a state is a people permanently occupying a fixed territory, bound together into one body politic by common subjection to some definite authority exercising, through the medium of an organised government, a control over all persons and things within its territory, capable of maintaining relations of peace and war, and free from political external control.

state aids A term used in Community law for any assistance granted by a Member State (*q.v.*) or any form of aid through state resources which distorts or threatens to distort competition by favouring certain undertakings or the production of certain goods. Insofar as they affect trade between Member States they are incompatible with the Common Market, art.87(1) of the EC Treaty (*q.v.*). Certain state aids are subject to express derogation in order to protect certain economic and social objectives.

state liability The principle of (Member) State liability established by the European Court of Justice (*q.v.*) in *Francovich and Bonifaci v Italy* (C–6/ 90 and C–9/90), [1991] E.C.R. I-5357 in which a Member State (*q.v.*) may be liable in damages to an individual whose rights have been infringed by a breach of Community law for which the Member State is responsible. The right may arise from a provision of the EC Treaty (*q.v.*) or from Community legislation (*q.v.*). It need not be a directly effective right. There must be a causal link between the breach and the damage suffered. The breach by the Member State must be sufficiently serious. See DIRECT EFFECT.

statement of case The statement of case contains the outline of the claimant's case and includes (CPR r.2.3(1)): (a) a claim form; (b) particulars of claim (where these are not included in the claim form); (c) defence; (d) counterclaims (see CPR r.20.2(1)); or (e) reply to defence; and also (f) any further information given in relation to these, either voluntarily, or ordered by the court under CPR r.18.1. The statement of case replaces what were previously the pleadings. Every statement of case must be verified by a statement of truth (*q.v.*).

statement of claim Formerly a written or printed statement by the plaintiff in an action in the High Court. Now replaced by particulars of claim (*q.v.*).

statement of compatibility See ACT OF PARLIAMENT; HUMAN RIGHTS.

statement of defence See DEFENCE.

statement of truth Under CPR r.22(1)(1)(a) every statement of case (*q.v.*) must be verified by a statement of truth. The statement of truth will be signed by the party putting forward the documents and will state that he believes the facts stated to be true (r.22.1.(4)). A statement of truth may be contained in the document it verifies, or it may be a separate document served at a later date (Practice Direction 22, 1.5). It is also possible for the legal representative of the party to make a statement of truth verifying the document put forward by the party. A person who makes, or causes to be made a false statement in a document verified by a statement of truth, without an honest belief in its truth, is guilty of contempt of court (r.32.14(1)).

statement of value Where a claimant is making a claim for money in a statement of case (*q.v.*) the claim form must contain a statement of value (CPR r.16.2(1)). The statement of value enables the court to allocate the case to the appropriate track (*q.v.*). A statement of value does not limit the power of the court to give judgment for the amount which it considers the claimant to be entitled (r.16.3(7)). See TRACK ALLOCATION.

status The legal position or condition of a person, e.g. a minor, married woman, bankrupt, or British national. The status of a person is an index to his legal rights and duties, powers and disabilities.

status de manerio [The state of a manor] The assembly of the tenants in the court of the lord to do suit.

status quo The state in which things are, or were.

statute An Act of Parliament (*q.v.*). See STATUTORY INTERPRETATION.

statute law The body of enacted law or legislation together with the accompanying body of judicial decisions, explanatory of the individual statutes (*q.v.*) (Bennion, *Statute Law*).

statute law revision Statute Law Revision Acts were passed every few years in the period from 1861 to remove Acts, or parts of Acts, which had become obsolete. However, the Law Commissions Act of 1965 inaugurated a departure by setting up a full-time Law Commission. The functions of the Commission extend to keeping under review all of the law with a view to its systematic development and reform, including in particular the codification of such law, the elimination of anomalies, the repeal of obsolete and unnecessary enactments and generally the simplification and modernisation of the law. See LAW COMMISSION.

statute merchant A bond acknowledged before the chief magistrate of some trading town pursuant to the statute De Mercatoribus, (13 Edw. 1).

Statute of Frauds 1677 (29 Car. 2 c.3). Passed for the prevention of frauds and perjuries in cases relating to land. It enacted (ss.1 and 2) that leases of lands, tenements or hereditaments (except leases not exceeding three years, reserving a rent of at least two-thirds the value of the land) shall have the force of leases at will only, unless they are put in writing and signed by the parties or their agents. Section 3 required assignments and surrenders of leases and interests in land (not being copyholds, etc.) to be in writing. Section 4 enacted that no action shall be brought upon any special promise by an executor or administrator to answer damages out of his own estate, or upon a guarantee, or upon an agreement made in consideration of marriage, or upon any contract for sale of lands, etc. or any interest in or concerning them, or upon any agreement that is not to be performed within a year, unless the agreement is in writing and signed by the party to be charged, or his agent (see *Actionstrength Ltd v International Glass Engineering* [2003] UKHL 17). Sections 7 and 9 required declarations or creations of trusts of lands, etc. and all assignments of trusts, to be in writing, signed by the party, but s.8 exempted trusts arising by implication of law. Sections 10 and 11 made the lands of a cestui que trust, when in the hands of his real representative, liable to his judgments and obligations.

It is now largely repealed and replaced by later enactments.

Statute of Uses 1535 (27 Hen. 8 c.10.). Repealed by Law of Property Act 1925. See USE.

Statute of Westminster 1931 Passed to define the constitutional position of the Dominions. In regard to legislation, by s.2 no Dominion legislation after 1931 is void or inoperative on the ground of repugnancy to the law of England, and a Dominion Parliament has power to repeal Imperial legislation insofar as it is part of the law of the Dominion (*q.v.*). By s.4 no Imperial legislation was to extend to a Dominion as part of the law of the Dominion, unless it was expressly declared in the Act that the Dominion had requested and consented to the enactment but this provision has been repealed.

statute staple A bond acknowledged before the mayor of the staple (*q.v.*) to provide a speedy remedy for recovering debts.

statutes of distribution See DISTRIBUTION.

statutes of limitation See LIMITATION, STATUTE OF.

statutory charge Where public funding has been received in respect of a legal action and property has been recovered or preserved by the assisted party, the Community Legal Service (*q.v.*) has a statutory charge on the monies recovered or preserved in respect of the costs paid from the fund to the extent that the costs are not met by the other party to the claim. See Access to Justice Act 1999 s.10(7).

statutory declaration A written statement of facts which is signed by the declarant and which is solemnly declared to be true before a solicitor (*q.v.*) or magisterial officer under the Statutory Declarations Act 1835 which substitutes declarations for oaths in many cases. See COMMISSIONERS OF OATHS.

statutory demand A demand in the prescribed form served on a debtor by a creditor requiring the debtor to pay the amount owed or to secure or compound for it to the creditor's satisfaction. Failure to comply with the statutory demand within three weeks of service where the amount of the debt is £750 or more (the bankruptcy level) is evidence that the debtor appears to be unable to pay the debt and may found the basis for a bankruptcy petition by the creditor, Insolvency Act 1986 ss.267, 268. See BANKRUPTCY.

The equivalent process in company liquidation, where a written demand is served on a company, is dealt with under ibid. s.123.

statutory derivative action Under the Companies Act 2006 s.260, a claim brought in the name of a claimant member but a claim which belongs to the company. The Act imposes various procedural safeguards and restricts claims to those "arising from an actual or proposed act or omission involving negligence, default, breach of duty or breach of trust by a director of the company". The company is joined as a nominal defendant even though those running the company may have refused to take the action in the company's name. Derivative claims can only be brought under the new statutory procedure or by court order on the grounds of unfair prejudice (ibid. s.994). See FRAUD ON THE MINORITY; DERIVATIVE ACTION.

statutory duty A duty, or liability, imposed by some statute (*q.v.*).

statutory instrument Where a power to make orders, rules, regulations and other subordinate legislation is conferred on Her Majesty in Council or on any minister of the Crown by Order in Council or by statutory instrument, any document by which that power is exercised shall be known as a statutory instrument (Statutory Instruments Act 1946 s.1(1)). Provision is also made in the Act (s.1(2)) for the term to apply to certain statutory rules made under primary legislation which was in force prior to the 1946 Act. Statutory instruments are often referred to as Regulations. See DELEGATED LEGISLATION.

statutory interpretation In fulfilling their task of applying the law to the facts before them, the courts frequently have to interpret (i.e. decide the meaning of) statutes. Whilst it is true to say that the intention of Parliament should prevail, the courts have adopted a number of conventional practices to resolve ambiguities. The contemporary approach, approved by the House of Lords in *Maunsell v Olins* [1975] A.C. 373, is the unified contextual approach devised by Professor Cross. This approach still gives primacy to the literal meaning of words within the context, to be established by a preliminary reading of the Act as a whole and permitted external aids to interpretation. Recourse to *Hansard* is now permitted, see *Pepper v Hart* [1992] 3 W.L.R. 1032, HL.

An overriding requirement is now contained in the Human Rights Act 1998 s.3, in that, so far as it is possible to do so, legislation must be read to give effect in a way which is compatible with the European Convention on Human Rights.

statutory maternity pay A sum paid by an employer to pregnant employees who satisfy various conditions including a minimum of 26 weeks' continuous service ending with the week immediately preceding the 14th week before the expected week of confinement. Payment (which normally runs from the eleventh week before the expected week of confinement) will not exceed 39 weeks (due to be raised eventually to 52 weeks), the first six to be paid at nine-tenths of the employee's normal pay (the earnings-related rate), the remainder at whatever is the lower of the earnings-related rate and the prescribed weekly rate. (See Social Security Contributions and Benefits Act 1992 Pt XII as supplemented by regulations and amended by the Employment Act 2002 and the Work and Families Act 2006.) See MATERNITY LEAVE.

statutory nuisance An act or omission to act categorised or treated by statute as a nuisance (*q.v.*). For example, under the Environment Protection Act 1990 Pt III, the following, amongst others, are stated as constituting statutory nuisance: any premises in such state as to be prejudicial to health or a nuisance; smoke emitted from premises so as to be prejudicial to health or a nuisance; any animal kept in such place or manner as to be prejudicial to health or a nuisance; noise emitted from premises so as to be prejudicial to health or a nuisance; artificial light emitted from premises so as to be prejudicial to health or a nuisance (as added by the Clean Neighbourhoods and Environment Act 2005). The 2005 Act repeals parts of the Noise and Statutory Nuisance Act 1993 and provides powers for local authorities to deal with the disturbance and annoyance caused by audible intruder alarms. See ABATEMENT; ABATEMENT NOTICE; ALARM NOTIFICATION AREAS; NOMINATED KEY-HOLDERS.

statutory objective A section or subsection included in an Act of Parliament setting out the objectives to be attained by the Act or part of the Act. Such a statutory objective was set out in the Legal Aid Act 1988 s.1 and the Courts and Legal Services Act 1990 s.17(1) and (3). In fact the former was repealed by the Access to Justice Act 1999 and in the latter case this provision is due to be repealed by the Legal Services Act 2007. Section 1 of the Legal Aid Act 1988 was added as an "appropriate fanfare" at the beginning of the Act, but the section did not impose any specific duty on the Lord Chancellor.

An overriding requirement is now contained in the Human Rights Act 1998 s.3, in that, in so far as it is possible to do so, legislation must be read and given effect in a way which is compatible with Convention rights (*q.v.*). See STATUTORY INTERPRETATION.

statutory owner In respect of settled land, the trustees of the settlement (except where they have power to convey in the name of the tenant for life) or other persons who, during a minority, or when there is no tenant for life, have the powers of a tenant for life (Settled Land Act 1925 s.117(1); Land Registration Rules 2003 Sch.7, para.16(1)).

No new settlements can be created on or after January 1, 1997, see Trusts of Land and Appointment of Trustees Act 1996 ss.2(1) and 27(2).

statutory rules and orders Delegated legislation (*q.v.*) made by a minister under statutory authority which is not either a statutory instrument (*q.v.*) or an Order in Council (*q.v.*). Such rules and orders are not regulated by the Statutory Instruments Act 1946.

statutory sick pay Payable to employees at a prescribed flat rate by employers during the first 28 weeks of any period of incapacity for work due to illness (Social Security Act 1975 and Social Security Contributions and Benefits Act 1992). The first seven days of absence may be self-certified but thereafter a medical certificate is required. See INCAPACITY BENEFIT; EMPLOYMENT AND SUPPORT ALLOWANCE.

statutory tenant Any person whose security of tenure is maintained as a result of a statutory provision. A statutory tenant has no estate or property as a tenant, but has a personal right to possession of the property. See Rent Act 1977. See ASSURED TENANCY.

statutory trusts Trusts created by statute, either expressly or by implication, e.g. those set out in Schs 1 and 2 to the Trusts of Land and Appointment of Trustees Act 1996.

Statutum de Mercatoribus The Statute of Acton Burnel, which established the Statute Merchant (*q.v.*).

stay of execution A judgment debtor who is unable to pay or alleges that it is otherwise inexpedient to enforce an order may apply for a stay of execution which, if granted, suspends the operation of a judgment or order.

stay of proceedings Suspension of the whole or any part of any proceedings, which may be permanent or temporary, until something requisite or ordered is done, CPR 1998 r.3.1. Under the Supreme Court Act 1981 s.49(3) the Supreme Court has a general power to stay any proceedings. Proceedings are stayed when an offer or payment is accepted or may be stayed pending proceedings where, in the interests of the efficient progress of the proceedings it is desirable to grant a stay. The court may impose a stay as a means of enforcing compliance with its orders. While a stay is in place, the proceedings remain alive but no action may be taken to progress the claim other than applying to lift the stay.

stealing See THEFT.

stet processus [Stay of proceedings] An entry on the record in an action in the old common law courts.

steward Formerly an officer of the Crown, or of a feudal lord, who acted as keeper of a court of justice; as, for example, the Lord High Steward (*q.v.*), or the steward of a lord of a manor.

stint A limit, as in the right to pasture a limited number of animals on land.

stipendiary magistrate Formerly a full-time salaried magistrate appointed from amongst solicitors or barristers of at least seven years' standing. A stipendiary magistrate could try a case by himself, whereas two lay magistrates are required for a summary trial (*q.v.*). Replaced by District Judge (Magistrates' Courts) (*q.v.*).

stipulatio [Roman law] A verbal contract formed by question and answer. One party proposed a question (*stipulatio*) and the other responded to it (*promissio*). In the time of Gaius it was necessary to use a certain solemn form of words; but before Justinian, the question and answer could be embodied in any words to express the meaning of the parties. The contract was unilateral, the promissor only being bound, and the parties had to be present when the contract was entered into.

stirpes Stocks or families. See PER STIRPES.

stock (1) A family.

(2) Fixed interest loan capital raised by the government or a local authority (*q.v.*).

(3) The capital of a company (*q.v.*) was formerly called its "joint-stock", meaning the common or joint fund contributed by its members.

(4) A fund or capital which is capable of being divided into and held in any irregular amount.

(5) A business supplier's goods that are available for sale may be referred to as stock in trade.

Under the Companies Act 2006 s.618 a company can convert all or any of its fully paid shares into stock, a single block, which then represents the nominal value of those shares. See also DEBENTURE.

Stock Exchange The London Stock Exchange is an investment market for the buying and selling of UK and international listed securities. The Main Market allows the listing and trading of equity, debt and other securities via either a primary listing (one requiring the highest standards of regulation and disclosure) or a secondary listing with lesser requirements.

The Financial Services Authority (FSA) (*q.v.*) is designated as the UK Listing Authority (UKLA) (*q.v.*) for supervision of admission to the Official List (*q.v.*). Public companies (*q.v.*) must comply with the Listing Rules (*q.v.*) made by UKLA before their shares are admitted onto the Official List and their shares are admitted to trading on the Stock Exchange.

There is also an Alternative Investment Market (AIM) (*q.v.*) which has less stringent admission requirements and is provided for young and growing public companies. Such companies must comply with the Prospectus and Listing Rules and the AIM Rules.

Investors who wish to deal on the Stock Exchange usually do so through market intermediaries who are members of the Stock Exchange and who act as market makers (*q.v.*), brokers (*q.v.*) or matching brokers. See CREST; COMPANY.

stock transfer form In share transfers (*q.v.*) it is a form used for the transfer of fully paid shares (*q.v.*) which attracts stamp duty. See the Stock Transfer Act 1963. See SHARE TRANSFER.

stockbroker A securities firm which provides advice and acts as an agent for investors who want to buy or sell securities on the Stock Exchange. The commission on a deal is the broker's profit. The firm may also deal on its own account.

Brokers may also act as "matching brokers" when they represent themselves as willing to attempt to buy or sell a particular security whenever they are asked to do so. See MARKET MAKER.

stockjobber The former name for a market maker (*q.v.*).

stop and search The police have a general power to stop and search a person without arresting that person, where they have a reasonable suspicion that a stolen or prohibited article, e.g. an offensive weapon, may be found, Police and Criminal Evidence Act 1984 Pt I. New powers to stop and search persons suspected of carrying prohibited fireworks are due to be introduced into PACE by the Serious Organised Crime and Police Act 2005 s.115. See SEARCH OF THE PERSON.

There are specific powers of search under various other statutes, e.g. Misuse of Drugs Act 1971.

stop notice (1) Where an enforcement notice (*q.v.*) has been served in respect of an alleged breach of development (*q.v.*) control, if the planning authority consider it expedient to prevent the carrying out of any activity, before the expiry of the compliance period, a stop notice may be served (Town and Country Planning Act 1990 s.183).

(2) Under the Charging Orders Act 1979 s.5, it means a notice requiring any person or body on whom it is duly served to refrain from taking, in respect of any of the securities specified in the notice (e.g. land, stock or funds in court), specified steps such as registering a transfer or paying a dividend without first notifying the person by whom, or on whose behalf, the notice was served. See also CPR Pt 73.16.

stop order Under the Charging Orders Act 1979 s.5, it means an order of the court prohibiting the taking, in respect of any of the securities specified in the order, (e.g. land, stock or funds in court), certain steps such as registering a transfer or paying a dividend. See also CPR Pt 73.11.

stoppage in transit If a buyer becomes insolvent, an unpaid seller (*q.v.*) has a right to stop goods in the course of transit and resume possession of the goods until payment, see Sale of Goods Act 1979 ss.44–48.

stranding Does not occur when a vessel takes the ground in the ordinary and usual course of navigation, so that she will float again on the flow of the tide; but it occurs if the vessel takes the ground by reason of some unusual or accidental occurrence, e.g. in consequence of an unknown and unusual obstruction, or on being driven on to rocks.

stranger One not party or privy to an act or transaction.

strict liability Liability without fault. In civil law the concept applies where a person is liable despite the absence of fault or negligence; the vicarious liability (*q.v.*) of an employer is strict. In criminal law there is said to be strict liability when there is liability even in the absence of *mens rea* (*q.v.*) and even though his ignorance is not attributable to any default or negligence on his part, e.g. under s.1 of the Trade Descriptions Act 1968, a person is guilty of an offence merely by reason of selling goods, in the course of a business, to which a false trade description has been applied.

strict settlement See MARRIAGE SETTLEMENT; SETTLEMENT.

strike Any concerted stoppage of work (Trade Union and Labour Relations (Consolidation) Act 1992 s.246) usually involving a partial or complete withdrawal of labour by workers. Such action will normally constitute a breach of contract, entitling the employer at common law to dismiss summarily or to sue for damages (*Simmons v Hoover Ltd* [1977] I.C.R. 483; *British Telecommunications Plc v Ticehurst* [1992] I.C.R. 383 CA). In addition strikers may suffer further disabilities, e.g. loss of state benefits. In some circumstances, however, an employee is still protected against unfair dismissal (*q.v.*) and may bring a complaint to an employment tribunal (*q.v.*) despite the employer's common law right of dismissal (see Trade Union and Labour Relations (Consolidation) Act 1992, ss.237–239, as amended by the Employment Relations Acts 1999 and 2004).

striking out In civil proceedings the court has the power to order the whole or any part of a statement of case (*q.v.*) to be struck out. The court may strike out a statement of case where it appears to the court that the case discloses no reasonable grounds for bringing or defending the claim; that the case is an abuse of the court's process (*q.v.*) or is likely to obstruct the just disposal of the proceedings; or there has been a failure to comply with a rule, practice direction or court order (CPR r.3.4). Either party to the proceedings may apply to the court to strike out or the court may do so of its own initiative. See CIVIL PROCEDURE RULES.

stuprum [Roman law] Any connection between a man and an unmarried free woman otherwise than in concubinage.

sub colore juris [Under colour of the law]

sub judice [In course of trial]

sub modo [Under condition or restriction]

sub nom.: sub nomine [Under the name]

sub voce [Under the title]

subduct To withdraw or take away.

subinfeudation The grant of the whole or part of his land by a tenant in fee simple to another, to hold of him as his tenant, so that the relation of tenure with its incidents of fealty, etc. was created between them. Subinfeudation was abolished by the Statute Quia Emptores (*q.v.*) (18 Edw. 1 c.1).

subject access request A request under the Freedom of Information Act 2000 for personal information about the individual making the request which is treated as a request made under the Data Protection Act 1998.

subject to contract An acceptance made "subject to contract" means that no legally binding agreement is formed until further formalities are completed.

submission A statement made by a lawyer in court in support of the client's case. See SUBMISSION OF NO CASE TO ANSWER.

submission of no case to answer After the case for a claimant has been made the defendant may make a submission of no case to answer on the basis that on the evidence adduced by the claimant the claim cannot succeed.

subordinate legislation Legislation made by a person or body on whom or which powers have been conferred by Act of Parliament (*q.v.*). See DELEGATED LEGISLATION; ORDER IN COUNCIL; STATUTORY INSTRUMENT.

subornation of perjury The offence of procuring a person to commit perjury, punishable as perjury (*q.v.*).

subpoena A writ issued in the High Court if it appears to the court that it is proper to compel the personal attendance at any trial of a witness who may not be within the jurisdiction of the court. The court may issue a *subpoena ad testificandum* (to compel a witness to attend court and give evidence) or a *subpoena duces tecum* (to compel a witness to attend court and also bring with him certain documents in his possession as specified in the subpoena).

In civil proceedings a witness summons (*q.v.*) is used to secure the attendance of a witness, CPR 1998 r.34. Subpoenas are not issued in criminal proceedings for the purpose of which a witness summons or a witness order may be issued, Criminal Procedure (Attendance of Witnesses) Act 1965 (as amended).

subrogation The substitution of one person or thing for another, so that the same rights and duties which attached to the original person or thing attach to the substituted one. If one person is subrogated to another, he is said to "stand in that other's shoes", e.g. creditors are subrogated to the executors' right of indemnity against the estate where a business is carried on under the authority of the will; a person paying the premium on a policy of insurance belonging to another may be subrogated to that other; and an insurer is subrogated to the rights of the insured on paying his claim.

subscribe To "write under"; to sign or attest; to apply for shares, etc.

subsidiarity The principle adopted in European Community Law and enshrined in art.5, EC of the Treaty (*q.v.*) (by the Treaty on European Union). By art.5 the Community can only act within the powers conferred by the Treaty. In areas which do not fall within the exclusive competence of the Community, the Community shall only take action in accordance with the principle of subsidiarity. Thus the Community shall only take action if the objectives of the proposed action cannot be sufficiently achieved by the Member States (*q.v.*) and can therefore, by reason of the scale or effects of the proposed action, be better achieved by the Community. Lord Mackenzie Stuart, the first UK judge on the European Court of Justice, opined that the wording of the Treaty would give rise to prolonged and frequent litigation.

subsidiary company Under the Companies Act 2006 s.1159, a company is a subsidiary of another company, its holding company (*q.v.*), if that other company:
    (a) holds a majority of the voting rights in it; or
    (b) is a member of it and has the right to appoint or remove a majority of its directors; or
    (c) is a member of it and controls alone, as a consequence of a shareholder agreement, a majority of the voting rights in it. A subsidiary company also includes a company which is a subsidiary of a subsidiary company.

subsidy Assistance; aid in money.

substantive law The actual law, as opposed to adjectival (*q.v.*) or procedural law.

substratum [Bottom or basis] It is a ground for winding up a company that its "substratum" has gone, i.e. that it is impossible to carry on the business for which the company was incorporated.

subtraction The neglect or refusal to perform a duty or service, e.g. pay a tithe.

succession Succeeding or following after. Ownership may be acquired by succession, for example under a will or intestacy. See INTESTATE SUCCESSION.

sue To bring an action, suit or other civil proceeding against a person.

sufficient interest test A court may not grant leave to apply for judicial review (*q.v.*) unless it considers the applicant has a sufficient interest in the matter to which the application relates, see Supreme Court Act 1981 s.31. The question of what constitutes a sufficient interest is a mixture of fact and law. Where the applicant is a victim of a human rights (*q.v.*) violation then they have sufficient interest, Human Rights Act 1998 s.7. See LOCUS STANDI; STANDING.

suggestio falsi An active misrepresentation, as opposed to a *suppressio veri*, or passive misrepresentation (*q.v.*).

sui generis [Of its own kind; the only one of its kind] The European Community is said to be sui generis.

sui juris [Roman law] One of full legal capacity. An independent person not subject to any of the three forms of authority, *potestas, manus, mancipium* In English law, a person who can validly contract and bind himself by legal obligation uncontrolled by any other person.

suicide Formerly the felony of self-murder. By the Suicide Act 1961 the rule of law whereby it is a crime for a person to commit suicide was abrogated, and the offence was created of complicity, whereby a person who aids, abets, counsels or procures the suicide of another, or an attempt by another to commit suicide, is punishable by 14 years' imprisonment.

suicide pact Where two or more persons make a common agreement to bring about the death of all, whether or not each is to take his own life. Any survivor who killed another party to the pact in pursuance of it is guilty of manslaughter (Homicide Act 1957 s.4).

suing and labouring clause The clause in a policy of marine insurance, as follows: "In case of any loss or misfortune, it shall be lawful to the assured, their factors, servants, and assigns, to sue labour, and travel for, in, or about the defence, safeguard, and recovery of the said goods, and merchandises, and ship, etc., or any part thereof, without prejudice to the insurance; to the charges whereof we will contribute each one according to the rate and quantity of his sum herein insured" (see Marine Insurance Act 1906 s.78).

The object of the suing and labouring clause is to encourage the assured person to take all necessary steps for the preservation of the property insured in case of accident.

suit Any legal proceeding of a civil kind brought by one person against another; an action, particularly in equity or for divorce. A bond or recognisance given to a public officer as security is said to be put in suit when proceedings are taken to enforce it.

summary assessment When a court makes a cost order it may make a summary assessment of the amount payable by way of costs immediately after making its order. Generally the court will make a summary assessment at the end of a fast track (*q.v.*) trial and also in interim hearings that last less than one day. The parties to the proceedings are required to file and serve statements of costs not less than 25 hours before the hearing (Practice Direction 44). Unless otherwise ordered costs assessed summarily are payable within 14 days of the order, CPR r.44.8.

summary judgment A court may give a summary judgment against a claimant or defendant on the whole of a claim or on a particular issue if it considers that the claim or defence has no real prospect of success and there is no other compelling reason why the case or issue should be disposed of at a trial (CPR r.24.2). The court may give summary judgment against a claimant in any type of proceedings. The court may not give judgment against a defendant in proceedings for possession of residential premises against a tenant, a mortgagor or a person holding over even after the end of his tenancy or in proceedings for an admiralty claim in rem (CPR Pt 24). Former restrictions in relation to the type of proceedings where summary judgment could be obtained have largely been removed. See CIVIL PROCEDURE RULES.

summary proceedings A summary trial is a trial in a magistrates' court, where the offence is a summary offence or an offence which is triable either way but which the magistrates have decided, with the accused's consent, to try summarily.

summer time For the purposes of the Summer Time Act 1972 is the period beginning at one o'clock, Greenwich mean time, in the morning of the last Sunday in March and ending at one o'clock, Greenwich mean time, in the morning of the last Sunday in October.

summing-up A recapitulation by the judge of the evidence adduced in an action, drawing the attention of the jury to the salient points. A defective summing-up in a criminal case may be a ground for the Court of Appeal quashing the conviction.

summons Formerly a document issued from the office of a court of justice, calling upon the person to whom it is directed to attend before a judge or officer of the court. In civil proceedings a summons to commence proceedings is now replaced by a claim form (*q.v.*). A relevant witness may be compelled to attend court by a witness summons (*q.v.*). See CLAIM FORM.

summum jus summa injuria [Extreme law is extreme injury] The rigour of the law, untempered by equity, is not justice but the denial of it.

super visum corporis [Upon view of the body] See CORONER.

superficies solo cedit [Whatever is attached to the land forms part of it] Actual physical attachment is not essential, e.g. a dry stone wall is part of the land. Corporeal hereditaments consist of the surface of the land and everything attached to the land.

superior court Defined in the Contempt of Court Act 1981 s.19 as the Court of Appeal, the High Court, the Crown Court, the Courts Martial Appeal Court, the Restrictive Practices Court, the Employment Appeal Tribunal, and any other court exercising powers equivalent to those of the High Court, including the House of Lords in its appellate capacity. See also SUPREME COURT.

supersedeas A writ of *supersedeas* was formerly issued to stay or put an end to proceedings.

superstitious uses A trust which has for its object the propagation of the rites of a religion not tolerated by the law, and which is therefore void. It is otherwise if the trust is for saying masses for the dead (*Bourne v Keane* [1919] A.C. 815; *Re Caus* [1934] Ch. 162).

supervision and treatment order Where a special verdict is returned that the accused is not guilty by way of insanity, or findings have been made that the accused is under a disability and that he did the act or made the omission charged against him, the court shall make, in respect of the accused, a hospital order (*q.v.*), a supervision order (*q.v.*) or an order for his absolute discharge, Criminal Procedure (Insanity) Act 1964 s.5 as substituted by Domestic Violence, Crime and Victims Act 2004 s.24(1). See ADMISSION ORDER.

supervision order An order placing a minor under the supervision of a designated supervisor (normally a local authority in whose area the child resides or will reside, or a probation officer), Children Act 1989 s.31(1). Such an order may be made if the court is satisfied that the child is suffering, or likely to suffer, significant harm and that the harm, or likelihood of harm, is attributable to the care, not being what it would be reasonable to expect a parent to give to the child, or the child's being beyond parental control.

supply of goods and services Contracts which involve the supply of goods and also the provision of labour or services. If the main substance of the contract is not the sale of the relevant goods then the contract should be classified as one for goods and services. See Supply of Goods and Services Act 1982 for terms implied into such contracts.

support, right of Every proprietor of land is entitled to so much lateral support from his neighbour's land as is necessary to keep his soil at its natural level, that is, his neighbour must not excavate so close to the boundary as to cause the land to fall or subside. Similarly the owner of the surface is entitled to vertical support as against the owner of the subsoil, that is, the owner of the subjacent land must not cause subsidence of the surface unless he has an easement entitling him to do so. The right does not extend to the case of land, the weight of which has been increased by buildings, unless it can be shown that the land would have sunk if there had been no buildings on it, or unless an easement has been acquired by 20 years' uninterrupted enjoyment. See *Dalton v Angus* (1881) 6 App. Cas. 740; *Barley Main Colliery Co v Mitchell* (1886) 11 App. Cas. 127. The common law rules are now largely superseded by the Party Wall, etc. Act 1996. See PARTY WALL.

suppressio veri [Suppression of the truth] Passive misrepresentation (*q.v.*). See SUGGESTIO FALSI.

supra [Above]

Supreme Court Established under the Constitutional Reform Act 2005, once that Act is in force (expected to be in late 2009), with a President and Deputy President, its remaining judges being styled "Justices of the Supreme Court". Initially the existing Lords of Appeal in Ordinary will fill this position. The Court will function as the highest court in the United Kingdom, effectively taking over from the House of Lords (*q.v.*) and the Judicial Committee of the Privy Council. One of its 12 Justices may be appointed President. In any proceedings the Court will normally be duly constituted if it consists of an uneven number of judges and at least three (ibid. s.42). The Court is to have a Chief Executive whose duties will include the non-judicial functions of the Court (ibid. s.48). See CHANCELLOR, LORD HIGH; JUDICIAL COMMITTEE; PRIVY COUNCIL.

Supreme Court Costs Office Formerly the Supreme Court Taxing Office, it consists of costs judges appointed to assess costs arising from legal proceedings. Under CPR 1998 r.44.7, when a court makes a cost order, it may either make a summary assessment (*q.v.*) or order detailed assessment by a costs officer.

Supreme Court of Judicature The court formed by the Judicature Act 1873, whose constitution and jurisdiction are now defined by the Supreme Court Act 1981. The Supreme Court consists of the Court of Appeal, the High Court of Justice and the Crown Court (Act of 1981 s.1(1)). It is due to be renamed the Senior Courts of England and Wales under the Constitutional Reform Act 2005 (expected to be late 2009).

sur [Upon] Used to point out on what the old real actions were founded, e.g. "sur disseisin", was to recover the land from a disseisor.

surcharge (1) To surcharge a common is to put more cattle thereon than the pasture and herbage will sustain, or than the commoner has a right to do.

(2) In taking or auditing accounts, to surcharge is to disallow an unauthorised item of expenditure and make the accounting party liable for it personally.

(3) Where any tax remains unpaid following the expiry of a certain period, the taxpayer is liable to a surcharge. See also ACCOUNT SETTLED.

sureties of the peace and good behaviour A person may be ordered to find sureties for his keeping the peace or to be of good behaviour on a complaint being made under s.115 of the Magistrates' Courts Act 1980, in addition to his own recognisances (*q.v.*). There is no upper limit to the surety which may exceed the maximum fine for the relevant offence (*Sandbach Justices Ex p. Williams* [1935] 2 K.B. 192). This process is called "binding over" (*q.v.*).

surety A person who binds himself, usually by deed, to satisfy the obligation of another person, if the latter fails to do so; a guarantor. If a surety satisfies the obligation for which he has made himself liable, he is entitled to recover the amount from the principal debtor. If one of several sureties is compelled to pay the whole amount or more than his share, he is entitled to contribution (*q.v.*) from his co-sureties. A surety is entitled to the benefit of all the securities which the creditor has against the principal. If the creditor releases the principal debtor, this will discharge the surety from liability, unless the creditor reserves his right against the surety. See BAIL.

surplus assets What is left of a company's property after payment of debts and repayment of the whole of the preference and ordinary capital. Whether the preference shareholders are entitled to share in surplus assets is a question of construction, but the courts will not readily hold that the preference shareholders have bartered away their rights as contributories (*q.v.*).

surplusage A superfluity or excess; in pleading the allegation of unnecessary matter. In civil proceedings the claim form and particulars of claim must be concise (CPR rr.16.2 and 16.4). See STATEMENT OF CASE; STRIKING OUT; PLEADINGS.

surprise This may be a ground for setting aside a contract, judgment or order if substantial injustice has been done.

surrebutter; surrejoinder Formerly a type of pleading.

surrender The voluntary yielding up of a limited estate in or lease of land, so that it merges in the remainder or reversion. Surrender may be by deed, or by operation of law, e.g. if a lessee accepts a new lease incompatible with his existing lease, this operates as a surrender in law of the latter. A mortgagee or mortgagor in possession has power to accept surrender of leases, subject to the conditions in s.100(5) of the Law of Property Act 1925.

surrogacy A process under which a woman, the surrogate mother (*q.v.*), carries a child under an arrangement made before the birth of the child with a view to handing over that child after birth so that other persons assume parental responsibility for that child, usually an infertile couple who have made the arrangement with the surrogate mother. Surrogacy can be full or partial. In deciding whether such an arrangement has been made, the circumstances as a whole can be looked at, in particular whether there was any promise of payment to the surrogate mother. No surrogacy arrangement (*q.v.*) is enforceable by or against any of the parties to the arrangement, see the Surrogacy Arrangements Act 1985 as amended. It is an offence to advertise surrogacy services and also for commercial agencies to engage women to act as surrogate mother. See PARTIAL SURROGACY.

surrogacy arrangement An arrangement under which, if the woman to whom the arrangement relates were to carry a child in pursuance of it, she would be a surrogate mother (*q.v.*), Surrogacy Arrangements Act 1985 s.1.

surrogate mother A woman who carries a child in pursuance of an arrangement made before she began to carry the child and made with a view to any child carried in pursuance of it being handed over to, and parental responsibility being met by, another person or other persons.

survivorship The right of a person to acquire absolute ownership of property by reason of his having survived another person who had an interest in it, e.g. on the death of one of two joint tenants, the whole property passes to the survivor. See COMMORIENTES.

sus. per coll. (suspendatur per collum) [Let him be hanged by the neck]

suspended sentence A court which passes a sentence of imprisonment for a term of at least 28 weeks but not more than 51 weeks may order that the imprisonment is not to take effect immediately but only on the happening of another event within a specified period. For example, conviction for another offence whether or not punishable by imprisonment during the "operational period" or failure to comply with a requirement imposed by and specified in the order during the "supervision period". The supervision period and operational period must each be a period of not less than six months and not more than two years beginning with the date of the order.

sustainable development Defined in the Bruntland Report of the World Commission on Environment and Development (1987) as "development that meets the needs of the present without compromising the ability of future generations to meet their own needs". Widely accepted as the most important principle of environmental law at the international, European and domestic level. Sustainable development is the primary objective of the European Community's Fifth Environmental Action Programme where it is defined as a policy and strategy for continued economic and social development without detriment to the environment and the natural resources on the quality of which continued activity and further development depend.

sweat test See SALIVA TEST.

syndic A person appointed by a corporation to act for it as regards a particular matter.

synod An ecclesiastical council.

T

TEU Treaty on European Union (*q.v.*).

ToA Treaty of Amsterdam 1997 (*q.v.*).

TOLATA Trusts of Land and Appointment of Trustees Act 1996. See TRUST OF LAND.

TUPE The Transfer of Undertakings (Protection of Employment) Regulations 1981 were enacted to implement the Acquired Rights Directive (77/187 replaced by 2001/23). The Regulations provide, inter alia, for automatic transfer of the contracts of employment between the transferor employer and the transferee employer of those employed in the undertaking where a "relevant transfer" (*q.v.*) has taken place. The 1981 Regulations were replaced by a new set of regulations in 2006.

Table A Companies limited by shares can adopt a model set of articles of association (*q.v.*) set out in Table A (Companies (Tables A to F) Regulations 1985). These articles will be deemed to have been adopted by a company unless excluded or modified by a bespoke set of articles of association (*q.v.*) adopted on incorporation (*q.v.*) or later by special resolution (*q.v.*). The 1985 Regulations were amended in 2007 to ensure compliance with the Companies Act 2006. A new set of model articles is due in 2009.

tabula in naufragio [Plank in the shipwreck] In the doctrine of tacking (*q.v.*) the legal estate was the plank on which the third mortgagee could save himself in the shipwreck while the second mortgagee was drowned.

tabulae [Roman law] Tablets.

tabularius [Roman law] A public notary.

tacking The priority of mortgagees over the same property is determined by the order in which the mortgages were made. Prior to 1926, this order might be disturbed by the process of adding a subsequent mortgage to an earlier mortgage or a further advance by the earlier mortgagee to his mortgage, when both would take the priority of the earlier, provided there was no notice of intervening mortgages at the time the subsequent mortgage was made. This was known as tacking. Thus a third mortgagee, who had no notice of a second mortgage at the time his mortgage was made, might subsequently acquire the first mortgage and the legal estate and squeeze out or postpone the second mortgagee. By s.94 of the Law of Property Act 1925 tacking was abolished, except that a prior mortgagee has the right to make further advances to rank in priority to subsequent mortgages, where such is made (a) by arrangement with the subsequent mortgagees; or (b) he had no notice of the subsequent mortgages at the time the further advance was made; or (c) the mortgage imposes an obligation on him to make further advances.

tagging, electronic See CURFEW ORDER.

tail See ENTAIL; ESTATE.

takeover The process by which one company (*q.v.*) acquires control of another company by buying all, or a majority of, its shares. This is usually brought about by means of a takeover bid (*q.v.*). Takeovers are regulated by Pt 28 of the Companies Act 2006.

takeover bid An offer by one company to the shareholders of a second company to acquire their shares. The offer may be for cash or for shares in the company making the bid, and will usually be conditional on acceptance by the holders of all the shares affected, or by a certain percentage so that the provisions of the Companies Act 2006 may be used. See TAKEOVER.

talaq An Islamic divorce.

tales [Such] Where a jury was summoned and found to be insufficient in number, the judge was empowered to award a *tales de circumstantibus*, that is, to command the sheriff to return so many other men duly qualified as should be present or could be found. The jurors so added were called talesmen. By the Juries Act 1974 ss.6, 11(2) as amended by the Criminal Justice Act 1988 (s.170(1), Sch.15), the court itself has power to make up the required numbers of a full jury from any persons in the vicinity of the court.

tallage Taxes.

tally A stick of rectangular section across one side of which were cut notches denoting payments. The stick being split lengthwise so that on each half there was half of each notch, the debtor retained one half of the stick as evidence of the payment and the creditor kept the other half as a record. They were used in the Exchequer (*q.v.*) from the earliest times.

tangible property Property that is physical in nature, such as land and chattels. See INTANGIBLE PROPERTY.

tattooing It is an offence punishable by fine on summary conviction to tattoo ("the insertion into the skin of any colouring material designed to leave a permanent mark") a person under the age of 18 years except for medical reasons (Tattooing of Minors Act 1969).

tax year The income tax (*q.v.*) year or year of assessment runs from April 6 to the following April 5. Companies pay corporation tax (*q.v.*) on a financial year (*q.v.*) which runs from April 1 to March 31.

taxation The imposition of duties for the raising of revenue. Direct taxes are imposed upon the individual, usually according to his ability to pay, e.g. income tax; indirect taxes are levied upon certain articles of popular consumption; e.g. customs and excise duties. See also VALUE ADDED TAX.

taxation of costs The process of examining and, if necessary, reducing the bill of costs of a solicitor. See DETAILED ASSESSMENT; SUMMARY ASSESSMENT; SUPREME COURT COSTS OFFICE.

Technology and Construction Court This is a specialist court dealing particularly with construction law disputes. It is part of the Queen's Bench Division of the High Court and replaces the work previously done by the Official Referees' Court. The court was established in 1998 and is presided over by a High Court judge who tries cases. Cases are also tried before circuit judges. A Technology and Construction Court claim is one which involves issues or questions which are technically complex or for which a trial by a judge of the Technology and Construction Court is for any other reason desirable (*Practice Direction—Technology and Construction Court*). This means that a Technology and Construction Court judge may try any case within the business of the Chancery and Queen's Bench divisions of the High Court.

technology transfer agreement Under EC Regulation 772/2004 (originally 240/96) an agreement that deals with the licensing of intellectual property rights. It may cover patent licensing agreements, know-how licensing agreements or mixed agreements.

tellers (1) Four officers of the Exchequer who received all moneys due to the King. (2) Counters of votes.

temporalities The properties and possessions of a bishop in his see.

tenancy deposit scheme An authorised scheme made for the purpose of safeguarding tenancy deposits paid in connection with shorthold tenancies (*q.v.*) and facilitating the resolution of disputes which have arisen in connection with such deposits, see Housing Act 2004.

tenancy in common A state of concurrent ownership by two or more persons, each having a distinct but "undivided" share in the property. No one person is entitled to exclusive title or use, each being entitled to occupy the whole in common with the others. Also known as "undivided shares" (see BULK GOODS). Since 1925 a tenancy in common in land can only exist as an equitable interest under a trust: See the Law of Property Act 1925 ss.1(6), 34. A legal tenancy in common can exist in a chose in possession but, as with land, a tenancy in common in a chose in action can only be equitable. See JOINT TENANCY.

tenant A holder (of land). All subjects hold land of the Crown, whether freehold (*q.v.*) or leasehold (*q.v.*) and are properly called tenants. Most commonly, however, the term applies to a person holding under a lease (*q.v.*) (the lessee).

tenant at sufferance One who has originally come into possession of land by a lawful title and continues such possession after his interest has determined. The tenant continues in possession without statutory authority and without the landlord's permission. See HOLDING OVER.

tenant at will A lessee of land at the will of himself and of the lessor, either of whom may withdraw the willingness to continue the arrangement at any time. The status is a hybrid between that of tenant and licensee.

tenant by copy of court roll A copyholder. See COPYHOLD.

tenant by curtesy See TENURE BY CURTESY OF ENGLAND.

tenant for life One who is entitled to land for the term of his own life: a life interest. Since 1925 a life interest can only exist in equity. A tenant for life is entitled to the rents and profits of the land during his life but is not entitled to commit voluntary waste (*q.v.*) unless made unimpeachable for waste.
Under s.19(1) of the Settled Land Act 1925 the person of full age, who is for the time being beneficially entitled under a settlement to possession of settled land for his life, is, for the purposes of that Act, the tenant for life of that land and entitled to have the legal estate in the settled land vested in him.

tenant for years One who holds for a term of years certain; a lessee.

tenant from year to year A tenant of land whose tenancy can only be determined by a notice to quit expiring at that period of the year at which it commenced. In the case of ordinary tenancies from year to year (in the absence of any provision to the contrary) a six months' notice to quit is required, or two quarters' notice where the term begins on one of the quarter days. Whenever one person holds land of another, and there is no express limitation or agreement as to the term for which it is to be held then, if the rent is payable with reference to divisions of the year (e.g. quarterly), the tenancy is deemed to be a tenancy from year to year. See NOTICE TO QUIT.

tenant in tail See ENTAIL.

tenant in tail after possibility of issue extinct Where land is given to a man and his wife in special tail, if one of them dies without issue, the survivor is tenant in tail after possibility of issue extinct, because there is no possibility of issue being born capable of inheriting the land. Such a tenant cannot bar the entail (*q.v.*) and is not impeachable for waste (Fines and Recoveries Act 1833 s.18; continued permanently in force by the Expiring Laws Act 1925). See Law of Property Act 1925 s.176(2). See ESTATE.

tenant pur autre vie A tenant for the life of another. If A granted land to B during the life of C and B died before C, then there was no one entitled to the land because A had parted with his right during C's life. Anyone might enter and occupy during C's life and was called a "general occupant". But B's heir might enter and occupy, and was called the "special occupant". By the Statute of Frauds s.12, however, a tenant *pur autre vie* might dispose of his interest by will; otherwise it formed part of his personal estate (see Wills Act 1837 s.3). Since 1926, a tenancy *pur autre vie* can only exist in equity, and on the death of the tenant *pur autre vie* during the life of the *cestui que vie*, the property is held in trust for the person entitled to the deceased's property, whether under his will or on intestacy, as the case may be. See CESTUI QUE VIE.

Tenant-in-chief One who held land directly from the King; it was normally held by knight's service (*q.v.*).

tenant-right The right of a tenant, despite determination of his tenancy, to the benefit of his toil on the land if need be by entry. Now generally supplanted by the security provisions of the Agricultural Holdings Act 1986 and the provisions for compensation. See EMBLEMENTS.

tenant to the praecipe One against whom a *praecipe* (*q.v.*) or writ was issued in a real action. See RECOVERY.

tender (1) An offer, e.g. by a debtor to his creditor, of the exact amount of the debt. The offer must be in money, which must be actually produced to the creditor, unless by words or acts he waives production. If a debtor has made a tender and continues ready to pay, he is exonerated from liability for the non-payment, but the debt is not discharged. See LEGAL TENDER; PAYMENT INTO COURT.

(2) An offer to supply or buy goods or services. In some situations the tender is a bid to supply goods or services submitted by a person in response to an invitation by another, e.g. a local authority, for the supply of those goods and services. At common law the bid will normally constitute an offer (*q.v.*) which will not bind the bidder until accepted by the party inviting the tender. Requests for tenders are a common form of negotiation for commercial contracts.

tenement (1) A thing which is the subject of tenure (*q.v.*), i.e. land.

(2) A house, particularly a house let in different apartments.

tenendum [To be held] The clause in a deed of conveyance of land indicating of whom the land is to be held. See HABENDUM.

tenor (1) The general import of a document.

(2) The period of time, as expressed in a bill of exchange (*q.v.*), after which it is payable.

Tenterden's Act (Lord) The Statute of Frauds Amendment Act 1828, which enacted that there must be in writing and signed a promise to pay, or an acknowledgement of a debt (s.1), and any representation as to the character of means of another with the intent that such person may obtain credit, money or goods (s.6).

tenths (1) The tenth part of the annual profit of an ecclesiastical benefice. See ANNATES; QUEEN ANNE'S BOUNTY.

(2) The tax consisting of one-tenth of every man's whole personal property, formerly levied by the Crown.

tenure An element of the feudal system of landholding, tenure denotes the type of holding of land, as in free (hold) tenure which indicates that no service is required of the owner for the use of the land.

tenure, security of The right of a tenant or licensee of land to remain in possession under a statutory provision after determination of the contractual tenancy or licence.

term (1) A portion of the year during which alone judicial business could be transacted. By the Judicature Acts 1873 and 1875 the division of the year into terms was abolished, the year being divided into sittings (*q.v.*) and vacations (*q.v.*).

(2) The fixed period for which a right is to be enjoyed.

(3) "Keeping Term" is the dining in hall of an Inn of Court the requisite number of times, in the course of qualifying for call to the bar.

(4) Any undertaking, express or implied, in a contract being either a condition (*q.v.*), a warranty (*q.v.*), or an innominate term (*q.v.*).

term of years An estate or interest in land limited to a fixed number of years, as in the case of a lease for seven years. A term of years includes a term for less than a year or for a year or years and a fraction of a year or from year to year (Law of Property Act 1925 s.205). A term of years absolute is one of the only two corporeal interests in land which, since 1925, are capable of subsisting or being conveyed or created at law (ibid. s.1(1)). See LEASEHOLDS.

terminus a quo [The starting point]

terminus ad quem [The finishing point]

termor One who holds land for a term of years.

terra Land.

terre-tenant [Land holder] One who has the seisin of land.

territorial limits The geographical area over which an Act of Parliament extends, including in the United Kingdom, the territorial waters (*q.v.*) up to the 12-mile limit.

territorial waters Such parts of the sea adjacent to the coast of a country as are deemed by international law to be within the territorial sovereignty of that country. The Territorial Waters Jurisdiction Act 1878 enacted that an offence committed by any person within territorial waters should be an offence within the Admiral's jurisdiction, although committed on a foreign ship. The Territorial Sea Act 1987 provides that the breadth of the territorial sea adjacent to the United Kingdom shall be 12 nautical miles. British fishing limits have been extended to 200 miles from the baselines from which the breadth of the territorial sea adjacent to the United Kingdom, the Channel Islands and the Isle of Man is measured (Fishery Limits Act 1976 s.1).

territoriality The principle of international law that states should not exercise jurisdiction outside the area of their own territory. The territory of a state includes its ships and aircraft. See TERRITORIAL LIMITS; TERRITORIAL WATERS.

terrorism The use or threat of action designed to influence the government or an international governmental organisation or intimidate the public or a section of the public in order to advance a political, religious or ideological cause. Proscribed actions include action involving serious violence against a person, serious damage to property, creating a serious risk to public health and safety and serious disruption or interference with an electronic system. See the Terrorism Act 2000; Suppression of Terrorism Act 1978; Taking of Hostages Act 1982; Extradition Act 2003; Prevention of Terrorism Act 2005; Terrorism Act 2006.

terrorist The Terrorism Act 2000 defines a terrorist as a person who commits any of the various offences under the Act or who is, or has been, concerned in the commission, preparation or instigation of acts of terrorism (*q.v.*).

test case A claim the result of which is applicable to other similar cases which are not litigated.

testament A will (*q.v.*). Technically a testament deals with the disposition of personal property while a will deals with real property. A formal will usually begins: "This is the last will and testament of me, A. B. etc.", but "testamentary power" applies generally to the power to make a valid will.

testamentary capacity The legal capacity to make a valid will. The testator (*q.v.*) is required to possess "a sound and disposing mind and memory" (*Banks v Goodfellow* (1870) L.R. 5 Q.B. 549).

testamentary expenses A term used when administering estates to cover costs arising from death. The estate must bear the expenses which arise from the proper performance of the duties of the personal representative (*q.v.*) in that capacity.

testamentary freedom The ability to leave one's property on death to whomsoever one wishes.

testamentary guardian The appointment of a guardian (*q.v.*) for the testator's (*q.v.*) minor (*q.v.*) children by the terms of a will (*q.v.*), effective on death.

testamentary trust A trust (*q.v.*) set up by the terms of a will (*q.v.*) and effective on death.

testate Having made a valid will (*q.v.*).

testator One who makes a will (*q.v.*).

testatum The opening words of the operative part of a deed (*q.v.*) "Now this deed witnesseth."

testimonium The clause at the end of a deed or will which commences "In witness, etc.".

testimony The evidence of a witness (*q.v.*) usually given in court and usually under oath.

textbooks Books of expert opinion on the current state of the law. Citation of textbooks to a court may be of assistance in the interpretation of the law but such texts are of no authority as a source of law. "Books of Authority", such as those of Bracton, Blackstone, Coke, Glanvil or Littleton are given the same authoritative status as cases of the same period.

theft A person is guilty of theft contrary to the Theft Act 1968 s.1, if he dishonestly appropriates property belonging to another with the intention of permanently depriving the other of it. A person guilty of theft is liable to imprisonment for a term not exceeding seven years (1968 Act s.7, as amended by the Criminal Justice Act 1991 s.26(1)).

thesaurus non competit regi, nisi quando nemo scit qui abscondit thesaurum [Treasure does not belong to the King, unless no one knows who hid it] See TREASURE TROVE (now abolished); TREASURE.

thing See CHOSE.

third party One who is stranger to a transaction or proceeding.
(1) Under the Civil Procedure Rules 1998, where a defendant to an existing claim, in turn claims to be entitled to a contribution or indemnity from another person (a third party) who is not a party to an action, or some question or issue

between the claimant and defendant should properly be determined between the claimant, defendant and third party, the defendant may issue a CPR Pt 20 claim (*q.v.*) (formerly a third-party notice) against such third-party.

(2) A "third party risk policy" is a policy of insurance against liability in respect of injury caused by the insured or others to the property or persons of another.

See the Road Traffic Act 1988, Pt VI. A motorcar owner is liable in damages to an injured third party for breach of the statutory duty to insure.

(3) Under the doctrine of privity of contract, a third part cannot, in principle, enforce rights under a contract, but see now Contracts (Rights of Third Parties) Act 1999.

threatening behaviour The Public Order Act 1986 ss.4 and 5 introduced a series of offences, relating to conduct which threatens another. For example, it is an offence to use threatening, abusive or insulting words or behaviour, or disorderly behaviour, or to display anything which is threatening, abusive or insulting within the sight of anyone likely to be harassed, alarmed or distressed by it.

threats The common law offence of obtaining property by threats was abolished by the Theft Act 1968 s.32. See BLACKMAIL. Threats to destroy or damage property constitute an offence. See CRIMINAL DAMAGE.

threshold criteria The criteria which must be met before the court can make a care order (*q.v.*) or supervision order (*q.v.*). The criteria include that the child is suffering or likely to suffer significant harm and that the harm, or likelihood of it, is attributable to the care given to the child.

tidal water Any part of the sea and any part of a river within the ebb and flow of the tide at ordinary spring tide and not being a harbour, Merchant Shipping Act 1995 s.255.

tied-house A public-house subject to a covenant, made with the freeholder or lessor of the premises, to obtain all supplies of alcoholic liquor from a particular brewer.

timber Properly only oak, ash and elm of mature age; but timber now includes all trees used for building. Timber is part of the realty until severed. Cutting timber is waste (*q.v.*). Under the Forestry Act 1967 s.3(4), timber includes all forest products. See ESTOVERS.

time The rules for computing any time limit contained in the CPR (*q.v.*), any practice direction (*q.v.*) or any judgment or order of the court are set out in CPR, Pt 2 r.2.8. A period of days expressed as a number of days is computed as clear days. A clear day means (a) that the day on which the period begins is not included; and (b) if the end of the period is defined by reference to an event, the day on which that event occurs is not included, ibid. rr.2.8.2–3.

time bargain An option (*q.v.*).

time charter A charterparty (*q.v.*) for a specified period.

time immemorial Term used to denote a time before legal memory. The Statute of Westminster 1275 fixed it at 1189.

time is of the essence A phrase indicating that performance of a contractual obligation, e.g. delivery of goods, within the stipulated time is a condition of the contract. See *Hartley v Hymans* [1920] 3 K.B. 475.

timeshare accommodation Any living accommodation, in a building or caravan, in the United Kingdom or elsewhere, used or intended to be used, wholly or partly, for leisure purposes by a class of persons (timeshare users) all of whom have rights to use, or participate in arrangements, under which they may use, that accommodation or accommodation within a pool of accommodation to which that accommodation belongs, for a specified or ascertained period of the year, Timeshare Act 1992 s.1, as amended SI 1997/1081. See TIMESHARE AGREEMENT; TIMESHARE RIGHTS.

timeshare agreement A contract which entitles a person to spend a certain period of time each year in a holiday property, the timeshare accommodation (*q.v.*). Defined under the Timeshare Act 1992, as amended by SI 1997/1081, as an agreement under which timeshare rights (*q.v.*) are conferred, or purport to be conferred, on any person.

Timeshare purchasers must be provided with information about their rights before entering into the contract and in the contract itself. There is a cooling-off period during which the timeshare contract and any associated credit contract can be cancelled.

timeshare rights Rights by virtue of which a person becomes or will become a timeshare user, being rights exercisable during a period of not less than three years, Timeshare Act 1992, s.1 as amended SI 1997/1081. See TIMESHARE AGREEMENT; TIMESHARE ACCOMMODATION.

tipstaff An officer, in the nature of a constable, attached to the Supreme Court. Since the abolition of imprisonment on mesne process, the functions of the tipstaves have been confined to arresting persons guilty of contempt of court.

tithe The payment due by the inhabitants of a parish for the support of the parish church and which was generally payable to the parson of the parish. Originally tithe was payable in kind and consisted of the tenth part of all yearly profits; from the soil (praedial tithes), from farm stock (mixed tithes), and from personal industry (personal tithes). Rectorial or great tithe was payable to the rector, vicarial or little tithe to the vicar, and lay tithe to a layman. Ecclesiastical tithe was attached to a benefice or ecclesiastical corporation. When land came into the hands of the monasteries the tithe was appropriated and the cure of souls was deputed to a vicar. The Tithe Act 1925 vested ecclesiastical tithe in Queen Anne's Bounty (*q.v.*).

Tithes generally were commuted for rentcharges, formerly varying with the price of corn. However, by the Tithe Act 1936, all tithe rentcharges were extinguished and replaced by "redemption annuities" payable to the Crown for 60 years, the owners of the tithe rentcharges being compensated by issues of Government Stock. The Finance Act 1962 s.32 provided for the compulsory redemption of tithe annuities charged on land whenever the land was sold. Tithe rentcharge annuities under the Act of 1936 as amended were finally abolished by the Finance Act 1977 s.56.

tithing A local division or district forming part of a hundred (*q.v.*), and so called because every tithing formerly consisted of 10 freeholders with their families. The tithing man was the chief member of a tithing. See FRANKPLEDGE.

title (1) Generally the term "title" signifies a right to property and is considered with reference either to the manner in which the right has been acquired or as to its capacity of being effectively transferred. A title may be: (a) original, where the person entitled does not take from any predecessor e.g. a patent or copyright; or (b) derivative, where the person entitled takes the place of a predecessor, by act of the parties or by operation of law. See ABSOLUTE TITLE; ABSTRACT OF TITLE; COVENANTS FOR TITLE.

(2) An appellation or address of honour or dignity.

(3) A description or heading, e.g. of a claim at law.

title-deeds The documents conferring or evidencing the title to land. They "savour of the realty" and pass with the land under a conveyance except deeds relating to the part of the estate retained by the vendor. In such case the vendor must acknowledge the buyer's right to production, and undertake their safe custody (Law of Property Act 1925 s.64). See also LAND REGISTRATION.

title information document Document issued by the Land Registry on the completion of an application for registration which confirms that the application has been completed. It will include a copy of the register and, if a new title plan has been prepared, a copy of that plan. It has no legal status. See land registration.

title, long See LONG TITLE It refers to an Act of Parliament.

title, short See SHORT TITLE It refers to an Act of Parliament.

toll A payment for passing over a highway, bridge, ferry, etc. The right to demand tolls frequently forms part of franchise (*q.v.*).
   Toll traverse was a sum payable for passing over the private soil of another; toll thorough for passing over the public highways.

Tomlin order An order, named after Mr Justice Tomlin who laid down the practice principles, which records that an action is stayed by the agreement of the parties under the terms set out in a schedule to the order.

tonnage (1) A former duty on imported wines, payable to the Crown. The duty was at the rate of so much for every tun or cask of wine. See POUNDAGE.
   (2) The burden that a ship will carry (Merchant Shipping Act 1995).

tonnage-rent The rent reserved by a mining lease or the like consisting of a royalty on every ton of minerals won from the mine.

tontine A financial agreement under which each of the subscribers to a loan fund receives an annuity for life. However, the right of survivorship applies so that the surviving subscribers receive increasing amounts as the others die. Eventually the sole surviving subscriber, until his death, receives the benefit of the total amount of the annuities.

Torrens Title A title to land under the system of registration of title which was introduced in South Australia, in 1858, by Sir Robert Torrens, the first Premier. It was subsequently adopted in the rest of Australia, and in Canada, and is the foundation of the system of registration of title established in England under the Land Transfer Acts. See LAND REGISTRATION.

tort [Crooked (conduct); a wrong]
   "A civil wrong for which the remedy is a common law action for unliquidated damages, and which is not exclusively the breach of a contract, or the breach of a trust or other merely equitable obligation" (Salmond).
   A tort is a civil wrong, the victim of which, is entitled to some form of redress, e.g. damages for harm suffered or an injunction to prevent harm occurring or the infringement of a legal right.
   The most common form of tort is an action in negligence resulting from a breach of a legal duty of care. Others include defamation (*q.v.*), nuisance (*q.v.*) and trespass (*q.v.*).

tortfeasor One who commits a tort. See TORT; JOINT TORTFEASORS.

tortious Wrongful. As in tortious conduct.

torture The offence of torture is committed by (a) a public official or person acting in an official capacity who, in the performance or purported performance of official duties, intentionally inflicts severe pain or suffering on another; or (b) someone who, at the instigation of or with the consent or acquiescence of such person, does such an act, Criminal Justice Act 1988 s.134. Article 3 of the European Convention on Human Rights (*q.v.*) provides that no one shall be subject to torture or inhuman or degrading treatment or punishment. This includes both physical and mental suffering.

total loss In marine insurance the total loss of the subject-matter insured (as opposed to partial loss) may be either actual or constructive. Actual total loss arises where the ship or cargo is totally destroyed or damaged so that it ceases to have its original identity. Where a ship is missing and no news is received after lapse of a reasonable time, there is a presumption of actual total loss. There is a constructive total loss where the subject-matter insured is reasonably abandoned on account of its actual total loss appearing to be unavoidable, or because it could not be preserved from actual total loss without an expenditure which would exceed its total loss value (Marine Insurance Act 1906 s.60). See abandonment.

toties quoties As often as something happens.

totting up Term applied to the procedure for disqualification from driving for repeated driving offences whereby each offence carries certain penalty points and disqualification must normally follow on the reaching of a certain number of points (Road Traffic Offenders Act 1988). See PENALTY POINTS.

towage Remuneration for towing a vessel which may be decreed in an Admiralty action.

town A collection of houses which has, or has had, a church and celebration of divine service, sacraments and burials.
A parish may, by resolution, take on itself the status of a town (Local Government Act 1972 s.245).

town and country planning See DEVELOPMENT; DEVELOPMENT PLANS; NEW TOWNS; PLANNING.

tracing The right of beneficiaries to follow assets to which they are entitled, or other assets into which they have been converted, into the hands of those who hold them. The equitable, but not the common law, rules allow tracing into a mixed fund, e.g. a bank account. The right is not restricted to misappropriation of trust funds but may arise from abuse of a fiduciary relationship, e.g. a company director misappropriating company funds.

track Under the Civil Procedure Rules 1998, each defended case is allocated by the courts to one of three case tracks, small claims track (*q.v.*), fast track (*q.v.*) or multi-track (*q.v.*). See track allocation.

track allocation An aspect of active case management by the courts under the Civil Procedure Rules 1998. It involves the allocation of defended cases to one of the three case management tracks. These consist of (1) small claims track (*q.v.*) for claims with a value of not more than £5,000; typically, for example, consumer disputes, minor injury cases; (2) fast track (*q.v.*) for cases expected to last one day or less, with a monetary value of £5,000 to £15,000; (3) multi-track (*q.v.*) for claims exceeding £15,000 and/or where the trial is expected to last more than one day. Usually the procedural judge will allocate a case when an allocation questionnaire has been returned by the parties or the time for filing such questionnaires has expired.

trade The business of selling, with a view to profit, goods which the trader has either manufactured or himself purchased.

Trade, Board of Originally a committee of the Privy Council (Interpretation Act 1889 s.12) but it never met and in practice was an administrative Government Department presided over by a President. The Secretary of State retained the title of the President within the Department of Trade and Industry. In 2007 the DTI became the Department for Business, Enterprise and Regulatory Reform.

trade description Under the Trade Descriptions Act 1968 it is an offence for a person in the course of a trade or business to apply a false trade description to products or to supply or offer to supply products to which such a description has been attached (e.g. "clocking" or turning back a car's odometer). A false trade description is one which is false or misleading in a material respect as regards the goods to which it is applied. The Act elaborately but exhaustively defines a "trade description". It is defined as an indication, direct or indirect, and by whatever means given of a list of matters in s.2(1), e.g. quality, size or gauge; fitness for purpose, strength, performance, behaviour or accuracy; place or date of manufacture, production, processing or reconditioning. Also proscribed by the 1968 Act are certain false or misleading statements as to services, accommodation or facilities. The Consumer Protection Act 1987 deals with misleading prices (*q.v.*).

The Property Misdescriptions Act 1991 extends similar proscription to the making of a false or misleading statement about a prescribed matter (any matter relating to land which is specified in an order made by the Secretary of State for Trade and Industry) in the course of an estate agency business or property development business. This criminal offence cannot be committed when a person is "providing conveyancing services". See also ESTATE AGENTS.

trade dispute A dispute between workers and their employer which relates wholly or mainly to one or more of a number of matters, including terms and conditions of employment, allocation of work as between workers and negotiating or consultation machinery (Trade Union and Labour Relations (Consolidation) Act 1992 s.244(1)). Certain acts taken "in contemplation or furtherance of a trade dispute" (*q.v.*) (the golden formula) may be granted immunity from liability in tort (ibid. ss.219–220). See PICKETING; SECONDARY ACTION.

trade mark A trade mark is a property right and is defined in Trade Marks Act 1994 s.1 as:
"any sign capable of being represented graphically which is capable of distinguishing goods or services of one undertaking from those of other undertakings".
It may consist, for example, of words, letters, a logo, colour, numerals, the shape or packaging of goods. It may be that sounds or even smells which can be represented graphically, for example, by musical notation or a chemical formula, may amount to a trade mark. A trade mark must be distinctive in order to be registered under the Act and it must not be deceptive. Registration in the United Kingdom is through the Trade Marks Registry and the registered owner of a mark has exclusive rights to the use of that mark. Protection from unauthorised use of a trade mark may be obtained through injunctions, damages, accounting for profits. An action for passing off (*q.v.*) may also be brought in certain circumstances. Some activities involving the unauthorised use of a trade mark, such as the sale of counterfeit goods, may also amount to a criminal offence.

There is also a European Community trade mark registration system. Registration of a community trade mark (CTM) is through the Community Trade Mark Office (CTMO) in Alicante.

trade mark agent The exclusive use of the title "registered trade mark agent" is preserved for those on the register of qualified trade mark agents (Copyright, Designs and Patents Act 1988 s.283). See REGISTERED TRADE MARK AGENT; TRADE MARK.

trade secret See CONFIDENTIALITY.

trade unions Originally friendly societies consisting of artisans engaged in a particular trade, such as carpenters, bricklayers, etc.; they in course of time acquired the character of associations for the protection of the interests of workmen. Being in restraint of trade they were illegal associations at common law, but, by the Trade Union Act 1871, this stigmatisation was abolished.

Since this early development the industrial scene has witnessed a continuous progression of legislation designed either to constrain or enhance the activities of trade unions; this legislation was brought together in the Trade Union and Labour Relations (Consolidation) Act 1992. Under s.1 of the 1992 Act a trade union includes:

"an organisation ... which consists wholly or mainly of workers of one or more descriptions and whose principal purposes include the regulation of relations between workers ... and employers".

Registration of trade unions is conducted by the certification officer (*q.v.*) who maintains a list of such organisations. The 1992 Act also makes provision for the control of union funds and property.

trader Any person who in relation to a commercial practice (*q.v.*) is acting for purposes relating to his business, and any one acting in the name of or on behalf of a trader (Consumer Protection from Unfair Trading Regulations 2008 reg.2).

trading certificate A public company once registered cannot start to do business or exercise any borrowing powers until the registrar of companies has issued it with a trading certificate. This is issued when the registrar is satisfied that the nominal value of the company's allotted share capital is not less than the authorised minimum, currently £50,000 (Companies Act 2006 s.761).

trading standards departments Trading standards departments, originally known as weights and measures departments (*q.v.*), provide a comprehensive enforcement and advice service and administer a whole range of laws governing metrology as well as fair trading, foodstuffs and consumer protection. They are part of the machinery of local authorities.

trainee solicitor A person who has entered a training contract in order to qualify as a solicitor (formerly known as an articled clerk). See SOLICITOR.

transaction at an undervalue The trustee in bankruptcy of the bankrupt's estate may apply to the court for an order re-opening a transaction entered into with any person at an undervalue within the relevant time, Insolvency Act 1986 ss.339–342. The administrator or liquidator of a company may make a similar application where the company has entered into a transaction at an undervalue within the relevant time, ibid. ss.238–241. See also PREFERENCE.

transactional decision Any decision taken by a consumer concerning whether, how and on what terms to purchase, make payment for, retain or dispose of a product or to exercise a contractual right in relation to a product (Consumer Protection from Unfair Trading Regulations 2008 reg.2).

transcript (1) An official copy of proceedings in a court, e.g. an account; (2) the transcription of the shorthand note of the proceedings at a hearing.

transfer The passage of a right from one person to another (i) by virtue of an act done by the transferor with that intention, as in the case of a conveyance or assignment by way of sale or gift, etc.; or (ii) by operation of law, as in the case of forfeiture, bankruptcy, descent, or intestacy. A transfer may be absolute or conditional, by way of security, etc. See BLANK TRANSFER; SHARE TRANSFER.

transfer of claims The transfer of claims between county courts (*q.v.*) and within the High Court is regulated by CPR, Pt 30.

transfer of risk in goods Subject to agreement to the contrary, under the Sale of Goods Act 1979 s.20, the risk of accidental loss or damage to goods is transferred from the seller to the buyer at the time ownership in the goods is transferred.

transfer of shares See SHARE TRANSFER.

transfer of undertakings See RELEVANT TRANSFER; TUPE.

transire The pass issued by the Commissioners of Customs and Excise for the goods loaded in a coasting ship in port, giving clearance of the ship from port and without which the ship is not to sail (Customs and Excise Management Act 1979 s.71.)

transit in rem judicatam [It passes into (or becomes) a res judicata] When a person has obtained a judgment in respect of a given right of action, he cannot bring another action for the same right, but must take proceedings to enforce his judgment. See MERGER.

transmission of shares See SHARE TRANSMISSION.

transportation The former punishment for felonies consisting of sending the convict to, e.g. Australia, to be kept there in hard labour.

transsexual A person who has the physical characteristics of one sex but who believes they are the other sex. See GENDER REASSIGNMENT.

travaux preparatoires [French] The material which has formed the background for legislation, e.g. Royal Commission Reports. Such material may be used as an aid to statutory interpretation so as to discover the mischief where legislation is not clear. See now *Pepper v Hart* [1992] 3 W.L.R. 1032, HL, holding that exceptionally *Hansard* (*q.v.*) may also be used. The European Court of Justice will frequently refer to legitimate proposals and parliamentary debates in the Member States (*q.v.*) as an aid to interpretation.

traverse To deny an allegation of fact in pleading. See NEGATIVE PREGNANT.

treason Breach of allegiance. There existed formerly both high treason and petty treason. Under the Treason Act 1351 high treason was limited to:
(1) compassing or imagining the death of the King, or of his Queen, or of their eldest son and heir;
(2) violating the King's consort, or the King's eldest unmarried daughter, or the wife of the King's eldest son and heir;
(3) levying war against the King in his realm;
(4) adhering to the King's enemies in his realm, giving them aid or comfort in the realm, or elsewhere;
(5) slaying the Chancellor or the judges.
In all prosecutions for treason some overt act must be alleged and proved. In view of the doctrine of constructive treason (*q.v.*), treason was further defined by the Treason Act 1795 to include compassing, etc. the death, or any harm tending to the death, wounding, imprisonment or restraint of the King.
Petty treason was where a servant killed his master, a wife her husband, or an ecclesiastical person his superior. It was converted into the crime of murder by the statute (9 Geo. 4 c.31, s.2).

treason felony The Treason Felony Act 1848 provides that treason felony consists in an intention to depose or levy war upon the Sovereign or compel him to change his measures or counsels, or to intimidate either House of Parliament, or to incite any foreigner to invade the King's dominions, coupled with an expression of such intention by any printing or writing or by open and advised speech or by any overt act. The maximum penalty is imprisonment for life.

treasure Any object: (1) at least 300 years old when found which is not a coin but has a metallic content of at least 10 per cent precious metal, or which, when found, is one of at least two coins in the same find which have that percentage of precious metal, or which, when found, is one of at least 10 coins in the same find;
(2) at least 200 years old in a designated class;
(3) which would previously have been classed as treasure trove (*q.v.*);
(4) which is part of the same find as any of the above whether found at the same time or earlier, Treasure Act 1996 s.1. Unworked natural objects or

415

minerals as extracted from a natural deposit or which belong to a designed class are not treasure, nor is wreck (*q.v.*).

Subject to any prior rights, treasure, when found, will belong to the franchisee, if there is one, otherwise to the Crown (subject to the rules on what would have been treasure trove) (ibid. s.4). Anyone who finds treasure or what he reasonably believes to be treasure has a duty to notify the coroner for the district in which the find is made (ibid. s.8).

treasure trove Abolished by the Treasure Act 1996. Defined as any money, coin, plate or bullion found hidden in the earth or other private place which contained a substantial amount of gold or silver. If it did not contain a substantial amount of gold or silver it was not treasure trove; this was an issue of fact for the Coroner's Jury to decide in each case (*Att Gen of the Duchy of Lancaster v G.E. Overton (Farms) Ltd* [1982] 1 All E.R. 524, CA). Treasure trove belonged to the Crown unless the owner appeared to claim it. The right of the Crown was not an incident of the Sovereign by virtue of the Royal Prerogative (*Lord Advocate v Aberdeen University* [1963] S.L.T. 361).

treasury Or the Lord Commissioners of the Treasury. The Treasury is the Government Department which administers the revenue of the State in accordance with the votes of the House of Commons. The political heads of the Treasury are the Chancellor of the Exchequer, the Paymaster-General, the Chief Secretary, the Parliamentary Secretary, the Financial Secretary and the Economic Secretary. The Parliamentary Secretary is the Chief Whip. See EXCHEQUER; PRIME MINISTER; WHIPS.

Treasury Bills Under the Treasury Bills Act 1877 the Treasury, when authorised by any other Act to raise money, may do so by means of bills (known as Treasury Bills) payable not more than 12 months after date. See also National Loans Act 1968.

Treasury Solicitor The legal adviser to the Treasury and certain other Government Departments. The post is held normally by a barrister (See the Treasury Solicitor Act 1876). He is a corporation sole. The Treasury Solicitor is also Her Majesty's Procurator-General (proctor) who acts for the Crown in the Prize Court, and the Queen's Proctor (*q.v.*).

treaty (1) The negotiations prior to and leading up to a contract or agreement.

(2) An agreement between the governments of two (bilateral treaty) or more States (multilateral treaty). The treaty-making power is part of the Royal Prerogative, but the private rights of a subject of this country are not affected by a treaty unless its terms are embodied in an Act of Parliament.

Treaty of Amsterdam The Treaty of Amsterdam 1997 amended both the EC Treaty and also the Treaty on European Union 1992 (*q.v.*).

Treaty of Rome Signed in Rome on March 25, 1957, the Treaty of Rome founded the EEC (*q.v.*) and the European Atomic Energy Community.

Treaty on European Union (TEU) The Treaty on European Union 1992, commonly known as the Maastricht Treaty, amended the Treaty of Rome (*q.v.*) 1957 and resulted in the renaming of the European Economic Community (EEC) (*q.v.*) as the European Community (EC) (*q.v.*). The Treaty on European Union also established the European Union (EU) (*q.v.*) and those provisions relating to the EU are now contained in a stand alone TEU, as amended by the Treaty of Amsterdam (*q.v.*) 1997 and the Treaty of Nice 2000. It is due to be further amended by the Treaty of Lisbon 2007 but not until this has been ratified by all member states.

tree preservation order An order made under the Town and Country Planning (*q.v.*) legislation prohibiting, in the interests of amenity, felling, lopping, uprooting or other wilful damage or destruction of trees without consent. Trees are not statutorily defined but see *Kent County Council v Batchelor* (1976) 33 P. & C.R. 185, where Lord Denning opined that in a woodland a tree "ought to be something over seven or eight inches in diameter" (doubted in *Bullock v S of S for the Environment* (1980) 40 P. & C.R. 246). Bushes, shrubs and hedges, as such, may not be the subject of an order, although an order over a hedgerow would cover the trees in it.

trespass Although originally in the nature of a criminal proceeding, trespass is now primarily a civil wrong or tort (*q.v.*) which may take one of three forms, namely trespass to the person, trespass to goods and trespass to land. Trespass will lie only in respect of a direct interference and there is authority to support the view that the interference must be intentional (*Letang v Cooper* [1965] 1 Q.B. 232).

trespass ab initio [Trespass from the beginning] He who enters on the land of another, by authority of law (not of a party), and is subsequently guilty of an abuse of that authority by committing a wrong or misfeasance against that other person, is deemed to have entered without authority, and is therefore liable as a trespasser ab initio for the entry itself and for all things done thereunder not otherwise justified.

trespasser A person who intentionally goes on to land in the possession of another without lawful authority.

trespassory assembly An assembly of 20 or more persons held on land without the permission of the owner or exceeding the extent of his permission. Such assemblies may be the subject of a banning order by virtue of s.14A of the Public Order Act 1986 if they might result in serious disruption to the life of the community or significant damage to land, buildings, etc. which are of historic, scientific or archaeological significance.

trial The examination of and decision on a matter of law or fact by a court of law.
  (1) Civil trial. Trial by judge and jury (*q.v.*) is the characteristic feature of the English legal system, however it is now rare in civil actions. Almost all cases are heard by one or more judges. A party can apply for trial by jury in certain actions such as fraud, defamation, malicious prosecution or false imprisonment and a jury trial will be ordered unless the court is of opinion that the trial requires any prolonged examination of documents or accounts or any scientific or local investigation which cannot conveniently be made with a jury. The court has an absolute discretion as to whether any civil case is heard by jury (see Supreme Court Act 1981 s.69). The details regarding the form and length of a civil trial will depend, in part, on which track (*q.v.*) the case has been allocated to. The claimant may make a short opening speech though this can be dispensed with. The claimant's evidence is then heard; in most cases written statements will stand as evidence in chief. Following cross-examination there may be a re-examination. The defence will then present its evidence; finally there will be closing speeches by the defendant's then the claimant's lawyers. The judge may deliver judgment immediately, after a short break or at a later date. See SMALL CLAIMS TRACK; FAST TRACK; MULTI TRACK.
  (2) Criminal trial. The majority of criminal proceedings are held in the magistrates' courts, see summary proceedings. Where the offence is serious, the trial may be in the Crown Court (*q.v.*). In the Crown Court a trial by jury consists of the operation of calling and swearing the jury; of a speech by the advocate for the prosecution; the examination, cross-examination and re-examination of the prosecution witnesses; a speech by the advocate for the defendant, followed by examination, cross-examination and re-examination of his witnesses; a closing speech by both sides before the summing up of the whole case by the judge for the jury; and, last, the jury's verdict.

trial at bar Formerly a trial before several judges and a jury; a trial by a Divisional Court.

trial by battle See APPEAL OF FELONY; BATTLE, TRIAL BY.

tribunal of inquiry A tribunal of inquiry may be established by a government minister under the Inquiries Act 2005 where particular events have caused, or are capable of causing, public concern or there is public concern that any particular events may have occurred (s.1). The minister must inform the relevant Parliament or Assembly of the inquiry, its chairperson and its terms of reference (s.6).

tribunals Bodies with judicial or quasi-judicial functions set up by statute and existing outside the usual judicial hierarchy of the Supreme Court and county courts, e.g. social security appeal tribunals (*q.v.*). They usually, but not necessarily, determine claims between an individual and a government department. The reasons for tribunals were said by Lord Pearce, in *Anisminic v Foreign Compensation Commission* [1969] 2 W.L.R. 964, to be "speed, cheapness and expert knowledge". In most cases tribunals are chaired by a barrister or solicitor appointed by the Lord Chancellor and sit with lay representatives with special interests.

The whole system of tribunals has been reformed following the Leggatt Review and the administration of tribunals centralised under the Tribunals Service (*q.v.*). From November 2008 the jurisdiction of individual tribunals is to be brought together under the First-tier Tribunal (*q.v.*) and the Upper Tribunal (*q.v.*). In the future, members of tribunals will be expected to sit across different jurisdictions. The legally qualified members will be referred to as judges. See MINISTRY OF JUSTICE, SENIOR PRESIDENT OF TRIBUNALS; ADMINISTRATIVE JUSTICE & TRIBUNALS COUNCIL.

Tribunals Service An agency of the Ministry of Justice (*q.v.*) charged with supporting the tribunals system. See SENIOR PRESIDENT OF TRIBUNALS; FIRST-TIER TRIBUNAL; UPPER TRIBUNAL.

Trinity House The Corporation of the Trinity House of Deptford Strond. It received its charter from Henry VIII in 1514. It has been entrusted with many duties relating to pilotage and lighthouses, beacons and sea marks. The Masters of Trinity House are known as Elder Brethren, and they may sit as assessors in the Admiralty Court.

trover A species of action on the case (*q.v.*), which originally lay for the recovery of damages against a person who has found another's goods and wrongfully converted them to his own use. Subsequently the allegation of the loss of the goods by the plaintiff (*q.v.*) and the finding of them by the defendant was merely fictitious, until the Common Law Procedure Act 1852 abolished these fictitious allegations and substituted a new form of declaration: "that the defendant converted to his own use, or wrongfully deprived the plaintiff of the use and possession of the plaintiff's goods". The action then became the remedy for any wrongful interference with or detention of the goods of another, and was called the action of conversion. See CONVERSION.

In an action of trover the plaintiff could recover only the value of the goods, not the goods themselves. See TRESPASS.

Truck Acts The Truck Acts 1831, 1887, 1896, 1940, were all passed to abolish the "truck" system, or the practice of employers paying their employees in tokens exchangeable for goods. Under these Acts, the full amount of a workman's wages was to be actually paid to him in cash, without any unauthorised deductions, and any contract as to the manner in which any part of the wages was to be expended was illegal. The Wages Act 1960, however, provided that it might be agreed between an employer and employee that wages (*q.v.*) should be paid into a bank account, or by cheque, postal, or money order. The Truck Acts, the Payment of Wages Act 1960 and related legislation (together with the Wages Councils Act 1979), were repealed by the Wages Act 1986. Part I of the Act (now Pt II of the Employment Rights Act 1996) concerns the payment of wages and provides protection for workers as regards deductions from wages. The general principle is that an employer must not make any deduction from any wages of a worker, nor receive any payments from him, unless the deduction or payment is required or authorised to be made under any statutory provision or any relevant provision of the worker's contract or with the worker's written agreement. See WAGES COUNCIL.

trust A trust exists when a person, or persons (the trustee, or trustees if more than one) has a duty to administer property for the benefit of another or others (the beneficiary or beneficiaries). The word "trust" is also used to describe the duties incident to the office of a personal representative (s.68(17) of the Trustee Act 1925). The trustee may have a beneficial interest in the property (s.68 of the Trustee Act 1925).

Instead of holding for a beneficiary, the trustee may have a duty to hold the property for a particular purpose (for example, a charitable purpose). With some exceptions, trusts for private non-charitable purposes are invalid.

Every kind of property, legal or equitable, can be the subject of a trust (provided the purpose of the trust is not illegal, or contrary to public policy, and the trust fulfils the principles of property law).

Trusts can be created expressly, by a declaration of trust, or impliedly by law. No special words are needed to create an express trust, but the words that are used must impose an obligation on the trustee to apply the property for the benefit of the beneficiary or for the purposes of the trust. The property subject to the trust, and the objects or persons to be benefited, must be certain. Express trusts of equitable interests must comply with s.53(1)(c) of the Law of Property Act 1925; and a declaration of trust regarding land, or any interest therein, must comply with s.53(1)(b) of the Law of Property Act 1925.

Examples of trusts created impliedly are resulting trusts (*q.v.*) and constructive trusts (*q.v.*). There are no formalities relating to the creation of such trusts (Law of Property Act 1925 s.53(2)).

trust corporation The Public Trustee or a corporation either appointed by the court in any particular case to be a trustee, or entitled by the rules made under the Public Trustee Act 1906 s.4 to act as custodian trustee (Trustee Act 1925 s.68; Law of Property Act 1925 s.205(1)): extended to include the Treasury Solicitor (*q.v.*), the Official Solicitor (*q.v.*), trustee in bankruptcy (*q.v.*), companies incorporated in the United Kingdom or in a Member State (*q.v.*) to undertake trust business.

trust for sale In relation to land, means an immediate binding (i.e. imperative) trust for sale, whether or not exercisable at the request or with the consent of any person, and with or without a power or discretion to postpone sale (Trustee Act 1925 s.68; Law of Property Act 1925 s.205(1)). See *Re Parker* [1928] Ch. 247.

All trusts for sale now take effect as trusts of land (*q.v.*), Trusts of Land and Appointment of Trustees Act 1996 s.1(2).

trust instrument A deed vesting property in trustees for the benefit of the beneficiaries specified in the deed. For settled land it is the instrument under which the trustees of the settlement are appointed; powers of the appointment are set out; and it bears any ad valorem stamp duty payable in respect of the settlement (Settled Land Act 1925).

trust of land Under the Trusts of Land and Appointment of Trustees Act 1996 s.1(1), which came into force on January 1, 1997, a trust of land is any trust property which consists of, or includes, land. The trust of land replaces the previous system of trusts for sale, bare trusts and settlements. The Act is applicable to trusts for sale (q.v.) which were created or arose before 1997 but does not apply to land which was settled land prior to 1997 or to certain university property.

trustee A trustee is a person who has a duty (either alone or with others) to administer property for the benefit of other(s), or for a purpose recognised as creating a valid trust. Certain people are excluded from being trustees, for example, a minor (q.v.) (s.20 of the Law of Property Act 1925). There are particular restrictions on who may be a trustee of a charity or an occupational pension fund (s.72 of the Charities Act 1993 (as amended) and s.29 of the Pensions Act 1995).

The appointment and retirement of the trustees of an express trust may be governed by the terms of the trust instrument. Sections 36(1) and 39(1) of the Trustee Act 1925 provide for the retirement generally of trustees and also the appointment of subsequent trustees.

Trustees have a range of powers and duties implied by equity and statute (especially the Trustee Act 1925 and the Trustee Act 2000). In the case of express trusts, reference should first be made to the trust instrument for any express provision varying or excluding the implied duties. In addition, trustees of pension funds and charities have particular duties (under the Pensions Act 1995 and the Charities Act 1993 respectively).

trustee de son tort One who intermeddles in a trust without authority, and is held liable to account as a trustee. See CONSTRUCTIVE TRUSTEE.

trustee in bankruptcy A person in whom the property of a bankrupt (q.v.) is vested for the creditors; his duty is to discover, realise and distribute it among the creditors, and for that purpose to examine the bankrupt's property, accounts, etc. to investigate proofs (q.v.) made by creditors, and to admit, reject or reduce them according to circumstances (Insolvency Act 1986 Pt IX).

trustee of land In relation to land in the trust, trustees of land have all the powers of an absolute owner (Trusts of Land and Appointment of Trustees Act, 1996 s.6). They have power to purchase land for any purpose and they have power to partition the land amongst beneficiaries of full age. These powers may be restricted by the disposition creating the trust.

turbary, common of A profit à prendre (q.v.). The right of digging peat or turf for fuel upon another person's land. See ESTOVERS.

turpis causa See EX TURPI CAUSA NON ORITUR ACTIO.

tutela [Roman law] Tutelage; guardianship. The public and unpaid duty imposed by the civil law on one or more persons of managing the affairs of a person under the age of puberty.

tutor [Roman law] A person on whom the civil law has imposed the duty of *tutela* There were the following varieties:

(a) *Atilianus* or *Juliatitianus* A tutor given to a pupil without one.

(b) *Dativus* A tutor appointed by an authorised magistrate.

(c) *Fiduciarius* A tutor holding office as if on a trust committed to him by the father. If a paterfamilias emancipated a descendant, and then died, leaving male descendants alive, such male descendants became the fiduciary tutors of those emancipated.

(d) *Honorarius* Tutors excluded from the actual administration of a pupil's property.

(e) *Legitimus* A statutory tutor who succeeded to the office under the provisions of some statute or the Twelve Tables.

(f) *Onerarius* A tutor who actually administered a pupil's property.

(g) *Testamentarius* A tutor appointed by will.

U

UKLA United Kingdom Listing Authority (*q.v.*).

UNCITRAL The United Nations Commission on International Trade Law which aims to help remove barriers to international trade. For example it promotes acceptance of international trade terms and prepares and promotes conventions and model laws, e.g. the United Nations Convention on Contracts for the Sale of Goods, Vienna, 1980. See INCOTERMS.

UNIDROIT The International Institute for the Unification of Private Law. Concerned with research and drafting and promoting conventions in relation to private law. See, e.g. Unidroit Convention on Agency in International Sale of Goods, Geneva, 1983.

uberrimae fidei [Of the utmost good faith] A contract is said to be *uberrimae fidei* when the promisee is bound to communicate to the promisor every fact and circumstance which may influence him in deciding to enter into the contract or not. Contracts of insurance of every kind are of this class. To a certain extent contracts for the sale of land, for family settlements, for the allotment of shares in companies, and (after the relationship has been entered into), contracts of suretyship and partnership, are also within this principle.

ubi jus ibi remedium [Where there is a right, there is a remedy] See, e.g. *Ashby v White* (1703) 2 Ld.Raym. 955.

ubi remedium ibi jus [Where there is a remedy there is a right] The maxim of early law before development.

ultra vires [Beyond the power] An act in excess of the authority conferred by law, and therefore invalid. For example:
(1) a registered company's powers were limited to the carrying out of its objects as set out in its memorandum of association (*q.v.*), including anything incidental to or consequential upon those authorised objects, and the shareholders could not, by any purported ratification of the company's acts, make any other contract valid; any such contract was, at common law, ultra vires and void (*Ashbury Railway Carriage Co v Riche* (1875) L.R. 7 H.L. 653). However, the ultra vires doctrine was modified in relation to companies by statute with the Companies Act 1985 s.35, as substituted by the Companies Act 1989, effectively abolishing it. From October 2009 the Companies Act 2006 s.31 will provide that unless a company's articles of association specifically restrict the objects of the company, its objects are unrestricted. Moreover, under s.39 the validity of an act done by a company will not be called into question on the ground of lack of capacity. See ASSOCIATION, ARTICLES OF.
(2) In the area of public or administrative law the ultra vires doctrine covers the validity of delegated legislation (*q.v.*), decisions of inferior courts or administrative tribunals (*q.v.*) and the decisions of administrative bodies (such as those taken by government ministers, local authorities or other bodies). Under the guise of the ultra vires doctrine the courts will examine, for example, whether delegated legislation deals with matters outside the enabling statute and whether procedural requirements as to the exercise of a legislative power have been observed. Decisions of inferior courts, administrative bodies and tribunals are also challengeable on grounds of illegality and irrationality. See JUDICIAL REVIEW.

umpire In an arbitration, the umpire is the person who decides the matter in the absence of agreement between arbitrators (Arbitration Act 1996).

unascertained goods In a sale of goods contract goods will be classified as unascertained goods if they are not identified and agreed on at the time the contract is made. They may be purely generic goods or unascertained goods but from an identified bulk or source. See SPECIFIC GOODS; ASCERTAINED GOODS; BULK GOODS.

uncertainty Failure to define or limit with sufficient exactitude; a gift by will, or a trust, will be void for uncertainty.

A claim may be struck out under CPR, r.3.4, for example, if it sets out no facts indicating what the claim is about, or if it is incoherent or makes no sense (Practice Direction 3).

unchastity An imputation of unchastity to a woman or girl is actionable per se (Slander of Women Act 1891). See DEFAMATION; SLANDER.

uncollected goods, disposal of A person in possession of goods belonging to another as a voluntary bailee, may give that person written notice that the goods are ready for delivery and specify the amount payable by that person in respect of the goods. If notice is given and the owner is not traced provision is made for the sale of the goods (Torts (Interference with Goods) Act 1977 s.12). See also UNSOLICITED GOODS.

unconscionable bargain A catching bargain (*q.v.*). For example, a contract where the terms are grossly unfair. In certain situations a surety may be able to set aside a charge directly against a creditor if the charge amounts to an unconscionable bargain. See EXTORTIONATE.

uncontrollable impulse Irresistible impulse does not in itself affect criminal liability, but may be evidence of insanity; but it may be taken into account in trials for murder in determining the diminished responsibility of the accused under the Homicide Act 1957 s.2.

unde nihil habet [Whence she has nothing] See DOWER, WRIT OF.

underlease A lease granted by a lessee or tenant for years; the latter is called the underlessor, and the person to whom the underlease is granted is called the underlessee. The underlessee is not liable to the original lessor on the covenants, etc. of the original lease. By the Law of Property Act 1925 s.146(5)(d) "underlease" includes an agreement for an underlease where the underlessee has become entitled to have his underlease granted.

undertaking (1) A promise, especially a promise in the course of legal proceedings by a party or his counsel, which may be enforced by attachment or otherwise in the same manner as an injunction.

(2) A word used in EC competition policy (*q.v.*) to describe a company, firm or economic entity.

undertaking for safe custody of documents When given, in writing, by a person retaining documents of title, it imposes on every possessor of the documents, so long as he has possession or control of them, an obligation to keep them safe, whole, uncancelled and undefaced, unless prevented from doing so by fire, or other inevitable accident (Law of Property Act 1925 s.64(9)).

underwriter (1) A person who joins with others in entering into a policy of insurance as insurer. Except where an insurance is effected with a company, a policy of marine insurance is generally entered into by a number of persons, each of whom makes himself liable for a certain sum, so as to divide the risk; they subscribe or underwrite the policy in lines one under the other.

(2) Subscribers to a public issue of shares by a company, who offer to take shares not taken up by the public in consideration of a commission at a rate disclosed in the prospectus. Thus the company is guaranteed that the issue of shares will raise a specific amount of funds.

undischarged bankrupt See BANKRUPT; BANKRUPTCY.

undisclosed principal An agent (*q.v.*) may act for an undisclosed principal, i.e. where the third party is unaware of the existence of the principal and believes that the agent is acting as a principal in his own right. In certain circumstances the principal may intervene and enforce the contract against the third party, equally once the principal's existence is known the third party may choose to enforce the contract against the agent or the principal.

undivided share The interest of a tenant in common. Where property belongs to two or more persons as tenants in common, each has ownership of an undivided share in the property. See also BULK GOODS.

undue influence The equitable doctrine that where a person enters into an agreement or makes a disposition of property under such circumstances as to show (actual undue influence) or give rise to the presumption that he has not been allowed to exercise a free and deliberate judgment on the matter, the court will set it aside. Such a presumption chiefly arises in cases where the parties stand in a relation implying mutual confidence, e.g. parent and child, guardian and ward, trustee and *cestui que trust*, legal adviser and client. But it may normally be rebutted by showing that the transaction was in fact reasonable and entered into in good faith, upon independent advice (see *Allcard v Skinner* (1887) 36 Ch.D. 145). See *Royal Bank of Scotland Plc v Etridge (No 2)* [2002] 2 A.C. 773.

It is not the law that in no circumstances can a solicitor who prepared a will for a testator take a benefit under it, but that fact creates a suspicion: it may be slight and easily dispelled; but it may be so grave that it can hardly be removed (*Wintle v Nye* [1959] 1 W.L.R. 284).

unemployment benefit See Jobseeker's Allowance (*q.v.*) under the Jobseeker's Act 1995.

unenforceable That which cannot be proceeded for, or sued on, in the courts, e.g. a contract may be good, but incapable of proof owing to want of form. At common law the effect is that as the contract, although unenforceable, is valid and subsisting, a transferee of property under such a contract might obtain a good title, and a deposit paid might be retained. The principal classes of contract subject to a requirement as to form were contracts of guarantee (Statute of Frauds 1677) and contracts for the sale or other disposition of an interest in land (Law of Property Act 1925 s.40). Under the Law of Property (Miscellaneous (Provisions) Act 1989 s.2, s.40 is repealed and a contract for the sale of land entered into orally on or after September 21, 1989 will not be valid, for the Act provides that such a contract "can only be made in writing", i.e. the requirement of writing is no longer merely evidential.

Contracts may be expressed by statute to be unenforceable for lack of form, e.g. the Consumer Credit Act 1974 s.65, provides that an improperly-executed agreement (*q.v.*) is unenforceable against the debtor except if the court makes an enforcement order in accordance with s.127 of that Act.

unfair commercial practice A practice that (a) contravenes the requirements of professional diligence (*q.v.*) and materially distorts the economic behaviour of the average consumer with regard to the product or (b) is a misleading action or omission or (c) is an aggressive practice (*q.v.*) (Consumer Protection from Unfair Trading Regulations 2008 regs.3-7).

unfair contract terms By the Unfair Contract Terms Act 1977 the right of the parties to a contract to avoid or limit their liability under the contract or otherwise may be limited. Thus, liability for negligently causing the death of or personal injury to any person may not be excluded or restricted (s.2(1)). In the case of other loss or damage exclusion may be effective if the reasonableness test is satisfied. The reasonableness test requires any term which it governs to be fair and reasonable in the circumstances which were, or ought reasonably to have been, known to or in the contemplation of the parties when the contract was made. The Act is generally restricted in its scope to business liability and often makes separate provision for "consumer" (*q.v.*) and "non-consumer" transactions.

The Unfair Terms in Consumer Contracts Regulations 1999 apply to contracts between a consumer and a business seller or supplier and provide that a term which is assessed as unfair will not be binding on the consumer. A contractual term which has not been individually negotiated will be regarded as unfair if, contrary to the requirement of good faith, it causes significant imbalance in the parties' rights and obligations arising under the contract, to the detriment of the consumer.

unfair dismissal When an employee can prove that he has been dismissed (see DISMISSAL OF EMPLOYEE) the burden of proving the reason for the dismissal is on the employer (Employment Rights Act 1996 s.98(1)). The determination of whether the dismissal was fair or unfair depends upon whether, having regard to the reason shown by the employer, the employer acted reasonably or unreasonably in treating it as a sufficient reason for dismissing the employee.

Certain reasons for dismissal are automatically unfair, including those related to membership or non-membership of a trade union, pregnancy, exercising rights under Working Time Regulations, or asserting a statutory right.

Claims for unfair dismissal are dealt with by employment tribunals (*q.v.*). Remedies are reinstatement, re-engagement and compensation.

unfair prejudice Conduct in the running of the affairs of a company which may entitle members of that company to a remedy (Companies Act 2006 ss.994–996). The legislation is designed to provide protection for minority shareholders. A member of a company may petition the court for an order that the affairs of the company are being, or have been, conducted in a manner which is unfairly prejudicial to the interests of the members generally, or some part of the members (including the claimant), or that an act or proposed act or omission is or would be so prejudicial. The court may make such order as it thinks fit. The usual remedy is the purchase of the petitioning member's shares.

unfitness to plead The test for fitness to plead was set down in *R. v Pritchard* (1836) 7 C. & P. 303. An accused may be said to be unfit to plead if he or she is not of sufficient intellect to comprehend the course of the proceedings so as to make a proper defence or to understand the difference between a guilty and a not guilty plea. The procedure for determining whether the accused is unfit to plead is set out in the Criminal Procedure (Insanity) Act 1964 as amended by the Criminal Procedure (Insanity and Unfitness to Plead) Act 1991. The procedure applies only to proceedings in the Crown Court. See INSANITY.

unified business rate Local government tax paid by businesses. See RATE.

Uniformity, Act of See ACT OF UNIFORMITY.

unilateral contract A contract under which only one party makes a promise. A common example is an offer to pay a reward in return for an act, such as returning lost property. The promise to pay becomes a binding obligation only if the act is performed; the person performing the act, however, makes no counter promise to so perform. For an example of a unilateral contract see *Carlill v Carbolic Smoke Ball Co* [1893] 1 Q.B. 256.

unilateral mistake See MISTAKE.

unincorporated body A body which does not have separate legal personality distinct from that of its members, e.g. a partnership (*q.v.*). See INCORPORATION; COMPANY.

union membership agreement See CLOSED SHOP.

unit trust A trust under which investments in a diversity of companies, etc. are vested in trustees with a view to small investors purchasing units (or interests) in the whole fund. The trustees enter into a trust deed with the managers of the fund under which the managers manage the fund and sell units to investors who thereby become entitled to an interest in the fund proportionate to their investment.

United Kingdom England, Wales, Scotland and Northern Ireland, but not including the Channel Islands or the Isle of Man.

United Kingdom Listing Authority (UKLA) The Financial Services Authority (FSA) (*q.v.*) acts in the capacity of a "competent authority" and is the United Kingdom Listing Authority. It is responsible for the maintenance of the Official List (*q.v.*) and the admission of companies that comply with the Listing Rules (*q.v.*) to the List. It has taken over this role from the Stock Exchange (*q.v.*). See FINANCIAL SERVICES AND MARKETS.

United Nations Established by Charter at San Francisco on June 26, 1945. It is based on the sovereign equality of all its Members and establishes machinery to enable them to settle their disputes, maintain international peace and co-operate together for the general welfare. Power is given to Her Majesty by the United Nations Act 1946 to give effect by Order in Council to measures not involving the use of armed force, including the apprehension, trial and punishment of persons offending against the Order. See INTERNATIONAL LAW.

universal succession In Roman law, the succession of the heir to all the deceased had. It is now used where one corporation succeeds entirely to another.

universitas [Roman law] A corporate body. *Universitas juris* was the totality of the rights and duties inhering in any individual man, and passing to another as a whole at once; an estate or inheritance.

University Courts Courts held by the Universities of Oxford and Cambridge pursuant to Royal Charters confirmed by (13 Eliz. 1 c.29).

unjust enrichment A term associated with the law on restitution which is most fully developed as the law of quasi-contract (*q.v.*).

unlawful assembly A common law misdemeanour consisting of the assembly of three or more persons with intent to commit by open force a crime, or in such a manner as to give just ground to apprehend a breach of the peace. The Public Order Act 1986 replaced unlawful assembly with the offence of violent disorder (*q.v.*).

unlawful wounding The offences of wounding and wounding with intent, Offences against the Person Act 1861 ss.18, 20.

unlimited company See COMPANY.

unliquidated damages Unascertained, e.g. damages left to a court to determine.

unpaid seller of goods Under the Sale of Goods Act 1979 s.38, a seller is unpaid when the whole of the price has not been paid or tendered or when a bill of exchange (*q.v.*) or other negotiable instrument (*q.v.*) has been received as conditional payment, and the condition on which it was received has not been fulfilled. An unpaid seller may have rights against the goods, e.g. lien (*q.v.*) and rights against the buyer, e.g. an action for the price.

unreasonable behaviour The somewhat misleading shorthand expression which was used to denote the fact set out in s.1(2)(b) of the Matrimonial Causes Act 1973 upon which a divorce petition could be based, i.e. "that the respondent has behaved in such a way that the petitioner cannot reasonably be expected to live with the respondent." Behaviour may be relevant, e.g. in respect of making a financial order under the Domestic Proceedings and Magistrates' Courts Act 1978. See DIVORCE; IRRETRIEVABLE BREAKDOWN.

unregistered company A company incorporated otherwise than by registration under the Companies Acts. See COMPANY.

unregistered land Land the title to which is not registered at HM Land Registry. See LAND REGISTRATION.

unsecured creditor A creditor who lends money without the benefit of security (*q.v.*).

unsolicited goods A form of inertia selling. Goods sent to any person without any prior request made by him or on his behalf. See the Unsolicited Goods and Services Acts 1971 and 1975. Consumers who receive unsolicited goods are entitled in certain circumstances to treat the goods as unconditional gifts. It is an offence to demand payment, etc. for such goods unless the business has reasonable cause to believe it has a right to payment.

unsound mind See PATIENT.

unsworn evidence See WITNESS.

unsworn statement A statement made from the dock by the accused whilst not under oath. The right to make such a statement was abolished by the Criminal Justice Act 1982.

Upper Tribunal Established as part of the unification of the tribunal appeal system under the Tribunals, Courts and Enforcement Act 2007 primarily to hear appeals from the newly formed First-tier Tribunal (*q.v.*), it also has an original jurisdiction. Appeals from the Upper Tribunal go to the relevant appellate court. It is a superior court of record (*q.v.*). See ADMINISTRATIVE JUSTICE & TRIBUNALS COUNCIL; SENIOR PRESIDENT OF TRIBUNALS.

urban development corporation. A non-departmental public body established under the Local Government, Planning and Land Act 1980 to secure the regeneration of a designated area. The original corporations were abolished by the mid 1990s but more recently new bodies have been set up, including one in East London to develop the area surrounding sites for the Olympic Games.

urban regeneration area Under the Leasehold Reform, Housing and Urban Development Act 1993 Pt III, the Secretary of State for the Environment has the power to designate certain areas which he considers suitable for urban development as urban regeneration areas. The aim of such a designation is to secure the regeneration of the area by the Urban Regeneration Agency which is the local planning authority for the area specified in the order. Urban regeneration areas replace the urban development areas (*q.v.*).

usage. An established uniformity of conduct of persons in a particular trade or business with regard to the same act or matter. A usage may harden into custom (*q.v.*).

usance A bill of exchange drawn at a fixed or determinable future time is known as a term or usance bill. The tenor of the bill gives the period of time on which or after which the bill is payable.

use The technical noun "use" is derived from the Latin opus (benefit). It is a word which has mistaken its own origin (Maitland).

Before 1536, if A conveyed land by feoffment to B, with the intention, express or implied, that B should not hold it for his own benefit, but for the benefit of a third person C, or of A himself, then B was said to hold the land "to the use," that is, for the benefit, of C or A. At common law the feoffee to uses (B) was the owner of the land, the seisin or legal estate being in him. In the Court of Chancery, on the other hand, he was merely the nominal owner; he was bound to allow the *cestui quo use* (C), or the feoffor (A), to have the profits and benefit of the land. The "use" or beneficial ownership was treated like an estate. It was devisable by will, although the land was not. A conveyance to uses enabled interests in land to be created and transferred with a flexibility and secrecy unknown to the common law; and it enabled the owners of land to evade inconvenient incidents of tenure.

The Statute of Uses was passed (27 Hen. 8 c.10) in 1536 to abolish uses by providing that where a person was seised of an estate of freehold to the use of another, the use should be converted into the legal estate, and the *cestui quo use* should become the legal owner. But the Statute failed to destroy uses and equitable interests, owing to the decision in *Jane Tyrrel's Case* (1557) Dyer 155a, where it was held that if there was a use following on a use, the Statute executed the first use, and was then exhausted, so that the legal estate vested in the first *cestui que use*, who held on behalf of the second, who still had an equitable estate. The second use came to be known as a trust. A use had only to be expressed to shift the legal estate without formality.

An executed use is one which takes effect immediately, as where land is conveyed to A and his heirs to the use of B and his heirs. An executory use is one which is to take effect at some future time. A springing use is an executory use which is to come into existence on the happening of some event, e.g. to A and his heirs to the use of B and his heirs on the death of C. A shifting use is an executory use which shifts from one person to another on the happening of some event, e.g. to A and his heirs to the use of B and his heirs, and on the death of C, to X and his heirs. The Statute of Uses was repealed by the Law of Property Act 1925.

use and occupation A claim for use and occupation arises where a person has used and occupied the land of another with his permission, but without any actual lease or agreement for a lease at a fixed rent.

use classes For the purposes of the Town and Country Planning Act 1990, a material change in the use of any buildings or other land is development (s.55) requiring planning permission. The Town and Country Planning (Use Classes) Order 1987 as amended, has effect as though made under s.55(2)(f) of the 1990 Act and provides that land, etc. used for a purpose within a certain class may be used for another purpose within the same class without the need to apply for planning permission as the change of use is deemed not to be a material change (e.g. a change of use from one type of shop to another or an office to another office use does not require planning permission).

user The use, enjoyment, or benefit of a thing, (*q.v.*) usage.

usher An official appointed to keep silence and order in a court and attend upon the judge. See BLACK ROD.

usufruct [Roman law] The right of using and taking the fruits of something belonging to another. It was understood to be given for the life of the receiver, the usufructuary, unless a shorter period was expressed, and then it was to be restored to the owner in as good condition as when it was given except for ordinary wear and tear.

usurpation The use by a subject of a royal franchise without lawful warrant.

usury Originally meant interest. By Acts of Parliament known as the Usury Laws (repealed in 1854) interest above certain rates was prohibited. Usury hence came to mean only illegal or excessive interest.

ut res magis valeat quam pereat [It is better for a thing to have effect than to be made void] See *Roe v Tranmarr* (1757) Willes 682.

uterine Born of the same mother, but not of the same father.

utmost good faith See UBERRIMAE FIDEI.

utter To attempt to pass off a forged document, die or seal, etc. or counterfeit coin, as genuine when it is known to be forged. See FORGERY.

utter barrister [Outer barrister] A junior barrister who has not been called within the bar of the court, i.e. is not a Queen's Counsel.

V

vacation The periods of the year during which the courts are not sitting, and chambers of the Supreme Court of Judicature are closed for ordinary business. There are, however, certain kinds of business which may be transacted during vacation and for this purpose two, or if need be more, High Court judges are selected to be available each year to act as vacation judges. Provision is made for the trial or hearing during the Long Vacation of urgent matters and appeals. (See Civil Procedure Rules 1998.) See SITTINGS; LONG VACATION.

vadium [Roman law] A pledge or security. In English law, a *vivum vadium* was a mortgage in which the lender took the rents and profits of the land in satisfaction of both the principal and interest of his loan: a *mortuum vadium* was a mortgage in which he took them in satisfaction of the interest only.

vagabond or vagrant Wanderers or idle fellows. The term used in the various Acts known as the Vagrancy Acts 1824 1889 and 1935. The term includes:

(1) idle and disorderly persons: e.g. persons who refuse to work, unlicensed pedlars, beggars, etc.;

(2) rogues and vagabonds: e.g. fortune-tellers, persons without visible means of subsistence, sellers of obscene prints, etc.;

(3) incorrigible rogues: e.g. persons twice convicted of being rogues and vagabonds, persons who escape from imprisonment as rogues and vagabonds, etc.;

(4) persons gaming or betting in a public street;

(5) persons persistently soliciting in public places for immoral purposes;

(6) those who, while lodging, cause damage to property or infection by vermin, etc.

value Valuable consideration, as in "purchaser for value", etc.

value added tax This tax (VAT) was introduced by the Finance Act 1972. It is a tax payable in effect by the ultimate consumer of goods or services. Some supplies of goods or services are exempt and some, such as books and food are zero-rated (*q.v.*). The amount of the tax payable is a percentage of the value of the goods or services supplied (currently fifteen percent for the majority of supplies) and the liability for tax arises at the time of the supply. Any person, firm or organisation making regular taxable supplies above a specified, but regularly revised, annual value must register with HM Revenue and Customs (HMRC) whose duty it is to administer the tax. The registered business is required to collect the appropriate tax from those supplied (the output tax). This collected tax is paid to HMRC but the business is entitled to reclaim tax that the business has itself paid (the input tax).

valued policy Where the value of the insured property is specifically agreed between the parties. See POLICY OF ASSURANCE.

Van Oppen order A procedural order for the administration of an insolvent estate (See *Re Van Oppen* [1935] W.N. 51).

variation of class rights Rights attached to different classes of company shares, such as voting rights or dividend rights can be varied with the consent of the requisite majority of members in that class, subject to minority protection safeguards. See Companies Act 2006 ss.630-635.

variation of trusts Under the Variation of Trusts Act 1958 the court may approve any arrangement varying or revoking a trust or the powers of the trustees of that trust provided that it would be of benefit to the beneficiaries of the trust.

Beneficiaries of the entire equitable interest who are of full age and sound mind may choose to have the trust property transferred to them and terminate the trust.

vastum Waste (*q.v.*).

veil of incorporation Once it is incorporated a company (*q.v.*) has its own separate legal personality distinct from that of its members. It is said that there is a veil of incorporation between the company and the identity of its members. In some situations the courts are prepared to "lift the veil" of incorporation and have regard to the identity of the membership of the company or to treat the rights and liabilities of the company as those of its members. The courts may lift the veil, e.g. to prevent the company being used as a means of fraud or evasion of legal responsibilities.

See also statutory provisions such as Companies Act 2006 ss.82-84; Insolvency Act 1986 s.213.

vendor Seller, particularly of land.

venire de novo The Court of Appeal (Criminal Division) has jurisdiction to issue a writ of *venire de novo*, that an appellant attend and be tried again on the indictment in question, where it holds that an appellant's trial has been a mistrial and so is a nullity. The conviction is set aside.

The writ may be issued if there has been an irregularity in procedure which meant that the trial was never validly started or where there was not a valid verdict from a properly constituted jury (See Supreme Court Act 1981 s.53). In civil cases this procedure is replaced by that relating to new trial (*q.v.*). For guidance as to the circumstances in which the Court of Appeal may order a *venire de novo*, see *R. v Rose* [1982] 2 All E.R. 731, HL.

verba accipienda sunt secundum subjectum materiem [Words are to be interpreted in accordance with the subject-matter]

verba cartarum fortius accipiuntur contra proferentem [The words of deeds are to be interpreted most strongly against him who uses them]

verba cum effectu accipienda sunt [Words are to be interpreted in such a way as to give them some effect]

verba fortius accipiuntur contra proferentem [Words must be construed strongly against those who use them]

verba generalia restringuntur ad habilitatem rei vel aptitudinem personae [General words are restricted to the nature of the subject-matter or the aptitude of the person]

verba intentioni, non e contra, debent inservire [Words ought to be made subservient to the intent, and not the other way about]

verba ita sunt intelligenda ut res magis valeat quam pereat [Words are to be understood that the object may be carried out and not fail]

verba posteriora, propter certitudinem addita, ad priora, quae certitudine indigent, sunt referenda [Subsequent words, added for the purpose of certainty, are to be referred to preceding words which need certainty]

verba relata hoc maxime operantur per referentiam ut in eis inesse videntur [Words to which reference is made in an instrument have the same operation as if they were inserted in the instrument referring to them]

verbatim Exactly; word for word.

verborum obligatio [Roman law] A verbal obligation, contracted by means of a question and answer; *stipulatio* (*q.v.*).

verdict The answer of a jury (*q.v.*) on a question of fact in civil or criminal proceedings (*vere dictum*–truly said). In civil cases the verdict of a jury need not be unanimous and the parties can agree to accept a majority verdict (Juries Act 1974 s.17). In criminal cases majority verdicts may be accepted in certain circumstances (Juries Act 1974 s.17).

Juries in civil or criminal cases may give general or special verdicts. A general verdict is where, in a civil case, there is a finding for the claimant or defendant. In a criminal case, the finding is either guilty or not guilty. A special verdict is where certain facts are found proved but the application of the law to the facts so found is left to the court. Such special verdicts are only to be returned in the most exceptional cases (*R. v Bourne* (1953) 34 Cr.App.R. 125).

A person may be found guilty of an offence other than the one specifically charged, i.e. an alternative verdict, where the offence charged in the indictment expressly or by implication includes an allegation of another offence (see Criminal Law Act 1967 s.6). On appeal against conviction, where the appellant was convicted of an offence and the jury on the indictment, could have found him guilty of another offence, the Court of Appeal, instead of allowing or dismissing the appeal, has power to substitute a verdict of guilty in relation to the other offence, see the Criminal Appeal Act 1968 ss.3(1)-(2) and 3A.

The jury may return a special verdict that the accused is not guilty by reason of insanity (Criminal Procedure (Insanity) Act 1964).

When the prosecution offers no evidence the judge may order that a verdict of not guilty be recorded (Criminal Justice Act 1967 s.17).

A coroner's inquest will give a verdict as to the cause of death of a person. An open verdict may be returned if the evidence does not fully disclose the cause of death.

verge The compass of the King's Court within which the coroner of the county had no jurisdiction.

versus (v) Against. In criminal proceedings, *v* is read as "against". In civil proceedings it is read as "and".

vertical agreements Agreements between businesses operating at different levels in the market, e.g. between manufacturers and retailers or between suppliers and distributors. Such agreements may contravene EC and UK competition rules if they contain anti-competitive terms, e.g. an exclusive distribution agreement. (See art.81 EC Treaty and the Competition Act 1998.) The European Commission has published a block exemption (reg.2790/79 [1999] O.J. L336) which applies to vertical agreements. Compare with horizontal agreements (*q.v.*). See COMPETITION POLICY.

vertical effect In European Community (*q.v.*) law it has been established that many of the provisions of the EC Treaty have direct effect (*q.v.*), e.g. arts 28–30, free movement of goods. Some treaty obligations have only vertical direct effect. This gives individuals rights enforceable against the state, reflecting the vertical nature of the relationship between the individual and the state. Contrast with the principle of horizontal effect (*q.v.*) where Treaty obligations may also be invoked by individuals against other individuals. See COMMUNITY LEGISLATION; CONTRAST HORIZONTAL EFFECT; INDIRECT EFFECT.

vest (or vest in) To clothe with legal rights.

vested An estate is said to be vested in possession when it gives a present right to the immediate possession of property; while an estate which gives a present right to the future possession of property is said to be vested in interest.

vesting assent The instrument whereby a personal representative, after the death of a tenant for life or statutory owner, vests settled land in a person entitled as tenant for life or statutory owner (Settled Land Act 1925 s.117(1)(xxxi)).

vesting declaration (1) A declaration in a deed of appointment of new trustees by the appointor that any estate or interest in the trust property is to vest in the new trustees. After 1881 the declaration operated to vest the property without any further conveyance. In a deed appointing new trustees made after 1925 the effect is the same even if there is no such declaration, except in the case of mortgages, shares in companies, and land held subject to a covenant not to assign the lease (Trustee Act 1925 s.40).

(2) When a compulsory purchase order has come into operation, a public authority may acquire the land by a vesting declaration (Compulsory Purchase (Vesting Declarations) Act 1981) referred to in the governing legislation as a general vesting declaration.

vesting deed An instrument whereby settled land is conveyed to, or vested in, a tenant for life or statutory owner (Settled Land Act 1925 s.117(1)(xxxi)). A vesting deed for giving effect to a settlement, or for conveying settled land to a tenant for life, is called a principal vesting deed. It contains:

(1) a description of the settled land;

(2) a statement that the settled land is vested in the person or persons to whom it is conveyed (or in whom it is declared to be vested) upon the trusts from time to time affecting the settled land;

(3) the names of the trustees of the settlement;

(4) any additional powers conferred by the trust instrument, which operate as powers of a tenant for life;

(5) the name of the person for the time being entitled to appoint new trustees (Settled Land Act 1925, s.5(1)).

vesting instrument A vesting deed, a vesting assent, or where the land affected remains settled land, a vesting order (Settled Land Act 1925 s.117(1)(xxxi)).

vesting order In cases, e.g. where trust property cannot be transferred by a vesting declaration (*q.v.*), the court may make a vesting order transferring the relevant property, Trustee Act 1925 ss.44–56.

vestry The assembly of the whole of a parish for the dispatch of the affairs and business of the parish, the repair of the church, etc. formerly commonly held in the vestry adjoining to or belonging to the church. The local governmental functions of the vestries have been transferred to parish meetings and councils, and other local authorities.

The work of the vestry relating to the affairs of the church is now performed by parochial church councils (*q.v.*).

Vetera Statuta The *Antiqua Statuta* (*q.v.*).

veto [I forbid] The power or right to prevent or reject some proposal or action.

vetting, jury See JURY VETTING.

vexatious actions The court may strike out a statement of case if it appears to the court that it discloses no reasonable grounds for bringing or defending the claim or is an abuse of the court's process. The court also has inherent jurisdiction to stay proceedings where there is an abuse of process. For example, this power will be exercised where the proceedings are shown to be frivolous, vexatious or harassing. See also vexatious litigant; abuse of process; striking out.

vexatious litigant A person who, with no reasonable prospect of success, persistently and without reasonable grounds, sues or prosecutes others. The Attorney-General (*q.v.*) may apply to the High Court for an order, a civil proceedings order, preventing anyone who has habitually and persistently without any reasonable grounds instituted vexatious legal proceedings or made vexatious applications in any legal proceedings from instituting or continuing any legal proceedings without leave of the court (Supreme Court Act 1981 s.42). The High Court may also, on application of the Attorney-General, make a "criminal proceedings order" restraining that person from instituting further prosecutions.

vi et armis [With force and arms] See TRESPASS.

vicar (1) A delegate or one who performs the functions of another.
(2) The incumbent of a parish church not being a rector (*q.v.*).

vicarious liability Liability which falls on one person (A) as a result of the action of another person (B) which has caused injury to a third person (C). Liability falls on A, not because of any breach of duty owed by A to C, but because B has breached a duty which he owed to C. The most common example of such liability is that owed by an employer (*q.v.*) for the acts or omissions of his employees committed during the course of employment. In contrast an employer will not normally be liable for the torts of an independent contractor (*q.v.*) but may be so liable where the employer is subject to a non-delegable duty. In the latter circumstances the employer will be bound because of a breach of his primary liability.

Vice-Admiralty Courts Courts having Admiralty jurisdiction in British possessions overseas. They acted under commissions from the Crown authorising governors of colonies to exercise such powers as in England appertained to the Lord High Admiral. The Colonial Courts of Admiralty Act 1890 provided for the establishment of Colonial Courts of Admiralty with a right of appeal to the Queen in Council in all British possessions to which it was applied by Order in Council.

Vice-Chancellor (1) The first Vice-Chancellor was appointed in 1813 to relieve the Lord Chancellor of some of his duties as a judge of first instance of the Court of Chancery; in 1841 two more Vice-Chancellors were appointed. The Vice-Chancellors were transferred to the Chancery Division of the High Court of Justice by the Judicature Act 1873.
The title was revived in favour of the senior judge of the Chancery Division in 1970 and the Vice-Chancellor is now vice-president of the Chancery Division (the Lord Chancellor being President) (Supreme Court Act 1981 s.5(1)(a)) and *ex-officio* a judge of the Court of Appeal (ibid. s.2(2)(g)).
(2) Formerly, a judge of the Palatine Courts (*q.v.*).

victim, code of practice A code of practice detailing services to be provided to victims of criminal conduct by persons exercising functions relating to victims of criminal conduct or to the criminal justice system. Issued in 2006 by the Home Secretary under the Domestic Violence, Crime and Victims Act 2004 s.32, it replaces the Victims' Charter.

videlicet [Namely; that is to say]

video evidence See WITNESS.

view of frankpledge See FRANKPLEDGE.

vigilantibus, non dormientibus, jura subveniunt [The laws give help to those who are watchful and not to those who sleep] See LACHES.

vill A township or parish.

villein Serf. (Latin, *villanus*, appertaining to a *villa*, or farm.) They belonged principally to lords of manors, and were either villeins regardant, that is, annexed to the manor or land, or else they were in gross, or at large, that is, annexed to the person of the lord; thus, where a lord granted a villein regardant by deed to another person, he became a villein in gross. Villeins could not leave their lord without his permission, nor acquire any property; but they could sue anyone except their lord, and were protected against atrocious injuries by him.

villein tenure See SERVICE; TENURE.

vindicatio [Roman law] A real action, especially the real action by which a title to real property could be made out, brought by the owner (*dominus*) against the person in possession.

violent disorder An offence committed when three or more persons, present together, use or threaten unlawful violence and the conduct of them (taken together) is such as would cause a person of reasonable firmness present at the scene to fear for their personal safety, Public Order Act 1986 s.2. Violent disorder may be committed in private as well as public places. See RIOT; AFFRAY; THREATENING BEHAVIOUR.

violent offender order A civil order of two to five years' duration designed to protect the public from the risk of serious violent harm (whether physical or psychological) posed by specific offenders. To be subject to a VOO an offender must be aged 18 or more, have committed a specified offence such as manslaughter (*q.v.*), grievous bodily harm (*q.v.*) or malicious wounding and been subject to (a) a custodial sentence of at least 12 months, (b) a hospital order (with or without a restriction order), or (c) a finding of not guilty on the grounds of insanity or a finding that they are disabled but in either case have had a hospital or supervision order imposed upon them (Criminal Justice and Immigration Act 2008 ss.98-117).

violenta praesumptio aliquando est plena probatio [Violent presumption is often proof]

VIPER parades See IDENTIFICATION PARADE.

vis major Irresistible force; e.g. a storm, earthquake, or armed forces. One of the "excepted perils" in a policy of marine insurance.

viscount The fourth in rank of the peers; he ranks above a baron and below an earl. The title dates from 1440.

viz Videlicet (*q.v.*).

vocatio in jus [Roman law] A summons before a magistrate.

void Of no legal effect; a nullity; e.g. an agreement for an immoral consideration. A contract may be void on the face of it, or evidence may be required to show that it is void.

voidable Capable of being set aside. An agreement or other act which one of the parties to it is entitled to rescind and which, until that happens, has full legal effect; e.g. in case of fraud in a contract. If, however, the party entitled to rescind the contract affirms the contract, or fails to exercise his right of rescission within a reasonable time, so that the position of the parties becomes altered, or if he takes a benefit under the contract or if third parties acquire rights under it, he will be bound by it. See UNENFORCEABLE.

voire dire A preliminary examination of a witness or witnesses by the judge in the absence of the jury in order to determine collateral matters such as admissibility of a confession.

volenti non fit injuria [That to which a man consents cannot be considered an injury] The voluntary assumption of risk. It is a defence to a claim in tort, particularly in respect of the defendant's negligence. No act is actionable as a tort at the suit of any person who has expressly or impliedly assented to it; no one can enforce a right which he has voluntarily waived or abandoned.

433

The maxim applies to (1) intentional acts which would otherwise be tortious, e.g. taking part in a boxing match; (2) running the risk of accidental harm which would otherwise be actionable as negligence.

Consent (*q.v.*), express or implied, may negative the existence of *mens rea* in crime; thus a person can effectively consent to certain acts being done, e.g. a surgical operation which would otherwise be a criminal act. But if an act is itself unlawful and criminal it cannot be rendered lawful because the person to whose detriment it is done consents to the injury or risk of injury, e.g. harm caused by sado-masochistic activities. No person can license another to commit a crime (*R. v Donovan* [1934] 2 K.B. 498 at 507; *R. v Brown* [1994] 1 A.C. 212).

Consent must be real, and given without force, fear, or fraud, because fraud vitiates consent. There is no consent where a man acts under the compulsion of legal or moral duty (*Haynes v Harwood* [1935] 1 K.B. 146). Mere knowledge of a risk does not amount to consent; the maxim is *volenti*—not *scienti*—*non fit injuria* Where a term in a contract or notice purports to exclude or restrict liability for negligence a person's agreement to or awareness of such term is not of itself to be taken as indicating his voluntary acceptance of any risk (Unfair Contract Terms Act 1977 s.2(3)).

voluntary Without valuable consideration. A voluntary gift, conveyance, or contract was valid if under seal and will be valid if executed as a deed (See the Law of Property (Miscellaneous Provisions) Act 1989 s.1, reforming the law on sealing and deeds). The Law of Property Act 1925 s.173 provides that the voluntary disposition of land with intent to defraud a subsequent purchaser is voidable at the instance of a purchaser for value.

The Insolvency Act 1986 ss.238, 339, provides for the adjustment or reopening of prior transactions where an insolvent company or a bankrupt have entered into a transaction at an undervalue (*q.v.*) or without any consideration. Application for a court order may be made by the administrator or liquidator of a company or by the trustee in bankruptcy of an individual.

voluntary arrangement Where a company (*q.v.*) is in financial difficulties, but not in liquidation or administration, the directors may propose a voluntary arrangement to the company's members and creditors. This may be a composition (*q.v.*) in satisfaction of its debts or a scheme of arrangement (*q.v.*) of its affairs.

A qualified insolvency practitioner must be nominated who must submit a report to the court stating whether or not the proposal should be put to the members and creditors for approval. If the relevant approval is given the proposal will be binding on all unsecured creditors and will be overseen by a supervisor. See Insolvency Act 1986, Pt I. Directors of an eligible company who intend to propose a voluntary arrangement may take steps to obtain a moratorium for the company on any creditor action, e.g. a petition for a winding-up order, Insolvency Act 1986 as amended by the Insolvency Act 2000.

If the company is in liquidation or administration the liquidator (*q.v.*) or administrator (*q.v.*) may make a similar proposal to the members and creditors without reporting to the court.

The equivalent process exists for an insolvent debtor who may propose a composition or scheme of arrangement as an individual voluntary arrangement (*q.v.*). See Insolvency Act 1986, Pt XIII as amended by Insolvency Act 2000.

A compromise or arrangement may be proposed between a company and its members and creditors in order to facilitate an arrangement or reconstruction, Companies Act 2006, ss.895-901.

voluntary conveyance A conveyance which is not made for valuable consideration.

voluntary indictment An indictment preferred by the direction or with the consent of a High Court judge.

voluntary winding-up A company (*q.v.*) may be voluntarily wound up by resolution of its members under a members' voluntary winding-up or a creditors' voluntary winding-up, Insolvency Act 1986 s.84. A members' voluntary winding-up occurs when the company directors are able to make a statutory declaration of solvency in respect of the company. If the directors cannot make such a declaration, it is a creditors' voluntary winding-up, ibid. s.90. See WINDING UP.

volunteer (1) A person who gives his services without any express or implied promise of remuneration.

(2) A person who is an object of bounty under a will or settlement as opposed to one who gives valuable consideration. Equity does not assist volunteers (see *Ellison v Ellison* (1802) 6 Ves. 656).

voting In meetings of a registered company, members usually vote on a resolution put to the meeting by a show of hands, where each person present and entitled to vote has one vote (Companies Act 2006 s.284). In certain circumstances there is a right to demand a poll (ibid. s.321). On a poll (*q.v.*) or a written resolution (*q.v.*), members vote according to the number of voting shares they hold.

On the notice calling a company meeting, members must be informed that they have a right to attend in person or to appoint a proxy (*q.v.*) to attend and vote instead (ibid. ss.324-5). Such communications may be conducted in electronic form (ibid. Sch.4-5).

In the case of a company formed before October 1, 2007, its articles of association may provide that, where there is an equality of votes in a company meeting, the chairman has a casting vote. See RESOLUTIONS; ASSOCIATION, ARTICLES OF.

vouch To call upon or summon. A voucher is a document which evidences a transaction, e.g. a receipt for money. As to "voucher to warranty", see RECOVERY.

voyage charter A charterparty (*q.v.*) for a specified voyage(s) in contrast to a time charter (*q.v.*).

voyeurism An offence which includes a person obtaining sexual gratification from observing or recording another person engaged in a private act, such as a sexual act, knowing that the person being observed does not consent to such observation, Sexual Offences Act 2003 ss.67–68. See SEXUAL OFFENCES.

W

WIPO World Intellectual Property Organisation (*q.v.*).

WTO World Trade Organisation (*q.v.*).

wager A promise to give money or money's worth upon the determination or ascertainment of an uncertain event; the consideration for such a promise is either something given by the other party to abide the event, or a promise to give upon the event determining in a particular way (Anson). The essence of gaming and wagering is that one party is to win and the other to lose upon a future event, which at the time of the contract is of an uncertain nature—that is to say, if an event turns out one way A will lose, but if it turns out the other way he will win (*Thacker v Hardy* (1878) 4 Q.B.D. 685 at 695). See BETTING; GAMING.

At common law, wagers were enforceable, unless it would have been contrary to public policy to enforce them, e.g. wagers as to the sex of a person; but wagers were rendered void by the Gaming Act 1845 s.18, which provided that no action should be brought to recover any money or thing won upon a wager. The 1845 Act has been repealed by the Gambling Act 2005 which provides that gambling contracts are enforceable like any other contract.

wager of law Compurgation (*q.v.*).

wagering policy A policy effected on a ship, etc. in which the insurer has no insurable interest and the contract is entered into with no expectation of acquiring such an interest. Every contract of marine insurance by way of gaming or wagering is void, Marine Insurance Act 1906 s.4. See INTEREST; PPI.

wages Money payable by an employer to an employee in respect of services at set intervals, for example weekly or monthly. For the purposes of regulating deductions from wages under Pt II of the Employment Rights Act 1996 (formerly Wages Act 1986) wages are defined as "any sums payable to the worker in connection with his employment" (s.27). Certain categories are included within this definition, for example fees and holiday pay, and others excluded, for example pension or redundancy payments. See also TRUCK ACTS.

wages council A statutory body, tracing its origins to 1909 trade boards, empowered to prescribe minimum rates of pay in a particular industry and to regulate deductions in respect of accommodation. Councils were composed of representatives of employers and employees in that industry together with independent members. Councils were normally established for industries where the collective bargaining power of employees was weak and trade union presence slight. Wages councils powers were weakened by the Wages Act 1986 and councils eventually abolished by the Trade Union Reform and Employment Rights Act 1993. The one surviving example of statutory wage fixing machinery of this type being that for agriculture. See NATIONAL MINIMUM WAGE.

wages, minimum See NATIONAL MINIMUM WAGE; LOW PAY COMMISSION.

waifs (*bona waviata*) Goods found but claimed by nobody. That to which everyone waives a claim. Blackstone indicated that stolen goods which are waived or thrown away in flight are given by law to the sovereign as a punishment for the owner not pursuing the felon and taking back the goods.

waive; waiver Abandonment of a legal right. A person is said to waive a benefit when he renounces or disclaims it, and he is said to waive a tort or breach of contract when he abandons the remedy which the law gives him for it. For example, a party might expressly waive a right to forfeit a lease where there has been a breach of covenant or may impliedly waive the right by accepting rent.

walking possession A procedure by which goods remain in the possession of a debtor, subject to a bailiff's right to return and remove the goods.

wall, party See PARTY WALL.

wapentake A hundred (*q.v.*).

war This is the legal categorisation of the state of affairs existing between states when force is used to vindicate rights or settle disputes between them. The power to declare war or to terminate war is part of the Royal Prerogative. As to the existence of a state of war, the certificate of the Secretary of State (on behalf of the Crown) that Her Majesty is still in a state of war with a named country is conclusive and binding even though hostilities may have ceased. During a state of war any trading or dealings, etc. with the enemy are prohibited except under licence. The effect of war on a contract with an enemy is to abrogate any right to further performance of the contract, other than the right to the payment of a liquidated sum of money which is treated as a debt which survives the war. Accrued rights are not affected, although the right to sue is suspended. Under international law the laws of wars will apply where there is a state of armed conflict as an alternative to there being a state of war. See GENEVA CONVENTION; INTERNATIONAL LAW.

war crimes War crimes include violation of the laws and customs of war and crimes against humanity. Under international law, national courts have the right to try alleged war criminals. Alternatively an international court may be established by treaty, or by the Security Council of the United Nations for the trial of certain war criminals. See GENEVA CONVENTION; INTERNATIONAL LAW; INTERNATIONAL CRIMINAL COURT.

ward of court A ward is a minor who is under the care of a guardian (*q.v.*). The Supreme Court Act 1981 s.41, provides that a minor (*q.v.*) can be made a ward of court only by virtue of an order of the court to that effect; except that where an application is made for such an order, the minor thereupon becomes a ward of court, but ceases to be so if no order is made in accordance with the application. Proceedings in relation to the wardship of minors are assigned to the Family Division of the High Court.

A ward of court cannot be taken out of the jurisdiction of the court, nor can any change be made in his or her position in life, without permission of the court. Thus, to marry a ward of court without the consent of the court is a contempt. As in all proceedings relating to the upbringing of a child or administration of his property, the court must regard the minor's welfare as the paramount consideration *Re B (a minor: sterilisation)* [1988] A.C. 199.

Wardship is used less commonly since the introduction of the Children Act 1989 which restricted the use of it by local authorities. In practice, it is now more common to apply for s.8 orders under the Children Act 1989, in particular, a prohibited steps order (*q.v.*) or a specific issue order (*q.v.*).

wardmote Formerly a court of the wards of the City of London.

wards Local government divisions. See the Local Government Act 1972 ss.6, 16, Sch.2, para.7.

wardship The status or condition of being a ward. Anciently, wardship was the right to the custody of the land or of the person of an infant heir of land. See WARD OF COURT.

warehouse receipt A document of title to goods lying in a warehouse, signed or certified by or on behalf of the warehouse keeper.

warrant A written authority used in executing process in civil and criminal cases. For example, information may be laid with the magistrates who may issue a warrant ordering some person to be arrested and brought before the court. The offence must be indictable or punishable with imprisonment, or the person's address must be insufficiently established for a summons to be served; or magistrates may issue a search warrant (*q.v.*) empowering the police to enter premises and search; or a warrant of execution may be issued against the goods of a judgment debtor (*q.v.*) who has failed to pay a judgment debt in whole or in part.

warranty (1) A promise or assurance. An agreement, for example, with reference to goods which are the subject of a contract of sale, but collateral to the main purpose of such contract, the breach of which gives rise to a claim for damages, but not to a right to reject the goods and treat the contract as repudiated (Sale of Goods Act 1979 s.61(1)).

Whether a stipulation in a contract of sale is a condition, the breach of which may give rise to a right to treat the contract as repudiated, or a warranty, depends in each case on the construction of the contract; a stipulation may be a condition though called a warranty in the contract (ibid. s.11(3)).

For implied warranties in contracts for the sale of goods, see ibid. s.12.

In insurance law a warranty by the insured is in fact a condition, breach of which entitles the insurer to treat the contract as discharged.

An action for breach of warranty of authority may be brought against an agent who acts in excess of authority granted him by his principal (*Collen v Wright* (1857) 8 E. & B. 647).

Formerly warranty was a covenant by the feoffor or donor of land to defend the feoffee or donee in the possession of the land, and to give him land of equal value if he was evicted from it.

(2) A common usage of the term is to refer to a manufacturer's written promise or guarantee as to the extent to which he will repair, replace or otherwise compensate for defective goods.

warren The privilege of keeping and killing hares and rabbits on a piece of ground. Franchises of free warren were abolished by the Wild Creatures and Forest Laws Act 1971.

waste (1) Generally, any alteration of a tenanted property which is attributable to the tenant's action or neglect. Types of waste are voluntary waste, permissive waste, equitable waste and ameliorating waste. Voluntary waste is an offence of commission, such as pulling down a house, converting arable land into pasture, opening new mines or quarries, etc. Permissive waste is one of omission, such as allowing a house to fall for want of necessary repairs. A landlord can take action against a tenant who commits impeachable waste.

If a limited owner is given power to commit waste, he is said to be unimpeachable for waste. Wanton destruction, e.g. cutting down ornamental timber or destruction of the manor house (*Vane v Lord Barnard* (1716) 2 Vern. 738), by a tenant for life unimpeachable for waste may be restrained as equitable waste (see Law of Property Act 1925 s.135). Ameliorating waste consists in altering the property by improvements.

(2) Uncultivated land, e.g. manorial waste or that part of a manor subject to the tenant's rights of common.

(3) Household waste, commercial waste, industrial waste (see Environmental Protection Act 1990 s.75. For the statutory duty of care in respect of waste, see ibid. s.34).

See DIRECTIVE WASTE; CONTROLLED WASTE.

Waste, directive See DIRECTIVE WASTE; CONTROLLED WASTE.

waste management licence A waste management licence was a licence granted by the Environment Agency (*q.v.*) authorising the treatment, keeping or disposal of any specified description of controlled waste (*q.v.*) in or on specified land or the treatment or disposal of any specified description of controlled waste by means of specified mobile plant (s.35 of the Environmental Protection Act 1990). The system of granting such licences has been replaced and simplified by one of granting environmental permits (*q.v.*) (see Environmental Permitting (England and Wales) Regulations 2007).

wasted costs order Costs which result from improper, unreasonable or negligent acts or omissions by a legal representative which the court considers it would be unreasonable for a party to pay. The order provides that the legal representative must pay the wasted costs personally. An order may be made on application by a party or initiated by the court, Civil Procedure Rules 1998 r.48.7; Prosecution of Offences Act 1985 s.19A and inherent Crown jurisdiction.

wasting assets (1) Property with only a limited existence; e.g. leaseholds. Where residuary personalty is given by will to trustees on trust for persons in succession, it is the duty of the trustees (unless the will shows a contrary intention) to sell such parts of the estate as are wasting, perishable, or unauthorised by the will or the general law, or reversionary, and invest the proceeds in authorised investments. This is the rule in *Howe v Lord Dartmouth* (1802) 7 Vest. 117, the object of which is to secure that successive beneficiaries should enjoy the same thing.

(2) For the purposes of capital gains tax mean in general assets with a predictable life not exceeding 50 years.

watch and ward The duty of the early constables was to keep "watch and ward", watch being the duty to apprehend rioters and robbers by night and ward being that by day.

watch committee A term correctly used in relation to the police committee of borough police forces (now abolished). It is loosely used to refer to the police authority for the county forces. This authority is charged with maintaining adequate and efficient forces and with appointing a chief constable. See POLICE AUTHORITIES.

water All riparian owners (*q.v.*) have a common law right to receive water in a stream or river coming to their property in both its natural state and its natural quantity, *Young v Bankier Distillery* [1893] A.C. 691. The right to receive water is protected by the tort of nuisance. The control of water resources (abstraction, drought and flood defences and fisheries) and the pollution of the water environment is principally the responsibility of the Environment Agency (*q.v.*) which subsumed the National Rivers Authority in 1996. The Water Resources Act 1991 (as amended by the Water Act 2003) contains provisions relating to the pollution of "controlled water" (*q.v.*) (Water Resources Act 1991 s.104). It is an offence to cause or knowingly permit the pollution of controlled waters (ibid. 1991 s.85). The privatised water companies in England and Wales act as water undertakers (the supply of water) and as sewerage undertakers (the treatment of sewage). The Water Services Regulation Authority (OFWAT) exercises regulatory control of the water companies in respect of their statutory functions. See CONTROLLED WATERS.

water, controlled See CONTROLLED WATERS.

water discharge consent A person shall not be guilty of an offence under s.85 of the Water Resources Act (causing or knowingly permitting the entry of polluting matter into controlled water (*q.v.*) if the entry is made under and in accordance with a water discharge consent granted under the terms of the Water Resources Act 1991). A water discharge consent is granted by the Environment Agency (*q.v.*). Schedule 10 to the WRA 1991 deals with the procedure governing applications for water discharge consents. It is a criminal offence (s.85(6) of the WRA 1991) to contravene any conditions of a water discharge consent.

water gavel A rent paid for water or for fishing rights.

water quality objectives Statutory water quality objectives for specific stretches of controlled water (*q.v.*) may be set by the Secretary of State following publication of the proposed classification and consultation with the Environment Agency (*q.v.*), s.83 of the Water Resources Act 1991. The Environment Agency is under a statutory duty to achieve, so far as practicable, any water quality objectives that have been set. Central to achieving these standards is the system of "permissions" to pollute controlled water under the auspices of Pts I and III of the Environmental Protection Act 1990, Pollution Prevention Control Act 1999 and also water discharge consents (*q.v.*) under the Water Resources Act 1991. See WATER QUALITY STANDARDS.

water quality standards A system for classifying the quality standards that waters must reach in order to come within certain classifications (such as abstraction for drinking or bathing water) (Water Resources Act 1991 s.82). Water quality standards enable the Secretary of State to comply with certain EC water objectives. See WATER QUALITY OBJECTIVES.

water-bailiff An official who enforces the Salmon Fishery Acts, etc.

watercourse The right of watercourse is the right of receiving or discharging water through another person's land and is an easement. By s.221 of the Water Resources Act 1991, a watercourse includes all rivers, streams, ditches, drains, cuts, culverts, dykes, sluices, sewers and passages through which water flows, except mains and other pipes which belong to the Environment Agency (*q.v.*) or a water undertaker (*q.v.*); or are used by a water undertaker or any other person for the purposes of only providing a supply of water to any premises. In *R. v Dovermoss Ltd* 159 J.P. 448; [1995] 11 L.S. Gaz. R 37, it was held that the words "through which water flows" in the definition of watercourses in the 1991 Act, governed only sewers and passages, not streams. Watercourses did not cease to be watercourses simply because they were dry. See CONTROLLED WATER.

waveson Floating wreckage: flotsam (*q.v.*). See WRECK.

way See RIGHT OF WAY.

waybill A document used in international sales of goods contracts. The waybill acts as a receipt for the goods but is not a document of title. Possession of goods is released to the person named in the waybill.

way-going crop A crop which has been sown or planted during a tenancy, but is not ready for gathering until after its expiration. A custom that the tenant should have the way-going crop, where not repugnant to the lease, has been considered to be good (*Wigglesworth v Dallison* (1779) 1 Doug. 201). See EMBLEMENTS.

wayleave A right of way over or through land for the carriage of minerals from a mine or quarry, or wires on pylons, or the like; generally created by express grant or by reservation.

wedding presents In the absence of evidence to the contrary, it may be assumed that wedding presents originating from one side of the family were intended for the husband and those from the other side were intended for the wife (*Samson v Samson* [1960] 1 W.L.R. 190). By the Law Reform (Miscellaneous Provisions) Act 1970, conditional gifts exchanged in contemplation of marriage are to be returned if the condition (express or implied) is not satisfied and are recoverable even by the party responsible for the marriage failing to take place. However, the gift of an engagement ring is presumed to be an absolute gift.

weight of evidence Where the evidence given at a hearing inclines in favour of one party, and the jury find in favour of the other party, the verdict is said to be against the weight of the evidence. The jury's verdict will not be disturbed, however, unless the jury could not properly, on a reasonable view of the evidence, have found as they did.

weights and measures Units and standards of measurement in the United Kingdom, Weights and Measures Act 1985 Pt 1. Responsibility for the enforcement of weights and measures legislation rests with local authority trading standards departments (*q.v.*).

welfare of the child The child's welfare is the paramount consideration for a court when determining any question in respect of the upbringing of a child or the administration of a child's property or the application of any income arising from it, Children Act 1989 s.1(1). A child is anyone under the age of 18. A statutory checklist is set out in s.1(3) which indicates some of the issues which may be relevant to the issue of a child's welfare. These include the ascertainable wishes and feelings of the child in the light of the child's age and understanding; the child's physical, emotional and educational needs; any harm the child has suffered or is at risk of suffering; how capable each of the child's parents or any other relevant person is of meeting the child's needs.

welfare report Under the Children Act 1989 the court can call for a welfare report when considering any matter under the Act relating to a child. With some exceptions such a report, when obtained, is for the use of the court and the parties only; to publish or reveal its contents to a third party may constitute contempt of court and may give rise to proceedings for defamation. From April

1, 2001, a new service, the Child and Family Court Advisory and Support Service (CAFCASS) (*q.v.*), has operated. It incorporates the functions of the court welfare service, the guardian *ad litem* (*q.v.*), reporting officer panels and the functions of the Official Solicitor in so far as they relate to the representation of children. The court welfare officer is now generally known as the children and family reporter (*q.v.*).

Welsh Assembly The National Assembly for Wales was established under the Government of Wales Act 1998 and has taken over the powers of the Welsh Office. Unlike the Scottish parliament it has no power to pass primary legislation.

Welsh language The Welsh language may be spoken by any party, witness or other person in any legal proceedings in Wales subject to such prior notice as may be required by rules of court (Welsh Language Act 1993 s.22).

Welsh mortgage The conveyance of an estate as security for a loan, redeemable at any time on payment of the debt without payment of interest by the borrower, or account of the rents and profits receivable by the lender, who is let into possession from the beginning, and who takes the rents in lieu of interest.

wer; wergild [Anglo-Saxon] Compensation for personal injury.

Westminster, Statute of (1931) See Statute of Westminister 1931.

Westminster the First, Statute of The 51 chapters passed in 1275.

Westminster the Second, Statute of The 50 chapters passed in 1285, the first of which is the statute De Donis, etc. See ESTATE.

Westminster the Third, Statute of Passed in 1290, commencing *quia emptores* (*q.v.*).

whipping A form of common law punishment for misdemeanours: abolished by the Criminal Justice Act 1948.

whips (From the hunting term "whipper-in" of a pack of hounds). The party officials whose duty it is to see that their party is as fully represented as possible at parliamentary divisions (i.e. when a vote is taken).
A "three-line whip" is an urgent, imperative call to a member to attend the House and vote.

whistleblower At common law a worker (*q.v.*) who discloses her employer's confidential information or practices faces an action for breach of confidentiality (*q.v.*). Under statute there is protection for a worker who makes public to prescribed persons, information which in his reasonable belief tends to show a criminal offence, a failure to comply with a legal obligation, a miscarriage of justice, a health and safety danger, environmental damage, or deliberate concealment of any of the foregoing (see ss.43A–43L of the Employment Rights Act 1996 (inserted by the Public Information Disclosure Act 1998)). A worker must not be subjected to any detriment because he has made a protected disclosure (see s.47(B) and s.48(1A)). An employee (but not a worker) who is dismissed for making such a protected disclosure will be automatically unfairly dismissed and will qualify to bring an unfair dismissal claim without needing the usual one year's continuous employment (s.103A and s.108). See EMPLOYER and EMPLOYEE for the distinction between employee and worker.

Whit Monday The Monday following the seventh Sunday after Easter. Formerly a bank holiday, the last Monday in May was substituted as a bank holiday by the Banking and Financial Dealings Act 1971 and is known as the "Spring Holiday".

White Book Colloquial description of a book published periodically containing (inter alia) the Civil Procedure Rules and Practice Directions.

441

white-collar crime A colloquial phrase used to refer to financial crimes, such as fraud (*q.v.*) or insider dealing (*q.v.*), committed primarily by persons at management level.

white paper See COMMAND PAPERS.

wild animals See ANIMALS.

wilful default See ACCOUNT ON THE FOOTING OF WILFUL DEFAULT.

wilful refusal to consummate See NULLITY OF MARRIAGE.

will A disposition or declaration by which the person making it (the testator) provides for the distribution or administration of property after his death. It is effective on death and is therefore revocable by him up until death.

The testator must be 18 years or over and have mental capacity to make a will. The testator must also have the intention to make that particular will. To be valid a will must in ordinary cases comply with the formal requirements of the Wills Act 1837 as amended. The will must be in writing, signed by the testator (or someone else in his presence and by his direction), and be attested by two witnesses (the signature must be either made or acknowledged by the testator in the presence of the two witnesses present at the same time). A devise (*q.v.*) or bequest (*q.v.*) to an attesting witness, or to his or her wife or husband, does not affect the validity of the will, but the gift is void (Wills Act 1837 s.15). See ATTESTATION CLAUSE.

However, a privileged will (a nuncupative will (*q.v.*)) can be made without formality and whatever the age of the testator (by a soldier or seaman on active service (See the Wills (Soldiers and Seamen) Act 1918 and the Navy and Marines (Wills) Act 1953)). See PROBATE.

A will may be revoked by: (a) a later will; (b) destruction, burning or tearing by the testator, or by some person in his presence and by his direction, with the intention of revoking it (Wills Act 1837 s.20); (c) marriage (ibid. s.18), unless the will is expressed to be made in contemplation of marriage; (d) dissolution or annulment of marriage. The Wills Act 1837 s.18A, as amended revokes a gift to a former spouse and treats as omitted an appointment of a former spouse as an executor (*q.v.*). See PROBATE.

winding-up Companies are wound up under the Insolvency Act 1986 as follows: compulsory winding-up by the court under s.122 or voluntary under s.84. A voluntary winding-up (*q.v.*) may be a members' voluntary winding-up or a creditors' voluntary winding-up (s.90). Certain companies may be struck off or dissolved without a winding-up (Companies Act 2006 ss.900 and 1000).

Wisby, Laws of The code of maritime law drawn up at the Hanse town of Wisby, in the island of Gotland, about the 14th century.

witchcraft A capital offence: abolished by the Witchcraft Act 1735, itself repealed by the Fraudulent Mediums Act 1951. See MEDIUMS; CONJURATION.

wite [Anglo-Saxon] A penalty for murder, etc. See BLODWYTE.

witenagemot The mote or meeting of the wise men. In Anglo-Saxon times it was the great council, consisting of bishops, abbots, ealdermen and other notables, which was associated with the King in the government of the country. See GREAT COUNCIL.

with costs An order by the court that the successful party in an action is awarded the legal costs of the action against the unsuccessful party.

withdrawal See DISCONTINUANCE.

withernam [A taking again] See CAPIAS IN WITHERNAM.

without notice An application in a judicial proceeding made: (1) by an interested person who is not a party; (2) by one party in the absence of the other. Formerly called an "ex parte" application (*q.v.*).

without prejudice When negotiations, either oral or in writing, are "without prejudice", nothing said or done is admissible in evidence in any subsequent trial should the negotiations fail. The use of the words themselves are unnecessary, the protection will apply provided the negotiations take place as part of a genuine attempt to settle the dispute. It is the purpose of the activity that counts. The rationale behind the protection is to encourage parties to settle disputes without fear of their discussions being disclosed in court.

Without prejudice statements are admissible in two circumstances: (1) the protection can be waived with the consent of both parties; (2) if a concluded compromise is reached as a result of without prejudice negotiations, the negotiations are admissible as evidence of that compromise.

without recourse to me An agent who so indorses a bill of exchange protects himself from liability. See SANS RECOURS.

witness A person who gives evidence to a court or tribunal usually in person and under oath. In some situations evidence may be given by television live link or by video recording, see the Criminal Justice Act 1988 ss.32; Youth Justice and Criminal Evidence Act 1999 ss.24,27,28; Criminal Justice Act 2003 s.51; Civil Procedure Rules 1998 r.32.3. Usually witnesses must be sworn before their evidence is given, unless they choose to make a solemn affirmation. The general rule, at common law, is that all persons are competent to give evidence, provided they have sufficient mental understanding.

In criminal proceedings, under the Youth Justice and Criminal Evidence Act 1999 Pt II, Ch.V a witness who does not understand the oath may still be competent to give evidence. Under the 1999 Act, children under the age of 14 cannot give *sworn* evidence in criminal proceedings but may still be competent. Children in civil proceedings may be competent to take the oath or, if not, may be competent to give unsworn evidence, Children Act 1989 s.96.

Most witnesses have a right to refuse to answer questions the answers to which would have a tendency to expose them to criminal proceedings, or to a forfeiture or penalty. The most important exception to this rule is that the accused in a criminal trial may be asked incriminating questions, Criminal Evidence Act 1898 s.1. See AFFIRM; EVIDENCE; HOSTILE WITNESS; OATHS.

witness anonymity order An order made by a court that requires such specified measures to be taken in relation to a witness in criminal proceedings as the court considers appropriate to ensure that the identity of the witness is not disclosed in or in connection with the proceedings (Criminal Evidence (Witness Anonymity) Act 2008 s.2).

witness statement Defined under the Civil Procedure Rules 1998 r.32.4(1) as a statement signed by a person which contains the evidence which that person would be allowed to give orally. The witness statement must contain a statement of truth (r.22.1(1)(c)). Witness statements may be used, e.g. at trial, or to support applications for interim remedies (*q.v.*).

witness summary A summary of evidence which, if known, would otherwise be included in a witness statement (*q.v.*) or a summary of the matters about which the party serving the summary will question the witness (*q.v.*), CPR, r.32.9(2). A party who is required to serve a witness statement but is unable to obtain one can apply to serve a witness summary instead, CPR, r.32.9(1). It may be used, for example, when a witness is unco-operative or hostile, or the whereabouts is unknown.

witness summons A document issued by the court requiring a witness to attend court to give evidence or produce a document to the court, CPR, r.34.2(1).

witnessing part The *testatum* (*q.v.*).

Woolf Report The report by Lord Woolf on the civil justice system. The Interim Report, Access to Justice, was issued in 1995. The Final Report, with related Draft Rules, was published in July 1996. The report led to reform of the civil justice system with the Civil Procedure Rules 1998 (CPR) (*q.v.*).

Woolsack The Lord Chancellor sits on the Woolsack when acting as Speaker of the House of Lords. It is not technically part of the House. When the Lord Chancellor (*q.v.*) votes as a peer, he votes from the Woolsack but if he wishes to speak as a peer, he leaves the Woolsack and goes to his place in the House.

words of art Words which have acquired an established legal meaning.

words of limitation Words in a conveyance or will which have the effect of marking out the duration of an estate. Thus, in a grant to A and his heirs, the words "and his heirs" are words of limitation. Formerly these words were essential to pass the fee simple, both in legal and equitable interests (*Re Bostock* [1921] 2 Ch. 469). The Conveyancing Act 1881, s.51 authorised the use of the words "in fee simple", but any other words, including "in fee", passed only a life estate (*Re Ethel and Mitchell* [1901] 1 Ch. 945). No words of limitation are necessary since 1925: a conveyance passes the whole interest of the grantor, unless a contrary intention is expressed (Law of Property Act 1925 s.60).
  To create an estate tail by deed, it was necessary that "words of procreation" should be used as "to A and the heirs of his body". Since 1925 an entailed interest may be created by way of trust in any property by the use of like words (Law of Property Act 1925 s.130).

words of purchase Words in a conveyance which denote the person who is to take an estate or interest in land in his own right. They are to be contrasted with words of limitation (*q.v.*). See PURCHASE.

work and materials, contract for See SUPPLY OF GOODS AND SERVICES.

work of equal value The provision of the amended Equal Pay Act 1970 which was introduced after a ruling of the ECJ that the United Kingdom had failed to properly implement the Equal Pay Directive (75/117) (See *EC Commission v UK* [1982] I.C.R. 578). Prior to this change a woman could only claim equal pay for work of equal value if an employer had voluntarily carried out a job evaluation study (*q.v.*) and her job had been given an equal rating with that of a man in the same employment. Under the revised provisions a woman may bring a claim, even though her work is not like work or work rated as equivalent with that of a man, where she is employed on work which:
  "is, in terms of the demands made on her (for instance under such headings as effort, skill decision), of equal value to that of a man in the same employment", ibid. s.1(2)(c).
  Such claims are subject to a special procedure in an employment tribunal which may involve job evaluations being undertaken by an independent expert. Claims are often complex and time consuming. See EQUALITY CLAUSE.

worker A term used in employment legislation to encompass both an employee (*q.v.*) working under a contract of service and an independent contractor working under a contract for services. Thus, for example, the Employment Rights Act 1996 s.230(3) defines a "worker" as:
  "an individual who has entered into or works under ... (a) a contract of employment, or (b) any other contract, whether expressed or implied ... whereby the individual undertakes to do or perform personally any work or services for another party to the contract whose status is not ... that of a client or customer of any profession or business undertaking carried on by the individual".
  Increasingly under employment legislation, rights are extended to workers and not provided merely for employees, e.g. the right to the national minimum

wage (*q.v.*) and to protection against unlawful deduction from wages (*q.v.*) and to protection for whistleblowing (*q.v.*). Article 39 of the EC Treaty (*q.v.*) establishes the freedom of movement of workers within the European Union (*q.v.*). Workers have the right to seek and take up employment in another Member State on the same terms as a national of the "host" State. The European Court of Justice (*q.v.*) has held that the term worker is a Community concept and should be given a broad Community meaning. A worker has been defined as a person who is engaged in a genuine and effective economic activity, under the direction and control of another, for which the worker receives remuneration. The term worker has also been held to include job seekers.

working tax credit A means-tested or income-related payment, administered by the Inland Revenue, for working households facing low income, including those in which a worker has a disability or in which there is a dependent child or young person (see Tax Credits Act 2002).

working time regulations These came into force on October 1, 1998 and enact the Working Time Directive. The 1998 Regulations introduce statutory controls on the number of hours in the working week, the length of night work and rest breaks and provide for paid annual holidays.

workmen's compensation The system of workmen's compensation was superseded by the National Insurance (Industrial Injuries) Act 1946 (repealed), and the industrial injuries scheme (*q.v.*) is now part of the general social security system, see the Social Security Contributions and Benefits Act 1992.

World Intellectual Property Organisation (WIPO) A specialised agency of the United Nations (*q.v.*) with a mandate to promote the protection of intellectual property (*q.v.*) throughout the world. It conducts international consultations and reviews on intellectual property issues and publishes reports, e.g. WIPO1 on registration of domain names (*q.v.*) which led to the Uniform Domain Name Dispute Resolution Policy (UDRP) concerning abusive registration of trade marks as domain names.

World Trade Organisation A global international organisation dealing with the rules of trade between nations. Created by the Uruguay Round negotiations (1986–1994), the WTO began operating on January 1, 1995, replacing GATT. Its functions include administering WTO trade agreements, acting as a forum for trade negotiations and monitoring national trade policies. At July 23, 2008 153 countries were members of the WTO. See GENERAL AGREEMENT ON TARIFFS AND TRADE.

world wide web (www) A collection of documents accessible on the internet (*q.v.*). This term is also used interchangeably with the word "internet".

wounding In the offences of unlawful wounding (*q.v.*) under the Offences against the Person Act 1861 ss.18 and 20, a wound requires a breaking of all the layers of the skin (*J.C.C. v Eisenhower* [1984] Q.B. 331).

wreck Defined under the Merchant Shipping Act 1995 s.255, as including jetsam (*q.v.*), flotsam (*q.v.*), lagan (*q.v.*) and derelict (*q.v.*) found in or on the shores of the sea or any tidal water. Fishing boats or fishing gear lost or abandoned at sea may also be treated as wreck. When a receiver takes possession of a wreck he must make a record describing the wreck and give notice of the description of the wreck. It is the duty of a receiver of wreck to preserve wreck, and if it is not claimed by the owner within a year, then to sell it and pay the proceeds to the Crown. Wreck (or shipwreck) is also used as meaning the destruction of a ship during a voyage so that she can no longer continue the voyage.

Wreck Commissioners Persons appointed by the Lord Chancellor (*q.v.*) under the Merchant Shipping Act 1995 to hold investigations into shipping casualties.

writ (1) A document in the Queen's name and under the seal of the Crown, a court or an officer of the Crown, commanding the person to whom it is addressed to do or forbear from doing some act.

(2) An original writ was anciently the mode of commencing every action at common law. Prior to the introduction of the Civil Procedure Rules 1998 a writ was used to begin an action in the High Court. All civil actions are now commenced using a claim form. The main form of writ now in common use is the writ of execution (*q.v.*) used in civil proceedings to enforce a judgment (CPR 1998, Sch.1, RSC Ord. 46); a writ is still used in an application for habeas corpus (*q.v.*) (CPR 1998, Sch.1, RSC Ord. 54). See EXECUTION; ENFORCEMENT; CLAIM FORM; PREROGATIVE WRITS; JUDICIAL REVIEW.

writ of execution Used in civil proceedings to enforce a judgment, it includes a writ of *fieri facias*, a writ of possession, a writ of delivery, a writ of sequestration (CPR 1998, Sch.1, RSC Ord. 46). See EXECUTION.

writ of right A real action which was formerly used to recover lands in fee simple, unjustly withheld from the rightful owner. It might be brought in any case of disseisin. There were also writs in the nature of writs of right, such as the writ of dower (*q.v.*).

writ of summons Prior to the introduction of the Civil Procedure Rules 1998, the writ of summons was the way in which an action in the High Court was commenced. It was issued at the instance of the plaintiff for the purpose of giving the defendant notice of the claim made against him and of compelling him to acknowledge service and answer it if he did not admit it.

written resolution See RESOLUTION.

written statement Part 1 of the Employment Rights Act 1996 requires an employer (*q.v.*) to provide an employee with a statement of the main particulars of employment within two months of the commencement of employment. The particulars to be provided include the names of the parties, the date of commencement of employment and information relating to pay, hours of work and notice entitlement.

The statement is not itself the contract of employment but only evidence of the terms of the contract (see *Turriff Construction v Bryant* (1967) 2 I.T.R. 292).

wrong A violation or infringement of a right. A private wrong or tort (*q.v.*) is an offence against an individual; a public wrong or crime (*q.v.*) is an offence against the community.

wrongful dismissal At common law an employee has a claim in damages for dismissal without proper notice. An employee who has been dismissed without notice is said to have been summarily dismissed. An employee also has a statutory right not to be unfairly dismissed. See UNFAIR DISMISSAL.

wrongful interference with goods See CONVERSION.

wrongful life A disabled child (by its next friend) sued a doctor and Area Health Authority on the ground that the mother should have been advised to have an abortion and claimed damages for wrongful entry into life, i.e. for allowing it to have been born. It was held that the statement of claim would be struck out and that English law did not recognise such a cause of action (*McKay v Essex Health Authority* [1982] 2 All E.R. 922, CA).

wrongful trading Under the Insolvency Act 1986, s.214, on an application by a liquidator, a court may order that a director of a company be made personally liable to contribute to the company's assets if the company has gone into insolvent liquidation and at some time before liquidation the director knew, or ought to have concluded, that there was no reasonable prospect that the company could avoid insolvent liquidation and yet the company continued to trade.

X

xenotransplantation Transplanting organs, e.g. a heart, from one species to another.

Y

year A year consists of 12 calendar months; that is, 365 days in an ordinary year, and 366 in a leap-year.

(1) The historical year has for a very long period begun on January 1.

(2) The civil, ecclesiastical and legal year, used by the Church and all public instruments, began at Christmas, until the end of the 13th century. In and after the 14th century, it commenced on March 25, and so continued until January 1, 1753 (Calendar (New Style) Act 1750).

(3) The regnal year commences on the Sovereign's accession. See TABLE OF REGNAL YEARS, BELOW.

(4) Where a year or more has elapsed since the last proceeding in a cause or matter, the party who desires to proceed must give to every other party not less than one month's notice of his intention to proceed.

(5) The income tax year, or year of assessment, runs from April 6 to the following April 5. The financial year for corporation tax runs from April 1 to March 31 (Income and Corporation Taxes Act 1988).

Year Books A series of anonymous reports of cases written in the Anglo-Norman language, commencing in the 13th century and existing either in manuscript copies or in print from 1290 to 1535, with very few gaps. The reports are grouped under the regnal years in which the cases were decided. It is generally agreed that they were notes of cases taken by apprentices to the law.

year, day, and waste The right which the Crown had to hold the lands of felons for a year and a day, and commit waste (*q.v.*) thereon.

yeoman He that hath free land of forty shillings by the year: who was anciently thereby qualified to serve on juries, vote for knights of the shire, and do any other act where the law requires (Blackstone).

yield To perform a service due by a tenant to his lord. It survives in the phrase "yielding and paying" the rent reserved in a lease.

York-Antwerp Rules The rules of adjustment of general average (a system for spreading the risk in sea transport) drawn up at conferences of the International Law Association at York (1864), and Antwerp (1877). They have been revised on several occasions, most recently in 2004. The application of the York–Antwerp Rules, if desired, must be stipulated in the contract.

Yorkshire Deed Registry A registry of deeds and wills relating to land in each of the three ridings of Yorkshire. If a deed or will was not registered, it was void as against a subsequent purchaser for value, who had registered his deed. By the Law of Property Act 1925 s.11, instruments which did not deal with the legal estate did not require registration; and land registered under the Land Registration Act 1925 was exempt from the local county registry. The Yorkshire deeds registries were closed by the Law of Property Act 1969 s.16.

young offender A offender aged under 21 but over 14 years of age. Distinguish from the term "juvenile" (a defendant who is 10 or over but under 18 years). The custodial sentences available for a young offender are: (1) a sentence of custody for life; (2) detention in a young offender institution; (3) detention under the provisions of the Children and Young Persons Act 1933 s.53; (4) a detention and training order (*q.v.*) under the provisions of the Crime and Disorder Act 1998.

young offender institution A facility run either by the Prison Service or a private sector contractor to which persons between the ages of 15 and 18 may be sent under a detention and training order (*q.v.*). Such facilities provide less specialised support than is available at secure training centres (*q.v.*) or secure children's homes (*q.v.*). Some institutions also accommodate those aged up to 21.

youth courts Formerly known as juvenile courts but renamed by the Criminal Justice Act 1991 s.70. These special courts sit apart from the ordinary criminal courts and are composed of persons whose names are on a special youth court panel. They deal with the trial of children and young persons. The attendance at court of a parent or guardian may be required and such person may be ordered to pay any fine and costs. The youth courts have enhanced powers of sentencing under the Crime and Disorder Act 1998.

youth default order An order imposing an unpaid work requirement, curfew requirement or attendance requirement on a young offender instead of an unpaid fine (Criminal Justice and Immigration Act 2008 s.39).

youth detention accommodation Facilities in which the custodial part of a detention and training order is to be served, including young offenders institutions (*q.v.*), secure training centres (*q.v.*) and secure children's homes (*q.v.*) (see Powers of Criminal Courts (Sentencing) Act 2000 s.107, as amended).

Youth Justice Board An executive non-departmental public body established under the Crime and Disorder Act 1998. It is responsible for monitoring and advising the Home Secretary on the operation of the youth justice system, for drawing up standards for those working in the system and for overseeing reforms to the system.

youth offending team Drawn from a range of services, such as police, probation, social services, health and education, so as to provide comprehensive coverage of the needs of young offenders and to identify suitable programmes to prevent reoffending. Every local authority in England and Wales has a team.

youth rehabilitation order A form of community sentence (*q.v.*) imposed upon a young person under 18 convicted of an offence (Criminal Justice and Immigration Act 2008 s.1). An order may impose one or more of several requirements including activity, supervision, attendance centre, curfew, drug testing and treatment, and education requirements (see further Sch.1 of the Act).

Z

zero rating Supplies of goods or services on which no valued added tax (VAT) (*q.v.*) is charged (Value Added Tax Act 1994 s.30 and Sch.8). A business making zero-rated supplies may still be able to recover input VAT.

zero tolerance A phrase used to describe a policy of non-tolerance and rigorous prosecution of even minor offences.

zones See ENTERPRISE ZONE; SIMPLIFIED PLANNING ZONE.

LAW REPORTS AND JOURNALS

AND THEIR ABBREVIATIONS

This list contains the abbreviations of the principal law reports and journals published in the United Kingdom, the British Commonwealth, and the Republic of Ireland. For historical law reports, the list shows the corresponding volume of the English Reports, or the Revised Reports in which the various series may be found. In the last column the English Reports volume appears without brackets, while the Revised Reports volume is indicated by a square bracket.

The supplementary list of abbreviations compiled by Professor Glanville Williams, with references to the English Reports (7 C.L.J. 262) has been incorporated in this list.

ABBR.	REPORTS/JOURNALS	PERIOD	E.R. [R.R.]
A. & E.	Adolphus & Ellis	1834–1840	110–3
A. & E.(N.S.)	See Q.B.		
A. & H.	Arnold & Hodges	1840–1841	—
A. & N.	Alcock & Napier (Ir.)	1831–1833	—
A. & S.L.	Air and Space Law	1975–date	—
A. Moo.	1 Bosanquet & Puller 471 ff.	1796–1797	126
A.A. & L.	Art Antiquity and Law	1996–date	—
A.A.L.R.	Australian Argus Law Reports	1960–1973[1]	—
A.B.	Anonymous at end of "Benloe"	1515-1628	73
A.B.C.	Australian Bankruptcy Cases	1928–1964	—
A'Beckett	Judgments of the Supreme Court of New South Wales for the District of Port Phillip – A'Beckett	1846–1851	—
A.C.	See "Law Reports".		
A.C.D.	Administrative Court Digest	2001–date[2]	
A.C.L. Rev.	Asian Commercial Law Review	1996–date	—
A.D.I.L.	Annual Digest of International Law	1919-1949[3]	—
A.D.R.L.J.	Arbitration and Dispute Resolution Law Journal	1992–[2001?]	—
A.D.R.L.N.	Arbitration and Dispute Resolution Law Newsletter	1992–2000[4]	—
A.E.R.	All England Law Reports	1936–date	—
A.I. & L.	Artificial Intelligence and Law	1992–date	—
A.I.A.J.	Asian International Arbitration Journal	2003–date	—
A.I.P.J.	Australian Intellectual Property Journal	1992–date	—
A.J.R.	Australian Jurist Reports, Victoria	1870-1874	—
A.L.E.R.	American Law and Economic Review	1999–date	—
A.L.J.	Australian Law Journal	1927–date	—
A.L.J.R.	Australian Law Journal Reports	1958–date[5]	—

[1] For previous volumes see Argus Law Reports (Aus.) (A.L.R.). Subsequent volumes continued by Australian Law Reports (A.L.R.).
[2] For previous volumes see Crown Office Digest (C.O.D.).
[3] For subsequent volumes see International Law Reports (I.L.R.).
[4] For subsequent volumes see Arbitration Law Monthly (Arb. L.M.).

A.L.M.D.	Australian Legal Monthly Digest	1947–date	—
A.L.Q.	Arab Law Quarterly	1985–date	—
A.L.R.	Adelaide Law Review	1960–date	—
A.L.R.	Aden Law Reports	1937–[?]	—
A.L.R.	Argus Law Reports (Aust.)	1895–1959[6]	—
A.L.R.	Australian Law Reports	1895–date[7]	—
A.L.T.	Australian Law Times, Victoria	1879–1928	—
A.M. & O.	Armstrong, Macartney & Ogle (Ir.)	1840–1842	—
A.P.J.E.L.	Asia Pacific Journal of Environmental Law	1996–date	—
A.P.J.H.R.L.	Asia-Pacific Journal on Human Rights and the Law	1999–date	—
A.P.L.R.	Asia Pacific Law Review	1992–date	—
A.R.	Appeal Reports, Upper Canada	1846–1866	—
A.R. (N.S.W.)	Industrial Arbitration Reports, New South Wales	1902–[?]	—
A.T.C.	Annotated Tax Cases	1922–1975	—
A.T.D.	Australian Tax Decisions	1930–1942	—
AVMA M. & L.J.	Action for Victims of Medical Accidents Medical and Legal Journal	1990–1994	—
Abr. Ca. Eq.	Equity Cases Abridged	1667–1744	21–2
Abr. Cas.	Crawford & Dix's Abridged Cases (Ir.)	1837–1838	—
Act.	Acton	1809–1811	12
Ad. & E.	Adolphus & Ellis	1834–1840	110–3
Adam	Adam (Sc.)	1893–1916	—
Add. E.R.	Addams	1822–1826	162
Adm. & Ecc.	See L.R. Adm. & Ecc.		
Admin. L.R.	Administrative Law Reports	1989–2000	—
Agri. Law	Agricultural Law	1990–date	—
Al.	Aleyn	1646–1649	82
Al. & N.	Alcock & Napier (Ir.)	1831–1833	—
Alc. Reg. C.	Alcock (Ir.)	1832–1841	—
Aleyn	Aleyn	1646–1649	82
All E.R.	All England Law Reports	1936–date	—
All E.R. (Comm)	All England Law Reports (Commercial Cases)	1999–date	—
All E.R. (EC)	All England Law Reports (European Cases)	1995–date	—
All E.R. Rep.	All England Law Reports Reprint	1558–1935	—
All E.R. Rev.	All England Law Reports Annual Review	1982–date	—
All I.R.	All India Reporter	1914–date	—
All. N.B.	Allen's Reports, New Brunswick	1848–1866	—
Alta. L.R.	Alberta Law Reports	1908–1932	—
Amb. (Ambl.)	Ambler	1737–1784	27
Amicus Curiae	Amicus Curiae	1997–date	—
And.	Anderson	1534–1606	123
And.	Andrews	1737–1738	95
Anglo-Am. L.R.	Anglo-American Law Review	1972–2000[8]	—
Ann.	Cases, temp. Hardwicke	1733–1738	95
Anst.	Anstruther	1792–1797	145
App. Cas.	See L.R. App. Cas.		
App. Comp. & Comm. L.	Applied Computer and Communications Law	1985–1992[9]	—
App. R.N.Z.	Appeal Reports, New Zealand; Johnston	1867–1877	—

[5] The Australian Law Journal Reports are part of the Australian Law Journal (A.L.J.).
[6] For subsequent volumes see Australian Argus Law Reports (A.A.L.R.).
[7] Since 1974 have included the Australian Argus Law Reports (A.A.L.R).
[8] For subsequent volumes see Common Law World Review (C.L.W. Rev., or C.L.W.R.).
[9] For subsequent volumes see IT Law Today (IT L.T.).

App. Rep.	Appeal Reports, Ontario	1876–1900	—
Arb. L.M.	Arbitration Law Monthly	2001–date[10]	—
Arbitration	Arbitration: Journal of the	1954–date	—
	Chartered Institute of Arbitrators		
Arbitration Int.	Arbitration International	1985–date	—
Arch. L.R.	Architects' Law Reports	1904–1909	—
Arch. News	Archbold News	1993–date	—
Arch P.L.C.	Archbold's Poor Law Cases	1842–1858	—
Arg. L.R.	Argus Law Reports (Aust.)	1895–1959[11]	—
Ark.	Arkley (Sc.)	1846–1848	—
Arm. M. & O.	Armstrong, Macartney & Ogle (Ir.)	1840–1842	—
Arn.	Arnold	1838–1839	[50]
Arn. & H.	Arnold & Hodges	1840–1841	—
Arnot Cr. C.	Arnot's Criminal Cases (Sc.)	1536–1784	—
Asp. Mar. Law Cas.	Aspinall's Maritime Law Cases	1870–1940	—
Atk.	Atkyns	1736–1755	26
Aust.	Austin	1867–1869	—
Aust. Jur.	Australian Jurist	1870–1874	—
Aust. L.J.	Australian Law Journal	1927–date	—
Aust. L.J. Rep.	Australian Law Journal Reports	1958–date[12]	—
B.	Beavan	1838–1866	48–55
B. & A.	Barnewall & Alderson	1817–1822	106
B. & Ad.	Barnewall & Adolphus	1830–1834	109–10
B. & Arn.	Barron & Arnold	1843–1846	—
B. & Aust.	Barron & Austin	1842	—
B. & B.	Ball and Beatty (Irish)	1807–1814	—
B. & B.	Broderip & Bingham	1819–1822	129
B. & C.	Barnewall & Cresswell	1822–1830	107–9
B. & C. Pr. Cas.	British & Colonial Prize Cases	1914–1922	—
B. & C.R.	Bankruptcy and Companies	1918–1941	—
	(Winding-up) Cases		
B. & F.	Broderick & Freemantle	1840–1864	—
B. & G.	Brownlow & Goldesborough	1569–1624	123
B. & I.	Bankruptcy and Insolvency Cases	1853–1855	—
B. & L.	Browning & Lushington	1863–1865	167
B. & Mac.	Browne & Macnamara (see Ry. &		
	Cam. Tr. Cas.)		
B. & P.	Bosanquet & Puller	1796–1804	126–7
B.& P., N.R.	Bosanquet & Puller, New Reports	1804–1807	127
B. & S.	Best & Smith	1861–1871[13]	121–2
B. Moore	Moore	1817–1827	[19–29]
B.B. & F.L.R.	Butterworths Banking and Financial	1987	—
	Law Review		
B.C.	British Columbia Law Reports	1867–1947	—
B.C. (N.S.W.)	New South Wales Bankruptcy Cases	1890–1899	—
B.C.C.	Bail Court Cases (by Lowndes &	1852–1854	—
	Maxwell)		
B.C.C.	British Company Cases	1990–date[14]	—
B.C.C.	British Company Law Cases	1983–1989[15]	—
B.C.C.	Brown Chancery Cases (by Belt)	1778–1794	28–9
B.C.L.C.	Butterworths Company Law Cases	1983–date	—
B.C.R.	Bail Court Reports (by Saunders &	1846–1848	[82]
	Cole)		
B.C.R.	Lowndes & Maxwell	1852–1854	—
B.D. & O.	Blackham, Dundas & Osborne (Ir.)	1846–1848	—
B.G.	British Guiana Law Reports	1890–1896	—

---

[10] For previous volumes see Arbitration and Dispute Resolution Law Newsletter (A.D.R.L.N.).
[11] For subsequent volumes see Australian Argus Law Reports (A.A.L.R.).
[12] The Australian Law Journal Reports are part of the Australian Law Journal (A.L.J.).
[13] Vols. 7–10 do not appear in the E.R., being after 1865.
[14] For previous volumes see British Company Law Cases (B.C.C.).
[15] For subsequent volumes see British Company Cases (B.C.C.).

B.H.C.	Bombay High Court Reports	1862–1875	—
B.H.R.C.	Butterworths Human Rights Cases	1997–date	—
B.J.A.L.	British Journal of Administrative Law	1954–1957[16]	—
B.J.I.B. & F.L.	Butterworths Journal of International Banking and Financial Law	1986–date	—
B.L.E.	Business Law Europe	1994–1998	—
B.L.G.R.	Butterworths Local Government Reports	1999–date[17]	—
B.L.R.	Bengal Law Reports	1868–1875	—
B.L.R.	Building Law Reports	1975–date	—
B.M.	Burrow	1756–1772	97–8
B.M.C.R.	Butterworths Merger Control Review	1991–date	—
B.M.L.R.	Butterworths Medico-Legal Reports	1992–date	—
B.N.C.	Bingham New Cases	1834–1840	131–3
B.N.C.	Brooke's New Cases	1515–1558[18]	73
B.P.C.	Brown's Parliamentary Cases	1702–1801	1–3
B.P.I.L.S.	Butterworths Personal Injury Litigation Service	1998–date	—
B.P.I.R.	Bankruptcy and Personal Insolvency Reports (Jordans)	1996–date	—
B.P.L.	British Pension Lawyer	1989–1995[19]	—
B.P.N.R.	Bosanquet & Puller's New Reports	1804–1807	127
B.R.A.	Butterworth's Rating Appeals	1913–1931	—
B.R.H.	Cases, temp. Hardwicke	1733–1738	95
B.S.	Brown's Supp. to Dictionary of Decisions (Sc.)	1622–1780	—
B.S.L.R.	BIO-Science Law Review	1997–date	—
B.T.C.	British Tax Cases	1982–date	—
B.T.R.	British Tax Review	1956–date	—
B.T.R.L.R.	Brewing Trade Review Licensing Law Report	1913–1957	—
B.V.C.	British Value Added Tax Reporter	1985–date	—
B.W.C.C.	Butterworth's Workmen's Compensation Cases	1908–1947[20]	—
B.Y.B.I.L.	British Year Book of International Law	1920–date	—
Bac. Abr.	Bacon's Abridgment	——	—
Bac. Rep.	Bacon's Decisions by Ritchie	1617–1621	—
Bah. L.R.	Bahamas Law Reports	1900–1906	—
Bail Ct. Rep.	Bail Court Reports (by Saunders & Cole)	1846–1848	[82]
	See Lownd. & M.	1852–1854	—
Ball & B.	Ball & Beatty, temp. Manners (Ir.)	1807–1814	[12]
Bank. L.R.	Banking Law Reports	1992–1997[21]	—
Bank. Law	Bankers' Law	2007–date	—
Banks. & Ins.	Bankruptcy & Insolvency	1853–1855	—
Bar. & Arn.	Barron & Arnold	1843–1846	—
Bar. & Aust.	Barron & Austin	1842	—
Bar Review	Bar Review (Ir.)	1996–date	—
Barn.	Barnardiston	1726–1735	94
Barn.	Barnardiston, temp. Hardwicke	1740–1741	27
Barn. & Adol.	Barnewall & Adolphus	1830–1834	109–10

[16] Subsequently incorporated into Public Law (P.L.).
[17] Also referred to as Local Government Law Reports (L.G.L. Rep., or L.G.L.R.). For previous volumes see Local Government Reports (L.G.R.).
[18] The volume called "Brooke's New Cases" in the E.R. should for preference be designated "March Brook" (Mar. Br.). It is a translation of "Brooke's New Cases" (otherwise called "Bellewe's Petit Brook, Cases tempore H.VIII"), but it is arranged alphabetically, whereas the original work is arranged chronologically.
[19] For subsequent volumes see Pension Lawyer (Pen. Law.).
[20] For previous editions see Workmen's Compensation Cases (W.C.C.).
[21] For subsequent volumes see Lloyd's Law Reports: Banking (Lloyd's Rep. Bank.).

Barn. & Ald.	Barnewall & Alderson	1817–1822	106
Barn. & Cress.	Barnewall & Cresswell	1822–1830	107–9
Barn. C.	Barnardiston, temp. Hardwicke	1740–1741	27
Barnard.	Barnardiston	1726–1735	94
Barnard. Ch.	Barnardiston, temp. Hardwicke	1740–1741	27
Barnard Ch. Rep.	Barnardiston, temp. Hardwicke	1740–1741	27
Barnard. K.B.	Barnardiston	1726–1735	94
Barnes	Barne's Notes of Cases	1732–1760	94
Batt.	Batty (Ir.)	1825–1826	—
Beat.	Beatty (Ir.) temp. Manners and Hart	1813–1830	—
Beav.	Beavan	1838–1866	48–55
Beav. & W.	Beavan & Walford	1846	—
Bel.	Bellewe	1378–1400	72
Bell	Bell (Sc.)	1842–1850	—
Bell App.	Bell (Sc.)	1842–1850	—
Bell C.	Bell (Sc.)	1790–1792	—
Bell C.C.	Bell	1858–1860	169
Bell. Cas. t. Hen. VIII	Brooke's New Cases	1515–1558[22]	73
Bell. Cas. t. R. II	Bellewe's Richard II	1378–1400	72
Bell Fol.	Bell (Sc.)	1794–1795	—
Bell Oct.	Bell (Sc.)	1790–1792	—
Bellewe's Ca., temp. Hen. VIII	Brooke's New Cases	1515–1558[23]	73
Bellewe's Ca., temp. R. II	Bellewe's Richard II	1378–1400	72
Bell's Dict.	Bell's Dictionary of Decisions (Sc.)	1808–1833	—
Belt Bro.	Browne Vesey (by Belt)	1778–1794	28–9
Belt Supp.	Senior Supp.	1747–1756	28
Ben. & D.	Benloe & Dalison	1486–1580	123
Ben. in Keil	Benloe	1531–1628	73
Bendl.	Benloe	1515–1628	73
Benl.	Benloe	1531–1628	73
Benl.	Benloe & Dalison	1486–1580	123
Benl. & Dal.	Benloe & Dalison	1486–1580	123
Benne	7 Modern Reports	1702–1745	87
Beor.	Queensland Law Reports	1876–1878	—
Ber.	Berton's Reports, New Brunswick	1835–1839	—
Bern.	Bernard Church Cases (Ir.)	1870–1875	—
Bidd.	Bidder's Locus Standi Reports	1920–1936	—
Bing.	Bingham	1822–1834	130–1
Bing., N.C.	Bingham, New Cases	1834–1840	131–3
Bitt. Cha. Cas.	Bittleston's Chamber Cases	1883–1884	—
Bl., D. & Osb.	Blackham, Dundas & Osborne (Ir.)	1846–1848	—
Bl. H.	Blackstone H.	1788–1796	126
Bl. R. (Bl. W.)	Blackstone, W.	1746–1780	96
Bla.	Blackstone, W.	1746–1780	96
Black.	Blackerby	1327–1716	—
Black.	Blackstone, W.	1746–1780	96
Black. H.	Blackstone, H.	1788–1796	126
Black R. (Black W.)	Blackstone, W.	1746–1780	96
Blackst.	Blackstone, W.	1746–1780	96
Bli.	Bligh	1818–1821	4
Bli., N.S.	Bligh, New Series	1827–1837	4–6
Bli., O.S.	Bligh	1818–1821	4
Bomb. L.R.	Bombay Law Reporter	1899–[?]	—
Bos. & Pul.	Bosanquet & Puller	1796–1804	126–7
Bos. & Pul. N.R.	Bosanquet & Puller, New Reports	1804–1807	127
Bosw.	Boswell Reports on Literary Properties (Sc.)	1773	—

[22] See note to Brooke's New Cases (B.N.C.).
[23] See note to Brooke's New Cases (B.N.C.).

Bott.	Bott	1761–1827	—
Bott's P.L.	Bott	1560–1833	—
Br. & Col. Pr. Cas.	British and Colonial Prize Cases	1914–1919	—
Br. J. Admin. L.	British Journal of Administrative Law	1954–1957[24]	—
Br. Sup.	Brown's Supp. to Dictionary of Decisions (Sc.)	1622–1780	—
Br. Syn.	Brown's Synopsis of Decisions (Sc.)	1540–1827	—
Brac.	Bracton's Note Book	1217–1240	—
Brac. L.J.	Bracton Law Journal	1965–date	—
Bracton L.J.	Bracton Law Journal	1965–date	—
Bridg.	Bridgman, J.	1613–1621	123
Bridg. O.	Bridgman, O.	1660–1667	124
Brit. J. Admin. Law	British Journal of Administrative Law	1954–1957[25]	—
Brit. J. Criminol.	British Journal of Criminology	1961–date	—
Brit. J. Law & Soc.	British Journal of Law and Society	1974–1981[26]	—
Brit. Y.B. Int. L.	British Yearbook of International Law	1920–date	—
Brn.	Brownlow & Goldesborough	1569–1624	123
Bro. & Mac.	Brown & Macnamara	1855	—
Bro. C.C.	Brown's Chanc. Rep.	1778–1794	28–9
Bro. Ch.	Brown's Chanc. Rep.	1778–1794	28–9
Bro. N.C.	Brooke's New Cases	1515–1558[27]	73
Bro. P.C.	Brown's Parliamentary Cases	1702–1800	1–3
Bro. Syn.	Brown's Synopsis of Decisions (Sc.)	1540–1827	—
Brod. & B.	Broderip & Bingham	1819–1822	129
Brod. & Frem.	Broderick & Fremantle	1840–1864	—
Broker	The Broker	1977–date	—
Brooke	Brooke	1850–1872	—
Broun	Broun (Sc.)	1842–1845	—
Brown. & Lush.	Browning & Lushington	1863–1865	167
Brownl.	Brownlow & Goldesborough	1569–1624	123
Bruce	Bruce (Sc.)	1714–1715	—
Buch.	Buchanan (Sc.)	1800–1813	—
Buch.	Buchanan Supreme Court, Cape of Good Hope, Reports	1868–1879	—
Buck	Buck	1816–1820	—
Build. L.M.	Building Law Monthly	1983–date	—
Bulst.	Bulstrode	1610–1625	80–1
Bunb.	Bunbury	1713–1741	145
Burr.	Burrow	1756–1772	97–8
Burr. S.C.	Burrow	1732–1776	—
Burrell	Burrell	1584–1839	167
Burt. Cas.	Burton's Cases with Opinions	1700–1795	—
Bus. L.B.	Business Law Bulletin	1993–date	—
Bus. L. Rev.	Business Law Review	1980–date	—
Bus. L.R.	Business Law Review	1980–date	—
Butt. C. & E.E.B.L.B.	Butterworths Central and East European Business Law Bulletin	1992– [199?][28]	—
Butt. W.C.C.	Butterworth's Workmen's Compensation Cases	1908–1947[29]	—
Butt. Work. Comp. Cas.	Butterworth's Workmen's Compensation Cases	1908–1947[30]	—

---

[24] Subsequently incorporated into Public Law (P.L.).
[25] Subsequently incorporated into Public Law (P.L.).
[26] For subsequent volumes see Journal of Law and Society (J. Law & Soc.).
[27] See note to Brookes New Cases (B.N.C.).
[28] Also referred to as Central and Eastern European Business Law Bulletin (C. & E.E.B.L.B.). For previous volumes see [Butterworths] Soviet and East European Business Law Bulletin (S. & E.E.B.L.B.).
[29] For previous volumes see Workmen's Compensation Cases (W.C.C.).
[30] For previous volumes see Workmen's Compensation Cases (W.C.C.).

Buyer	The Buyer	1979–date	—
C. & A.	Cooke & Alcock (Ir.)	1833–1834	—
C. & D.	Corbett & Daniell	1819	—
C. & D.C.C.	Crawford & Dix Circuit Reports (Ir.)	1839–1846	—
C. & E.	Cababé & Ellis	1882–1885	—
C. & E.E.B.L.B.	Central and East European Business Law Bulletin	1992–[199?][31]	—
C. & E.L.	Construction and Engineering Law	1996–date	—
C. & F.	Clark & Finnelly	1831–1846	6–8
C. & F.L.	Credit and Finance Law	1989–date	—
C. & F.L.U.	Child and Family Law Update (Ir.)	1998–date	—
C. & J.	Crompton & Jervis	1830–1832	148–9
C. & K.	Carrington & Kirwan	1843–1850	174–5
C. & L.	Connor & Lawson, temp. Sugden (Ir.)	1841–1843	—
C. & M.	Carrington & Marshman	1841–1842	174
C. & M.	Crompton & Meeson	1832–1834	149
C. & P.	Carrington & Payne	1823–1841	171–3
C. & P.	Craig & Phillips, temp. Cottenham	1840–1841	41
C. & R.	Clifford & Rickards	1873–1884	—
C. & R.	Cockburn & Rowe	1833	—
C. & S.	Clifford & Stephens	1867–1872	—
C. Home	Clerk Home (Sc.)	1735–1744	—
C. McK. Env. L.B.	Cameron McKenna Environmental Law Bulletin	1988–date	—
C. Rob.	Robinson, Christopher	1799–1808	165
C.A.R.	Commonwealth Arbitration Reports (Aus.)	1905–[date?]	—
C.B.	Common Bench	1845–1856	135–9
C.B., N.S.	Common Bench, New Series	1856–1865	140–4
C.B.R.	Canadian Bankruptcy Reports, Fourth Series	1920–date	—
C.C.	See L.R.C.C.R.		
C.C. Chron.	County Courts Chronicle	1847–1920	—
C.C.C.	Canadian Criminal Cases	1898–date	—
C.C.C.	Choyce Cases in Chancery	1557–1606	21
C.C.C.	Cox's Criminal Cases	1843–1941	—
C.C.C.(2d)	Canadian Criminal Cases, Second Series	1971–83	—
C.C.C.(3d)	Canadian Criminal Cases, Third Series	1983–date	—
C.C.C. Sess. Pap.	Central Criminal Ct. Sessions Papers	1834–1913	—
C.C.L.	Commercial Conflict of Laws	2001–date	—
C.C.L. Rep.	Community Care Law Reports	1997–date	—
C.C.L. Rev.	Carbon and Climate Law Review	2007–date	—
C.C.L.R.	Community Care Law Reports	1997–date	—
C.C.L.R.	Community Credit Law Reports	1976–[date?]	—
C.C.R.	See L.R.C.C.R.		
C.E.C.	European Community Cases	1989–date	—
C.F.I.L.R.	Company Financial and Insolvency Law Review	1997–2000	—
C.F.L.Q.	Child and Family Law Quarterly	1995–date[32]	—
C.H.R.L.D.	Commonwealth Human Rights Law Digest	1996–date	—
C.I.L.	Contemporary Issues in Law	1995–date	—
C.I.L.L.	Construction Industry Law Letter	1983–date	—
C.I.P.A.J.	Chartered Institute of Patent Agents Journal	1971–date	—
C.J.	Contract Journal	1979–date	—

---

[31] Also referred to as Butterworth's Central and East European Business Law Bulletin (Butt. C. & E.E.B.L.B.). For previous volumes see [Butterworths] Soviet and East European Business Law Bulletin (S. & E.E.B.L.B.).

[32] For previous volumes see Journal of Child Law (J.C.L.).

C.J. Europe	Criminal Justice Europe	1991–1996	—
C.J.Q.	Civil Justice Quarterly	1982–date	—
C.J.R.B.	Commercial Judicial Review Bulletin	1995–date	—
C.L.	Commercial Lawyer	1995–date	—
C.L.	Company Lawyer	1980–date	—
C.L.	Current Law Monthly Digest	————	—
C.L. & P.	Computer Law and Practice	1984–1995[33]	
C.L. & P.R.	Charity Law and Practice Review	1992–date	—
C.L. Pract.	Commercial Law Practitioner (Ir.)	1994–date	—
C.L.B.	Commonwealth Law Bulletin	1974–date	—
C.L.C.	Commercial Law Cases	1994–date	—
C.L.C.	Current Law Consolidation (1947–1951)	1947–1951	—
C.L.D.	Company Lawyer Digest	1979–1993	—
C.L.E.	Commercial Laws of Europe	1978–date	—
C.L.J.	Cambridge Law Journal	1921–date	—
C.L.J.	Canada Law Journal	1855–1922	—
C.L.L.	Corporate Legal Letter	1978–1992	—
C.L.L.R.	Commercial Liability Law Review	2000–date	—
C.L.L. Rev.	Commercial Liability Law Review	2000–date	—
C.L.M.	Company Law Monitor	1993–1996	—
C.L.M.D.	Current Law Monthly Digest	————	—
C.L.N.	Construction Law Newsletter	1997–[date?]	—
C.L.P.	Current Legal Problems	1948–date	—
C.L.R.	Canada Law Reports	1923–1970	—
C.L.R.	Common Law Reports	1853–1855	—
C.L.R.	Commonwealth Law Reports (Aus.)	1903–date	—
C.L.R.	Cyprus Law Reports	1883–[?]	—
C.L.R.(Can.)	Canada Law Reports	1923–1970	—
C.L.S.	Current Law Statutes	1948–1950[34]	—
C.L.S.A.	Current Law Statutes Annotated	1951–date[35]	—
C.L.S.R.	Computer Law and Security Report	1985–date	—
C.L.T.	Canadian Law Times	1881–1922	—
C.L.W.	Current Law Week	1993–date	—
C.L.W. Rev.	Common Law World Review	2001–date[36]	—
C.L.W.R.	Common Law World Review	2001–date[37]	—
C.L.Y.	Current Law Yearbook	1952–date	—
C.L.Y.B.	Current Law Year Book	1952–date	—
C.M.	Compliance Monitor	1988–1996	—
C.M. & H.	Cox, Macrae & Hertslet	1847–1858	—
C.M. & R.	Crompton, Meeson & Roscoe	1834–1835	149–50
C.M.L. Rev.	Common Market Law Review	1963–date	—
C.M.L.J.	Capital Markets Law Journal	2006–date	—
C.M.L.R.	Common Market Law Reports	1962–date	—
C.M.L.R.	Common Market Law Reports: Anti-Trust Reports	1988–date	—
C.M.L.R.(A.R.)	Common Market Law Reports: Anti-Trust Reports	1988–date	—
C.O.D.	Crown Office Digest	1988–2000[38]	—
C.P.	See L.R.C.P.		
C.P. Rep.	Civil Procedure Law Reports (Online)	1999–date	—
C.P. Rep.	Civil Procedure Reports	2005–date	—
C.P.C.	Cooper, C.P., Practice Cases	1837–1838	47
C.P.D.	See L.R.C.P.D.		

---

[33] Merged with Journal of Media Law and Practice (J.M.L. & P.) to form Communications Law (Comms. Law).
[34] For subsequent volumes see Current Law Statutes Annotated (C.L.S.A.).
[35] For previous volumes see Current Law Statutes (C.L.S.).
[36] For previous volumes see Anglo-American Law Review (Anglo-Am. L.R.).
[37] For previous volumes see Anglo-American Law Review (Anglo-Am. L.R.).
[38] For subsequent volumes see Administrative Court Digest (A.C.D.).

C.P.D.	Cape Provincial Division S.A.	1910–1946	—
C.P.L.	Current Property Law	1952–1953[39]	—
C.P.L.J.	Conveyancing and Property Law Journal (Ir.)	1996–date	—
C.P.L.R.	Civil Practice Law Reports	1999–date	—
C.P.N.	Civil Procedure News	2000–date	—
C.S. & P.	Craigie, Stewart & Paton (Sc.)	1726–1821	—
C.S.R.	Company Secretary's Review	1993–date	—
C.T.L.R.	Computer and Telecommunications Law Review	1995–date	—
C.t. N.	Eden	1757–1766	28
C.W.	Copyright World	1998–date	—
C.W.N.	Calcutta Weekly Notes	1896–[?]	—
C.Y.E.L.S.	Cambridge Yearbook of European Legal Studies	1998–date	—
Ca. Prac. C.P.	Cooke's Practice Cases	1706–1747	125
Ca. Sett.	Cases of Settlement and Removals	1710–1742	—
Ca. temp. F.	Cases temp. Finch	1673–1681	23
Ca. temp. Hard.	Cases temp. Hardwicke	1733–1738	95
Ca. temp. Holt.	11 Modern Reports	1702–1710	88
Ca. temp. King	See Sel. Cas. Ch.		
Ca. temp. Lee	Cases temp. Lee	1752–1758	—
Ca. temp. Talbot	Cases temp. Talbot	1733–1738	25
Cab. & Ell.	Cababé & Ellis	1882–1885	—
Cairns Dec.	Cairn's Decisions Albert Assurance Arbitration	1871–1875	—
Cal.	Calthrop's Customs and Liberties of London	1609–1618	80
Cal. L.J.	Calcutta Law Journal	1905–[?]	—
Cal. W.N.	Calcutta Weekly Notes	1896–[?]	—
Cald.	Caldecott	1776–1785	—
Camb. L.J.	Cambridge Law Journal	1921–date	—
Cambr. L.J.	Cambridge Law Journal	1921–date	—
Cambrian L.R.	Cambrian Law Review	1970–date	—
Cambridge L.J.	Cambridge Law Journal	1921–date	—
Camp.	Campbell	1807–1816	170–1
Can. B. Rev.	Canadian Bar Review	1923–date	—
Can. Com. R.	Canadian Commercial Law Reports	1901–1903	—
Can. Cr. Cas.	Canadian Criminal Cases	1898–date	—
Can. Crim. Cas.	Canadian Criminal Cases	1898–date	—
Can. Ex. R.	Canadian Exchequer Reports	1875–1922	—
Can. L. Rev.	Canadian Law Review	1901–1907	—
Can. L.J.	Canada Law Journal	1855–1922	—
Can. L.R.	Canada Law Reports	1923–1970	—
Can. L.T.	Canadian Law Times	1881–1922	—
Can. Sup. Ct.	Canada Supreme Court Reports	1923–date	—
Car. & K.	Carrington & Kirwan	1843–1850	174–5
Car. & M.	Carrington & Marshman	1841–1842	174
Car. & P.	Carrington & Payne	1823–1841	171–3
Carp. P.C.	Carpmael	1602–1842	—
Cart.	Carter	1664–1675	124
Cart B.N.A.	Cartwright's Constitutional Cases, Canada	1868–1896	—
Carth.	Carthew	1687–1701	90
Cartm.	Cartmell's Trade Mark Cases	1876–1892	—
Cary	Cary	1557–1604	21
Cas. B.R. t. W. III	12 Modern Reports	1690–1702	88
Cas. C.R.	12 Modern Reports	1690–1702	88
Cas. Ch.	9 Modern Reports	1722–1755	88
Cas. Eq. Abr.	Equity Cases Abridged	1667–1744	21–2

---

[39] Merged with Journal of Planning Law (J.P.L.) to become Journal of Planning and Property Law (J.P.L.).

Cas. K.B. t. Hard	Kelynge (W.)	1730–1734	25
Cas. L. Eq.	10 Modern Reports	1710–1725	88
Cas. Sett.	Cases of Settlements	1710–1742	—
Cas. t. Hard.	Cases temp. Hardwicke	1733–1738	95
Cas. t. Maccl.	10 Modern Reports	1710–1725	88
Cas. t. Q. Anne	11 Modern Reports	1702–1731	88
Cas. t. Talb.	Talbot, Cases in Equity	1733–1738	25
Cass. L.G.B.	Casson's Local Government Board Decisions	1902–1916	—
Ch.	See L.R. Ch.		
Ch. App.	See L.R. Ch. Appeals		
Ch. Ca.	Cases in Chancery	1660–1697	22
Ch.D.	See L.R. Ch.D.		
Cham. Rep.	Chambers Reports, Upper Canada	1846–1852	—
Chan. Cas.	Cases in Chancery	1660–1697	22
Chan. Chamb.	Chancery Chambers Reports, Upper Canada	1857–1872	—
Chan. Rep. C.	Reports in Chancery	1615–1710	21
Charl. Cha. Ca.	Charley's Chamber Cases	1875–1876	—
Charl. Pr. Ca.	Charley's New Practice Cases	1875–1881	—
Chip.	Chipman's Reports, New Brunswick	1825–1838	—
Chit.	Chitty	1770–1822	[22–3]
Cho. Ca. Ch.	Choyce Cases in Chancery	1557–1606	21
Civ. Lit.	Civil Litigation	1999–date	—
Civ. P.B.	Civil Practice Bulletin	1995–date	—
Cl. & F.	Clark & Finnelly	1831–1846	6–8
Clay.	Clayton's York Assizes	1631–1650	—
Cliff.	Clifford's Southwark	1796	—
Cliff. & Rick	Clifford & Rickards	1873–1884	—
Cliff. & Steph.	Clifford & Stephens	1867–1872	—
Co.	Coke	1572–1616	76–7
Co. Ct. Chr.	County Courts Chronicle	1847–1920	—
Co. Ct. Rep.	County Courts Reports	1860–1920	—
Co., G.	Cooke's Practice Cases	1706–1747	125
Co. L. Dig.	Company Law Digest	1979–1993[40]	—
Co. L.J.	Commercial Litigation Journal	2005–date	—
Co. Law.	Company Lawyer	1980–date	—
Co. Rep.	Coke	1572–1616	76–7
Coch.	Cochran, Nova Scotia Reports	1859	—
Cockb. & R.	Cockburn & Rowe	1833	—
Col. C.C.	Collyer, temp. Bruce, V.-C.	1844–1846	63
Col. N.C.	Collyer, temp. Bruce, V.-C.	1844–1845	63
Coll., P.C.	Colles (Supp. vol. to Bro. P.C.)	1697–1713	1
Colles, P.C.	Colles (Supp. vol. to Bro. P.C.)	1697–1713	1
Colly.	Collyer, temp. Bruce, V.-C.	1844–1845	63
Colquit	1 Modern Reports	1669–1670	86
Colt.	Coltman	1879–1885	—
Com.	Comyns	1695–1741	92
Com. Cas.	Commercial Cases	1895–1941[41]	—
Com. Jud. J.	Commonwealth Judicial Journal	1973–date	—
Com. L.L.	Commonwealth Law Librarian	1992–1994	—
Com. Law. Rep.	Common Law Reports	1853–1855	—
Com. Lawyer	Commonwealth Lawyer	1984–date	—
Com. Rep.	Comyns	1695–1741	92
Comb.	Comberbach	1685–1698	94
Comm. A.R.	Commonwealth Arbitration Reports, Australia	1905–[date?]	—
Comm. L.J.	Commercial Law Journal	1998–date	—
Comm. Law.	Commercial Lawyer	1995–date	—
Comm. Lawyer	Commonwealth Lawyer	1984–date	—

[40] Merged with Company Lawyer (C.L., or Co. Law.).
[41] Incorporated into the Times Law Reports (T.L.R., or Times L. Rep., or Times L.R.).

Comm. Leases	Commercial Leases	1987–date	—
Comm. Prop.	Commercial Property	1994–date	—
Comms. Law	Communications Law	1996–date[42]	—
Comp. & Law	Computers and Law	1974–date	—
Comp. L.I.	Competition Law Insight	2003–date[43]	—
Comp. L.J.	Competition Law Journal	2002–date	—
Comp. L.M.	Competition Law Monitor	2001–2003[44]	—
Comp. Law	Competition Law Journal	2002–date	—
Comp. Law E.C.	Competition Law in the European Communities	1978–date	—
Comp. Law.	Company Lawyer	1980–date	—
Comps. & Law	Computers and Law	1974–date	—
Con. & L.	Connor & Lawson (Ir.), temp. Sugden	1841–1843	—
Con. L.D.	Construction Law Digest	1982–[2000?]	—
Con. L.R.	Construction Law Reports	1985–date	—
Conr.	Conroy's Custodiam Reports	1652–1788	—
Cons. & Mar. Law	Consumer and Marketing Law	1987–1994	—
Cons. L. Today	Consumer Law Today	1977–date	—
Cons. Law	Construction Law	1992–date[45]	—
Cons. Law	Constructional Law	1990–1992[46]	—
Const. L.J.	Construction Law Journal	1984–date	—
Consum. L.J.	Consumer Law Journal	1993–2000	—
Conv. (N.S.)	Conveyancer and Property Lawyer (New Series)	1936–date	—
Coo. & Al.	Cooke & Alcock (Ir.)	1833–1834	—
Cooke	Cooke's Practice Cases	1706–1747	125
Coop.	Cooper, G., temp. Eldon	1815	35
Coop., C.C.	Cooper, C.C. temp. Cottenham	1846–1848	47
Coop., G.	Cooper, G., temp. Eldon	1815	35
Coop. P.C.	Cooper, C.P., Practice Cases	1837–1838	47
Coop., temp. Brough	Cooper, C.P., temp. Cottenham	1833–1834	47
Coop., temp. Cott.	Cooper, C.P., temp. Cottenham	1846–1848	47
Corb. & Dan.	Corbett & Daniell	1819	—
Corp. Brief.	Corporate Briefing : Legal and Regulatory Developments Affecting Company Strategy	1986–date	—
Corp. C.	Corporate Counsel	1997–date	—
Costs L.R.	Costs Law Reports	1997–date	—
Counsel	Counsel	1986–date	—
Coup.	Couper (Sc.)	1868–1885	—
Cowp.	Cowper	1774–1778	98
Cox	Cox's Equity	1783–1796	29–30
Cox & Atk.	Cox & Atkinson	1843–1846	—
Cox & M'C.	Cox, Macrae & Hertslet	1847–1858	—
Cox C.C.	Cox's Criminal Cases	1843–1941	—
Cox Cty. Ct. Cas.	Cox County Court Cases	1860–1919	—
Cox Jt. Stk.	Cox's Joint Stock Cases	1864–1872	—
Cox M.C.	Cox's Magistrates' Cases	1859–1920	—
Cr. & Dix	Crawford & Dix's Irish Circuit Reports	1839–1846	—
Cr. & Dix Ab. Ca.	Crawford & Dix's Notes of Cases (Ir.)	1837–1838	—
Cr. & Ph.	Craig & Phillips', temp. Cottenham	1840–1841	41
Cr. S. & P.	Craigie, Stewart & Paton (Sc.)	1726–1821	—
Cr. App. R.	Criminal Appeal Reports	1908–date	—

[42] Formed from a merger between Computer law and Practice (C.L. & P.) and Journal of Media Law and Practice (J.M.L. & P.).
[43] For previous volumes see Competition Law Monitor (Comp. L.M.).
[44] For subsequent volumes see Competition Law Insight (Comp. L.I.).
[45] For previous volumes see Constructional Law (C.L.).
[46] For subsequent volumes see Construction Law (C.L.).

Law Reports, Journals

Cr. App. R.(S.)	Criminal Appeal Reports (Sentencing)	1979–date	—
Creasy	Creasy's Reports, Ceylon	1859–1870	—
Cress.	Cresswell	1827–1829	—
Crim. L.B.	Criminal Law Bulletin	1993–date	—
Crim. L.J.	Criminal Law Journal	1977–date	—
Crim. L.R.	Criminal Law Review	1954–date	—
Crim. L.W.	Criminal Law Week	1997–date	—
Crim. Law.	Criminal Lawyer	1989–date	—
Criminologist	Criminologist	1967–1975; 1987–date	—
Cripps' Cas.	Cripps' Church and Clergy	1847–1850	—
Cro. Car. (3)	Croke	1625–1641	79[47]
Cro. Eliz. (1)	Croke	1582–1603	78[47]
Cro. Jac. (2)	Croke	1603–1625	79[47]
Crockford	Crockford, Maritime Law Reports	1860–1871	—
Croke	See "Cro.Car., Eliz. And Jac."		
Croke	Keilway	1496–1531	72
Cromp.	Crompton Star Chamber Cases	1881	—
Cromp. & Jer.	Crompton & Jervis	1830–1832	148–9
Cromp. & M.	Crompton & Meeson	1832–1834	149
Cromp., M. & R.	Crompton, Meeson & Roscoe	1834–1835	149–50
Crow	Crowther's Reports, Sri Lanka	1863	—
Ct. of S.	See Sess. Cas.		
Cunn.	Cunningham, temp. Hardwicke	1734–1736	94
Curt.	Curteis	1834–1844	163
D.	Denison	1844–1852	169
D.	Dyer, ed. Vaillant	1513–1582	73
D.	Session Cases, 2nd Series [Dunlop] (Sc.)	1838–1862	—
D. & B.	Dearsley & Bell	1856–1858	169
D. & C.	Dow & Clark's Appeals	1827–1832	6
D. & Ch.	Deacon & Chitty	1832–1835	—
D. & E.	Durnford & East's Term Reports	1785–1800	99–101
D. & G.	Diprose and Gammon, Reports of Law Affecting Friendly Societies	1801–1897	—
D. & J.	De Gex & Jones, Chancery	1857–1859	44–45
D. & J.B.	De Gex & Jones' Bankruptcy Reports	1857–1859	—
D. & L.	Dowling & Lowndes	1843–1849	[67–82]
D. & Mer.	Davison & Merivale	1843–1844	[64]
D. & R.	Dowling & Ryland King's Bench	1821–1827	[23–30]
D. & R.M.C.	Dowling & Ryland Magistrates	1822–1827	—
D. & R.N.P.	Dowling & Ryland	1822–1823	171
D. & S.	Drewry & Smale, temp. Kindersley	1860–1865	62
D. & Sm.	De Gex & Smale, temp. Knight-Bruce & Parker	1846–1852	63–4
D. & W.	Drury & Walsh (Ir.)	1837–1840	—
D. & W.	Drury & Warren (Ir.)	1841–1843	—
D.C.R.	District Court Reports	1988–date[48]	—
D.D. & R.M.	Due Diligence and Risk Management	2000–date[49]	—
D.E.J.	Digital Evidence Journal	2006–date[50]	—

[47] "According to the lettering on the spines of Volumes 78 and 79, '1 & 2 Cro.' are Cro. Eliz., '3 Cro.' is Cro. Jac., and '4 Cro.' is Cro. Car. But this has never been the standard mode of citation. Originally Cro. Jac. and Cro. Car. were published before Cro. Eliz., and the three volumes were therefore labelled '1,' '2,' '3,' in that order. Later, however, the regnal order of time asserting itself, they become '2,' '3,' and '1' respectively. It was not until 1790–1792 that Cro. Eliz. was published as two volumes, and I cannot find that this has since affected the mode of citation." –7 C.L.J., vii, p.262.
[48] For previous volumes see New Zealand District Court Reports (N.Z.D.C.R.).
[49] For previous volumes see Environmental Due Diligence and Risk Management (E.D.D. & R.M.).
[50] Incorporates E-Signature Law Journal (E.S.L.J.).

D.F. & J.	De Gex, Fisher & Jones, Chancery	1860–1862	45
D.F. & J.B.	De Gex, Fisher & Jones, Bankruptcy	1859–1861	—
D.G.	De Gex, Bankruptcy	1844–1850	—
D.J. & S.	De Gex, Jones & Smith, Chancery	1862–1866	46
D.J. & S.B.	De Gex, Jones & Smith, Bankruptcy	1862–1865	—
D.L.R.	Discrimination Law Reports	1999–date	—
D.L.R.	Dominion Law Reports (Can.)	1912–date	—
D.L.R.(2d)	Dominion Law Reports, Second Series (Can.)	1956–1968	—
D.L.R.(3d)	Dominion Law Reports, Third Series (Can.)	1969–1984	—
D.L.R.(4d)	Dominion Law Reports, Fourth Series (Can.)	1984–date	—
D.M.	Davison & Merivale	1843–1844	[64]
D.M. & G.	De Gex, Macnaghten & Gordon, Chancery	1851–1857	42–44
D.M. & G.B.	De Gex, Macnaghten & Gordon, Bankruptcy	1851–1857	—
D.N.S.	Dowling's New Series	1841–1842	[63–5]
D.P. & P.P.	Data Protection and Privacy Practice	1999–date	—
D.P.C.	Dowling's Practice Cases	1830–1841	[36–61]
D.P.L. & P.	Data Protection Law and Policy	2004–date	—
D.R.A.	De-Rating Appeals	1930–1961[51]	
D.U.L.J.	Dublin University Law Journal	1976–date	—
Dal.	Benloe & Dalison	1486–1580	123
Dal. In Keil.	Dalison's Reports in Keilway	1533–1664	—
Dale	Dale's Judgements	1868–1871	—
Dalr.	Dalrymple (Sc.)	1698–1718	—
Dan.	Daniell (Equity). temp. Richards	1817–1823	159
Dan. & L.	Danson & Lloyd	1828–1829	[34]
Das.	Dassent's Bankruptcy Reports	1853–1855	—
Dav. P.C.	Davies	1785–1816	—
Davies (Davis or Davy)	Davis (Ir.)	1604–1612	80
Day Elect. Cas	Day's Election Cases	1892–1893	—
De Coly	De Colyar, County Court Cases	1867–1882	—
De G. & J.	De Gex & Jones, Chancery	1857–1859	44–5
De G. & J. By.	De Gex & Jones' Chancery Appeals	1857–1859	—
De G. & Sm.	De Gex & Smale, temp. Knight-Bruce & Parker	1846–1852	63–4
De G.F. & J.	De Gex, Fisher & Jones, temp. Campbell	1860–1862	45
De G.F. & J. By.	De Gex, Fisher & Jones, Bankruptcy	1859–1861	—
De G.J. & S.	De Gex, Jones & Smith, Chancery	1862–1866	46
De G.J. & S. By.	De Gex, Jones & Smith's Bankruptcy Reports	1862–1865	—
De G.M. & G.	De Gex, Macnaghten & Gordon, Chancery	1851–1857	42–44
De G.M. & G. By	De Gex, Macnaghten & Gordon, Bankruptcy	1851–1857	—
De Gex	De Gex, Bankruptcy	1844–1850	—
De Voil I.T.I.	De Voil Indirect Tax Intelligence	1996–date	—
Dea. & Ch.	Deacon & Chitty	1832–1835	—
Dea. & Sw.	Deane & Swabey	1855–1857	164
Deac.	Deacon	1835–1840	—
Deane. Ecc. Rep. B.	Deane & Swabey	1855–1857	164
Dear. & B.C.C.	Dearsley & Bell	1856–1858	169
Dears. C.C.	Dearsley	1852–1856	169
Deas & And.	Deas & Anderson (Sc.)	1829–1833	—
Del.	Delane's Decisions	1832–1835	—

[51] For subsequent volumes see Rating Appeals (RA).

Den. & P.	Denison and Pearce	1844–1852	169
Den. C.C.	Denison and Pearce	1844–1852	169
Denning L.J.	Denning Law Journal	1986–date	—
Dick.	Dickens	1599–1798	21
Dirl.	Dirleton (Sc.)	1665–1677	—
Disc. L.R.	Discrimination Law Reports	1999–date	—
Dod. (Dods.)	Dodson, temp. Scott	1811–1822	165
Dom. L.R.	Dominion Law Reports (Can.)	1912–date	—
Donn.	Donnelly	1836–1837	47
Donn. Ir. Land Cas.	Donnell, Irish Land Cases (Ir.)	1871–1876	—
Dor.	Dorion's Reports, Quebec	1880–1886	—
Doug.	Douglas, Election	1774–1776	—
Doug.	Douglas, King's Bench	1778–1785	99
Dow	Dow	1812–1818	3
Dow. (Dow. P.C.; Dow. P.R.)	Dowling's Practice Cases	1830–1841	[36–61]
Dow & Cl.	Dow & Clark's Appeals	1827–1832	6
Dow. & L.	Dowling & Lowndes	1843–1849	[67–82]
Dow. & Ry.	Dowling & Ryland, King's Bench	1821–1827	[24–30]
Dow. & Ry. N.P.	Dowling & Ryland, Nisi Prius	1822–1823	171
Dow. & Ry. M.C.	Dowling & Ryland, Magistrates	1822–1827	—
Dow N.S.	Dow & Clark's Appeals	1827–1832	6
Dow N.S.	Dowling's New Series	1841–1843	[63–5]
Dr.	Drewry's Reports, temp. Kindersley	1852–1859	61–2
Dr. & Sm. (Drew. & Sm.)	Drewry & Smale, temp. Kindersley	1860–1865	62
Dr. & Wal.	Drury & Walsh (Ir.)	1837–1840	—
Dr. & War.	Drury & Warren (Ir.)	1841–1843	—
Dr. t. Nap.	Drury, temp. Napier (Ir.)	1858–1859	—
Dr. t. Sug.	Drury, temp. Sugden (Ir.)	1843–1844	—
Draper	Draper's Upper Canada King's Bench Reports	1829–1831	—
Drew.	Drewry Reports, temp. Kindersley	1852–1859	61–2
Drink.	Drinkwater	1840–1841	[60]
Dublin U.L.J.	Dublin University Law Journal	1976–date	—
Dunc.Mer.Cas	Duncan, Mercantile Cases	1885–1886	—
Dunlop	Session Cases, 2nd Series (Sc.)	1838–1862	—
Dunning	Dunning	1753–1754	—
Durie	Durie (Sc.)	1621–1642	—
Durn. & E.	Durnford & East's Term Reports	1785–1800	99–101
Dy.	Dyer, ed. Vaillant	1513–1582	73
E.	East's Term Reports	1800–1912	102–4
E. & A.	Ecclesiastical and Admiralty Reports (Spinks)	1853–1855	164
E. & A.R.	Error and Appeal Reports, Ontario	1846–1866	—
E. & B.	Ellis & Blackburn	1852–1858	118–120
E. & E.	Ellis & Ellis	1858–1861	120–1
E. & I. App.	Law Reports, English & Irish Appeals	1866–1875	—
E. and L.	Education and the Law	1989–date	—
E. & P.	International Journal of Evidence and Proof	1996–date	—
E. & S.L.J.	Entertainment and Sports Law Journal	2005–date	—
E. & Y.	Eagle & Young	1204–1825	—
E. St. A.L.	European State Aid Law Quarterly	2002–date	—
E-Law Rev.	E-Law Review	2001–date	—
E.A.	East African Law Reports	1957–1967	—
E.A.C.A.	East Africa Court of Appeal Reports	1934–1956	—
E.A.L.R.	East Africa Law Reports	1897–1915	—
E.B. & E.	Ellis, Blackburn & Ellis	1858	120
E.B. & F.L.J.	European Banking and Financial Law Journal	2007–date	—
E.B.L.	Electronic Business Law	1999–date	—

E.B.L. Rev.	European Business Law Review	1988–date	—
E.B.L.R.	Electronic Business Law Reports	2001–date	—
E.B.L.R.	European Business Law Review	1988–date	—
E.B.O.R.	European Business Organization Law Review	2000–date	—
E.C. C.P.N.	European Commission Competition Policy Newsletter	[?]–date	—
EC. F.L.M.	EC Food Law Monthly	1992–1994	—
E.C. Law	European Company Law	2002–date	—
E.C.A.	Elderly Client Adviser	1995–date	—
E.C.C.	European Commercial Cases	1978–date	—
E.C.D.R.	European Copyright and Design Reports	1999–date	—
E.C.F.R.	European Company and Financial Law Review	2004–date	—
E.C.J.	Environmental Claims Journal	1988–date	—
E.C.L.	European Corporate Lawyer	1994–1998	—
E.C.L. & P.	E-Commerce Law and Policy	1999–date	—
E.C.L. Rep.	E-Commerce Law Reports	2001–date	—
E.C.L. Rev.	Electronic Communication Law Review	2002–date[52]	—
E.C.L. Review	European Constitutional Law Review	2005–date	—
E.C.L.R.	European Competition Law Review	1980–date	—
E.C.R.	European Court Reports	1954–date	—
E.C.R. – S.C.	European Court Reports – Reports of European Staff Cases	1994–date	—
E.D.C.	Eastern District Court Reports, Cape of Good Hope	1880–1909	—
E.D.D. & R.M.	Environmental Due Diligence and Risk Management	1999–2000[53]	—
EDI L.R.	EDI Law Review, also titled Electronic Data Interchange Law Review	1994–2001[54]	—
E.D.L.	Eastern District's Local Division Reports (S.Afr.)	1910–1946	—
E.E.B.L.	East European Business Law	1991–1998	—
E.E.E.L.R.	European Energy and Environmental Law Review	2008–date[55]	—
E.E.L.R.	European Environmental Law Review	1992–2007[56]	—
E.F.A. Rev.	European Foreign Affairs Review	1996–date	—
E.F.F.L.R.	European Food and Feed Law Review	2006–date	—
E.F.P.L. & P.	E-Finance and Payments Law and Policy	2006–date	—
E.F.S.L.	European Financial Services Law	1994–[2003?]	—
E.G.	Estates Gazette	1858–date	—
E.G.C.S.	Estates Gazette Case Summaries	1988–date	—
E.G.D.	Estates Gazette Digest of Cases	1902–1984	—
E.G.D.C.	Estates Gazette Digest of Cases	1902–1984	—
E.G.L.R.	Estates Gazette Law Reports	1858–date	—
E.H.L.R.	Environmental Health Law Reports	1998–date	—
E.H.R.L.R.	European Human Rights Law Review	1995–date	—
E.H.R.R.	European Human Rights Reports	1979–date	—
E.I.P.R.	European Intellectual Property Review	1978–date	—

[52] For previous volumes see E.D.I. Law Review (EDI L.R.).
[53] For subsequent volumes see Due Diligence and Risk Management (D.D. & R.M.).
[54] For subsequent volumes see Electronic Communication Law Review (E.C.L. Rev.).
[55] For previous volumes see European Environmental Law Review (E.E.L.R.).
[56] For subsequent volumes see European Energy and Environmental Law Review (E.E.E.L.R.).

E.J.C.	European Journal of Criminology	2004–date	—
E.J.C.L.	Electronic Journal of Comparative Law	1997–date	—
E.J.E.L. & P.	European Journal for Education Law and Policy	1997–date	—
E.J.H.L.	European Journal of Health Law	1994–date	—
E.J.I.L.	European Journal of International Law	1990–date	—
E.J.L.E.	European Journal of Legal Education	2001–date	—
E.J.L.R.	European Journal of Law Reform	1999–2002	—
E.J.M.L.	European Journal of Migration and Law	1999–date	—
E.J.R.B.	Environmental Judicial Review Bulletin	1994	—
E.L.	Equitable Lawyer	1999	—
E.L. Rev.	European Law Review	1975–date	—
E.L.A. Briefing	Employment Lawyers Association Briefing	1999–date	—
E.L.B.	Environment Law Brief	1990–date	—
E.L.D.	European Law Digest	1973–1991[57]	—
E.L.F.	Elder Law and Finance	2001–date	—
E.L.J.	European Law Journal	1995–date	—
E.L.M.	Environmental Law and Management	1993–date[58]	—
E.L.R.	Eastern Law Reporter, Canada	1906–1914	—
E.L.R.	Education Law Reports	1994–date	—
E.L.R.	Environmental Law Review	1998–date	—
E.L.R.	European Law Review	1975–date	—
E.L.R.I.	Employment Law Review – Ireland	2005–date	—
E.M.L.R.	Entertainment and Media Law Reports	1993–date	—
E.O.R.	Equal Opportunities Review	1985–date	—
E.O.R. Dig.	Equal Opportunities Review Discrimination Case Law Digest	1989–2001	—
E.P.C.	English Prize Cases (Ed. Roscoe)	1745–1859	—
E.P. & L.	Environmental Policy and Law	1975–date	—
E.P.I.S.	EMIS Personal Injury Service	2005–date	—
E.P.L.	European Public Law	1995–date	—
E.P.L.I.	Education, Public Law, and the Individual	1995–date	—
E.P.O.R.	European Patent Office Reports	1986–date	—
E.P.P.P.L.R.	European Public Private Partnership Law Review	2006–date	—
E.P.S.	EMIS Property Service	2003–date	—
E.R.	English Reports	1220–1865	1–176
E.R.P.L.	European Review of Private Law	1993–date	—
E.S.L.J.	E-Signature Law Journal	2004–2005[59]	—
E.R.C.L.	European Review of Contract Law	2005–date	—
E.T.M.R.	European Trade Mark Reports	1996–date	—
EWCA Civ. number	Media neutral citation from the Court of Appeal (Civil Division)	2001–date	—
EWCA Crim. number	Media neutral citation from the Court of Appeal (Criminal Division)	2001–date	—
EWCST number	Media neutral citation from the Care Standards Tribunal	[2002]–date	—
EWHC number (Admin.)	Media neutral citation from the High Court (Administrative Court)	2001–date	—

---

[57] For subsequent volumes see European Current Law (Euro. C.L.).
[58] For previous volumes, see Land Management and Environmental Law Report (L.M.E.L.R.).
[59] From 2006 incorporated in Digital Evidence Journal (D.E.J.).

EWHC number (Admlty.)	Media neutral citation from the High Court (Admiralty Court)	2002–date	—
EWHC number (Ch.)	Media neutral citation from the High Court (Chancery Division)	2002–date	—
EWHC number (Comm.)	Media neutral citation from the High Court (Commercial Court)	2002–date	—
EWHC number (Costs)	Media neutral citation from the Supreme Court Cost Office	[2000]–date	—
EWHC number (Fam.)	Media neutral citation from the High Court (Family Division)	2002–date	—
EWHC number (Pat.)	Media neutral citation from the High Court (Patents Court)	2002–date	—
EWHC number (QB)	Media neutral citation from the High Court (Queen's Bench Division)	2002–date	—
EWHC number (TCC)	Media neutral citation from the High Court (Technology and Construction Court)	2002–date	—
Ea. (East)	East's Term Reports	1800–1812	102–4
Ec. & Mar.	Notes of Cases in Ecclesiastical and Maritime Courts	1841–1850	
Ecc. & Ad.	Spinks	1853–1855	164
Ecc. L.J.	Ecclesiastical Law Journal	1987–date	—
Ed.	Eden	1757–1766	28
Ed. C.R.	Education Case Reports	1998–date	—
Ed. L.M.	Education Law Monitor	1994–date	—
Ed. Law.	Education Law Journal	2000–date	—
Edgar	Edgar (Sc.)	1724–1725	—
Edin. L.R.	Edinburgh Law Review	1996–date	—
Edw.	Edwards	1808–1812	165
El. & Bl.	Ellis & Blackburn	1851–1858	118–20
El. & El.	Ellis & Ellis	1858–1861	120–1
El. B. & El.	Ellis, Blackburn & Ellis	1858	120
Elch.	Elchies (Sc.)	1733–1754	—
EMIS E.L.S.	EMIS E-Law Service	2003–date	—
Emp. Law	Employers' Law	1997–date	—
Emp. Law	Employment Law	1994–2003	—
Emp. L. & L.	Employment Law and Litigation	1996–date	—
Emp. L. Brief	Employment Law Briefing	1993–1999	—
Emp. L.B.	Employment Law Bulletin	1992–date	—
Emp. L.J.	Employment Law Journal	1999–date	—
Emp. L.N.	Employment Law Newsletter	1993–date	—
Emp. Lit.	Employment Litigation	1996–2000	—
Employ. L.	Employers' Law	1997–date	—
Eng. Judg.	English Judges (Sc.)	1665–1661	—
Ent. Law	Entertainment Law	2002–date	—
Ent. L.R.	Entertainment Law Review	1990–date	—
Env. L. Rev.	Environmental Law Review	1999–date	—
Env. L.R.	Environmental Law Review	1999–date	—
Env. L.B.	Environmental Law Bulletin	1994–date	—
Env. L.M.	Environmental Law Monthly	1992–date	—
Env. L.R.	Environmental Law Reports	1992–date	—
Env. Law	Environmental Law	1994–date	—
Env. Liability	Environmental Liability	1993–date	—
Eq.	See L.R.Eq.		
Eq. Ab.	Equity Cases Abridged	1667–1744	21–2
Eq. Ca. Abr.	Equity Cases Abridged	1667–1744	21–2
Eq. Cas.	9 Modern Reports	1722–1755	88
Eq. Rep.	Common Law and Equity Reports	1853–1855	—
Eq. Rep.	Gilbert, Equity Reports	1705–1727	25
Esp.	Espinasse	1793–1807	170
Eu. L.F.	European Legal Forum	2000–date	—
Eu. L.R.	European Law Reports	1997–date	—
Eur. Ass. Arb.	European Assurance Arbitration	1872–1875	—

Eur. Counsel	European Counsel	1996–2000[60]	—
Eur. Envtl. L. Rev.	European Environmental Law Review	1992–date	—
Eur. J. Crime Cr. L. Cr. J.	European Journal of Crime, Criminal Law and Criminal Justice	1993–date	—
Eur. L. Rev.	European Law Review	1975–date	—
Euro. C.J.	European Competition Journal	2005–date	—
Euro. C.L.	European Current Law	1992–date[61]	—
Euro. L.B.	European Legal Business	1998–date	—
Euro. L.M.	European Law Monitor	1993–date	—
Euro. Law	European Lawyer	2000–date	—
Euro. T.L.	European Transport Law	1966–date	—
Evans	Evans	1756–1788	—
Ex.	Exchequer Reports (Welsby, Hurlstone & Gordon)	1847–1856	154–6
Ex.	See L.R.Ex.		
Exch. Rep., W., H. & G.	Exchequer Reports (Welsby, Hurlstone & Gordon)	1847–1856	154–6
F.	Session Cases, 5th Series [Frasier] (Sc.)	1898–1906	—
F. & C.L.	Finance and Credit Law	1987–date	—
F. & D.I.B.	Food and Drink Industry Bulletin	2002–2003[62]	—
F. & D.L.M.	Food and Drink Law Monthly	2003–date[63]	—
F. & D.L.R.	Futures and Derivatives Law Review	1994–1996	—
F. & F.	Foster & Finlason	1858–1867	175–6
F. & S.	Fox & Smith (Ir.)	1822–1824	—
F. & S.	Fox & Smith	1886–1895	—
F.B.C.	Fonblanque	1849–1852	—
F.B.R.	Full Bench Rulings-Bengal: North West Provinces		
F.C.	Faculty Collection (Sc.)	1738–1841	—
F.C.R.	Family Court Reporter	1987–date	—
F.D. & D.I.B.	Food, Drinks and Drugs Industry Bulletin	1997–2001[64]	—
F.L.	Family Law	1971–date	—
F.L.R.	Family Law Reports	1980–date	—
F.L.R.	Federal Law Reports (Aust.)	1956–date	—
F.L.R.	Fiji Law Reports	1875–1959	—
F.L.R. Rep.	Family Law Reports Reprint 1864–1980	1864–1980	—
F.L.T.	Family Law Today	1992–1996	—
F.M.S.R.	Federated Malay States Reports	1899–1941	—
F.O.I.	Freedom of Information	2004–date	—
F.S.L.J.	Financial Services Law Journal	1997–2001	—
F.S.L.L.	Financial Services Law Letter	1988–1996	—
F.S.R.	Fleet Street Reports	1978–date[65]	—
F.S.R.	Fleet Street Reports of Patent Cases	1963–1978[66]	—
FTLR	Financial Times Law Reports	1981–[?]	—
Falc.	Falconer (Sc.)	1744–1751	—
Falc. & Fitz.	Falconer & Fitzherbert	1835–1838	—
Fam. L. Rep.	Family Law Reports	1980–date	—
Fam. L.B.	Family Law Bulletin	2001–date[67]	—
Fam. L.J.	Family Law Journal	1993–date	—

---

[60] For subsequent volumes see Global Counsel (Global Counsel).
[61] For previous volumes see European Law Digest (E.L.D.).
[62] For previous volumes see Food, Drink and Drugs Industry Bulletin (F.D. & D.I.B.).
[63] Formed from a merger between Food Law Monthly (Food L.M.) and Food and Drink Industry Bulletin (F. & D.I.B.).
[64] For subsequent volumes see Food and Drink Industry Bulletin (F. & D.I.B.).
[65] Previously titled Fleet Street Reports of Patent Cases (F.S.R.).
[66] Subsequently titled Fleet Steet Reports (F.S.R.).
[67] For previous volumes see Family Matters (Fam. M.).

Fam. L.R.	Family Law Reports	1980–date	—
Fam. L.R.	Green's Family Law Reports (Sc.)	1997–date	—
Fam. Law	Family Law	1971–date	—
Fam. M.	Family Matters	1993–2000[68]	—
Fam. Med.	Family Mediation	1991–date	—
Farm Law	Farm Law	1992–1997	—
Farresley	7 Modern Reports	1733–1745	87
Fem. L.S.	Feminist Legal Studies	1993–date	—
Ferg.	[Ferguson of] Kilkerran's Session Cases (Sc.)	1738–1752	—
Ferg.	Ferguson Consistorial Decisions (Sc.)	1811–1817	—
Fin. Dig.	Finlay's Irish Digest	1769–1771	—
Fin. L.R.	Financial Law Reports	1984–1989	—
Fin. Pr.	Finch's (T.) Precedents	1689–1723	24
Fin. T.	Finch's (T.) Precedents	1689–1723	24
Fin.(Fin.H.)	Reports, temp. Finch.	1673–1681	23
Finch Cas. Contr.	Finch's Cases on Contract	1886	—
Fitzg.	Fitzgibbon	1727–1732	94
Fl. & K.	Flanagan & Kelly (Ir.)	1840–1842	—
Fol. Dic.	Folio Dictionary (Kames & Woodhouselee) (Sc.)	1540–1796	—
Fol. P.L.C.	Foley's Poor Law Cases	1556–1730	—
Fonbl.	Fonblanque New Reports	1849–1852	—
Food L.M.	Food Law Monthly	1981–2003[69]	—
Foord	Foord's Supreme Court Reports, Cape Colony	1880	—
For.	Forrester's Chancery Reports	1733–1738	25
Forbes	Forbe's Decisions (Sc.)	1705–1713	—
Forr.	Forrest	1800–1801	145
Forr.	Talbot, Cases in Equity	1734–1738	25
Fors. Cas. & Op.	Forsyth, Cases And Opinions on Constitutional Law	1704–1856	—
Fort. (Fortes.)	Fortescue	1695–1738	92
Fost. & Fin.	Foster & Finlason	1856–1867	175–6
Fost. (Foster)	Foster	1743–1761	168
Fount.	Fountainhall (Sc.)	1678–1712	—
Fox	Fox Registration Cases	1886–1895	—
Fox. & S.	Fox & Smith (Ir.)	1822–1824	—
Fox & Sm. R.C.	Fox & Smith	1886–1895	—
Fr. E.C.	Fraser	1776–1777	—
Free.	Freeman (ed. By Hovenden)	1660–1706	22
Free. Ch.	Freeman (ed. By Hovenden)	1660–1706	22
Free. K.B.	Freeman (ed. By Smirke)	1670–1704	89
Fult.	Fulton's Supreme Court Reports, Bengal	1842–1844	—
G.	Gale	1835–1836	—
G. & D.	Gale & Davison	1841–1843	[55–62]
G. & J.	Glyn & Jameson	1819–1828	—
G.C.D.C.	Gold Coast Divisional Court Reports	1921–1931	—
G.C.L.R.	Global Competition Litigation Review	2008–date	—
G.C.R.	Global Competition Review: the International Journal of Competition Policy and Regulation	1997–date	—
G.I.L.S.I.	Gazette, Incorporated Law Society of Ireland	1964–date	—
G.L. & B.	Global Law and Business	1994–1996[70]	—

---

[68] For subsequent volumes see Family Law Bulletin (Fam. L.B.).
[69] Merged with Food and Drink Industry Bulletin (F. & D.I.B.) to form Food and Drink Law Monthly (F. & D.L.M.).
[70] From 1994 incorporates Lawyers in Europe (Law. in Eur.).

G.L.J.	Guernsey Law Journal	1986–[1997?]—	
G.W.D.	Green's Weekly Digest (Sc.)	1986–date	—
G.W.L.	South Africa Law Reports Griqualand West	1910–1946	—
Gal. & Dav.	Gale & Davison	1841–1843	[55–62]
Gaz. Bank.	Gazette of Bankruptcy	1861–1863	—
Gaz. L.R.	Gazette Law Reports, New Zealand	1898–1953	—
Gazette	Gazette (Law Society, Great Britain)	1990–date[71]	—
Geld. & Ox.	Geldert & Oxley, Decisions, Nova Scotia	1866–1875	—
Geld. & R.	Geldert & Russell Reports, Nova Scotia	1895–1910	—
Gil. & Fal.	Gilmour & Falconer (Sc.)	1661–1666	—
Gif. (Giff.)	Giffard	1857–1865	65–6
Gil. (Gilb.)	Gilbert, Equity Reports	1705–1726	25
Gil. (Gilb.)	Gilbert, Cases in Law and Equity	1713–1714	93
Gl. & J.	Glyn & Jameson	1819–1828	—
Glan. El. Cas.	Glanville, Election Cases	1623–1624	—
Glas.	Glascock (Ir.)	1831–1832	—
Global Counsel	Global Counsel	2001–date[72]	—
Godb.	Godbolt	1574–1638	78
Good. Pat.	Goodeve, Abstract of Patent Cases	1785–1883	—
Gould. (Gold., Goldes.)	Gouldsborough	1586–1601	75
Gow	Gow's Cases	1818–1820	171
Grant	Grant's Upper Canada Chancery Reports	1849–1882	—
Grant E. & A.	Grant's Error and Appeal Reports, Ontario	1846–1866	—
Green Sc. Cr. Cas.	Green, Criminal Cases (Sc.)	1820	—
Greer	Greer, Irish Land Cases	1872–1903	—
Greg.	Gregorowski High Court Reports, Orange Free State	1883–1887	—
Gren.	Grenier's Reports (Sri Lanka)	1872–1874	—
Grif. P.L.C.	Griffith, London Poor Law Cases	1821–1831	—
Grif. Pat. C.	Griffin's Patent Cases	1866–1887	—
Guth. Sh. Cas.	Guthrie (Sc.)	1861–1885	—
Gwil.	Gwillim, Tithe Cases	1224–1824	—
H.	Hare, temp. Wigram, Turner & Page-Wood	1841–1853	66–8
H. & B.	Hudson & Brooke (Ir.)	1827–1831	—
H. & C.	Hurlstone & Coltman	1862–1866	158–9
H. & H.	Horn & Hurlstone	1838–1839	[51]
H. & J.	Hayes & Jones (Ir.)	1832–1834	—
H. & M.	Hay & Marriott	1776–1779	165
H. & M.	Hemming & Miller	1862–1865	71
H. & N.	Hurlstone & Norman	1856–1862	156–8
H. & P.	Hopwood & Philbrick	1863–1867	—
H. & R.	Harrison & Rutherford	1865–1866	—
H. & S.I.B.	Health and Safety Information Bulletin	1976–date	—
H. & S.L.	Health and Safety Law	2002–date	—
H. & S.M.	Health and Safety Monitor	1978–date	—
H. & T. (H. & Tw.)	Hall & Twells, temp. Cottenham	1849–1850	47
H. & W.	Harrison & Wollaston	1835–1836	[47]
H. & W.	Hurlstone & Walmsley	1840–1841	[58]
H.B. (H.Bl.)	Blackstone, H.	1788–1796	126
H.C.L.M.	High Court Litigation Manual	1990–date	
H.C.R.	High Court Reports, India	1910–1913	—
H.C.R., N.W.F.	High Court Reports, North West Frontier		

---

[71] For previous volumes see Law Society's Gazette (L.S.G., or L.S. Gaz.).
[72] For previous volumes see European Counsel (Eur. Counsel).

H.K. Law Reports	Hong Kong Law Reports	1905–1995	—
H.K.L.J.	Hong Kong Law Journal	1971–date	—
H.K.L.R.	Hong Kong Law Reports	1905–1995	—
H.L.	See L.R.H.L.		
H.L. Cas.	House of Lords Cases (Clark)	1847–1866	9–11
H.L.J.	Hibernian Law Journal (Ir.)	2000–date	—
H.L.M.	Housing Law Monitor	1994–date	—
H.L.R.	Housing Law Reports	1976–date	—
H.R.	Human Rights	2001–date	—
H.R. & I.L.D.	Human Rights and International Legal Discourse	2007–date	—
H.R. & U.K. P.	Human Rights and UK Practice	1999–date	—
H.R.C.D.	Human Rights Case Digest	1990–date	—
H.R.L. Rev.	Human Rights Law Review	2001–date	—
H.R.L.R.	Human Rights Law Reports – UK Cases	2000–date	—
H.R.L.R.	Human Rights Law Review	2001–date	—
H.S.I.	Halsbury's Statutory Instruments		
H.S.I.B.	Health & Safety Information Bulletin	1976–date	—
Ha.	Hare, temp. Wigram, Turner and Page-Wood	1841–1853	66–8
Ha. & Tw.	Hall & Twells, temp. Cottenham	1849–1850	47
Had.	Haddington's Reports (Sc.)	1592–1624	—
Hag. Adm.	Haggard (Admiralty)	1822–1838	166
Hag. Con.	Haggard (Consistory)	1789–1821	161
Hag. Ecc.	Haggard (Ecclesiastical)	1827–1833	162
Hailes	Hailes (Sc.)	1766–1791	—
Hale Ecc.	Hale's Ecclesiastical Reports	1583–1736	—
Hale Prec.	Hale's Precedents in Ecclesiastical Cases	1475–1640	—
Halsbury S.	Halsbury's Statutes		
Han.	Hanson Bankruptcy	1915–1917	—
Hann.	Hannay's Report, New Brunswick	1867–1871	—
Har. & Ruth.	Harrison & Rutherford	1865–1866	—
Har. & Woll.	Harrison & Wollaston	1835–1836	[47]
Harc.	Harcase (Sc.)	1681–1691	—
Hard.	Hardres	1655–1669	145
Hard.	Kelynge, W.	1730–1734	25
Hardw.	Cases, temp. Hardwicke	1733–1738	95
Hare	Hare	1841–1853	66–8
Hare (App.)	Hare (Appendix)	1852–1853[73]	68
Harm.	Harman's Upper Canada Common Pleas Reports	1850–1882	—
Harr. & Hodge.	Harrison & Hodgin's Upper Canada Municipal Reports	1845–1851	—
Harr. & Woll.	Harrison & Wollaston	1835–1836	[47]
Hats.	Hatsell Parliamentary Precedents	1290–1818	—
Hav. Ch. Rep.	Haviland's Chancery Reports, Prince Edward Island	1850–1872	—
Haw.	Hawarde, Star Chamber Cases	1593–1609	—
Hay	Hayes (Ir.)	1830–1832	—
Hay. & J.	Hayes & Jones (Ir.)	1832–1834	—
Hay & M.	Hay & Marriott	1776–1779	165
Hayes	Hayes (Ir.)	1830–1832	—
Health Law	Health Law for Healthcare Professionals	1996–date	—
Hem. & M.	Hemming & Miller	1862–1865	71
Hemmant.	Hemmant Sel. Cases in the Exchequer Chamber, (Seldon Society)	1377–1460	—

[73] Appendices will be found in vols. 9 and 10.

Herm.	Hermand Consistorial Decisions (Sc.)	1684–1777	—
Het. (Hetl.)	Hetley	1627–1631	124
Ho. Lords C.	House of Lords Cases (Clark)	1847–1866	9–11
Hob. (Hob. R.)	Hobart	1603–1625	80
Hodg.	Hodgin, Election Cases, Ontario	1871–1879	—
Hodges	Hodges	1835–1837	[42–3]
Hog.	Hogan, temp. M'Mahon (Ir.)	1816–1834	—
Hold. L.R.	Holdsworth Law Review	1980–date	—
Holt	Holt's Judgments in *Ashby* v. *White* and *Re Patey et al.*	1704–1705	—
Holt Adm. Ca.	Holt's Admiralty Cases	1863–1867	—
Holt Eq.	Holt	1845	71
Holt N.P.	Holt	1815–1817	171
Home (Cl.)	Clerk Home (Sc.)	1735–1744	—
Hong Kong L.J.	Hong Kong Law Journal	1971–date	—
Hong Kong L.R.	Hong Kong Law Reports	1905–date	—
Hop. & C.	Hopwood & Coltman	1868–1878	—
Hop. & Ph.	Hopwood & Philbrick	1863–1867	—
Horn. & H.	Horn & Hurlstone	1838–1839	[51]
Hous. L.R.	Green's Housing Law Reports (Sc.)	1996–date	—
Hov. Supp.	Hovenden's Supplement. See Ves. Jr.	1789–1817	34
How. C.	Howard, Chancery Practice (Ir.)	1775	—
How. Po. Ca.	Howard, Popery Cases (Ir.)	1720–1773	—
How. St. Tr.	State Trials (Cobbett & Howell)	1163–1820	—
Hub.	Hobart, King's Bench	1603–1625	80
Hud. & Br.	Hudson & Brooke (Ir.)	1827–1831	—
Hume	Hume (Sc.)	1781–1822	—
Hunt's A.C.	Hunt's Annuity Cases	1776–1796	—
Hurl. & Colt.	Hurlstone & Coltman	1862–1866	158–9
Hurl. & Gord.	Hurlstone & Gordon	1854–1856	156
Hurl. & Nor.	Hurlstone & Norman	1856–1862	156–8
Hurl. & Walm.	Hurlstone & Walmsley	1840–1841	[58]
Hut. (Hutt.)	Hutton	1612–1639	123
Hyde	Hyde's Reports, Bengal	1862–1864	—
I. & C.T.L.	Information and Communications Technology Law	1992–date[74]	—
I. & N.L. & P.	Immigration and Nationality Law and Practice	1986–1992[75]	—
I. Bull.	Interights Bulletin	1985–date	—
I. Prop.	Intellectual Property	1996–1997	—
I.A.	Law Reports, Indian Appeals	1872–1950	—
I.A.N.L.	Immigration, Asylum and Nationality Law	2001–2002[76]	—
I.A.N.L.	Journal of Immigration, Asylum and Nationality Law	2003–date[77]	—
I.B.F.L.	International Banking and Financial Law	1991–1998[78]	—

[74] For previous volumes see Law, Computers and Artificial Intelligence (L.C. & A.I.).
[75] For subsequent volumes see Immigration Law and Practice, also known as Tolley's Immigration Law and Practice (I.L. & P.).
[76] Also known as Tolley's Immigration, Asylum and Nationality Law. For previous volumes see Immigration Law and Practice, also known as Tolley's Immigration Law and Practice (I.L. & P.). For subsequent volumes see Journal of Immigration, Asylum and Nationality Law, also known initially as Tolley's Journal of Immigration, Asylum and Nationality Law, but subsequently also as Tottel's Journal of Immigration, Asylum and Nationality Law (I.A.N.L., or J.I.A.N.L.).
[77] Initially, also known as Tolley's Journal of Immigration, Asylum and Nationality Law, but subsequently also as Tottel's Journal of Immigration, Asylum and Nationality Law. For previous volumes see Immigration, Asylum and Nationality Law, also known as Tolley's Immigration, Asylum and Nationality Law (I.A.N.L.).
[78] For previous volumes see International Banking Law (I.B.L.).

I.B.L.	International Banking Law	1982–1991[79] —
I.B.L.J.	International Business Law Journal	1985–date —
I.B.L.Q.	Irish Business Law Quarterly	2005–date —
I.B.L.	International Business Lawyer	1973–date —
I.C. Lit.	International Commercial Litigation	1995– — [200?][80]
I.C.C.L.J.	International and Comparative Corporate Law Journal	1999–date —
I.C.C.L.R.	International Company and Commercial Law Review	1990–date —
I.C.J.R.	International Court of Justice Law Reports	1947–[?] —
I.C.J. Reports	International Court of Justice Law Reports	1947–[?] —
I.C.J. Rev.	International Commission of Jurists Review	1969–date —
I.C.L.	International Corporate Law	1990–1995[81] —
I.C.L. Rev.	International Construction Law Review	1983–date —
I.C.L.B.	International Corporate Law Bulletin	1998–2000 —
I.C.L.J.	Irish Criminal Law Journal	1991–date —
I.C.L.M.D.	Irish Current Law Monthly Digest	
I.C.L.Q.	International & Comparative Law Quarterly	1952–date[82] —
I.C.L.R.	International Construction Law Review	1983–date —
I.C.L.S.A.	Irish Current Law Statutes Annotated	1984–date —
I.C.R.	Industrial Cases Reports	1974–date[83] —
I.C.R.	Industrial Court Reports	1971–1974[84] —
I.C.R.	Irish Circuit Reports	1841–1843 —
IDS Brief	IDS Brief, Employment Law and Practice	1972–2005[85] —
IDS Emp. L. Brief	IDS Employment Law Brief	2005–date[86] —
IDS P.L.R.	IDS Pensions Law Reports	1989–date —
I.E.L.J.	Irish Employment Law Journal	2003–date —
I.E.L.R.	International Energy Law Review	2008–date[87] —
I.E.L.T.R.	International Energy Law and Taxation Review	2000–date[88] —
I.F.L.	International Family Law	1997–date —
I.F.L. Rev.	International Financial Law Review	1982–date —
I.F.L. Review	International Financial Law Review	1982–date —
I.F.L.J.	International Family Law Journal	1987–1997[89] —
I.F.L.R.	International Financial Law Review	1982–date —
I.H.L.	In-House Lawyer	1992–date —
I.H.R.R.	International Human Rights Reports	1994–date —
I.I.C.	International Review of Industrial Property and Copyright Law	1970–2003[90] —

[79] For subsequent volumes see International Banking and Financial Law.
[80] Incorporates International Corporate Law (I.C.L.).
[81] Subsequently incorporated into International Commercial Litigation (I.C. Lit.).
[82] Formed from a merger between Journal of Comparative Legislation and International Law (J.C.L. & I.L.) and International Law Quarterly (I.L.Q.).
[83] For previous volumes see Industrial Court Reports (I.C.R.).
[84] For subsequent volumes see Industrial Cases Reports (I.C.R.).
[85] For subsequent volumes see IDS Employment Law Brief (IDS Emp. L. Brief).
[86] For previous volumes see IDS Brief, Employment Law and Practice (IDS Brief).
[87] For previous volumes see International Energy: Law and Taxation Review (I.E.L.T.R.).
[88] For previous volumes see Oil and Gas: Law and Taxation Review (O.G.L.T.R.). For subsequent volumes see International Energy Law Review (I.E.L.R.).
[89] For subsequent volumes see International Journal of Law, Policy and the Family (I.J.L.P.F.).
[90] For subsequent volumes see International Review of Intellectual Property and Competition Law (I.I.C.).

I.I.C.	International Review of Intellectual Property and Competition Law	2004–date[91]	—
I.I.E.L.	Immigration and International Employment Law	2000–date	—
I.I.L. Review	International Internet Law Review	2000–2001[92]	
I.I.L.R.	Irish Insurance Law Review	1997–date	—
I.I.P.R.	Irish Intellectual Property Review	1997–date	—
I.I.R.	International Insolvency Review	1992–date	—
I.J.	Irish Jurist	1849–1866	—
I.J.	Irish Jurist	1935–date	—
I.J.B.L.	International Journal of Biosciences and the Law	1996–2003[93]	—
I.J.C.L.	International Journal of Constitutional Law	2002–date	—
I.J.C.L.E.	International Journal of Clinical Legal Education	2000–date	—
I.J.C.L.P.	International Journal of Communications Law and Policy	1998–date	—
I.J.D.G.	International Journal of Disclosure and Governance	2003–date	—
I.J.D.L.	International Journal of Discrimination and the Law	1995–date	—
I.J.E.C.L.	International Journal of Estuarine and Coastal Law	1986–1992[94]	—
I.J.E.L.	Irish Journal of European Law	1992–date	—
I.J.F.D.L.	International Journal of Franchising and Distribution Law	1999–2002[95]	—
I.J.F.L.	International Journal of Franchising Law	2003–date[96]	—
I.J.F.L.	Irish Journal of Family Law	1998–date	—
I.J.H.R.	International Journal of Human Rights	1997–date	—
I.J.I.L.	International Journal of Insurance Law	1994–[199?]	—
I.J.L. & I.T.	International Journal of Law and Information Technology	1993–date	—
I.J.L.C.J.	International Journal of Law, Crime and Justice	2008–date[97]	—
I.J.L.P.	International Journal of the Legal Profession	1994–date	—
I.J.L.P.F.	International Journal of Law, Policy and the Family	1998–date[98]	—
I.J.M.C.L.	International Journal of Marine and Coastal Law	1993–date[99]	—
I.J.O.S.L.	International Journal of Shipping Law	1996–[200?]	—
I.J.R.L.	International Journal of Refugee Law	1989–date	—

[91] For previous volumes see International Review of Industrial Property and Copyright Law (I.I.C.).

[92] For subsequent volumes see International Technology Law Review (I.T.L.R.).

[93] For subsequent volumes see Law Science and Policy (L.S. & P.).

[94] For subsequent volumes see International Journal of Marine and Coastal Law (I.J.M.C.L., or T.I.J.M.C.L.).

[95] For previous volumes see Journal of International Franchising and Distribution Law (J.I.F.D.L.). For subsequent volumes see International Journal of Franchising Law (I.J.F.L.).

[96] For previous volumes see International Journal of Franchising and Distribution Law (I.J.F.D.L.).

[97] For previous volumes see International Journal of the Sociology of Law (Int. J. Soc. L., or Int. J. Sociol. Law.).

[98] For previous volumes see International Family Law Journal (I.F.L.J.).

[99] For previous volumes see International Journal of Estuarine and Commercial Law (I.J.E.C.L.).

I.J.R.L. & P.	International Journal of Regulatory Law & Practice	1992–1993	—
I.J.S.L.	International Journal for the Semiotics of Law	1988–date	—
I.J.T.J.	International Journal of Transitional Justice	2007–date	—
I.L. & P.	Insolvency Law and Practice	1985–date	—
I.L. & P.	Immigration Law and Practice	1993–2000[1]	—
I.L. Pr.	International Litigation Procedure	1990–date	—
I.L.D.	Immigration Law Digest	1997–date	—
I.L.F.M.	International Law Firm Management	1993–[date?]	—
I.L.J.	Industrial Law Journal	1972–date	—
I.L.P.	International Legal Practitioner	1980–date	—
I.L.Q.	International Law Quarterly	1947–1951[2]	—
I.L.R.	Indian Law Reports- Allahabad: Bombay: Calcutta: Lahore: Lucknow: Madras: Nagpur: Patna: Rangoon.	various	—
I.L.R.	International Law Reports	1950–date[3]	—
I.L.R.M.	Irish Law Reports Monthly	1978–date	—
I.L.T.	Irish Law Times	1867–date	—
I.L.T.R.	Irish Law Times Reports	1867–date[4]	—
I.M.L.	International Maritime Law	1994–2002[5]	—
I.M.L.	International Media Law	1982–date	—
I.N.L.	Internet Newsletter for Lawyers	1995–[date?]	—
I.N.L.P.	Immigration and Nationality Law and Practice	1986–1992[6]	—
I.N.L.R.	Immigration and Nationality Law Reports	1997–date	—
I.O.L.R.	International Organizations Law Review	2004–date	—
I.P.	Intellectual Property	1996–1997[7]	—
I.P. & I.T. Law	Intellectual Property and Information Technology Law	1998–date[8]	—
I.P. & T.	Butterworths Intellectual Property and Technology Cases	1999–date	—
I.P. News.	Intellectual Property Newsletter	1979–date	—
I.P.D.	Intellectual Property Decisions	1978–date	—
I.P.E.L.J.	Irish Planning and Environmental Law Journal	1994–date	—
I.P.J.	Intellectual Property Journal (Canada)	1984–date	—
I.P.L.	International Pension Lawyer	1989–1991	—
I.P.Q.	Intellectual Property Quarterly **First Series**	1997–date	—
I.R.	Irish Reports	1838–date	—
I.E.R.	Irish Equity Reports	1838–1850	—

---

[1] Also known as Tolley's Immigration Law and Practice. For previous volumes see Immigration and Nationality Law and Practice (I. & N.L. & P., or I.N.L.P.). For subsequent volumes see Immigration, Asylum and Nationality Law, also known as Tolley's Immigration, Asylum and Nationality Law (I.A.N.L.).

[2] Merged with Journal of Comparative Legislation and International Law (J.C.L. & I.L.) to form International and Comparative Law Quarterly (I.C.L.Q., or Int. Comp. L.Q., or Int. Comp. Law Quart.).

[3] For previous volumes see Annual Digest of International Law (A.D.I.L.).

[4] Appear as part of the Irish Law Times (I.L.T.).

[5] For subsequent volumes see Journal of International Maritime Law (J.I.M.L.).

[6] For subsequent volumes see Immigration Law and Practice, also known as Tolley's Immigration Law and Practice (I.L. & P.).

[7] For subsequent volumes see Intellectual Property and Information Technology Law (I.P. & I.T. Law).

[8] For previous volumes see Intellectual Property (I.P.).

I. Eq. R.	Irish Equity Reports	1838–1850	—
I.L.R.	Irish Law Reports	1838–1850	—
	Second Series		
I.C.L.R.	Irish Common Law Reports	1850–1866	—
I. Ch. R.	Irish Chancery Reports	1850–1866	—
Ir. Ch. Rep.	Irish Chancery Reports	1850–1866	—
	Third Series		
I.R.C.L.	Irish Reports, Common Law	1866–1878	—.
I.R. Eq.	Irish Reports, Equity	1866–1878	—
	Fourth Series		
L.R. Ir.	Law Reports, Ireland	1878–1893	—
	Fifth Series		
I.R.	Irish Reports	1894–date	—
I.R.L.A.	Insurance and Reinsurance Alert	1999–date[9]	—
I.R.L.B.	Industrial Relations Law Bulletin	1993–date[10]	—
I.R.L.C.T.	International Review of Law, Computers and Technology	1996–date[11]	—
I.R.L.I.B.	Industrial Relations Legal Information Bulletin	1973–1992[12]	—
I.R.L.N.	Insurance and Reinsurance Law Newsletter	1995–1998[13]	—
I.R.L.R.	Industrial Relations Law Reports	1972–date	—
I.R.R.R.	Industrial Relations Review and Report	1971–1994[14]	—
IRS Emp. Law	IRS Employment Law	1995–date	—
IRS Emp. Trends	IRS Employment Trends	1995–date[15]	—
I.R.S.R.	Insurance and Reinsurance Solvency Report	1986–[199?]	—
I.S.L. Rev.	Irish Student Law Review	1991–date	—
I.S.L.J.	International Sports Law Journal	2003–date	—
I.S.L.L.	International Survey of Legal Decisions on Labour Law	1925–1938	—
I.S.L.R.	International Sports Law Review	2002–date	—
I.T. & C.L.J.	Information Technology and Communications Law Journal	1998–2000[16]	—
I.T. & C.L.R.	IT and Communications Law Reports	1998–date	—
I.T. & Comm. News	Information Technology and Communications Newsletter	1998[17]	—
I.T.E.L.R.	International Trust and Estate Law Reports	1998–date	—
I.T. L.T.	IT Law Today	1993–date[18]	—
I.T.L.J.	International Travel Law Journal	1997–date[19]	—
I.T.L.Q.	International Trade Law Quarterly	1997–[200?]	—
I.T.L.R.	International Technology Law Review	2001–[?][20]	—
I.T.R.	Industrial Tribunal Reports	1966–1978	—

---

[9] For previous volumes see Insurance and Reinsurance Law Newsletter (I.R.L.N.).
[10] For previous volumes see Industrial Relations Legal Information Bulletin (I.R.L.I.B.).
[11] For previous volumes see International Yearbook of Law, Computers and Technology (I.Y.L.C.T.).
[12] For subsequent volumes see Industrial Relations Law Bulletin (I.R.L.B.).
[13] For subsequent volumes see Insurance and Reinsurance Law Alert (I.R.L.A.).
[14] For subsequent volumes see IRS Employment Trends (IRS Emp. Trends).
[15] For previous volumes see Industrial Relations Review and Report (I.R.R.R.).
[16] Law Journal For previous volumes see Information Technology and Communications Newsletter (I.T. & Comm.News).
[17] For subsequent volumes see Information Technology and Communications Law Journal (I.T. & C.L.J.).
[18] For previous volumes see Applied Computer and Communications Law (App. Comp. & Comm. L.).
[19] For previous volumes see Travel Law Journal (T.L.J.).
[20] For previous volumes see International Internet Law Review (I.I.L. Review).

I.Y.L.C.T.	International Yearbook of Law, Computers and Technology	1992–1995[21] —
Imm. A.R.	Immigration Appeal Reports	1970–date —
In Comp.	In Competition	1993–date —
In-House L.	In-House Lawyer	1992–date —
Ind. C.	Industrial Court Awards	1970-[?] —
Ind. App.	See L.R. Ind. App	
Ind. L.J.	Industrial Law Journal	1972–date —
Ind. Sol.	Independent Solicitor	1983–[199?] —
Ind. Trib. R.	Industrial Tribunal Reports	1966–1978 —
Indust. L. Rev.	Industrial Law Review	1972–date —
Info. & Comm. Tech. L.	Information and Communications Technology Law	1991–date —
Info. T.L.R.	Information Technology Law Reports	1997–date —
Ins. & Reins. Law Int.	Insurance and Reinsurance Law International	1983–date —
Ins. L. & C.	Insurance Law and Claims	1992–date —
Ins. L. & P.	Insurance Law and Practice	1991–1995 —
Ins. L.J.	Insurance Law Journal	1988–date —
Ins. L.M.	Insurance Law Monthly	1989–date —
Insolv. Int.	Insolvency Intelligence	1988–date —
Insolv. L.	Insolvency Lawyer	1991–date —
Insolv. L. & P.	Insolvency Litigation and Practice	1996–date —
Insolv. P.	Insolvency Practitioner	1991–1999 —
Int. A.L.R.	International Arbitration Law Review	1997–date —
Int. Bank. L.	International Banking Law	1982–1991 —
Int. C.L. Rev.	International Community Law Review	2006–date[22] —
Int. C.L.R.	International Criminal Law Review	2001–date —
Int. Comp. L.Q.	International and Comparative Law Quarterly	1952–date[23] —
Int. Comp. Law Quart.	International and Comparative Law Quarterly	1952–date[24] —
Int. I.L.R.	International Insurance Law Review	1993–date —
Int. J. Comp. L.L.I.R.	International Journal of Comparative Labour Law and Industrial Relations	1985–date —
Int. J. Criminol.	International Journal of Criminology and Penology	1973–1978[25] —
Int. J. Law & Fam.	International Journal of Law and the Family	1987–1997[26] —
Int. J. Law & Fam.	International Journal of Law, Policy and the Family	1998–date[27] —
Int. J. Soc. L.	International Journal of the Sociology of Law	1979–date[28] —
Int. J. Sociol. Law	International Journal of the Sociology of Law	1979–date[29] —

[21] For previous volumes see Yearbook of Law, Computers and Technology (Y.L.C.T.). For subsequent volumes see International Review of Law, Computers and Technology (I.R.L.C.T.).

[22] Formed from a merger between International Law Forum du Droit International (1999-2006, no abbreviation), and Non-State Actors and International Law (N.S.A.I.L.).

[23] Formed from a merger between Journal of Comparative Legislation and International Law (J.C.L. & I.L.), and International Law Quarterly (I.L.Q.).

[24] Formed from a merger between Journal of Comparative Legislation and International Law (J.C.L. & I.L.) and International Law Quarterly (I.L.Q.).

[25] For subsequent volumes see International Journal of the Sociology of Law (Int. J. Soc. L., or Int. J. Sociol. Law).

[26] For subsequent volumes see International Journal of Law, Policy and the Family (I.J.L.P.F., or Int. J.L.P.F.).

[27] For previous volumes see International Journal of Law and the Family (Int. J. Law & Fam).

[28] For previous volumes see International Journal of Criminology and Penology (Int. J. Criminol.).

[29] For previous volumes see International Journal of Criminology and Penology (Int. J. Criminol.).

Int. J.F.L.	International Journal of Franchising Law	2003–date[30]	—
Int. J.L.C.	International Journal of Law in Context	2005–date	—
Int. J.L.P.F.	International Journal of Law, Policy and the Family	1998–date[31]	
Int. M.L.	International Maritime Law	1994–date	—
Int. Rev. Law & Econ.	International Review of Law and Economics	1981–date	—
Int. T.L.R.	International Trade Law and Regulation	1995–date	—
Intell. Prop. J.	Intellectual Property Journal (Canada)	1984–date	—
Intl. J. Cult. Prop.	International Journal of Cultural Property	1992–2002;2005–date	—
Int'l. Rev. L. Computers & Tech.	International Review of Law, Computers and Technology	1996–date[32]	—
Ir. B.L.	Irish Business Law	1998–date	—
Ir. Cir.	Irish Circuit Reports	1841–1843	—
Ir. Eccl.	Milward, Irish Reports	1819–1843	—
Ir. L. Rec.	Irish Law Recorder, First Series	1827–1831	—
Ir. L.T.	Irish Law Times	1867–date	—
Ir. Law Rec., N.S.	Law Recorder, New Series (Ir.)	1833–1838	—
Ir. R. Reg. App.	Irish Reports, Registration Appeals	1868–1876	—
Ir. W.L.R.	Irish Weekly Law Reports	1895–1902	—
Irish Jurist	Irish Jurist	1848–date	—
Irv.	Irvine (Sc.)	1851–1868	—
IT L.T.	IT Law Today	1984–date	—
J.	Scottish Jurist (Sc.)	1829–1873	—
J. Afr. L.	Journal of African Law	1957–date	—
J. & C.	Jones & Cary (Ir.)	1838–1839	—
J. & H.	Johnson & Hemming	1859–1862	70
J. & La T.	Jones & La Touche (Ir.)	1844–1846	—
J. & S.	Jebb & Symes (Ir.)	1838–1841	—
J. & S.	Judah and Swan Reports, Jamaica	1839	—
J. & W.	Jacob & Walker	1819–1821	37
J. Assoc. L. Teachers	Journal of the Association of Law Teachers	1967–1970	—
J. Bridg.	Bridgman J.	1613–1621	123
J. Bus. L.	Journal of Business Law	1957–date	—
J. Civ. Lib.	Journal of Civil Liberties	1996–date	——
J. Comm. Mar. St.	Journal of Common Market Studies	1962–date	—
J. Crim. L.	Journal of Criminal Law	1937–date	—
J. En. & Nat. Res. L.	Journal of Energy and Natural Resources Law	1983–date	—
J. Env. L.	Journal of Environmental Law	1989–date	—
J. Int. Arb.	Journal of International Arbitration	1984–date	—
J. Int. P.	Journal of International Trust and Corporate Planning	1993–date	—
J. Kel.	Kelyng, Sir John	1662–1669	84
J. Law & Soc	Journal of Law and Society	1982–date[33]	—
J. Leg. Hist.	Journal of Legal History	1980–date	—
J. Plan. & Environ. L.	Journal of Planning and Environment Law	1973–date[34]	—
J. Priv. Int. L.	Journal of Private International Law	2005–date	—

[30] For previous volumes see International Journal of Franchising and Distribution Law (I.J.F.D.L.).
[31] For previous volumes see International Journal of Law and the Family (Int. J. Law & Fam.).
[32] For previous volumes see International Yearbook of Law, Computers and Technology (I.Y.L.C.T.).
[33] For previous volumes see British Journal of Law and Society (Brit. J. Law & Soc.).
[34] For previous volumes see Journal of Planning and Property Law (J.P.L.).

J. Shaw	John Shaw (Sc.)	1848–1852	—
J. Soc. Pub. T.L.	Journal of the Society of Public Teachers of Law	1924–1938 1947– 1980[35]	—
J. Soc. Wel. & Fam. L.	Journal of Social Welfare and Family Law	1995–date[36]	—
J. Soc. Wel. L.	Journal of Social Welfare Law	1978–1994[37]	—
J. World Tr.	Journal of World Trade	1988–date[38]	—
J. World. Tr. L.	Journal of World Trade Law	1967–1987[39]	—
J. World Trade L.	Journal of World Trade Law	1967–1987[40]	—
J.A.C.L.	Journal of Armed Conflict Law	1996–1999[41]	—
J.A.L.	Journal of African Law	1957–date	—
J.B.F.L.P.	Journal of Banking and Finance Law and Practice	1990–date	—
J.B.L.	Journal of Business Law	1957–date	—
J.B.R.	Journal of Banking Regulation	2006–date[42]	—
J.C.	Justiciary Cases (Sc.)	1916–date	—
J.C. & S.L.	Journal of Conflict and Security Law	2000–date[43]	—
J.C.I. Arb.	Arbitration: Journal of the Chartered Institute of Arbitrators	1954–date	—
J.C.L.	Journal of Child Law	1989–1995[44]	—
J.C.L.	Journal of Criminal Law	1937–date	—
J.C.L. & E.	Journal of Competition Law and Economics	2005–date	—
J.C.L. & I.L.	Journal of Comparative Legislation and International Law	1896–1951[45]	—
J.C.L.L.E.	Journal of Commonwealth Law and Legal Education	2001–date	—
J.C.L.P.	Journal of Competition Law and Policy	1999–date	—
J.C.L.S.	Journal of Corporate Law Studies	2001–date	—
J.C.P.	Journal of Consumer Policy	1983–date	—
J.C.P.P.	Journal of Civil Practice and Procedure	2004–date	—
J.E.C.L. & P.	Journal of Electronic Commerce Law and Practice	2000–date	—
J.E.E.P.L.	Journal for European Environmental and Planning Law	2004–date	—
J.E.L.P.	Journal of Employment Law and Practice	1994–1995	—
J.E.L.S.	Journal of Empirical Legal Studies	2004–date	—
J.E.R.L.	Journal of Energy and Natural Resources Law	1983–date	—
J.F.R.C.	Journal of Financial Regulation and Compliance	1992–date	—
J.H.L.	Journal of Housing Law	1997–date	—
J.I.A.N.L.	Journal of Immigration, Asylum and Nationality Law	2003–date[46]	—

---

[35] For subsequent volumes see Legal Studies (L.S.).
[36] For previous volumes see Journal of Social Welfare Law (J. Soc. Wel. L., or J.S.W.L.).
[37] For subsequent volumes see Journal of Social Welfare and Family Law (J. Soc. Wel. & Fam. Law).
[38] For previous volumes see Journal of World Trade Law (J. World Tr. L., or J. World Trade L.).
[39] For subsequent volumes see Journal of World Trade (J. World Tr.).
[40] For subsequent volumes see Journal of World Trade (J. World Tr.).
[41] For subsequent volumes see Journal of Conflict and Security Law (J.C. & S.L.).
[42] For previous volumes see Journal of International Banking Regulation (J.I.B.L.R.).
[43] For previous volumes see Journal of Armed Conflict Law (J.A.C.L.).
[44] For subsequent volumes see Child and Family Law Quarterly (C.F.L.Q.).
[45] Merged with International Law Quarterly (I.L.Q.) to form International and Comparative Law Quarterly (I.C.L.Q., or Int. Comp. L.Q., or Int. Comp. Law Quart.).
[46] For previous volumes see Immigration, Asylum and Nationality Law (I.A.N.L.). This title initially also known as Tolley's Journal of Immigration, Asylum and Nationality Law, but subsequently also as Tottel's Journal of Immigration Asylum and Nationality Law, (I.A.N.L., or J.I.A.N.L.).

J.I.B. Law	Journal of International Biotechnology Law	2004–date	—
J.I.B.L.	Journal of International Banking Law	1986–2003[47]	—
J.I.B.L.	Journal of International Biotechnology Law	2004–date	—
J.I.B.L.R.	Journal of International Banking Law and Regulation	2004–date[48]	—
J.I.B.R.	Journal of International Banking Regulation	1999–2005[49]	—
J.I.C.J.	Journal of International Criminal Justice	2003–date	—
J.I.C.L.	Journal of International Commercial Law	2002–date	—
J.I.E.L.	Journal of International Economic Law	1998–date	—
J.I.F.D.L.	Journal of International Franchising and Distribution Law	[1986–1999][50]	—
J.I.F.M.	Journal of International Financial Markets: Law and Regulation	1998–date	—
J.I.L.T.	Journal of Information, Law and Technology	1996–date[51]	—
J.I.M.L.	Journal of International Maritime Law	2003–date[52]	—
J.I.P.L.P.	Journal of Intellectual Property Law and Practice	2005–date	—
J.I.T.C.P.	Journal of International Trust and Corporate Planning	1994–date[53]	—
J.J.	Justice Journal	2004–date	—
J.L.E. & O.	Journal of Law, Economics and Organization	1985–date	—
J.L.G.L.	Journal of Local Government Law	1998–date	—
J.L.R.	Jamaica Law Reports	1933–date	—
J.L.R.	Jersey Law Reports	1985–date	—
J.L.S.	Journal of the Law Society of Scotland	1956–date	—
J.L.S.	Journal of Legislative Studies	1995–date	—
J.L.S.S.	Journal of the Law Society of Scotland	1956–date	—
J.M.D.D.U.	Journal of the Medical and Dental Defence Unions	1995–1996[54]	—
J.M.D.U.	Journal of the MDU [Medical Defence Union]	1996–date[55]	—
J.M.D.U.	Journal of the Medical Defence Union	1985–1995[56]	—
J.M.H.L.	Journal of Mental Health Law	1999–date	—
J.M.L. & P.	Journal of Media Law and Practice	1980–1991[57]	—

---

[47] For subsequent volumes see Journal of International Banking Law and Regulation (J.I.B.L.R.).
[48] For previous volumes see Journal of International Banking Law (J.I.B.L.).
[49] For subsequent volumes see Journal of Banking Regulation (J.B.R.).
[50] For subsequent volumes see International Journal of Franchising and Distribution Law (I.J.F.D.L.).
[51] For previous volumes see Law Technology Journal (L.T.J.).
[52] For previous volumes see International Maritime Law (I.M.L.).
[53] For previous volumes see Journal of International Planning (1992-1993, no abbreviation).
[54] For previous volumes see Journal of the Medical Defence Union (J.M.D.U.), also known as the Medical Defence Union Journal (M.D.U. J.). For subsequent volumes see Journal of the MDU (J.M.D.U.).
[55] For previous volumes see Journal of the Medical Defence Unions (J.M.D.D.U.).
[56] Also referred to as the Medical Defence Union Journal (M.D.U. Jour.). For subsequent volumes see Journal of the Medical and Dental Defence Unions (J.M.D.D.U.).
[57] Merged with Computer Law and Practice (C.L. & P.) to form Communications Law (Comms. L.).

J.O. & R.	Journal of Obligations and Remedies	2001-2004	—
J.O.R.	Journal of Obligations and Remedies	2001–2004	—
J.P.	Justice of the Peace	1837–1926	—
J.P.	Justice of the Peace and Local Government Review	1837–date	—
J.P.	Justice of the Peace Reports	1837–date	—
J.P. Rep.	Justice of the Peace and Local Government Law Reports	1837–date	—
J.P. Sm.	J.P. Smith, King's Bench	1803–1806	[7–8]
J.P.I. Law	Journal of Personal Injury Law	2000-date[58]	
J.P.I.L.	Journal of Personal Injury Litigation	1994-2000[59]	—
J.P.L.	Journal of Planning and Environment Law	1973–date[60]	—
J.P.L.	Journal of Planning and Property Law	1954–1972[61]	—
J.P.L.	Journal of Planning Law	1948–1953[62]	—
J.P.N.	Justice of the Peace	1837–1926	—
J.P.N.	Justice of the Peace Reports	1837–date	—
J.P.N.	Justice of the Peace and Local Government Law	1993–date	—
J.R.	Judicial Review	1996–date	—
J.R.	N.Z. Jurist Reports	1873–1875	—
J.R.(N.S.)	N.Z. Jurist Reports, New Series	1875–1878	—
J.S.B.J.	Judicial Studies Board Journal	1997–date	—
J.S.P.T.L.	Journal of the Society of Public Teachers of Law	1924–1938, 1947– 1980[63]	—
J.S.S.L.	Journal of Social Security Law	1994–date	—
J.S.W.L.	Journal of Social Welfare Law	1978–1993[64]	—
J.W.E.L.B.	Journal of World Energy Law and Business	2008–	
J.W.I.P.	Journal of World Intellectual Property	1998–date	—
J.W.L.	Journal of Water Law	2003–date[65]	—
J.W.T.	Journal of World Trade	1988–date[66]	—
J.W.T.L.	Journal of World Trade Law	1967–1987[67]	—
Jac.	Jacob	1821–1822	37
Jac. & W.	Jacob & Walker	1819–1921	37
James & Mont.	Jameson & Montagu Bankruptcy Reports	1821–1828	—
James Sel. Cas.	James' Select Cases, Nova Scotia	1853–1855	—
Jebb	Jebb (Ir.)	1822–1840	—
Jebb & B.	Jebb & Burke (Ir.)	1841–1842	—
Jebb & S.	Jebb & Symes (Ir.)	1838–1841	—
Jenk.	Jenkins	1220–1623	145
Jer. Dig.	Jeremy's Digest	1817–1823 1838–1849	—

[58] For previous volumes see Journal of Personal Injury Litigation (J.P.I.L.).
[59] For subsequent volumes see Journal of Personal Injury Law (J.P.I. Law).
[60] For previous volumes see Journal of Planning and Property Law (J.P.L.).
[61] Formed from a merger between Current Property Law (C.P.L.) and Journal of Planning Law (J.P.L.). For subsequent volumes see Journal of Planning and Environment Law (J. Plan. & Environ. L. or (J.P.L.).
[62] Merged with Current Property Law (C.P.L.) to become Journal of Planning and Property Law (J.P.L.).
[63] For subsequent volumes see Legal Studies (L.S.).
[64] For subsequent volumes see Journal of Social Welfare and Family Law (J. Soc. Wel. & Fam. Law).
[65] For previous volumes see Water Law (W.L.).
[66] For previous volumes see Journal of World Trade Law (J.W.T.L.).
[67] For subsequent volumes see Journal of World Trade (J.W.T.).

Jersey L.R.	Jersey Law Review	1997–date	—
Jo.	Jones (Ir.)	1834–1838	—
Jo. & La T.	Jones & La Touche (Ir.)	1844–1846	—
Johns. (John.; Johns (V.C.))	Johnson, Ch. Rep.	1859	70
Johns. & Hem.	Johnson & Hemming	1860–1862	70
Jon. & Car	Jones & Cary (Ir.)	1838–1839	—
Jon. Ex.	Jones (Ir.)	1834–1838	—
Jones	Jones (Ir.)	1834–1838	—
Jones	Jones' Upper Canada Common Pleas Reports	1850–1882	—
Jones (1)	Jones, Sir Wm	1620–1641	82
Jones (2)	Jones, Sir Thos.	1667–1685	84
Jones, T.	Jones, Sir Thos.	1667–1685	84
Jones, W.	Jones, Sir Wm.	1620–1641	82
Jour. P.I.L.	Journal of Private International Law	2005–date	—
Jud. & Sw.	Judah & Swan Reports, Jamaica	1839	—
Jur.	Jurist Reports	1837–1854	—
Jur. N.S.	Jurist Reports, New Series	1855–1866	—
Jur. Rev.	Juridical Review (Sc.)	1889–date	—
Jurid. Rev.	Juridical Review (Sc.)	1889–date	—
Juta.	Juta's Reports Supreme Court, Cape of Good Hope	1880–1910	—
K.	Kenyon	1753–1759	96
K.	Kotze's High Court Reports, Transvaal	1877–1881	—
K. & B.	Kotze's and Barber High Court Reports, Transvaal	1885–1888	—
K. & G.	Keane & Grant's Appeals	1854–1862	—
K. & J.	Kay & Johnson	1854–1858	69–70
K. & O.	Knapp & Ombler	1834–1835	—
K. & W. Dic.	Kames & Woodhouselee's folio Dictionary (Sc.)	1540–1796	—
K.B.	See L.R.K.B.		
K.C.	King's Counsel	1936–1939; 1948– 1989[68]	—
K.C.L.J.	King's College Law Journal	1990–2006[69]	—
K.I.L.R.	Knight's Industrial Law Reports	1975[70]	—
K.I.R.	Knight's Industrial Reports	1966–1974[71]	—
K.L.G.R.	Knight's Local Government Reports	1902–1998[72]	—
K.L.J.	King's Law Journal	2007–date[73]	—
K.L.R.	Kenya Law Reports	1919–[date?]	—
Kam. Rem.	Kame's Remarkable Decisions (Sc.)	1716–1752	—
Kam. Sel.	Kames' Select Decisions (Sc.)	1752–1768	—
Kay	Kay	1853–1854	69
Kay & J.	Kay & Johnson	1854–1858	69–70
Ke.	Keen	1836–1838	48
Keane & Gr.	Keane & Grant's Appeals	1854–1862	—
Keb.	Keble	1661–1679	83–4
Keil. (Keilw.)	Keilway	1496–1578	72
Kel. (1)	Kelyng, Sir John	1662–1669	84
Kel. (2)	Kelynge, W., temp. Hardwicke	1730–1734	25

[68] For subsequent volumes see King's College Law Journal (K.C.L.J.)
[69] For previous volumes see King's Counsel (K.C. or King's Counsel). For subsequent volumes see King's Law Journal (K.L.J.).
[70] For previous volumes see Knight's Industrial Reports (K.I.R.). For subsequent volumes see Managerial Law (Man. L. or Man. Law).
[71] For subsequent volumes see Knight's Industrial Law Reports (K.I.L.R.).
[72] Also referred to as Local Government Reports (L.G.R.). For subsequent volumes see Butterworths Local Government Reports (B.L.G.R.).
[73] For previous volumes see King's College Law Journal (K.C.L.J.).

Kel. J.	Kelyng, Sir John	1662–1669	84
Kel. W.	Kelynge, W., temp. Hardwicke	1730–1734	25
Keny.	Kenyon	1753–1759	96
Kerr	Kerr's New Brunswick Reports	1840–1848	—
Keyl.	Keilway (Keylway)	1496–1578	72
Kilk.	Kilkerran (Sc.)	1738–1752	—
King	Select Cases, temp. King, ed. Macnaghten	1724–1733	25
Kings Counsel	Kings Counsel	1936–1939; 1948–1989[74]	—
Kingston L.R.	Kingston Law Review	1968–1985	—
Kn. & O.	Knapp & Ombler	1834–1835	—
Kn. (Kn. A. C.)	Knapp's Appeal Cases	1829–1836	12
Knox	Knox's Reports New South Wales	1877	—
Konst. & W. Rat. App.	Konstam & Ward's Rating Appeals	1909–1912	—
Konst. Rat. App.	Konstam's Rating Appeals	1904–1908	—
Kotze	Kotze High Court Reports, Transvaal	1877–1881	—
L. & C.	Leigh & Cave	1861–1865	169
L. & F.M.R.	Law and Financial Markets Review	2007–date	—
L. & G. t. Plunk	Lloyd & Goold, temp. Plunkett (Ir.)	1834–1839	—
L. & G. t. Sug	Lloyd & Goold, temp. Sugden (Ir.)	1835	—
L. & H.	Law and Humanities	2007–date	—
L. & M.	Lowndes & Maxwell	1852–1854	—
L. & P.	Law and Practice of International Courts and Tribunals	2002–date	—
L. & T.	Longfield & Townsend (Ir.)	1841–1842	—
L. & T.R.	Landlord and Tenant Reports	1998–date	—
L. & T. Review	Landlord and Tenant Law Review	1996–date	—
L. & W.	Lloyd and Welsby Commercial Cases	1829–1830	—
L. Ex.	Legal Executive	1963–date	—
L. Notes	Law Notes	1885–1994	—
L. (T.C.)	Tax Cases Leaflets	1938–[date?]	—
LAG Bull.	Legal Action Group Bulletin	1979–1984[75]	—
L.A.L.	Local Authority Law	1992–1997	—
L.C.	Scottish Land Court Reps. (Sc.)	1913–date	—
L.C. & A.I.	Law, Computers and Artificial Intelligence	1992–1995[76]	—
L.C.C. (N.S.W.)	Land Court Cases, New South Wales	1890–1921	—
L.C.J.	Lower Canada Jurist, Montreal	1848–1891	—
L.C.L.J.	Lower Canada Law Journal, Montreal	1865–1868	—
L.C.R.	Lower Canada Reports	1850–1867	—
L.E.	Lawyers' Europe	1990–1997	—
L.F.	Litigation Funding	1999–date	—
L.F.M.R.	Law and Financial Markets Review	2007–date	—
L.G. and L.	Local Government and Law	1991–date	—
L.G.D.	Law, Social Justice and Global Development	2000–date	—
L.G. Rev.	Local Government Review Reports	1993–1996[77]	—
L.G.L. Rep.	Local Government Law Reports	1999–date[78]	—
L.G.L.R.	Local Government Law Reports	1999–date[79]	—

[74] For subsequent volumes see King's College Law Journal (K.C.L.J.).
[75] For subsequent volumes see Legal Action (Legal Action).
[76] For subsequent volumes see Information and Communications Technology Law (I. & C.T.L.).
[77] Subsequently incorporated into Justice of the Peace (J.P. or J.P.N.).
[78] Also referred to as Butterworths Local Government Reports (B.G.L.R.). For previous volumes see Knight's Local Government Reports (K.L.G.R.), also known as Local Government Reports (L.G.R.).
[79] Also referred to as Butterworths Local Government Reports (B.G.L.R.). For previous volumes see Knight's Local Government Reports (K.L.G.R.), also known as Local Government Reports (L.G.R.).

L.G.R.	Local Government Reports	1902–1998[80]	—
L.G.R.	Local Government Law Reports, New South Wales	1911–1956	—
L.G.R.A.	Local Government Reports, Australia	1956–1992	—
L.I.E.I.	Legal Issues of Economic Integration	1999–date[81]	—
L.I.E.I.	Legal Issues of European Integration	1974–1999[82]	—
L.I.M.	Legal Information Management	2001–date[83]	—
L.J.	Law Journal	1866–1965[84]	—
L.J. Rep., N.S.	Law Journal Reports, New Series (see L.J.R.)	1831–1949	—
L.J. Adm.	Law Journal Reports, Admiralty	1865–1875	—
L.J. Bcy.	Law Journal Reports, Bankruptcy	1832–1880	—
L.J. Ch.	Law Journal Reports, Chancery	1831–1946	—
L.J. Ecc.	Law Journal Reports, Ecclesiastical Cases	1866–1875	—
L.J.C.C.A.	Law Journal Newspaper County Court Appeals	1935	—
L.J.C.C.R.	Law Journal Reports, County Court Reports	1912–1933	—
L.J.C.P.	Law Journal Reports, Common Pleas	1831–1875	—
L.J.H.L.	Law Journal Reports, House of Lords	1831–1949	—
L.J.I.L.	Leiden Journal of International Law	1988–date	—
L.J.K.B.	Law Journal Reports, King's Bench	1831–1946	—
L.J.M.C.	Law Journal Reports, Magistrates' Cases	1831–1946	—
L.J.N.C.C.R.	Law Journal Newspaper County Court Reports	1934–1947	—
L.J.O.S.	Law Journal Reports, Old Series	1822–1831	—
L.J.P.	Law Journal Reports, Probate, Divorce and Admiralty	1875–1946	—
L.J.P.C.	Law Journal Reports, Privy Council	1865–1946	—
L.J.P. & M.	Law Journal Reports, Probate and Matrimonial	1858–1859	—
		1866–1875	—
L.J.P.D. & A.	Law Journal Reports, Probate, Divorce and Admiralty	1875–1946	—
L.J.Q.B.	Law Journal Reports, Queen's Bench	1831–1946	—
L.J.R.	Law Journal Reports	1947–1949	—
L.L.R.	Licensing Law Reports	2001–date	—
L.L.R.	London Law Review	2005–date	—
L.M. & P.	Lowndes, Maxwell & Pollock	1850–1851	[86]
L.M.C.L.Q.	Lloyd's Maritime and Commercial Law Quarterly	1974–date	—
L.M.E.L.R.	Land Management and Environmental Law Report	1989–1992[85]	—
L.M.L.N.	Lloyd's Maritime Law Newsletter	1979–date	—
L.N.	Law Notes	1885–1994	—
L.O.	Legal Observer	1830–1856	—
L.P. & R.	Law, Probability and Risk	2002–date	—
L.P. & Risk	Law Probability and Risk	2002–date	—
L.P.I.C.T.	Law and Practice of International Courts and Tribunals	2002–date	—
L.Q.R.	Law Quarterly Review	1885–date	—

---

[80] Also referred to as Knight's Local Government Reports (K.L.G.R.). For subsequent volumes see Butterworths Local Government Reports (B.L.G.R.).
[81] For previous volumes see Legal Issues of European Integration (L.I.E.I.).
[82] For subsequent volumes see Legal Issues of Economic Integration (L.I.E.I. or Legal I.E.I.).
[83] For previous volumes see Law Librarian (Law Lib.).
[84] For subsequent volumes see New Law Journal (N.L.J.).
[85] For subsequent volumes, see Environmental Law and Management (E.L.M.).

L.R.	Law Reports		
	First Series	1865–1875	—
L.R. A. & E.	Admiralty and Ecclesiastical Cases	1865–1875	—
L.R. C.C.R.	Crown Cases Reserved	1865–1875	—
L.R. C.P.	Common Pleas Cases	1865–1875	—
L.R. Ch. App.	Chancery Appeal Cases	1865–1875	—
L.R. Eq.	Equity Cases	1866–1875	—
L.R. Ex.	Exchequer Cases	1865–1875	—
L.R. H.L.	English and Irish Appeals	1866–1875	—
L.R. P. & D.	Probate and Divorce Cases	1865–1875	—
L.R. P.C.	Privy Council Appeals	1865–1875	—
L.R. Q.B.	Queen's Bench	1865–1875	—
L.R. Sc. & Div.	Scotch and Divorce Appeals	1866–1875	—
—	Statutes	1866–1875	—
	Second Series		
App.Cas.	Appeal Cases	1875–1890	—
Ch.D.	Chancery Division	1875–1890	—
C.P.D.	Common Pleas Division	1875–1880	—
Ex. D.	Exchequer Division	1875–1880	—
P.D.	Probate Division	1875–1890	—
Q.B.D.	Queen's Bench Division	1875–1890	—
—	Statutes	1876–1890	—
	Third Series		
A.C.	Appeal Cases	1891–date	—
Ch.	Chancery Division	1891–date	—
Fam.	Family Division	1971–date[86]	—
K.B. (Q.B.)	King's (Queen's) Bench	1891–date	—
P.	Probate Division	1891–1971[87]	—
—	Statutes	1891–date	—
L.R. (N.S.W.)	Law Reports, New South Wales	1880–1900	—
L.R. R.P.C.	Restrictive Practice Cases	1958–1972	—
L.R.B.G.	Law Reports, British Guiana	1890–1955	—
L.R.E.A.	Law Reports, East Africa	1897–1921	—
L.R. Ind. App.	Law Reports, Indian Appeals	1872–1950	—
L.R.Ir.	See I.R.		
L.R.L.R.	Lloyd's Reinsurance Law Reports	1995–1997[88]	—
L.S.	Legal Studies	1981–date[89]	—
L.S. & P.	Law Science and Policy	2004–date[90]	—
L.S. Gaz.	Law Society's Gazette	1903–1989[91]	—
L.S.G.	Law Society's Gazette	1903–1989[92]	—
L.S.R.	Locus Standi Reports	1936–1960	—
L.T.	Law Times Reports	1859–1947	—
L.T. Jour.	Law Times Newspapers	1843	—
L.T.I.	Legal Technology Insider	1995–d ate	—
L.T.J.	Law Technology Journal	1991–1996[93]	—
L.T.O.S.	Law Times, Old Series	1843–1859	—
L.T.R.	Law Times Reports	1859–1947	—
L.T.R.A.	Lands Tribunal Rating Appeals	1950–[1961?]—	
L.V.R.	Land and Valuation Court Reports (New South Wales)	1922–1970[94]	—

[86] For previous volumes see Probate Division (P.).
[87] For subsequent volumes see Family Division (Fam.).
[88] Merged with Reinsurance Law Reports (Re. L.R.) to form Lloyds Law Reports: Insurance and Reinsurance (Lloyd's Rep. I.R.).
[89] For previous volumes see Journal of the Society of Public Teachers of Law (J. Soc. Pub. T.L., or J.S.P.T.L.).
[90] For previous volumes see International Journal of Biosciences and Law (I.J.B.L.).
[91] For subsequent volumes see Gazette (Law Society, Great Britain) (Gazette).
[92] For subsequent volumes see Gazette (Law Society, Great Britain) (Gazette).
[93] For subsequent volumes see Journal of Information Law and Technology (J.I.L.T.).
[94] Also known as New South Wales Land and Valuation Court Reports (N.S.W.L.V.R.). Merged with New South Wales State Reports (N.S.W.S.R.) and absorbed by New South Wales Law Reports (N.S.W.L.R.).

La (Lane)	Lane	1605–1611	145
Lah.	Indian Law Reports, Lahore	1920–1947	—
Lap. Dec.	Laperriere's Speaker's Decisions, Canada	1841–1872	—
Lat. (Latch)	Latch	1625–1628	82
Law and Crit.	Law and Critique	1990–date	—
Law & Just.	Law and Justice	1962–date	—
Law & Pol.	Law and Policy	1979–date	—
Law & Tax R.	Law and Tax Review	1982–1992	—
Law for Bus.	Law for Business	1988–1992	—
Law. in Eur.	Lawyers in Europe	1990–1994[95]	—
Law J.	Law Journal	1866–1965[96]	—
Law J.	Law Journal Reports	1822–1831; 1832–1949	—
Law Jour.	Law Journal	1866–1965[97]	—
Law Jour.	Law Journal Reports	1822–1831; 1832–1949	—
Law Lib.	Law Librarian	1970–2000[98]	—
Law Mag.	Law Magazine	1997–1998	—
Law Rec., N.S.	Law Recorder, New Series (Ir.)	1833–1838	—
Law Rec. (O.S.)	Law Recorder (Ir.)	1827–1831	—
Law Teach.	Law Teacher	1971–date	—
Laws. Reg. Cas.	Lawson's Irish Registration Cases	1885–1914	—
Lawyer	Lawyer	1987–date	—
Lawyer 2B	Lawyer 2B	2001–date	—
Ld. Ken.	Kenyon	1753–1759	96
Ld. Ray.	Raymond, Lord	1694–1732	91–2
Le. & Ca.	Leigh & Cave	1861–1865	169
Leach	Leach	1730–1815	168
Lee	Lee	1752–1758	161
Lee & H.	Cases, temp. Hardwicke	1733–1738	95
Lee t. Hard.	Cases, temp. Hardwicke	1733–1738	95
Lef. & Cass.	Lefroy and Cassel's Practice Cases, Ontario	1881–1883	—
Leg.	Legisprudence	2007–date	—
Leg. News	Legal News, Montreal	1878–1897	—
Leg. Ob.	Legal Observer	1830–1856	—
Leg. Rep.	Legal Reporter (Ir.)	1840–1843	—
Legal Action	Legal Action	1985–date[99]	—
Legal Bus.	Legal Business	1990–date	—
Legal Ethics	Legal Ethics	1998–date	—
Legal I.E.I.	Legal Issues of Economic Integration	1999–date[1]	—
Legal IT	Legal IT	2000–date	—
Legal Theory	Legal Theory	1995–date	—
Legal Times	Legal Times	1994–1996	—
Legal Week	Legal Week	1999–date	—
Legge	Legge's Supreme Court Cases, New South Wales	1825–1862	—
Leigh	Ley's Reports	1608–1629	80
Leigh & C.	Leigh & Cave	1861–1865	169
Leo.	Leonard	1540–1615	74
Lev.	Levinz	1660–1697	83
Lew.	Lewin	1822–1838	168
Ley	Ley	1608–1629	80
Lil	Lilly, Assize	1688–1693	170

---

[95] From 1994 incorporated in Global Law and Business (G.L. & B.).
[96] For subsequent volumes see New Law Journal (N.L.J.).
[97] For subsequent volumes see New Law Journal (N.L.J.).
[98] For subsequent volumes see Legal Information Management (L.I.M.).
[99] For previous volumes see Legal Action Group Bulletin (LAG Bull).
[1] For previous volumes see Legal Issues of European Integration (L.I.E.I.).

Lit.	Litigation	1981–date	—
Lit. L.	Litigation Letter	1981–date	—
Lit. (Litt.)	Littleton	1626–1632	124
Litigator	Litigator	1994–1997	—
Little Brooke	Brooke's New Cases	1515–1558[2]	73
Liverpool L.R.	Liverpool Law Review	1979–date	—
Ll. & G. t. P.	Lloyd & Goold, temp. Plunkett (Ir.)	1834–1839	—
Ll. & G. t. S.	Lloyd & Goold, temp. Sugden (Ir.)	1835	—
Ll. & W.	Lloyd & Welsby Commercial Cases	1829–1830	—
Ll. L.R.	Lloyd's List Law Reports	1919–1950[3]	—
Ll.M.C.L.Q.	Lloyd's Maritime and Commercial Law Quarterly	1974–date	—
Ll. Pr. Cas.	Lloyd's Reports of Prize Cases	1914–1924	—
Ll. Pr. Cas. N.S.	Lloyd's Reports of Prize Cases, 2nd Series	1939–1953	—
Ll. Rep.	Lloyd's List Reports	1919–1950[4]	—
Lloyd's Rep.	Lloyd's Law Reports	1951–date[5]	—
Lloyd's Rep. Bank.	Lloyd's Law Reports: Banking	1999–date[6]	—
Lloyd's Rep. I.R.	Lloyd's Law Reports: Insurance and Reinsurance	1998–date[7]	—
Lloyd's Rep. Med.	Lloyd's Law Reports: Medical	1998–date[8]	—
Lloyd's Rep. P.N.	Lloyds Law Reports: Professional Negligence	1999–2003[9]	—
Lofft	Lofft	1772–1774	98
Longff. & T.	Longfield & Townsend (Ir.)	1841–1842	—
Lorenz	Lorenz Reports (Sri Lanka)	1856–1859	—
Low. Can. Jur.	Lower Canada Jurist	1848–1891	—
Low. Can. Rep.	Lower Canada Reports	1850–1867	—
Lownd. & M.	Lowndes & Maxwell	1852–1854	—
Lownd. M. & P.	Lowndes Maxwell & Pollock	1850–1851	[86]
Luc.	Modern Cases. Temp. Lucas (10 Modern Reports)	1710–1725	88
Lud. El. Cas.	Luder's Cases	1784–1787	—
Lum. (P.L.C.)	Lumley's Poor Law Cases	1834–1842	—
Lush.	Lushington	1859–1862	167
Lut. R.C.	A.J. Lutwyche	1843–1853	—
Lutw.	E. Lutwyche	1682–1704	125
Lyne (Wall.)	Wallis' Select Cases, ed. by Lyne (Ir.)	1766–1791	—
M.	Session Cases, 3rd Series [Macpherson] (Sc.)	1862–1873	—
M.	Menzies Supreme Court Reports, Cape of Good Hope	1828–1849	—
M.	Morison's Dictionary of Decisions (Sc.)	1540–1808	—
M. Advocate	Maritime Advocate	1997–date	—
M. & A.	Montagu & Ayrton	1833–1838	—
M. & A. Ins. Rep.	Marine and Aviation Insurance Report	1984–1993[10]	—
M. & B.	Montagu & Bligh	1832–1833	—
M. & C.	Montagu & Chitty	1838–1840	—
M. & C.	Mylne & Craig	1835–1851	140–1

[2] See note to Brooke's New Cases (B.N.C.).
[3] For subsequent volumes see Lloyd's Law Reports (Lloyd's Rep.).
[4] For subsequent volumes see Lloyd's Law Reports (Lloyd's Rep.).
[5] For previous volumes see Lloyd's List Law Reports (Ll. Rep., or Ll. L.R.).
[6] For previous volumes see Banking Law Reports (Bank. L.R.).
[7] Formed from a merger between Lloyd's Reinsurance Law Reports (L.R.L.R.) and Reinsurance Law Reports (Re. L.R.). From 2003 incorporates Lloyd's Law Reports: Professional Negligence (Lloyd's Rep. P.N.).
[8] For previous volumes see Medical Law Reports (Med. L.R.).
[9] Subsequently incorporated into Lloyd's Law Reports: Insurance and Reinsurance (Lloyd's Rep. I.R.).
[10] For subsequent volumes see Marine Insurance Report (Marine I.R.).

Law Reports, Journals

M. & G.	Macnaghten & Gordon	1849–1851	41–2
M. & G.	Maddock & Geldart	1815–1822	56
M. & G.	Manning & Granger	1840–1844	133–5
M. & H.	Murphy & Hurlstone	1836–1837	[51]
M. & K.	Mylne & Keen	1832–1835	39–40
M. & M.	Moody & Malkin	1826–1830	173
M. & M'A	Montagu & MacArthur	1828–1829	—
M. & P.	Moore & Payne	1827–1831	[29–33]
M. & R.	Maclean & Robinson (Sc.)	1839	9
M. & R.	Manning & Ryland, King's Bench	1827–1830	[31–4]
M. & R.	Moody & Robinson	1830–1844	174
M. & R.M.C.	Manning & Ryland, Magistrates' Cases	1827–1830	—
M. & S.	Manning & Scott	1845–1856	135–9
M. & S.	Maule & Selwyn	1813–1817	105
M. & S.	Moore & Scott	1831–1834	[34–8]
M. & W.	Meeson & Welsby	1836–1847	150–3
M.A.L.Q.R.	Model Arbitration Law Quarterly Reports	1995–date	
M.A.R.	Municipal Association Reports, New South Wales	1886–1911	—
M.C.	Magistrates Cases. See L.J.M.C.		
M.C.C.	Moody	1824–1844	168–9
M.C.P.	Magistrates' Court Practice	1997–date	—
M.C.R.	Magistrates' Reports, New Zealand	1939–1979[11]	—
M.D. & D. (M.D. & De G.)	Montague, Deacon & De Gex	1840–1844	—
M.D.U. Jour.	Medical Defence Union Journal	1985–1995[12]	—
M.E.C.L.R.	Middle East Commercial Law Review	1995–date	—
M.G. & S.	Common Bench (Manning Granger & Scott) Reports	1845–1856	135–9
M.I.A.	Moore's Indian Appeals	1836–1871	18–20
M.J.	Maastricht Journal of European and Comparative Law	1994–date	—
M.J.L.S.	Mountbatten Journal of Legal Studies	1997–date	—
M.L.J.	Madras Law Journal	1891–[?]	—
M.L.J.	Malaya Law Journal	1932–[?]	—
M.L.J.I.	Medico-Legal Journal of Ireland	1995–date	—
M.L.N.	Media Lawyer Newsletter	1996–date	—
M.L.R.	Malayan Law Review	1959–1990[13]	—
M.L.R.	Modern Law Review	1937–date	—
M.P.C.	Moore, E.F.	1836–1862	12–15
M.P.R.	Maritime Provinces Reports, Canada	1930–1968	—
M.R.	Mauritius Decisions	1861–[?]	—
M.R.I.	Maritime Risk International	2005–date[14]	—
M.W.N.	Madras Weekly Notes	1910–[?]	—
Maastricht J.	Maastricht Journal of European and Comparative Law	1994–date	—
Mac.	Macassey's Reports, New Zealand	1861–1872	—
Mac. & G.	Macnaghten & Gordon	1848–1851	41–2
Mac. & H.	Cox, Macrae & Hertslet	1847–1858	—
Mac. & H.	Macrae & Hertslet	1847–1852	—
Mac. & R.	Maclean & Robinson (Sc.)	1839	9
Mac. C.C.	MacGillivray's Copyright Cases	1901–1949	—
Mac. P.C.	Macrory	1847–1860	—
MacCarthy	MacCarthy's Irish Land Cases	1887–1892	—

[11] Superseded by the New Zealand District Court Reports (N.Z.D.C.R.).
[12] Also referred to as Journal of the Medical Defence Union (J.M.D.U.). For subsequent volumes see Journal of the Medical and Dental Defence Unions (J.M.D.D.U.).
[13] For subsequent volumes see Singapore Journal of Legal Studies (S.J.L.S.).
[14] For previous volumes see P. & I International (P. & I. Int.).

Maccl.	Modern Cases, temp. Macclesfield (10 Modern Reports)	1710–1724	88
MacDev.	MacDevitt's Irish Land Cases	1882–1884	—
Macf.	Macfarlane	1838–1839	—
Macl. Rem. Cas.	Maclaurin's Remarkable Cases (Sc.)	1670–1773	—
Macph.	Session Cases, 3rd Series [Macpherson] (Sc.)	1862–1873	—
Macq.	Macqueen (Sc.)	1851–1865	—
Macr.	Macrory	1847–1860	—
Macr. & H.	Macrae & Hertslet	1847–1852	—
Macr. P. Cas.	Macrory	1847–1860	—
Mad. & Gel.	Maddock & Geldart	1821–1822	56
Madd.	Maddock	1815–1822	56
Madd. & G.	Maddock & Geldart	1821–1822	56
Mag. Cas.	See L.J.M.C.		
Magistrate	Magistrate: the Bulletin of the Magistrates Association	1921–1954[15]	—
Magistrate	Magistrate: the Journal of the Magistrates Association	1955–date[16]	—
Man.	Manning's Revision Cases	1832–1835	—
Man. & G.	Manning & Granger	1840–1844	133–5
Man. & Ry.	Manning & Ryland, King's Bench	1827–1830	[31–4]
Man. & Ry. M.C.	Manning & Ryland, Magistrates' Cases	1827–1830	—
Man. & Sc.	Manning, Granger & Scott, Common Bench Reports	1845–1856	135–9
Man. Gr. & S.	Manning, Granger & Scott, Common Bench Reports	1845–1856	135–9
Man. L.	Managerial Law	1975–date[17]	—
Man. L.J.	Manitoba Law Journal	1966–date	—
Man. L.R.	Manitoba Law Reports	1884–1963	—
Man. Law	Managerial Law	1975–date[18]	—
Man. R.	Manitoba Reports	1884–date	—
Manson	Manson	1894–1914	—
Mar.	March	1639–1642	82
Mar. L.C.	Maritime Law Cases	1870–1940[19]	—
(Mr. L.R.)	(Crockford)	1860–1871	—
Mar. L.C., N.S.	Aspinall's Maritime Law Cases	1870–1940[20]	—
March [N.C.]	March's Translation of Brook's New Cases	1515–1558[21]	73
March N.C.	March's New Cases	1639–1642	82
Marine I.R.	Marine Insurance Report	1993–date[22]	—
Marr.	Marriott	1776–1779	165
Marsh.	Marshall	1813–1816	[15, 17]
Marsh.	Marshall, W. High Court Reports, Bengal	1862–1863	—
	Marshall C. Judgments Supreme Court Ceylon (Sri Lanka)	1833–1836	—
Masons C.L.R.	Masons Computer Law Reports	1994–1999	—
Mau. & Sel.	Maule & Selwyn	1813–1817	105
Mayn.	Maynard's Reports	1273–1326	—
McCle (McCl.)	M'Cleland	1824	148

---

[15] For subsequent volumes see Magistrate: the Journal of the Magistrates Association (Magistrate).
[16] For previous volumes see Magistrate: the Bulletin of the Magistrates Association (Magistrate).
[17] For previous volumes see Knight's Industrial Law Reports (K.I.L.R.).
[18] For previous volumes see Knight's Industrial Law Reports (K.I.L.R.).
[19] Also known as Aspinall's Maritime Law Cases (Mar. L.C., N.S.).
[20] Also known as Maritime Law Cases (Mar. L.C.).
[21] See note to Brooke's New Cases (B.N.C.).
[22] For previous volumes see Marine and Aviation Insurance Report 1984 – 1993 (M. & A. Ins. Rep.).

McCle. & Yo.	M'Cleland & Younge	1824–1825	148
Med. L. Int	Medical Law International	1993–date	—
Med. L. Mon	Medical Law Monitor	1994–date	—
Med. L. Rev.	Medical Law Review	1993–date	—
Med. L.J.	Medico-Legal Journal	1947–date	—
Med. L.R.	Medical Law Reports	1989–1998[23]	—
Med. Leg. J.	Medico-Legal Journal	1947–date	—
Med. Lit.	Medical Litigation	1998–date	—
Med. Sci. Law	Medicine, Science and the Law	1960–date	—
Mees. & Wels.	Meeson & Welsby	1836–1847	150–3
Megone	Megone's Company Cases	1888–1890	—
Melb. Univ. L.R.	Melbourne University Law Review	1957–date	—
Menz.	Menzies Reports, Cape of Good Hope	1828–1849	—
Mer.	Merivale	1815–1817	35–6
Milw. Ir. Ecc. Rep.	Irish Reports by Milward	1819–1843	—
Mo.	Modern Reports (ed. Leach)	1669–1755	86–8
Mo.	Moore, E.F.	1836–1862	12–15
Mo.	Moore, E.F., Indian Appeals	1836–1872	18–20
Mo.	Moore, Sir Francis	1512–1621	72
Mo.	Moore, J.B.	1817–1827	[19–29]
Mo. & R.	Moody & Robinson	1830–1844	174
Mo. & Sc.	Moore & Scott	1831–1834	[34–38]
Mo. I.A.	Moore, E.F., Indian Appeals	1836–1872	18–20
Mod.	Modern Reports	1669–1755	86–8
Mod. Ca.L. & Eq.	8 & 9 Modern Reports	1721–1755	88
Mod. Ca. Per Far.	7 Modern Reports	1702–1745	87
Mod. Ca. t. Holt	7 Modern Reports	1702–1745	87
Mod. Cas.	Modern Cases	1702–1745[24]	87–8
Mod. L. Rev.	Modern Law Review	1937–date	—
Mod. L.R.	Modern Law Review	1937–date	—
Mod. Rep.	Modern Reports	1669–1755	86–8
Modern L. Rev.	Modern Law Review	1937–date	—
Modern L.R.	Modern Law Review	1937–date	—
Mol. (Moll.)	Molloy (Ir.)	1827–1831	—
Mont.	Montagu	1829–1832	—
Mont. & Ayr.	Montagu & Ayrton	1833–1838	—
Mont. & Bl.	Montagu & Bligh	1832–1833	—
Mont. & C.	Montagu & Chitty	1838–1840	—
Mont. & MacA	Montagu & MacArthur	1828–1829	—
Mont. Cond. Rep.	Montreal Condensed Reports	1853–1854	—
Mont. D. & De. G.	Montagu, Deacon & De Gex	1840–1844	—
Mont. L.R.	Montreal Law Reports	1885–1891	—
Moo.	Moody	1824–1844	168–9
Moo.	Moore, E.F.	1836–1862	12–15
Moo.	Moore, Sir Francis	1512–1621	72
Moo.	Moore, J.B.	1817–1827	[19–29]
Moo. & M.	Moody & Malkin	1826–1830	173
Moo. & Pay.	Moore & Payne	1827–1831	[29–33]
Moo. & Rob.	Moody & Robinson	1831–1844	174
Moo. & Sc.	Moore & Scott	1831–1834	[34–8]
Moo. A.	1 Bosanquet & Puller, 471 ff	1796–1797	126
Moo. C.C.	Moody	1824–1844	168–9
Moo. F.	Moore, Sir Francis	1512–1621	72
Moo. Ind. App.	Moore, E.F., Indian Appeals	1836–1872	18–20
Moo. K.B.	Moore, Sir Francis	1512–1621	72
Moo. N.S.	Moore, E.F., New Series	1862–1873	15–17
Moo. P.C.	Moore, E.F.	1836–1862	12–15
Mor.	Morris's Reports, Jamaica	1836–1884	—
Mor. Dic.	Morison's Dictionary of Decisions (Sc.)	1540–1808	—

[23] For subsequent volumes see Lloyd's Law Reports: Medical (Lloyd's Rep. Med.).
[24] Mod. Cases = 6,7 Mod.; 2 Mod. Cas. sometimes = 7 Mod., sometimes 8 Mod.

Mor. Syn.	Morison's Synopsis (Sc.)	1808–1816	—
Morr.	Morrell	1884–1893	—
Mos.	Mosley	1726–1730	25
Mumf.	Mumford's Reports, Jamaica	1838	—
Mun.	Munitions Appeal Reports	1916–1920	—
Mun. App. Sc.	Munitions of War Acts, Scottish Appeals	1916–1920	—
Mundy	Mundy's Abstracts of Star Chamber	1550–1558	—
Mur. (Murr.)	Murray (Sc.)	1815–1830	—
Mur. & Hurl.	Murphy & Hurlestone	1836–1837	[51]
Myl. & Cr.	Mylne & Craig	1835–1841	40–1
Myl. & K.	Mylne & Keen	1832–1835	39–40
N. & M.	Nevile & Manning, King's Bench	1832–1836	[38–43]
N. & M.M.C.	Nevile & Manning, Magistrates' Cases	1832–1836	—
N. & McN.	Nevile & Macnamara	1855–1950	—
N. & P.	Nevile & Perry, King's Bench	1836–1838	[44–5]
N. & P.M.C.	Nevile & Perry, Magistrates' Cases	1836–1837	—
N. & S.	Nicholls & Stops. Reports, Tasmania	1897–1904	—
N. Ir. L.Q.	Northern Ireland Legal Quarterly	1936–date	—
N. Ir. L.R.	Northern Ireland Law Reports	1925–date	—
N.A.C.	Native Appeal Cases, South Africa	1894–1929	—
N.B. Eq. R.	New Brunswick Equity Reports	1894–1912	—
N.B.R.	New Brunswick Reports	1825–1929	—
N. Ben	Benloe	1515–1628	73
N.C.	Bingham, New Cases	1834–1840	131–3
N.C.	Notes of New Cases (ed. Thornton)	1841–1850	—
N.C.C.	Younge & Collyer	1841–1844	62–3
N.C. Str.	Strange's Notes of Cases, Madras	1798–1816	—
N.F.	Newfoundland Law Reports	1817–1946	—
N.H. & C.	Nicholl, Hare, & Carrow	1835–1854	—
N.I.	Northern Ireland Law Reports	1925–date	—
N.I.J.	New Irish Jurist (Ir.)	1900–1905	—
N.I.L.Q.	Northern Ireland Legal Quarterly	1936–date	—
N.I.L.R.	Netherlands International Law Review	1953–date	—
N.I.L.R.	Northern Ireland Law Reports	1925–date	—
N.J.I.L.	Nordic Journal of International Law	1930–date	—
N.L.J.	New Law Journal	1965–date[25]	—
N.L.R.	New Law Reports of Cases Decided by the Supreme Court of Ceylon (afterwards Sri Lanka)	1896–1977[26]	—
N.L.R.	Natal Law Reports (S. Afr.)	1879–1910	—
N.L.R.	Newfoundland Law Reports	1817–1946	—
N.L.R.	Nigeria Law Reports	1881–[?]	—
N.L.R.	Nyasaland Law Reports	1922–[?]	—
N.P.C.	New Practice Cases	1844–1848	—
N.P.C.	New Property Cases	1986–date	—
N.P.D.	Natal Province Division, South African Law Reports	1910–1946	—
N.Q.H.R.	Netherlands Quarterly of Human Rights	1995–date	—
N.R.	Bosanquet & Puller, New Reports	1804–1807	127
N.R.	New Reports	1862–1865	—
N.R.L.R.	Northern Rhodesia Law Reports	1931–1955	—
N.S.A.I.L.	Non-State Actors and International Law	1999–2006[27]	—
N.S. Dec.	Nova Scotia Decisions	1867–1874	—

[25] For previous volumes see Law Journal (L.J., or Law J., or Law Jour.).
[26] For subsequent volumes see Sri Lanka Law Reports (S.L.L.R.).
[27] Merged with International Law Forum du Droit International (1999 – 2006, no abbreviation), to form International Community Law Review (Int. C.L. Rev.).

N.S.C.	New Sessions Cases by Carrow, Hamerton & Allen	1844–1851	—
N.S.L.R.	Nova Scotia Law Reports	1834–1852	—
N.S.W.A.R.	New South Wales Arbitration Reports	1902–[?]	—
N.S.W.L.R.	New South Wales Law Reports	1880–1900	—
N.S.W.L.R.	New South Wales Law Reports	1971–date[28]	—
N.S.W.L.V.R.	New South Wales Land and Valuation Court Reports	1922–1970[29]	—
N.S.W.S.R.	New South Wales State Reports	1901–1970[30]	—
N.S.W.W.C.R.:	New South Wales Workmen's Compensation Reports	1926–[?]	—
N.S.W.W.N.	New South Wales Weekly Notes	1884–1970[31]	—
N.W.T.R.	North West Territories Reports, Canada	1885–1907	—
N.Y.I.L.	Netherlands Yearbook of International Law	1970–date	—
N.Z.	New Zealand Law Reports	1883–date	—
N.Z.B.L.Q.	New Zealand Business Law Quarterly	1995–date	—
N.Z. Jur.	New Zealand Jurist	1873–1875	—
N.Z.D.C.R.	New Zealand District Court Reports	1980–date[32]	—
N.Z.L.J.	New Zealand Law Journal	1925–date	—
N.Z.L.R.	New Zealand Law Reports	1883–date	—
N.Z.U.L.R.	New Zealand Universities Law Review	1963–date	—
Nell	Nell's Reports, Ceylon	1845–1855	—
Nels. (Nels. 8vo)	Nelson	1625–1693	21
Nels. (Nels. Fol.)	Finch's Reports (ed. By Nelson)	1673–1681	23
Nelson's Rep.	Nelson t. Finch	1673–1681	23
Nev. & M.M.C.	Nevile & Manning, Magistrates'	1832–1836	—
Nev. & Man	Nevile & Manning, King's Bench	1832–1836	[38–43]
Nev. & McN.	Railway, Canal and Road Traffic Cases	1885–1949	—
	Traffic Cases, New Series (with Vol. 30)	1952–[?]	—
Nev. & P.	Nevile & Perry, King's Bench	1836–1838	[44–5]
Nev. & P. Mag. Cas.	Nevile & Perry, Magistrates'	1836–1837	—
New Benl.	Benloe	1531–1628	73
New Cas. Eq.	Modern Cases (8 & 9 Modern Reports)	1721–1755	88
New Mag. Cas.	Magistrates' Cases	1844–1851	—
New Pr. Cas.	New Practice Cases	1844–1848	—
New Rep.	New Reports	1862–1865	—
New Sess. Cas.	New Sessions Cases by Carrow, Hamerton & Allen (Sc.)	1844–1851	—
Newf. Sel. Cas.	Newfoundland Select Cases	1817–1828	—
Nic. Ha. C.	Nicholl, Hare & Carrow	1835–1855	—
Nig. L.R.	Nigeria Law Reports	1881–1955	—
Nolan	Nolan's Magistrates' Cases	1791–1792	—
Not. Cas.	Notes of Cases, ed. Thornton	1841–1850	—
Nott. L.J.	Nottingham Law Journal	1992–date	—
Noy	Noy	1559–1649	74

---

[28] Supersedes the New South Wales Weekly Notes (N.S.W.W.N. or W.N.(N.S.W.)), and New South Wales State Reports (N.S.W.S.R.), and includes the merged New South Wales Land and Valuation Court Reports (N.S.W.L.V.R.), also known as Land and Valuation Court Reports (New South Wales) (L.V.R.).

[29] Also known as Land and Valuation Court Reports (New South Wales) (L.V.R.). Merged with New South Wales State Reports (N.S.W.S.R.) and absorbed by New South Wales Law Reports (N.S.W.L.R.).

[30] Superseded by the New South Wales Law Reports (N.S.W.L.R.).

[31] Superseded by the New South Wales Law Reports (N.S.W.L.R.).

[32] Supersedes the Magistrates' Reports, New Zealand (M.C.R.). For subsequent volumes see District Court Reports (D.C.R.).

Ny. L.R.	Nyasaland Law Reports	1922–[?]	—
O. Benl.	Benloe & Dalison	1486–1580	123
O. Bridg.	Bridgman, O.	1660–1667	124
O.A.R.	Ontario Appeal Reports	1876–1900	—
O.B. & F.	Ollivier, Bell & Fitzgerald's Reports, New Zealand	1878–1880	—
O.B.S.P.	Old Bailey, Sessional Papers	1715–1834	—
O.D. and I.L.	Ocean Development and International Law	1973–date	—
O.F.S.	Orange Free State High Court Reports	1879–1883	—
O.G.L.T.R.	Oil and Gas: Law and Taxation Review	1982–1999[33]	—
OJ	Official Journal of the European Communities	1952–date	—
O.J.L.S.	Oxford Journal of Legal Studies	1981–date	—
O.L.R.	Ontario Law Reports	1901–1931	—
O'M. & H.	O'Malley & Hardcastle	1869–1929	—
O.P.D.	South Africa Law Reports, Orange Free State Province Division	1910–1946	—
O.P.L.R.	Occupational Pensions Law Reports	1992–date	—
O.P.R.	Ontario Practice Reports	1850–1900	—
O.R.	Ontario Reports	1882–1900 1931–date	—
O.S.S. Bull	Office for the Suspension of Solicitors Bulletin	1996–1999	—
O.U.C.L.J.	Oxford University Commonwealth Law Journal	2001–date	—
O.W.N.	Ontario Weekly Notes	1909–1962	—
O.W.R.	Ontario Weekly Reporter	1902–1914	—
Old Benloe	Benloe & Dalison	1486–1580	123
Oldr.	Oldright's Reports, Nova Scotia	1860–1867	—
Oll. B. & F.	Ollivier Bell & Fitzgerald's Reports, New Zealand	1878–1880	—
Ont.	Ontario Reports	1882–1900	—
Ont. App.	Ontario Appeal Reports	1876–1900	—
Ont. Elect.	Ontario Election Cases	1884–1900	—
Ont. L.R.	Ontario Law Reports	1901–1931	—
Ont. Pr. Rep.	Ontario Practice Reports	1850–1900	—
Ont. W.R.	Ontario Weekly Reporter	1902–1914	—
Ow.	Owen	1556–1615	74
Ox. J.L.S.	Oxford Journal of Legal Studies	1981–date	—
Oxley	Young's Vice-Admiralty Decisions, Nova Scotia, by Oxley	1865–1880	—
P		See L.R.P.	
P. & C.R.	Planning and Compensation Reports	1949–1967[34]	—
P. & C.R.	Property and Compensation Reports	1968–1987[35]	—
P. & C.R.	Property, Planning and Compensation Reports	1988–date[36]	—
P. & D.	Perry & Davison	1838–1841	[48–54]
P. & D.	See L.R.P.D.		
P. & D.P.	Privacy and Data Protection	2000–date	—
P. & I. Int.	P & I International	1987–2004[37]	—
P. & K.	Perry & Knapp	1833	—

[33] For subsequent volumes see International Energy Law and Taxation Review (I.E.L.T.R.).
[34] For subsequent volumes see Property and Compensation Reports (P. & C.R.).
[35] For previous volumes see Planning and Compensation Reports (P. & C.R.). For subsequent volumes see Property, Planning and CompensationReports (P & C.R.).
[36] For previous volumes see Property and Compensation Reports (P & C.R.).
[37] For subsequent volumes see Marine Risk International (M.R.I.).

Law Reports, Journals

P. & M.I.L.L.	Personal and Medical Injuries Law Letter	1985–2003[38]	—
P. & P.	Practice and Procedure	1996–date	—
P. & R.	Pigott & Rodwell	1843–1845	—
P. & T.	Pugsley and Trueman Reports, New Brunswick	1882–1883	—
P. Cas.	British and Colonial Prize Cases (Trehern & Grant)	1914–1922	—
P. Injury	Personal Injury (EMIS)	1996–1997[39]	—
P. Shaw	Patrick Shaw (Sc.)	1819–1831	—
PAD	Planning Appeal Decisions	1985–date	—
P.A.D.	Planning Appeal Decisions	1985–date	—
P.C.	See "Law Reports."		
P.C. & L.	Psychology, Crime and Law	1994–date	—
P.C.B.	Private Client Business	1992–date	—
PCC	Palmers Company Cases	1985–1989	—
P.C.L.B.	Practitioners' Child Law Bulletin	1989–2000	—
P.C.L.J.	Practitioners' Child Law Journal	1988–1999	—
P.C.P.	Private Client Practitioner	2006–date[40]	—
P.D.	See L.R.P.D.		
P.E.B.L.	Perspectives on European Business Law	1999–date	—
P.E.I. Rep.	Prince Edward Island Reports	1850–1872	—
P.E.L.B.	Planning and Environment Law Bulletin	1991–date	—
P.I.	Personal Injury (Wiley)	1996–[1997?]	—
P.I. Comp.	Personal Injury Compensation	2004–date[41]	—
P.I.B.U.	Personal Injury Brief Update Law Journal	2007–date	—
P.I.B.U.L.J.	Personal Injury Brief Update Law Journal	2007–date	—
P.I.C.	Palmer's In Company	1992–date	—
P.I.L.J.	Personal Injury Law Journal	2001–date	—
P.I.L.M.R.	Personal Injury Law and Medical Review	1994–1996[42]	—
P.I.Q.R.	Personal Injuries and Quantum Reports	1992–date	—
P.L. & B.	Privacy Laws and Business	1987–1994[43]	—
P.L.	Public Law	1956–date[44]	—
P.L. & B.I.N.	Privacy Laws and Business International Newsletter	1998–date[45]	—
P.L. & B.N.	Privacy Laws and Business Newsletter	1995–1998[46]	—
P.L. & B.U.K.N.	Privacy Laws and Business United Kingdom Newsletter	1998–date[47]	—
P.L. Mag	Poor Law Magazine (Sc.)	1858–1930	—
P.L.B.	Property Law Bulletin	1980–date	—
P.L.C.	Practical Law for Companies	1990–date	—
P.L.C.R.	Planning Law Case Reports	1998–1999	—
P.L.I.	Product Liability International	1979–1996	—
P.L.J.	Property Law Journal	1998–date	—

[38] For subsequent volumes see Personal Injury Compensation (P.I. Comp.).
[39] For previous volumes see Personal Injury Law and Medical Review (P.I.L.M.R.).
[40] For previous volumes see Trust and Estates Practitioner (T. & E.P.).
[41] For previous volumes see Personal and Medical Injuries Law Letter (P. & M.I.L.L.).
[42] For subsequent volumes see Personal Injury (P.I.).
[43] For subsequent volumes see Privacy Laws and Business Newsletter (P.L. & B.N.).
[44] Incorporates British Journal of Administrative Law (B.J.A.L., or Brit. J. Admin. Law).
[45] For previous volumes see Privacy Laws and Business Newsletter (P.L. & B.N.).
[46] For previous volumes see Privacy Laws and Business (P.L. & B.). For subsequent volumes see Privacy Laws and Business International Newsletter (P.L. & B.I.N.), and Privacy Laws and Business United Kingdom Newsletter (P.L. & B.U.K.N.).
[47] For previous volumes see Privacy Laws and Business Newsletter (P.L. & B.N.).

P.L.R.	Planning Law Reports	1988–date	—
P.L.T.	Professional Liability Today	1986–1996	—
P.N.	Professional Negligence	1985–date	—
P.N. & L.	Professional Negligence and Liability	1997	—
P.N.L.R.	Professional Negligence and Liability Reports	1996–date	—
P.N.P.	Peake	1790–1794	170
P.O. Cas.	Perry's Oriental Cases, Bombay	1843–1852	—
P.P.L.	Practical Planning Law	1996–date	—
P.P.L.R.	Public Procurement Law Review	1992–date	—
P.P.M.	Professional Practice Management	1986–1999	—
P.R. & D.	Power, Rodwell & Dew	1847–1856	—
P.R.U.C.	Practice Reports, Upper Canada	1850–1900	—
P.S.P.	Police Station Practice	1998–date	—
P.W.	Patent World	1987–date	—
P.W. (P. Wms.)	Peere Williams	1695–1735	24
Pal.(Palm.)	Palmer	1619–1629	81
Park.	Parker	1743–1767	145
Pat. & Mur.	Paterson and Murray's Reports, New South Wales	1870–1871	—
Pat. Abr.	Paterson's Abridgement of Poor Law Cases	1857–1863	—
Pat. App.	Paton's Appeals (Sc.)	1726–1821	—
Pat. Cas.	Reports of Patent, Design and Trade Mark Cases	1884–date	—
Paters. App.	Paterson Appeals (Sc.)	1851–1873	—
Patr. Elect. Cas	Patrick's Election Cases, Upper Canada	1824–1849	—
Pea. (2)	Peake's Additional Cases	1795–1812	170
Pea. (Peake)	Peake	1790–1794	170
Peck	Peckwell	1802–1806	—
Peere Wms.	Peere Williams	1695–1735	24
Pelham	Pelham's Reports, South Australia	1865–1866	—
Pens. L.R.	I.D.S. Pensions Law Reports	1989–date	—
Pen. Law.	Pension Lawyer	1995–date[48]	—
Per. & Dav.	Perry & Davison	1838–1841	[45–54]
Per. Or. Cas.	Perry Oriental Cases. Bombay	1843–1852	—
Perry Ins.	Perry's Insolvency Cases	1831	—
Pet.	Peters' Prince Edward Island Reports	1850–1872	—
Pet. Br.	Brooke's New Cases	1515–1558[49]	73
Ph. (Phil.)	Phillimore's Reports	1809–1821	161
Ph. (Phil.)	Phillips	1841–1849	41
Ph. (Phil.)	Phillips' Election Cases	1780–1781	—
Pharm. L.I.	Pharmaceutical Law Insight	2005–date	—
Phil. Ecc. Judg.	Phillimore's Judgments	1867–1875	—
Phil. Ecc. R.	Phillimore's Reports	1809–1821	161
Phil. El. Cas.	Phillips' Election Cases	1780–1781	—
Phil. Judg.	Phillimore's Judgments	1867–1875	—
Pig. & R.	Pigott & Rodwell	1843–1845	—
Pist.	Piston's Reports, Mauritius	1861–1862	—
Pitc.	Pitcairn Criminal Trials (Sc.)	1488–1624	—
Pl.	Plowden's Commentaries	1550–1580	75
Pl. & Pr. Cas.	Pleading and Practice Cases	1837–1838	—
Plac. Angl. Nor.	Placita Anglo-Normannica	1066–1195	—
Pol.	Pollexfen	1669–1685	86
Pop. (Poph.)	Popham	1592–1627	79
Pow. R. & D.	Power, Rodwell & Dew	1847–1856	—

[48] For previous volumes see British Pension Lawyer (B.P.N.).
[49] See note to Brooke's New Cases (B.N.C.).

Pr.	Price	1814–1824	145–7
Pr. Ch.	Precedents in Chancery (Finch)	1689–1722	24
Pr. Exch.	Price	1814–1824	145–7
Prac. Law.	Practical Lawyer	1989–date	—
Pract. Today	Practice Today	1985–1986	—
Pratt	Pratt's Supplement to Bott's Poor Laws	1833	—
Pres. Fal.	Falconer's Decisions (Sc.)	1744–1751	—
Price, P.C.	Price Practice Cases	1830–1831	—
Prid. & C.	Prideaux and Cole's Reports (New Sessions Cases), Volume 4	1850–1851	—
Prof. L.	Professional Lawyer	1990–1992	—
Prop. L. Bull.	Property Law Bulletin	1980–date	—
Pugs.	Pugsley's Reports, New Brunswick	1872–1877	—
Pugs. & Bur.	Pugsley & Burbridge's Reports, New Brunswick	1878–1882	—
Pugs. & Tru.	Pugsley and Trueman's Reports, New Brunswick	1882–1883	—
Pyke	Pyke's Lower Canada King's Bench Reports	1809–1810	—
Q.B.	See L.R.Q.B.		
Q.B. (Q.B.R.)	Queen's Bench Reports (Adolphus & Ellis, N.S.)	1841–1853	113–18
Q.B.U.C.	Queen's Bench Reports, Upper Canada	1844–1882	—
Q.C.L.L.R.	Crown Lands Law Report (Queensland)	1859–1973[50]	—
Q.C.R.	Queensland Criminal Reports	1860–1907	—
Q.J.P.	Queensland Justice of the Peace and Local Authorities Journal	1907–1969[51]	—
Q.J.P.R.	Queensland Justice of the Peace and Reports	1907–1972[52]	—
Q.L.	Queensland Lawyer	1973–[date?][53]	—
Q.L.C.R.	Queensland Land Court Reports	1974–date[54]	—
Q.L.J.	Queensland Law Journal	1879–1901	—
Q.L.R.	Quebec Law Reports	1874–1891	—
Q.L.R.	Queensland Law Reporter	1908–[?]	—
Q.L.R.	Queensland Law Reports	1876–1878	—
Q.O.R.	Quebec Official Reports	1892–date	—
Q.P.R.	Quebec Practice Reports	1897–1982	—
Q.R.S.C.	Quebec Reports, Superior Court	1892–date	—
Q.S.C.R.	Queensland Supreme Court Reports	1860–1881	—
Q.S.R.	State Reports (Queensland)	1902–1957[55]	—
Q.U.L.J.	Queensland University Law Journal	1948–date	—
Q.W.M.	Queensland Law Reporter & Weekly Notes	1908–1972	—
Q.W.N.	Weekly Notes, Queensland	1908–1972	—
Qd. R.	Queensland Reports	1958–date[56]	—
Queens. L.J. & R.	Queensland Law Journal and Reports	1879–1901[57]	—
R.	The Reports	1893–1895	—
R.	Session Cases, 4th Series [Rettie] (Sc.)	1873–1898	—

[50] Superseded by the Queensland Land Court Reports (Q.L.C.R.).
[51] or subsequent volumes see Queensland Justice of the Peace and Reports (Q.J.P.R.).
[52] For previous volumes see Queensland Justice of the Peace and Local Authorities Journal (Q.J.P.). For subsequent volumes see Queensland Lawyer (Q.L.).
[53] Incorporates Queensland Justice of the Peace and Reports (Q.J.P.R.).
[54] Supersedes the Crown Lands Law Report (Queensland), (Q.C.L.L.R.).
[55] For previous volumes see Queensland Law Journal and Reports (Queens. L.J. & R.). For subsequent volumes see Queensland Reports (Qd. R.).
[56] For previous volumes see State Reports, Queensland (Q.S.R., or S.R.Q.).
[57] For subsequent volumes see State Reports, Queensland (Q.S.R., or S.R.Q.).

R. & C.	Russell & Chesley Reports, Nova Scotia	1875–1879	—
R. & G.	Russell & Geldert Equity Reports, Nova Scotia	1879–1895	—
R. & I.T.	Rating and Income Tax Reports	1924–1960[58]	—
R. & M.	Russell & Mylne	1829–1831	39
R. & M.	Ryan & Moody	1823–1826	171
R. & McG.	Income Tax Decisions of Australasia, Ratcliffe McGrath	1891–1930	—
R. & McG. Ct. of Rev.	Court of Review Decisions, Ratcliffe Ratcliffe and McGrath, N.S.W.	1913–1927	—
R. & N.	Rhodesia and Nyasaland Law Reports	1956–1964	—
R. & R.C.C.	Russell & Ryan	1799–1824	168
R. & V.R.	Rating and Valuation Reporter	1961–date[59]	—
R. Pat. Cas.	Reports of Patent, Design and Trade Mark Cases	1884–date	—
RA	Rating Appeals	1962–date[60]	—
R.A.C.	Ramsay's Appeal Cases, Canada	1873–1886	—
R.A.D.I.C.	African Journal of International and Comparative Law	1988–2000	—
R.A.L.Q.	Receivers, Administrators and Liquidators Quarterly	1994–date	—
R.C.	Nicholl, Hare & Carrow	1835–1855	—
R.C. & C.R.	Revenue Civil and Criminal Reporter, Calcutta	1866–1868	—
R.E.C.I.E.L.	Review of European Community and International Environmental Law	1992–date	—
R.E.D.	Reserved and Equity Decisions, New South Wales	1845	—
R.H.C.	Road Haulage Cases	1950–[?]	—
R.J.	Judgments of the Supreme Court of N.S.W. for the district of Port Philip. A'Beckett	1846–1851	—
R.J.O.	Rapports Judiciaires Officiels, Quebec	1892–date	—
R.L. & S.	Ridgway, Lapp & Schoales (Ir.)	1793–1795	—
R.L. & W.	Robert, Leaming and Wallis	1849–1851	—
R.L., N.S.	Revue Legale, New Series Quebec	1895–1942	—
R.L.R.	Restitution Law Review	1993–date	—
R.P.C.	Reports of Patent Design and Trade Mark Cases	1884–date	—
R.P.D.T.M.C.	Reports of Patent Design and Trade Mark Cases	1884–date	—
R.R.	Revised Reports	1785–1866	—
R.R.C.	Ryde's Rating Cases	1956–1979	—
R.R.L.R.	Rent Review and Lease Renewal	1981–date	—
R.T.I.	Road Traffic Indicator	1993–1999	—
R.T.L.B.	Road Traffic Law Bulletin	1984–1988	—
R.T.R.	Road Traffic Reports	1968–date	—
R.V.R.	Rating and Valuation Reporter	1961–date[61]	—
R.W.L.R.	Rights of Way Law Review	1990–date	—
Rams. App.	Ramsey's Appeal Cases, Quebec	1873–1886	—
Ratio Juris	Ratio Juris	1988–date	—
Ray. Ti. Cas	Rayner's Tithe Cases	1575–1782	—
Raym.	Raymond, Lord	1694–1732	91–2
Raym.	Raymond, Sir T.	1660–1684	83
Rayn.	Rayner's Tithe Cases	1575–1782	—

[58] Superseded by Rating and Valuation Reporter (R. & V.R., or R.V.R.).
[59] Supersedes Rating and Income Tax Reports (R. & I.T.).
[60] For previous volumes see De-Rating Appeals (D.R.A.).
[61] Supersedes Rating and Income Tax Reports (R. & I.T.).

Re. L.R.	Reinsurance Law Reports	1993–1997[62]	—
Real Prop. Cas.	Real Property Cases	1843–1847	—
Regulator	Regulator and Professional Conduct Quarterly	1995–date	—
Rep.	Coke	1572–1616	76–7
Rep. B.	Reparation Bulletin (Sc.)	1995–date	—
Rep. Cas. Eq.	Gilbert, Equity Reports	1705–1727	25
Rep. Ch.	Reports in Chancery	1615–1712	21
Rep. Com. Cas.	Reports of Commercial Cases	1895–1941	—
Rep. Eq.	Gilbert, Equity Reports	1705–1727	25
Rep. in Ch.	Reports in Chancery	1615–1712	21
Rep. in Cha.	Bittleston's Chamber Cases	1883–1884	—
Rep. L.R.	Reparation Law Reports (Sc.)	1996–date	—
Rep. of Sel. Cas in Ch.	Kelygne, W., temp. Hardwicke	1730–1736	125
Rep. Pat. Cas.	Reports of Patent, Design and Trade Mark Cases	1884–date	—
Rep. Q.A.	Cases temp. Queen Anne (11 Modern Reports)	1702–1710	88
Rep. t. F.	Reports, temp. Finch	1673–1681	23
Rep. t. Hard.	Cases temp. Hardwicke (ed. Lee)	1733–1738	95
Res. & Eq. J.	Reserved and Equity Judgments, New South Wales	1845	—
Res Publica	Res Publica	1995–date	—
Reserv. Cas.	Reserved Cases (Ir.)	1860–1864	—
Restric. Prac.	Reports of Restrictive Practices Cases	1957–1972	—
Rett.	Session Cases, 4th Series [Rettie] (Sc.)	1873–1898	—
Rev. C.E.E. Law	Review of Central and East European Law	1995–date[63]	—
Rev. Lég.	La Revue Légale, Quebec	1869–1892	—
Rev. Lég. N.S.	La Revue Légale, New Series, Quebec	1895–date	—
Rev. Soc. L.	Review of Socialist Law	1975–1994[64]	—
Rick. & M.	Rickards & Michael	1885–1889	—
Rick. & S.	Rickards & Saunders	1890–1894	—
Ridg. (Ridg. t. Hard.)	Ridgeway, temp. Hardwicke, King's Bench	1733–1736	94
Ridg. (Ridg. t. Hard.)	Ridgeway, temp. Hardwicke, Chancery	1733–1745	27
Ridg. L. & S.	Ridgeway, Lapp & Schoales (Ir.)	1793–1795	—
Ridge. P.C.	Ridgeway's Parliamentary Reports (Ir.)	1784–1796	—
Ritch.	Ritchie, Reports by Francis Bacon	1617–1621	—
Ritch.	Ritchie's Equity Reports Nova Scotia	1872–1882	—
Road L.	Road Law	1985–1993[65]	—
Road L.R.	Road Law Reports	1992–1993[66]	—
Road L.R.	Road Law and Road Law Reports	1994–1995[67]	—
Rob.	Robertson's Appeal (Sc.)	1707–1727	—
Rob.	Robinson's Appeals (Sc.)	1840–1841	—
Rob.	Robinson, Christopher	1799–1808	165
Rob.	Robinson, William	1838–1853	166
Rob. A.	Robinson, Christopher	1799–1808	165
Rob. App.	Robinson's Appeals (Sc.)	1840–1841	—

[62] Merged with Lloyd's Reinsurance Law Reports (L.R.L.R.) to form Lloyd's Law Reports: Insurance and Reinsurance (Lloyd's Rep. I.R.).
[63] For previous volumes see Review of Socialist Law (Rev. Soc. L.).
[64] For subsequent volumes see Review of Central and East European Law (Rev. C.E.E. Law).
[65] Merged with Road Law Reports (Road L.R.) to form Road Law and Road Law Reports (Road L.R.).
[66] Merged with Road Law (Road L.) to form Road Law and Road Law Reports (Road L.R.).
[67] Formed from a merger between Road Law (Road L.) and Road Law Reports (Road L.R.).

Rob. Cas.	Robertson's Appeals (Sc.	1707–1727	—
Rob. Chr.	Robinson, Christopher	1799–1808	165
Rob. E.	Robertson	1844–1853	163
Rob. Jun.	Robinson, William	1838–1853	166
Rob. Sc. App.	Robertson's Appeals (Sc.)	1707–1727	—
Rob. U.C.	Robinson's Reports, Upper Canada	1844–1882	—
Robin. Sc. App.	Robinson's Appeals (Sc.)	1840–1841	—
Robinson	Robinson, Christopher	1799–1808	165
Robinson	Robinson, William	1838–1852	166
Roche D. & K.	Roche, Dillon and Kehoe Irish Land Reports	1881–1882	—
Roll. (Rolle)	Rolle	1614–1625	81
Rom.	Romilly's Notes of Cases	1767–1787	—
Rose	Rose	1810–1816	—
Rose, P.C.	Roscoe's Price Cases	1745–1859	—
Ross, L.C.	Ross Leading Cases (Sc.)	1638–1849	—
Rot. Cur. Regis	Rotuli Curiae Regis (by Palgrave)	1194–1199	—
Rul. Cas.	Ruling Cases, edited Campbell	1894–1908	—
Russ.	Russell	1823–1829	38
Russ. & Ches.	Russell & Chesley's Reports, Nova Scotia	1875–1879	—
Russ. & Geld.	Russell & Geldert's Reports, Nova Scotia	1879–1895	—
Russ. & M.	Russell & Mylne	1829–1831	39
Russ. & R.	Russell & Ryan	1799–1824	168
Russ. Elect. Cas.	Russell's Election Cases, Nova Scotia	1874	—
Ry. & Can. Tr. Cas.	Railway, Canal and Road Traffic Cases	1885–1949[68]	—
Ry. & M.	Ryan & Moody	1823–1826	171
Ry. Cas.	Railway Cases	1835–1854	—
Ryde	Ryde's Rating Appeals	1871–1893[69]	—
Ryde & K.	Ryde and Konstam Rating Appeals	1894–1904[70]	—
S.	Session Cases, 1st Series [Shawl] (Sc.)	1821–1838	—
S.	Shaw's Appeals (Sc.)	1821–1824	—
S. & A.	Saunders & Austin	1895–1904	—
S. & B.	Saunders & Bidder	1905–1919	—
S. & B.	Smith & Batty (Ir.)	1824–1825	—
S. & C.	Saunders & Cole	1846–1848	[82]
S. & C.L.	Sports and Character Licensing	1999–date	—
S. & D.	Session Cases, 1st Series (Shaw & Dunlop) (Sc.)	1821–1838	—
S. & E.E.B.L.B.	[Butterworths] Soviet and East European Business Law Bulletin	1990–1991[71]	—
S. & G.	Smale & Giffard	1852–1857	65
S. & L.	Schoales & Lefroy (Ir.)	1802–1806	—
S. & L.J.	Sport and the Law Journal	1993–date	—
S. & L.S.	Social and Legal Studies	1992–date	—
S. & M.	Shaw & Maclean (Sc.)	1835–1838	—
S. & S.	Sausse & Scully (Ir.)	1837–1840	—
S. & S.	Simons & Stuart	1822–1826	57
S. & Sm.	Searle & Smith	1859–1860	—
S. & T.	Swabey & Tristram	1858–1865	164
S. & T.L.I.	Shipping and Transport Lawyer International	1998–date	—
S. News	Sentencing News	1991–date	—

[68] For subsequent volumes see Traffic Cases, New Series (Traff. Cas.).
[69] For subsequent volumes see Ryde and Konstam Rating Appeals (Ryde & K.).
[70] For previous volumes see Ryde's Rating Appeals (Ryde).
[71] For subsequent volumes see Butterworths Central and East European Business Law Bulletin (Butt. C. & E.E.B.L.B.), also known as Central and East European Business Law Bulletin (C. & E.E.B.L.B.)

Law Reports, Journals

S.A.I.R.	South Australian Industrial Reports	1916–[date?]	—
S.A.L.J.	South African Law Journal	1884–date	—
S.A.L.R.	South African Law Reports	1947–date	—
S.A.L.R.	South Australian Law Reports	1865–1892	—
		1899–1920	—
S.A.R.	South Australian Industrial Court Reports	1916–[date?]	—
S.A.S.R.	South Australian State Reports	1867–date	—
S.Bell	Bell (Sc.)	1842–1850	—
S.C.	Supreme Court Reports, Cape of Good Hope	1880–1910	—
S.C.	Session Cases (Sc.) [and see "Sess. Cas."]	1906–date	—
S.C. (H.L.)	Sessions Cases (House of Lords) (Sc.)	1850–date	—
S.C. (J.)	Session Cases (Justiciary Reports) (Sc.)	1907–1916	—
S.C.A.L. & P.	Scottish Constitutional and Administrative Law and Practice	1999–date	—
S.C.C.	Select Cases in Chancery temp. King, ed. Macnaghten	1724–1733	25
S.C.C.R.	Scottish Criminal Cases Reports	1981–date	—
S.C.L. Rev.	Scottish Construction Law Review	2001–date	—
S.C.L.R.	Scottish Civil Law Reports	1987–date	—
S.C.P. News	Supreme Court Practice News	1994–date	—
S.C.R.	Supreme Court Reports, Canada	1876–1922	—
S.C.R. (N.S.W.)	Supreme Court Reports, New South Wales	1862–1879	—
S.C.R. (N.S.)(N.S.W.)	Supreme Court Reports, New Series, New South Wales	1878–1879	—
S.H.R.J.	Scottish Human Rights Journal	2000–date	—
S.J.	Scottish Jurist	1829–1873	—
S.J.	Solicitors' Journal	1857–date	—
S.J.L.S.	Singapore Journal of Legal Studies	1991–date[72]	—
S.L. & F.	Sports Law and Finance	1992–1996[73]	—
S.L. Rev.	Student Law Review	1990–date	—
S.L.A. & P	Sports Law Administration and Practice	1997–date[74]	—
S.L.A. & P.	Sports Law Administration and Practice	1997–date	—
S.L. Rev.	Scottish Law Review	1885–1963	—
S.L.B.	Sports Law Bulletin	1998–date	—
S.L.C.	Stuart's Appeals, Lower Canada	1810–1853	—
S.L.C.R.	Scottish Land Court Reports	1913–[date?]	—
S.L.G.	Scottish Law Gazette	1933–date	—
S.L.L.P.	Scottish Licensing Law and Practice	1995–date	—
S.L.L.R.	Sri Lanka Law Reports	1978–[date?][75]	—
S.L.P.Q.	Scottish Law and Practice Quarterly	1995–date	—
S.L.R.	Scottish Land Court Reports	1913–[date?]	—
S.L.R.	Scottish Law Reporter	1865–1925	—
S.L.R.	Student Law Review	1990–date	—
S.L.R.	Sydney Law Review (Aus.)	1953–date	—
S.L.T.	Scots Law Times	1893–date	—
SLT (Lands Tr.)	Scottish Law Times Lands Tribunal Reports	1971–[date?]	—
S.L.T. (Land Ct.)	Scottish Land Court Reports	1964–[date?]	—

---

[72] For previous volumes see the Malayan Law Review (M.L.R.).
[73] For subsequent volumes see Sports Law, Administration and Practice (S.L.A. & P.).
[74] For previous volumes see Sports Law and Finance (S.L. & F.).
[75] For previous volumes see New Law Reports of Cases Decided by the Supreme Court of Ceylon (afterwards Sri Lanka), (N.L.R.).

S.L.T. (Lyon Ct.)	Scots Law Times (Lyon Court)	1950–[date?]	—
S.L.T. (Notes)	Scots Law Times (Notes)	1946–[date?]	—
S.L.T. (Sh. Ct.)	Scots Law Times (Sheriff Court)	1893–[date?]	—
S.N.	Session Notes	1925–1948	—
S.P.E.L.	Scottish Planning and Environmental Law	1993–date	—
S.P.L.P.	Scottish Planning Law and Practice	1980–1993	—
S.P.T.L. Reporter	Society of Public Teachers of Law Reporter	1990–date	—
S.R., H.C.R.	Southern Rhodesia High Court Reports	1911–1955	—
S.R. (N.S.W.)	State Reports, New South Wales	1901–1972	—
S.R.Q.	State Reports, Queensland	1902–1957[76]	—
S.T.	State Trials	1163–1820	—
S.T.C.	Simon's Tax Cases	1972–date	—
S.T.C. (SCD)	Simons Tax Cases: Special Commissioners Decisions	1995–date	—
S.T.L.	Shipping and Trade Law	2000–date	—
S.V.A.R.	Stuart's Vice Admiralty Reports, Quebec	1836–1874	—
S.W.A.	South West Africa Reports	1920–1945	—
S.W.T.I.	Simon's Weekly Tax Intelligence	1973–date	—
Salk.	Salkeld	1689–1712	91
Sask.	Saskatchewan Law Reports	1908–1931	—
Saund.	Saunders (ed. Williams)	1666–1673	85
Saund. & C.	Saunders & Cole	1846–1848	[82]
Saund. B.C.	Saunders & Cole	1846–1848	[82]
Sausse & Sc.	Sausse & Scully (Ir.)	1837–1840	—
Sav.	Savile	1580–1594	123
Say.	Sayer	1751–1756	96
Sc.	Scott	1834–1840	[41–54]
Sc. & Div.	See L.R. Sc. & Div.		
Sc. N.R.	Scott's New Reports	1840–1845	[56–66]
Sch. & Lef.	Schoales & Lefroy (Ir.)	1802–1806	—
Schalk	Schalk's Reports, Jamaica	1855–1876	—
SCOLAG	SCOLAG (Sc.)	1975–date	—
Scot. Jur.	Scottish Jurist (Sc.)	1829–1873	—
Scot. L.T.	Scots Law Times	1893–date	—
Scots. L.T.	Scots Law Times	1893–date	—
Searle	Searle's Supreme Court Reports, Cape Colony	1850–1867	—
Searle & Sm.	Searle & Smith	1859–1860	—
Seign. Rep.	Seigniorial Reports, Lower Canada	1856	—
Sel. Cas. Ch.	Select Cases in Chancery temp. King, ed. Macnaghten	1724–1733	25
Sel. Cas. N.F.	Select Cases, Newfoundland	1817–1828	—
Sel. Cas. t. King	Select Cases in Chancery temp. King, ed. Macnaghten	1724–1733	25
Sess. Ca. (Sess. Cas.)	Sessions Cases, K.B.	1710–1748	93
Sess. Cas.	Session Cases (Sc.) -		
S.	1st Series [Shaw]	1821–1838	—
D.	2nd Series [Dunlop]	1838–1862	—
M.	3rd Series [Macpherson]	1862–1873	—
R.	4th Series [Rettie]	1873–1898	—
F.	5th Series [Fraser]	1989–1906	—
Sess. Cas. (6 Ser.)	6th Series (See "S.C.")	1906–date	—
Sess. Pap. C.C.	Sessional Papers, Central Criminal Court	1834–1913	—
Sett. & Rem.	Cases of Settlements and Removals	1710–1742	—

---

[76] For previous volumes see Queensland Law Journal and Reports (Queens. L.J. & R.). For subsequent volumes see Queensland Reports (Qd. R.).

Sh.	Shower (ed. Butt)	1678–1695	89
Sh.	Shower's Parliamentary Cases	1694–1699	1
Sh. & Macl.	Shaw & Maclean (Sc.)	1835–1838	—
Sh. App.	Shaw's Appeals (Sc.)	1821–1824	—
Sh. Ct. Rep.	Sheriff Court Reports (Sc.)	1885–1963	—
Sh. Teind. Ct.	Shaw's Teind Court Decisions (Sc.)	1821–1831	—
Shaw, J.	John Shaw (Sc.)	1848–1852	—
Shaw, P.	Patrick Shaw (Sc.)	1819–1831	—
Shill. W.C.	Irish Workmen's Compensation Cases	1934–1938	—
Show.	Shower (ed. Butt)	1678–1695	89
Show. K.B.	Shower (ed. Butt)	1678–1695	89
Show. P.C.	Shower's Parliamentary Cases	1694–1699	1
Sid.	Siderfin	1657–1670	82
Sim.	Simons	1826–1850	57–60
Sim. & St.	Simons & Stuart	1822–1826	57
Sim. N.S.	Simons, New Series	1850–1852	61
Six Circ.	Cases on the Six Circuits (Ir.)	1841–1843	—
Skin	Skinner	1681–1698	90
Sm. (Smith)	Smith, J.P.	1803–1806	[7–8]
Sm. & Bat.	Smith & Batty (Ir.)	1824–1825	—
Sm. & G.	Smale & Giffard	1852–1857	65
Smith Reg. Cas.	Smith, Registration Cases	1895–1914	—
Smy. (Smythe)	Smythe (Ir.)	1839–1840	—
Smy. & B.	Smythe and Bourke, Irish Marriage Cases	1842	—
Soc. L.	Socialist Lawyer	1987–date	—
Sol.	The Solicitor	1934–1961	—
Sol. J.	Solicitors' Journal	1857–date	—
Sol. Jo.	Solicitor's Journal	1857–date	—
Solic. J.	Solicitor's Journal	1857–date	—
Sp.	Spinks	1853–1855	164
Sp.	Spinks, Prize Cases	1854–1856	164
Sp. & Sel. Cas.	Special and Selected Law Cases	1648	—
St. Brown	Stewart-Brown, Cases in the Court of the Star Chamber	1455–1547	—
St. Tr.	State Trials (Cobbett & Howell)	1163–1820	—
St. T., N.S.	State Trials, New Series	1820–1858	—
Stair	Stair (Sc.)	1661–1681	—
Star. (Stark.)	Starkie	1814–1823	171
Stat. L. Rev.	Statute Law Review	1980–date	—
Stat. L.R.	Statute Law Review	1980–date	—
Stew. Adm.	Stewart's Vice-Admiralty Reports, Nova Scotia	1803–1813	—
Stil.	Stillingfleet	1698–1704	—
Sto. & G.	Stone and Graham, Private Bill Decisions	1865	—
Stock.	Stockton's Vice-Admiralty Reports, New Brunswick	1879–1891	—
Str.	Strange. J. (ed. By Nolan)	1716–1749	93
Str. Ev.	Strange, Cases of Evidence	1698–1732	—
Stu. Adm.	Stuart's Vice-Admiralty Reports, Lower Canada	1836–1874	—
Stu. K.B.	Stuart's Lower Canada Reports	1810–1853	—
Stu. M. & P.	Stuart, Milne and Peddie's Reports (Sc.)	1851–1853	—
Stuart, M. & P.	Stuart, Milne & Peddie (Sc.)	1851–1853	—
Stud. L.R.	Students' Law Reporter	1970–1988	—
Sty. (Style)	Style	1646–1655	82
Suth. W.R.	Sutherlands Weekly Reporter (India)	1864–1876	—
Sw.	Swabey	1855–1859	166
Sw.	Swanston	1818–1819	36
Sw. & Tr.	Swabey & Tristram	1858–1865	164
Swab.	Swabey	1855–1859	166

Swan.	Swanston	1818–1819	36
Swin.	Swinton (Sc.)	1835–1841	—
Swin. Reg. App.	Swinton Registration Appeals (Sc.)	1835–1841	—
Syd. L.R.	Sydney Law Review	1953–date	—
Syme	Syme (Sc.)	1826–1830	—
T. & E.L.J.	Trusts and Estates Law Journal	1998–2004[77]	—
T. & E.P.	Trust and Estates Practitioner	2003–2006[78]	—
T. & G.	Tyrwhitt & Granger	1835–1836	[46]
T. & M.	Temple & Mew's Cases	1848–1851	169
T. & R.	Turner & Russell	1822–1824	37
T. & T.	Trusts and Trustees	1996–date	—
T. Raym.	Raymond, Sir T.	1660–1684	83
T.C.	Reports of Tax Cases	1875–date	—
T.C.L.R.	Technology and Construction Law Reports	1999–2002	—
T.E.L. & P.	Tolley's Employment Law and Practice	1996–1998[79]	—
T.E.L. & T.J.	Trusts and Estates Law and Tax Journal	2004–date[80]	—
T.E.L.L.	Tolley's Employment Law-Line	1998–2001[81]	—
T.E.L.L.N.	Tolley's Employment Law-Line Newsletter	2001–date[82]	—
T.I.J.M.C.L.	The International Journal of Marine and Coastal Law	1993–date[83]	—
T.J.E.L. & P.	Tolley's Journal of Employment Law and Practice	1993–1996[84]	—
T.Jo.	Jones, Sir Thomas	1667–1685	84
T.L. & P.	Trust Law and Practice	1986–1990	—
T.L.J.	Travel Law Journal	1994–1996[85]	—
T.L.P.	Transport Law and Policy	1997–date	—
T.L.R.	Tanganyika Law Reports	1921–1952	—
T.L.R.	Tasmanian Law Reports	1905–1940[86]	—
T.L.R.	Times Law Reports	1884–1952; 1990–date[87]	—
T.L.T.	Telecoms Law Today	2001–date	—
T.P.D.	Transvaal Province Division South Africa	1910–1946	—
T.R.	Taxation Reports	1939–1982	—
T.R.	Term Reports (by Durnford & East)	1785–1800	99–101
T.R.N.S.	East	1801–1812	102–4
T.W.	Trademark World	1986–date	—
Tal. (Talb.)	Talbot, Cases In Equity, ed. Williams	1733–1738	25
Tam.	Tamlyn	1829–1830	48
Tarl.	Tarleton Term Reports (New South Wales)	1881–1883	—
Tas. L.R.	Tasmanian Law Reports	1905–1940[88]	—

[77] For previous volumes see Trusts and Estates (Tr. & Est.). For subsequent volumes see Trusts and Estates Law and Tax Journal (T.E.L. & T.J.).
[78] For subsequent volumes see Private Client Practitioner (P.C.P.).
[79] For previous volumes see Tolley's Journal of Employment Law and Practice (T.J.E.L. & P.). For subsequent volumes see Tolley's Employment Law-Line (T.E.L.L.).
[80] For previous volumes see Trusts and Estates Law Journal (T. & E.L.J., or Tr. & Est. L.J.).
[81] For previous volumes see Tolley's Employment Law and Practice (T.E.L. & P.) For subsequent volumes see Tolley's Employment Law-Line Newsletter (T.E.L.L.N.).
[82] For previous volumes see Tolley's Employment Law-Line (T.E.L.L.).
[83] For previous volumes see International Journal of Estuarine and Coastal Law (I.J.E.C.L.).
[84] For subsequent volumes see Tolley's Employment Law and Practice (T.E.L. & P.).
[85] For subsequent volumes see International Travel Law Journal (I.T.L.J.).
[86] For subsequent volumes see Tasmanian State Reports (Tas. S.R.).
[87] Although different abbreviations – T.L.R. and Times L. Rep. and Times L.R. – have been used and are given for the two different time periods (1884–1952, and 1990–date), the 1990–date reports should be cited T.L.R.
[88] For subsequent volumes see Tasmanian State Reports (Tas. S.R.).

Tas. R.	Tasmanian Reports	1979–date[89]	—
Tas. S.R.	Tasmanian State Reports	1941–1978[90]	—
Tas. Univ. L. Rev.	Tasmanian University Law Review	1959–1963[91]	—
Taun. (Taunt.)	Taunton	1807–1819	127–9
Tax Cas.	Tax Cases	1875–date	—
Tay.	Taylor's Reports, Ontario	1823–1827	—
Temp. & M.	Temple & Mews' Cases	1848–1851	169
Term.	Term Reports (by Durnford & East)	1785–1800	99–101
Terr. L.R.	Territories Law Reports, Canada	1885–1907	—
Thom. Dec.	Nova Scotia Reports	1834–1851	—
Times L. Rep.	Times Law Reports	1884–1952 1990–date[92]	—
Times L.R.	Times Law Reports	1884–1952 1990–date[93]	—
To. Jo.	Jones, Sir Thomas	1667–1685	84
Toml. Supp Br.	Supplement to Brown's Parliamentary Cases by Tomlin	1689–1795	—
Tot. (Toth.)	Tothill	1559–1646	21
Town. St. Tr.	Townsend Modern State Trials	1850	—
Tr. & Est.	Trusts and Estates	1987–1997[94]	—
Tr. & Est. L.J.	Trusts and Estates Law Journal	1998–2004[95]	—
Tr. Consist. J.	Tristram's Consistory Judgments	1872–1890	—
Tr. L.R.	Trading Law Reports	1983–1993[96]	—
Tr. L.R.	Trinidad Law Reports	1893–[?]	—
Tr. Law	Trading Law and Trading Law Reports	1994–1999[97]	—
Trad. L.	Trading Law	1981–1993[98]	—
Traff. Cas.	Railway, Canal and Road Traffic Cases	1885–1949[99]	—
Traff. Cas.	Traffic Cases, New Series (with Vol. 30)	1952–[?][1]	—
Trans. L. & P.	Transport Law and Policy	1997–date	—
Trent L.J.	Trent Law Journal	1977–1987	—
Tribunals	Tribunals	1994–date	—
Tru.	Trueman's Equity Cases, New Brunswick	1876–1893	—
Tru. & E.L.J.	Trusts and Estates Law Journal	1998–2004[2]	—
Tru. L.I.	Trust Law International	1990–date[3]	—

[89] For previous volumes see Tasmanian State Reports (Tas. S.R.).
[90] For previous volumes see Tasmanian Law Reports (T.L.R., or Tas. L.R.). For subsequent volumes see Tasmanian Reports (Tas. R.).
[91] For subsequent volumes see the University of Tasmania Law Review (Univ. T.L.R.).
[92] Although different abbreviations – T.L.R. and Times L. Rep. and Times L.R. – have been used and are given for the two different time periods (1884–1952, and 1990–date), the 1990–date reports should be cited T.L.R.
[93] Although different abbreviations – T.L.R. and Times L. Rep. and Times L.R.. – have been used and are given for the two different time periods (1884–1952 and 1990–date), the 1990–date reports should be cited T.L.R.
[94] For subsequent volumes see Trusts and Estates Law Journal (T. & E.L.J., or Tr. & Est. L.J., or Tru. & E.L.J.)
[95] For previous volumes see Trusts and Estates (Tr. & Est.). For subsequent volumes see Trusts and Estates Law and Tax Journal (T.E.L. & T.J.).
[96] Merged with Trading Law (Trad. Law) to form Trading Law and Trading Law Reports (Tr. Law).
[97] Formed from a merger between Trading Law (Trad. Law) and Trading Law Reports (Tr. L.R.).
[98] Merged with Trading Law Reports (Tr. L.R.) to form Trading Law and Trading Law Reports (Tr. Law).
[99] For subsequent volumes see Traffic Cases, New Series (Traff. Cas.).
[1] For previous volumes see Railway, Canal and Road Traffic Cases (Ry. & Can. Tr. Cas., or Traff. Cas.).
[2] For previous volumes see Trusts and Estates (Tr. & Est.). For subsequent volumes see Trusts and Estates Law and Tax Journal (T.E.L. & T.J.).
[3] For previous volumes see Trust Law and Practice (Trust L. & P.).

Trust L. & P.	Trust Law and Practice	1986–1990[4]	—
Tuck.	Tucker's Select Cases, Newfoundland	1817–1828	—
Tupp.	Tupper Reports, Ontario	1876–1900	—
Tur. & Rus.	Turner & Russell	1822–1824	37
Tyr. (Tyrw.)	Tyrwhitt	1830–1835	[35–40]
Tyr. & G.	Tyrwhitt & Granger	1835–1836	[46]
U.C. Ch.	Upper Canada Chancery Reports	1849–1882	—
U.C. Chamb.	Upper Canada Chambers Reports	1846–1852	—
U.C. Jur.	Upper Canada Jurist	1844–1848	—
U.C. Pr. R.	Upper Canada Practice Reports	1850–1900	—
U.C.C.P.	Upper Canada Common Pleas Reports	1850–1882	—
U.C.E. & A.	Upper Canada Error and Appeal Reports	1846–1866	—
U.C.K.B.	Upper Canada King's Bench Reports, Old Series	1831–1844	—
U.C.L.J.	Upper Canada Law Journal	1855–1922	—
U.C.O.S.	Upper Canada King's Bench Reports (Old Series)	1831–1844	—
U.C.Q.B.	Upper Canada Queen's Bench Reports	1844–1881	—
UKHL number	Media neutral citation from the House of Lords	2001–date	—
UKPC number	Media neutral citation from the Privy Council	2001–date	—
U.K.C.L.R.	UK Competition Law Reports	1999–date	—
U.K.H.R.R.	United Kingdom Human Rights Reports	2000–date	—
U.L.R.	Uganda Law Reports	1904–1973	—
U.L.R.	Utilities Law Review	1990–date	—
U.S.	United States Supreme Court Reports	1790–date	—
Udal	Udal's Reports (Fiji) Vol. 1	1875–1897	—
Uniform L.R.	Uniform Law Review	1973–date	—
Univ. Q.L.J.	University of Queensland Law Journal	1948–date	—
Univ. T.L.R.	University of Tasmania Law Review	1964–date[5]	—
Univ. W.A.L.R.	University of Western Australia Law Review	1960–date[6]	—
Util. L.R.	Utilities Law Review	1990–date	
Util. Law Rev.	Utilities Law Review	1990–date	
V. & B.	Vesey & Beames	1812–1814	35
V. & D.R.	Value Added Tax and Duties Tribunals Reports	1995–date[7]	—
V. & S.	Vernon & Scriven (Ir.)	1786–1788	—
V.A.T. Trib. Rep.	Value Added Tax Tribunal Reports	1973–1994[8]	—
V.A.T.T.R.	Value Added Tax Tribunal Reports	1973–1994[9]	—
V.C. Adm.	Victoria Reports, Admiralty (Aust.)	[?]	
V.C. Eq.	Victoria Reports, Equity (Aust.)	[?]	
V.L.R.	Victorian Law Reports (Aust.)	1875–1956[10]	—
V.L.T.	Victorian Law Times (Aust.)	1856–1857	—
V.R.	Victorian Reports (Aust.)	1957–date[11]	—

---

[4] For subsequent volumes see Trust Law International (Tru. L.I.).
[5] For previous volumes see Tasmanian University Law Review (Tas. Univ. L. Rev.).
[6] For previous volumes see Western Australia University Law Review (W.A.U.L.R.).
[7] For previous volumes see Value Added Tax Tribunal Reports (V.A.T. Trib. Rep., or V.A.T.T.R.).
[8] For subsequent volumes see Value Added Tax and Duties Tribunals Reports (V. & D.R.).
[9] For subsequent volumes see Value Added Tax and Duties Tribunals Reports (V. & D.R.).
[10] For subsequent volumes see Victorian Reports (V.R.).
[11] For previous volumes see Victorian Law Reports (V.L.R., or Vict. L.R.).

V.R.	Victorian Reports, Webb, etc. (Aust.)	1870–1872	—
Van K.	Van Koughwet's Reports, Upper Canada	1864–1871	—
Vanderst.	Vanderstraaten's Reports (Ceylon)	1869–1871	—
Vaug. (Vaugh.)	Vaughan	1665–1674	124
Vent.	Ventris	1668–1688	86
Vern.	Vernon	1681–1720	23
Vern. & Sc.	Vernon & Scriven (Ir.)	1786–1788	—
Ves. & Bea.	Vesey & Beames	1812–1814	35
Ves. Jr.	Vesey Junior	1789–1817	30–34
Ves. Sen.	Vesey Senior (ed. by Belt)	1747–1756	27–8
Ves. Sen. Sup.	Vesey Senior (Belt's Supplement)	1747–1756	28
Ves. Supp.	Supplement to Vesey Junior by Hovenden	1789–1817	34
Vict. L.R.	Victorian Law Reports (Aust.)	1875–1956[12]	—
W.	Watermayer's Supreme Court Reports, Cape of Good Hope	1857	—
W. & B.	Wolferstan & Bristowe	1859–1864	—
W. & D.	Wolferstan & Dew	1856–1858	—
W. & S.	Wilson & Shaw (Sc.)	1825–1835	—
W. & W.	Wyatt & Webb's Reports, Victoria (Aust.)	1861–1863	—
W. Comp	World Competition	1987–date	—
W. Jones	Sir William Jones' Reports	1620–1641	82
W. Rob.	W. Robinson's Reports	1838–1852	166
W.A.A.R.	Western Australian Arbitration Reports	1901–1920	—
W.A.'B & W.	Webb, A'Beckett & Williams Reports, Victoria	1870–1872	—
W.A.C.A.	West Africa Court of Appeal Reports	1930–1955	—
W.A.L.R.	Western Australian Law Reports	1898–1959[13]	—
W.A.R.	Western Australian Reports	1960–date[14]	—
W.A.U.L.R.	Western Australia University Law Review	1948–1959[15]	—
W.B.	Welfare Benefits	1996–date	—
W.Bl.	Blackstone, W.	1746–1780	96
W.C. & I.R.	Workmen's Compensation and Insurance Reports	1912–1933	—
W.C.C.	Workmen's Compensation Cases	1898–1907[16]	—
W.C.R. (N.S.W.)	Worker's Compensation Reports (New South Wales)	1926–[date?]	—
W.H.C.	Witwatersrand High Court Reports, South Africa	1910–1946	—
W.I.R.	West Indian Reports	1959–date	—
W.L.	Journal of Water Law	2003–date[17]	—
W.L.	Water Law	1990–2002[18]	—
W.L.D.	Witwatersrand Local Division, South Africa Law Reports	1910–1946	—
W.L.L.R.	World Licensing Law Reports	1999–date	—
W.L.R.	Weekly Law Reports	1953–date[19]	—
W.L.R.	Western Law Reporter, Canada	1905–1916	—
W.L.T.	Western Law Times, Canada	1889–1895	—
W.N.	Weekly Notes (Reports)	1866–1952[20]	—

[12] For subsequent volumes see Victorian Reports (V.R.).
[13] For subsequent volumes see Western Australian Reports (W.A.R.).
[14] For previous volumes see Western Australian Law Reports (W.A.L.R.).
[15] For subsequent volumes see University of Western Australia Law Review (Univ. W.A.L.R.).
[16] For subsequent volumes see Butterworths Workmen's Compensation Cases (Butt. W.C.C., or Butt. Work. Comp. Cas.).
[17] For previous volumes see Water Law (W.L.).
[18] For subsequent volumes see Journal of Water Law (W.L.).
[19] Supersedes Weekly Notes (W.N.) and Weekly Notes (Miscellaneous) (W.N. Misc.).
[20] Superseded by Weekly Law Reports (W.L.R.).

W.N. (Calc.)	Weekly Notes (Calcutta)	1896–1941	—
W.N. Misc.	Weekly Notes (Miscellaneous)	1866–1952[21]	—
W.N. (N.S.W.)	Weekly Notes, New South Wales	1884–1970[22]	—
W.O.G.L.R.	World Online Gambling Law Report	2002–date	—
W.R.	Weekly Reporter	1853–1906	—
W.R.	West's Reports, temp. Hardwicke	1736–1739	25
W.R.N.L.R.	Western Region of Nigeria Law Reports	1955–[?]	—
W.R.T.L.B.	Wilkinson's Road Traffic Law Bulletin	1989–date	—
W.S.L.R.	World Sport Law Report	2003–date	—
W.T.L.R.	Wills and Trusts Law Reports	2000–date	—
W.T.R.	World Trade Review	2002–date	—
W.W.	Wyatt and Webb's Reports (Victorian) (Aust.)	1861–1863	—
W.W. & A'B.	Wyatt, Webb & A'Beckett's Reports Victoria (Aust.)	1864–1869	—
W.W. & D.	Willmore, Wollaston & Davison	1837	[52]
W.W. & H.	Willmore, Wollaston & Hodges	1838–1839	[52]
W.W.R.	Western Weekly Reports	1911–date	—
Wales L.J.	Wales Law Journal	2001–date	—
Wall.	Wallis' Reports (Ir.)	1766–1791	—
Wall. Lyn.	Wallis's Select Cases by Lyne (Ir.)	1766–1791	—
Wat.	Watermeyer's Supreme Court Reports, Cape of Good Hope	1857	—
Web J.C.L.I.	Web Journal of Current Legal Issues	1995–date	—
Web. P.C.	Webster	1601–1855	—
Welsb. H. & G.	Exchequer Reports (Welsby, Hurlestone & Gordon)	1847–1856	154–6
Welsh	Welsh (Ir.)	1832–1840	—
West	West	1839–1841	9
West	West's Reports, temp. Hardwicke	1736–1739	25
West. A.U.L.R.	Western Australia University Law Review	1948–1959[23]	—
West. L.R.	Western Law Reporter, Canada	1905–1916	—
West. L.T.	Western Law Times, Canada	1889–1895	—
West. Ti. Cas.	Western's Tithe Cases	1535–1822	—
White	White (Sc.)	1886–1893	—
Wight.	Wightwick	1810–1811	145
Wilk. & Ow.	Wilkinson and Owen Reports, New South Wales	1862–1865	—
Will.	Willes (ed. Durnford)	1737–1760	125
Will. Saund.	Notes to Saunders' Reports, by Williams	1666–1673	85
Will. Woll. & D.	Willmore, Wollaston & Davison	1837	[52]
Will. Woll. & H.	Willmore, Wollaston & Hodges	1838–1839	[52]
Willes	Willes (ed. Durnford)	1737–1760	125
Williams	Peere Williams' Reports	1695–1735	24
Williams P.	Peere Williams' Reports	1695–1735	24
Wilm.	Wilmot's Notes of Cases	1757–1770	97
Wils.	Wilson	1818–1819	37
Wils.	Wilson's King's Bench Reports	1742–1774	95
Wils. & Sh.	Wilson & Shaw (Sc.)	1825–1835	—
Wils. Exch.	Wilson's Reports	1805–1817	159
Win. (Winch)	Winch	1621–1625	124
Wm. Bl.	Sir William Blackstone	1746–1780	96
Wm. Rob.	W. Robinson's Reports	1838–1852	166
Wms. P.	Peere Williams' Reports	1695–1735	24

[21] Superseded by Weekly Law Reports (W.L.R.).
[22] Superseded by the New South Wales Law Reports (N.S.W.L.R.).
[23] For subsequent volumes see University of Western Australia Law Review (Univ. W.A.L.R.).

Wms. Saund.	Saunders' Reports, annotated by Williams	1666–1673	85
Wol. (Woll.)	Wollaston	1840–1841	—
Wolf. & B.	Wolferstan & Bristow	1859–1864	—
Wolf. & D.	Wolferstan & Dew	1856–1858	—
Wood. Tit. Cas.	Wood's Tithe Cases	1650–1798	—
World I.L.R.	World Internet Law Report	1999–date	—
World T.R.	World Trade Review	2002–date	—
Worldlaw Bus.	Worldlaw Business	1999–date	—
Wyatt, W. & A'B.	Wyatt, Webb & A'Beckett's Reports, Victoria	1864–1869	—
Y. & C. Ch.	Younge & Collyer, temp. Bruce	1841–1843	62–3
Y. & C. Ex.	Younge & Collyer	1834–1842	160
Y. & J.	Younge & Jervis	1826–1830	148
Y.B.	Year Books (ed. Dieser)	1388–1389	—
Y.B.	Year Books (ed. Maynard)	1367–1537	—
Y.B. (R.S.)	Year Books (ed. Horwood) (Roll Series)	1292–1307	—
Y.B. (R.S.)	Year Books (ed. Horwood & Pike) (Rolls Series)	1337–1346	—
Y.B. (S.S.)	Year Books (Selden Society)	1307–1319	—
Y.B. Rich II.	Bellewe's Richard II	1378–1400	72
Y.C. & M.L.	Yearbook of Copyright and Media Law	1999–date	—
Y.E.L.	Yearbook of European Law	1981–date	—
Y.L.C.T.	Yearbook of Law, Computers and Technology	1984–1991[24]	—
Y.M.E.L.	Yearbook of Media and Entertainment Law	1995–1998	—
Yb. Int'l. Env. L.	Yearbook of International Environmental Law	1990–date	—
Yrbk. Intl. Hum. L.	Yearbook of International Humanitarian Law	1998–date	—
Yel. (Yelv.)	Yelverton	1602–1613	80
You. (Younge)	Younge	1830–1832	159
Young Adm.	Young's Nova Scotia Admiralty Cases	1865–1880	—
Z.L.R.	Zanzibar Law Reports	1919–1950	—

[24] For subsequent volumes see International Yearbook of Law, Computers and Technology (I.Y.L.C.T.).

THE REGNAL YEARS
OF
ENGLISH SOVEREIGNS

	FROM	TO	YEARS
William I	Oct. 14, 1066	Sept. 9, 1087	21
William II	Sept. 26, 1087	Aug. 2, 1100	13
Henry I	Aug. 5, 1100	Dec. 1, 1135	36
Stephen	Dec. 26, 1135	Oct. 25, 1154	19
Henry II	Dec. 19, 1154	July 6, 1189	35
Richard I	Sept. 3, 1189	Apr. 6, 1199	10
John	May 27, 1199	Oct. 19, 1216	18
Henry III	Oct. 28, 1216	Nov. 16, 1272	57
Edward I	Nov. 20, 1272	July 7, 1307	35
Edward II	July 8, 1307	Jan. 20, 1327	20
Edward III	Jan. 25, 1327	June 21, 1377	51
Richard II	June 22, 1377	Sept. 29, 1399	23
Henry IV	Sept. 30, 1399	Mar. 20, 1413	14
Henry V	Mar. 21, 1413	Aug. 31, 1422	10
Henry VI	Sep. 1, 1422	Mar. 4, 1461	39
Edward IV[1]	Mar. 4, 1461	Apr. 9, 1483	23
Edward V	Apr. 9, 1483	June 25, 1483	1
Richard III	June 26, 1483	Aug. 22, 1485	3
Henry VII	Aug. 22, 1485	Apr. 21, 1509	24
Henry VIII	Apr. 22, 1509	Jan. 28, 1547	38
Edward VI	Jan. 28, 1547	July 6, 1553	7
Mary[2]	July 6, 1553	Nov. 17, 1558	6
Elizabeth I	Nov. 17, 1558	Mar. 24, 1603	45
James I	Mar. 24, 1603	Mar. 27, 1625	23
Charles I	Mar. 27, 1625	Jan. 30, 1649	24
Charles II[3]	Jan. 30, 1649	Feb. 6, 1685	37
James II	Feb. 6, 1685	Dec. 11, 1688	4
William and Mary[4]	Feb. 13, 1689	Mar. 8, 1702	14
Anne	Mar. 8, 1702	Aug. 1, 1714	13
George I	Aug. 1, 1714	June 11, 1727	13
George II	June 11, 1727	Oct. 25, 1760	34
George III[5]	Oct. 25, 1760	Jan. 29, 1820	60
George IV	Jan. 29, 1820	June 26, 1830	11
William IV	June 26, 1830	June 20, 1837	7
Victoria	June 20, 1837	Jan. 22, 1901	64
Edward VII	Jan. 22, 1901	May 6, 1910	10
George V	May 6, 1910	Jan. 20, 1936	26
Edward VIII[6]	Jan. 20, 1936	Dec. 11, 1936	1
George VI	Dec. 11, 1936	Feb. 6, 1952	17
Elizabeth II	Feb. 6, 1952		

[1] Henry VI (restored)–Oct. 9, 1470, to about Apr. 1471.
[2] Jane–July 6 to July 17, 1553. Mary married Philip, July 25, 1554.
[3] Not king *de facto* until May 29, 1660.
[4] Mary died Dec. 27, 1694.
[5] Regency from Feb. 5, 1811.
[6] Executed an Instrument of Abdication on December 10, 1936 which took effect on December 11, 1936 (His Majesty's Declaration of Abdication Act, 1936; 1 Edw. 8, c.3).